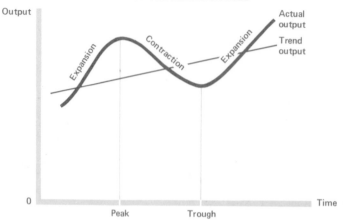

STAGES OF THE BUSINESS CYCLE

U.S. BUSINESS CYCLES SINCE THE GREAT DEPRESSION

Peak	Trough	DURATION IN MONTHS		Unemployment rate at trough, percent	Decline in industrial production, percent
		Peak to trough	Trough to peak		
Aug. 1929	Mar. 1933	43	50		51.8
May 1937	June 1938	13	80		31.7
Feb. 1945	Oct. 1945	8	37		31.4
Nov. 1948	Oct. 1949	11	45	7.9	9.9
July 1953	May 1954	10	39	5.9	8.9
Aug. 1957	April 1958	8	24	7.4	12.6
April 1960	Feb. 1961	10	106	6.9	6.1
Dec. 1969	Nov. 1970	11	36	5.9	5.8
Nov. 1973	Mar. 1975	16	58	8.6	15.1
Jan. 1980	July 1980	6	12	7.8	8.3
July 1981	Dec. 1982	18		10.8	12.2

U.S. INFLATION (GNP DEFLATOR), 1930–1989

GROWTH IN INDUSTRIALIZED COUNTRIES, 1960–1987 (percent per year)

	Growth	Growth per capita	Labor productivity
United States	3.2	2.1	1.2
Japan	6.5	5.5	5.4
Germany	3.0	2.7	3.1
United Kingdom	2.4	2.0	3.9
Canada	4.4	3.0	1.8
OECD	3.7	2.7	2.6

SOURCE: OECD, *Historical Statistics.*

macroeconomics

MACROECONOMICS

fifth edition

RUDIGER DORNBUSCH

Department of Economics
Massachusetts Institute of Technology

STANLEY FISCHER

The World Bank
and
Department of Economics
Massachusetts Institute of Technology

McGraw-Hill Publishing Company

New York   St. Louis   San Francisco   Auckland
Bogotá   Caracas   Hamburg   Lisbon   London
Madrid   Mexico   Milan   Montreal   New Delhi
Oklahoma City   Paris   San Juan   São Paulo
Singapore   Sydney   Tokyo   Toronto

MACROECONOMICS
INTERNATIONAL EDITION

1 2 3 4 5 6 7 8 9 0 KKP UPE 9 4 3 2 1 0

This book was set in Century Old Style by Progressive
Typographers, Inc.
The editors were Scott D. Stratford and Larry Goldberg.
The designer was Joan Greenfield.
The production supervisor was Janelle S. Travers.

Library of Congress Cataloging-in-Publication Data

Dornbusch, Rudiger.
    Macroeconomics / Rudiger Dornbusch, Stanley Fischer.
    ---5th ed.
    p.   cm.
    Rev. ed. of: Macroeconomics. 4th ed. c1987.
    ISBN 0–07–017787–2
    1. Macroeconomics.   I. Fischer, Stanley.
    II. Dornbusch, Rudiger.
Macroeconomics.   III. Title
HB172.5.D67   1990   89–27589
339--dc20

When ordering this title use ISBN 0–07–100696–6

Printed in Singapore

ABOUT THE AUTHORS

RUDIGER DORNBUSCH did his undergraduate work in Switzerland and holds a Ph.D. from the University of Chicago. He has taught at Chicago, Rochester, and since 1975 at MIT. His research is primarily in international economics, with a major macroeconomic component. His special research interests are the behavior of exchange rates, high inflation and hyperinflation, and the international debt problem. He visits and lectures extensively in Europe and in Latin America, where he takes an active interest in problems of stabilization policy, and has held visiting appointments in Brazil and Argentina. His writing includes *Open Economy Macroeconomics* and, with Stanley Fischer and Richard Schmalensee, *Economics.* His interests in public policy take him frequently to testify before Congress and to participate in international conferences. He regularly contributes newspaper editorials on current policy issues here and abroad.

STANLEY FISCHER was an undergraduate at the London School of Economics and has a Ph.D. from MIT. He taught at the University of Chicago while Rudi Dornbusch was a student there, starting a long friendship and collaboration. From 1973 to 1987 he has taught at MIT and spent several leaves at the Hebrew University in Jerusalem. On leave from MIT since January 1988, he is currently Vice President, Development Economics and Chief Economist, The World Bank, Washington, D.C. His main research interests are in economic growth and development, inflation and stabilization, indexation, and international and macroeconomics. He has published widely in these areas and participates regularly in scholarly meetings. He is the editor of the *NBER Macroeconomics Annual,* initiated by the National Bureau of Economic Research to bridge the gap between theory and policy in the macroeconomic area.

To Eliana and Rhoda

CONTENTS

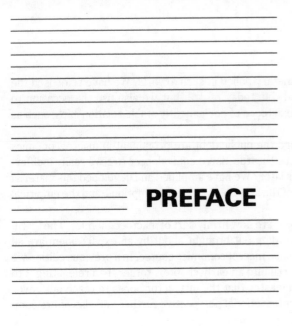

PREFACE

The fifth edition is the most ambitious working over of *Macroeconomics* since the book was first published. Every new edition offers the opportunity to add material, round out arguments, and update information and case studies. But occasionally it is essential to make a complete evaluation of progress in the field, rethink issues, and restate arguments in the light of new findings and new ways of thinking. When the first edition came out, in 1978, today's New Keynesians had barely finished their first degrees, rational expectations was only starting to flourish, and the real business cycle approach had not even seen the light of day. Today it is impossible to write seriously in macroeconomics without integrating the challenges, the findings, and the perspective of those approaches. The present edition accomplishes this task.

Beyond the general recognition of these important developments in macroeconomics, we have in particular expanded material on such topics as credit rationing, efficiency wages, the Lucas supply curve, and credibility and time consistency. Interestingly, we have been able to incorporate the emphasis given by the new approaches without abandoning the structure and, indeed, much of the argument of earlier editions. The Lucas supply curve, for example, is developed as an aggregate supply curve that fits easily into the introductory material on aggregate supply and demand, but yields the extra insight of distinguishing between anticipated and unanticipated monetary changes.

THREE MAJOR AREAS OF CHANGE

We have very substantially rewritten material in three areas. First, the money market is today dominated by the fact that most money pays interest. That changes much of the argument in traditional treatments of money demand and raises the interesting question of what happens to monetary policy in such a world. We have refocused the chapters to highlight the central role today of $M2$, but we also use the occasion to caution against believing in the existence of permanently stable relationships, such as the stability of $M2$ velocity.

Issues of budget deficits and the public debt are prominent in macroeconomics today: Do deficits matter? Is there Ricardo-Barro equivalence? Are we really indifferent between taxes now and taxes later? We have amplified and developed this material to give an up-to-date evaluation of the arguments, the presumptions, and the empirical evidence.

International economic issues are now firmly part of macroeconomics. The "twin deficits," the dollar, and the crowding out brought about by an export boom are all topics that belong today in a balanced macroeconomics course. In a previous edition we already moved some of this material into an early chapter, rather than relegating it to those classes at the end of the semester that the instructor hopes to reach but never does. This edition develops the international perspective further and also offers comparisons of international data for key issues.

OTHER SIGNIFICANT IMPROVEMENTS

Data and case studies are essential in grasping what the macroeconomic issues are all about. Accordingly, we have now provided significantly more material of the case study variety in boxes and in the text. We have also added data appendixes for key chapters. These data allow students to go ahead and form their own judgment about the arguments advanced in the book.

If macroeconomics is in a state of flux, awareness of alternative approaches is important. We have not only stated and developed these in the text, but also go further by providing substantial bibliographical information. We refer in footnotes not only to literature of the very useful survey kind, but also to more difficult articles that mark the frontiers of current academic debate.

GENERAL APPROACH

As to our general approach, we repeat here what we said in the preface to earlier editions. We have remained faithful to our basic approach, presenting the relevant theory and at the same time showing both its empirical relevance and policy applications. We have, of course, stayed with our generally eclectic outlook on macroeconomics.

Although there are major changes from earlier editions, the book remains recognizably the same in that it develops, and teaches students to use, a broad-based, critical, and useful macroeconomics. Our overriding objective is to explain how modern macroeconomics is used in understanding important economic issues, and to help readers analyze macroeconomic issues for themselves. The book provides full coverage of all major topics in macroeconomics. No important topic has been omitted because it is too difficult, but we have taken great pains to make nothing more difficult than it need be.

TEACHING AIDS

An *Instructor's Manual* and *Test Bank* to accompany the text have been prepared by Professor Juergen Fleck of Hollins College. The *Instructor's Manual* has been substantially updated and includes chapter summaries, learning objectives, solutions to the end-of-chapter problems, and many additional problems (and their solutions) to be used for class discussion, homework assignments, or examination questions. The *Test Bank* has been expanded and now includes more than 750 questions. The *Study Guide* by Professor Richard Startz of the University of Washington, Seattle, has also been revised and brought up to date.

Also, there is now available a software program, *PC-Macroeconomics,* developed by Professors F. Gerard Adams and Eugene Kroch of the University of Pennsylvania, which provides an important tool to put macroeconomics in action. The software follows the sequencing in the text and patiently builds the analytical framework by using empirical data that allow students to understand macroeconomics in a step-by-step integration of text, data, and graphics. Students can either view the analysis in a demonstration mode, choose to interact within the parameters, or even change those parameters as desired. It uses the Lotus 1-2-3 application program (version 2.0 or higher) for IBM-PCs and most compatibles.

Ben Bernanke of Princeton, one of the profession's best teachers, has prepared a book of case studies and readings to accompany *Macroeconomics.*

ACKNOWLEDGMENTS

In writing this book in its various editions we have had much help from friends, present and former students, and colleagues who advised us on how to improve the book. We wish to thank especially Andrew Abel, Richard Anderson, Yves Balcer, Robert Bishop, Olivier Blanchard, Cary Brown, Eliana Cardoso, Jacques Cremer, Allen Drazen, Robert Feldman, Jeffrey Frankel, Jacob Frenkel, Ronald Jones, Paul Joskow, Edi Karni, Tim Kehoe, Don Patinkin, Robert Pindyck, Donald Richter, David Romer, Michael Rothschild, Paul Samuelson, Michael Schmid, Steven Sheffrin, Robert Solow, Richard Startz, Charles Steindel, Larry Summers, Peter Temin, Hal Varian, and Michael Veall.

Many readers and users of our book have given us the benefit of their teaching experience and particular suggestions. We would like to thank especially Eskarder Alvi, Joseph Aubareda, Alan Auerbach, Francis Bator, Samuel Bentolila, Frank Bonello, Thomas Bonsor, Hua-Cheng Chang, Carl Christ, David Colander, Giacomo Costa, Kevin Davis, Jim Devine, Akiva Dickstein, Clifford B. Donn, Paul Duda, Gerald V. Egerer, Robert Eisner, Liang-Shing Fang, George Feiwel, Rendigs Fels, Benjamin Friedman, Joanna Froyden, James Gale, Charles C. Gillete, Micha Gisser, Kalmon Goldberg, Stephen Goldfeld, Robert J. Gordon, Stephen Groninger, Nachum Gross, Joseph Guerin, John Haltiwanger, Raundi Halvorson, Dennis J. Hanseman, Brian Horrigan, O. Houkalehto, Mike Jacobson, James Johannes, Yoshiaki Kaoru, S. W. Kardasz, John Kareken, Pari Kasliwal, M. P. Kidd, David Laidler, Douglas Lamdin, Kathleen Langley, David Levhari, Stephen Lewis, Michael Lopez, Barry A. Love, David McClain, Jaime Marquez, Erwin Miller, Richard Miller, Douglas W. Mitchell, Masanori

Morita, Robert Murphy, John Naylor, Norman Obst, Edward Akiva Offenbacher, Athanasios Orphanides, Patricia Pando, Fai-Nan Perng, Lochlan H. Rose, Thomas Russell, Walter Salant, Robert Schenk, Edward Shapiro, Masaki Shinbo, Luigi Spaventa, Richard Startz, Edward Steinberg, Kirker Stevens, Houston Stokes, M.A. Taslim, Earl Thompson, James Tobin, Hal Varian, David H. Vrooman, Shinichi Watanabe, Ken West, Randy Williams, Moojin Yoo, and Jong S. You.

We owe a special debt to reviewers of various editions who prepared very detailed comments and suggestions. We would like to mention especially Roland Artle, Lloyd Atkinson, Michael Babcock, Ben Bernanke, Shirley Brow, the late Arnold Collery, Alan Deardorff, James Duga, Michael Edgmand, Don Heckerman, William Hosek, Timothy Kersten, Charles Knapp, Charles Lieberman, Thomas Mayer, Hajime Miyazaki, Andrew Policano, William Poole, Aris Protopapadakis, Steven Shapiro, and Stephen Van der Ploeg. McGraw-Hill and the authors would like to thank the following reviewers for their useful suggestions: George S. Bohler, Embry-Riddle Aeronautical University; William Dickens, University of California; Donald Dutkowsky, Syracuse University; David Findlay, Colby College; John Huizinga, University of Chicago; John T. Imness, Lehigh University; Beth Ingram, University of Iowa; and Daniel Richards, Tufts University.

Over the years we have enjoyed and benefited from the most competent and dedicated research assistance. We would like to thank particularly David Modest and Carl Shapiro, who helped us with the first two editions, and Michael Gavin and Patricia Mosser, who did the work for the third edition. Carolyn Dedutis, Nancy Johnson, Carol McIntire, Liz Walb, and Barbara Ventresco have at different times performed valiant and cheerful feats in handling drafts of chapters. For this edition we are grateful for the very generous assistance of Carol McIntire (once more), Caterina Nelson, and Athanasios Orphanides.

TO THE STUDENT

Macroeconomics is not cut and dried. There are disputes over basic issues — for instance, over whether the government should try actively to fight unemployment. That makes macroeconomics unsatisfying if you are looking for clear-cut, definite answers to all the economy's problems. But it should also make the subject more interesting because you have to think hard and critically about the material being presented.

Despite the disagreements, there is a substantial basic core of macroeconomics theory that we present in this book and that will continue to be useful in understanding the behavior of the economy. We have not hesitated to say where we think theories are incomplete, or where the evidence on a question is not yet decisive. But we have not hesitated, either, to describe the many areas in which macroeconomic theory does a good job of explaining the real world.

Because we have not shied away from important topics even if they are difficult, parts of the book require careful reading. There is no mathematics except simple algebra. Some of the analysis, however, involves sustained reasoning. Careful reading should therefore pay off in enhanced understanding. Chapter 1 gives you suggestions on how to learn from this book. The single most important suggestion is that you learn actively. Some of the chapters (such as Chapter 12) are suitable for bedtime reading, but most are not. Use pencil and paper to be sure you are following the argument. See if you can find reasons to disagree with arguments we make. Work the problem sets! Be sure you understand the points contained in the summaries to each chapter. Follow the economic news in the press, and see how that relates to what you are learning. Try to follow the logic of the budget or any economic packages the administration may present. Occasionally, the chairpersons of the Federal Reserve Board or the Council of Economic Advisers testify before Congress. Read what they have to say, and see if it makes sense to you.

A *Study Guide,* by Richard Startz of the University of Washington–Seattle, is available to accompany this edition. The *Study Guide* contains a wide range of questions, starting from the very easy and progressing in each chapter to material that will challenge the more advanced student. It is a great help in studying, particularly since active learning is so important in mastering new material. Also, *PC-Macroeconomics,* a software program that is new to this edition, is designed to give hands-on practice with empirical data and will be a valuable part of your learning experience.

Rudiger Dornbusch
Stanley Fischer

macroeconomics

part one

INTRODUCTION

M acroeconomics is concerned with the behavior of the economy as a whole — with booms and recessions, the economy's total output of goods and services and the growth of output, the rates of inflation and unemployment, the balance of payments, and exchange rates. Macroeconomics deals with the increase in output and employment over long periods of time — that is, economic growth — and with the short-run fluctuations that constitute the business cycle.

Macroeconomics focuses on the economic behavior and policies that affect consumption and investment, the dollar and the trade balance, the determinants of changes in wages and prices, monetary and fiscal policies, the money stock, the federal budget, interest rates, and the national debt. In brief, macroeconomics deals with the major economic issues and problems of the day.

Macroeconomics is interesting because it deals with important issues. But it is fascinating and challenging too, because it reduces complicated details of the economy to manageable essentials. *Those essentials lie in the interactions among the goods, labor, and assets markets of the economy and in the interactions among national economies that trade with each other.*

In dealing with the essentials, we go beyond details of the behavior of individual economic units, such as households and firms, or the determination of prices in particular markets. These are the subject matter of microeconomics. In macroeconomics we deal with the market for goods as a whole, treating all the markets for different goods — such as the markets for agricultural products and for medical services — as a single market. Similarly, we deal with the labor market as a whole, abstracting from differences between the markets for, say, migrant labor and doctors. We deal with the assets markets as a whole, abstracting from differences between the markets for IBM shares and for Rembrandt paintings. The cost of the abstraction is that omitted details sometimes matter. The benefit of the abstraction is increased understanding of the vital interactions among the goods, labor, and assets markets. Passing over the details of thousands of individual markets allows us to focus more clearly on these key markets.

Despite the contrast between macroeconomics and microeconomics, there is no conflict between them. On the contrary, the economy in the aggregate is nothing but the sum of its submarkets. The difference between microeconomics and macroeconomics is, therefore, primarily one of emphasis and exposition. In studying price determination in a single industry, it is convenient for microeconomists to assume that prices in other industries are given. In macroeconomics, in which we study the price level, it is for the most part sensible to ignore changes in relative prices of goods among different industries. In microeconomics, it is convenient to assume that the total income of all consumers is given and to then ask how consumers divide their spending of that income among different goods. In macroeconomics, by contrast, the aggregate level of income or spending is among the key variables to be studied.

The great macroeconomists have always enjoyed a keen interest in the application of macrotheory to policy. This was true in the case of John Maynard Keynes and is true of modern American leaders in the field, especially the older Nobel laureate generation, such as Milton Friedman of the University of Chicago and the Hoover Institution, Franco Modigliani and Robert Solow of the Massachusetts Institute of Technology, and James Tobin of Yale University. But even the younger leaders, such as Robert Barro and Martin Feldstein of Harvard University, Robert Lucas of the University of Chicago, and Robert Hall, Thomas Sargent, and John Taylor of Stanford University, despite being more — and in some cases altogether — skeptical about the wisdom of active government policies, do analyze policy issues. The fundamental questions are, *Can* the government and *should* the government intervene in the economy to improve its performance?

Indeed, developments in macrotheory are closely related to the economic problems of the day. *Keynesian* economics developed during the great depression of the 1930s and showed the way out of such depressions. *Monetarism* developed during the 1960s, promising a way of solving the inflation problem. *Supply-side economics* became the fad of the early 1980s, promising an easy way out of the economic mess of the time by cutting taxes. But supply-side economics overpromised, and there was no easy way out. Today an influential school of thought, led by Robert Lucas, questions the effectiveness of policy. Even so, the scope for and limits of policy remain at the center of debate. Beyond a questioning of policy effectiveness, the 1980s have also brought a renewed interest by macroeconomists in *economic growth*: The basic questions here are, What factors help explain the increase in a country's standard of living over time, and what role can economic policies play in speeding up economic progress?

Because macroeconomics is closely related to the economic problems of the day, it does not yield its greatest rewards to those whose primary interest is theoretical. The need for compromise between the comprehensiveness of the theory and its manageability inevitably makes macrotheory a little untidy at the edges. And the emphasis in macroeconomics is on the manageability of the theory and on its applications. This book uses macroeconomics to illuminate economic events from the great depression through the 1980s. We refer continually to real world events to elucidate the meaning and the relevance of the theoretical material.

1-1 CONTROVERSIES AND THE RESEARCH AGENDA

There are three central issues on the research agenda in macroeconomics. First, how do we explain periods of high and persistent unemployment? For example, in the 1930s unemployment was over 20 percent for several years, and the postwar period has also seen high unemployment rates on several occasions. In the United States, unemployment reached 10.6 percent in 1982 and averaged nearly 9 percent from 1982 to 1984; by early 1989 the unemployment rate was down to 5 percent. Several European economies, including the United Kingdom and France, suffered double-digit unemployment during much of the eighties.

Macroeconomic research focuses on persistent unemployment as a central question. There are many theories of why persistent high unemployment is possible, and we shall develop the most important in this book. There is also the research question of what should be done about unemployment. Some say not much: that the government should put in place appropriate unemployment compensation schemes[1] and otherwise not undertake any special policies — for instance, cutting taxes — to deal with unemployment. This view, which may seem extraordinary to someone new to economics (and even to someone who has spent a life in the field), is maintained, for example, by Robert Lucas, one of the leaders in the profession.[2] Others argue that the government should pursue an active fiscal policy, for instance by cutting taxes and/or raising government spending when unemployment is high.

A second major research issue is how to explain inflation: Why did prices in the United States rise by more than 10 percent a year in 1979 and 1980, and by less than 2 percent in 1986? And what causes hyperinflations, when prices rise by more than 1,000 percent per year, as for instance, the more than 11,000 percent increase in prices in Bolivia in 1985? The policy issues here are how to keep inflation low; and, if it is high, how to reduce it without raising unemployment.

The third major research question is, What determines the rate of growth of output? Why has output per person risen more or less steadily in the United States at an annual rate of 1.7 percent, doubling every 40 years? And why has output grown more rapidly in Japan than in the United States over the past century? Will the Japanese economy keep growing more rapidly than the U.S. economy when income per person reaches the U.S. level — as, by some measures, it already has?

---

[1] That is, schemes that make some payments to unemployed workers as compensation to them for losing their jobs; the worker is required to look for a new job, and the compensation usually lasts for a specified period, such as 26 weeks. After that if the worker still does not have a job and needs income, he or she has to go on welfare.

[2] See Robert Lucas, *Models of Business Cycles* (Oxford, England: Basil Blackwell, 1987).

The questions of whether the government *can* and *should* do something about unemployment and *what* is best to do have been at the center of macroeconomics for a long time. These questions continue to divide the profession, and every generation develops its own debate, reinterpreting past events, such as the great depression of the 1930s and more recent episodes. Similarly, views about inflation differ among economists. Some believe that inflation can be controlled by keeping money growth low and that the way to stop rapid inflation is to stop the money growth that certainly accompanies the inflation; others argue that the links between money and inflation are at best imprecise, and that merely cutting money growth in a high inflation economy will also cause a recession that could be avoided by more sophisticated policies. There are still many unresolved questions but fewer controversies about the causes of growth.

We introduce here briefly the major schools of thought. In doing so we must bear in mind that while the unemployment, inflation, and growth issues are central problems of macroeconomics, there are many others, important and less so. Among the important issues are the international dimensions of macroeconomics, as the world economy becomes increasingly integrated and a stock market crash one day in New York spreads almost instantly to London, Tokyo, Frankfurt, Sydney, Hong Kong, Mexico City, and every other stock market. Among the apparently less important issues is the question of why wages are so "sticky," why they change slowly, rather than quickly as does the price of fish. But even the answers to such an apparently unimportant question may help in understanding how unemployment can emerge.

Schools of Thought

There have long been two main intellectual traditions in macroeconomics. One school of thought believes that markets work best if left to themselves; another believes that government intervention can significantly improve the operation of the economy. In the 1960s, the debate on these questions involved *monetarists,* led by Milton Friedman, on one side and *Keynesians,* including Franco Modigliani and James Tobin, on the other side. In the 1970s, the debate on much the same issues brought to the fore a new group — the *new classical macroeconomists.*

THE NEW CLASSICAL SCHOOL

The new classical macroeconomics, which developed in the 1970s, remained influential in the 1980s. This school of macroeconomics, which includes among its leaders Robert Lucas, Thomas Sargent, Robert Barro, and Edward Prescott and Neil Wallace of the University of Minnesota, shares many policy views with Friedman. It sees the world as one in which individuals act rationally in their self-interest in markets that adjust rapidly to changing conditions. The government, it is claimed, is likely only to make things worse by intervening. That model is a challenge to traditional macroeconomics, which sees a role for useful government action in an economy that is viewed as adjusting sluggishly, with slowly adjusting prices, poor information, and social customs impeding the rapid clearing of markets.

The central working assumptions of the new classical school are three:

- Economic agents *maximize*. Households and firms make *optimal* decisions. This means that they use all available information in reaching decisions and that those decisions are the best possible in the circumstances in which they find themselves.

- Decisions are *rational* and are made using all the relevant information. Expectations are rational when they are statistically the best predictions of the future that can be made using the available information. Indeed, the new classical school is sometimes described as the *rational expectations school*, even though rational expectations is only one part of the theoretical approach of the new classical economists.[3] The rational expectations implication is that people eventually will come to understand whatever government policy is being used, and thus that it is not possible to fool most of the people all the time or even most of the time.

- *Markets clear*. There is no reason why firms or workers would not adjust wages or prices if that would make them better off. Accordingly prices and wages adjust in order to equate supply and demand; in other words, markets clear. Market clearing is a powerful assumption, as we shall see presently.

One dramatic implication of these assumptions, which seem so reasonable individually, is that there is no possibility for *involuntary* unemployment. Any unemployed person who really wants a job will offer to cut his or her wage until the wage is low enough to attract an offer from some employer. Similarly, anyone with an excess supply of goods on the shelf will cut prices so as to sell. Flexible adjustment of wages and prices leaves all individuals *all the time* in a situation in which they work as much as they want and firms produce as much as they want.

The essence of the rational expectations equilibrium approach is the assumption that markets are continuously in equilibrium. In particular, new classical macroeconomists regard as incomplete or unsatisfactory any theory that leaves open the possibility that private individuals could make themselves better off by trading among themselves. As Lucas put it, "there are no $50 bills lying on the sidewalk," meaning that if there were ways in which individuals could improve their material position, they would do so.

Adherents of the new classical school do not doubt that the great depression did take place, and they recognize that the measured unemployment rate occasionally reaches more than 10 percent. Their explanations for these observations, which are consistent with the view that people are at all times doing what is best for them, will be discussed in Chapter 13.

---

[3] Many economists who are not members of the new classical school assume that expectations are rational.

THE NEW KEYNESIANS

The new classical group remains highly influential in today's macroeconomics. But a new generation of scholars, the *new Keynesians,* mostly trained in the Keynesian tradition but moving beyond it, has emerged in the 1980s. The group includes among others George Akerlof and Janet Yellen of the University of California–Berkeley, Olivier Blanchard of the Massachusetts Institute of Technology, Greg Mankiw and Larry Summers of Harvard, and Ben Bernanke of Princeton University. They do not believe that markets clear all the time but seek to understand and explain exactly why markets can fail.

The new Keynesians argue that markets sometimes do not clear even when individuals are looking out for their own interests. Both information problems and costs of changing prices lead to some price rigidities and, as a result, create a possibility for macroeconomic fluctuations in output and employment. For example, in the labor market, firms that cut wages not only reduce the cost of labor, but are also likely to wind up with a poorer-quality labor force. Thus they will be reluctant to cut wages. If it is costly for firms to change the prices they charge and the wages they pay, the changes will be infrequent; but if all firms adjust prices and wages infrequently, the economy-wide level of wages and prices may not be flexible enough to avoid occasional periods of even high unemployment.

ECONOMIC CONTROVERSY

This description of the two main strands in macroeconomics may suggest that the field is little more than the battleground between implacably opposed schools of thought. There is no denying that there are conflicts of opinion and even theory between different camps. And because macroeconomics is about the real world, the differences that exist are sure to be highlighted in political and media discussions of economic policy.

It is also the case, though, that there are significant areas of agreement and that the different groups, through discussion and research, continually evolve new areas of consensus and a sharper idea of where precisely the differences lie. For instance, there is now a consensus emerging on the importance of information problems for wage and price setting and economic fluctuations. In this book we do not emphasize the debate, preferring to discuss the substantive matters, but we do indicate alternative views of an issue whenever that is relevant.

In the remainder of this chapter we present an overview of the key concepts with which macroeconomics deals. Section 1-2 examines key concepts: output, prices, growth, and inflation. Relationships among the main macroeconomic variables are discussed in Section 1-3. Section 1-4 presents a diagrammatic introduction to aggregate demand and supply and their interaction; it gives a very general perspective on the fundamentals of macroeconomics and the organization of this book. Section 1-5 introduces stabilization policy. Then, in Section 1-6, we outline the approach of the book to the study of macroeconomics and of macropolicy making and present a preview of the order in which topics are taken up. Section 1-7 contains brief remarks on how to use the book.

1-2 KEY CONCEPTS

Gross National Product

Gross national product (GNP) is the value of all final goods and services produced in the economy in a given time period (quarter or year). GNP is the basic measure of economic activity.

Three important distinctions must be made:

- *Nominal* versus *real* GNP
- *Levels* of GNP, nominal or real, versus the *growth* of GNP
- GNP versus GNP *per capita*

We now examine each of these distinctions. Figure 1-1 shows two measures of GNP — *nominal,* or *current dollar,* GNP and *real,* or *constant dollar,* GNP.[4] Nominal GNP measures the value of output at the prices prevailing in the period during which the output is produced, while real GNP measures the output produced in any one period at the prices of some base year. Real GNP, which values the output produced in different years at the *same* prices, implies an estimate of the real or physical change in production or output between any specified years. At present, 1982 serves as the base year for real output measurement, but the base year will be changed to 1987 in 1990.

In Table 1-1, nominal GNP is equal to $4,864 billion in 1988 and $1,598 billion in 1975 (see, too, Figure 1-1). Thus nominal GNP grew at an average rate of 8.9 percent during the period 1975–1988. Real GNP was $3,996 billion in 1988 and $2,695 billion in 1975, implying an average annual growth rate of real GNP of only 3.1 percent per year over the period.

Another measure of real GNP looks at income *per capita*, adjusting the value of output by the size of the population. If we divide total real GNP by population — 246 million people in 1988 — we obtain *per capita* real GNP, which was $16,244 per member of the population.

INFLATION AND NOMINAL GNP

Figure 1-1 shows that nominal GNP has risen much more rapidly than real GNP. The difference between the growth rates of real and nominal GNP occurs because the prices of goods have been rising, or there has been *inflation.* The inflation rate is the percentage rate of increase of the level of prices during a given period.

Real GNP grew at an average annual rate of 3.1 percent over the 13 years from 1975 to 1988, while nominal GNP grew at an average annual rate of 8.9 percent.

---

[4] Notice that the scale for GNP in Fig. 1-1 is not linear. The scale is logarithmic, which means that equal ratios are represented by equal distances. For instance, the distance from 900 to 1,800 is the same as the distance from 1,200 to 2,400, since GNP doubles in both cases. On a logarithmic scale, a variable growing at a constant rate (e.g., 4 percent per annum) is represented by a straight line.

Because real GNP is calculated holding the prices of goods constant, the difference is entirely due to inflation, or rising prices. Over the 13-year period, prices were on average rising at 5.8 percent per year. In other words, the average rate of inflation over that period was 5.8 percent per year.

With 1982 as the base year for the prices at which output is valued, we observe in Figure 1-1 two implications of the distinction between nominal and real GNP. First, in 1982 the two are equal, because in the base year, current and constant dollars are the same. Second, with inflation, nominal GNP rises faster than real GNP, and therefore, after 1982, nominal GNP exceeds real GNP. The converse is, of course, true before 1982.

FIGURE 1-1

REAL AND NOMINAL GNP, 1960–1988. Nominal GNP measures the output of final goods and services produced in the economy in a given period, using the prices of that period. Real GNP measures the value of the output using the prices of a *given* year, in this case 1982. Nominal GNP has risen more rapidly than real GNP because prices have been rising. (SOURCE: DRI/McGraw-Hill.)

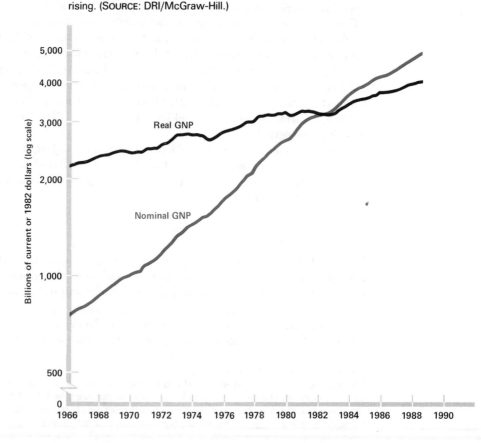

TABLE 1-1
ALTERNATIVE MEASURES OF GNP (dollars in billions)

	Nominal GNP	Real GNP*	Per capita real GNP*
1975	$1,598	$2,695	$12,479
1982	3,166	3,166	13,617
1988	4,864	3,996	16,244
Growth rate per year, 1975–1988	8.9%	3.1%	2.0%

* Measured in 1982 prices.

SOURCE: DRI/McGraw-Hill.

GROWTH AND REAL GNP

We turn next to the reasons for the growth of real GNP. The *growth rate* of the economy is the rate at which real GNP is increasing. Anytime we refer to growth or the growth rate without any other qualifying word, we mean the growth rate of real GNP. On average, most economies grow by a few percentage points per year over long periods. For instance, U.S. real GNP grew at an average rate of 3.1 percent per year from 1960 to 1988. But this growth has certainly not been smooth, as Figure 1-1 confirms.

What causes real GNP to grow over time? The first reason real GNP changes is that the available amount of resources in the economy changes. The resources are conveniently split into capital and labor. The labor force, consisting of people either working or looking for work, grows over time and thus provides one source of increased production. The capital stock, including buildings and machines, likewise has been rising over time, providing another source of increased output. Increases in the availability of factors of production—the labor and capital used in the production of goods and services—thus account for part of the increase in real GNP.

The second reason for real GNP to change is that the efficiency with which factors of production work may change.[5] Over time, the same factors of production can produce more output. These increases in the efficiency of production result from changes in knowledge, including learning by doing, as people learn through experience to perform familiar tasks better.

Table 1-2 shows a comparison of growth rates of real per capita income in different countries. Studies of the sources of growth across countries and history seek to explain which factors make a country like Brazil grow very rapidly, while Ghana, for example, has had very little growth. Ghana's income in 1980 was only 20 percent

---

[5] These efficiency improvements are called productivity increases.

TABLE 1-2
PER CAPITA REAL INCOME GROWTH RATES,
1913–1980 (average annual growth rate)

Country	Growth rate	Country	Growth rate
Argentina	1.1	India	0.6
Brazil	2.9	Spain	1.9
China	1.5	U.K.	1.4
France	2.2	U.S.	1.7
Ghana	0.3		

SOURCE: A. Maddison, "A Comparison of GDP Per Capita Income Levels in Developed and Developing Countries, 1700–1980," *Journal of Economic History*, March 1983, table 2.

higher than in 1913, while Brazil's income had increased more than fivefold. Obviously, it would be well worth knowing what policies, if any, can raise a country's average growth rate over long periods of time.

Employment and Unemployment

The third source of change in real GNP is a change in the employment of the given resources available for production. Not all the capital and labor available to the economy is actually used at all times.

The *unemployment rate* is the fraction of the labor force that cannot find jobs. For example, in 1982, a reduction in the employment of labor, or a rise in unemployment, shows up in Figure 1-1 as a fall in real GNP. Indeed, in that year unemployment rose to 10.6 percent, the highest unemployment rate in the post-World War II period. More than one person out of every ten who wanted to work could not find a job. Such unemployment levels had not been experienced since the great depression of the 1930s.

Inflation, Growth, and Unemployment: The Record

Macroeconomic performance is judged by the three broad measures we have introduced: the *inflation* rate, the *growth* rate of output, and the rate of *unemployment*. News of these three variables makes the headlines because these issues affect our daily lives. They also dominate the research agenda in macroeconomics.

During periods of inflation, the prices of goods people buy are rising. Partly for this reason, inflation is unpopular, even if people's incomes rise along with the prices. Inflation is also unpopular because it is often associated with other disturbances to the economy — such as the oil price increases of the 1970s — that would make people worse off even if there were no inflation. Inflation is frequently a major political issue, as it was, for instance, in the 1980 presidential election between Jimmy Carter and Ronald Reagan, when the high rate of inflation contributed to Reagan's victory. And again, in 1988, low inflation (and high growth over several years) helped the election of President Bush.

When the growth rate is high, the production of goods and services is rising, making possible an increased standard of living. With the high growth rate typically go lower unemployment and the availability of more jobs. High growth is a target and hope of most societies.

The growth rate of real GNP per person is the most important of all the macroeconomic indicators by which to judge the economy's long-run performance. Per capita GNP doubles every 35 years if it grows at 2 percent per year. In that case, each generation could look forward to a material standard of living double that of its parents. If per capita GNP grows at only 1 percent per annum, it takes 70 years to double. Over long periods, small differences in growth rates thus mount up to big differences in the standard of living that a country can achieve.

High unemployment rates are a major social problem. Jobs are difficult to find. The unemployed suffer a loss in their standard of living, personal distress, and sometimes a lifetime deterioration in their career opportunities. When unemployment reaches double-digit percentages — and even well short of that — it becomes the number-one social and political issue.

Macroeconomic Performance, 1952–1989

Table 1-3 shows that economic performance in the United States deteriorated sharply from the decade of the sixties to the seventies. Inflation and unemployment increased, and growth fell.

TABLE 1-3
MACROECONOMIC PERFORMANCE, 1952–1989

Period	Inflation, % p.a.	Growth, % p.a.	Unemployment rate, % of the labor force
1952–1962	1.3	2.9	5.1
1962–1972	3.3	4.0	4.7
1972–1982	8.7	2.2	7.0
1981–1982	6.1	−1.9	9.7
1982–1989	3.6	3.8	7.2

NOTE: Unemployment rate is average of rates for years shown; inflation rate is for CPI, year over year; "p.a." means per annum.

SOURCE: *Economic Report of the President, 1989* and DRI/McGraw-Hill.

The table also shows the radical change in inflation performance since 1982. As the economy recovered from high unemployment in 1981–1982, the unemployment rate began to fall, growth increased, and inflation stayed low for some time. Many hoped that the economy was in for another high-growth, low-inflation decade like the sixties. Collapsing oil prices in 1985–1986 reinforced that expectation. Indeed, until 1988, when unemployment had declined to as little as 5 percent, inflation was not a major issue. But by 1989 the inflation issue was back. Even so, the period from 1982 to 1989 was more like the sixties than the seventies.

As we develop macroeconomics in this book, we are looking for answers to the questions that recent macroeconomic performance raises. Why did the inflation rate rise from the fifties to the seventies and then fall rapidly? Will the growth rate return to the high levels of the sixties? Can the unemployment rate be reduced below 5 percent? And, of course, what economic policies, if any, can produce low inflation, low unemployment, and high growth all at the same time?

The Business Cycle and the Output Gap

Inflation, growth, and unemployment are related through the *business cycle*. The business cycle is the more or less regular pattern of expansion (recovery) and contraction (recession) in economic activity around the path of trend growth. At a cyclical *peak*, economic activity is high relative to trend; and at a cyclical *trough*, the low point in economic activity is reached. Inflation, growth, and unemployment all have clear cyclical patterns, as we will show below. For the moment we concentrate on measuring the behavior of output or real GNP relative to trend over the business cycle.

The black line in Figure 1-2 shows the trend path of real GNP. The trend path of GNP is the path GNP would take if factors of production were fully employed. Over time, real GNP will change for two reasons, as we already noted. First, more resources become available: The size of the population increases, firms acquire machinery or build plants, land is improved for cultivation, the stock of knowledge increases as new goods and new methods of production are invented and introduced. This increased availability of resources allows the economy to produce more goods and services, resulting in a rising trend level of output.

But, second, factors are not fully employed all the time. Full employment of factors of production is an economic, not a physical, concept. Physically, labor is fully employed if everyone is working 16 hours per day all year. In economic terms, there is full employment of labor when everyone who wants a job can find one within a reasonable amount of time. Because the economic definition is not precise, we typically define full employment of labor by some convention, for example, that labor is fully employed when the unemployment rate is 5.5 percent. Capital similarly is never fully employed in a physical sense; for example, office buildings or lecture rooms, which are part of the capital stock, are used only part of the day.

Output is not always at its trend level, that is, the level corresponding to (economic) full employment of the factors of production. Rather output fluctuates around the trend level. During an *expansion* (or *recovery*) the *employment* of factors of

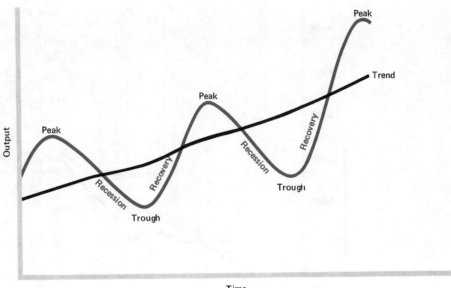

FIGURE 1-2

THE BUSINESS CYCLE. Output, or GNP, does not grow at its trend rate. Rather, it fluctuates irregularly around trend, showing business cycle patterns from trough through recovery to peak, and then from peak through recession and back to the trough. Business cycle output movements are not regular in timing or in size. Nor is the trend growth rate constant; it varies with changes in technical knowledge and the growth of supplies of factors of production.

production increases, and that is a source of increased production. Output can rise above trend because people work overtime and machinery is used for several shifts. Conversely, during a *recession* unemployment develops and less output is produced than can in fact be produced with the existing resources and technology. The wavy line in Figure 1-2 shows these cyclical departures of output from trend. Deviations of output from trend are referred to as the *output gap*. The output gap measures the gap between actual output and the output the economy could produce at full employment given the existing resources. Full-employment output is also called *potential output*.

$$\text{Output gap} \equiv \text{potential output} - \text{actual output} \qquad (1)$$

The output gap allows us to measure the size of the cyclical deviations of output from potential output or trend output (we use these terms interchangeably). Figure 1-3

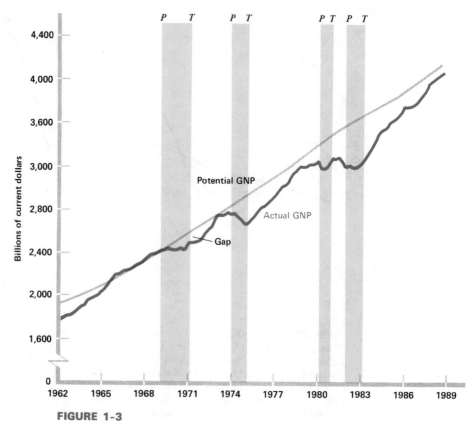

FIGURE 1-3

ACTUAL AND POTENTIAL OUTPUT, 1960–1988. Potential output is the full-employment level of output. It grows like trend output in Figure 1-2. Actual GNP fluctuates around potential, falling below during recession, and rising up toward the potential level during recoveries. Shaded areas represent recessions. (SOURCE: DRI/McGraw-Hill.)

shows actual and potential output for the United States. The shaded lines represent recessions, with the letters *P* and *T* denoting cyclical peaks and troughs.[6]

The figure shows that the output gap grows during a recession, such as in 1982. More resources become unemployed, and actual output falls below potential output. Conversely, during an expansion, most strikingly in the long expansion of the 1960s, the gap declines and ultimately even becomes negative. A negative gap means that there is overemployment, overtime for workers, and more than the usual rate of

---

[6] Dating of the business cycle is done by the National Bureau of Economic Research (NBER). The NBER is a private, nonprofit research organization based in Cambridge, Massachusetts.

utilization of machinery. It is worth noting that the gap is sometimes very sizable. For example, in 1982 it amounted to as much as 10 percent.

Establishing the level of potential output is a difficult problem. In the 1960s it was believed that full employment corresponded to a measured rate of unemployment of 4 to 4.5 percent of the labor force. Changes in the composition of the labor force including increases in the proportion of younger workers and female workers, who change jobs more frequently, raised the estimate of the full-employment rate of unemployment to a range around 5.5 percent in the 1980s.

The potential output data are calculated in a number of ways. One procedure, used by the Bureau of Economic Analysis (BEA) of the U.S. Department of Commerce, identifies as potential GNP the level of output that would exist if the unemployment rate were 6 percent. The series is a benchmark for calculating what potential output or full-employment output is, but it is only a benchmark, not a rigid, undebatable rule. Even so, the GNP gap provides an important indicator of how the economy is performing and in which direction policies should try to move the economy's level of activity.[7] Other series use different benchmark unemployment rates, some as low as 5 percent. In the series shown in Figure 1-3, for example, in 1988 the economy still has a positive gap — potential output exceeds actual output by 2.2 percent — even though the unemployment rate averaged 5.5 percent.[8] Differences among various estimates of potential output highlight the fact that there is no precise measure of full employment. An important part of the difference in estimates is the result not only of the benchmark unemployment rate used but also of judgments about the extent of capacity utilization that corresponds to full employment of plant and equipment.

Much of recent history can be read from the GNP gap. In the Kennedy-Johnson years (1961 – 1968) the output gap declined under the impact of expansionary government policies. The policies were successful in reducing the gap, but did so at the cost of building up inflationary pressures. The first Nixon administration (1969 – 1973) inherited this inflation problem and decided to fight it by tight policies that led to a recession and thus a growing gap. In 1972 – 1973, highly expansionary monetary policies of the Federal Reserve System led to recovery and even overemployment; these are shown by a near-zero gap, with actual output equaling potential output. In 1973 – 1974, tight policies together with the huge increases in oil prices threw the economy into a deep recession. Recovery in the 1976 – 1979 period was too fast and led to sharp increases in inflation.

With another rapid rise in oil prices in 1979, inflation had come to exceed 10 percent by 1980, and again tight policies drove the unemployment rate steadily upward. By mid-1989, the economy was back to full employment, and there were signs of a resurgence of inflation. At that point, the recovery had been under way for nearly 34 quarters, since the fall of 1982. The longest previous postwar expansion was that of 1962 – 1969, which had lasted 38 quarters. The question that naturally arises is

---

[7] The BEA does not use the term *potential output* so that the bureau will not be seen as suggesting that the economy *should* have a 6 percent unemployment rate.

[8] The estimate of potential output in Fig. 1-3 is calculated by DRI/McGraw-Hill.

whether expansions succumb inevitably to old age, or whether they are instead brought to an end by policy mistakes. As we shall see, often a long expansion reduces unemployment too much, causes inflationary pressures, and therefore triggers policies to fight inflation — and such policies usually create recessions.

1-3 RELATIONSHIPS AMONG MACROECONOMIC VARIABLES

The preliminary look at the data presented above and our discussion of the business cycle suggest — correctly — that we should expect to find simple relationships among the major macroeconomic variables of growth, unemployment, and inflation. There are indeed such relationships, as we now document.

Growth and Unemployment

We have already noted that changes in the employment of factors of production provide one of the sources of growth in real GNP. We would then expect high GNP growth to be accompanied by declining unemployment. That is indeed the case, as we observe from Figure 1-4. On the vertical axis, Figure 1-4 shows the growth rate of real output in a particular year, and on the horizontal axis the change in the unemployment rate in that year. For example, in 1984, the growth rate of output was 6.8 percent and the reduction in the unemployment rate was 2.1 percentage points. Thus we plot the point labeled 1984 in the upper left-hand region. That region corresponds to a period of expansion and falling unemployment rates.

By contrast, in the lower right-hand region, points such as those labeled 1980 and 1982 are periods of recession — low growth and rising unemployment rates. Note that even when there is some growth, such as in 1981, unemployment rates may be rising. It takes growth rates above about 2.5 percent to cause unemployment rates to come down. The year 1984 stands out as having the most rapid growth and largest reduction in unemployment in 20 years.

OKUN'S LAW

A relationship between real growth and changes in the unemployment rate is known as *Okun's law*, named after its discoverer, the late Arthur Okun of the Brookings Institution, former chairperson of the Council of Economic Advisers (CEA). Okun's law says that the unemployment rate declines when growth is above the trend rate of 2.5 percent. Specifically, for every percentage point of growth in real GNP above the trend rate that is sustained for a year, the unemployment rate declines by 0.4 percentage points. This relationship is stated in equation (2) where Δu denotes the change in the unemployment rate, y is the growth rate of output, and 2.5 is the trend growth of output. To show the use of the formula, suppose growth in a given year is 4 percent. That would imply an unemployment rate reduction of 0.52 [$= 0.4(4 - 2.7)$] percentage points.

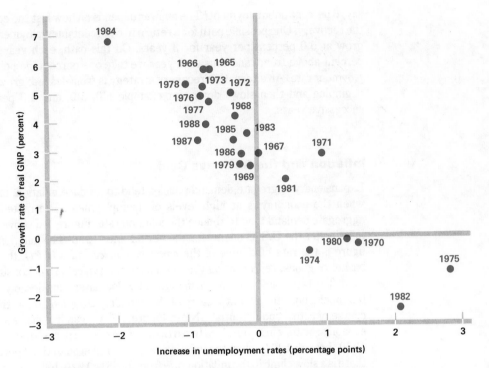

FIGURE 1-4

GROWTH AND THE CHANGE IN THE UNEMPLOYMENT RATE, 1962–1988.
High rates of growth cause the unemployment rate to fall, and low or
negative rates of growth are accompanied by increases in the
unemployment rate. The relationship shown by the scatter of the points
in this figure is summarized by *Okun's law*, which links the growth rate
to the change in the unemployment rate.

$$\Delta u = -0.4(y - 2.5) \tag{2}$$

The formula can also be used to ask how much growth is required to reduce the unemployment rate by one percentage point. The answer is 5 percent [$-1 = -0.4(5 - 2.5)$]. With 7.5 percent growth maintained for a year, the unemployment rate would be cut by two percentage points. Okun's law, the status of which is somewhat exaggerated by calling it a law rather than an empirical regularity, provides a rule of thumb for assessing the implications of real growth for unemployment. While the rule is only approximate and will not work very precisely from year to year, it still gives a sensible translation from growth to unemployment.

Okun's law is a useful guide to policy because it allows us to ask how a particular growth target will affect the unemployment rate over time. Suppose we were in a deep recession with 9 percent unemployment. How many years would it take us to return to, say, 6 percent unemployment? The answer depends on how fast the economy grows in the recovery. One possible path for a return to 6 percent unemployment is for output to grow at 5.0 percent per year for 3 years. On this path, each year we grow at 2.5 percent above trend, and thus each year we take one percentage point off the unemployment rate. An alternative recovery strategy is front-loaded: growth is high at the beginning and then slows down, for example 6.0, 5.0, and 4.0 percent growth in successive years.

Inflation and the Business Cycle

Expansionary aggregate demand policies tend to produce inflation, unless they occur when the economy is at high levels of unemployment. Protracted periods of low aggregate demand tend to reduce the inflation rate. Figure 1-5 shows one measure of inflation for the U.S. economy for the period since 1960. The inflation measure in the figure is the rate of change of the *consumer price index* (*CPI*), the cost of a given basket of goods, representing the purchases of a typical urban consumer.[9]

The rate of inflation shown in Figure 1-5 fluctuates considerably. Just as we could tell much about the recent history of the economy from looking at the picture of the course of actual and potential GNP in Figure 1-3, we can likewise see much of recent economic history in Figure 1-5. In particular, there is the period of steady inflation from 1960 through 1964, when the inflation rate hovered around the 2 percent level. Then there is a slow climb in the inflation rate from 1965 to 1970, followed by a slowing down till mid-1972. And finally there are the inflationary bursts from 1972 to 1974 and 1978 to 1981 as the inflation rate rose to 12 percent and above. In 1982–1983 inflation was again down, under the impact of a deep recession. This time, into 1987, the inflation rate stayed low even as the economy grew fast out of the recession. Only by 1989 was the inflation rate back to 5 percent.

Figure 1-5 shows the *rate of increase* of prices. We can also look at the *level* of prices. All the inflation of the 1960s and 1970s adds up to a large increase in the price level. In the period from 1960 to 1989, the price level more than quadrupled. A product that cost $1 in 1960 cost $4.19 by 1989. Most of that increase in prices took place after the early 1970s.

Inflation, like unemployment, is a major macroeconomic problem. However, the costs of inflation are much less obvious than those of unemployment. In the case of unemployment, potential output is going to waste, and it is therefore clear why the reduction of unemployment is desirable. In the case of inflation, there is no obvious loss of output. As we noted above, consumers in part dislike inflation because it is often associated with disturbances, such as the oil price shocks, that reduce their real incomes. It is also argued that inflation upsets familiar price relationships and reduces the efficiency of the price system. Whatever the reasons, policy makers have been

---

[9] By contrast, the measure of inflation obtained in Fig. 1-1 by comparing nominal and real GNP is the rate of change of the *GNP deflator*. The CPI rate of inflation is the most frequently used, and the GNP deflator is the next most popular. Chapter 2 presents more details on the different price indexes.

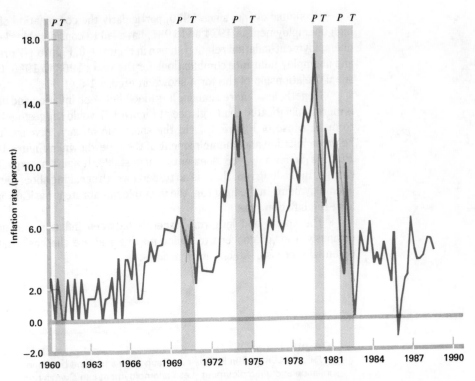

FIGURE 1-5
THE RATE OF INFLATION IN CONSUMER PRICES, 1960–1988. The inflation
rate falls during and after recessions, and then—over the period
shown—tends to rise later in the recovery. (SOURCE: DRI/McGraw-Hill.)

willing to increase unemployment in an effort to reduce inflation—that is, to trade off
some unemployment for less inflation.

Inflation-Unemployment Tradeoffs

The *Phillips curve* describes an empirical relationship between wage and price inflation and unemployment: the higher the rate of unemployment, the lower the rate of
inflation. It was made famous in the 1950s in Great Britain and has since become a
cornerstone of macroeconomic discussion. Figure 1-6 presents a typical downward-
sloping Phillips curve showing that high rates of unemployment are accompanied by
low rates of inflation and vice versa. The curve suggests that less unemployment can
always be attained by incurring more inflation and that the inflation rate can always be
reduced by incurring the costs of more unemployment. In other words, the curve
suggests there is a tradeoff between inflation and unemployment.

Economic events since 1970, particularly the combination of high inflation and high unemployment in 1974 and 1981, have led to considerable skepticism about the unemployment-inflation relation shown in Figure 1-6. Figure 1-7 presents the inflation and unemployment rate combinations for the years 1963 to 1985. Clearly, there is no simple relationship of the form shown in Figure 1-6.

Nonetheless, there remains a tradeoff between inflation and unemployment that is more sophisticated than a glance at Figure 1-6 would suggest and that will enable us to make sense of Figure 1-7. In the short run of, say, 2 years, there is a relation between inflation and unemployment of the type shown in Figure 1-6. The *short-run Phillips curve*, however, does not remain stable. It shifts as expectations of inflation change. In the long run, there is no tradeoff worth speaking about between inflation and unemployment. In the long run, the unemployment rate is basically independent of the long-run inflation rate.

The short- and long-run tradeoffs between inflation and unemployment are obviously a major concern of policy making and are the basic determinants of the potential success of stabilization policies.

FIGURE 1-6

A PHILLIPS CURVE. The Phillips curve suggests a tradeoff between inflation and unemployment: Less unemployment can always be obtained by incurring more inflation — or inflation can be reduced by allowing more unemployment. The combination of high inflation *and* high unemployment in years such as 1975 and 1981 led to skepticism about the Phillips curve. It nonetheless remains useful, as we shall show later.

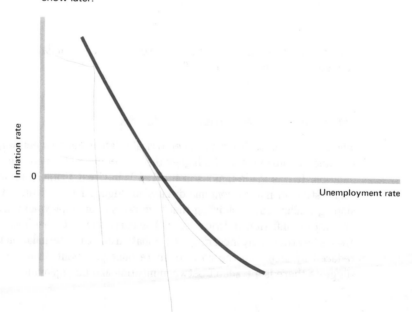

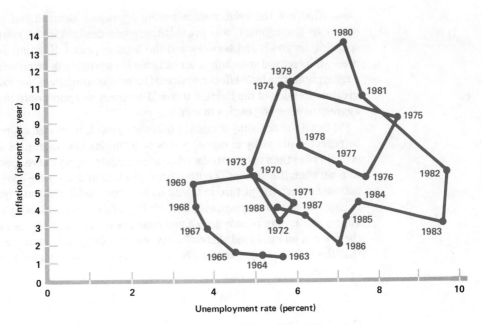

FIGURE 1-7

INFLATION AND UNEMPLOYMENT, 1960–1988. The actual history of
inflation and unemployment in the United States since 1960 shows no
simple Phillips curve relationship. There are periods, for instance,
1963–1969, 1976–1979, and 1980–1982, that fit the general shape
of the Phillips curve, but in between there are periods when inflation
and unemployment both increase or sometimes (e.g., 1984–1985)
decrease.

1-4 AGGREGATE DEMAND AND SUPPLY

The key overall concepts in analyzing output, inflation, growth, and the role of policy
are *aggregate demand* and *aggregate supply*. In this section we provide a brief preview
of those concepts and of their interaction, with the aims of showing where we are
heading.

The level of output and the price level are determined by the interaction of
aggregate demand and aggregate supply. Under some conditions, employment depends only on total spending, or aggregate demand. At other times, supply limitations
are an important part of the policy problem and have to receive major attention. From
the 1930s to the later 1960s, macroeconomics was very much demand-oriented.

But in recent years the emphasis has shifted, and aggregate supply and *supply-
side economics* have gained in importance. This shift of emphasis and interest was no
doubt fostered by the slow growth and high inflation experienced by the industrialized
countries in the 1970s.

What are the relationships among aggregate demand and aggregate supply, output or employment, and prices? Aggregate demand is the relationship between spending on goods and services and the level of prices. If output limitations are not present, increased spending or an increase in aggregate demand will raise output and employment with little effect on prices. Under such conditions, for example, during the great depression of the thirties, it would certainly be appropriate to use expansionary aggregate demand policies to increase output.

But if the economy is close to full employment, increased aggregate demand will be reflected primarily in higher prices or inflation. The aggregate supply side of the economy has then to be introduced. The aggregate supply curve specifies the relationship between the amount of output firms produce and the price level. The supply side not only enters the picture in telling us how successful demand expansions will be in raising output and employment, but also has a role of its own. Supply disturbances, or *supply shocks*, can reduce output and raise prices, as was the case in the 1970s when the price of oil increased sharply. Conversely, policies that increase productivity, and thus the level of aggregate supply at a given price level, can help reduce inflationary pressures.

Graphical Analysis

Figure 1-8 shows aggregate demand and supply curves. The vertical axis P is the price level, and the horizontal axis Y is the level of real output or income. Although the curves look like the ordinary supply and demand curves of microeconomics, an understanding of the curves in the figure will not be reached until Chapter 7.

Aggregate demand is the total demand for goods and services in the economy. It depends on the aggregate price level, as shown in Figure 1-8. It can be shifted by monetary and fiscal policy. The aggregate supply curve shows the price level associated with each level of output. It can, to some extent, be shifted by fiscal policy.

Aggregate supply and demand interact to determine the price level and output level. In Figure 1-8, P_0 is the equilibrium price level and Y_0 the equilibrium level of output. If the *AD* curve in the figure shifts upward to the right, then the extent to which output and prices, respectively, are changed depends on the steepness of the aggregate supply curve.[10] If the *AS* curve is very steep, then a given increase in aggregate demand mainly causes prices to rise and has very little effect on the level of output. If the *AS* curve is flat, a given change in aggregate demand will be translated mainly into an increase in output and hardly at all into an increase in the price level.

One of the crucial points about macroeconomic adjustment is that the aggregate supply curve is not a straight line. Figure 1-9 shows that at low levels of output, below potential output Y^*, the aggregate supply curve is quite flat. When output is below potential, there is very little tendency for prices of goods and factors (wages) to fall. Conversely, for output above potential, the aggregate supply curve is steep and prices

---

[10] Experiment with graphs like Fig. 1-8 to be sure you understand this fact.

tend to rise continuously. The effects of changes in aggregate demand on output and prices therefore depend on the level of actual relative to potential output.

All these observations are by way of a very important warning. In Chapters 3 through 6 we focus on aggregate demand as the determinant of the level of output. We shall assume that prices are given and constant and that output is determined by the level of demand — that there are no supply limitations. We are thus talking about the very flat part of the aggregate supply curve, at levels of output below potential.

The suggestion that output rises to meet the level of demand without a rise in prices leads to a very activist conception of policy. Under these circumstances, without any obvious tradeoffs, policy makers would favor very expansionary policies to raise demand and thereby cause the economy to move to a high level of employment and output. There are circumstances in which such a policy view is altogether correct. The early 1960s are a case in point. Figure 1-3 shows that in those years output was substantially below potential. There were unused resources, and the problem was a deficiency of demand. By contrast, in the late 1960s and the late 1980s the economy

FIGURE 1-8

AGGREGATE DEMAND AND SUPPLY. The basic tools for analyzing output, the price level, inflation, and growth are the aggregate supply and demand curves. Shifts in either aggregate supply or aggregate demand will cause the level of output to change — thus affecting growth — and will also change the price level — thus affecting inflation. Through Okun's law, changes in output are linked to changes in the unemployment rate. For the first six chapters, we concentrate on aggregate demand. Then in the later chapters, we introduce the aggregate supply curve, thereby completing the analysis.

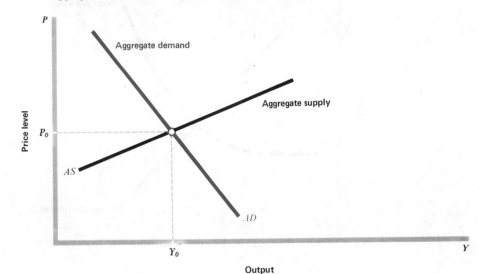

was operating at full employment. There was no significant GNP gap. An attempt to expand output or real GNP further would run into supply limitations and force up prices rather than the production of goods. In those circumstances, a model that assumes that output is demand-determined and that increased demand raises output and *not* prices is simply inappropriate.

Should we think that the model with fixed prices and demand-determined output is very restricted and perhaps artificial? The answer is no. There are two reasons for this. First, the circumstances under which the model is appropriate — those of high unemployment — are neither unknown nor unimportant. Unemployment and down-ward price rigidity are continuing features of the U.S. economy. Second, even when we come to study the interactions of aggregate supply and demand in Chapter 7 and later, we need to know how given policy actions *shift* the aggregate demand curve at a given level of prices. Thus all the material of Chapters 3 through 6 on aggregate demand plays a vital part in our understanding of the effects of monetary and fiscal policy on the

FIGURE 1-9

AGGREGATE DEMAND AND NONLINEAR AGGREGATE SUPPLY. A key fact about the aggregate supply curve is that it is not linear. At low levels of output, prices do not change much on the aggregate supply schedule, implying that more output will be supplied without much increase in prices. But as the economy gets close to full employment or potential output, further increases in output will be accompanied by increased prices.

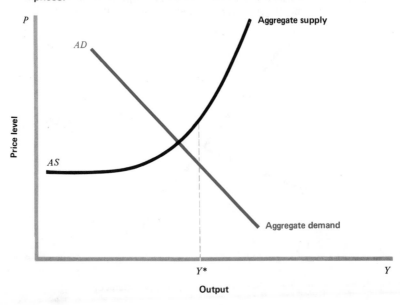

price level as well as on output in circumstances in which the aggregate supply curve is upward-sloping.

What, then, is the warning of this section? It is simply that the very activist spirit of macroeconomic policy under conditions of unemployment must not cause us to overlook the existence of supply limitations and price adjustment when the economy is near full employment.

1-5 MACROECONOMIC POLICY

The aggregate demand and supply framework suggests that under specified conditions there is room for macroeconomic policy to expand demand or to contract it. Policy makers have at their command two broad classes of policies that potentially affect the economy. *Monetary policy* is controlled by the Federal Reserve System (the Fed). The instruments of monetary policy are changes in the stock of money, changes in the interest rate — the discount rate — at which the Fed lends money to banks, and some controls over the banking system. *Fiscal policy* is under the control of the Congress and usually is initiated by the executive branch of the government. The instruments of fiscal policy are tax rates and government spending.

One of the central facts of policy is that the effects of monetary and fiscal policy on the economy are not fully predictable in their *timing* or in the *extent* to which they affect demand or supply. These two uncertainties are at the heart of the problem of stabilization policy. *Stabilization policies* are monetary and fiscal policies designed to moderate the fluctuations of the economy — in particular, fluctuations in the rates of growth, inflation, and unemployment.

Figure 1-7, which shows large fluctuations of the rates of inflation and unemployment, suggests strongly that stabilization policy has not been fully successful in keeping them within narrow bounds. The failures of stabilization policy are due both to uncertainty about the way it works and to limits on the effects of policy on the economy.

However, questions of political economy are also involved in the way stabilization policy has been operated. The speed at which to proceed in trying to eliminate unemployment, at the risk of increasing inflation, is a matter of judgment about both the economy and the costs of mistakes. Those who regard the costs of unemployment as high relative to the costs of inflation will run greater risks of inflation to reduce unemployment than will those who regard the costs of inflation as primary and unemployment as a relatively minor misfortune.

Political economy affects stabilization policy in more ways than through the costs that policy makers of different political persuasions attach to inflation and unemployment and the risks they are willing to take in trying to improve the economic situation. There is also the so-called *political business cycle*, which is based on the observation that election results are affected by economic conditions. When the economic situation is improving and the unemployment rate is falling, incumbent presidents tend to be reelected. There is thus the incentive for policy makers running for reelection, or who wish to affect the election results, to use stabilization policy to produce booming economic conditions before elections.

Stabilization policy is also known as *countercyclical policy,* that is, policy to moderate the trade cycle or business cycle. Figure 1-3 shows that cycles in the past 20 years have been far from regular. The behavior, and even the existence, of the trade cycle is substantially affected by the conduct of stabilization policy. Successful stabilization policy smooths out the cycle, while unsuccessful stabilization policy may worsen the fluctuations of the economy. Indeed, one of the tenets of monetarism is that the major fluctuations of the economy are a result of government actions rather than the inherent instability of the economy's private sector.

Monetarists and Activists

Many of the debates in macroeconomics can be understood in terms of this aggregate demand and supply framework. The discussion focuses on which factors produce disturbances in the economy and what, if any, are the appropriate policy responses.

We noted above that there is controversy over the existence of a tradeoff between inflation and unemployment. That controversy arose around 1967 – 1968 in the context of the debate in macroeconomics between monetarists and nonmonetarists, or fiscalists. We have already identified some of the major participants in the debate as Milton Friedman on the monetarist side and Franco Modigliani and James Tobin on the nonmonetarist side. But macroeconomists cannot be neatly classified into one camp or the other. Instead, there is a spectrum of views. There are monetarists who make Friedman look like a Keynesian, and Keynesians who make Modigliani look like a monetarist. Not only that; there is no compelling unity in the views that are identified with monetarism, and the balanced economist is likely to accept some monetarist arguments and reject others. Nor is the debate one in which there is no progress. For example, both theory and empirical evidence have been brought to bear on the issue of the inflation-unemployment tradeoff, and it is no longer central to the monetarist-fiscalist debate.

Another major point of contention is the relation between *money* and *inflation. Monetarists* tend to argue that the quantity of money is the prime determinant of the level of prices and economic activity, that excessive monetary growth is responsible for inflation, and that unstable monetary growth is responsible for economic fluctuations. Since they contend that variability in the growth rate of money accounts for the variability in real growth, they are naturally led to argue for a monetary policy of low and constant growth in the money supply — a constant money growth rule. *Activists,* by contrast, point out that there is no close relationship between monetary growth and inflation in the short run and that monetary growth is only one of the factors affecting aggregate demand. Activists maintain that policy makers are — or at least can be — sufficiently careful and skillful to be able to use monetary and fiscal policy to control the economy effectively.

The skill and care of the policy makers are important because monetarists raise the issue of whether aggregate demand policies might not worsen the performance of the economy. Monetarists point to episodes such as the inflationary policies followed by the Fed in the 1970s to argue that policy makers cannot and do not exercise sufficient caution to justify using activist policy. Here the activists are optimists, suggesting that we can learn from our past mistakes. They point to periods of high growth and low inflation, such as 1982 – 1989, to support the view that skillful, active monetary policy can help keep the economy growing smoothly.

A further issue that divides the two camps concerns the proper role of government in the economy. This is not really an issue that can be analyzed using macroeconomic theory, but it is difficult to follow some of the debate without being aware that the issue exists.

Monetarists tend to be conservatives who favor small government and abhor budget deficits and a large public debt. They favor tax cuts during recessions and cuts in public spending during booms, with the net effect of winding up with government having a smaller share of the economy. Activists, by contrast, tend to favor an active role for government and are therefore quite willing to use increased government spending and transfers as tools of stabilization policy. Differences between monetarists and activists must, therefore, be seen in a much broader perspective than in terms of their particular disagreements about the exact role of money in the short run.

New Classical Macroeconomics and Activism

The monetarist challenge to Keynesian activism warmed up in the 1960s and still continues today. But its importance has been superseded by the more fundamental and theoretically innovative *new classical macroeconomics* that we discussed earlier.

The new classical school, as we have seen, asserts that firms and households are rational and make whatever adjustments are needed to improve their economic well-being. As a consequence, there cannot be involuntary unemployment. This view severely limits the desirability of using stabilization policy to affect the unemployment rate.

New classical macroeconomists, like monetarists, tend to be conservatives, who see only a relatively small role for active government policy in the economy. This follows from the view that markets are mostly in equilibrium and that people look after their own interests, leaving little for the government to do to improve the situation. The new classicists argue also that activist policy is difficult to carry out successfully because the reactions of rational and optimizing firms and consumers to government actions depend on what the private sector thinks the government is trying to achieve and may be difficult to predict.

Although they share many policy views, new classical macroeconomists are not necessarily monetarists. We discuss the equilibrium approach, rational expectations, and the new classical macroeconomics throughout the book and, in detail, in Chapter 13.

The New Keynesians

The policy views of the new Keynesians are similar to those of the original Keynesians. They tend to believe that activist policy can and should be used to try to stabilize the economy. They differ from the original Keynesians in accepting the challenge of the new classicists to provide a theoretical explanation for the slow adjustment of wages and prices on which the possibility of useful stabilization policy is built.

1-6 OUTLINE AND PREVIEW OF THE TEXT

We have sketched the major issues we shall discuss in the book. We now outline our approach to macroeconomics and the order in which the material will be presented. The key overall concepts, as already noted, are aggregate demand and aggregate supply. Aggregate demand is influenced by monetary policy, primarily via interest rates and expectations, and by fiscal policy. Aggregate supply is affected by fiscal policy and also by disturbances such as changes in the supply of oil.

The coverage by chapters starts in Chapter 2 with national income accounting, emphasizing data and relationships that are used repeatedly later in the book. Chapters 3 through 6 are concerned with aggregate demand. Chapter 7 introduces aggregate supply and shows how aggregate supply and demand interact to determine both real GNP and the price level. Chapters 8 through 11 present material that clarifies and deepens the understanding of aggregate demand and of the ways in which monetary and fiscal policies affect the economy. Chapters 12 through 19 perform a similar service for aggregate supply and the interactions of aggregate supply and demand. Chapter 20 extends the Chapter 6 discussion of the role of international trade in macroeconomics.

1-7 PREREQUISITES AND RECIPES

In concluding this introductory chapter we offer a few words on how to use this book. First, we note that there is no mathematical prerequisite beyond high school algebra. We do use equations when they appear helpful, but they are not an indispensable part of the exposition. Nevertheless, they can and should be mastered by any serious student of macroeconomics.

The technically harder chapters or sections can be skipped or dipped into. Either we present them as supplementary material, or we provide sufficient nontechnical coverage to help the reader get on without them later in the book. The reason we do present more advanced material or treatment is to afford a complete and up-to-date coverage of the main ideas and techniques in macroeconomics. Even though you may not be able to grasp every point of such sections on first reading — and should not even try to — these sections should certainly be read to get the main message and an intuitive appreciation of the issues that are raised.

The main problem you will encounter will come from trying to comprehend the interaction of several markets and many variables, as the direct and feedback effects in the economy constitute a quite formidable system. How can you be certain to progress efficiently and with some ease? The most important thing is to ask questions. Ask yourself, as you follow the argument, Why is it that this or that variable should affect, say, aggregate demand? What would happen if it did not? What is the critical link?

There is no substitute whatsoever for *active learning*. Reading sticks at best for 7 weeks. Are there simple rules for active study? The best way to study is to use pencil and paper and work through the argument by drawing diagrams, experimenting with flowcharts, writing out the logic of an argument, working out the problems at the end of each chapter, and underlining key ideas. The *Study Guide*, by Richard Startz of the University of Washington, contains both much useful material and problems that will help in your studies. Another valuable exercise is to take issue with an argument or position, or to spell out the defense for a particular view on policy questions. Beyond that, if you get stuck, read on for half a page. If you are still stuck, go back five pages.

You should also learn to use the index. Several concepts are discussed at different levels in different chapters. If you come across an unfamiliar term or concept, check the index to see whether and where it was defined and discussed earlier in the book.

As a final word, this chapter is designed for reference purposes. You should return to it whenever you want to check where a particular problem fits or to what a particular subject matter is relevant. The best way to see the forest is from Chapter 1.

KEY TERMS

Monetarists	Recovery or expansion
Keynesians	Recession
New classical macroeconomists	Output gap
Rational expectations	Okun's law
GNP, nominal and real	Phillips curve
Inflation	Monetary policy
Growth	Fiscal policy
Unemployment	Stabilization policies
Business cycle	Activists
Trend or potential output	Aggregate demand and supply
Peak	Supply-side economics
Trough	Supply shocks

NATIONAL INCOME ACCOUNTING

Macroeconomics is ultimately concerned with the determination of the economy's total output, the price level, the level of employment, interest rates, and the other variables discussed in Chapter 1. A necessary step in understanding how these variables are determined is *national income accounting*.

The national income accounts give us regular estimates of GNP, the basic measure of the economy's performance in producing goods and services. The first part of this chapter discusses the measurement and meaning of GNP, nominal and real. But the national income accounts are useful also because they provide us with a conceptual framework for describing the relationships among three key macroeconomic variables: output, income, and spending. Those relationships are described in the second part of this chapter.

We start, in Section 2-1, by examining GNP and its measurement. Section 2-2 returns to the distinction between real and nominal GNP, a distinction that is necessary because of inflation. Section 2-3 compares alternative measures of inflation. Then we move, in Sections 2-4 and 2-5, to the relationships among output, income, and spending. Section 2-6 develops relationships that are central to understanding the links among the budget, saving, investment, and the external balance. Section 2-7 introduces balance sheets and reinforces international aspects of national accounts.

2-1 GROSS NATIONAL PRODUCT AND NET NATIONAL PRODUCT

Calculating Gross National Product

GNP is the value of all final goods and services produced by domestically owned factors of production within a given period. It includes the value of goods produced, such as houses and bourbon, and the value of services, such as brokers' services and economists' lectures. The output of each of these is valued at its market price, and the values are added together to give GNP. GNP accounts for the U.S. economy since 1929 are available on a systematic basis. There are a variety of estimates for earlier periods. In 1989 the value of GNP in the U.S. economy was more than $5,000 billion.

There are a number of subtleties in the calculation of GNP.

FINAL GOODS AND VALUE ADDED

GNP is the value of *final* goods and services produced. The insistence on final goods and services is simply to make sure that we do not double-count. For example, we would not want to include the full price of an automobile in GNP and then also include as part of GNP the value of the tires that were sold to the automobile producer to put on the car. The components of the car that are sold to the manufacturers are called *intermediate* goods, and their value is not included in GNP. Similarly, the wheat that goes into bread is an intermediate good. We count only the value of the bread as part of GNP; we do not count in the value of the wheat sold to the miller and the value of the flour sold to the baker.

In practice, double counting is avoided by working with the *value added*. At each stage of the manufacture of a good, only the value added to the good at that stage of manufacture is counted as part of GNP. The value of the wheat produced by the farmer is counted as part of GNP. Then the value of the flour sold by the miller minus the cost of the wheat is the miller's value added. If we follow this process along, we will see that the sum of value added at each stage of processing will be equal to the final value of the bread sold.[1]

CURRENT OUTPUT

GNP consists of the value of output *currently produced*. It thus excludes transactions in existing commodities, such as old masters or existing houses. We count the construction of new houses as part of GNP, but we do not add trade in existing houses. We do, however, count the value of realtors' fees in the sale of existing houses as part of GNP. The realtor provides a current service in bringing buyer and seller together, and that is appropriately part of current output.

MARKET PRICES

GNP values goods at *market prices*. The market price of many goods includes indirect taxes such as the sales tax and excise taxes, and thus the market price of goods is not the same as the price the seller of the goods receives. The net price, the market price minus indirect taxes, is the *factor cost*, which is the amount received by the factors of production that manufactured the good. GNP is valued at market prices and not at

---

[1] How about the flour that is directly purchased by households for baking in the home? It is counted as a contribution toward GNP since it represents a final sale.

factor cost. This point becomes important when we relate GNP to the incomes received by the factors of production.[2]

Valuation at market prices is a principle that is not uniformly applied, because there are some components of GNP that are difficult to value. There is no very good way of valuing the services of homemakers, or a self-administered haircut, or, for that matter, the services of the police force or the government bureaucracy. Some of these activities are simply omitted from currently measured GNP, as, for instance, homemakers' services. Government services are valued at cost, so the wages of government employees are taken to represent their contribution to GNP. There is no unifying principle in the treatment of these awkward cases, but rather a host of conventions is used.

GNP and Gross Domestic Product

There is a distinction between GNP and *gross domestic product,* or *GDP.* GDP is the value of final goods produced within the country. What is the difference between GNP and GDP? Part of GNP is earned abroad. For instance, the income of an American citizen working in Japan is part of U.S. GNP. But it is not part of U.S. GDP because it is not earned in the United States. On the other side, the profits earned by Honda from its U.S. manufacturing operations are part of Japanese GNP and not U.S. GNP. But they are part of U.S. GDP because they are earned in the United States.

When GNP exceeds GDP, residents of a given country (say the United States) are earning more abroad than foreigners are earning in that country (in this case, the United States). In the United States, GNP exceeded GDP for the post-World War II period until 1988. During that period, U.S. corporations and residents who owned factories or worked abroad earned more in foreign countries than foreign firms and individuals earned in the United States. However, after 1988 foreigners earned more in the United States than U.S. residents earned abroad. The change is a result of the large balance of payment deficits the United States has been running during the 1980s and will not be reversed unless the United States starts running surpluses in its current account.

2-2 REAL AND NOMINAL GNP

Nominal GNP measures the value of output in a given period in the prices of that period, or, as it is sometimes put, in *current dollars.*[3] Thus 1990 nominal GNP measures the value of the goods produced in 1990 at the market prices prevailing in

---

[2] The value of output measured at factor cost is referred to as *national income.* On this point see Appendix 2-2 at the end of this chapter.

[3] National income account data are regularly reported in the *Survey of Current Business (SCB).* Historical data are available in the September issue of *SCB;* in the Commerce Department's *Business Statistics,* a biennial publication; and in the annual *Economic Report of the President.*

box 2-1 GNP MEASUREMENT

Two particular (unrelated) problems of GNP measurement are the possibility that large parts of economic activity escape being counted in GNP and that the data are frequently and quite substantially revised. We take up the two problems in turn.

THE UNDERGROUND ECONOMY

By some estimates, as much as 30 percent of U.S. GNP may not be measured in the GNP accounts. Here are examples of transactions that generate goods and services that might not make it into measured GNP: working at a second job for cash, illegal gambling, working as an illegal immigrant, working while collecting unemployment benefits, illegal drug dealing, working for tips that are not fully reported, selling home-grown tomatoes for cash.*

There are two main types of transactions that people attempt to conceal: transactions that are not inherently illegal, but for which people are not complying with tax or immigration laws or other government regulations; and transactions that are themselves illegal, such as drug dealing. The U.S. national income accounts do not include the value of illegal activities in GNP as a matter of principle, so part of the underground economy would not count even if it could be measured. But many other countries and economists have no objection to including illegal activities if they can be measured.

The remaining activities in the underground economy occur mainly because people are trying to keep from losing some government benefit or avoid paying taxes, and these activities should be included in GNP.

How large is the underground economy, and how can it be measured? Of course, by their nature these are difficult data to estimate. Estimates range widely. For the United States, conservative numbers are 3 to 4 percent of GNP, with a radical number of 33 percent of GNP. Estimates for foreign countries are similar; for instance, for Canada, estimates range from 4 to 22 percent of GNP, and for Italy, from 8 to 33 percent.

The largest estimates for the United States were based on the holdings of currency, on the argument that black-market transactions are undertaken mainly using currency. The ratio of currency holdings to bank deposits has risen from 25 percent in 1959 to 40 percent in 1984, and it is argued that the reason is the increasing share of underground economic activity. However, the ratio of currency to bank deposits has fallen since 1984. Alternative estimates are based on inconsistencies in the GNP accounts, for instance, differences between total spending and total income. The Bureau of Economic Analysis, which creates the GNP accounts, believes the underground economy is 3 percent of GNP or less, while the Internal Revenue Service has come up with an estimate as high as 8 percent of GNP. The evidence in favor of really large corrections, say, more than 10 percent, is weak.

What problems does the underground economy pose for GNP measurement? The main problem is that the relative importance of underground activities may have

---

* A more complete list is provided in the excellent survey article by Carol S. Carson, "The Underground Economy: An Introduction," *Survey of Current Business*, May 1984; see also part II of the same article, in the July 1984 *Survey of Current Business*. There was an explosion of research on the underground economy in the mid-1980s; for a review of three books on the topic see Peter M. Gutman, *Journal of Economic Literature*, March 1983, pp. 117–120.

been changing. If, say, the underground economy was always equal to 10 percent of reported GNP, then measured GNP would show accurately the *rate* at which output *changes* over time. But if the underground economy grows relative to the measured economy, then the measured growth rate of output is below the true growth rate. It was the claim that the underground economy had been growing rapidly, and that therefore slow economic growth in the seventies was in large part a statistical illusion, that spurred research on the topic. But because of the difficulty of getting data on the underground economy, this research has not been conclusive.

GNP REVISIONS AND THE ACCURACY OF GNP ESTIMATES

There are several estimates of GNP for a given period. First to be reported is the so-called *advance* estimate for a given quarter, which appears about 3 weeks after the end of the quarter. These data are then revised a month later (the preliminary estimate) and once more a month after that (the final estimate). The data are then revised each July for the next 3 years, and thereafter a comprehensive revision of all GNP data (a so-called *benchmark* revision) is carried out every 5 years.

It is thus clear that GNP data are not, when they first appear, firm estimates; nor, for that matter, is any GNP figure for any year ever guaranteed not to change at some future date. The reason is that many of the data are not measured directly but rather are based on surveys and guesses. Considering that GNP is supposed to measure the value of *all* production of goods and services in the economy, it is not surprising that not all the data are available within a few weeks after the period of production. The data are revised as new figures come in and as the Bureau of Economic Analysis improves its data collection and estimation methods.

Data revisions may be quite large. The estimate of how fast GNP grew from one quarter to the next can sometimes change by 2 to 3 percent (at an annual rate) between the first and third estimates of GNP. But changes in the benchmark year for calculating real GNP also introduce important revisions. The next revision of the GNP benchmark year is to be undertaken in 1990 when the base year is moved to 1987. Preliminary estimates of the new GNP series in 1987 dollars will differ substantially from the data currently available. As Table 1 shows, the more recent base year shows smaller growth.

TABLE 1
GNP BENCHMARK REVISION (annual real GNP growth rate)

	1987 dollars	1982 dollars
1983	3.5	3.6
1984	6.0	6.8
1985	3.0	3.4
1986	3.0	2.8
1987	3.2	3.4
1988	3.5	3.9

SOURCE: Allan H. Young, "Alternative Measures of Real GNP," *Survey of Current Business,* April 1989.

1990, and 1976 nominal GNP measures the value of goods produced in 1976 at the market prices that prevailed in 1976.

Nominal GNP changes from year to year for two reasons. The first reason is that the physical output of goods changes. The second is that market prices change. As an extreme and unrealistic example, one could imagine the economy producing exactly the same output in 2 years between which all prices have doubled. Nominal GNP in the second year would be twice the nominal GNP in the first year, even though the physical output of the economy had not changed at all.

Real GNP measures changes in *physical* output in the economy between different time periods by valuing all goods produced in the two periods *at the same prices,* or in *constant dollars.* Real GNP is now measured in the national income accounts in the prices of 1982. That means that, in calculating real GNP, today's physical output is multiplied by the prices that prevailed in 1982 to obtain a measure of what today's output would have been worth had it been sold at the prices of 1982.[4]

In Table 2-1 we present a simple example that illustrates the calculation of nominal and real GNP. The hypothetical outputs and prices of bananas and oranges in 1982 and 1990 are shown in the first two columns of Table 2-1. Nominal GNP in 1982 was $14, and nominal GNP in 1990 was $21, or an increase in nominal GNP of 50 percent. However, much of the increase in nominal GNP is purely a result of the increase in prices between the 2 years and does not reflect an increase in physical output. When we calculate real GNP in 1990 by valuing 1990 output at the prices of 1982, we find real GNP equal to $17.20, which is an increase of 23 percent rather than 50 percent. The 23 percent increase is a better measure of the increase in physical output of the economy than is the 50 percent increase.

We see from the table that the output of bananas rose by 33 percent from 1982 to 1990, while the output of oranges increased by 20 percent. We should thus expect our measure of the increase in real output to be somewhere between 20 and 33 percent, as it is.[5]

Figure 2-1 shows the behavior of real and nominal GNP over the period since 1972. Note particularly that in some periods real GNP fell while nominal GNP kept on rising. That happened in the recessions of 1973–1975, 1980, and 1981–1982. The recession periods, shaded in the figure, stand out as years of low or negative real GNP growth.

It would clearly be a mistake to regard the increases in *nominal* GNP as

---

[4] The shift from the prices of 1972 to those of 1982 for calculating real GNP was made at the end of 1985. In 1990, the base year will be changed to 1987. See Box 2-1.

[5] The calculated increase in real GNP depends on the prices used in the calculation. If you have a calculator, you might want to compare the increase in real GNP between 1982 and 1990 if the prices of 1990 are used to make the comparison. (Using 1990 prices, real GNP rises 23.5 percent from 1982 to 1990, compared with 22.9 percent using 1982 prices.) The ambiguities that arise in comparisons using different prices to calculate real GNP are an inevitable result of the attempt to use a single number to capture the increase in output of both bananas and oranges when those two components did not increase in the same proportion. However, the ambiguity is not a major concern when there is inflation at any substantial rate, and that is precisely when we most want to use real (rather than nominal) GNP to study the performance of the economy.

TABLE 2-1

REAL AND NOMINAL GNP, AN ILLUSTRATION

	1982 nominal GNP		1990 nominal GNP		1990 real GNP*	
Bananas	15 at $0.20	$ 3.00	20 at $0.30	$ 6.00	20 at $0.20	$ 4.00
Oranges	50 at 0.22	11.00	60 at 0.25	15.00	60 at 0.22	13.20
		$14.00		$21.00		$17.20

* Measured in 1982 prices.

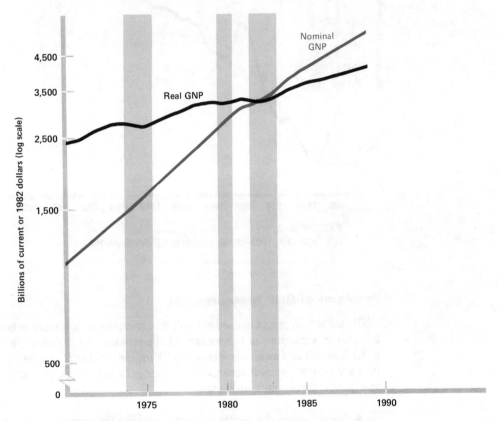

FIGURE 2-1

U.S. REAL AND NOMINAL GNP, 1972–1988. (SOURCE: DRI/McGraw-Hill.)

indicating that the performance of the economy in producing goods and services was improving from, say, 1981 to 1982. So we look at real rather than nominal GNP as the basic measure for comparing output in different years. Figure 2-2 shows U.S. real GNP for the period since 1929.

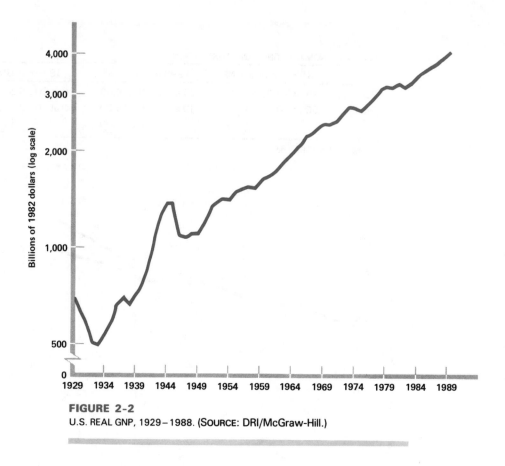

FIGURE 2-2
U.S. REAL GNP, 1929–1988. (SOURCE: DRI/McGraw-Hill.)

Problems of GNP Measurement

GNP data are, in practice, used not only as a measure of how much is being produced, but also as a measure of the welfare of the residents of a country. Economists and politicians talk as if an increase in real GNP means that people are better off. But GNP data are far from perfect measures of either economic output or welfare. There are, specifically, three major problems:

- Some outputs are poorly measured because they are not traded in the market. Specific examples include government services, nonmarket activities such as volunteer work, and do-it-yourself activities in the home.

- It is difficult to account correctly for improvements in the quality of goods. This has been the case particularly for computers, whose quality has improved dramatically while their price has fallen sharply.[6] The national income accountants

---

[6] When the base year for calculating real GNP was changed from 1972 to 1982, new estimates of computer

box 2-2

FACTOR SHARES IN NATIONAL INCOME

Table 1 shows how national income is split (*factor shares*) among different types of incomes. The most striking fact in the table is the very large share of wages and salaries—compensation of employees—in national income. This accounts for 73 percent of national income. Proprietors' income is income from unincorporated businesses. Rental income of persons includes the *imputed* income of owner-occupied housing* and income from ownership of patents, royalties, and so on. The net interest category consists of interest payments by domestic businesses and the rest of the world to individuals and firms who have lent to them.

The division of national income into various classes is not too important for our macroeconomic purposes. It reflects, in part, answers to such questions as whether corporations are financed by debt or equity, whether a business is or is not incorporated, and whether the housing stock is owned by persons or corporations—which, in turn, are owned by persons.† ■

TABLE 1
NATIONAL INCOME AND ITS DISTRIBUTION, 1988

	$ billions	Percent
National income	3,968.4	100
Compensation of employees	2,904.7	73.2
Proprietors' income	324.5	8.2
Rental income of persons	19.3	0.5
Corporate profits	328.4	8.3
Net interest	391.5	9.9

NOTE: Numbers may not sum to totals because of rounding.
SOURCE: *Survey of Current Business.*

* GNP includes an estimate of the services homeowners receive by living in their homes. This is estimated by calculating the rent on an equivalent house. Thus the homeowner is treated as if she pays herself rent for living in her home.

† You might want to ask how Table 1 would be modified for each of the possibilities described in this sentence.

attempt to adjust for improvements in quality, but the task is not easy, especially when new models and types of goods are being invented.

prices were introduced as well. Whereas it was initially assumed that there had been no improvement in computer quality from 1972 to 1984, it was later assumed that the price of computers had effectively been falling 14 percent per year. This meant that the $3.5 billion spent on computers in 1972 corresponded to only $0.9 billion of real spending on computers in 1982 dollars. Why? Because computers were much more expensive in 1972 than they were in 1982, a dollar spent on computers in 1972 bought less computer than a dollar spent in 1982. For details, see *Survey of Current Business*, December 1985, pp. 1–19; for subsequent information, see *Survey of Current Business*, November 1988, pp. 22–23.

- Some activities measured as adding to real GNP in fact represent the use of resources to avoid or contain "bads" such as crime or risks to national security.

Attempts have been made to construct an *adjusted* GNP series that takes account of some of these difficulties, moving closer to a measure of welfare. The most comprehensive of these studies, by Robert Eisner of Northwestern University, estimates an adjusted GNP series in which the level of real GNP is about 50 percent higher than the official estimates.[7] Interestingly, while the adjusted level of GNP by far exceeds the official series, the estimated *growth rate* of real GNP over the 1946–1981 period is almost identical to the official estimate. This suggests that official estimates give a reasonably good idea of the rate of change in the level of economic activity over time even if their level is inaccurate.

2-3 PRICE INDEXES

The GNP Deflator

The calculation of real GNP gives us a useful measure of inflation known as the *GNP deflator*. Returning to the hypothetical example of Table 2-1, we can get a measure of inflation between 1982 and 1990 by comparing the value of 1990 GNP in 1990 prices and 1982 prices. The ratio of nominal to real GNP in 1990 is 1.22 (= 21/17.2). In other words, output is 22 percent higher in 1990 when it is valued using the higher prices of 1990 than valued in the lower prices of 1982. We ascribe the 22 percent increase to price increases, or inflation, over the 1982–1990 period.

The GNP deflator is the ratio of nominal GNP in a given year to real GNP, and it is a measure of inflation from the period for which the base prices for calculating the real GNP are taken to the current period. Since the GNP deflator is based on a calculation involving all the goods produced in the economy, it is a widely based price index that is frequently used to measure inflation.

The Consumer Price Index

The *consumer price index* (CPI) measures the cost of buying a fixed basket of goods and services representative of the purchases of urban consumers.[8] The GNP deflator differs in three main ways from the CPI. First, the deflator measures the prices of a

---

[7] Eisner presents his data in "The Total Incomes System of Accounts," *Survey of Current Business,* January 1985, and offers detailed discussion in "Extended Accounts for National Income and Product," *Journal of Economic Literature,* December 1988. See, too, William Nordhaus and James Tobin, "Is Growth Obsolete?" in National Bureau of Economic Research, *Fiftieth Anniversary Colloquium* (New York: Columbia University Press, 1972).

[8] Occasionally the basket of goods is changed to remain representative of actual consumption patterns.

much wider group of goods than the CPI does. CPI prices are measured by field-workers who go into shops and make phone calls to discuss the prices of the goods being sold by firms. Second, the CPI measures the cost of a given basket of goods, which is the same from year to year. The basket of goods included in the GNP deflator, however, differs from year to year, depending on what is produced in the economy in each year. When corn crops are large, corn receives a relatively large weight in the computation of the GNP deflator. By contrast, the CPI measures the cost of a fixed basket of goods that does not vary over time. Third, the CPI directly includes prices of imports, whereas the deflator includes only prices of goods *produced* in the United States.[9]

The two main indexes used to compute inflation, the GNP deflator and the CPI, accordingly differ in behavior from time to time. For example, at times when the price of imported oil rises rapidly, the CPI is likely to rise faster than the deflator.

The Producer Price Index

The *producer price index* (PPI) is the third price index that is widely used. Like the CPI, this is a measure of the cost of a given basket of goods. It differs from the CPI partly in its coverage, which includes, for example, raw materials and semifinished goods. It differs, too, in that it is designed to measure prices at an early stage of the distribution system. Whereas the CPI measures prices where urban households actually do their spending — that is, at the retail level — the PPI is constructed from prices at the level of the first significant commercial transaction.

This difference makes the PPI a relatively flexible price index and one that signals changes in the general price level, or the CPI, some time before they actually materialize. For this reason the PPI, and more particularly, some of its subindexes, such as the index of "sensitive materials," serve as one of the business cycle indicators that are closely watched by policy makers.

Table 2-2 shows the CPI, the PPI, and the GNP deflator for the past 38 years. Both the PPI and the GNP deflator use 1982 as their base year. The CPI uses prices from the period 1982–1984 as base prices. The GNP deflator expresses prices in the current year relative to 1982 prices, using quantities of the current year as weights. Note from the table that all three indexes have been increasing throughout the period. This is a reflection of the fact that the average price of goods has been rising, whatever basket we look at. Note, too, that the cumulative increase ("1988 price/1950 price") differs across indexes. These differences occur because the indexes represent the prices of different commodity baskets.

Although the indexes do not change at the same rate over the entire period, all of them show substantial — and reasonably close — annual rates of inflation. There is no

---

[9] Until 1983 there was a fourth difference: through the seventies and until 1982 the CPI badly miscalculated housing costs and gave too much weight to interest rate changes. The index was revised in 1983 to improve its measurement of housing costs. The mechanics of price indexes are briefly described in Appendix 2-1. Detailed discussion of the various price indexes can be found in Bureau of Labor Statistics *Handbook of Methods* and in the Commerce Department's biennial *Business Statistics*.

TABLE 2-2

IMPORTANT PRICE INDEXES

	CPI, 1982–84 = 100	PPI, 1982 = 100	GNP deflator, 1982 = 100
1950	24.1	28.2	23.9
1960	29.6	33.4	30.9
1970	38.8	39.3	42.0
1980	82.4	88.0	85.7
1985	107.6	104.7	110.9
1988	118.1	108.0	121.7
Increase:			
1988 price/1950 price	4.90	3.83	5.09
Average annual inflation rate	4.3%	3.6%	4.4%

SOURCE: DRI/McGraw-Hill.

sense in which one of the indexes is "correct" while the others are not. The indexes measure changing prices of different baskets of goods. We tend to focus on the deflator or the CPI, the deflator because it measures the prices of a very broad range of goods, and the CPI because the concept it tries to measure — the cost of buying a given basket of goods for the consumer — is a useful one.

We now return to the relationships between income and spending.

2-4 GNP AND PERSONAL DISPOSABLE INCOME

GNP is a measure of the output produced in the economy. Corresponding to this output is the income received by the owners of the factors of production — labor, capital, and land — that are used to produce the output. *Personal disposable income* is the level of income available for spending and saving by households in the economy. A number of adjustments have to be made to GNP to arrive at the level of personal disposable income; the relationship is described in some detail in Appendix 2-2, which includes a number of further definitions.

Three Adjustments

The need for these adjustments stems from three complications:

- Most obviously, the government enters the picture in two ways: the government collects taxes and makes transfer payments. Transfer payments are payments that do not represent compensation for current productive activities. Examples of transfers are pensions and unemployment compensation. Taxes (income taxes, Social Security taxes, excise taxes, etc.) reduce household income relative to GNP, while transfer payments raise it relative to GNP.

■ The business sector emerges as another complication. Businesses do not distribute to households all the income they receive. To the extent that businesses retain earnings rather than paying them out to their shareholders, household income falls short of GNP. Businesses also make transfer payments to households and thus, just as in the case of government, raise household income relative to GNP.

■ Not all of GNP is available as income for households because part of output has to be set aside to maintain the economy's productive capacity. The production of GNP (and the sheer passage of time) causes wear and tear on the existing capital stock. *Depreciation* is a measure of the part of GNP that would have to be set aside to maintain the economy's productive capacity. Net national product (NNP) is defined as GNP minus depreciation. The depreciation allowance amounts to about 11 percent of GNP in the U.S. economy.

In summary, we can write a definition[10] of personal disposable income as follows:

$$\text{Personal disposable income} \equiv \text{GNP} - \text{depreciation} - \text{retained earnings} \\ + \text{transfers} - \text{taxes} \qquad (1)$$

Note that this definition looks at the income households actually receive. But households own the firms and therefore also own the undistributed profits of firms. Some economists argue that a more meaningful definition of household income simply cuts through the "veil" of a business sector and thus includes even undistributed profits.

The Allocation of Personal Disposable Income

Personal disposable income is the amount households have available to spend or save. Table 2-3 shows how households allocate their disposable income. By far the largest outlay is for personal consumption. Most of the remainder is saved. Small amounts of personal disposable income are used to make interest payments and to make transfers to foreigners.

The U.S. personal saving rate is among the world's lowest. We shall see later why this worries some economists.

---

[10] Throughout the book we distinguish identities from equations. Identities are statements that are *always* true because they are directly implied by definitions of variables or accounting relationships. They do not reflect any economic behavior but are extremely useful in organizing our thinking. Identities, or definitions, are shown with the sign $\equiv$, and equations with the usual equality sign $=$.

TABLE 2-3
THE ALLOCATION OF PERSONAL DISPOSABLE INCOME, 1988

	$ billions	$ billions	Percent of disposable income
Personal disposable income		3,471.8	100
Personal outlays		3,327.5	95.8
Personal consumption spending	3,227.5		
Interest paid by consumers	98.9		
Transfers to foreigners	1.0		
Personal savings		144.3	4.2

SOURCE: *Survey of Current Business.*

2-5 OUTLAYS AND COMPONENTS OF DEMAND

In the previous section, we examined the link between GNP and the income of households in the economy, in effect asking how much of the value of goods and services produced actually gets into the hands of households. In this section we present a different perspective on GNP by asking who buys the output, rather than who receives the income. More technically, we look at the demand for output and speak of the *components* of the aggregate demand for goods and services.

Total demand for domestic output is made up of four components: (1) consumption spending by households; (2) investment spending by businesses and households; (3) government (federal, state, and local) purchases of goods and services; and (4) foreign demand. We now look more closely at each of these components.

Consumption

Table 2-4 presents a breakdown of the demand for goods and services in 1988 by components of demand. The table shows that the chief component of demand is *consumption* spending by the household sector. This includes anything from food to golf lessons, but involves also, as we shall see in discussing investment, consumer spending on durable goods such as automobiles — spending that might be regarded as investment rather than consumption.

Government

Next in importance we have *government purchases* of goods and services. This includes such items as national defense expenditures, road paving by state and local governments, and salaries of government employees.

TABLE 2-4
GNP AND COMPONENTS OF DEMAND, 1988

	$ billions	Percent
Personal consumption expenditures	3,227.5	66.4
Gross private domestic investment	766.5	15.8
Government purchases of goods and services	964.9	19.8
Net exports of goods and services	−94.6	−2.0
Gross national product	4,864.3	100.0

NOTE: Numbers do not sum to totals because of rounding.

SOURCE: *Survey of Current Business.*

We draw attention to the use of certain words in connection with government spending. We refer to government spending on goods and services as *purchases* of goods and services, and we speak of *transfers plus purchases* as *government expenditure.* The federal government budget, of the order of $1,000 billion ($1 trillion), refers to federal government expenditure. Less than half that sum is for federal government purchases of goods and services; most of it is for transfers.

Investment

Gross private domestic investment requires some definitions. First, throughout this book, *investment* means additions to the physical stock of capital. As we use the term, investment does *not* include buying a bond or purchasing stock in General Motors. Practically, investment includes housing construction, building of machinery, construction of factories and offices, and additions to a firm's inventories of goods.

If we think of investment more generally as any current activity that increases the economy's ability to produce output in the future, we would include not only physical investment but also what is known as investment in human capital. Human capital is the knowledge and ability to produce that is embodied in the labor force. Education can be regarded as investment in human capital.[11]

The classification of spending as consumption or investment remains to a significant extent a matter of convention. From the economic point of view, there is little difference between a household's building up an inventory of peanut butter and a grocery store's doing the same. Nevertheless, in the national income accounts, the individual's purchase is treated as a personal consumption expenditure, whereas the

---

[11] In the total incomes system of accounts (TISA) referred to in footnote 7 above, the definition of investment is broadened to include investment in human capital, which means that total investment in that system is more than one-third of GNP. But in this book we mean by investment only additions to the physical capital stock.

store's purchase is treated as investment in the form of inventory investment. Although these borderline cases clearly exist, we can apply a simple rule of thumb: Investment is associated with the business sector's adding to the physical stock of capital, including inventories.[12]

Similar issues arise in the treatment of household sector expenditures. For instance, how should we treat purchases of automobiles by households? Since automobiles usually last for several years, it would seem sensible to classify household purchases of automobiles as investments. We would then treat the *use* of automobiles as providing consumption services. (We could think of imputing a rental income to owner-occupied automobiles.) However, the convention is to treat all households' expenditures as consumption spending. This is not quite so bad as it might seem, since the accounts do separate households' purchases of *durable goods* like cars and refrigerators from their other purchases.[13]

In passing, we note that in Table 2-4 investment is defined as "gross" and "domestic." It is gross in the sense that depreciation is not deducted. Net investment is gross investment minus depreciation. The term *domestic* means that this is investment spending by domestic residents but is not necessarily spending on goods produced within this country. It may well be an expenditure on foreign goods. Similarly, consumption and government spending may also be partly for imported goods. On the other hand, some of domestic output is sold to foreigners.

Net Exports

The item "net exports" appears in Table 2-4 to show the effects on the aggregate demand for domestic output of domestic spending on foreign goods and of foreign spending on domestic goods. The total demand for the goods we produce includes exports, that is, the demand from foreigners for our goods. It excludes imports, the part of our domestic spending that is not for our own goods. Accordingly, the difference between exports and imports, called *net exports,* is a component of the total demand for our goods. Net exports were negative for much of the 1980s, as shown in Figure 2-3, reflecting a high level of imports and a low level of exports.

The point can be illustrated with an example. Assume that personal sector spending was higher by $20 billion. How much higher would GNP be? If we assume that

---

[12] The GNP accounts record as investment *business sector* additions to the stock of capital. Some government spending, for instance, for roads or schools, also adds to the capital stock. Estimates of the capital stock owned by government are available in the *Survey of Current Business,* for instance, August 1988, p. 87; this source also provides references to estimates of government investment.

[13] The convention that is adopted with respect to the household sector's purchases of houses also deserves comment. The accounts treat the building of a house as investment by the business sector. When the house is sold to a private individual, the transaction is treated as the transfer of an asset, and not as an act of investment. Even if a house is custom-built by the owner, the accounts treat the builder who is employed by the owner as undertaking the act of investment in building the house. The investment is thus attributed to the business sector.

government and investment spending remained unchanged, we might be tempted to say that GNP would have been $20 billion higher. That is correct if all the additional spending had fallen on our goods. The other extreme, however, is the case in which all the additional spending falls on imports. In that event, consumption would be up $20 billion *and* net exports would be down $20 billion, with *no* net effect on GNP.

Final Sales

As we have just seen, total spending by domestic residents may not be equal to GNP because spending can exceed output when net imports are positive or can fall short of output when net exports are positive. In the national income accounts, total spending by domestic residents is called *gross domestic purchases* and is defined as follows:

$$\text{Gross domestic purchases} \equiv \text{GNP} + \text{imports} - \text{exports}$$

Although gross domestic purchases refers to *total* spending by domestic residents, it is also useful to have a concept of spending that nets out changes in invento-

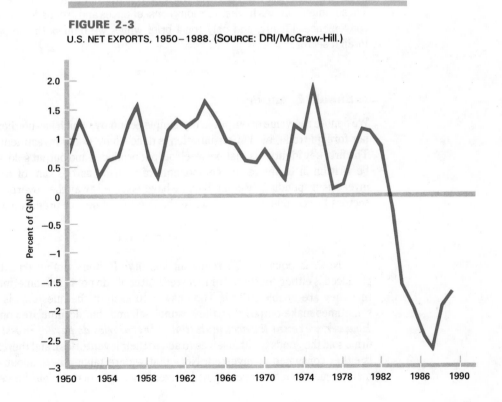

FIGURE 2-3

U.S. NET EXPORTS, 1950–1988. (SOURCE: DRI/McGraw-Hill.)

ries. This is *final sales to domestic purchasers,* or *final sales* for short, and is defined as

$$\text{Final sales} \equiv \text{GNP} + \text{imports} - \text{exports} - \text{inventory change}$$

The definition of final sales is useful because it reminds us that total sales of goods are not exactly equal to GNP, and also points to the sources of the discrepancy between final sales of goods and GNP. These comprise net exports and changes in inventories.

2-6 SOME IMPORTANT IDENTITIES

In this section we summarize the discussion of the preceding sections by writing down a set of national income relationships that we use extensively in Chapter 3. We introduce here some notation and conventions that we follow throughout the book.

For analytical work in the following chapters, we simplify our analysis by omitting the distinction between GNP and national income. For the most part we disregard depreciation and thus the difference between GNP and NNP as well as the difference between gross and net investment. We refer simply to investment spending. We also disregard indirect taxes and business transfer payments. With these conventions in mind, *we refer to national income and GNP interchangeably as income or output.* These simplifications have no serious consequences and are made only for expositional convenience. Finally, and only for a brief while, we omit both the government and foreign sector.

A Simple Economy

We denote the value of output in our simple economy, which has neither a government nor foreign trade, by Y. Consumption is denoted by C and investment spending by I. The first key identity is that between output produced and output sold. Output sold can be written in terms of the components of demand as the sum of consumption and investment spending. (Remember, we have assumed away the government and foreign sectors.) Accordingly, we can write the identity of output produced and output sold:

$$Y \equiv C + I \tag{2}$$

Now, is equation (2) really an identity? Is it inevitably true that all output produced is either consumed or invested? After all, do not firms sometimes make goods that they are unable to sell? The answer to each of the questions is yes. Firms do sometimes make output that they cannot sell and that accumulates on their shelves. *However, we count the accumulation of inventories as part of investment* (as if the firms sold the goods to themselves to add to their inventories), and therefore, all output is either consumed or invested. Note that we are talking here about *actual* investment, which includes investment in inventories that firms might be very unhappy to make. Because of the way investment is defined, output produced is identically equal to output sold.

The next step is to draw up a relation among saving, consumption, and GNP. For that purpose, it is convenient to ignore the existence of corporations and consolidate, or add together, the entire private sector. Using this convention, we know that private sector income is Y, since the private sector receives as income the value of goods and services produced. Why? Because who else would get it? There is no government or external sector yet.

Now the private sector receives, as disposable personal income, the whole of income Y. How will that income be allocated? Part will be spent on consumption, and part will be saved. Thus we can write

$$Y \equiv S + C \tag{3}$$

where S denotes private sector saving. Identity (3) tells us that the whole of income is allocated to either consumption or saving. Next, identities (2) and (3) can be combined to read

$$C + I \equiv Y \equiv C + S \tag{4}$$

The left-hand side of identity (4) shows the components of demand, and the right-hand side shows the allocation of income. The identity emphasizes that output produced is equal to output sold. The value of output produced is equal to income received, and income received, in turn, is spent on goods or saved.

Identity (4) can be slightly reformulated to let us look at the relation between saving and investment. Subtracting consumption from each part of identity (4), we have

$$I \equiv Y - C \equiv S \tag{5}$$

Identity (5) is an important result. It shows first that in this simple economy, saving is identically equal to income less consumption. This result is not new, since we have already seen it in identity (4). The new part concerns the identity of the left and right sides: *Investment is identically equal to saving.*

One can think of what lies behind this relationship in a variety of ways. In a very simple economy, the only way the individual can save is by undertaking an act of physical investment — for example, by storing grain or building an irrigation channel. In a slightly more sophisticated economy, one could think of investors financing their investing by borrowing from individuals who save.

However, it is important to recognize that equation (5) expresses the identity between investment and saving and that some of the investment might well be undesired inventory investment, occurring as a result of mistakes by producers who expected to sell more than they actually did. The identity is really only a reflection of our definitions — output less consumption is investment, output is income, and income less consumption is saving. Even so, we shall find that identity (5) plays a key role in Chapter 3.

Reintroducing the Government and Foreign Trade

We can now reintroduce the government sector and the external sector.[14] First, for the government we denote purchases of goods and services by G and all taxes by TA. Transfers to the private sector (including interest) are denoted by TR. Net exports (exports minus imports) are denoted by NX.

We return to the identity between output produced and sold, taking account now of the additional components of demand, G and NX. Accordingly, we restate the content of Table 2-4 by writing

$$Y \equiv C + I + G + NX \tag{6}$$

Once more we emphasize that in identity (6) we use actual investment in the identity and thus do not rule out the possibility that firms might not at all be content with the investment. Still, as an accounting identity, equation (6) will hold.

Next we turn to the derivation of the very important relation between output and disposable income. Now we have to recognize that part of income is spent on taxes and that the private sector receives net transfers (TR) in addition to national income. Disposable income (YD) is thus equal to income plus transfers less taxes:

$$YD \equiv Y + TR - TA \tag{7}$$

Disposable income, in turn, is allocated to consumption and saving:

$$YD \equiv C + S \tag{8}$$

Combining identities (7) and (8) allows us to write consumption as the difference between income, plus transfers minus taxes, and saving:

$$C + S \equiv YD \equiv Y + TR - TA \tag{9}$$

or

$$C \equiv YD - S \equiv Y + TR - TA - S \tag{9a}$$

Identity (9a) states that consumption is disposable income less saving or, alternatively, that consumption is equal to income plus transfers less taxes and saving. Now we use the right-hand side of equation (9a) to substitute for C in identity (6). With some rearrangement, we obtain

$$S - I \equiv (G + TR - TA) + NX \tag{10}$$

---

[14] *Government* throughout this chapter means the federal government plus state and local governments. A breakdown among these entities can be found in the *Economic Report of the President.*

Saving, Investment, the Government Budget, and Trade

Identity (10) cannot be overemphasized. Its importance arises from the fact that the first set of terms on the right-hand side $(G + TR - TA)$ is the *government budget deficit.* $(G + TR)$ is equal to government purchases of goods and services (G) plus government transfer payments (TR), which is total government spending. TA is the amount of taxes received by the government. The difference $(G + TR - TA)$ is the excess of government spending over its receipts, or its budget deficit. The second term on the right-hand side is the excess of exports over imports, or the *net exports of goods and services,* or net exports for short.

Thus, identity (10) states that the excess of savings over investment $(S - I)$ of the private sector is equal to the government budget deficit plus the trade surplus. The identity suggests — correctly — that there are important relations among the excess of private saving over investment $(S - I)$, the government budget $(G + TR - TA)$, and the external sector. For instance, if, for the private sector, saving is equal to investment, then the government's budget deficit (surplus) is reflected in an equal external deficit (surplus).

Table 2-5 shows the significance of identity (10). To fix ideas, suppose that private sector saving S is equal to $750 (billion). In the first two rows we assume that exports are equal to imports, so that the trade surplus is zero. In row 1, we assume the government budget is balanced. Investment accordingly has to equal $750 billion. In the next row we assume the government budget deficit is $150 billion. *Given the level of saving* of $750 billion and a zero trade balance, it has to be true that investment is now lower by $150 billion. Row 3 shows how this relationship is affected when there is a trade surplus.

To interpret these relationships, realize that any sector that spends more than it receives in income has to borrow to pay for the excess spending. The private sector has three ways of disposing of its saving. It can make loans to the government, which thereby pays for the excess of its spending over the income it receives from taxes. Or the private sector can lend to foreigners, who are buying more from us than we are buying from them. They therefore are earning less from us than they need in order to pay for the goods they buy from us, and we have to lend to cover the difference. Or it can lend to business firms, which use the funds for investment.

The last row of Table 2-5 is relevant to the change in the U.S. budget and trade

---

TABLE 2-5

THE BUDGET DEFICIT, TRADE, SAVING, AND INVESTMENT (billions of dollars)

Saving (S)	Investment (I)	Budget deficit (BD)	Net exports (NX)
750	750	0	0
750	600	150	0
750	650	0	100
750	770	150	-130

deficits between 1981 and 1988. Between those years the government budget deficit increased. Private saving did not increase much, and private investment did not fall. Accordingly, as a matter of arithmetic, the United States had to be running a trade deficit. That is what happened. Between 1981 and 1988 the government deficit increased by $59 billion while net exports fell by $127 billion.

2-7 BALANCE SHEETS

The discussion so far has focused on *flows* such as income or spending. Flows are measured as dollars per unit time, as for example imports, which in 1988 took place at a rate of $614.4 billion per year. We next turn briefly to another important concept, namely *stocks*, or asset positions. A *balance sheet* is a statement of the assets and liabilities of an economic unit, such as a household, a firm, or a country.

The Household Balance Sheet

For any household we can draw up a balance sheet that shows on the asset side the various forms in which the household holds its wealth: real estate, bank deposits, a car, consumer durables, and corporate stock, to name the most important. Table 2-6 shows such a hypothetical household balance sheet. The liabilities side includes all loans outstanding to the household's creditors, for example a mortgage, a car loan, or a student loan. Also appearing on the liabilities side is *net worth*, the net value of household assets. Net worth is equal to the excess of assets over other liabilities. Its inclusion on the liability side makes the two sides of the balance sheet equal.

From the definition of net worth as the balancing item we derive the central accounting identity for balance sheets:[15]

$$\text{Assets} \equiv \text{liabilities} + \text{net worth} \tag{11}$$

---

[15] Another way of looking at identity (11) is as a definition of net worth. We could then write it as:
$$\text{Net worth} \equiv \text{assets} - \text{liabilities}$$

TABLE 2-6
A HYPOTHETICAL HOUSEHOLD
BALANCE SHEET

Assets	Liabilities
Deposits in banks	Mortgage
Consumer durables	Student loans
Automobile	Net worth
Equity	
Home	

TABLE 2-7
NATIONAL NET WORTH (billions of dollars)

	1950	1970	1980	1988
National net worth	$892.3	$2,908.4	$9,726.7	$14,601.7
National net worth/GNP	3.09	2.86	3.56	3.0

SOURCE: Board of Governors of the Federal Reserve, *Balance Sheets for the U.S. Economy,*
1948–88 and *Economic Report of the President.*

The National Balance Sheet

Just as we can draw up a balance sheet for the household, we can list assets and liabilities and thus create balance sheets for the economy as a whole and for each sector in the economy: government, business, and the external sector. The balance sheet for the U.S. external sector describes the foreign assets held by U.S. residents and the liabilities of U.S. residents to foreigners.

In drawing up balance sheets, as in GNP accounting, we have to avoid double counting. In GNP accounting we avoid double counting by focusing on value added. In drawing up a balance sheet for a particular sector of the economy, we avoid double counting by canceling the assets and corresponding liabilities that are confined solely to that sector. For instance, in drawing up the balance sheet of your family, the debt you owe your mother is a liability of yours and an asset of hers, but that asset and liability cancel out when we list the assets and liabilities of the family as a whole. Similarly, in drawing up a balance sheet for the United States we would cancel out the debts you owe the banks and the corresponding assets (for example, your mortgage that the bank owns) owned by the banks.

It is a formidable task to estimate the country's GNP, and it may be even more difficult to estimate the national wealth (or net worth) of a country.[16] But estimates are available for the United States, and Table 2-7 shows the data for selected years.[17] *National net worth* for the U.S. economy for 1988 was estimated to be near $15,000 billion, about 3 times the value of GNP.

Since national net worth is arrived at by canceling or offsetting all national intersectoral claims, it essentially cuts through the financial structure to leave only *tangible assets* (and net claims on foreigners). For instance, in consolidating the

---

[16] Just as we distinguish between GDP and GNP, we have to distinguish between *national* wealth, the wealth of the residents of the country, and *domestic* wealth, the wealth located in the country. A Manhattan skyscraper may be owned by British or Japanese interests and hence not be part of U.S. national wealth. The distinction between national and domestic wealth has become increasingly important in recent years as foreigners have purchased U.S. assets on a large scale.

[17] The data are reported by the Federal Reserve Board. The methodology is under revision, mainly because of concerns that the data do not accurately measure *national* wealth, both because the ownership of assets in the United States may not be accurately known and because the value of assets held abroad is not measured well.

business and the household sectors, households' equity assets (your shares in IBM) are canceled out by the equity liabilities of firms (IBM accounts treat your shares in IBM as a liability); however, the plant, machinery, and inventories of IBM are not canceled out and remain as part of national net worth. Thus national net worth represents the land, plant and equipment, and consumer durables owned by residents. Consumer durables, items such as cars, stereos, washing machines, and home computers, make up 12 percent of national net worth.

The ratio of national net worth to GNP changes over time, though for the United States it has generally been around 3. The main reason the ratio fluctuates is that the value of assets can change. For example, an increase in land prices raises the value of land relative to the flow of income produced in the economy.[18] In addition, the ratio of national net worth to GNP declines when we sell our assets to foreigners. For example, the decline in the U.S. ratio of net worth to GNP in the 1980s in part reflects this effect since current account deficits were financed by selling assets to foreigners.[19]

Net Foreign Investment Position

The growing internationalization of the U.S. economy and, indeed, the world economy, in the 1980s can also be seen in balance sheets. Table 2-8 shows the *international investment position* of the United States. The balance sheet shows U.S. claims on foreigners (government or private) and foreign claims on the United States.

Countries that on balance have net positive foreign assets are called (net) *creditor countries*; correspondingly, *debtor countries* are those, like the United States today, that (again in net terms) own fewer foreign assets than foreigners own in their country.

Table 2-8 and Figure 2-4 show that the United States moved from being a creditor country (indeed, in 1980, the largest net creditor) to net debtor status in the 1980s. Today we owe more abroad than we have claims on the rest of the world. The reason is that the United States has spent more than its income throughout much of the 1980s. The excess of spending over income is financed by selling to foreigners assets located in the United States or U.S. assets located abroad. Countries with large external surpluses, notably Japan, are on the other side of the transaction. As Figure 2-4 shows, their net international investment position has improved sharply in the 1980s. The most visible counterpart is Japanese purchases not only of U.S. govern-

---

[18] The ratio of national net worth to GNP for Japan is higher than that in the United States, being close to 5, in large part because the total value of land in Japan is so high: the total value of land in Japan exceeds that in the United States, even though GNP in Japan is about half that in the United States and the total area of the United States is 25 times that of Japan.

[19] Of course, when an asset is sold to a foreigner, the income earned by that asset is no longer part of GNP. Thus external deficits reduce both GNP and net worth. But given a rate of return on assets of around 15 percent and a ratio of net worth to GNP of 3, a sale of assets would, other things equal, reduce the ratio of net worth to GNP.

TABLE 2-8
U.S. INTERNATIONAL INVESTMENT POSITION (billions of dollars)

	1980	1988
Net international investment position	106.3	−532.5
U.S. assets abroad	607.1	1,253.6
Private assets	516.6	1,205.8
Foreign assets in U.S.	500.8	1,786.2
Private assets	324.8	1,464.1

SOURCE: *Economic Report of the President* and *Survey of Current Business.*

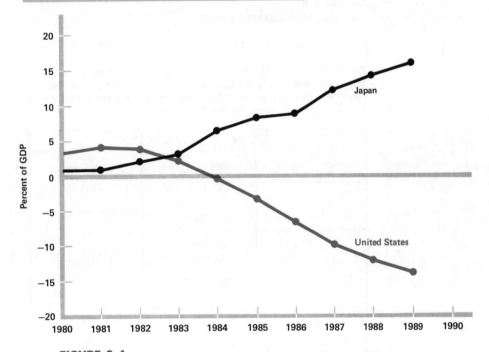

FIGURE 2-4
THE NET INTERNATIONAL INVESTMENT POSITION: THE UNITED STATES AND JAPAN, 1980–1988. (SOURCE: International Monetary Fund.)

ment bonds but also of real estate in Hawaii, Los Angeles, and New York as well as the establishment of Japanese automobile plants in the south and in California. However, so far it is Europeans and not the Japanese who are the largest foreign investors in the United States.

2-8 SUMMARY

1. Nominal GNP is the value, measured at market prices, of the output of final goods and services produced by domestically owned factors of production.
2. Gross domestic product is the value of output produced within the country. It differs from GNP because some of our GNP is produced abroad and because some of our domestic production is produced by foreign-owned factors of production.
3. Real GNP is the value of the economy's output measured in the prices of some

FIGURE 2-5
THE BASIC MACROECONOMIC IDENTITY

$$C + G + I + NX \equiv Y \equiv YD + (TA - TR) \equiv C + S + (TA - TR) \qquad (12)$$

The left-hand side is the demand for output by components; it is identically equal to output supplied. Output supplied is equal to GNP. Disposable income is equal to GNP plus transfers less taxes. Disposable income is allocated to saving and consumption.

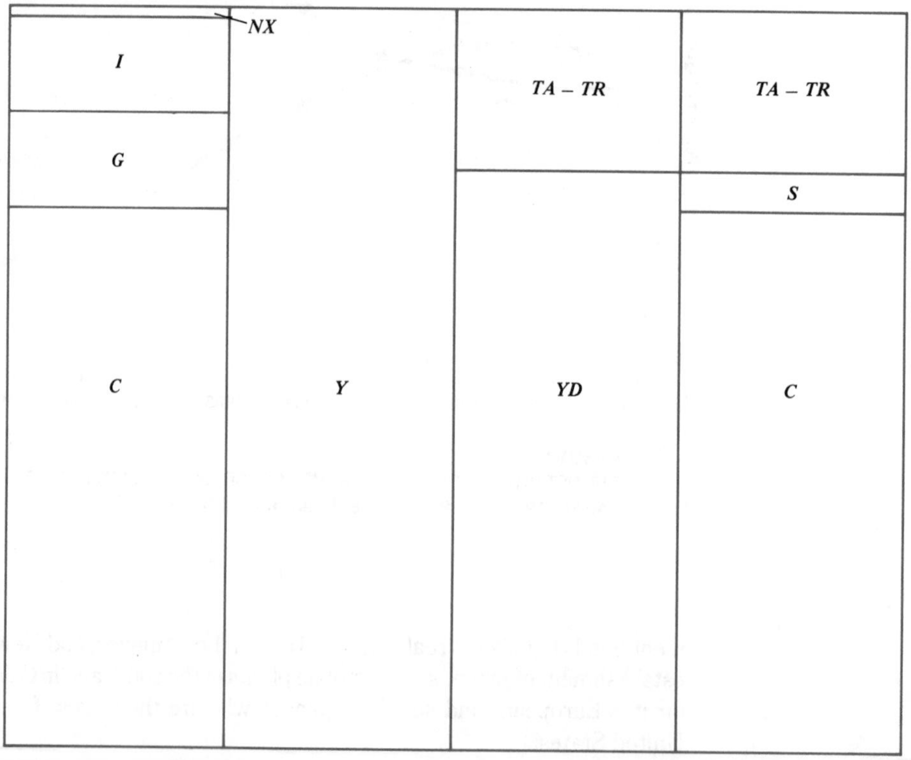

	NX		
I		TA − TR	TA − TR
G			
			S
C	Y	YD	C

base year. Real GNP comparisons, which are all based on the same set of prices for valuing output, provide a better measure of the change in the economy's physical output than nominal GNP comparisons, which also reflect inflation.

4. The GNP deflator is the ratio of nominal to real GNP. It reflects the general rise in prices from the base date at which real GNP is valued. Other frequently used price indexes are the consumer and producer price indexes.

5. Spending on GNP is divided into consumption, investment, government purchases of goods and services, and net exports. The division between consumption and investment in the national income accounts is somewhat arbitrary at the edges.

6. The excess of the private sector's saving over investment is equal to the sum of the budget deficit and the foreign trade surplus.

7. For the remainder of the book we use a simplified model for expositional convenience. We assume away depreciation, indirect taxes, business transfer payments, and the difference between households and corporations. For this simplified model, Figure 2-5 and equation (12) review the *basic macroeconomic identity:*

$$C + G + I + NX \equiv Y \equiv YD + (TA - TR) \equiv C + S + (TA - TR) \quad (12)$$

The left-hand side is the demand for output by components and is identically equal to output supplied. Output supplied is equal to GNP. Disposable income is equal to GNP plus transfers less taxes. Disposable income is allocated to saving and consumption.

8. Balance sheets record the assets, liabilities, and net worth of a sector or country. Net national worth is equal to the net value of the assets of a country's residents.

9. The net international investment position represents a country's net claims on the rest of the world. The United States became a net debtor country in the 1980s.

KEY TERMS

Final goods
Value added
Market prices
Gross domestic product (GDP)
Net national product (NNP)
Depreciation
The illegal economy
GNP deflator
Consumer price index (CPI)
Producer price index (PPI)
Transfers
Disposable personal income

Consumption
Government purchases
Government expenditure
Investment
Net exports
Gross domestic purchases
Final sales
Consumer durables
Government budget deficit
Balance sheets
National net worth
Net international investment position

PROBLEMS

1. Show from national income accounting that:
   (a) An increase in taxes (while transfers remain constant) must imply a change in the trade balance, government purchases, or the saving-investment balance.
   (b) An increase in disposable personal income must imply an increase in consumption or an increase in saving.
   (c) An increase in both consumption and saving must imply an increase in disposable income.
   [For both (b) and (c) assume there are no interest payments by households or transfer payments to foreigners.]

2. The following is information from the national income accounts for a hypothetical country:

GNP	$4,800
Gross investment	800
Net investment	300
Consumption	3,000
Government purchases of goods and services	960
Government budget surplus	30

What is
   (a) NNP?
   (b) net exports?
   (c) government taxes-transfers?
   (d) disposable personal income?
   (e) personal saving?

3. What would happen to GNP if the government hired unemployed workers, who had been receiving amount TR in unemployment benefits, as government employees to do nothing, and now paid them $TR?$ Explain.

4. What is the difference in the national income accounts between
   (a) A firm's buying an auto for an executive and the firm's paying the executive additional income to buy the automobile herself?
   (b) Your hiring your spouse (who takes care of the house) rather than having him or her do the work without pay?
   (c) Your deciding to buy an American car rather than a German car?

5. Explain the following terms: (a) value added, (b) inventory investment, (c) GNP deflator, (d) national net worth.

6. The following discussion deals with GNP and GDP.
   (a) In 1988, U.S. GNP was $4,864.3 billion; GDP was $4,839.2 billion. Why is there a difference?
   (b) In 1988, U.S. GNP was $4,864.3 billion; NNP was $4,357.9 billion. What accounts for the difference? How typical is the 1988 difference as a fraction of GNP?

7. This question deals with price index numbers. Consider a simple economy in which only three items are in the CPI: food, housing, and entertainment (fun). Assume in the base period, say, 1982, the household consumed the following quantities at the then prevailing prices:

	Quantity	Price, $ per unit	Expenditure, $
Food	5	14	70
Housing	3	10	30
Fun	4	5	20
Total			120

(a) Define the consumer price index.

(b) Assume that the basket of goods that defines the CPI is as given in the table. Calculate the CPI for 1990 if the prices prevailing in 1990 are as follows: food, $30 per unit; housing, $20 per unit; and fun, $6 per unit.

*(c) Show that the change in the CPI relative to the base year is a weighted average of the individual price changes, where the weights are given by the base year expenditure shares of the various goods.

8. Use Appendix 2-2 and the following 1987 GNP data (in billions) to answer this question:
GNP = $4,527
NNP = $4,047
Indirect taxes = $366
Other (net) = −$2
(a) What are (i) depreciation and (ii) national income?
(b) Why are indirect taxes deducted from NNP to get national income?

9. Assume that GNP is $5,000, personal disposable income is $4,100, and the government budget deficit is $200. Consumption is $3,800, and the trade deficit is $100.
(a) How large is saving *(S)*?
(b) What is the size of investment *(I)*?
(c) How large is government spending *(G)*?

10. Figure 2-4 shows that Japan is a net creditor. How does a country become a net creditor? Is Latin America a net debtor or a net creditor?

11. Show that a country that spends more than its income must have an external deficit.

APPENDIX 2-1: PRICE INDEX FORMULAS

Both the PPI and CPI are price indexes that compare the current and base year cost of a basket of goods of *fixed* composition. If we denote the base year quantities of the various goods by q_0^i and their base year prices by p_0^i, the cost of the basket in the base year is $\Sigma p_0^i q_0^i$, where the summation (Σ) is over all the goods in the basket. The cost of a basket of the *same* quantities but at today's prices is $\Sigma p_t^i q_0^i$, where p_t^i is today's price. The CPI or PPI is the ratio of today's cost to the base year cost, or

$$\text{Consumer or producer price index} = \frac{\Sigma p_t^i q_0^i}{\Sigma p_0^i q_0^i}$$

This is a so-called *Laspeyres*, or *base-weighted*, price index.

The GNP deflator, by contrast, uses the weights of the *current* period to calculate the price index. Let q_t^i be the quantities of the different goods produced in the current year.

---

* An asterisk denotes a more difficult problem.

$$\text{GNP deflator} = \frac{\text{GNP measured in current prices}}{\text{GNP measured in base year prices}}$$

$$= \frac{\Sigma p_t^i q_t^i}{\Sigma p_0^i q_t^i} \times 100$$

This is known as a *Paasche,* or *current-weighted,* price index.

Comparing the two formulas we see that they differ only in that q_0^i, or the base year quantities, appears in both numerator and denominator of the CPI and PPI formula, whereas q_t^i appears in the formula for the deflator. In practice, the CPI, PPI, and GNP deflator indexes differ also because they involve different collections of goods.

PROBLEM: Calculate both the Laspeyres and Paasche price indexes for the information in Table 2-1.

APPENDIX 2-2: RELATION BETWEEN GNP AND PERSONAL DISPOSABLE INCOME

This appendix sets out the steps that are needed to calculate the level of personal disposable income, starting from GNP. The necessity for these adjustments arises from four sources: depreciation, transfers, taxes and subsidies, and the presence of a business sector that retains some profits.

The first step is to move from GNP to NNP, from "gross" to "net," in order to reflect depreciation. Thus net national product, or NNP, is GNP less depreciation.

Table A2-1 summarizes the remaining steps from NNP to personal disposable income.

TABLE A2-1
GNP AND PERSONAL DISPOSABLE INCOME, 1988 (billions of dollars)

Gross national product			4,864.3
Less	Capital consumption allowance	506.4	
Equals	Net national product		4,357.9
Less	Indirect taxes	389.0	
	Other (net)	0.5	
Equals	National income		3,968.4
Less	Corporate profits	328.4	
	Social insurance contributions	444.7	
Plus	Government and business transfers to persons	586.1	
	Interest adjustment	184.4	
	Dividends	96.3	
Equals	Personal income		4,062.1
Less	Personal tax and nontax payments	590.3	
Equals	Disposable personal income		3,471.8

SOURCE: *Survey of Current Business.*

INCOME AND SPENDING

*O*ne of the central questions in macroeconomics is why output fluctuates. We saw in Chapter 1 that over the past 60 years output has grown at an *average* annual rate of 3.0 percent. But that growth has been uneven; in some years, for example, the great depression in the 1930s, output actually fell. In other years, especially in recovery periods, output grew more rapidly than the trend rate. Figure 3-1 shows the behavior of real GNP in 1978–1984. Both in 1980–1981 and in 1982 real GNP declined. By contrast, in 1983 output grew rapidly. This chapter offers a first theory of these fluctuations in real GNP. The cornerstone of this model is the interaction between output and spending: Spending determines output and income, but output and income determine spending.[1]

Before developing this *Keynesian* model of income determination we make some brief comments that place this simple first model in the context of the more comprehensive model of income and price determination that will be developed in later chapters.

A student of microeconomics would have a ready answer to the question, What happens if there is an increase in the demand for a particular good, say shoes? We are likely to get one of three answers:

- Firms will produce more.
- Firms will raise the price.
- Firms will sell from the stock of inventories they hold.

In most cases the adjustment to a demand disturbance will involve all three reactions.

---

[1] Because output is equal to income received in the economy, economists tend to use the terms income and output interchangeably when discussing the level of economic activity.

The importance of each reaction will depend on a host of factors: Is the increase in demand permanent or only transitory? How easy is it to change the level of production? Are inventories high or low?

We can ask the same question in macroeconomics. What happens if there is an increase in *aggregate* demand, the total amount of goods and services demanded in the economy? The model developed in this chapter provides part of the answer to that question.

In Figure 3-2 we show the economy's aggregate demand curve, introduced in Chapter 1, as well as the aggregate supply schedule. The increase in demand is shown by a rightward shift of the demand schedule, so at each level of prices the quantity demanded is now higher. If the initial market equilibrium was at *E*, then after the shift in demand the market clears at *E'*, at which point both output and prices have risen.

Many of the questions raised in this book have to do with what we see in Figure 3-2. We highlight two in particular: First, what factors cause the *aggregate* demand or supply curve to shift? Second, given a shift in the aggregate demand or supply curve, is the adjustment made mostly by price changes or mostly by changes in output?

In this chapter we develop a first model of macroeconomic adjustment. The

FIGURE 3-1
FLUCTUATIONS IN REAL GNP, 1978–1984. (SOURCE: DRI/McGraw-Hill.)

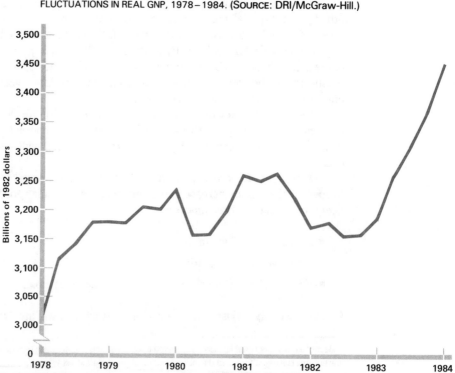

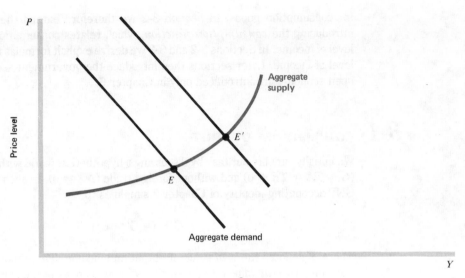

FIGURE 3-2
THE EFFECT OF A SHIFT IN AGGREGATE DEMAND. In Chapter 1 we
introduced aggregate demand and supply schedules. An increase in
aggregate demand is shown as a rightward shift of the demand
schedule. The effect of increased demand is to raise both output and
the price level.

model is extreme in that it assumes that firms are willing to sell *any* amount of output
at a given level of prices P_0 so that the aggregate supply curve is entirely flat.[2] In this
case shifts in aggregate demand affect only output. Of course, this is an extreme case
because it assumes prices are fixed, and in later chapters we allow price adjustments.
But the lack of realism pays off. An important point of the model is to show that when
output adjusts in response to a change in demand, the increases in output and income
have a feedback effect on demand. An increase in demand raises output, but the
increases in output and income feed back to demand and cause further rounds of
adjustment. We will now study how the equilibrium level of output is determined in this
case.

The key concept of *equilibrium output* is introduced immediately, in Section
3-1. We assume initially that the demand for goods is *autonomous*—that is, independent of the level of income.[3] In fact, though, increases in income increase the demand

---

[2] The assumption that prices are constant is made in order to simplify the exposition of Chaps. 3 and 4. In
later chapters, starting with Chap. 7, we use the theory of aggregate demand developed here to study the
factors that determine the price level and cause it to change over time.

[3] The terms *autonomous* and *induced* are traditionally used to indicate spending that is independent of
the level of income and dependent on the level of income, respectively. More generally, autonomous
spending is spending that is independent of the other variables explained in a given theory.

for consumption goods. In Section 3-2 we therefore extend the basic analysis by introducing the *consumption function,* which relates consumption spending to the level of income. In Sections 3-2 and 3-3 we derive explicit formulas for the equilibrium level of income. Later sections then introduce the government sector. Issues of the open economy are introduced only in Chapter 6.

3-1 EQUILIBRIUM OUTPUT

We initially simplify our task by discussing a hypothetical world without a government ($G \equiv TA \equiv TR \equiv 0$) and without foreign trade ($NX \equiv 0$). In such a world, the basic GNP accounting identity of Chapter 2 simplifies to

$$C + I \equiv Y \equiv C + S \tag{1}$$

where Y denotes the *real* value of output and income. Throughout this chapter we refer only to *real* values. For instance, when we speak of a change in consumption spending, we mean a change in real consumption spending.

What would determine the level of output if firms could supply any amount of output at the prevailing level of prices? *Demand* must enter the picture. Firms would produce at a level just sufficient to meet demand. To develop this point, we define the concepts of *aggregate demand* and *equilibrium output.*

Aggregate Demand

Aggregate demand is the total amount of goods demanded in the economy. In general, the quantity of goods demanded, or aggregate demand, depends on the level of income in the economy and — as we shall see later — on interest rates. But for now we shall assume that the amount of goods demanded is constant, independent of the level of income.

Aggregate demand is shown in Figure 3-3 by the horizontal line *AD.* In the diagram, aggregate demand is equal to 300 (billion dollars). This means that the total amount of goods demanded in the economy is $300 billion, independent of the level of income.

But if the quantity of goods demanded is constant, independent of the level of income, what determines the actual level of income? We have to turn to the concept of equilibrium output.

Equilibrium Output

Output is at its *equilibrium* level when the quantity of output produced is equal to the quantity demanded. An equilibrium situation is one which no forces are causing to change. We now explain why output is at its equilibrium level when it is equal to aggregate demand.

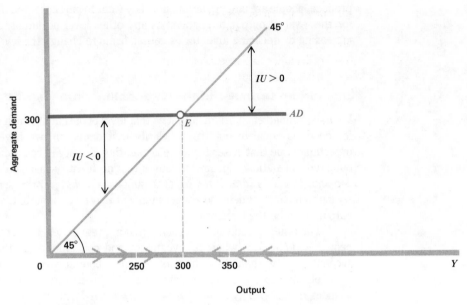

FIGURE 3-3

EQUILIBRIUM WITH CONSTANT AGGREGATE DEMAND. Aggregate demand is shown by the *AD* line and is equal to 300. Output is at its equilibrium level when it is equal to aggregate demand, which equals 300. Thus the equilibrium is at point *E*, as shown. At any other output level, inventories are changing in a way that causes firms to change their production in a direction that moves output toward the equilibrium level.

In Figure 3-3 we show the level of output on the horizontal axis. The 45° line serves as a reference line that translates any horizontal distance into an equal vertical distance. For any given level of output (*Y*) on the horizontal axis, the 45° line gives the level of aggregate demand on the vertical axis that is equal to that level of output. For instance, at point *E*, both output and aggregate demand are equal to 300.

Point *E* is the point of equilibrium output, at which the quantity of output produced is equal to the quantity demanded. To understand why this should be the equilibrium level of output, suppose that firms were producing some other amount, say 350 units. Then output would exceed demand. Firms would be unable to sell all they produce and would find their warehouses filling with inventories of unsold goods. They would then cut their output. This is shown by the horizontal arrow pointing left from the output level of 350.

Similarly, if output were less than 300, say 250, firms would either run out of goods or be running down their inventories. They would therefore increase output, as shown by the horizontal arrow pointing to the right from the output level of 250.

Thus at point *E*, the equilibrium level of output, firms are selling as much as they produce, people are buying the amount they want to purchase, and there is no tendency for the level of output to change. At any other level of output, the pressure from increasing or declining inventories causes firms to change the level of output.

Equilibrium Output and the National Income Identity

We have defined equilibrium output as that level of output at which aggregate demand for goods is equal to output. To clarify that definition, we have to dispose of an unsettling issue that arises from the accounting identity in equation (1), derived from our study of national income accounting. The identity in equation (1) states that demand, $C + I$, is *identically* equal to supply, Y, *whatever* the level of output. That seems to mean that demand equals supply at *any* level of output, so that any level of output could be the equilibrium level.

The issue is resolved by recalling that aggregate demand is the amount of goods people *want to buy*, whereas investment and consumption in the national income accounts are the amounts of the goods *actually* bought whether or not people wanted to or planned to buy them. In particular, the investment measured in equation (1) includes *involuntary*, or *unintended* (or *undesired*), inventory changes, which occur when firms find themselves selling more or fewer goods than they had planned to sell. Similarly, if households cannot buy all the goods they want, the consumption measured in equation (1) will differ from planned consumption.

We have to make a distinction between the actual aggregate demand that is measured in an accounting context and the relevant economic concept of planned (desired, intended) aggregate demand.

Actual aggregate demand $(C + I)$ is, by the accounting identity in equation (1), equal to the level of output (Y). The output level is determined by firms. In deciding how much to produce, firms calculate how much investment, including inventory investment, they want to undertake. They also produce to meet the demand for consumption they forecast will be forthcoming from households. *Planned aggregate demand* consists of the amount of consumption that households plan to carry out plus the amount of investment planned by firms.[4]

If firms miscalculate households' consumption demands, planned aggregate demand does not equal actual aggregate demand. Suppose first that firms overestimate consumption demand. In terms of Table 3-1, suppose that firms decide to produce 350 units of output, expecting to be able to sell that amount. However, aggregate demand is only 300. The firms thus sell 300 units of output. But they are left with 50, which they have to add to their inventories. It is as if they buy those extra 50 units of output themselves. In the national income accounts, additions to inventories count as investment. Of course, this is not *planned* or *desired* investment, but it does count as part of

---

[4] From now on we shall assume that actual consumption is equal to planned consumption, so that all differences between actual and planned aggregate demand are reflected in unintended inventory changes. In practical terms, this means we are not considering situations where firms put "Sold Out" signs in their windows and customers cannot buy what they want.

TABLE 3-1

EQUILIBRIUM OUTPUT AND INVOLUNTARY INVENTORY CHANGE

Output	Aggregate demand	Involuntary inventory changes
200	300	−100
250	300	−50
300	300	0
350	300	+50
400	300	+100

investment. Looking at the national income accounts of such an economy, we would see output equal to 350 and consumption plus investment equal to 350. But the equality of output and $(C + I)$ does not mean that 350 is the equilibrium level of output, because 50 units of investment were undesired additions to inventories.

When aggregate demand—the amount people want to buy—is not equal to output, there is unplanned inventory investment. We summarize this as

$$IU = Y - AD \tag{2}$$

where IU is unplanned additions to inventory.

In Figure 3-3, unplanned inventory investment is shown by the vertical arrows. When output exceeds 300, there is unplanned inventory investment. When output is less than 300, there are unplanned reductions in inventories. In Table 3-1, unplanned inventory investment is shown in the last column.

An alternative way of seeing the link between the national income accounting relations and the economic concepts is in equation (2a). Here we state that actual output is equal to planned spending, or aggregate demand, plus involuntary inventory adjustment

$$\text{Output} = \text{planned spending} + \text{involuntary inventory adjustment} \tag{2a}$$

The *equilibrium* level of income is the level of income (or output) at which planned spending is equal to actual output, so that there is no involuntary inventory accumulation or rundown.

Equilibrium Output and Demand

We can now define equilibrium output more formally, using equation (2). Output is at its equilibrium level when it is equal to aggregate demand, or when unplanned inventory accumulation is zero. That is, output is at its equilibrium level when

$$Y = AD \tag{3}$$

There are three essential notions in this section:

1. Aggregate demand determines the equilibrium level of output.
2. At equilibrium, unintended changes in inventories are zero, and households consume the amount they want to consume.
3. An adjustment process for output based on unintended inventory changes will actually move output to its equilibrium level.[5]

Note, too, that the definition of equilibrium implies that actual spending on consumption and investment equals planned spending. In equilibrium, aggregate demand, which is planned spending, equals output. Since output identically equals income, we see also that *in equilibrium, planned spending equals income.*

3-2 THE CONSUMPTION FUNCTION AND AGGREGATE DEMAND

The preceding section studied the equilibrium level of output (and income) on the assumption that aggregate demand was simply a constant. Now we move to a more realistic specification of aggregate demand and begin to examine the economic variables that determine it.

In our simplified model, which excludes both the government and foreign trade, aggregate demand consists of the demands for consumption and investment. The demand for consumption goods is not in practice autonomous, as we have so far assumed, but rather increases with income — families with higher incomes consume more than families with lower incomes, and countries where income is higher typically have higher levels of total consumption. The relationship between consumption and income is described by the *consumption function.*

The Consumption Function

We assume that consumption demand increases with the level of income:[6]

$$C = cY \qquad 0 < c < 1 \tag{4}$$

---

[5] You may have noticed that the adjustment process we describe raises the possibility that output will temporarily exceed its new equilibrium level during the adjustment to an increase in aggregate demand. This is the inventory cycle. Suppose firms desire to hold inventories which are proportional to the level of demand. When demand unexpectedly rises, inventories are depleted. In subsequent periods, the firms have to produce not only to meet the new, higher level of aggregate demand, but also to restore the depleted inventories and raise them to the new higher level. While firms are rebuilding their inventories and also producing to meet the higher level of demand, their total production will exceed the new higher level of aggregate demand.

[6] Equation (4) is special because consumption is proportional to income, implying that at a zero level of income consumption would be zero. Box 3-1 shows that this form is supported by the data. But one often sees discussion of a consumption function that includes a constant, $C = C' + cY$. Nothing substantive is changed by this alternative. Several of the problems at the end of the chapter use this form.

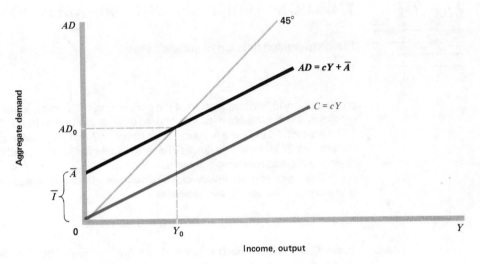

FIGURE 3-4

THE CONSUMPTION FUNCTION AND AGGREGATE DEMAND. The consumption function shows the level of consumption spending at each level of income. The consumption function is upward-sloping. The slope of the consumption function is the marginal propensity to consume, c. Aggregate demand is the sum of the demands for consumption and investment goods. Investment demand, I, is assumed constant and is added to consumption demand to obtain the level of aggregate demand at each level of income. The line AD shows how aggregate demand increases with income. Its slope is c, the marginal propensity to consume.

This consumption function is shown in Figure 3-4. The level of consumption is proportional to income; for every \$1 increase in income, consumption rises by \$$c$. For example, if c is 0.90, then for every \$1 increase in income, consumption rises by 90 cents. The *slope* of the consumption function is c. Along the consumption function the level of consumption rises with income. Box 3-1 shows that this relationship holds in practice.

The coefficient c is sufficiently important to have a special name, the *marginal propensity to consume.* The marginal propensity to consume is the increase in consumption per unit increase in income. In our case, the marginal propensity to consume is less than 1, which implies that out of a dollar increase in income, only a fraction, c, is spent on consumption.

Consumption and Saving

What happens to the rest, the fraction $(1 - c)$, that is not spent on consumption? If it is not spent, it must be saved. Income is either spent or saved; there are no other uses to which income can be put.

box 3-1

THE CONSUMPTION-INCOME RELATIONSHIP

The consumption function of equation (4),

$$C = cY$$

provides a good first description of the consumption-income relationship. Annual consumption and disposable personal income data for the United States for the years since 1948 are plotted in Figure 1. Recall from Chapter 2 that disposable personal income is the amount of income households have available for either spending or saving after paying taxes and receiving transfers.

The figure reveals a very close relationship between consumption and disposable income. The actual relationship is

$$C = 0.92\,YD$$

where C and YD are each measured in billions of real (1982) dollars. Although the relationship between consumption and disposable income is close, not all the points in Figure 1 lie exactly on the line. That means that something other than disposable income is affecting consumption in any given year. We turn our attention to those other factors determining consumption in Chapter 8. Meanwhile, it is reassuring that equation (4) is a quite accurate description of the real world's consumption-income relationship. ∎

More formally, look at equation (5) which says that income that is not spent on consumption is saved, or

$$S \equiv Y - C \qquad Y = C + S \tag{5}$$

Equation (5) tells us that by definition *saving is equal to income minus consumption.* This means that we cannot postulate an independent saving function in addition to the consumption function and still expect consumption and saving to add up to income.

The consumption function in equation (4) together with equation (5), which we call the *budget constraint*, imply a saving function. The saving function relates the

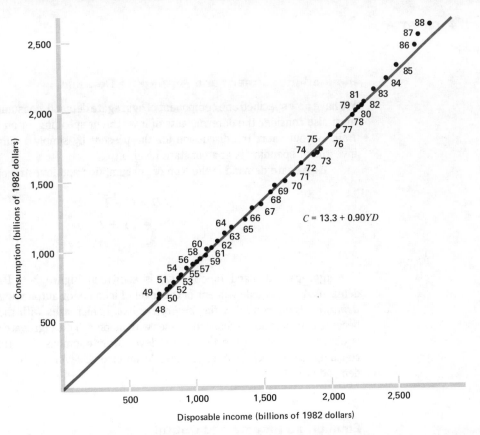

$C = 13.3 + 0.90YD$

FIGURE 1

THE CONSUMPTION-INCOME RELATION, 1948–1988. There is a close
relationship in practice between consumption spending and disposable
income. Consumption spending rises on average by 92 cents for every
extra dollar of disposable income. The colored line is the fitted
regression line that summarizes the relationship shown by the points
for the individual years.

level of saving to the level of income. Substituting the consumption function in equation
(4) into the budget constraint in equation (5) yields the saving function

$$S \equiv Y - C = Y - cY = (1 - c)Y \tag{6}$$

From equation (6), we see that saving is an increasing function of the level of income
because the *marginal propensity to save*, $s = 1 - c$, is positive. For instance, suppose the marginal propensity to consume, c, is 0.9, meaning that 90 cents out of each
extra dollar of income is consumed. Then the marginal propensity to save, s, is 0.10,
meaning that the remaining 10 cents of each extra dollar of income is saved (Box 3-1).

Planned Investment and Aggregate Demand

We have now specified one component of aggregate demand, consumption demand. We must also consider the determinants of investment spending, or an *investment function*. We cut short the discussion for the present by simply assuming that planned investment spending is at a constant level, $\bar{I}$.[7]

Aggregate demand is the sum of consumption and investment demands:

$$
\begin{aligned}
AD &= C + \bar{I} \\
&= cY + \bar{I} \\
&= \bar{A} + cY
\end{aligned}
\tag{7}
$$

The aggregate demand function (7) is shown in Figure 3-4. Part of aggregate demand, $\bar{A} = \bar{I}$, is independent of the level of income, or autonomous. But *aggregate demand also depends on the level of income*. It increases with the level of income because consumption demand increases with income. The aggregate demand schedule is obtained by adding (vertically) the level of autonomous investment spending to consumption at each level of income. At an income level Y_0 the level of aggregate demand is AD_0.

Equilibrium Income and Output

The next step is to use the aggregate demand function, AD, in Figure 3-4 and equation (7) to determine the equilibrium levels of output and income. We do this in Figure 3-5.

Recall the basic point of this chapter: The equilibrium level of income is such that aggregate demand equals output (which in turn equals income). The 45° line in Figure 3-5 shows points at which output and aggregate demand are equal. The aggregate demand schedule in Figure 3-5 cuts the 45° line at E, and it is accordingly at E that aggregate demand is equal to output (equals income). Only at E, and at the corresponding equilibrium levels of income and output (Y_0), does aggregate demand exactly equal output.[8] At those levels of output and income, planned spending precisely matches production.

The arrows in Figure 3-5 indicate once again how we reach equilibrium. If firms expand production whenever they face unintended decreases in their inventory holdings, then they increase output at any level below Y_0; this is because below Y_0, aggregate demand exceeds output and inventories are declining. Conversely, for output levels above Y_0, firms find inventories piling up and therefore cut production. This process leads to the output level Y_0, at which current production exactly matches planned aggregate spending and unintended inventory changes are therefore equal to

---

[7] In later chapters investment spending will become a function of the interest rate and will gain an important place in the transmission of monetary policy.

[8] We frequently use the subscript 0 to denote the equilibrium level of a variable.

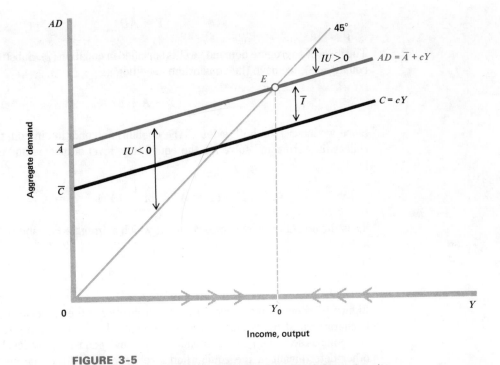

FIGURE 3-5
DETERMINATION OF EQUILIBRIUM INCOME AND OUTPUT. Output is at its
equilibrium level when aggregate demand is equal to output. This
occurs at point E, corresponding to the output (and income) level Y_0.
At any higher level of output, aggregate demand is below the level of
output, firms are unable to sell all they produce, and there is undesired
accumulation of inventories. Firms therefore reduce output, as shown
by the arrows. Similarly, at any level of output below Y_0, aggregate
demand exceeds output, firms run short of goods to sell, and they
therefore increase output. Only at the equilibrium output level, Y_0, are
firms producing the amount that is demanded, and there is no tendency
for the level of output to change.

zero. Again, the arrows in Figure 3-5 represent the dynamic process by which the
economy moves to the equilibrium level of output Y_0.[9]

THE FORMULA FOR EQUILIBRIUM OUTPUT

The determination of equilibrium output in Figure 3-5 can also be described using
equation (7) and the equilibrium condition in the goods market, which is that output is
equal to aggregate demand:

[9] Do you see that there is once more the possibility of an inventory cycle? Refer to footnote 5.

$$Y = AD \tag{8}$$

The level of aggregate demand, AD, is specified in equation (7). Substituting for AD in equation (8), we have the equilibrium condition as

$$Y = \overline{A} + cY \tag{9}$$

Since we have Y on both sides of the equilibrium condition in equation (9), we can collect the terms and solve for the equilibrium level of income and output, denoted by Y_0:

$$Y - cY = \overline{A} \quad \text{or} \quad Y(1 - c) = \overline{A}$$

Thus the equilibrium level of income, at which aggregate demand equals output, is

$$Y_0 = \frac{1}{1 - c} \overline{A} \tag{10}$$

Figure 3-5 sheds light on equation (10). The position of the aggregate demand schedule is characterized by its slope, c, and intercept, $\overline{A}$. The intercept, $\overline{A}$, is the level of autonomous spending, that is, spending that is independent of the level of income. The other determinant of the equilibrium level of income is the marginal propensity to consume, c, which is the slope of the aggregate demand schedule.

Given the intercept, a steeper aggregate demand function — as would be implied by a higher marginal propensity to consume — implies a higher level of equilibrium income. Similarly, for a given marginal propensity to consume, a higher level of autonomous spending — in terms of Figure 3-5, a larger intercept — implies a higher equilibrium level of income. These results, suggested by Figure 3-5, are easily verified using equation (10), which gives the formula for the equilibrium level of income.

Thus, the equilibrium level of output is higher, the larger the marginal propensity to consume, c, and the higher the level of autonomous spending, $\overline{A}$.

Saving and Investment

There is a useful alternative formulation of the equilibrium condition that aggregate demand is equal to output. In *equilibrium, planned investment equals saving*. This condition applies only to an economy in which there is no government and no foreign trade.

To understand this relationship, return to Figure 3-5. The vertical distance between the aggregate demand and consumption schedules in that figure is equal to planned investment spending, $\overline{I}$. Note also that the vertical distance between the consumption schedule and the 45° line measures saving ($S = Y - C$) at each level of income.

The equilibrium level of income is found where AD crosses the 45° line, at E.

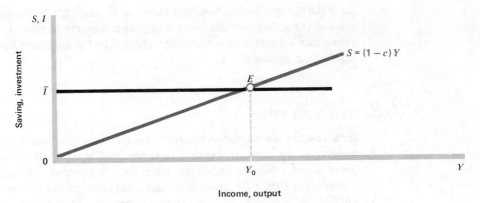

FIGURE 3-6

SAVING AND INVESTMENT. An alternative definition of the equilibrium level of output is that it occurs where saving is equal to (planned) investment. This is shown at point E, with corresponding output level Y_0. At higher levels of output, consumers want to save more than I. They do not buy all of output, inventories accumulate, and actual investment is made equal to saving because firms undertake undesired inventory investment. They therefore cut output, and the economy moves to output level Y_0.

Accordingly, at the equilibrium level of income — and only at that level — the two vertical distances are equal. Thus at the equilibrium level of income, saving equals (planned) investment. By contrast, above the equilibrium level of income, Y_0, saving (the distance between the 45° line and the consumption schedule) exceeds planned investment, while below Y_0, planned investment exceeds saving.

The equality between saving and investment at equilibrium is an essential characteristic of the equilibrium level of income. We can see that by starting with the basic equilibrium condition, equation (8), $Y = AD$. If we subtract consumption from both Y and AD, we realize that $Y - C$ is saving and $AD - C$ is planned investment. In symbols,

$$Y = AD$$
$$Y - C = AD - C \tag{11}$$
$$S = \bar{I}$$

Thus, the condition $S = \bar{I}$ is merely another way of stating the basic equilibrium condition.[10]

There is also a diagrammatic derivation of the equilibrium level of income in terms of the balance between saving and investment in equation (11). In Figure 3-6, we

---

[10] In problem 3 at the end of this chapter, we ask you to derive equation (10) for Y_0 by starting from $S = I$ and substituting for S from equation (6).

show the saving function. Saving is shown as increasing with the level of income. The slope of the saving function is the marginal propensity to save, $1 - c$. We also have drawn planned investment spending, indicated by the horizontal line with intercept $\bar{I}$. Equilibrium income is Y_0.

3-3   THE MULTIPLIER

In this section we develop an answer to the following question: By how much does a $1 increase in autonomous spending raise the equilibrium level of income?[11] There appears to be a simple answer. Since, in equilibrium, income equals aggregate demand, it would seem that a $1 increase in (autonomous) demand or spending should raise equilibrium income by $1. That answer is wrong. Let us now see why.

Suppose first that output increased by $1 to match the increased level of autonomous spending. This increase in output and income would in turn give rise to further *induced* spending as consumption rises because the level of income has risen. How much of the initial $1 increase in income would be spent on consumption? Out of an additional dollar of income, a fraction (c) is consumed. Assume then that production increases further to meet this induced expenditure, that is, that output and thus income increase by $1 + c$. That will still leave us with an excess demand, because the expansion in production and income by $1 + c$ will give rise to further induced spending. This story could clearly take a long time to tell. We seem to have arrived at an impasse at which an expansion in output to meet excess demand leads to a further expansion in demand without an obvious end to the process.

It helps to lay out the various steps in this chain more carefully. We do this in Table 3-2. We start off the first round with an increase in autonomous spending, ΔA. Next we allow an expansion in production to meet exactly that increase in demand. Production accordingly expands by ΔA. This increase in production gives rise to an equal increase in income and, therefore, via the consumption function, $C = cY$, gives rise in the second round to induced expenditures of size $c(\Delta A)$. Assume again that production expands to meet the increase in spending. The production adjustment this time is $c\Delta A$, and so is the increase in income. This gives rise to a third round of induced spending equal to the marginal propensity to consume times the increase in income $c(c\Delta A) = c^2\Delta A$. Careful inspection of the last term shows that induced expenditures in the third round are smaller than those in the second round. Since the marginal propensity to consume, c, is less than 1, the term c^2 is less than c. This can be seen also in the lower part of the table, where we assume $c = 0.6$ and show the steps corresponding to those in the upper part of the table.

If we write out the successive rounds of increased spending, starting with the initial increase in autonomous demand, we obtain

---

[11] Recall that autonomous spending, A, is spending that is independent of the level of income. Note also that the answer to this question is contained in equation (10). Can you deduce the answer directly from equation (10)? This section provides an explanation of that answer.

TABLE 3-2
THE MULTIPLIER

Round	Increase in demand this round	Increase in production this round	Total increase in income
1	$\Delta\overline{A}$	$\Delta\overline{A}$	$\Delta\overline{A}$
2	$c\Delta\overline{A}$	$c\Delta\overline{A}$	$(1+c)\Delta\overline{A}$
3	$c^2\Delta\overline{A}$	$c^2\Delta\overline{A}$	$(1+c+c^2)\Delta\overline{A}$
4	$c^3\Delta\overline{A}$	$c^3\Delta\overline{A}$	$(1+c+c^2+c^3)\Delta\overline{A}$
.	.	.	.
.	.	.	.
.	.	.	$\dfrac{1}{1-c}\Delta\overline{A}$
1	1.0	1.0	1.0
2	0.6	0.6	1.6
3	0.36	0.36	1.96
4	0.216	0.216	2.176
5	0.1296	0.1296	2.3056
.	.	.	.
.	.	.	.
.	.	.	2.5

$$\Delta AD = \Delta\overline{A} + c\Delta\overline{A} + c^2\Delta\overline{A} + c^3\Delta\overline{A} + \cdots$$
$$= \Delta\overline{A}(1 + c + c^2 + c^3 + \cdots) \tag{12}$$

For a value of $c < 1$, the successive terms in the series become progressively smaller. In fact, we are dealing with a geometric series, so the equation simplifies to

$$\Delta AD = \frac{1}{1-c}\Delta\overline{A} = \Delta Y_0 \tag{13}$$

From equation (13), therefore, we find that the cumulative change in aggregate spending is equal to a multiple of the increase in autonomous spending. This could also have been deduced from equation (10).[12] The multiple $1/(1-c)$ is called the *multiplier*. The multiplier is the amount by which equilibrium output changes when autonomous aggregate demand increases by one unit. Because the multiplier exceeds unity,

---

[12] If you are familiar with the calculus, you will realize that the multiplier is nothing other than the derivative of the equilibrium level of income, Y_0, in equation (10) with respect to autonomous spending. Use the calculus on equation (10) and later on equation (22) to check the statements in the text.

we know that a $1 change in autonomous spending increases equilibrium income and output by more than $1.[13]

The concept of the multiplier is sufficiently important to create new notation. Defining the multiplier as α, we have

$$\alpha \equiv \frac{1}{1-c} \tag{14}$$

Inspection of the multiplier in equation (14) shows that the larger the marginal propensity to consume, the larger the multiplier. With a marginal propensity to consume of 0.6, as in Table 3-2, the multiplier is 2.5; for a marginal propensity to consume of 0.8, the multiplier is 5. The reason is simply that a high marginal propensity to consume implies that a large fraction of an additional dollar of income will be consumed, and thereby added to aggregate demand. Accordingly, expenditures induced by an increase in autonomous spending are high and, therefore, so is the expansion in output and income that is needed to restore balance between income and demand (or spending).

Note that the relationship between the marginal propensity to consume, c, and the marginal propensity to save, s, allows us to write equation (14) in a somewhat different form. Remembering from the budget constraint that saving plus consumption adds up to income, we realize that the fraction of an additional dollar of income consumed plus the fraction saved must add up to a dollar, or $1 \equiv s + c$. Substituting $s \equiv 1 - c$ in equation (14), we obtain an equivalent formula for the multiplier in terms of the marginal propensity to save: $\alpha \equiv 1/s$.

The Multiplier in Pictures

Figure 3-7 provides a graphical interpretation of the effects of an increase in autonomous spending on the equilibrium level of income. The initial equilibrium is at point E with an income level Y_0. Now autonomous spending increases from $\overline{A}$ to $\overline{A}'$. This is represented by a parallel upward shift of the aggregate demand schedule to AD'. The upward shift means that now, at each level of income, aggregate demand is higher by an amount $\Delta \overline{A} \equiv \overline{A}' - \overline{A}$.

Aggregate demand now exceeds the initial level of income, Y_0, or output. Consequently, unintended inventory rundown is taking place at a rate equal to the increase in autonomous spending, or to the vertical distance $\Delta \overline{A}$. Firms will respond to that excess

---

[13] *Two warnings:* (1) The multiplier is necessarily greater than 1 in this very simplified model of the determination of income, but as we shall see in the discussion of "crowding out" in Chap. 4, there may be circumstances in which it is less than 1; (2) the term *multiplier* is used more generally in economics to mean the effect on some endogenous variable (a variable whose level is explained by the theory being studied) of a unit change in an exogenous variable (a variable whose level is not determined within the theory being examined). For instance, one can talk of the multiplier of a change in the income tax rate on the level of unemployment. However, the classic use of the term is as we are using it here — the effects of a change in autonomous spending on equilibrium output.

demand by expanding production, say to income level Y'. This expansion in production gives rise to induced expenditure, increasing aggregate demand to the level A'. At the same time, the expansion reduces the gap between aggregate demand and output to the vertical distance FG. The gap between demand and output is reduced because the marginal propensity to consume is less than 1.

Thus, a marginal propensity to consume that is positive but less than unity implies that a sufficient expansion in output will restore the balance between aggregate demand and output. In Figure 3-7 the new equilibrium is indicated by point E', and the corresponding level of income is Y'_0. The change in income required is therefore $\Delta Y_0 = Y'_0 - Y_0$.

The magnitude of the income change required to restore equilibrium depends on

FIGURE 3-7

GRAPHICAL DERIVATION OF THE MULTIPLIER. When there is an increase in autonomous aggregate demand, the aggregate demand schedule shifts up to AD'. The equilibrium moves from E to E'. The increase in equilibrium output $(Y'_0 - Y)$, which equals distance PE equal to PE', exceeds the increase in autonomous demand, $E'Q$. From the diagram we see that the excess is a result of the AD curve's having a positive slope rather than being horizontal. In other words, the multiplier exceeds 1 because consumption demand increases with output — any increase in output produces further increases in demand.

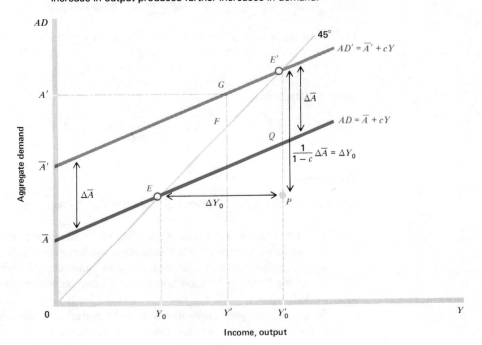

two factors. The larger the increase in autonomous spending, represented in Figure 3-7 by the parallel shift in the aggregate demand schedule, the larger the income change. Furthermore, the larger the marginal propensity to consume — that is, the steeper the aggregate demand schedule — the larger the income change.

As a further check on our results, we verify from Figure 3-7 that the change in equilibrium income exceeds the change in autonomous spending. For that purpose, we use the 45° line to compare the change in income $\Delta Y_0 (= EP = PE')$ with the change in autonomous spending that is equal to the vertical distance between the new and old aggregate demand schedule (QE'). It is clear from Figure 3-7 that the change in income, PE', exceeds the change in autonomous spending, QE'.

Another Derivation

Finally, there is yet another way of deriving the multiplier. Remember that in equilibrium, aggregate demand equals income or output. From one equilibrium to another, it must therefore be true that the change in income, ΔY_0, is equal to the change in aggregate demand, ΔAD:

$$\Delta Y_0 = \Delta AD \qquad (15)$$

Next we split up the change in aggregate demand into the change in autonomous spending, $\Delta \bar{A}$, and the change in expenditure induced by the consequent change in income, that is, $c\Delta Y_0$:

$$\Delta AD = \Delta \bar{A} + c\Delta Y_0 \qquad (16)$$

Combining equations (15) and (16), the change in income is

$$\Delta Y_0 = \Delta \bar{A} + c\Delta Y_0 \qquad (17)$$

or, collecting terms,

$$\Delta Y_0 = \frac{1}{1-c} \Delta \bar{A} = \alpha \Delta \bar{A} \qquad (18)$$

Summary

There are three points to remember from this discussion of the multiplier.

1. An increase in autonomous spending raises the equilibrium level of income.
2. The increase in income is a multiple of the increase in autonomous spending.
3. The larger the marginal propensity to consume, the larger the multiplier arising from the relation between consumption and income.

As a check on your understanding of the material of this section, you should develop the same analysis, and the same answers, in terms of Figure 3-6.

3-4 THE GOVERNMENT SECTOR

So far we have ignored the role of the government sector in the determination of equilibrium income. The government affects the level of equilibrium income in two separate ways. First, government purchases of goods and services, G, are a component of aggregate demand. Second, taxes and transfers affect the relation between output and income, Y, and the *disposable income*—income available for consumption or saving—that accrues to the private sector, YD. In this section, we are concerned with the way in which government purchases, taxes, and transfers affect the equilibrium level of income.

We start again from the basic national income accounting identities. The introduction of the government restores government purchases (G) to the expenditure side of equation (1) of this chapter, and taxes (TA) less transfers (TR) to the allocation of income side. We can accordingly rewrite the identity in equation (1) as

$$C + I + G \equiv S + (TA - TR) + C \tag{1a}$$

The definition of aggregate demand has to be augmented to include government purchases of goods and services — the purchases of military equipment and services of bureaucrats, for instance. Thus we have

$$AD \equiv C + \bar{I} + G \tag{7a}$$

Consumption will no longer depend on income, but rather on disposable income, YD.[14] Disposable income (YD) is the net income available for spending by households after receiving transfers from and paying taxes to the government. It thus consists of income plus transfers less taxes, $Y + TR - TA$. The consumption function is now

$$C = cYD = c(Y + TR - TA) \tag{4a}$$

A final step is a specification of fiscal policy. Fiscal policy is the policy of the government with regard to the level of government purchases, the level of transfers, and the tax structure. We assume that the government purchases a constant amount, $\bar{G}$; that it makes a constant amount of transfers, $\overline{TR}$; and that it collects a fraction, t, of income in the form of taxes:

$$G = \bar{G} \qquad TR = \overline{TR} \qquad TA = tY \tag{19}$$

With this specification of fiscal policy, we can rewrite the consumption function, after substitution from equation (19) for TR and TA in equation (4a), as

$$C = c(Y + \overline{TR} - tY)$$
$$= c\overline{TR} + c(1 - t)Y \tag{20}$$

---

[14] The consumption function in Box 3-1 relates consumption to disposable income.

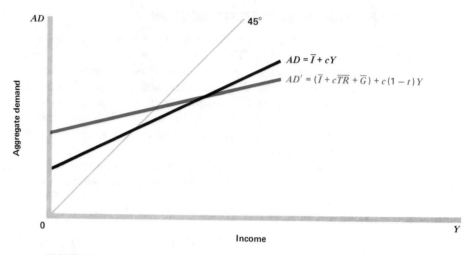

FIGURE 3-8

GOVERNMENT AND AGGREGATE DEMAND. Government affects aggregate demand through its own purchases, assumed here to be fixed at the autonomous level $\overline{G}$, through transfers $\overline{TR}$, and through taxes. Taxes are assumed to be a constant proportion, t, of income. Under these assumptions, the introduction of government shifts the intercept of the aggregate demand curve up and flattens the curve.

Note in equation (20) that the presence of transfers raises autonomous consumption spending by the marginal propensity to consume out of disposable income, c, times the amount of transfers.[15] The presence of income taxes, by contrast, lowers consumption spending at each level of income. That reduction arises because households' consumption is related to *disposable* income rather than income itself, and income taxes reduce disposable income relative to the level of income.

While the marginal propensity to consume out of disposable income remains c, now the marginal propensity to consume out of income is $c(1 - t)$, where $1 - t$ is the fraction of income left after taxes. For example, if the marginal propensity to consume, c, is 0.8 and the tax rate is 0.25, then the marginal propensity to consume out of income, $c(1 - t)$, is 0.6 [= 0.8 × (1 − 0.25)].

Combining (7 *a*), (19), and (20), we have now

$$AD = (c\overline{TR} + \overline{I} + \overline{G}) + c(1 - t)Y$$
$$= \overline{A} + c(1 - t)Y \tag{21}$$

The effects of the introduction of government on the aggregate demand schedule

---

[15] We are assuming no taxes are paid on transfers from the government. As a matter of fact, taxes are paid on some transfers, such as interest payments on the government debt, and not paid on other transfers, such as welfare benefits.

are shown in Figure 3-8. The new aggregate demand schedule, denoted AD' in the figure, starts out higher than the original schedule, AD, but has a flatter slope. The intercept is larger because it now includes both government spending, $\overline{G}$, and the part of consumption resulting from transfer payments by the government, $c\overline{TR}$. The slope is flatter because households now have to pay part of every dollar of income in taxes, and are left with only $(1 - t)$ of that dollar. Thus, as (21) shows, the marginal propensity to consume out of income is now $c(1 - t)$ instead of c.

Equilibrium Income

We are now set to study income determination when the government is included. We return to the equilibrium condition for the goods market, $Y = AD$, and using (21), write the equilibrium condition as

$$Y = \overline{A} + c(1 - t)Y$$

We can solve this equation for Y_0, the equilibrium level of income, by collecting terms in Y:

$$Y[1 - c(1 - t)] = \overline{A}$$

$$Y_0 = \frac{1}{1 - c(1 - t)}(\overline{G} + c\overline{TR} + \overline{I}) \tag{22}$$

In comparing equation (22) with equation (10), we see that the government sector makes a substantial difference. It raises autonomous spending by the amount of government purchases, $\overline{G}$, and by the amount of induced spending out of net transfers, $c\overline{TR}$.

INCOME TAXES AND THE MULTIPLIER

At the same time *income taxes lower the multiplier*. As can be seen from equation (22), if the marginal propensity to consume is 0.8 and taxes are zero, the multiplier is 5; with the same marginal propensity to consume and a tax rate of 0.25, the multiplier is cut in half to $1/[1 - 0.8(0.75)] = 2.5$. Income taxes reduce the multiplier because they reduce the induced increase of consumption out of changes in income. This can be seen in Figure 3-8, where the inclusion of taxes flattens the aggregate demand curve — recall from Figure 3-7 that the larger the multiplier, the steeper is the aggregate demand schedule.

Effects of a Change in Government Purchases

We now consider the effects of changes in fiscal policy on the equilibrium level of income. We distinguish three possible changes in fiscal variables: changes in government purchases, changes in transfers, and changes in the income tax. The simplest illustration is that of a change in government purchases. This case is shown in Figure 3-9, where the initial level of income is Y_0.

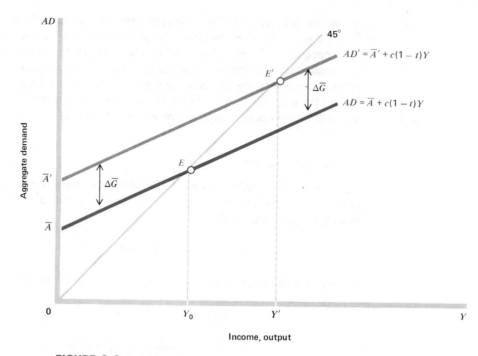

FIGURE 3-9
THE EFFECTS OF AN INCREASE IN GOVERNMENT PURCHASES. An increase in government spending shifts the aggregate demand schedule up from AD to AD'. Output rises from Y_0 to Y'. The multiplier is smaller now than it was in Figure 3-7.

An increase in government purchases is a change in autonomous spending and therefore shifts the aggregate demand schedule upward by an amount equal to the increase in government purchases. At the initial level of output and income, the demand for goods exceeds output, and accordingly, firms expand production until the new equilibrium, at point E', is reached.

By how much does income expand? Recall that the change in equilibrium income will equal the change in aggregate demand, or

$$\Delta Y_0 = \Delta \overline{G} + c(1 - t)\Delta Y_0$$

where the remaining terms ($\overline{TR}$ and $\overline{I}$) are constant by assumption. Thus, the change in equilibrium income is

$$\Delta Y_0 = \frac{1}{1 - c(1 - t)} \Delta \overline{G} = \overline{\alpha}\Delta \overline{G} \tag{23}$$

where we have introduced the notation $\overline{\alpha}$ to denote the multiplier in the presence of income taxes:

$$\bar{\alpha} \equiv \frac{1}{1 - c(1 - t)} \tag{24}$$

From equation (23) it is apparent that a \$1 increase in government purchases will lead to an increase in income in excess of a dollar. Thus, as we have already seen, with a marginal propensity to consume of $c = 0.8$ and an income tax rate of $t = 0.25$, we would have a multiplier of 2.5: a \$1 increase in government spending raises equilibrium income by \$2.50.

INCOME TAXES AS AUTOMATIC STABILIZERS

We have just seen that a proportional income tax reduces the multiplier. This means that if any component of autonomous demand changes, output will change by less if there is a proportional income tax than in the absence of such taxes. The proportional income tax is one example of the important concept of *automatic stabilizers*. An automatic stabilizer is any mechanism in the economy that reduces the amount by which output changes in response to a change in autonomous demand.

We shall see later that one explanation of the business cycle, the more or less regular movements of real GNP around trend, is that it is caused by shifts in investment demand. Sometimes, it is argued, investors are optimistic and investment is high — and so, therefore, is output. But sometimes they are pessimistic, and so both investment and output are low.

Swings in investment demand will have a smaller effect on output when automatic stabilizers are in place. This means that in the presence of automatic stabilizers we should expect output to fluctuate less than it would without them. Higher income tax rates in the post-World War II period are one reason that the business cycle has been less pronounced since 1945 than it was earlier.

The proportional income tax is not the only automatic stabilizer. Unemployment benefits enable the unemployed to continue consuming even if they do not have a job. This means that demand falls less when someone becomes unemployed than it would if there were no benefits. This too makes the multiplier smaller and output more stable. Unemployment benefits and a proportional income tax are two automatic stabilizers that keep the multiplier small, thereby stabilizing the economy by protecting it from responding strongly to every small movement in autonomous demand.[16]

Effects of Increased Transfer Payments

An increase in transfer payments increases autonomous demand, as can be seen in equation (21), in which autonomous demand includes the term $c\overline{TR}$. A \$1 increase in transfers therefore increases autonomous demand by the amount c. For instance, if the marginal propensity to consume, c, is 0.8, a \$1 increase in transfers increases autono-

---

[16] Automatic stabilizers are discussed by T. Holloway, "The Economy and the Federal Budget: Guide to Automatic Stabilizers," *Survey of Current Business,* July 1984.

mous demand by \$0.80. The increase is less than the full \$1 increase in transfers because part of the transfer—\$0.20 in this case—is saved.

Given that a \$1 increase in transfers increases autonomous demand by the amount c, it is clear that the multiplier for an increase in transfers is c times the multiplier for an increase in government spending. For instance, with c equal to 0.8, and a tax rate of 0.25, the government spending multiplier is 2.5. The multiplier for transfers is 0.8 times 2.5, or 2.0.

Effects of an Income Tax Change

The final fiscal policy question is on the effects of a reduction in the income tax rate. This is illustrated in Figure 3-10 by an increase in the slope of the aggregate demand function, because that slope is equal to the marginal propensity to spend out of income, $c(1 - t)$. At the initial level of income, the aggregate demand for goods now exceeds output because the tax reduction causes increased consumption. The new, higher equilibrium level of income is Y'.

To calculate the change in equilibrium income, we equate the change in income to the change in aggregate demand. The change in aggregate demand has two components. The first is the change in spending at the initial level of income that arises from the tax cut. This part is equal to the marginal propensity to consume out of disposable income times the change in disposable income due to the tax cut, $cY_0\Delta t$, where the term $Y_0\Delta t$ is the initial level of income times the change in the tax rate. The second component of the change in aggregate demand is the induced spending due to higher income. This is now evaluated at the new tax rate t' and has the value of $c(1 - t')\Delta Y_0$. We can therefore write[17]

$$\Delta Y_0 = -cY_0\Delta t + c(1 - t')\Delta Y_0 \tag{25}$$

or

$$\Delta Y_0 = -\frac{1}{1 - c(1 - t')} cY_0\Delta t \tag{26}$$

EXAMPLE: An example clarifies the effects of an income tax cut. Initially the level of income is $Y_0 = 100$, the marginal propensity to consume is $c = 0.8$, and the tax rate $t = 0.2$. Assume now a tax cut that reduces the income tax rate to only 10 percent, or $t' = 0.1$.

At the initial level of income, disposable income rises by $Y_0\Delta t = 100(t - t') = \$10$. Out of the increase in disposable income of \$10, a fraction $c = 0.8$ is spent on consumption, so that aggregate demand, at the initial level of income, increases by \$8. This corresponds to the first term on the right-hand side of equation (25). The increase in aggregate demand causes an expansion in output and income. Disposable income

---

[17] You should check equation (26) by using equation (22) to write out Y_0 corresponding to a tax rate of t, and Y_0' corresponding to t'. Then subtract Y_0 from Y_0' to obtain ΔY_0 as given in equation (26).

rises by a fraction $(1 - t')$ of the increase in income. Furthermore, of the increase in disposable income, only a fraction, c, is spent. Accordingly, induced consumption spending is equal to $c(1 - t')\Delta Y_0$, which is the second term in equation (25).

How much does the income tax cut achieve in terms of output expansion? Substituting our numbers into equation (26), we have

$$\Delta Y_0 = \frac{1}{1 - 0.8(1 - 0.1)} (0.8)(100)(0.2 - 0.1)$$

$$= 28.56$$

(26 a)

In our example, a cut in the tax rate such that taxes fall by $10 at the initial level of income raises equilibrium income by $28.56. Note, however, that although taxes are initially cut by $10, the government's total taxes received fall by less than $10. Why?

FIGURE 3-10

THE EFFECTS OF A DECREASE IN THE TAX RATE. A reduction in the income tax rate leaves the consumer with a larger proportion of every dollar of income earned. Accordingly, a larger proportion of every extra dollar of income is consumed. The aggregate demand curve swings upward, from AD to AD'. It becomes steeper because the income tax cut, in effect, acts like an increase in the propensity to consume. The equilibrium level of income rises from Y_0 to Y'.

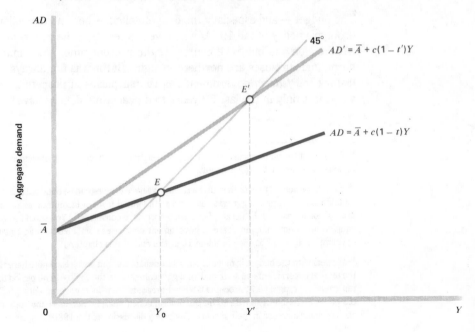

Income, output

The reason is that the government receives 10 percent of the induced increase in income, or $2.856, as taxes. Thus the final reduction in tax receipts by the government is not the initial $10, but rather $7.144.[18]

Summary and Implications

1. Government purchases and transfer payments act like increases in autonomous spending in their effects on equilibrium income.
2. A proportional income tax reduces the proportion of each extra dollar of output that is received as disposable income by consumers, and thus has the same effects on equilibrium income as a reduction in the propensity to consume.[19]
3. Changes in government spending and taxes affect the level of income. This raises the possibility that fiscal policy can be used to stabilize the economy. When the economy is in a recession, perhaps taxes should be cut or spending increased to get output to rise. And when the economy is booming, perhaps taxes should be increased or government spending cut to get back down to full employment.
4. Fiscal policy is in practice actively used to try to stablize the economy. Increases in government spending or a reduction in taxes are used to pull the economy out of a recession. Reduced spending or increased taxes are used to slow a boom.

3-5 THE BUDGET

The budget — and especially the budget deficit — became the major preoccupation of economic policy in the 1980s when, year after year, the government was borrowing $150 billion and more. Of course, at the present time, government deficits are the norm, and surpluses are nowhere in sight. But it was not always so. For most of its history the *federal* government has run surpluses in peacetime and deficits during wars. It is only in the last 20 years that peacetime deficits have become standard.[20]

---

[18] We leave it to you to calculate the multiplier relating the change in equilibrium income to the total change in taxes received by the government.

[19] It might be helpful to note that all the results we have derived can be obtained in a straightforward manner by taking the change in aggregate demand at the initial level of income times the multiplier. (Check this proposition for each of the fiscal policy changes we have considered.) You should consider, too, the effect on equilibrium income of an increase in government purchases combined with an equal reduction in transfer payments, $\Delta G = -TR$. (See problem 10 at the end of this chapter.)

[20] We deal with the budget in more detail in later chapters. But we already note here the distinction between the federal government and state and local governments. In the 1950–1980 period the federal government ran a deficit averaging 0.7 percent of GNP, whereas state and local governments actually showed a surplus of 0.2 percent of GNP. From 1980 on the federal deficit sharply increased and state and local governments showed some increase in their surplus. The policy discussion of the 1980s centers on correcting the federal deficit.

As very large, triple-digit deficits emerged in the first half of the 1980s, the prospect of continuing large deficits threatened unless taxes were raised or government spending cut. The fear that the economy could not prosper with the threat of large deficits hanging over it was strong. In 1985 Congress passed the Gramm-Rudman bill, requiring the budget to be balanced by 1991. But at the end of the 1980s it seemed unlikely that the deficit reduction targets would be met according to the agreed timetable.

The budget deficit on which the media and politicians focus is the federal budget deficit, which in 1988 was $155.1 billion. The concepts of government budget surplus and deficit that appear in the national income accounts are the *combined* deficits of the federal government and state and local governments. In 1988 their combined deficit was $99.2 billion, reflecting the small surplus of the state and local governments.

Why the concern? The fear was that the government's borrowing would make it difficult for private firms to borrow and invest, and thus would slow the economy's growth. Full understanding has to wait until later chapters, but we start now, dealing with the government budget, its effects on output, and the effects of output on the budget.

The first important concept is the *budget surplus*, denoted by *BS*. The budget surplus is the excess of the government's revenues, consisting of taxes, over its total expenditures, consisting of purchases of goods and services and transfer payments.

$$BS \equiv TA - \overline{G} - \overline{TR} \tag{27}$$

A negative budget surplus, an excess of expenditure over taxes, is a *budget deficit*.

Substituting in equation (27) the assumption of a proportional income tax that yields tax revenues $TA = tY$ gives us

$$BS = tY - \overline{G} - \overline{TR} \tag{27a}$$

In Figure 3-11 we plot the budget surplus as a function of the level of income for given $\overline{G}$, $\overline{TR}$ and income tax rate, t. At low levels of income, the budget is in deficit (the surplus is negative) because payments $\overline{G} + \overline{TR}$ exceed income tax collection. For high levels of income, by contrast, the budget shows a surplus, since income tax collection exceeds expenditures in the form of government purchases and transfers.

Figure 3-11 demonstrates that the budget deficit depends not only on the government's policy choices, reflected in the tax rate (t), purchases ($\overline{G}$), and transfers ($\overline{TR}$), but also on anything else that shifts the level of income. For instance, suppose there is an increase in investment demand that increases the level of output. Then the budget deficit will fall or the surplus will increase because tax revenues have risen. But the government has done nothing that changed the deficit.

We should accordingly not be surprised to see budget deficits in recessions. Those are periods when the government's tax receipts are low. And in practice, transfer payments, through unemployment benefits, also increase in recessions, even though we are taking $\overline{TR}$ as autonomous in our model.

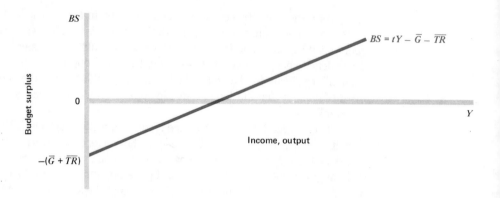

FIGURE 3-11

THE BUDGET SURPLUS. The budget surplus, or deficit, depends in part on the level of income. Given the tax rate, t, and $\overline{G}$ and $\overline{TR}$, the budget surplus will be high if income is high—because then the government takes in a lot of taxes. But if the level of income is low, there will be a budget deficit because government tax receipts are small.

The Effects of Government Purchases and Tax Changes on the Budget Surplus

Next we show how changes in fiscal policy affect the budget. In particular, we want to find out whether an increase in government purchases must reduce the budget surplus. At first sight, this appears obvious, because increased government purchases, from equation (27), are reflected in a reduced surplus or increased deficit. On further thought, however, the increased government purchases will cause an increase (multiplied) in income and, therefore, increased income tax collection. This raises the interesting possibility that tax collection might increase by more than government purchases.

A brief calculation shows that the first guess is right—increased government purchases reduce the budget surplus. From equation (23) we see that the change in income due to increased government purchases is equal to $\Delta Y_0 \equiv \alpha \Delta G$. A fraction of that increase in income is collected in the form of taxes, so that tax revenue increases by $t\alpha\Delta G$. The change in the budget surplus, using equation (24) to substitute for α, is therefore

$$\Delta BS = \Delta TA - \Delta \overline{G}$$
$$= t\overline{\alpha}\Delta \overline{G} - \Delta \overline{G}$$
$$= \left[\frac{t}{1 - c(1 - t)} - 1 \right] \Delta \overline{G} \tag{28}$$
$$= -\frac{(1 - c)(1 - t)}{1 - c(1 - t)} \Delta \overline{G}$$

which is unambiguously negative.

We have, therefore, shown that an increase in government purchases will reduce the budget surplus, although by considerably less than the increase in purchases. For instance, for $c = 0.8$ and $t = 0.25$, a \$1 increase in government purchases will create a \$0.375 reduction in the surplus.[21]

In the same way, we can consider the effects of an increase in the tax rate on the budget surplus. We know that the increase in the tax rate will reduce the level of income. It might thus appear that an increase in the tax rate, keeping the level of government spending constant, could reduce the budget surplus. In fact, an increase in the tax rate increases the budget surplus, despite the reduction in income that it causes, as you are asked to show in problem 7 at the end of this chapter.[22]

3-6 THE FULL-EMPLOYMENT BUDGET SURPLUS

A final topic to be treated here is the concept of the full-employment budget surplus.[23] Recall that increases in taxes add to the surplus and that increases in government expenditures reduce the surplus. Increases in taxes have been shown to reduce the level of income; and increases in government purchases and transfers, to increase the level of income. It thus seems that the budget surplus is a convenient, simple measure of the overall effects of fiscal policy on the economy. For instance, when the budget is in deficit, we would say that fiscal policy is expansionary, tending to increase GNP.

However, the budget surplus by itself suffers from a serious defect as a measure of the direction of fiscal policy. The defect is that the surplus can change because of changes in autonomous private spending, as we have seen. Thus, if the economy moves into a recession, tax revenue automatically declines and the budget deficit increases (or the surplus declines). Conversely, an increase in economic activity causes the budget surplus to increase (or the deficit to decline). These changes in the budget take place automatically for a given tax structure. This implies that we cannot simply look at the budget deficit as a measure of whether government fiscal policy is expansionary or deflationary. A given fiscal policy may imply a deficit if private spending is low and a surplus if private spending is high. Accordingly, an increase in the budget deficit does not necessarily mean that the government has changed its policy in an attempt to increase the level of income.

Since we frequently want to measure the way in which fiscal policy is being used to affect the level of income, we require some measure of policy that is independent of the particular position of the business cycle — boom or recession — in which we may

---

[21] In this case, $[\alpha = 1/[1 - 0.8(0.75)] = 2.5$. So $\Delta BS = -2.5(0.2)(0.75) = -0.375$.

[22] The theory that tax rate cuts would increase government revenue (or tax rate increases reduce government revenue) is associated with Arthur Laffer of Pepperdine University. Laffer's argument, however, did not depend on the aggregate demand effects of tax cuts but, rather, on the possibility that a tax cut would lead people to work more. This was a strand in supply-side economics, which we examine in Chap. 18.

[23] The concept of the full-employment surplus was first used by E. Cary Brown, "Fiscal Policy in the Thirties: A Reappraisal," *American Economic Review,* December 1956.

TABLE 3-3

THE FEDERAL BUDGET DEFICIT AND UNEMPLOYMENT IN THE 1980s

	BUDGET DEFICIT, % of GNP		Unemployment rate, %
	Actual	Full-employment	
1980	2.2	0.4	7.2
1981	2.1	0.0	7.6
1982	4.6	1.1	9.7
1983	5.2	2.1	9.6
1984	4.4	3.0	7.5
1985	4.9	3.9	7.2
1986	4.8	4.1	7.0
1987	3.5	3.0	6.2
1988	2.9	2.9	5.5

SOURCE: DRI/McGraw-Hill.

find ourselves. Such a measure is provided by the *full-employment surplus*, which we denote by *BS**. The full-employment budget surplus measures the budget not at the actual level of income but, rather, at the full-employment level of income or at potential output. Thus, a given fiscal policy summarized by $\overline{G}$, $\overline{TR}$, and *t* is assessed by the level of the surplus, or deficit, that it generates at full employment. Using *Y** to denote the full-employment level of income, we can write

$$BS^* = tY^* - \overline{G} - \overline{TR} \qquad (29)$$

Alternative names for the full-employment surplus have been proliferating. Included are the *cyclically adjusted surplus* (or deficit), the *high-employment surplus*, the *standardized employment surplus*, and the *structural surplus*. All these names refer to the same concept. The new names are intended to divert attention from the notion that there is a unique level of full-employment output that the economy has not yet reached. They suggest instead that the concept is merely a convenient measuring rod that fixes a given level of employment as the reference point. Given the difficulty of knowing exactly what is the full-employment level of output, the new names have some justification.[24]

To see the difference between the actual and the full-employment budgets, we subtract the actual budget in equation (27*a*) from equation (29) to obtain

$$BS^* - BS = t(Y^* - Y) \qquad (30)$$

---

[24] For a useful exposition, see Congressional Budget Office, *The Economic Outlook*, February 1984, Appendix B.

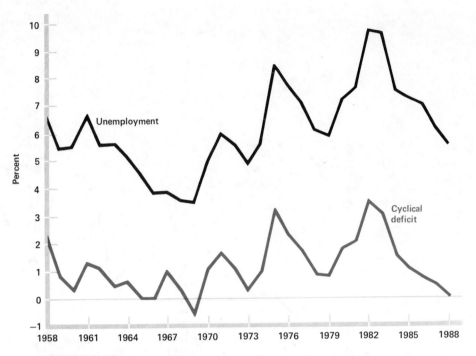

FIGURE 3-12

THE RELATION BETWEEN THE CYCLICAL BUDGET AND THE UNEMPLOYMENT RATE, 1958–1988. Note that the unemployment rate is measured as a percentage of the civilian labor force and the cyclical budget is defined as the difference between the actual and the full-employment budget, expressed as a percentage of GNP. (SOURCE: DRI/McGraw-Hill.)

The only difference arises from income tax collection.[25] Specifically, if output is below full employment, the full-employment surplus exceeds the actual surplus. Conversely, if actual output exceeds full-employment (or potential) output, the full-employment surplus is less than the actual surplus. The difference between the actual and the full-employment budget is the *cyclical* component of the budget. In a recession the cyclical component tends to show a deficit and in a boom there may even be a surplus.

Table 3-3 reports the actual budget deficit and the full-employment deficit, as well as the unemployment rate; and Figure 3-12 plots the latter two. It is clear from the

---

[25] In practice, transfer payments, such as welfare and unemployment benefits, are also affected by the state of the economy, so that *TR* also depends on the level of income. But the major cause of differences between the actual surplus and the full-employment surplus is taxes. Automatic movements in taxes caused by a change in income are about five times the size of automatic movements in spending. (See T. M. Holloway and J. C. Wakefield, "Sources of Change in the Federal Government Deficit, 1970–86," *Survey of Current Business,* May 1985.)

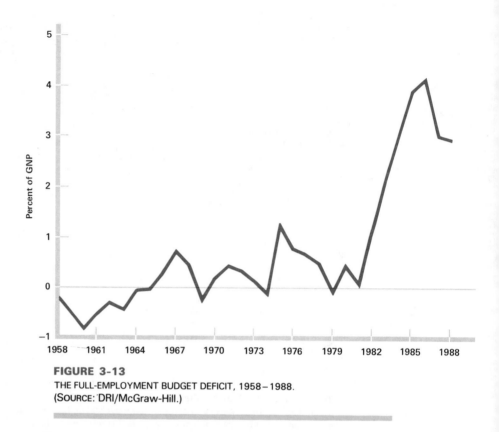

FIGURE 3-13
THE FULL-EMPLOYMENT BUDGET DEFICIT, 1958–1988.
(SOURCE: DRI/McGraw-Hill.)

graph that whenever the unemployment rate is high, as in the 1974–1975 or 1980–1982 recessions, the cyclical component of the budget shows a large deficit. By contrast when the economy is at full employment, as in 1988, the cyclical component of the deficit is zero.

We next look at the full-employment budget deficit shown in Figure 3-13. Public concern about the deficit mounted in the 1980s. For many economists, the behavior of the deficit during the high-unemployment years 1982 and 1983 was not especially worrisome. The actual budget is usually in deficit during recessions. But the shift toward deficit of the full-employment budget was regarded as an entirely different matter.

Two final words of warning. First, there is no certainty as to the true full-employment level of output. Various assumptions about the level of unemployment that corresponds to full employment are possible. The usual assumptions now are that full employment means an unemployment rate of about 5.0 to 5.5 percent, although when the actual unemployment rate was higher there were some estimates as high as 7 percent. The point is that estimates of the full-employment deficit or surplus will differ depending on the assumptions made about the economy at full employment.

Second, the high-employment surplus is a better measure of the direction of active fiscal policy than is the actual budget surplus. But it is not a perfect measure of the thrust of fiscal policy. The reason is that balanced budget increases in government purchases, for example, are themselves expansionary (see Box 3-2), so that an increase in government purchases matched by a tax increase that keeps the surplus constant leads to an increase in the level of income. Because fiscal policy involves the setting of a number of variables — the tax rate, transfers, and government purchases — it is difficult to describe the thrust of fiscal policy perfectly by a single number. But the high-employment surplus is nevertheless a useful guide to the direction of fiscal policy.

3-7 SUMMARY

1. Output is at its equilibrium level when the aggregate demand for goods is equal to the level of output.
2. Aggregate demand consists of planned spending by households on consumption, by firms on investment goods, and by government on its purchases of goods and services.
3. When output is at its equilibrium level, there are no unintended changes in inventories and all economic units are making precisely the purchases they had planned to. An adjustment process for the level of output based on the accumulation or rundown of inventories leads the economy to the equilibrium output level.
4. The level of aggregate demand is itself affected by the level of output (equal to the level of income) because consumption demand depends on the level of income.
5. The consumption function relates consumption spending to income. Consumption rises with income. Income that is not consumed is saved, so that the saving function can be derived from the consumption function.
6. The multiplier is the amount by which a $1 change in autonomous spending changes the equilibrium level of output. The greater the propensity to consume, the higher the multiplier.
7. Government purchases and government transfer payments act like increases in autonomous spending in their effects on the equilibrium level of income. A proportional income tax has the same effect on the equilibrium level of income as a reduction in the propensity to consume. A proportional income tax thus reduces the multiplier.
8. The budget surplus is the excess of government receipts over expenditures. When the government is spending more than it receives, the budget is in deficit. The size of the budget surplus (deficit) is affected by the government's fiscal policy variables — government purchases, transfer payments, and tax rates.
9. The actual budget surplus is also affected by changes in tax collection and transfers resulting from movements in the level of income that occur as a result of changes in private autonomous spending. The full-employment (high-employment) budget surplus is used as a measure of the active use of fiscal policy. The full-employment surplus measures the budget surplus that would exist if output were at its potential (full-employment) level.

box 3-2

A SIMULTANEOUS CHANGE IN TAXES AND PURCHASES

What happens when taxes and government purchases both change? We examine an example in Table 1. We assume a fiscal policy change that reduces the tax rate and government purchases. The reduction is such that at the initial equilibrium level of

TABLE 1

EFFECTS OF COMBINED TAX CUT AND GOVERNMENT SPENDING DECREASE

Parameters: Initial tax rate, $t = 0.2$

New tax rate, $t' = 0.1$

Initial level of income, $Y_0 = \$100$

Marginal propensity to consume, $c = 0.8$

Change in government spending, $\Delta \overline{G} = -10$

Multiplier: $\alpha = \dfrac{1}{1 - c(1 - t')} = \dfrac{1}{1 - 0.72} = 3.57$

Effects of tax cut [see equation (26)]:

Change in income: $-cY_0 \Delta t = -(3.57)(0.8)(100)(-0.1) = 28.56$

Effects of cut in government spending [see equation (23)]:

Change in income: $\overline{G} = -35.70$

Total effect on income: $Y_0 = -35.70 + 28.56$

$= -7.14$

Therefore: $Y_0' = 100 - 7.14 = 92.86$

Effect on tax receipts: Initial taxes $= 20$

Taxes in new situation $= 0.1 \times 92.86 = 9.29$

Therefore: Change in taxes, $TA = -10.71$

Effects on budget surplus: $BS = TA - \overline{G}$

$= -10.71 + 10.00$

$= -0.71$

KEY TERMS

Aggregate demand

Equilibrium output

Unintended (undesired) inventory accumulation

Planned aggregate demand

Consumption function

Marginal propensity to consume

Marginal propensity to save

Multiplier

Automatic stabilizer

Budget surplus

Budget deficit

Balanced budget multiplier

Full-employment (high-employment) surplus

income, 100, the cut in taxes is exactly equal to the cut in government purchases.

What effect would we expect such a fiscal policy to have? A first reaction would be that since taxes are being cut by the same amount as spending, there will be no effect. But the table shows that is not right. The combined effect of the two actions is actually to lower income.

Why? The reason is that part of the cut in taxes is saved, so that not all the tax cut goes to increase aggregate demand. But the entire cut in government spending reduces aggregate demand. Therefore, this fiscal policy actually reduces aggregate demand, and therefore income.

Notice also from the table that the budget deficit in the end increases slightly — as a result of the fall in income — even though at the initial level of income the cuts in taxes and spending are equal.

BALANCED BUDGET MULTIPLIER

In the previous example, the combined tax cut and reduction of government purchases raised the budget deficit. What would happen to the level of income if government purchases and taxes changed by exactly the same amount, so that the budget surplus remained unchanged between the initial and final level of income? The answer to this question is contained in the famous *balanced budget multiplier* result. The result is that the balanced budget multiplier is exactly 1. That is, an increase in government purchases, accompanied by an equal increase in taxes, increases the level of income by exactly the amount of the increase in purchases.* This interesting result is derived in the appendix at the end of this chapter.

The major points of the preceding discussion are that a balanced budget cut in government purchases lowers equilibrium income and that a dollar increase in government purchases has a stronger impact on equilibrium income than a dollar cut in taxes. A dollar cut in taxes leads only to a fraction of a dollar's increase in consumption spending, the rest being saved, while government purchases are reflected dollar for dollar in a change in aggregate demand.† ∎

---

* Note that the balanced budget multiplier may well be less than 1 in the more sophisticated models of Chap. 4, in which investment spending depends on the interest rate.

† Rather than go through the analysis of changes in transfer payments, we leave it to you, in problem 10 at the end of the chapter, to work through an example of the effects on the budget of a change in transfer payments.

PROBLEMS

1. Here we investigate a particular example of the model studied in Sections 3-2 and 3-3 with no government. Suppose the consumption function is given by $C = 100 + 0.8Y$, while investment is given by $I = 50$.

   (a) What is the equilibrium level of income in this case?

   (b) What is the level of saving in equilibrium?

   (c) If, for some reason, output were at the level of 800, what would the level of involuntary inventory accumulation be?

(d) If I were to rise to 100 (we discuss what determines I in later chapters), what would the effect be on equilibrium income?

(e) What is the value of the multiplier, α, here?

(f) Draw a diagram indicating the equilibria in both 1a and 1d.

2. Suppose consumption behavior were to change in problem 1 so that $C = 100 + 0.9Y$, while I remained at 50.

(a) Would you expect the equilibrium level of income to be higher or lower than in 1a? Calculate the new equilibrium level, Y', to verify this.

(b) Now suppose investment increases to $I = 100$, just as in 1d. What is the new equilibrium income?

(c) Does this change in investment spending have more or less of an effect on Y than in problem 1? Why?

(d) Draw a diagram indicating the change in equilibrium income in this case.

3. We showed in the text that the equilibrium condition $Y = AD$ is equivalent to the $S = I$, or saving = investment, condition. Starting from $S = I$ and the saving function, derive the equilibrium level of income, as in equation (10).

4. Suppose the consumption function is $C = C_0 + cY$, where C_0 is a constant.

(a) Draw a diagram of the consumption function.

(b) What is the saving function?

5. This problem relates to the so-called paradox of thrift. Suppose that $I = I_0$ and that $C = C_0 + cY$, where C_0 is a constant.

(a) What is the saving function, that is, the function that shows how saving is related to income?

(b) Suppose individuals want to save more at every level of income. Show, using a figure like Figure 3-6, how the saving function is shifted.

(c) What effect does the increased desire to save have on the new equilibrium level of saving? Explain the paradox.

6. Now let us look at a model that is an example of the one presented in Sections 3-4 and 3-5; that is, it includes government purchases, taxes, and transfers. It has the same features as the one in problems 1 and 2 except that it also has a government. Thus, suppose consumption is given by $C = 100 + 0.8YD$ and that $I = 50$, while fiscal policy is summarized by $G = 200$, $TR = 62.5$, and $t = 0.25$.

(a) What is the equilibrium level of income in this more complete model?

(b) What is the value of the new multiplier, α? Why is this less than the multiplier in problem 1e?

7. Using the same model as in problem 5, determine the following:

(a) What is the value of the budget surplus, BS, when $I = 50$?

(b) What is BS when I increases to 100?

(c) What accounts for the change in BS between 6b and 6a?

(d) Assuming that the full-employment level of income, Y^*, is 1,200, what is the full-employment budget surplus BS^* when $I = 50$? 100? (Be careful.)

(e) What is BS^* if $I = 50$ and $G = 250$, with Y^* still equal to 1,200?

(f) Explain why we use BS^* rather than simply BS to measure the direction of fiscal policy.

8. Suppose we expand our model to take account of the fact that transfer payments, TR, do depend on the level of income, Y. When income is high, transfer payments such as

unemployment benefits will fall. Conversely, when income is low, unemployment is high and so are unemployment benefits. We can incorporate this into our model by writing transfers as $TR = \bar{TR} - bY, b > 0$. Remember that equilibrium income is derived as the solution to $Y_0 = C + I + G = cYD + I + G$, where $YD = Y + TR - TA$ is disposable income.

(a) Derive the expression for Y_0 in this case, just as equation (22) was derived in the text.

(b) What is the new multiplier?

(c) Why is the new multiplier less than the standard one, α?

(d) How does the change in the multiplier relate to the concept of automatic stabilizers?

9. Now we look at the role taxes play in determining equilibrium income. Suppose we have an economy of the type in Sections 3-4 and 3-5, described by the following functions:

$$C = 50 + 0.8\,YD$$
$$\bar{I} = 70$$
$$\bar{G} = 200$$
$$\bar{TR} = 100$$
$$t = 0.20$$

(a) Calculate the equilibrium level of income and the multiplier in this model.

(b) Calculate also the budget surplus, BS.

(c) Suppose that t increases to 0.25. What is the new equilibrium income? The new multiplier?

(d) Calculate the change in the budget surplus. Would you expect the change in the surplus to be more or less if $c = 0.9$ rather than 0.8?

(e) Can you explain why the multiplier is 1 when $t = 1$?

10. Suppose the economy is operating at equilibrium, with $Y_0 = 1,000$. If the government undertakes a fiscal change so that the tax rate, t, increases by 0.05 and government spending increases by 50, will the budget surplus go up or down? Why?

11. Suppose Congress decides to reduce transfer payments (such as welfare), but to increase government purchases of goods and services by an equal amount. That is, it undertakes a change in fiscal policy such that $\Delta G = -\Delta TR$.

(a) Would you expect equilibrium income to rise or fall as a result of this change? Why? Check out your answer with the following example: Suppose that initially, $c = 0.8$, $t = 0.25$, and $Y_0 = 600$. Now let $\Delta G = 10$ and $\Delta TR = -10$.

(b) Find the change in equilibrium income, ΔY_0.

(c) What is the change in the budget surplus, ΔBS? Why has BS changed?

*12. We have seen in problem 10 that an increase in G accompanied by an equal decrease in TR does not leave the budget unchanged. What would the effect on equilibrium income be if TR and G change so as to leave the budget surplus, BS, fixed? [*Hint:* Notice that $BS = TA - TR - G$. We want

$$\Delta BS = \Delta TA - \Delta TR - \Delta G = 0 \tag{P1}$$

---

* An asterisk denotes a more difficult problem.

so that $\Delta TR = \Delta TA - \Delta G$. Since t is constant,

$$\Delta TA = t\Delta Y_0 \tag{P2}$$

We also know that $Y_0 = \alpha(C + I + G + cR)$ and

$$\Delta Y_0 = \alpha(\Delta G + c\Delta TR) \tag{P3}$$

Substituting equations (P1) and (P2) into equation (P3), derive an expression for ΔY in terms of ΔG. Simplify that expression, using the fact that $\alpha = 1/[1 - c(1 - t)]$, to obtain the balanced budget result in the case of changes in transfers and government spending.] If you have trouble with this problem, check the appendix to this chapter.

*13. In the preceding problem and in the appendix we derived the balanced budget multiplier result that is noted in Box 3-2. It states that if $\Delta G = \Delta TA$ from the initial to final equilibrium, then $\Delta Y = \Delta G$. Let us look at an example of this balanced budget multiplier in action.

Consider the economy described by the following functions:

$$C = 85 + 0.75\, YD$$
$$\bar{I} = 50$$
$$\bar{G} = 150$$
$$\overline{TR} = 100$$
$$t = 0.20$$

(a) Derive the multiplier, α, and the level of autonomous spending, A.
(b) From 12a calculate the equilibrium level of income and the budget surplus.
(c) Now suppose G rises to 250 while t increases to 0.28. Repeat 12a for the new fiscal policy.
(d) What are ΔTA, ΔG, ΔY, and ΔBS?
(e) In view of this result and that of problem 10, what do you think the effect on income would be if we had a balanced budget change such that $\Delta TR = \Delta TA$?

*14. Suppose the aggregate demand function is as in the following figure. Notice that at Y_0 the

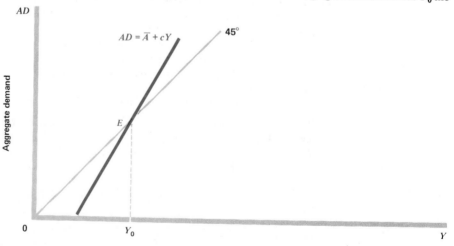

slope of the aggregate demand curve is greater than 1. (This would happen if $c > 1$.) Complete this picture as is done in Figure 3-2 to include the arrows indicating adjustment when $Y \neq Y_0$ and show what IU is for $Y < Y_0$ and $Y > Y_0$. What is happening in this example, and how does it differ fundamentally from Figure 3-2?

*15. This problem anticipates our discussion of the open economy in Chapter 6. It is hard, and only the ambitious student should try it. You are asked to derive some of the results that will be shown there. We start with the assumption that foreign demand for our goods is given and equal to X. Our demand for foreign goods or imports, denoted Q, is a linear function of income.

$$\text{Exports} = \bar{X} \qquad \text{Imports} = Q = \bar{Q} + mY$$

where m is the *marginal propensity to import.*

(a) The trade balance, or net exports, NX, is defined as the excess of exports over imports. Write an algebraic expression for the trade balance and show in a diagram net exports as a function of the level of income. (Put Y on the horizontal axis.)

(b) Show the effect of a change in income on the trade balance, using your diagram. Show also the effect of a change in exports on the trade balance, given income.

(c) The equilibrium condition in the goods market is that aggregate demand for *our* goods be equal to supply. Aggregate demand for our goods includes exports but excludes imports. Thus we have

$$Y = C + \bar{I} + NX$$

where we have added net exports (exports less imports) to investment and consumption. Using the expression for net exports developed in 14a and the consumption function $C = cY$, derive the equilibrium level of income, Y_0.

(d) On the basis of your expression for the equilibrium level of income in 14c, what is the effect of a change in exports, X, on equilibrium income? Interpret your result and discuss the multiplier in an open economy.

(e) Using your results in 14a and 14d, show the effect of an increase in exports on the trade balance.

APPENDIX: THE BALANCED BUDGET MULTIPLIER

This appendix considers the balanced budget multiplier result mentioned in Box 3-2. The balanced budget multiplier refers to the effects of an increase in government purchases accompanied by an increase in taxes such that, in the new equilibrium, the budget surplus is exactly the same as in the original equilibrium. The result is that the multiplier of such a policy change, the balanced budget multiplier, is 1.

A multiplier of unity implies that output expands by precisely the amount of the increased government purchases with no induced consumption spending. It is apparent that what must be at work is the effect of higher taxes that exactly offset the effect of the income expansion, thus maintaining disposable income, and hence consumption, constant. With no induced consumption spending, output expands simply to match the increased government purchases.

We can derive this result formally by noting that the change in aggregate demand ΔAD is equal to the change in government purchases plus the change in consumption spending. The latter is equal to the marginal propensity to consume out of disposable income, c, times the change in disposable income, ΔYD; that is, $\Delta YD = \Delta Y_0 - \Delta TA$, where ΔY_0 is the change in output. Thus,

$$\Delta AD = \Delta \overline{G} + c(\Delta Y_0 - \Delta TA) \tag{A1}$$

Since from one equilibrium to another the change in aggregate demand has to equal the change in output, we have

$$\Delta Y_0 = \Delta \overline{G} + c(\Delta Y_0 - \Delta TA)$$

or

$$\Delta Y_0 = \frac{1}{1-c}(\Delta \overline{G} - c\Delta TA) \tag{A2}$$

Next we note that by assumption the change in government purchases between the new equilibrium and the old one is exactly matched by a change in tax collection, so that $\Delta \overline{G} = \Delta TA$. It follows from this last equality, after substitution in equation (A2), that with this particular restriction on fiscal policy we have

$$\Delta Y_0 = \frac{1}{1-c}(\Delta \overline{G} - c\Delta \overline{G}) = \Delta \overline{G} = \Delta TA \tag{A3}$$

so that the multiplier is precisely unity.

Another way of deriving the balanced budget multiplier result is by considering the successive rounds of spending changes caused by government policy changes. Suppose each of government purchases and taxes increased by \$1. Let $c(1 - t)$, the induced increase in aggregate demand caused by a \$1 increase in income in the presence of taxes, be denoted by $\bar{c}$.

Table A3-1 shows the spending induced by the two policy changes. The first column shows the changes in spending resulting from the change in government purchases and its later

TABLE A3-1
THE BALANCED BUDGET MULTIPLIER

Spending round	CHANGE IN SPENDING RESULTING FROM		Net this round	Total
	$\overline{G} = 1$	$TA = 1$		
1	1	$-\bar{c}$	$1 - \bar{c}$	$1 - \bar{c}$
2	$\bar{c}$	$-\bar{c}^2$	$\bar{c} - \bar{c}^2$	$1 - \bar{c}^2$
3	$\bar{c}^2$	$-\bar{c}^3$	$\bar{c}^2 - \bar{c}^3$	$1 - \bar{c}^3$
4	$\bar{c}^3$	$-\bar{c}^4$	$\bar{c}^3 - \bar{c}^4$	$1 - \bar{c}^4$
.	.	.	.	.
.	.	.	.	.
.	.	.	.	.
n	$\bar{c}^{n-1}$	$-\bar{c}^n$	$\bar{c}^{n-1} - \bar{c}^n$	$1 - \bar{c}^n$

repercussions. The second column similarly gives the spending effects in successive rounds of the tax increase. The third column sums the two effects for each spending round, while the final column adds all the changes in spending induced so far. Since $\bar{c}$ is less than 1, $\bar{c}^n$ becomes very small as the number of spending rounds, n, increases, and the final change in aggregate spending caused by the balanced budget increase in governmental spending is just equal to $1.

Finally, the balanced budget multiplier can also be thought of from a somewhat different perspective. Consider the goods market equilibrium condition in terms of saving, taxes, transfers, investment, and government purchases:

$$S + TA - \overline{TR} = \bar{I} + \overline{G} \tag{A4}$$

Now, using the definition of the budget surplus,

$$BS = TA - \overline{TR} - \overline{G}$$
$$BS = \bar{I} - S \tag{A5}$$

If there is no change in the budget deficit or in investment, the equilibrium change in saving is zero. For saving not to change, disposable income must remain unchanged. This says that $\Delta YD = \Delta Y - \Delta T = 0$, and hence shows once more that the change in income equals the change in taxes. This in turn equals the change in government purchases.

Hence, the balanced budget multiplier, or more precisely, the multiplier associated with an unchanging budget surplus or deficit, is equal to unity. This perspective on the income determination process is very useful because it emphasizes the fact that a change in the surplus or deficit of one sector is matched by a corresponding change in the deficit or surplus of the remaining sectors. If the government surplus is constrained by fiscal policy to be unchanged, so too must be the private sector's surplus, $S - I$.

4

MONEY, INTEREST, AND INCOME

*T*he stock of money, interest rates, and the Federal Reserve seemingly have no place in the model of income determination developed so far. But money plays an important role in the determination of income and employment. Interest rates are a significant determinant of aggregate spending, and the Federal Reserve and monetary policy receive at least as much public attention as fiscal policy. For instance, the blame for the deep 1981–1982 recession and its extraordinarily high interest rates is often placed on the Federal Reserve's tight money policy. In 1989 rising interest rates were again expected to lead at least to a slowdown, if not an outright recession. This chapter introduces money and monetary policy, and builds an explicit framework of analysis in which to study the interaction of goods and assets markets.

This new framework leads to an understanding of the determination of interest rates and of their role in the business cycle. Figure 4-1 shows the interest rate on Treasury bills. The interest rate on Treasury bills represents the payment, per dollar per year, that someone who lends to the U.S. government receives. Thus, an interest rate of 10 percent means that someone who lends $100 to the government for 1 year will receive 10 percent, or $10, in interest. Figure 4-1 immediately suggests some questions: What factors cause the interest rate to increase, as occurred, for example, in 1980–1981; and what factors cause rates to decline, as they did in 1984–1987? Furthermore, when interest rates increase, what are the effects on output and employment?

The model we introduce in this chapter, the *IS-LM model*, is the core of modern macroeconomics. It maintains the spirit and, indeed, many details of the model of the previous chapter. The model is broadened, though, by introducing the interest rate as an additional determinant of aggregate demand. In Chapter 3, autonomous spending and fiscal policy were the chief determinants of aggregate demand. Now we add the

107

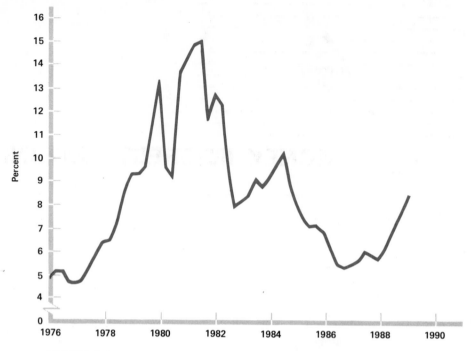

FIGURE 4-1
THE INTEREST RATE ON TREASURY BILLS (percent per year). (SOURCE: DRI/McGraw-Hill.)

FIGURE 4-2
THE STRUCTURE OF THE *IS-LM* MODEL. The *IS-LM* model emphasizes the interaction between the goods and assets markets. The model of Chapter 3 looks at income determination by arguing that income affects spending, which in turn determines output and income. Now we add the effects of interest rates on spending, and thus income, and the dependence of assets markets on income. Higher income raises money demand and thus interest rates. Higher interest rates lower spending and thus income. Spending, interest rates, and income are determined jointly by equilibrium in the goods *and* assets markets.

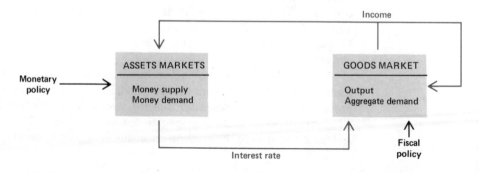

interest rate and argue that a reduction in the interest rate raises aggregate demand. This seems to be a minor extension which can readily be handled in the context of Chapter 3. This is not entirely correct, because we have to ask what determines the interest rate. That question extends our model to include the markets for financial assets and forces us to study the interaction of goods and assets markets. Interest rates and income are jointly determined by equilibrium in the goods and assets markets.

What is the payoff for that complication? The introduction of assets markets and interest rates serves three important purposes:

1. The extension shows how monetary policy works.
2. The analysis qualifies the conclusions of Chapter 3. Consider Figure 4-2, which lays out the logical structure of the model. So far we looked at the submodel of autonomous spending and fiscal policy as determinants of aggregate demand and equilibrium income. Now the inclusion of assets markets—money demand and supply—introduces an additional channel. An expansionary fiscal policy, for example, would in the first place raise spending and income. This increase in income would affect the assets markets by raising money demand and thereby raising interest rates. The higher interest rates in turn would reduce aggregate spending and thus, as we shall show, dampen the expansionary impact of fiscal policy. Indeed, under certain conditions, the increase in interest rates may be sufficient to offset *fully* the expansionary effects of fiscal policy. Clearly, such an extreme possibility is an important qualification to our study of fiscal policy in Chapter 3.
3. Even if the interest rate changes just mentioned only dampen (rather than offset fully) the expansionary effects of fiscal policy, they nevertheless have an important side effect. The *composition* of aggregate demand between investment and consumption spending will depend on the interest rate (i.e., investment versus consumption). Higher interest rates dampen aggregate demand mainly by reducing investment. Thus, an expansionary fiscal policy would tend to raise consumption through the multiplier, but would tend to reduce investment through the induced increase in interest rates. The side effects of fiscal expansion on interest rates and investment continue to be a sensitive and important issue in policy making. Because fiscal expansion tends to reduce investment, an influential view is that fiscal policy should not be used as a tool for demand management.

These three reasons justify the more complicated model we study in this chapter. The extended model also helps us understand the functioning of financial markets.

OUTLINE OF THE CHAPTER

We use Figure 4-2 once more to lay out the structure of this chapter. We start in Section 4-1 with a discussion of the link between interest rates and aggregate demand. Here we use the model of Chapter 3 directly, augmented to include the interest rate as a determinant of aggregate demand. We derive a key relationship—the *IS* curve—

that shows combinations of interest rates and levels of income for which the goods markets clear. In Section 4-2, we turn to the assets markets and in particular to the money market. We show that the demand for money depends on interest rates and income and that there are combinations of interest rates and income levels — the *LM* curve — for which the money market clears.[1] In Section 4-3, we combine the two schedules to study the joint determination of interest rates and income. Section 4-4 lays out the adjustment process toward equilibrium. Monetary policy is discussed in Sections 4-5 and 4-6. Fiscal policy and the important issue of the monetary-fiscal policy mix are reserved for Chapter 5. That material is in a separate chapter only to avoid making this chapter too long.

4-1 THE GOODS MARKET AND THE *IS* CURVE

In this section we derive a *goods market equilibrium schedule.* The goods market equilibrium schedule, or *IS* schedule, shows combinations of interest rates and levels of output such that planned spending equals income. The goods market equilibrium schedule is an extension of income determination with a 45°-line diagram. What is new here is that investment is no longer fully exogenous but is also determined by the interest rate. To appreciate the extension of Chapter 3 we briefly review what we found there.

In Chapter 3 we derived an expression for equilibrium income:

$$Y_0 = \frac{\overline{A}}{1 - \overline{c}} \qquad \overline{c} = c(1 - t) \tag{1}$$

Equilibrium income in this simple Keynesian model has two determinants: autonomous spending (A) and the propensity to consume out of income ($\overline{c}$). Autonomous spending includes government spending, investment spending, and autonomous consumption spending. The propensity to consume out of income, as seen from (1), depends on the propensity to consume out of disposable income (c) and on the fraction of a dollar of income retained after taxes ($1 - t$). The higher the level of autonomous spending and the higher the propensity to consume, the higher the equilibrium level of income.

Investment and the Interest Rate

So far, investment spending (I) has been treated as *entirely* exogenous — some number like $800 billion determined altogether outside the model of income determination. Now, as we make our macromodel more complete by introducing interest rates as a

---

[1] The terms *IS* and *LM* are shorthand representations, respectively, of the relationships investment equals saving (goods market equilibrium) and money demand (L) equals money supply (M), or money market equilibrium. The classic article that introduced this model is J. R. Hicks, "Mr. Keynes and the Classics: A Suggested Interpretation," *Econometrica*, 1937, pp. 147–159.

part of the model, investment spending, too, becomes endogenous. The desired or planned rate of investment is lower the higher the interest rate.

A simple argument shows why. Investment is spending on additions to the capital stock (machinery, structures, inventories). Such investment is undertaken with the aim of making profits in the future by operating machines and factories. Suppose firms borrow to buy the capital (machines and factories) that they use. Then the higher the interest rate, the more firms have to pay out in interest each year from the earnings they receive from their investment. Thus, the higher the interest rate, the less the profits to the firm after paying interest, and the less it will want to invest. Conversely, a low rate of interest makes investment spending profitable and is, therefore, reflected in a high level of planned investment.

The Investment Demand Schedule

We specify an investment spending function of the form[2]

$$I = \bar{I} - bi \qquad b > 0 \tag{2}$$

where i is the rate of interest and b measures the interest response of investment. $\bar{I}$ now denotes autonomous investment spending, that is, investment spending that is independent of both income and the rate of interest.[3] Equation (2) states that the lower the interest rate, the higher is planned investment, with the coefficient b measuring the responsiveness of investment spending to the interest rate.

Figure 4-3 shows the investment schedule of equation (2). The schedule shows for each level of the interest rate the amount which firms plan to spend on investment. The schedule is negatively sloped to reflect the assumption that a reduction in the interest rate increases the profitability of additions to the capital stock and therefore leads to a larger rate of planned investment spending.

The position of the investment schedule is determined by the slope — the term b in equation (2) — and by the level of autonomous investment spending, $\bar{I}$. If investment is highly responsive to the interest rate, a small decline in interest rates will lead to a large increase in investment, so that the schedule is almost flat. Conversely, if investment responds little to interest rates, the schedule will be more nearly vertical. Changes in autonomous investment spending, $\bar{I}$, shift the investment schedule. An increase in $\bar{I}$ means that at each level of the interest rate, firms plan to invest at a higher rate. This would be shown by a rightward shift of the investment schedule.

---

[2] Here and in other places in the book, we specify linear (straight-line) versions of behavioral functions. We use the linear specifications to simplify both the algebra and the diagrams. The linearity assumption does not lead to any great difficulties so long as we confine ourselves to talking about small changes in the economy. You should often draw nonlinear versions of our diagrams to be sure you can work with them.

[3] In Chap. 3, investment spending was defined as autonomous with respect to income. Now that the interest rate appears in the model, we have to extend the definition of autonomous to mean independent of *both* the interest rate and income. To conserve notation, we continue to use $\bar{I}$ to denote autonomous investment, but recognize that the definition is broadened.

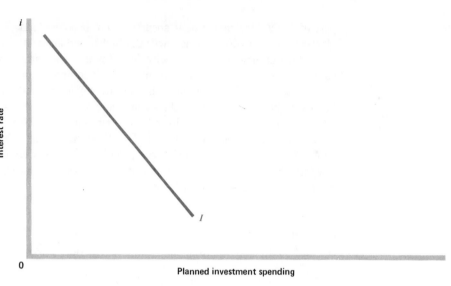

FIGURE 4-3

THE INVESTMENT SCHEDULE. The investment schedule shows the planned level of investment spending at each rate of interest. Because higher interest rates reduce the profitability of additions to the capital stock, higher interest rates imply lower planned rates of investment spending. Changes in autonomous investment shift the investment schedule.

The Interest Rate and Aggregate Demand: The *IS* Curve

We now modify the aggregate demand function of Chapter 3 to reflect the new planned investment spending schedule. [Aggregate demand still consists of the demand for consumption, investment, and government spending on goods and services, only now investment spending depends on the interest rate.] We have

$$AD \equiv C + I + G$$
$$= c\overline{TR} + c(1 - t)Y + \overline{I} - bi + \overline{G} \tag{3}$$
$$= \overline{A} + \overline{c}Y - bi$$

where $\quad \overline{A} \equiv c\overline{TR} + \overline{I} + \overline{G}$ $\tag{4}$

From equation (3) we observe that an increase in the interest rate reduces aggregate demand for a given level of income because an interest rate increase reduces investment spending. Note that the term $\overline{A}$, which is the part of aggregate demand unaffected by either the level of income or the interest rate, does include part of investment spending, namely, $\overline{I}$. As noted earlier, $\overline{I}$ is the *autonomous* component of investment spending, which is independent of the interest rate (and income).

At any given level of the interest rate, we can still proceed as in Chapter 3 to determine the equilibrium level of income and output. As the interest rate changes, however, the equilibrium level of income changes. Figure 4-4 is used to derive the *IS* curve.

For a given level of the interest rate, say, i_1, the last term of equation (3) is a constant (bi_1), and we can, in Figure 4-4*a*, draw the aggregate demand function of Chapter 3, this time with an intercept, $\overline{A} - bi_1$. The equilibrium level of income obtained in the usual manner is Y_1 at point E_1. Since that equilibrium level of income was derived for a given level of the interest rate (i_1), we plot that pair (i_1, Y_1) in the bottom panel as point E_1. We now have one point, E_1, on the *IS* curve.

Consider next a lower interest rate, i_2. At a lower interest rate, aggregate demand would be higher for each level of income because investment spending is higher. In terms of Figure 4-4*a*, that implies an upward shift of the aggregate demand schedule. The curve shifts upward because the intercept, $\overline{A} - bi$, has increased. Given the increase in aggregate demand, the equilibrium level of income rises to point E_2, with an associated income level Y_2. At point E_2, in the bottom panel, we record the fact that interest rate i_2 implies equilibrium level of income Y_2 — equilibrium in the sense that the goods market is in equilibrium (or that the goods market *clears*). Point E_2 is another point on the *IS* curve.

We can apply the same procedure to all conceivable levels of the interest rate and thereby generate all the points that make up the *IS* curve. They have in common the property that they are those combinations of interest rates and income (output) at which the goods market clears. That is why the *IS* curve is called the *goods market equilibrium schedule*.

Figure 4-4 shows that the *IS* curve is negatively sloped, reflecting the increase in aggregate demand associated with a reduction in the interest rate. We can also derive the *IS* curve by using the goods market equilibrium condition, that is, income equals planned spending, or

$$Y = AD \tag{5}$$
$$= \overline{A} + \overline{c}Y - bi$$

which can be simplified to

$$Y = \overline{\alpha}(\overline{A} - bi) \qquad \overline{\alpha} = \frac{1}{1 - \overline{c}} \tag{6}$$

where $\overline{\alpha}$ is the multiplier of Chapter 3. Equation (6) should now be compared with (1) at the beginning of this chapter. Note from equation (6) that a higher interest rate implies a lower level of equilibrium income for a given $\overline{A}$, as Figure 4-4 shows.

The construction of the *IS* curve is quite straightforward and may even be deceptively simple. We can gain further understanding of the economics of the *IS* curve by asking and answering the following questions:

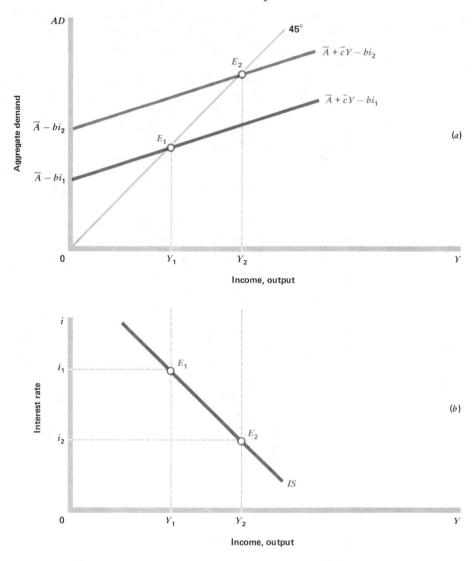

FIGURE 4-4
DERIVATION OF THE *IS* CURVE. At an interest rate i_1, equilibrium in the goods market is at point E_1 in the upper panel with an income level Y_1. In the lower panel this is recorded as point E_1, also. A fall in the interest rate to i_2 raises aggregate demand, increasing the level of spending at each income level. The new equilibrium income level is Y_2. In the lower panel, point E_2 records the new equilibrium in the goods market corresponding to an interest rate i_2.

- What determines the slope of the *IS* curve?
- What determines the position of the *IS* curve, given its slope, and what causes the curve to shift?
- What happens when the interest rate and income are at levels such that we are not on the *IS* curve?

The Slope of the *IS* Curve

We have already noted that the *IS* curve is negatively sloped because a higher level of the interest rate reduces investment spending, thereby reducing aggregate demand and thus the equilibrium level of income. The steepness of the curve depends on how sensitive investment spending is to changes in the interest rate and also on the multiplier, $\bar{\alpha}$, in equation (6).

Suppose that investment spending is very sensitive to the interest rate, so that b in equation (6) is large. Then, in terms of Figure 4-4, a given change in the interest rate produces a large change in aggregate demand, and thus shifts the aggregate demand curve in Figure 4-4a up by a large amount. A large shift in the aggregate demand schedule produces a correspondingly large change in the equilibrium level of income. If a given change in the interest rate produces a large change in income, the *IS* curve is very flat. This is the case if investment is very sensitive to the interest rate, that is, if b is large. Correspondingly, with b small and investment spending not very sensitive to the interest rate, the *IS* curve is relatively steep.

THE ROLE OF THE MULTIPLIER

Consider next the effects of the multiplier, $\bar{\alpha}$, on the steepness of the *IS* curve. Figure 4-5 shows aggregate demand curves corresponding to different multipliers. The coefficient $\bar{c}$ on the darker aggregate demand curves is smaller than the corresponding coefficient $\bar{c}'$ on the lighter aggregate demand curves. The multiplier is accordingly larger on the lighter aggregate demand curves. The initial levels of income, Y_1 and Y'_1, correspond to the interest rate i_1 on the lower pair of dark and light aggregate demand curves, respectively.

A given reduction in the interest rate, to i_2, raises the intercept of the aggregate demand curves by the same vertical distance, as shown in the top panel. However, the implied change in income is very different. For the lighter curve, income rises to Y'_2, while it rises only to Y_2 on the darker line. The change in equilibrium income corresponding to a given change in the interest rate is accordingly larger as the aggregate demand curve is steeper; that is, the larger the multiplier, the greater the rise in income. As we see from the lower figure, the larger the multiplier, the flatter the *IS* curve. Equivalently, the larger the multiplier, the larger the change in income produced by a given change in the interest rate.

We have thus seen that the smaller the sensitivity of investment spending to the interest rate and the smaller the multiplier, the steeper the *IS* curve. This conclusion is confirmed using equation (6). We can turn equation (6) around to express the interest rate as a function of the level of income:

$$i = \frac{\overline{A}}{b} - \frac{Y}{\overline{\alpha}b}$$

(6a)

FIGURE 4-5
EFFECTS OF THE MULTIPLIER ON THE STEEPNESS OF THE *IS* CURVE. The diagram shows that corresponding to a higher marginal propensity to spend and, hence, a steeper aggregate demand schedule, there is a flatter *IS* schedule.

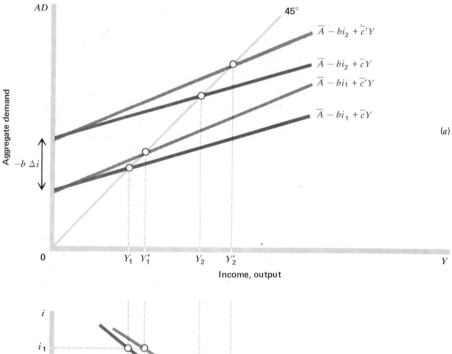

(a)

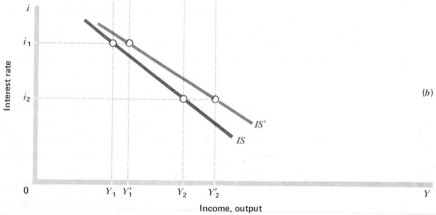

(b)

Thus, for a given change in Y, the associated change in i will be larger in size as b is smaller and as $\overline{\alpha}$ is smaller.

Given that the slope of the IS curve depends on the multiplier, fiscal policy can affect that slope. The multiplier, $\overline{\alpha}$, is affected by the tax rate: An increase in the tax rate reduces the multiplier. Accordingly, the higher the tax rate, the steeper is the IS curve.[4]

The Position of the IS Curve

Figure 4-6 shows two different IS curves, the lighter one of which lies to the right and above the darker IS curve. What might cause the IS curve to be at IS' rather than at IS? The answer is, An increase in the level of autonomous spending.

In Figure 4-6a we show an initial aggregate demand curve drawn for a level of autonomous spending $\overline{A}$ and for an interest rate i_1. Corresponding to the initial aggregate demand curve is the point E_1 on the IS curve in Figure 4-6b. Now, at the same interest rate, let the level of autonomous spending increase to $\overline{A}'$. The increase in autonomous spending increases the equilibrium level of income at the interest rate i_1. The point E_2 in Figure 4-6b is thus a point on the new goods market equilibrium schedule IS'. Since E_1 was an arbitrary point on the initial IS curve, we can perform the exercise for all levels of the interest rate and thereby generate the new curve, IS'. Thus, an increase in autonomous spending shifts the curve out to the right.

By how much does the curve shift? The change in income as a result of the change in autonomous spending can be seen from the top panel to be just the multiplier times the change in autonomous spending. That means that the IS curve is shifted horizontally by a distance equal to the multiplier times the change in autonomous spending, as in the lower panel.

The level of autonomous spending from equation (4) is

$$\overline{A} \equiv c\overline{TR} + \overline{I} + \overline{G}$$

Accordingly, an increase in government purchases or transfer payments will shift the IS curve out to the right, with the extent of the shift depending on the size of the multiplier. A reduction in transfer payments or in government purchases shifts the IS curve to the left.

Positions off the IS Curve

We can gain an understanding of the meaning of the IS curve by considering points off the curve. Figure 4-7 reproduces Figure 4-4 along with two additional points — the *dis*equilibrium points E_3 and E_4. Consider the question of what is true for points off the

---

[4] In problem 3 we ask you to relate this fact to the discussion of automatic stabilizers in Chap. 3.

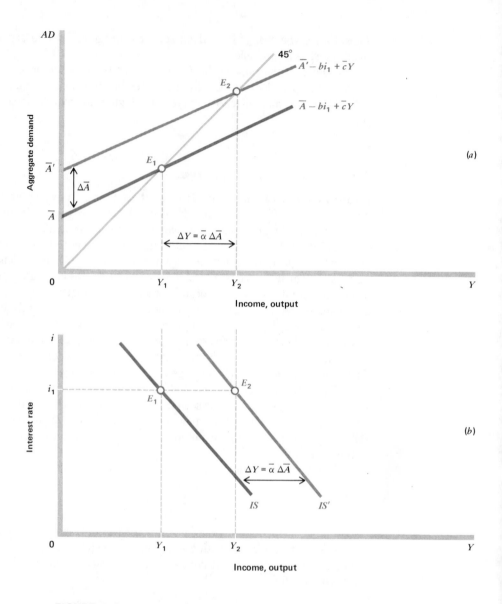

FIGURE 4-6

A SHIFT IN THE *IS* CURVE CAUSED BY A CHANGE IN AUTONOMOUS SPENDING.
An increase in aggregate demand due to higher autonomous spending
shifts the aggregate demand curve in part (*a*) up, raising the equilibrium
level of output at interest rate i_1. The *IS* schedule in part (*b*) shifts. At
each level of the interest rate, equilibrium income is now higher. The
horizontal shift of the *IS* schedule is equal to the multiplier times the
increase in autonomous spending.

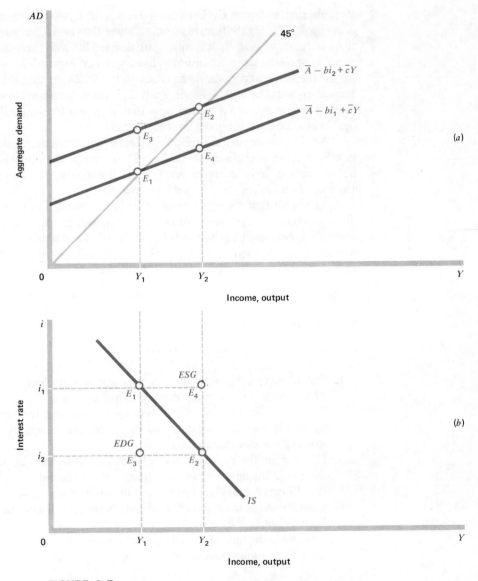

FIGURE 4-7

EXCESS SUPPLY (*ESG*) AND DEMAND (*EDG*) IN THE GOODS MARKET. Points above and to the right of the *IS* schedule correspond to an excess supply of goods, and points below and to the left to an excess demand for goods. At a point such as E_4, interest rates are higher than at E_2 on the *IS* curve. At the higher interest rates, investment spending is too low, and thus output exceeds planned spending and there is an excess supply of goods.

schedule, such as E_3 and E_4. In Figure 4-7b, at point E_3 we have the same interest rate i_2 as at point E_2, but the level of income is lower than at E_2. Since the interest rate i_2 at E_3 is the same as at E_2, the aggregate demand function corresponding to the two points must be the same. Accordingly, looking now at Figure 4-7a, we find both points are on the same aggregate demand schedule. At E_3 on that schedule, aggregate demand exceeds the level of output. Point E_3 is therefore a point of *excess demand for goods:* The interest rate is too low or output is too low for the goods market to be in equilibrium. Demand for goods exceeds output.

Next, consider point E_4 in Figure 4-7b. Here we have the same rate of interest i_1 as at E_1, but the level of income is higher. The corresponding point in Figure 4-7a is at E_4, at which we have an *excess supply of goods* since output is larger than aggregate demand, given interest rate i_1 and income level Y_2.

The preceding discussion shows that points above and to the right of the *IS* curve — points like E_4 — are points of excess supply of goods. This is indicated by *ESG* (excess supply of goods) in Figure 4-7b. Points below and to the left of the *IS* curve are points of excess demand for goods (*EDG*). At a point like E_3, the interest rate is too low and aggregate demand is therefore too high relative to output.

Summary

The major points about the *IS* curve are these:

1. The *IS* curve is the schedule of combinations of the interest rate and level of income such that the goods market is in equilibrium.
2. The *IS* curve is negatively sloped because an increase in the interest rate reduces planned investment spending and therefore reduces aggregate demand, thus reducing the equilibrium level of income.
3. The smaller the multiplier and the less sensitive investment spending is to changes in the interest rate, the steeper the *IS* curve.
4. The *IS* curve is shifted by changes in autonomous spending. An increase in autonomous spending, including an increase in government purchases, shifts the *IS* curve out to the right.
5. At points to the right of the curve, there is excess supply in the goods market; and at points to the left of the curve, there is excess demand for goods.

We turn now to examine behavior in the assets markets.

4-2 THE ASSETS MARKETS AND THE *LM* CURVE

In the preceding section, we discussed aggregate demand and the goods market. In the present section, we turn to the assets markets. The assets markets are the markets in which money, bonds, stocks, houses, and other forms of wealth are traded. Up to this point in the book, we have ignored the role of those markets in affecting the level of income, and it is now time to remedy the omission.

There is a large variety of assets, and a tremendous volume of trading occurs every day in the assets markets. But we shall simplify matters by grouping all available assets into two groups, *money* and *interest-bearing assets*.[5] By analogy with our treatment of the goods market, we proceed in the assets markets as if there are only two assets, money and all others. It will be useful to think of the other assets as marketable claims to future income such as *bonds*.

A bond is a promise to pay to its holder certain agreed-upon amounts of money at specified dates in the future. For example, a borrower sells a bond in exchange for a given amount of money today, say $100, and promises to pay a fixed amount, say $6, each year to the person who owns the bond, and to repay the full $100 (the principal) after some fixed period of time, such as 3 years. In this example, the interest rate is 6 percent, for that is the percentage of the amount borrowed that the borrower pays each year.

The Wealth Constraint

At any given time, an individual has to decide how to allocate his or her financial wealth between alternative types of assets. The more bonds held, the more interest received on total financial wealth. The more money held, the more likely the individual is to have money available when he or she wants to make a purchase. The person who has $1,000 in financial wealth has to decide whether to hold, say $900 in bonds and $100 in money, or rather, $500 in each type of asset, or even $1,000 in money and none in bonds. Decisions on the form in which to hold assets are *portfolio decisions*.

The example makes it clear that the portfolio decisions on how much money to hold and on how many bonds to hold are really the same decision. Given the level of financial wealth, the individual who has decided how many bonds to hold has implicitly also decided how much money to hold. There is a *wealth budget constraint* which states that the sum of the individual's demand for money and demand for bonds has to add up to that person's total financial wealth.

Real and Nominal Money Demand

At this stage we have to reinforce the crucial distinction between *real* and *nominal* variables. The nominal demand for money is the individual's demand for a given number of dollars, and similarly, the nominal demand for bonds is the demand for a given number of dollars' worth of bonds. The real demand for money is the demand for

---

[5] We assume in this section that certain assets, such as the capital that firms use in production, are not traded. That too is a simplification. A more complete treatment of the assets markets would allow for the trading of capital and would introduce a relative price for the capital operated by firms. This treatment is usually reserved for advanced graduate courses. For such a treatment of the assets markets, see James Tobin, "A General Equilibrium Approach to Monetary Theory," *Journal of Money, Credit and Banking,* February 1969, pp. 15–29, and by the same author, "Money, Capital, and Other Stores of Value," *American Economic Review,* May 1961, pp. 26–37.

box 4-1

ASSETS AND ASSET RETURNS

Assets fall into two broad categories, financial assets and tangible assets. A further subdivision identifies four main asset categories in the economy: money and other deposits (credit market instruments or bonds for short); equities, or stocks; and tangible, or real, assets. Table 1 shows the main categories of assets held by U.S. households in 1988. These asset holdings are reported by the Federal Reserve in *Balance Sheets for the US Economy*, March 1989. We now comment briefly on each category.

MONEY AND OTHER DEPOSITS

The money stock proper consists of assets that can be immediately used for making payments. Money includes currency (notes and coins) and also deposits on which checks can be written. At the end of 1988, currency and checkable deposits (a measure of money called $M1$) amounted to $790 billion. A broader measure of money (called $M2$) includes in addition to checkable deposits at banks also money market mutual funds and other deposits such as savings accounts. This measure of money was $3069 billion at the end of 1988.

From the 1930s until the mid-1970s, no interest was paid on checkable deposits. During that period, people held checkable deposits purely for the convenience. Now interest is paid on checkable deposits. Thus they are now held partly because they pay interest but also because they offer a convenient way of making payments.

BONDS

A bond is a promise by a borrower to pay the lender a certain amount (the principal) at a specified date (the maturity date of the bond) and to pay a given amount of interest per year in the meantime. Thus we might have a bond, issued by the U.S. Treasury, that pays $10,000 on June 1, 1999, and until that time pays 8 percent interest ($800) per year. Bonds are issued by many types of borrowers—governments, municipalities, and corporations. The interest rates on bonds issued by different borrowers reflect the differing risks of default. Default occurs when a borrower is unable to meet the commitment to pay interest or principal. Corporations sometimes default, and during the great depression of the 1930s, so did some cities. In the late 1970s there was fear that New York City would default, and in the 1980s there was fear that many foreign governments would do so.

By the end of 1988, individuals in the United States held a total of about $1.3 trillion in the form of bonds. Nearly $800 billion consisted of government bonds held by individuals. Households held relatively small amounts of corporate bonds—under $100 billion.

EQUITIES OR STOCKS

Equities or stocks are claims to a share of the profits of an enterprise. For example, a share in IBM entitles the owner to a share of the profits of that corporation. The shareholder, or stockholder, receives the return on equity in two forms. Most firms pay regular *dividends*, which means that stockholders receive a certain amount for each

TABLE 1
HOUSEHOLD ASSET HOLDINGS (percent of total household assets)

	1970	1988
Total household assets	100.0	100.0
Financial assets	68.1	64.9
Checkable deposits and currency	3.2	2.8
Other deposits	11.6	13.6
Credit market instruments (bonds)	6.8	6.9
Equities		
Corporate	19.9	12.0
Noncorporate	15.5	12.9
Life insurance and pension fund reserves	10.8	15.5
Tangible assets	31.9	35.1

share they own. Firms may also decide not to distribute profits to the stockholders, but rather retain the profits and reinvest them by adding to the firms' stocks of machines and structures. When this occurs, the shares become more valuable since they now represent claims on the profits from a larger capital stock. Therefore, the price of the stock in the market will rise, and stockholders can make *capital gains.* A capital gain is an increase, per period of time, in the price of an asset. Of course, when the outlook for a corporation turns sour, stock prices can fall and stockholders can make capital losses.

Thus the return on stocks, or the yield to a holder of a stock, is equal to the dividend (as a percent of price) plus the capital gain.

Suppose we look at 1989 and 1990 and consider the yield on a stock in an imaginary company, BioMiracles, Inc. In 1989 the stock traded for $15. In 1990, the stock pays a dividend of $0.75 and the stock price increases to $16.50. What is the yield on the stock? The yield per year is equal to 15.0 percent, which is the dividend as a percent of the initial price [5 percent = (0.75/15) × 100] plus 10.0 percent, which is the $1.50 capital gain as a percent of the initial price.

At the end of 1988, the value of equity held by households in the United States was $4.6 trillion. Slightly more than half of this equity was in noncorporate businesses.

REAL ASSETS

Real assets, or tangible assets, are the machines, land, and structures owned by corporations, and the consumer durables (cars, washing machines, stereos, etc.) and residences owned by households. These assets carry a return that differs from one asset to another. Owner-occupied residences provide a return to owners who enjoy living in them and not paying monthly rent; the machines a firm owns contribute to producing output and thus making profits. The assets are called *real* to distinguish them from *financial* assets (money, stocks, bonds). The total value of tangible assets at the end of 1988 was $6.5 trillion, or over $26,530 per person.

The value of equities and bonds held by individuals cannot be added to tangible wealth to get the total wealth of individuals. The reason is that the equities and bonds individuals hold are claims on the part of tangible wealth that is held by corporations. The equity share gives an individual a part ownership in the factory and machinery.

In macroeconomics, to make things manageable, we lump assets into two categories. On one side we have money, with the specific characteristic that it is the only asset that serves as a means of payment. On the other side we have all other assets. Because money offers the convenience of being a means of payment, it carries a lower return than other assets, but that differential depends on the relative supplies of assets. As we see in this chapter, when the Fed reduces the money stock and increases the supply of other assets (we say ''bonds''), the yield on other assets increases.

The appendix to Chapter 9 develops the relationship between interest rates and asset prices or present values. The appendix can be read independently of Chapter 9, and the interested student can study that material now. ∎

money expressed in terms of the number of units of goods that money will buy: it is equal to the nominal demand for money divided by the price level. If the nominal demand for money is $100 and the price level is $2 per good — meaning that the representative basket of goods costs $2 — then the real demand for money is 50 goods. If the price level later doubles to $4 per good and the demand for nominal money likewise doubles to $200, the real demand for money is unchanged at 50 goods.

Real money balances — real balances for short — are the quantity of nominal money divided by the price level, and the real demand for money is called the *demand for real balances.* Similarly, real bond holdings are the nominal quantity of bonds divided by the price level.

The wealth budget constraint in the assets markets states that the demand for real balances, which we denote L, plus the demand for real bond holdings, which we denote DB, must add up to the real financial wealth of the individual. Real financial wealth is, of course, simply nominal wealth, WN, divided by the price level, P:

$$L + DB \equiv \frac{WN}{P} \tag{7}$$

Note, again, that the wealth budget constraint implies, given an individual's real wealth, that a decision to hold more real balances is also a decision to hold less real wealth in the form of bonds. This implication turns out to be both important and convenient. It will allow us to discuss assets markets entirely in terms of the money market. Why? Because, given real wealth, when the money market is in equilibrium, the bond market will turn out also to be in equilibrium. We now show why that should be.

The total amount of real financial wealth in the economy consists of existing real money balances and real bonds. Thus, total real financial wealth is equal to

$$\frac{WN}{P} \equiv \frac{M}{P} + SB \tag{8}$$

where M is the stock of nominal money balances and SB is the real value of the supply of bonds. Total real financial wealth consists of real balances and real bonds. The distinction between equations (7) and (8) is that equation (7) is a constraint on the amount of assets individuals wish to hold, whereas equation (8) is merely an accounting relationship that tells us how much financial wealth there is in the economy. There is no implication in the accounting relationship in equation (8) that individuals are necessarily happy to hold the amounts of money and bonds that actually exist in the economy.

Now substitute equation (7) into equation (8) and rearrange terms to obtain

$$\left(L - \frac{M}{P}\right) + (DB - SB) \equiv 0 \tag{9}$$

Let us see what equation (9) implies. Suppose that the demand for real balances, L, is equal to the existing stock of real balances, $\overline{M}/\overline{P}$. Then the first term in parentheses in equation (9) is equal to zero, and therefore the second term in parentheses must also be zero. Thus, if the demand for real money balances is equal to the real money supply, the demand for real bonds, DB, must be equal to the supply of real bonds, SB.

Stating the same proposition in terms of "markets," we can say the following: The *wealth budget constraint* implies that when the money market is in equilibrium ($L = \overline{M}/\overline{P}$), the bond market, too, is in equilibrium ($DB = SB$). Similarly, when there is excess demand in the money market, so that $L > \overline{M}/\overline{P}$, there is an excess supply of bonds, that is, $DB < SB$. We can therefore fully discuss the assets markets by concentrating our attention on the money market.

The Demand for Money

We now turn to the money market and initially concentrate on the demand for real balances.[6] The demand for money is a demand for *real* balances because people hold money for what it will buy. The higher the price level, the more nominal balances a person has to hold to be able to purchase a given quantity of goods. If the price level doubles, then an individual has to hold twice as many nominal balances in order to be able to buy the same amount of goods.

The demand for real balances depends on the level of real income and the interest rate. It depends on the level of real income because individuals hold money to finance

---

[6] The demand for money is studied in depth in Chap. 10; here we only briefly present the arguments underlying the demand for money.

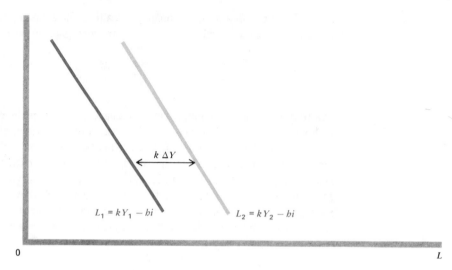

Demand for money

FIGURE 4-8
THE DEMAND FOR REAL BALANCES AS A FUNCTION OF THE INTEREST RATE
AND REAL INCOME. The demand for real balances is drawn as a function
of the rate of interest. The higher the rate of interest, the lower the
quantity of real balances demanded, given the level of income. An
increase in income raises the demand for money. This is shown by a
rightward shift of the money demand schedule.

their expenditures, which, in turn, depend on income. The demand for money depends also on the cost of holding money. The cost of holding money is the interest that is forgone by holding money rather than other assets. The higher the interest rate, the more costly it is to hold money rather than other assets and, accordingly, the less cash will be held at each level of income.[7] Individuals can economize on their holdings of cash when the interest rate rises by being more careful in managing their money and by making transfers from money to bonds whenever their money holdings reach any appreciable magnitude. If the interest rate is 1 percent, then there is very little benefit from holding bonds rather than money. However, when the interest rate is 10 percent, one would probably go to some effort not to hold more money than is needed to finance day-to-day transactions.

On these simple grounds, then, the demand for real balances increases with the

---

[7] As we discuss in Chap. 11, changes in financial regulations in the early 1980s led to the payment of interest on some forms of money holdings. In Chap. 10 we discuss the effects of such changes on the demand for money and on the *LM* curve. But there do remain sizable parts of money holding — including currency — on which no interest is paid, so that overall, money earns less interest than other assets and the analysis of this chapter is still applicable.

level of real income and decreases with the interest rate.] The demand for real balances is accordingly written[8]

$$L = kY - hi \qquad k, h > 0 \qquad (10)$$

The parameters k and h reflect the sensitivity of the demand for real balances to the level of income and the interest rate, respectively. A \$5 increase in real income raises money demand by $5k$ real dollars. An increase in the interest rate of one percentage point reduces real money demand by h real dollars.

The demand function for real balances, equation (10), implies that for a given level of income, the quantity demanded is a decreasing function of the rate of interest. Such a demand curve is shown in Figure 4-8 for a level of income Y_1. The higher the level of income, the larger is the demand for real balances, and therefore the further to the right the demand curve. The demand curve for a higher level of real income, Y_2, is also shown in Figure 4-8.

The Supply of Money, Money Market Equilibrium, and the *LM* Curve

Now we study equilibrium in the money market. For that purpose we have to say how the supply of money is determined. The nominal quantity of money, M, is controlled by the Federal Reserve System (Fed), and we take it as given at the level $\overline{M}$. We assume the price level is constant at the level $\overline{P}$, so that the real money supply is at the level $\overline{M}/\overline{P}$.[9]

In Figure 4-9, we show combinations of interest rates and income levels such that the demand for real balances exactly matches the available supply. Starting with the level of income, Y_1, the corresponding demand curve for real balances, L_1, is shown in Figure 4-9b. It is drawn, as in Figure 4-8, as a decreasing function of the interest rate. The existing supply of real balances, $\overline{M}/\overline{P}$, is shown by the vertical line, since it is given and therefore is independent of the interest rate. The interest rate, i_1, has the property that it clears the money market. At that interest rate, the demand for real balances equals the supply. Therefore, point E_1 is an equilibrium point in the money market. That point is recorded in Figure 4-9a as a point on the *money market equilibrium schedule,* or the *LM curve.*

Consider next the effect of an increase in income to Y_2. In Figure 4-9b, the higher level of income causes the demand for real balances to be higher at each level of the interest rate, and so the demand curve for real balances shifts up and to the right, to L_2. The interest rate increases to i_2 to maintain equilibrium in the money market at

---

[8] Once again, we use a linear equation to describe a relationship. You should experiment with an alternative form, for example, $L = kY + h'/i$, where k and h' are positive. How would the equivalent of Fig. 4-8 look for this demand function?

[9] Since, for the present, we are holding constant the money supply and price level, we refer to them as exogenous and denote that fact by a bar.

that higher level of income. Accordingly, the new equilibrium point is E_2. In Figure 4-9a, we record point E_2 as a point of equilibrium in the money market. Performing the same exercise for all income levels, we generate a series of points that can be linked to give us the *LM* schedule.

The *LM* schedule, or money market equilibrium schedule, shows all combinations of interest rates and levels of income such that the demand for real balances is equal to the supply. Along the *LM* schedule, the money market is in equilibrium.

The *LM* curve is positively sloped. An increase in the interest rate reduces the demand for real balances. To maintain the demand for real balances equal to the fixed supply, the level of income has to rise. Accordingly, money market equilibrium implies that an increase in the interest rate is accompanied by an increase in the level of income.

The *LM* curve can be obtained directly by combining the demand curve for real balances, equation (10), and the fixed supply of real balances. For the money market to be in equilibrium, demand has to equal supply, or

$$\frac{\overline{M}}{P} = kY - hi$$

(11)

FIGURE 4-9

DERIVATION OF THE *LM* CURVE. The right-hand panel shows the money market. The supply of real balances is the vertical line $\overline{M}/P$. The nominal money supply $\overline{M}$ is fixed by the Fed, and the price level $\overline{P}$ is assumed given. Demand for money curves L_1 and L_2 corresponds to different levels of income. When the income level is Y_1, L_1 applies, and the equilibrium interest rate is i_1. This gives point E_1 on the *LM* schedule in (a). At income level Y_2, greater than Y_1, the equilibrium interest rate is i_2, yielding point E_2 on the *LM* curve.

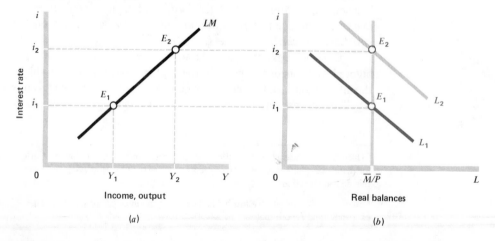

Solving for the interest rate:

$$i = \frac{1}{h}\left(kY - \frac{\overline{M}}{\overline{P}}\right)$$

(11*a*)

The relationship (11*a*) is the *LM* curve.

Next we ask the same questions about the properties of the *LM* schedule that we asked about the *IS* curve.

The Slope of the *LM* Curve

The larger the responsiveness of the demand for money to income, as measured by *k*, and the lower the responsiveness of the demand for money to the interest rate, *h*, the steeper the *LM* curve will be. This point can be established by experimenting with Figure 4-9. It can also be confirmed by examining equation (11*a*), where a given change in income, ΔY, has a larger effect on the interest rate *i*, the larger is *k* and the smaller is *h*. If the demand for money is relatively insensitive to the interest rate, so that *h* is close to zero, the *LM* curve is nearly vertical. If the demand for money is very sensitive to the interest rate, so that *h* is large, then the *LM* curve is close to horizontal. In that case, a small change in the interest rate must be accompanied by a large change in the level of income in order to maintain money market equilibrium.

The Position of the *LM* Curve

The real money supply is held constant along the *LM* curve. It follows that a change in the real money supply will shift the *LM* curve. In Figure 4-10, we show the effect of an increase in the real money supply. In Figure 4-10*b*, we draw the demand for real money balances for a level of income Y_1. With the initial real money supply, $\overline{M}/\overline{P}$, the equilibrium is at point E_1, with an interest rate i_1. The corresponding point on the *LM* schedule is E_1.

Consider the effect of an increase in the real money supply to $\overline{M}'/\overline{P}$, which is represented by a rightward shift of the money supply schedule. At the initial level of income and, hence, on the demand schedule L_1, there is now an excess supply of real balances. To restore money market equilibrium at the income level Y_1, the interest rate has to decline to i_2. The new equilibrium is, therefore, at point E_2. This implies that in Figure 4-10*a*, the *LM* schedule shifts to the right and down to *LM'*. At each level of income the equilibrium interest rate has to be lower to induce people to hold the larger real quantity of money. Alternatively, at each level of the interest rate the level of income has to be higher so as to raise the transactions demand for money and thereby absorb the higher real money supply. These points can be noted, too, from inspection of the money market equilibrium condition in equation (11).

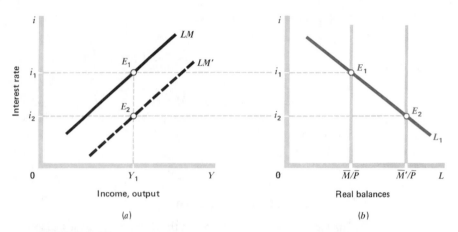

FIGURE 4-10

AN INCREASE IN THE SUPPLY OF MONEY FROM $\overline{M}$ TO $\overline{M}'$ SHIFTS THE *LM* CURVE TO THE RIGHT. An increase in the stock of real balances shifts the supply schedule in the right panel from $\overline{M}/\overline{P}$ to $\overline{M}'/\overline{P}$. At the initial income level Y_1, the equilibrium interest rate in the money market falls to i_2. In the left panel we show point E_2 as one point on the new *LM* schedule, corresponding to the higher money stock. Thus an increase in the real money stock shifts the *LM* schedule down and to the right.

Positions off the *LM* Curve

Next we consider points off the *LM* schedule in order to characterize them as points of excess demand or excess supply of money. For that purpose, look at Figure 4-11, which reproduces Figure 4-9 but adds the disequilibrium points E_3 and E_4. Look first at point E_1, where the money market is in equilibrium. Next assume an increase in the level of income to Y_2. This will raise the demand for real balances and shift the demand curve to L_2. At the initial interest rate, the demand for real balances would be indicated by point E_4 in Figure 4-11 b, and we would have an excess demand for money — an excess of demand over supply — equal to the distance $E_1 E_4$. Accordingly, point E_4 in Figure 4-11 a is a point of excess demand for money: the interest rate is too low and/or the level of income too high for the money market to clear. Consider, next, point E_3 in Figure 4-11 b. Here we have the initial level of income Y_1, but an interest rate that is too high to yield money market equilibrium. Accordingly, we have an excess supply of money equal to the distance $E_3 E_2$. Point E_3 in Figure 4-11 a therefore corresponds to an excess supply of money.

More generally, any point to the right and below the *LM* schedule is a point of excess demand for money, and any point to the left and above the *LM* curve is a point of excess supply. This is shown by the *EDM* and *ESM* notations in Figure 4-11 a.

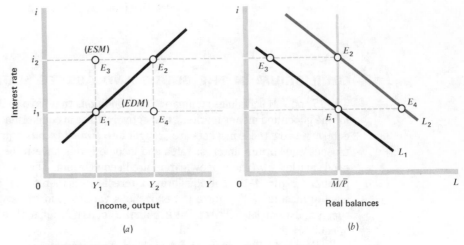

FIGURE 4-11

EXCESS DEMAND (*EDM*) AND SUPPLY (*EDM*) OF MONEY. Points above and to the left of the *LM* schedule correspond to an excess supply of real balances; points below and to the right, to an excess demand for real balances. Starting at point E_1 in the left panel, an increase in income takes us to E_4. At E_4 in the right panel, there is an excess demand for money—and thus at E_4 in the left panel there is an excess demand for money. By a similar argument, we can start at E_2 and move to E_3, at which the level of income is lower. This creates an excess supply of money.

Summary

The following are the major points about the *LM* curve:

1. The *LM* curve is the schedule of combinations of interest rates and levels of income such that the money market is in equilibrium.
2. When the money market is in equilibrium, so is the bond market. The *LM* curve is, therefore, also the schedule of combinations of interest rates and levels of income such that the bond market is in equilibrium.
3. The *LM* curve is positively sloped. Given the fixed money supply, an increase in the level of income, which increases the quantity of money demanded, has to be accompanied by an increase in the interest rate. This reduces the quantity of money demanded and thereby maintains money market equilibrium.
4. The *LM* curve is shifted by changes in the money supply. An increase in the money supply shifts the *LM* curve to the right.
5. At points to the right of the *LM* curve, there is an excess demand for money, and at points to its left, there is an excess supply of money.

We are now ready to discuss the joint equilibrium of the goods and assets markets.

4-3 EQUILIBRIUM IN THE GOODS AND ASSETS MARKETS

The IS and LM schedules summarize the conditions that have to be satisfied in order for the goods and money markets, respectively, to be in equilibrium. The task now is to determine how these markets are brought into *simultaneous* equilibrium. For simultaneous equilibrium, interest rates and income levels have to be such that *both* the goods market *and* the money market are in equilibrium. That condition is satisfied at point E in Figure 4-12. The equilibrium interest rate is therefore i_0 and the equilibrium level of income is Y_0, given the exogenous variables, in particular the real money supply and fiscal policy.[10] At point E, both the goods market and the assets markets are in equilibrium.

Figure 4-12 summarizes our analysis: The interest rate and the level of output are determined by the interaction of the assets (LM) and goods (IS) markets.

It is worth stepping back now to review our assumptions and the meaning of the equilibrium at E. The major assumption is that the price level is constant and that firms are willing to supply whatever amount of output is demanded at that price level. Thus, we assume the level of output Y_0 in Figure 4-12 will be willingly supplied by firms at the price level $\overline{P}$. We repeat that this assumption is one that is temporarily needed for the development of the analysis; it will be dropped in Chapter 7 when we begin to study the determinants of the price level.

At the point E in Figure 4-12, the economy is in equilibrium, given the price level, because both the goods and money markets are in equilibrium. The demand for goods is equal to the level of output on the IS curve. And on the LM curve, the demand for money is equal to the supply of money. That also means the supply of bonds is equal to the demand for bonds, as the discussion of the wealth budget constraint showed. Accordingly, at point E, firms are producing the amount of output they plan to (there is no unintended inventory accumulation or rundown), and individuals have the portfolio compositions they desire.

Changes in the Equilibrium Levels of Income and the Interest Rate

The equilibrium levels of income and the interest rate change when either the IS or the LM curve shifts. Figure 4-13, for example, shows the effects of an increase in the rate of autonomous investment on the equilibrium levels of income and the interest rate. Such an increase raises autonomous spending, $\overline{A}$, and therefore shifts the IS curve to

---

[10] Recall that exogenous variables are those whose values are not determined within the system being studied.

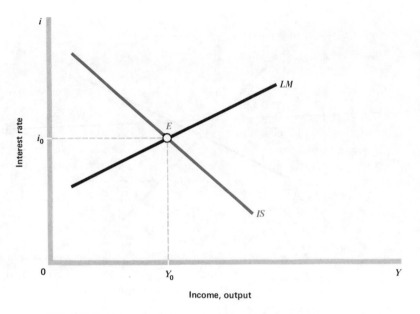

FIGURE 4-12

GOODS AND ASSETS MARKET EQUILIBRIUM. Goods and assets markets clear at point E. Interest rates and income levels are such that the public holds the existing stock of money and planned spending equals output.

the right. That results in a rise in the level of income and an increase in the interest rate at point E'.

Recall that an increase in autonomous investment spending, $\Delta \bar{I}$, shifts the *IS* curve to the right by the amount $\bar{\alpha}\Delta \bar{I}$ as we show in Figure 4-13. In Chapter 3, where we dealt only with the goods market, we would have argued that $\bar{\alpha}\Delta \bar{I}$ would be the change in the level of income resulting from the change of $\Delta \bar{I}$ in autonomous spending. But it can be seen in Figure 4-13 that the change in income here is only ΔY_0, which is clearly less than the shift in the *IS* curve, $\bar{\alpha}\Delta \bar{I}$.

What explains the fact that the increase in income is smaller than the increase in autonomous spending, $\Delta \bar{I}$, times the simple multiplier, $\bar{\alpha}$? Diagrammatically, it is clear that the explanation is the slope of the *LM* curve. If the *LM* curve were horizontal, there would be no difference between the extent of the horizontal shift of the *IS* curve and the change in income. If the *LM* curve were horizontal, then the interest rate would not change when the *IS* curve shifts.

What is the economics of what is happening? The increase in autonomous spending does tend to increase the level of income. But an increase in income increases the demand for money. With the supply of money fixed, the interest rate has to rise to

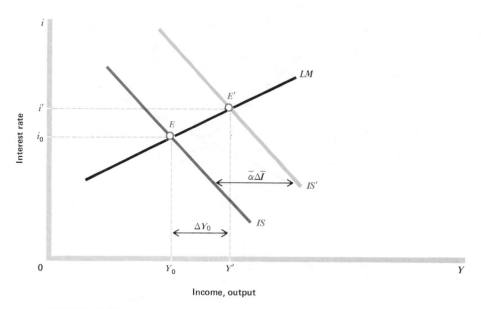

FIGURE 4-13

EFFECTS OF AN INCREASE IN AUTONOMOUS SPENDING ON INCOME AND THE INTEREST RATE. An increase in autonomous spending shifts the *IS* schedule out and to the right. Income increases, and the equilibrium income level rises. The increase in income is less than is given by the simple multiplier $\bar{\alpha}$. This is because interest rates increase and dampen investment spending.

ensure that the demand for money stays equal to the fixed supply. When the interest rate rises, investment spending is reduced because investment is negatively related to the interest rate. Accordingly, the equilibrium change in income is less than the horizontal shift of the *IS* curve, $\bar{\alpha}\Delta\bar{I}$.

We have now provided an example of the use of the *IS-LM* apparatus. That apparatus is very useful for studying the effects of monetary and fiscal policy on income and the interest rate, and we so use it in Sections 4-5 and 4-6 and Chapter 5. Before we do so, however, we discuss how the economy moves from one equilibrium, such as *E*, to another, such as *E'*.

4-4 ADJUSTMENT TOWARD EQUILIBRIUM

Suppose that the economy were initially at a point like *E* in Figure 4-13 and that one of the curves then shifted, so that the new equilibrium was at a point like *E'*. How would that new equilibrium actually be reached? The adjustment would involve changes in both the interest rate and the level of income. To study how they move over time, we make two assumptions:

1. Output increases whenever there is an excess demand for goods and declines whenever there is an excess supply of goods. This assumption reflects the adjustment of firms to undesired rundown and accumulation of inventories.
2. The interest rate rises whenever there is an excess demand for money and falls whenever there is an excess supply of money. This adjustment occurs because an excess demand for money implies an excess supply of other assets (bonds). In attempting to acquire more money, people sell off bonds and thereby cause bond prices to fall or their yields (interest rates) to rise.

A detailed discussion of the relationship between the price of a bond and its yield is presented in the appendix to Chapter 9. Here we give only a brief explanation. For simplicity, consider a bond that promises to pay the holder of the bond $5 per year forever. The $5 is known as the bond *coupon,* and a bond that promises to pay a given amount to the holder of the bond forever is known as a *perpetuity.* If the yield available on other assets is 5 percent, the perpetuity will sell for $100 because at that price it, too, yields 5 percent (= $5/$100). Now suppose that the yield on other assets rises to 10 percent. Then the price of the perpetuity will drop to $50 because only at that price does the perpetuity yield 10 percent; that is, the $5 per year interest on a bond costing $50 gives its owners a 10 percent yield on their $50. This example makes it clear that the price of a bond and its yield are inversely related, given the coupon.

In point 2 above we assumed that an excess demand for money causes asset holders to attempt to sell off their bonds, thereby causing bond prices to fall and their yields to rise. Conversely, when there is an excess supply of money, people attempt to use their money to buy up other assets, raising the prices of the other assets and lowering their yields.

In Figure 4-14 we apply the analysis to study the adjustment of the economy. Four regions are represented, and they are characterized in Table 4-1. We know from Figure 4-11 that there is an excess supply of money above the *LM* curve, and hence we show *ESM* in regions I and II in Table 4-1. Similarly, we know from Figure 4-7 that there is an excess demand for goods below the *IS* curve. Hence, we show *EDG* for regions II and III in Table 4-1. You should be able to explain the remaining entries of Table 4-1.

The adjustment directions specified in assumptions 1 and 2 above are represented by arrows. Thus, for example, in region IV we have an excess demand for money that causes interest rates to rise as other assets are sold off for money and their prices decline. The rising interest rates are represented by the upward-pointing arrow. There is also an excess supply of goods in region IV and, accordingly, involuntary inventory accumulation, to which firms respond by reducing output. Declining output is indicated by the leftward-pointing arrow. The adjustments shown by the arrows will lead ultimately, perhaps in a cyclical manner, to the equilibrium point E. For example, starting at E_1 we show the economy moving to E, with income and the interest rate increasing along the *adjustment path* indicated.

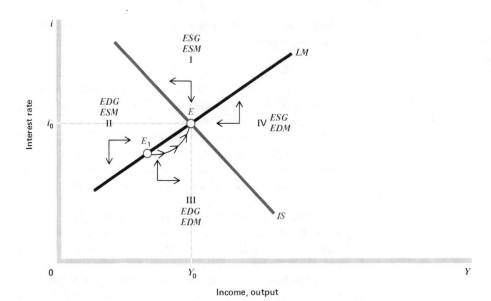

FIGURE 4-14
DISEQUILIBRIUM AND DYNAMICS IN THE GOODS AND MONEY MARKETS.
Income and interest rates adjust to the disequilibrium in goods markets
and assets markets. Specifically, interest rates fall when there is an
excess supply of money and rise when there is an excess demand.
Income rises when aggregate demand for goods exceeds output and
falls when aggregate demand is less than output. The system
converges over time to the equilibrium at E.

TABLE 4-1
DISEQUILIBRIUM AND ADJUSTMENT

| Region | GOODS MARKET | | MONEY MARKET | |
	Disequilibrium	Adjustment: output	Disequilibrium	Adjustment: interest rate
I	ESG	Falls	ESM	Falls
II	EDG	Rises	ESM	Falls
III	EDG	Rises	EDM	Rises
IV	ESG	Falls	EDM	Rises

Rapid Asset Market Adjustment

For many purposes it is useful to restrict the dynamics by the reasonable assumption that the money market adjusts very quickly and the goods market adjusts relatively slowly. Since the money market can adjust merely through the buying and selling of bonds, the interest rate adjusts rapidly and the money market effectively is always in equilibrium. Such an assumption implies that we are always on the *LM* curve: any departure from the equilibrium in the money market is almost instantaneously eliminated by an appropriate change in the interest rate. In disequilibrium, we therefore move along the *LM* curve, as is shown in Figure 4-15.

The goods market adjusts relatively slowly because firms have to change their production schedules, which takes time. For points below the *IS* curve, we move up along the *LM* schedule with rising income and interest rates, and for points above the *IS* schedule, we move down along the *LM* schedule with falling output and interest rates until point *E* is reached. The adjustment process is *stable* in that the economy does move to the equilibrium position at *E*.

The adjustment process shown in Figure 4-15 is very similar to that of Chapter 3. To the right of the *IS* curve, there is an excess supply of goods, and firms are therefore

FIGURE 4-15
ADJUSTMENT TO EQUILIBRIUM WHEN THE MONEY MARKET ADJUSTS QUICKLY. If the money market adjusts very rapidly, then the economy is always in monetary equilibrium. In the diagram this corresponds to always being on the *LM* schedule. When there is excess demand for goods, output and interest rates are rising, and when there is excess supply of goods, output and interest rates are falling.

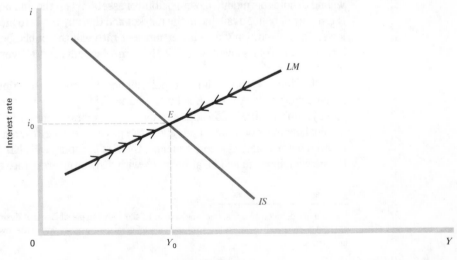

accumulating inventories. They cut production in response to their inventory buildup, and the economy moves down the *LM* curve. The difference between the adjustment process here and in Chapter 3 is the following: Here, as the economy moves toward the equilibrium level of income, with a falling interest rate, desired investment spending actually rises.[11]

Now that we have established that the economy does adjust toward its equilibrium position, we turn to examining the effects of monetary and fiscal policy on the equilibrium interest rate and level of income.

4-5 MONETARY POLICY

In this section, we are concerned with the effect of an increase in the real quantity of money on the interest rate and level of income. We break up that inquiry into two separate questions. First, what is the ultimate effect of the increase in the money supply when the new equilibrium is reached? Second, how is that new equilibrium reached, or what is the transmission mechanism?

Through monetary policy the Federal Reserve affects the quantity of money and thereby the interest rate and income. The chief instrument, studied in more detail in Chapter 12, is *open market operations.* In an open market operation, the Federal Reserve purchases bonds in exchange for money, thus increasing the stock of money, or it sells bonds in exchange for money paid by the purchasers of the bonds, thus reducing the money stock.

We take here the case of an open market purchase of bonds. The purchase is made by the Federal Reserve System, which pays for its purchases with money that it can create. One can usefully think of the Fed as printing money with which to buy bonds, even though that is not strictly accurate, as we shall see in Chapter 11. The purpose of an open market operation is to change the available *relative* supplies of money and bonds and thereby change the interest rate or yield at which the public is willing to hold this modified composition of assets. When the Fed buys bonds, it reduces the supply of bonds available in the market and thereby tends to increase their price, or lower their yield. Only at a lower interest rate will the public be prepared to hold a larger fraction of its given wealth in the form of money, and a lower fraction in the form of bonds.

In Figure 4-16 we show graphically how the open market purchase works. The initial equilibrium at point E is on the initial *LM* schedule that corresponds to a real money supply, $\overline{M}/P$. Consider next an open market operation that increases the nominal quantity of money and, given the price level, the real quantity of money. We showed before that, as a consequence, the *LM* schedule will shift to *LM'*. Therefore, the new equilibrium will be at point E' with a lower interest rate and a higher level of

---

[11] In a more detailed analysis, one would want to allow for the possibility that desired investment would be cut back in response to excess inventories. This again raises the possibility of the inventory cycle, referred to in Chap. 3.

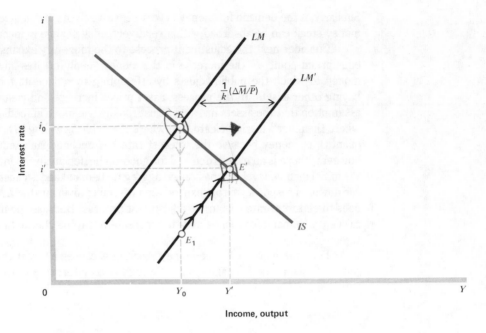

FIGURE 4-16
THE ADJUSTMENT PATH OF THE ECONOMY FOLLOWING AN INCREASE IN THE
MONEY STOCK. An increase in the real money stock shifts the *LM*
schedule down and to the right. Interest rates immediately decline from
E to E_1 and then, through their effect on investment, cause spending
and income to rise until a new equilibrium is reached at E'. Once all
adjustments have taken place, a rise in the real money stock raises
equilibrium income and lowers equilibrium interest rates.

income. The equilibrium level of income rises because the open market purchase
reduces the interest rate and thereby increases investment spending.

By experimenting with Figure 4-16, you will be able to show that the steeper the
LM schedule, the larger the change in income. If money demand is very sensitive to
the interest rate, then a given change in the money stock can be absorbed in the assets
markets with only a small change in the interest rate. The effects of an open market
purchase on investment spending would then be small. By contrast, if the demand for
money is not very sensitive to the interest rate, a given change in the money supply will
cause a large change in the interest rate and have a big effect on investment demand.[12]

---

[12] In problem 3, we ask you to provide a similar explanation of the role of the slope of the *IS* curve—which is
determined by the multiplier and the interest sensitivity of investment demand—in determining the effect
of monetary policy on income.

Similarly, if the demand for money is very sensitive to income, a given increase in the money stock can be absorbed with a relatively small change in income.

Consider next the adjustment process to the monetary expansion. At the initial equilibrium point, E, the increase in the money supply creates an excess supply of money to which the public adjusts by attempting to reduce its money holdings by buying other assets. In the process, asset prices increase and yields decline. By our assumption that the assets markets adjust rapidly, we move immediately to point E_1, where the money market clears, and where the public is willing to hold the larger real quantity of money because the interest rate has declined sufficiently. At point E_1, however, there is an excess demand for goods. The decline in the interest rate, given the initial income level Y_0, has raised aggregate demand and is causing inventories to run down. In response, output expands and we start moving up the LM' schedule. Why does the interest rate rise in the adjustment process? Because the increase in output raises the demand for money and that increase has to be checked by higher interest rates.

Thus the increase in the money stock first causes interest rates to fall as the public adjusts its portfolio and then — through lower interest rates — increases aggregate demand.

The Transmission Mechanism

Two steps in the *transmission mechanism* — the process by which changes in monetary policy affect aggregate demand — are essential. The first is that an increase in real balances generates a *portfolio disequilibrium,* that is, at the prevailing interest rate and level of income, people are holding more money than they want. This causes portfolio holders to attempt to reduce their money holdings by buying other assets, thereby changing asset prices and yields. In other words, the change in the money supply changes interest rates. The second stage of the transmission process occurs when the change in interest rates affects aggregate demand.

These two stages of the transmission process are essential in that they appear in almost every analysis of the effects of changes in the money supply on the economy. The details of the analysis will often differ — some analyses will have more than two assets and more than one interest rate; some will include an influence of interest rates on other categories of demand, in particular consumption and spending by local government.[13]

Table 4-2 provides a summary of the stages in the transmission mechanism.

---

[13] Some analyses also include a mechanism by which changes in real balances have a direct effect on aggregate demand through the real balance effect. The argument is that wealth affects consumption demand (as we shall see in Chap. 8) and that an increase in real balances increases wealth and therefore consumption demand. This effect would not apply in the case of an open market purchase, which merely exchanges one asset for another (bonds for money) without changing wealth. The real balance effect is not very important empirically because the relevant real balances are only a small part of wealth. The definitive book on the topic is Don Patinkin, *Money, Interest and Prices,* New York: Harper & Row, 1965.

TABLE 4-2
THE TRANSMISSION MECHANISM

(1)	(2)	(3)	(4)
Change in real money supply	Portfolio adjustments lead to a change in asset prices and interest rates	Spending adjusts to the change in interest rates	Output adjusts to the change in aggregate demand

There are two critical links between the change in real balances and the ultimate effect on income. First, the change in real balances, by bringing about portfolio disequilibrium, must lead to a change in interest rates. Second, that change in interest rates must change aggregate demand. Through those two linkages, changes in the real money stock affect the level of output in the economy. But that outcome immediately implies the following: If portfolio imbalances do not lead to significant changes in interest rates — for whatever reason — or if spending does not respond to changes in interest rates, the link between money and output does not exist.[14] We now study these linkages in more detail.

The Liquidity Trap

In discussing the effects of monetary policy on the economy, two extreme cases have received much attention. The first is the *liquidity trap,* a situation in which the public is prepared, at a given interest rate, to hold whatever amount of money is supplied. This implies that the *LM* curve is horizontal and that changes in the quantity of money do not shift it. In that case, monetary policy carried out through open market operations[15] has no effect on either the interest rate or level of income. In the liquidity trap, monetary policy is powerless to affect the interest rate.

There is a liquidity trap at a zero interest rate. At a zero interest rate, the public would not want to hold any bonds, since money, which also pays zero interest, has the advantage of being usable in transactions. Accordingly, if the interest rate ever, for some reason, were zero, increases in the quantity of money could not induce anyone to

---

[14] We refer to the responsiveness of aggregate demand — rather than investment spending — to the interest rate because consumption demand may also respond to the interest rate. Higher interest rates may lead to more saving and less consumption at a given level of income. Empirically, it has been difficult to isolate such an interest rate effect on consumption.

[15] We say "through open market operations" because an increase in the quantity of money carried out simply by giving the money away increases individuals' wealth and, through the real balance effect, has some effect on aggregate demand. An open market purchase, however, increases the quantity of money and reduces the quantity of bonds by the same amount, leaving wealth unchanged.

shift into bonds and thereby reduce the interest rate on bonds below zero. An increase in the money supply in case would have no effect on the interest rate or income, and the economy would be in a liquidity trap.

The belief that there was a liquidity trap at low positive (rather than zero) interest rates was quite prevalent during the forties and fifties. It was a notion associated with the followers and developers of the theories of the great English economist John Maynard Keynes — although Keynes himself did state that he was not aware of there ever having been such a situation.[16] The importance of the liquidity trap stems from its presenting a circumstance under which monetary policy has no effect on the interest rate and thus on the level of real income. Belief in the trap, or at least a strong sensitivity of the demand for money to the interest rate, was the basis of the Keynesian belief that monetary policy has no effect on the economy. There is no strong evidence that there ever was a liquidity trap, and there certainly is not one now.

The Classical Case

The polar opposite of the horizontal *LM* curve — which implies that monetary policy cannot affect the level of income — is the vertical *LM* curve. The *LM* curve is vertical when the demand for money is entirely unresponsive to the interest rate. Under these circumstances, any shift in the *LM* curve has a maximal effect on the level of income. Check this by moving a vertical *LM* curve to the right and comparing the resultant change in income with the change produced by a similar horizontal shift of a nonvertical *LM* curve.

The vertical *LM* curve is called the *classical case*. It implies that the demand for money depends only on the level of income and not at all on the interest rate. The classical case is associated with the classical *quantity theory of money*, which argues that the level of nominal income is determined solely by the quantity of money. We return to this view in Chapter 5. As we shall see, a vertical *LM* curve implies not only that monetary policy has a maximal effect on the level of income, but also that fiscal policy has no effect on income. The vertical *LM* curve, implying the comparative effectiveness of monetary over fiscal policy, is sometimes associated with the view that "only money matters" for the determination of output. Since the *LM* curve is vertical only when the demand for money does not depend on the interest rate, the interest sensitivity of the demand for money turns out to be an important issue in determining the effectiveness of alternative policies.

These two extreme cases, the liquidity trap and the classical case, suggest that the slope of the *LM* curve is a key determinant of the effectiveness of monetary policy in affecting output. The slope of the *LM* curve in turn depends on the interest sensitivity of money demand. The more sensitive to the interest rate is the quantity of money demanded, the flatter the *LM* curve.

---

[16] J. M. Keynes, *The General Theory of Employment, Interest and Money* (New York: Macmillan, 1936), p. 207.

4-6 AN APPLICATION OF MONETARY POLICY: THE 1979 POLICY SWITCH

From 1975 to 1979, the U.S. economy expanded rapidly under the impact of monetary and fiscal stimuli. The unemployment rate had been as high as 9 percent in 1975; by the middle of 1979 it was down to 5.6 percent. At the same time, the inflation rate had risen from an annual rate of 4.8 percent in 1976 to 13.3 percent in 1979.

With unemployment low, the Fed saw the rapid inflation as the prime problem facing the economy and decided to try to reduce inflation by reducing aggregate demand.[17] In October 1979, the Fed announced a major change in monetary policy, the ultimate aim of which was to bring much lower inflation to the U.S. economy. In terms of the *IS-LM* diagram in Figure 4-17, the *LM* schedule was shifted to the left.

Table 4-3 shows data on the growth rates of money and GNP, the Treasury bill rate, and the share of investment spending in GNP in the period from the second quarter of 1979 to the fourth quarter of 1980. The quantity of money was growing at more than 10 percent per year in the second and third quarters of 1979, with the Treasury bill rate below 10 percent. About 18 percent of GNP was being invested.

In the next three quarters the growth rate of money was cut back sharply. The interest rate rose to more than 13 percent by the first quarter of 1980. In response there was a fall in investment, from 18 percent of GNP in 1978–1979 to only 16 percent in early 1980. Correspondingly, GNP fell dramatically in the second quarter of 1980, creating a very sharp recession. As investment and GNP fell, the demand for money was reduced and the Treasury bill rate fell back to the 9 to 10 percent range in the second quarter of 1980, even though money growth was still slow.

Afraid of creating a massive recession, the Fed reversed direction drastically in the third quarter of 1980. The money stock was increased rapidly, and investment and GNP soon began to climb again. But so did inflation, with the result that just a year later monetary policy put the economy into another recession. The 1981–1982 recession lasted for over a year but this time did reduce the inflation rate substantially.

In terms of Figure 4-17, the Fed's policy switch shifted the *LM* curve from *LM* to *LM'*. The economy moved first from a point like *E* to *E'* in the fourth quarter of 1979 and first quarter of 1980. Under the pressure of high interest rates, investment and GNP fell, as did the interest rate when the economy went into a sharp slide in the second quarter of 1980. Then the Fed shifted policy, moving the *LM* curve to the right again, setting the stage for a recovery and rising interest rates.

Two important points emerge from this episode:

1. There is a *lag* between the time the Fed changes policy and the time the policy takes effect. The interest rate rose sharply in the fourth quarter of 1979, but it was not until the third quarter of 1980 that the full effect on investment was visible. Lags imply that monetary policy cannot work very quickly — say in the same quarter — on aggregate demand. Tight money, if sustained for some time,

---

[17] Although we have not yet studied inflation, it suffices for now to know that policies that reduce aggregate demand tend to reduce the inflation rate.

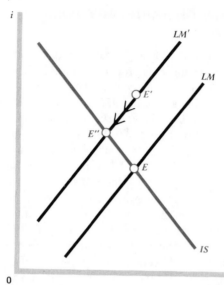

FIGURE 4-17

THE EFFECTS OF TIGHT MONEY. At the end of 1979 the Fed tightened monetary policy. The *LM* curve shifted to *LM'*. Interest rates rose, and then as the economy moved from *E'* to *E"*, real GNP fell.

TABLE 4-3

THE CHANGE IN MONETARY POLICY, 1979

	Money growth	Treasury bill rate	Investment/ GNP, %	GNP growth
1979:2	7.2	9.4	18.6	−0.4
1979:3	13.9	9.7	17.9	3.6
1979:4	4.4	11.8	17.3	−0.8
1980:1	4.2	13.4	17.2	4.0
1980:2	−6.0	9.6	15.8	−9.5
1980:3	19.5	9.2	14.8	0.3
1980:4	11.7	13.6	16.1	5.1

NOTE: All growth rates are quarter over quarter at annual rate, money stock is *M*1, and the investment share and GNP growth use real (1982 prices) data.

SOURCE: DRI/McGraw-Hill.

will reduce investment, but these effects can take well over half a year to become visible. The reason is that much of the investment spending that takes place in a given quarter is based on plans and even financing that were prepared some time ago. For instance, someone starting to build a house this quarter certainly drew up the plans earlier and probably arranged a loan some months back, too. Thus high interest rates today primarily affect investment for which plans are drawn up now but which will take place over months to come.

2. It follows that the Fed can easily miscalculate and make economic performance worse rather than better when it tries to stabilize the economy. In particular, many believe that the Fed overreacted in the second quarter of 1980, when it sharply reduced the growth rate of money and undertook other restrictive policies, precisely at a time when the economy was already going into a deep slide. And it may then have overreacted in the opposite direction in the third quarter of 1980 when it changed policy so rapidly. The analogy is to a driver who swings the wheel sharply to the left to avoid an obstacle, heads toward the ditch, then swings sharply to the right to avoid the ditch on the left, and ends up looking like a drunk driver and quite likely in the ditch as well.

4-7 SUMMARY

1. The *IS-LM* model presented in this chapter is the basic model of aggregate demand that incorporates the assets markets as well as the goods market. It lays particular stress on the channels through which monetary and fiscal policy affect the economy.

2. The *IS* curve shows combinations of interest rates and levels of income such that the goods market is in equilibrium. Increases in the interest rate reduce aggregate demand by reducing investment spending. Thus at higher interest rates, the level of income at which the goods market is in equilibrium is lower: the *IS* curve slopes downward.

3. The demand for money is a demand for *real* balances. The demand for real balances increases with income and decreases with the interest rate, the cost of holding money rather than other assets. With an exogenously fixed supply of real balances, the *LM* curve, representing money market equilibrium, is upward-sloping. Because of the wealth constraint, equilibrium of the money market implies equilibrium of the remaining assets markets — summarized here under the catchall phrase "bond market."

4. The interest rate and level of output are jointly determined by simultaneous equilibrium of the goods and money markets. This occurs at the point of intersection of the *IS* and *LM* curves.

5. Assuming that output is increased when there is an excess demand for goods and that the interest rate rises when there is an excess demand for money, the economy does move toward the new equilibrium when one of the curves shifts. Typically we think of the assets markets as clearing rapidly so that, in response to

a disturbance, the economy tends to move along the *LM* curve to the new equilibrium.

6. Monetary policy affects the economy in the first instance by affecting the interest rate, and then by affecting aggregate demand. An increase in the money supply reduces the interest rate, increases investment spending and aggregate demand, and thus increases equilibrium output.

7. There are two extreme cases in the operation of monetary policy. In the classical case the demand for real balances is independent of the rate of interest. In that case monetary policy is highly effective. The other extreme is the liquidity trap, the case in which the public is willing to hold *any* amount of real balances at the going interest rate. In that case changes in the supply of real balances have no impact on interest rates and therefore do not affect aggregate demand and output.

8. *A final warning:* We are assuming here that any level of output that is demanded can be produced by firms at the constant price level. Price level behavior, including inflation, is discussed in substantially more detail first in Chapter 6 and then in Chapters 13 and 14. Those chapters build on the analysis of the *IS-LM* model.

KEY TERMS

IS curve
LM curve
IS-LM model
Bond
Money
Portfolio decisions

Real balances (real money balances)
Wealth budget constraint
Open market operation
Transmission mechanism
Liquidity trap
Classical case

PROBLEMS

1. The following equations describe an economy. (Think of *C, I, G,* etc., as being measured in billions and *i* as a percentage; a 5 percent interest rate implies $i = 5$.)

$$C = 0.8(1 - t)Y \tag{P1}$$

$$t = 0.25 \tag{P2}$$

$$I = 900 - 50i \tag{P3}$$

$$\overline{G} = 800 \tag{P4}$$

$$L = 0.25Y - 62.5i \tag{P5}$$

$$\overline{M}/P = 500 \tag{P6}$$

(a) What is the equation that describes the *IS* curve?
(b) What is the general definition of the *IS* curve?
(c) What is the equation that describes the *LM* curve?

(d) What is the general definition of the *LM* curve?

(e) What are the equilibrium levels of income and the interest rate?

(f) Describe in words the conditions that are satisfied at the intersection of the *IS* and *LM* curves, and explain why this is an equilibrium.

2. Continue with the same equations.

    (a) What is the value of $\bar{\alpha}$, which corresponds to the simple multiplier (with taxes) of Chapter 3?

    (b) By how much does an increase in government spending of $\Delta\bar{G}$ increase the level of income in this model, which includes the assets markets?

    (c) By how much does a change in government spending of $\Delta\bar{G}$ affect the equilibrium interest rate?

    (d) Explain the difference between your answers to 2a and 2b.

3. (a) Explain in words how and why the multiplier $\bar{\alpha}$ and the interest sensitivity of aggregate demand affect the slope of the *IS* curve.

    (b) Explain why the slope of the *IS* curve is a factor in determining the working of monetary policy.

4. Explain in words how and why the income and interest sensitivities of the demand for real balances affect the slope of the *LM* curve.

5. (a) Why does a horizontal *LM* curve imply that fiscal policy has the same effects on the economy as we derived in Chapter 3?

    (b) What is happening in this case in terms of Figure 4-2?

    (c) Under what circumstances might the *LM* curve be horizontal?

6. We mentioned in the text the possibility that the interest rate might affect consumption spending. An increase in the interest rate could, in principle, lead to increases in saving and therefore a reduction in consumption, given the level of income. Suppose that consumption were in fact reduced by an increase in the interest rate. How would the *IS* curve be affected?

7. Suppose that the money supply, instead of being constant, increased (slightly) with the interest rate.

    (a) How would this change affect the construction of the *LM* curve?

    (b) Could you see any reason why the Fed might follow a policy of increasing the money supply along with the interest rate?

8. (a) How does an increase in the tax rate affect the *IS* curve?

    (b) How does the increase affect the equilibrium level of income?

    (c) How does the increase affect the equilibrium interest rate?

9. Draw a graph of how i and Y respond over time (that is, use time as the horizontal axis) to an increase in the money supply. You may assume that the money market adjusts much more rapidly than the goods market.

10. (a) Show that a given change in the money stock has a larger effect on output the less interest sensitive the demand for money.

    (b) How does the response of the interest rate to a change in the money stock depend on the interest sensitivity of money demand?

11. In 1988–1989 the interest rate increased from near 6 percent at the beginning of the period to more than 8.5 percent in early 1989. Show the effects of that monetary tightening with the same data analysis as Table 4-3 for the 1988–1990 period.

FISCAL POLICY, CROWDING OUT, AND THE POLICY MIX

Whenever governments run a budget deficit, borrowing to pay for the excess of their spending over the tax revenue they receive, the talk turns to *crowding out*. Crowding out occurs when expansionary fiscal policy causes interest rates to rise, thereby reducing private spending, particularly investment.

In this chapter, we focus on how fiscal policy works when the interdependence of goods and assets markets is taken into account. Our aim is to see how explicit consideration of interest rates affects the conclusions we reached in Chapter 3 about fiscal policy. Is it still the case that an increase in government spending raises output and employment? Do tax cuts still increase output? Or is it possible that the effects of fiscal policy on interest rates are so important that our previous conclusions about the effects of fiscal policy on the economy are reversed?

Figure 5-1 shows how fiscal policy fits into the *IS-LM* model. Fiscal policy affects aggregate demand directly. For instance, an increase in government spending increases aggregate demand, tending to raise output. But the higher output level raises the interest rate in the assets markets which dampens the effects of the fiscal policy on output. The higher interest rates reduce the level of investment spending or crowd out investment. Thus a fiscal policy that increases output may actually reduce the rate of investment.

Once we have discussed crowding out, we turn to the issue of the *monetary-fiscal policy mix*. The policy mix is the combination of monetary and fiscal policies. For instance, monetary policy may be easy, with rapid monetary growth, and fiscal policy may be tight or restrictive, with taxes being increased. We ask what various alternative mixes imply for the economy. The question of the appropriate mix is frequently at the center of political controversy.

Table 5-1 shows four possible combinations and indicates for each case when, in recent U.S. history, the combination prevailed.

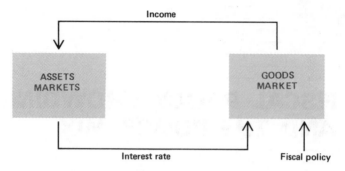

FIGURE 5-1
FISCAL POLICY IN THE *IS-LM* MODEL. Fiscal policy affects aggregate demand and thus has an impact on output and income. But changes in income affect the demand for money and thereby equilibrium interest rates in assets markets. These interest rate changes feed back to the goods market and dampen the impact of fiscal policy.

TABLE 5-1
MONETARY-FISCAL POLICY MIXES

| Fiscal policy | MONETARY POLICY | |
	Tightening	Easing
Tightening	1974, 1981, 1988–1989	1976–1977
Easing	1982	1982–1984

5-1 FISCAL POLICY AND CROWDING OUT

This section shows how changes in fiscal policy shift the *IS* curve, the curve that describes the goods market equilibrium. Recall from Chapter 4 that the *IS* curve slopes downward because a decrease in the interest rate increases spending for investment, thereby increasing aggregate demand and the level of output at which the goods market is in equilibrium. Recall also that changes in fiscal policy shift the *IS* curve. Specifically, a fiscal expansion shifts the *IS* curve out and to the right.

The equation of the *IS* curve, derived in Chapter 4, is repeated here for convenience:

$$Y = \overline{\alpha}(\overline{A} - bi) \qquad \overline{\alpha} = 1/[1 - c(1 - t)] \tag{1}$$

Note that $\overline{G}$, the level of government spending, is a component of autonomous spending, $\overline{A}$, in (1). The income tax rate, t, is part of the multiplier. Thus both government spending and the multiplier affect the IS schedule. We now show, in Figure 5-2, how fiscal expansion raises equilibrium income and the interest rate.

An Increase in Government Spending

At unchanged interest rates, higher levels of government spending will increase the level of aggregate demand. To meet the increased demand for goods, output must rise. In Figure 5-2, we show the effect of a shift in the IS schedule. At each level of the interest rate, equilibrium income must rise by $\overline{\alpha}$ times government spending. For example, if government spending rises by 100 and the multiplier is 2, then equilibrium income must increase by 200 at each level of the interest rate. Thus the IS schedule shifts to the right by 200.

FIGURE 5-2

EFFECTS OF AN INCREASE IN GOVERNMENT SPENDING. An increase in government spending raises aggregate demand at each level of the interest rate and thus shifts the IS schedule out and to the right, to IS'. At point E there is now an excess demand for goods. Output rises, and with it the interest rate, because the income expansion raises money demand. The new equilibrium is at point E'. The increase in income $(Y'_0 - Y_0)$ is less than the amount indicated by the simple multiplier $(Y'' - Y_0)$ because higher interest rates crowd out some investment spending.

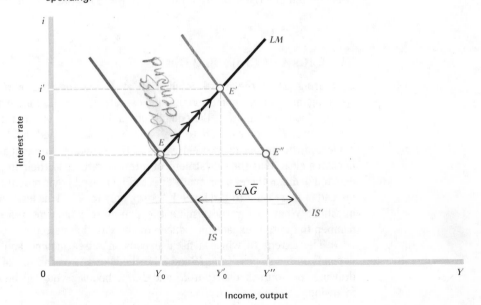

Income, output

If the economy is initially in equilibrium at point E and government spending rises by 100, we would move to point E'' *if the interest rate stayed constant*. At E'' the goods market is in equilibrium in that planned spending equals output. But the assets market is no longer in equilibrium. Income has increased, and therefore the quantity of money demanded is higher. At interest rate i_0, the demand for real balances now exceeds the given real money supply. Because there is an excess demand for real balances, the interest rate rises. But as interest rates rise, private spending is cut back. Firms' planned investment spending declines at higher interest rates, and thus aggregate demand falls off.

What is the complete adjustment, taking into account the expansionary effect of higher government spending and the dampening effects of higher interest rates on private spending? Figure 5-2 shows that only at point E' do *both* the goods and assets markets clear. Only at point E' is planned spending equal to income and, at the same time, the quantity of real balances demanded equal to the given real money stock. Point E' is therefore the new equilibrium point.

The Dynamics of Adjustment

We continue to assume that the money market clears quickly and continuously, while output adjusts only slowly. This implies that as government spending increases, we stay initially at point E, since there is no disturbance in the money market. The excess demand for goods, however, leads firms to increase output, and that increase in output and income raises the demand for money. The resulting excess demand for money, in turn, causes interest rates to be bid up, and we proceed up along the LM curve with rising output and rising interest rates, until we reach the new equilibrium at point E'.

The Extent of Crowding Out

Comparing E' to the initial equilibrium at E, we see that increased government spending raises both income and the interest rate. But another important comparison is between points E' and E'', the equilibrium in the goods market at unchanged interest rates. Point E'' corresponds to the equilibrium we studied in Chapter 3, when we neglected the impact of interest rates on the economy. In comparing E'' and E' it becomes clear that the adjustment of interest rates and their impact on aggregate demand dampen the expansionary effect of increased government spending. Income, instead of increasing to the level Y'', rises only to Y_0'. This leads us to the following question: What factors determine the extent to which interest rate adjustments dampen the output expansion induced by increased government spending?

The extent to which a fiscal expansion raises income and the interest rate depends on the slopes of the IS and LM schedules and on the size of the multiplier. By drawing for yourself different IS and LM schedules you will be able to show the following:

- Income increases more, and interest rates increase less, the flatter the *LM* schedule.
- Income increases less, and interest rates increase less, the flatter the *IS* schedule.
- Income and interest rates increase more the larger the multiplier, $\overline{\alpha}$, and thus the larger the horizontal shift of the *IS* schedule.

To illustrate these conclusions, we turn to the two extreme cases we discussed in connection with monetary policy, the liquidity trap and the classical case.

The Liquidity Trap

If the economy is in the liquidity trap, so that the *LM* curve is horizontal, an increase in government spending has its full multiplier effect on the equilibrium level of income. There is no change in the interest rate associated with the change in government spending, and thus no investment spending is cut off. There is therefore no dampening of the effects of increased government spending on income.

You should draw your own *IS-LM* diagrams to confirm that if the *LM* curve is horizontal, monetary policy has no impact on the equilibrium of the economy and fiscal policy has a maximal effect. Less dramatically, if the demand for money is very sensitive to the interest rate, so that the *LM* curve is almost horizontal, fiscal policy changes have a relatively large effect on output, while monetary policy changes have little effect on the equilibrium level of output.

So far, we have taken the money supply to be constant at the level $\overline{M}$. It is possible that the Fed might instead manipulate the money supply so as to keep the interest rate constant. In that case the money supply is responsive to the interest rate: the Fed increases the money supply whenever there are signs of an increase in the interest rate and reduces the money supply whenever the interest rate seems about to fall. The more responsive the money supply with respect to the interest rate, the flatter will be the *LM* curve, and fiscal policy will again have a large impact on the level of output.

The Classical Case and Crowding Out

If the *LM* curve is vertical, then an increase in government spending has *no* effect on the equilibrium level of income and only increases the interest rate. This case is shown in Figure 5-3 *a*, where an increase in government spending shifts the *IS* curve to *IS'* but has no effect on income. If the demand for money is not related to the interest rate, as a vertical *LM* curve implies, then there is a unique level of income at which the money market is in equilibrium.

Thus, with a vertical *LM* curve, an increase in government spending cannot change the equilibrium level of income and only raises the equilibrium interest rate. But

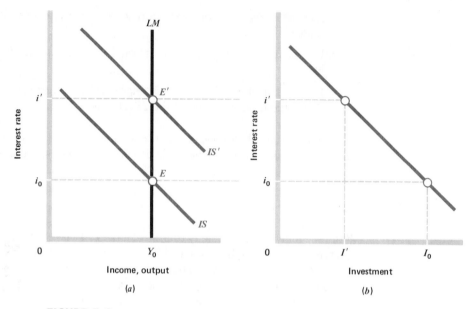

FIGURE 5-3

FULL CROWDING OUT. With a vertical *LM* schedule, a fiscal expansion, shifting out the *IS* schedule, raises interest rates, not income. Government spending displaces, or crowds out, private spending, one for one.

if government spending is higher and output is unchanged, there must be an offsetting reduction in private spending. The increase in interest rates *crowds out* private investment spending. Crowding out, as defined earlier, is the reduction in private spending (particularly investment) associated with the increase in interest rates caused by fiscal expansion. There will be full crowding out if the *LM* curve is vertical.[1]

In Figure 5-3 we show the crowding out in panel (*b*), where the investment schedule of Figure 4-3 is drawn. The fiscal expansion raises the equilibrium interest rate from i_0 to i' in panel (*a*). In panel (*b*), as a consequence, investment spending declines from the level I_0 to I'. Now it is easy to verify that if the *LM* schedule were positively sloped rather than vertical, interest rates would rise less with a fiscal expansion and, as a result, investment spending would decline less. The extent of crowding out thus depends on the slope of the *LM* curve and therefore on the interest responsiveness of money demand. The less interest-responsive money demand is, the more a fiscal expansion crowds out investment rather than raising output.

---

[1] Note that, in principle, consumption spending could be reduced by increases in the interest rate, and then both investment and consumption would be crowded out. Further, as we will see in Chap. 6, fiscal expansion can crowd out net exports, increasing the trade deficit.

The view that increased government spending crowds out private spending largely, or even completely, is held by most monetarists.[2] They believe money determines income or, as we saw above, that money demand does not depend on the interest rate, implying a vertical *LM* schedule. However, there is also another case in which crowding out can be complete, as we shall see in Chapter 7. If the economy is at full employment, so that output cannot expand, then, of course, increased purchases of goods and services by the government must mean that some other sector uses fewer goods and services. Interest rates increase to crowd out private spending by an amount exactly equal to the higher level of government spending.

Is Crowding Out Likely?

How seriously must we take the possibility of crowding out? Here three points must be made. First, in an economy with unemployed resources there will *not* be full crowding out because the *LM* schedule is not, in fact, vertical. A fiscal expansion will raise interest rates, but income will also rise. Crowding out is therefore a matter of degree. The increase in aggregate demand raises income, and with the rise in income, the level of saving rises. This expansion in saving, in turn, makes it possible to finance a larger budget deficit without *completely* displacing private borrowing or investment.

We can look at this proposition with the help of equation (2), which relates savings to investment as described in Chapter 3:[3]

$$S = I + (G + TR - TA) \tag{2}$$

Here the term $G + TR - TA$ is the budget deficit. Now from (2) an increase in the deficit, given saving, must lower investment. In simple terms, when the deficit rises, the government has to borrow to pay for its excess spending. That borrowing uses part of the resources households save and lend, leaving less available for firms to borrow for their investment plans. But it is equally apparent that if saving rises with a government spending increase because income rises, then there need not be a one-for-one decline in investment. In an economy with unemployment, crowding out is incomplete because the increased demand for goods raises real income and output; saving rises and interest rates do not rise enough (because of interest-responsive money demand) to choke off investment.

The second point is that with unemployment and, thus, a possibility for output to expand, interest rates need not rise at all when government spending rises, and there need not be any crowding out. This is true because the monetary authorities can

---

[2] We discuss monetarism in Chap. 11.

[3] In Chap. 6, in the open economy, the identity reads $S = I + (G + TR - TA) + NX$, where NX stands for net exports or net foreign lending. Thus, borrowing abroad can supplement saving to finance a budget deficit without the need for crowding out. This was particularly important in the United States from 1983 to 1990.

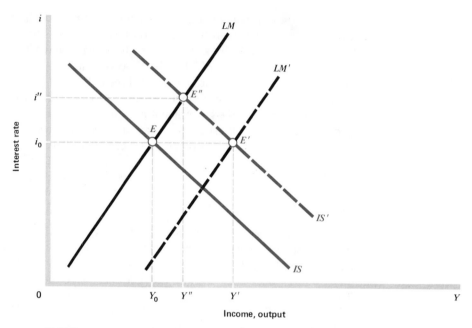

FIGURE 5-4

MONETARY ACCOMMODATION OF FISCAL EXPANSION. A fiscal expansion shifts the *IS* curve to *IS'* and moves the equilibrium of the economy from *E* to *E"*. Because the higher level of income has increased the quantity of money demanded, the interest rate rises from i_0 to $i"$, thereby crowding out investment spending. But the Fed can accommodate the fiscal expansion, creating more money and shifting the *LM* curve to *LM'*, and the equilibrium of the economy to *E'*. The interest rate remains at level i_0, and the level of output rises to *Y'*.

accommodate the fiscal expansion by an increase in the money supply. Monetary policy is *accommodating* when, in the course of a fiscal expansion, the money supply is increased in order to prevent interest rates from increasing. Monetary accommodation is also referred to as *monetizing budget deficits,* meaning that the Federal Reserve prints money to buy the bonds with which the government pays for its deficit.[4] When the Fed accommodates a fiscal expansion, both the *IS* and *LM* schedules shift to the right, as in Figure 5-4. Output will clearly increase, but interest rates need not rise. Accordingly, there need not be any adverse effects on investment. On some occasions, as in the 1960s, the Fed has been willing to accommodate, as we see in Section 5-3 below.

---

[4] The term *accommodation* is also used more generally. For instance, when oil prices increased in the 1970s, there was much discussion of whether the Fed should accommodate the higher prices by raising the money stock. The issue, and the meaning of *accommodation* in that context, is discussed in Chap. 14.

The third comment on crowding out is an important warning. So far we are assuming an economy with prices given. When we talk about fully employed economies in later chapters, crowding out becomes a much more realistic possibility, and an accommodating monetary policy may turn into an engine of inflation.

5-2 THE COMPOSITION OF OUTPUT

We have now seen that both monetary and fiscal policy can be used to expand aggregate demand and thus raise the equilibrium level of output. Since the liquidity trap and the classical case represent, at best, extremes useful for expositional purposes, it is apparent that policy makers can use either monetary or fiscal policy to affect the level of income.

Table 5-2 summarizes the effects of expansionary monetary and fiscal policy on output and the interest rate.

We now examine the policy choices for an economy that is in equilibrium with an output level, Y_0, that is below the full-employment level Y. What can be done to raise output? From the preceding analysis and Table 5-3, it is obvious that we could use an expansionary monetary policy. By increasing the money supply, we could shift the *LM* curve down and to the right, lower interest rates, and raise aggregate demand. Alternatively, we could use an expansionary fiscal policy to shift the *IS* curve up and to the right. Finally, we could use a combination of monetary and fiscal policy. What package should we choose?

The choice between monetary and fiscal policy as tools of stabilization policy is an important and controversial topic. One basis for decision is the flexibility and speed

TABLE 5-2

SUMMARY: POLICY EFFECTS ON INCOME AND INTEREST RATES

Policy	Equilibrium income	Equilibrium interest rate
Monetary expansion	+	−
Fiscal expansion	+	+

TABLE 5-3

ALTERNATIVE FISCAL POLICIES

	Interest rate	Consumption	Investment	GNP
Income tax cut	+	+	−	+
Government spending	+	+	−	+
Investment subsidy	+	+	+	+

with which these policies can be implemented and take effect. Here we do not discuss speed and flexibility, but rather look at what these policies do to the composition of aggregate demand.

In that respect, there is a sharp difference between monetary and fiscal policy. Monetary policy operates by stimulating interest-responsive components of aggregate demand, primarily investment spending. There is strong evidence that the earliest and strongest effect of monetary policy is on residential construction.

Fiscal policy, by contrast, operates in a manner that depends on precisely what goods the government buys or what taxes and transfers it changes. Here we might be talking of government purchases of goods and services such as defense spending, or a reduction in the corporate profits tax, sales taxes, or Social Security contributions. Each policy affects the level of aggregate demand and causes an expansion in output, but the composition of the output increase depends on the specific policy. An investment subsidy, discussed below, increases investment spending. An income tax cut has a direct effect on consumption spending. All expansionary fiscal policies will raise the interest rates if the quantity of money is unchanged.

An Investment Subsidy

Table 5-3 shows examples of the impact of different fiscal policies on key variables. One interesting case is an *investment subsidy,* shown in Figure 5-5. When the government subsidizes investment, it essentially pays part of the cost of each firm's investment. An investment subsidy shifts the investment schedule in panel (*a*). At each interest rate, firms now plan to invest more. With investment spending higher, aggregate demand increases.

In panel (*b*), the *IS* schedule shifts by the amount of the multiplier times the increase in autonomous investment brought about by the subsidy. The new equilibrium is at point E', where goods and money markets are again in balance. But note now that although interest rates have risen, we see, in panel (*a*), that investment is higher. Investment is at the level I'_0, up from I_0. The interest rate increase has only dampened but not reversed the impact of the investment subsidy. Here is an example in which both consumption, induced by higher income, and investment rise as a consequence of fiscal policy.

The Policy Mix

In Figure 5-6 we show the policy problem of reaching full-employment output, Y^*, for an economy that is initially at point E with unemployment. Should we choose a fiscal expansion, moving to point E_1 with higher income and higher interest rates? Or should we choose a monetary expansion, leading to full employment with lower interest rates at point E_2? Or should we pick a policy mix of fiscal expansion and accommodating monetary policy, leading to an intermediate position?

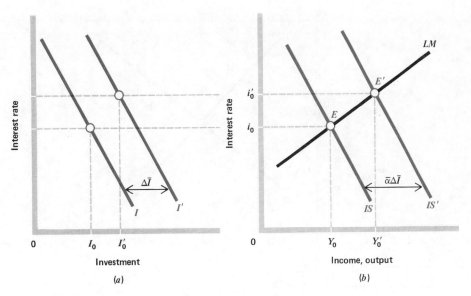

FIGURE 5-5

AN INVESTMENT SUBSIDY. An investment subsidy shifts the investment
schedule in panel (*a*) at each interest rate out and to the right. The
increase in planned investment shows in panel (*b*) as a shift of the *IS*
curve. Equilibrium income rises to Y'_0, and the interest rate increases to
i'_0. At the higher interest rate, investment is still higher, I'_0, than it was
initially. Thus an investment subsidy raises interest rates, income, and
investment.

Once we recognize that all the policies raise output but differ significantly in their
impact on different sectors of the economy, we open up a problem of political economy.
Given the decision to expand aggregate demand, who should get the primary benefit?
Should the expansion take place through a decline in interest rates and increased
investment spending, or should it take place through a cut in taxes and increased
personal spending, or should it take the form of an increase in the size of government?

Questions of speed and predictability of policies apart, the issues have been
settled by political preferences. Conservatives will argue for a tax cut anytime. They
will favor stabilization policies that cut taxes in a recession and cut government
spending in a boom. Over time, given enough cycles, the government sector becomes
very small, just as a conservative would want it to be. The counterpart view belongs to
those who believe that there is a broad scope for government spending on education,
the environment, job training and rehabilitation, and the like, and who, accordingly,
favor expansionary policies in the form of increased government spending. Growth-
minded people and the construction lobby argue for expansionary policies that operate
through low interest rates.

The recognition that monetary and fiscal policy changes have different effects on

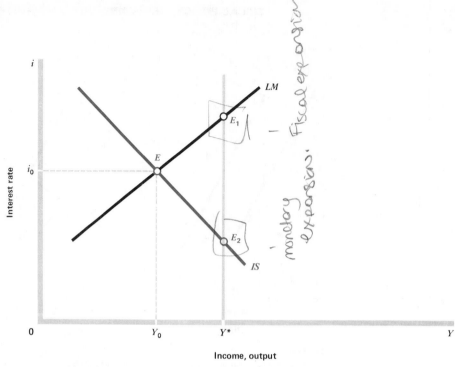

FIGURE 5-6

EXPANSIONARY POLICIES AND THE COMPOSITION OF OUTPUT. In an economy with output Y_0 below the full-employment level, Y^*, there is a choice of using monetary or fiscal expansion to move to full employment. Monetary expansion would move the LM curve to the right, putting the equilibrium at E_2. Fiscal expansion shifts the IS curve, putting the new equilibrium at E_1. The expansionary monetary policy reduces the interest rate, while the expansionary fiscal policy raises it. The lower interest rate in the case of monetary policy means that investment is higher at E_2 than at E_1.

the composition of output is important. It suggests that policy makers can choose a *policy mix* that will not only get the economy to full employment but also make a contribution to solving other policy problems. We anticipate here several subsequent discussions in which we point out two other targets of policy that have been taken into account in setting monetary and fiscal policy — growth and balance of payments equilibrium.

5-3 THE POLICY MIX IN ACTION

In this section we review several episodes of monetary and fiscal policy in recent U.S. economic history. We first look at the great economic expansion of the 1960s, originating in the 1964 tax cut. We conclude with the monetary-fiscal policy mix of the 1980s.

TABLE 5-4
THE 1964 TAX CUT

	1963	1964	1965
GNP gap, %	5.6	3.3	0.7
GNP growth, %	4.0	5.3	6.0
Full-employment surplus, % of GNP	0.5	0.1	0.1
Interest rate, %	4.3	4.5	4.5

SOURCE: DRI/McGraw-Hill.

The 1964 Tax Cut

In the early 1960s the U.S. economy was in a recession, with a GNP gap of 3.2 percent in 1963. To help the economy recover, the Kennedy-Johnson administration proposed a package of fiscal expansion. The program had two parts, a cut in the personal income tax rates and a cut in corporate-profit taxes. The program, enacted in February 1964, complemented an investment subsidy that went into effect in late 1962. The Revenue Act of 1964 provided for a permanent cut in income tax rates for all individual and corporate taxpayers. Personal taxes were cut by more than 20 percent and corporate taxes by about 8 percent. Before the cut, the marginal personal tax rates ranged from 20 to 91 percent; afterward, the range was 14 to 70 percent. For most corporations, the rate fell from 52 to 48 percent.

In terms of the *IS-LM* diagram, the fiscal expansion moves the *IS* schedule out and to the right. Monetary policy determines the extent to which interest rates rise. Table 5-4 summarizes some of the relevant data.

Note in Table 5-4 the large fiscal expansion, visible in the significant decline of the full-employment surplus. The effects of the fiscal expansion show up in high real growth and a declining GNP gap. To judge monetary policy we look at the behavior of interest rates. Interest rates in Table 5-4 are measured by the yield on high-quality corporate bonds. The interest rate moves up only very slightly. Thus monetary policy was accommodating on balance, keeping interest rates relatively constant. The fiscal expansion was therefore allowed to push up aggregate demand, without adverse side effects on interest rates that would lead to a decline in investment. This is precisely the policy combination shown in Figure 5-4.

In commenting on the monetary-fiscal policy mix in the period, Arthur Okun summarized the experience as follows:[5]

> In short, the strong economic expansion of 1964–65 would not have taken place in the face of a highly restrictive monetary strategy. Moreover, the job could in principle have been accomplished by a very expansionary monetary strategy without a stimulative fiscal

[5] *The Political Economy of Prosperity* (New York: Norton, 1970), p. 59.

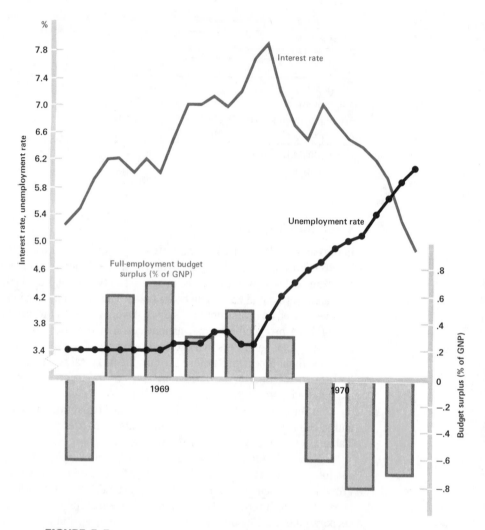

FIGURE 5-7

THE 1969–1970 CONTRACTION. The figure shows monthly data for the Treasury bill rate and the unemployment rate. Quarterly data are shown for the full-employment budget surplus, expressed as a fraction of GNP. (SOURCE: DRI/McGraw-Hill.)

policy. But the monetary policy that was actually pursued would not in itself have quickened the pace of the economy. It supplied a good set of tires for the economy to move on, but fiscal policy was the engine of growth.

The 1969–1970 Contraction

The expansion of economic activity in response to stimulative fiscal policy led to a significant reduction of unemployment over the 1960s. By 1968 the unemployment rate had fallen to only 3.4 percent. At that unemployment rate, output was above its full-employment level. The boom in activity not only reduced unemployment, but also increased the inflation rate. With unemployment no longer a problem and inflation uncomfortably high — 5 percent in 1968 and 1969, up from only 1 percent at the beginning of the 1960s — monetary and fiscal policy turned to restraint.

Figure 5-7 shows the policy changes. Fiscal policy moved to correct the budget deficits caused by stimulative fiscal policy and the defense spending associated with the Vietnam war. Monetary policy tightened, pushing up interest rates.

The fiscal contraction starting at the end of 1968 was a long delayed measure to help reduce the war-inflated budget deficits by increasing tax revenues. The Revenue and Expenditure Control Act of 1968, which became effective in June 1968, had been recommended by the administration in January 1967. The chief measure was a 10 percent surtax on personal and corporate income taxes. The surtax, for example, implied that an individual who had previously paid $1,000 in taxes would now have to pay $1,100. Fiscal revenues increased strongly, and the budget deficit declined. These surtaxes were supplemented by cuts in government spending. When the Nixon administration came into power in 1969, expenditure increases were sharply curtailed, further increasing the full-employment surplus.

In Figure 5-7 we show the effects of the monetary-fiscal policy mix. Tight money shows up in rising interest rates throughout 1969. The tightening of fiscal policy is indicated by the large shift in the full-employment budget. From the last quarter of 1968 to the first quarter of 1969, fiscal policy swings by a full percentage point of GNP, from a deficit of 0.6 percent to a surplus of that magnitude. If we compare annual averages (not shown in the figure), the shift is even larger: from a deficit that averaged 1.3 percent of GNP in 1968 to a surplus of 0.5 percent of GNP in 1969, a shift of nearly 2 percent. Clearly, fiscal policy took a decidedly restrictive course, thus complementing tight money.

Figure 5-7 also shows the unemployment rate for the period. It is interesting to observe the lags between the restrictive policies and their effects on unemployment. Throughout 1969, despite the tightening of policies, unemployment hardly changed. But by late 1969 the restraint of demand through increased taxes and high interest rates has clearly built up, and unemployment increased rapidly throughout 1970.

The 1980s Recession and Recovery

Economic policy in the early 1980s departed radically from the policies of the previous two decades. First, tight money was implemented at the end of 1979 to fight an inflation rate that had reached record peacetime levels; then, in 1981, an expansionary fiscal policy was put in place as President Reagan's program of tax cuts and increased defense spending began.

This subsection serves to discuss the highly unusual policy mix of the early 1980s and to introduce the problem of inflation. Systematic study of inflation begins in Chapter 7, when we introduce aggregate supply and drop the assumption that the price level is fixed.

For this subsection, we need to know that policies that reduce aggregate demand, such as reducing the growth rate of money or government spending, tend to reduce the inflation rate along with the level of output. An expansionary policy increases inflation together with the level of output. Recall also that inflation is unpopular, and that governments will generally try to reduce the inflation rate after it has risen.

In 1973 the United States and the rest of the world were hit by the first oil shock, in which the oil-exporting countries raised the price of oil fourfold. The oil price increase raised other prices and, in the United States, helped create inflation and also a recession in which unemployment increased to the then post-World War II record rate of 8.9 percent. The recession ended in 1975. Economic policy under the Carter administration (1977 – 1981) was generally expansionary; by 1979 unemployment was below 6 percent and thus perhaps below the full-employment level. Inflation increased with the expansionary policy over the period, and in 1979 inflation increased sharply as the second oil shock hit and the price of oil doubled.

The rising inflation was extremely unpopular, and in October 1979 the Fed acted, turning monetary policy in a highly restrictive direction. The monetary squeeze was tightened in the first half of 1980, at which point the economy went into a

TABLE 5-5

THE 1982 RECESSION AND THE RECOVERY (percent)

	1980	1981	1982	1983	1984
Monetary base growth*	8.4	4.2	7.6	10.3	6.8
Real interest rate†	3.0	8.6	8.0	5.2	7.4
Full-employment deficit	0.4	0.0	1.1	2.1	3.0
Unemployment rate	7.1	7.5	9.6	9.5	7.4
GNP gap	6.4	7.1	11.6	10.4	6.2
Inflation‡	10.0	7.4	4.3	3.8	2.9

* Fourth quarter to fourth quarter.

† Three-month CD (certificate of deposit) rate less inflation rate of the GNP deflator.

‡ GNP deflator.

Source: DRI/McGraw-Hill.

TABLE 5-6
THE POLICY MIX IN THE 1980s EXPANSION (percent)

	1984	1985	1986	1987	1988
Real interest rate*	7.4	5.6	3.1	4.2	3.0
Full-employment deficit†	3.0	3.9	4.1	3.0	2.9

* Three-month CD rate less the rate of inflation of the GNP deflator.

† Percent of GNP.

SOURCE: DRI/McGraw Hill.

minirecession. After a brief recovery, 1982 brought the deepest recession since the great depression.

The reason for the sharp decline in activity was tight money. Because inflation was still above 10 percent and the money stock was growing at only 5.1 percent in 1981, the real money supply was falling. Interest rates continued to climb (Table 5-5). Not surprisingly investment, especially construction, collapsed. The economy was dragged into a deep recession with a trough in December 1982.

Table 5-5 also shows the second component of the early 1980s policy mix: The full-employment deficit increased rapidly from 1981 to 1984. The 1981 tax bill cut tax rates for individuals, with the cuts coming into effect over the next 3 years, and increased investment subsidies for corporations. The full-employment deficits in those years are the largest in peacetime U.S. history.

With a policy mix of easy fiscal and tight monetary policy, the analysis of Figure 5-6 tells us to expect a rise in the interest rate.[6] With investment subsidies increased, Figure 5-5 tells us to look for the possibility that investment increases along with the interest rate.

The first element — a rise in the interest rate — indeed occurred. That may be a surprise if you look only at the CD rate in Box 5-1. But when there is inflation, the correct interest rate to consider is not the *nominal* rate but the *real* rate. The real interest rate is the nominal (stated) rate of interest minus the rate of inflation. Over the period 1981 to 1984 the *real* interest rate increased sharply even as the *nominal* rate declined. The real cost of borrowing went up although the nominal cost went down. Investment spending responded to both the increased interest rates, falling 13 percent between 1981 and 1982, and the investment subsidies and prospects of recovery, increasing 49 percent between 1982 and 1984.

The unemployment rate peaked at over 11 percent in the last quarter of 1982 and then steadily declined under the impact of the huge fiscal expansion. As Table 5-6 shows, in 1984 yet further fiscal expansion pushed the recovery of the economy forward, and the expansion continued throughout the 1980s.

---

[6] The policy mix had another important consequence: It strengthened the dollar, making imports cheap and reducing U.S. net exports. Understanding the mechanism through which the policy mix affected the exchange rate will have to wait till we open the economy to international trade, in Chapter 6.

NOMINAL AND REAL INTEREST RATES

In a world without inflation, changes in nominal interest rates can be used to judge changes in the cost of loans for firms or households. But when there is inflation, we need to make a sharp distinction between *nominal* interest rates and *real* interest rates. Investment decisions depend on inflation-adjusted or real interest rates. The real interest rate is the nominal (stated) rate of interest minus the rate of inflation.

To understand the distinction between real and nominal interest rates, realize that when prices are rising, when there is inflation, borrowers pay back in dollars that have lost value compared with the dollars they borrowed. If prices are rising 10 percent and we can borrow at 6 percent, then we can take the dollars we borrow, buy goods or invest, sell the goods a year later for 10 percent more dollars than we paid (because prices have risen 10 percent in the meantime), and pay back only the 6 percent interest. We would be ahead by 4 percent. In this case the real cost of borrowing is negative even though we are paying 6 percent nominal interest. To calculate the *real* cost of borrowing, deduct the inflation rate from the interest rate.

Let i continue to denote the nominal interest rate; π, the rate of inflation; and r, the (realized or actual) real interest rate. Our definition of the real interest rate then is

$$r = i - \pi$$

Figure 1 shows the rate of inflation of the GNP deflator and the interest rate on three-month certificates of deposit, which represents the rate at which major customers can borrow in the capital market. Note that in 1976–1978 the interest rate was almost equal to the rate of inflation so that real interest rates were zero or even negative. But in the 1980s real interest rates turned sharply positive. In 1981–1982 real interest rates reached a record level of more than 8 percent, causing a sharp recession. ■

Summary

The policy mix in the early 1980s featured highly expansionary fiscal policy and tight money. The tight money succeeded in reducing the inflation of the late 1970s and very early 1980s, at the expense of a serious recession. Expansionary fiscal policy then drove a recovery during which real interest rates increased sharply. By 1989 continuing high real interest rates and the tightening of fiscal policy brought about a situation much like that of 1969: Both monetary and fiscal policy were putting a squeeze on demand and the expansion was likely to come to an end.

*5-4 A FORMAL TREATMENT OF THE *IS-LM* MODEL

Our exposition so far has been a verbal and graphical one and has been supplemented by a look at several policy applications in recent U.S. history. We now round off the analysis with a more formal treatment that uses the equations of the *IS* and *LM* schedules to derive and discuss fiscal and monetary policy multipliers.

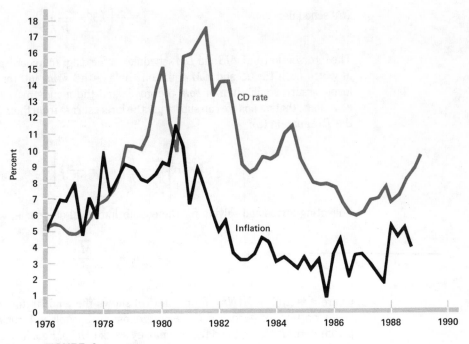

FIGURE 1
INTEREST RATES AND INFLATION. (SOURCE: DRI/McGraw-Hill.)

Equilibrium Income and the Interest Rate

The intersection of the *IS* and *LM* schedules determines equilibrium income and the equilibrium interest rate. We can derive expressions for these equilibrium values by using the equations of the *IS* and *LM* schedules. From Chapter 4 we remember the equation of the *IS* schedule or goods market equilibrium schedule as

IS schedule: $$Y = \overline{\alpha}(\overline{A} - bi) \qquad (3)$$

and the equation describing money market equilibrium as[7]

---

[7] To deal with the case in which liquidity preference is not only high but at some rate, say i', is *perfectly elastic*, we could rewrite the *LM* equation as $\overline{M/P} = kY - h(i - i')$, so that real money demand depends on the excess of the interest rate above some floor level i'. With this formulation, (4) becomes $i = i' + (1/h)(kY - \overline{M/P})$. If h is extremely high, the interest rate is $i = i'$ or the *LM* schedule is horizontal at the level i'.

LM schedule:
$$i = \frac{1}{h}\left(kY - \frac{\overline{M}}{\overline{P}}\right)$$
(4)

The intersection of the *IS* and *LM* schedules in the diagrams corresponds to a situation in which both the *IS* and *LM* equations hold—the *same* interest rate and income levels assure equilibrium in *both* the goods and the money market. In terms of the equations, that means we can substitute the interest rate from the *LM* equation (4) into the *IS* equation (3):

$$Y = \overline{\alpha}\left[\overline{A} - \frac{b}{h}\left(kY - \frac{\overline{M}}{\overline{P}}\right)\right]$$
(5)

Collecting terms and solving for the equilibrium level of income, we obtain

$$Y_0 = \gamma\overline{A} + \gamma\frac{b}{h}\frac{\overline{M}}{\overline{P}}$$
(5a)

where $\gamma = \overline{\alpha}/(1 + k\overline{\alpha}b/h)$. Equation (5a) shows the equilibrium level of income depends on two exogenous variables: autonomous spending $\overline{A}$, including fiscal policy parameters (I, G, TR), and the real money stock ($\overline{M}/\overline{P}$). Equilibrium income is higher the higher the level of autonomous spending, $\overline{A}$, and the higher the stock of real balances.

The equilibrium rate of interest, i_0, is obtained by substituting the equilibrium income level, Y_0, from (5a) into the equation of the *LM* schedule, (4):

$$i_0 = \frac{k}{h}\gamma\overline{A} - \frac{1}{h + kb\overline{\alpha}}\frac{\overline{M}}{\overline{P}}$$
(6)

Equation (6) shows that the equilibrium interest rate depends on the parameters of fiscal policy captured in the multiplier and the term $\overline{A}$ and on the real money stock. A higher real money stock implies a lower equilibrium interest rate.

For policy questions we are interested in the precise relation between changes in fiscal policy or changes in the real money stock and the resulting changes in equilibrium income. The *monetary* and *fiscal policy multipliers* provide the relevant information.

The Fiscal Policy Multiplier

The fiscal policy multiplier shows how much an increase in government spending changes the equilibrium level of income, holding the real money supply constant. Examine equation (5a) and consider the effect of an increase in government spending on income. The increase in government spending, $\Delta\overline{G}$, is a change in autonomous spending, so that $\Delta\overline{A} = \Delta\overline{G}$. The effect of the change in $\overline{G}$ is given by

$$\frac{\Delta Y_0}{\Delta \overline{G}} = \gamma \qquad \gamma = \frac{\overline{\alpha}}{1 + k\overline{\alpha}\,\dfrac{b}{h}} \tag{7}$$

The expression γ is the fiscal or government spending multiplier once interest rate adjustment is taken into account. Consider how this multiplier, γ, differs from the simpler expression $\overline{\alpha}$ that applied under constant interest rates. Inspection shows that γ is less than $\overline{\alpha}$ since $1/(1 + k\overline{\alpha}b/h)$ is a fraction. This represents the dampening effect of increased interest rates associated with a fiscal expansion in the *IS-LM* model.

We note that the expression in equation (7) is zero if h is very small and will be equal to $\overline{\alpha}$ if h approaches infinity. This corresponds, respectively, to vertical and horizontal *LM* schedules. Similarly, a large value of either b or k serves to reduce the effect of government spending on income. Why? A high value of k implies a large increase in money demand as income rises and hence a large increase in interest rates required to maintain money market equilibrium. In combination with a high b, this implies a large reduction in private aggregate demand. Equation (7) thus presents the algebraic analysis that corresponds to the graphical analysis of Figures 5-2 and 5-3.

The Monetary Policy Multiplier

The monetary policy multiplier shows how much an increase in the real money supply increases the equilibrium level of income, keeping fiscal policy unchanged. Using equation (5*a*) to examine the effects of an increase in the real money supply on income, we have

$$\frac{\Delta Y_0}{\Delta(\overline{M}/\overline{P})} = \frac{b}{h}\,\gamma \tag{8}$$

The smaller h and k and the larger b and $\overline{\alpha}$, the more expansionary the effect of an increase in real balances on the equilibrium level of income. Large b and $\overline{\alpha}$ correspond to a very flat *IS* schedule. Equation (8) thus corresponds to the graphical analysis presented in Figure 4-16.

The Classical Case and the Liquidity Trap

We now turn to two special cases that demonstrate the role of the demand function for real balances in the effectiveness of monetary and fiscal policies. Consider first the possibility that money demand does not depend at all on interest rates and is simply proportional to real income. This happens if parameter h is zero, so that real money demand is simply

$$L = kY \tag{9}$$

In this case monetary equilibrium, equating the demand and supply of money, leads to[8]

$$Y_0 = \frac{1}{k} \frac{\overline{M}}{\overline{P}} \tag{10}$$

This case is called the *classical case* because classical (that is, nineteenth-century) economists did not give much emphasis to the interest response of money demand. The case is important because it has the following implication: If money demand does not depend on the interest rate and depends only on the level of income, as in (9), the money supply alone determines income.

In this classical case, the level of nominal income, *PY,* is proportional to the nominal money stock. Changes in the nominal money stock lead to changes in income in the same proportion. Furthermore, while income does respond to money, it is *totally* unresponsive to fiscal policy. We also can see the point from (5*a*) by setting $h = 0$.

Interest Rates and Fiscal Policy

How is it possible that fiscal policy has no effect at all on income? After all, if the government were to spend more, how is it possible that the increased spending should *not* raise income? The reasoning is as follows. An increase in government spending does lead to an incipient rise in aggregate demand and income, but that immediately raises the demand for money. With the money supply unchanged, interest rates will shoot up to clear the money market. As interest rates rise because of the excess demand for money, investment spending declines. The fall in investment spending compensates exactly for the higher government spending, and the level of income is unchanged.

In problem 11c at the end of the chapter you are asked to show that the larger the value of *h,* the smaller will be the fraction of an extra dollar of government spending that is offset by reduced investment spending.

Liquidity Trap

The other extreme for monetary and fiscal policy is represented by a world where *h* is infinite. Then money and other assets are effectively perfect substitutes. In such a world, equation (5*a*) reduces to

$$Y = \overline{\alpha} \overline{A} \tag{11}$$

---

[8] The demand for real balances is $L = kY$ and the supply is $\overline{M}/\overline{P}$. Thus with demand equal to supply, $\overline{M}/\overline{P} = kY$, or $Y = (1/k)\overline{M}/\overline{P}$.

This is the "multiplier world" of Chapter 3, where autonomous spending entirely determines the level of real income. It occurs if the economy is in a liquidity trap.

In the liquidity trap, money does not matter for income determination because money demand is *so* responsive to interest rates. The smallest change in interest rates is sufficient to eliminate imbalances in the money market that might arise from changes in money supply or in income. And because these corrective changes in interest rates are so small, they do not even affect aggregate demand. The interest rate effect can be verified from (11). With h extremely high, investment spending is not influenced by either monetary or fiscal policy.

5-5 SUMMARY

1. Taking into account the effects of fiscal policy on the interest rate modifies the multiplier results of Chapter 3. Fiscal expansion, except in extreme circumstances, still leads to an income expansion. However, the rise in interest rates that comes about through the increase in money demand caused by higher income dampens the expansion.

2. Fiscal policy is more effective the smaller are the induced changes in interest rates and the smaller is the response of investment to these interest rate changes.

3. In the liquidity trap, the interest rate is constant because money demand is completely elastic with respect to the interest rate. Monetary policy has no effect on the economy, whereas fiscal policy has its full multiplier effect on output and no effect on interest rates.

4. In the classical case, the demand for money is independent of the interest rate. In that case, changes in the money stock change income. But fiscal policy has no effect on income — it affects only the interest rate. In this case there is complete crowding out of private spending by government spending.

5. Neither the liquidity trap nor the classical case applies in practice. But they are useful extremes to study to show what determines the magnitude of monetary and fiscal policy multipliers.

6. A fiscal expansion, because it leads to higher interest rates, displaces or crowds out some private investment. The extent of crowding out is a sensitive issue in assessing the usefulness and desirability of fiscal policy as a tool of stabilization policy.

7. In an economy that is less than fully employed, crowding out need not occur. The monetary authorities can provide an accommodating monetary policy that avoids the rise in interest rates associated with the output expansion.

8. The question of the monetary-fiscal policy mix arises because expansionary monetary policy reduces the interest rate while expansionary fiscal policy increases the interest rate. Accordingly, expansionary fiscal policy increases output while reducing the level of investment; expansionary monetary policy increases output and the level of investment.

9. Governments have to choose the mix in accordance with their objectives for economic growth, or increasing consumption, or from the viewpoint of their beliefs about the desirable size of the government.

10. The real interest rate is the nominal rate minus the inflation rate.

KEY TERMS

Crowding out
Monetary-fiscal policy mix
Monetary accommodation
Monetizing budget deficits
Composition of output

Investment subsidy
Monetary policy multiplier
Fiscal policy multiplier
Real interest rate

PROBLEMS

1. The economy is at full employment. Now the government wants to change the composition of demand toward investment and away from consumption without, however, allowing aggregate demand to go beyond full employment. What is the required policy mix? Use the *IS-LM* diagram to show your policy proposal.

2. Discuss the role of the parameters $\bar{\alpha}$, h, b, and k in the transmission mechanism linking an increase in government spending to the resulting change in equilibrium income. In developing the analysis use the following table:

(1)	(2)	(3)
Increase in $\bar{G}$ raises aggregate demand and output.	The increase in income raises money demand and hence interest rates.	The increase in interest rates reduces investment spending and hence dampens output expansion.

3. Suppose the government cuts income taxes. Show in the *IS-LM* model the impact of the tax cut under two assumptions: One, the government keeps interest rates constant through an accommodating monetary policy; two, the money stock remains unchanged. Explain the difference in results.

4. Discuss the circumstances under which the monetary and fiscal policy multipliers are each, in turn, equal to zero. Explain in words why this can happen and how likely you think this is.

5. Consider an economy in which the government considers two alternative programs for contraction. One is the removal of an investment subsidy; the other is a rise in income tax rates. Use the *IS-LM* schedule and the investment schedule, as shown in Figure 5-5, to discuss the impact of these alternative policies on income, interest rates, and investment.

*6. Suppose the parameters k and $\bar{\alpha}$ are 0.5 and 2, respectively. Assume there is an increase of $1 billion in government spending. By how much must the real money stock be increased to hold interest rates constant?

7. Discuss the circumstances whereby fiscal expansion leads to *full* crowding out.

8. In Figure 5-6 the economy can move to full employment by an expansion in either money or the full-employment deficit. Which policy leads to E_1 and which to E_2? How would you expect the choice to be made? Who would most strongly favor moving to E_1? to E_2? What policy would correspond to "balanced growth"?

9. "We can have the GNP path we want equally well with a tight fiscal policy and an easier monetary policy, or the reverse, within fairly broad limits. The real basis for choice lies in many subsidiary targets, besides real GNP and inflation, that are differentially affected by fiscal and monetary policies." What are some of the subsidiary targets referred to in the quote? How would they be affected by alternative policy combinations?

10. Explain why
    (a) A rise in interest rates reduces the quantity of real balances demanded.
    (b) A fall in interest rates raises investment spending.

11. Use the investment equation $I = \bar{I} - bi$ to derive an expression for the level of investment spending, given *IS-LM* equilibrium. To do so substitute the equilibrium interest rate, i_0, into the investment equation. Discuss then the determinants ($b, k, h, \bar{\alpha}$) of the extent of crowding out associated with an increase in government spending.

---

* An asterisk denotes a more difficult problem.

INTERNATIONAL LINKAGES

*E*conomic influences from abroad sometimes have a powerful effect on the U.S. economy. And even more, U.S. policies have substantial effects on foreign economies. Whether the U.S. economy grows or moves into recession makes a big difference to Japan or to Mexico, and whether other industrial countries shift to fiscal stimulus or, on the contrary, to budget surpluses, makes a difference to the U.S. economy. A tightening of U.S. monetary policy that raises interest rates not only affects the debt service payments owed by Latin America, but will also change the value of the dollar relative to other currencies, and thus affect U.S. competitiveness and worldwide trade and GNP.

In this chapter we present the key linkages among *open* economies — economies that trade with others — and introduce some first pieces of analysis. We present more detail on international aspects of macroeconomics in Chapter 20.

Any economy is linked to the rest of the world through two broad channels: *trade* (in goods and services) and *finance*. The *trade* linkage arises from the fact that some of a country's production is exported to foreign countries, while some goods that are consumed or invested at home are produced abroad and imported. In 1984–1989 U.S. exports of goods and services amounted to 11.3 percent of GNP, while imports were equal to 13.1 percent of GNP. By comparison with other countries the United States engages in relatively little international trade — or is a relatively closed economy. For the Netherlands, at the other extreme — a very open economy — imports and exports each amount to about 60 percent of GNP.

The trade linkages are nonetheless important for the United States. Spending on imports escapes from the circular flow of income, in the sense that part of the income spent by U.S. residents is not spent on domestically produced goods; by contrast, exports appear as an increase in the demand for domestically produced goods. Thus the basic *IS-LM* model of income determination must be amended to include international effects.

The trade channel also opens up an international influence on prices in the U.S. economy. We have not yet analyzed the determinants of the price level, but it is worthwhile noting here how trade linkages affect domestic prices and the demand for our goods. Foreign prices matter in two main respects. First, the prices of commodities or raw materials (tin, copper, agricultural products, and, especially, oil), which are inputs in production and an element of producers' costs, are heavily affected by worldwide supply and demand conditions. Changes in commodity prices affect costs and prices in the United States. The most striking examples are the oil price increases of the 1970s. When oil prices were increased dramatically by the oil producers' cartel in 1973–1974 and 1979–1980, U.S. inflation rose sharply. In the 1980s, disinflation in the United States was made easier by the sharp decline in oil prices.

Foreign prices matter in a second way. The prices of foreign manufactured goods, such as cars, VCRs, and machine tools, affect the demand for domestically produced goods. A decline in the dollar prices of our competitors, relative to the prices at which U.S. firms sell, shifts demand away from U.S. goods toward goods produced abroad. Our imports rise and exports fall. This is precisely what happened in the United States between 1980 and 1985 as the value of the dollar increased relative to foreign currencies. Conversely, when a decline in the value of the dollar relative to other countries raises foreign prices in dollars relative to our prices, demand here and abroad shifts toward our goods, exports rise, and imports decline.

There are also strong international links in the area of *finance*. U.S. residents, whether households, banks, or corporations, can hold U.S. assets such as Treasury bills or corporate bonds, or they can hold assets in foreign countries, say in Canada or in Germany. Most U.S. households, in fact, hold almost exclusively U.S. assets, but that is certainly not true for banks or large corporations. Portfolio managers will shop around the world for the most attractive yields, and they may well decide at a particular time that holding German government bonds, Yen bonds issued by the Japanese government, or Swiss bonds offers a better yield — all things considered — than U.S. bonds.

International investors seeking the best return on their assets link asset markets here and abroad together, and their actions have fundamental effects on the determination of income, exchange rates, and the ability of monetary policy to affect interest rates. We show in this chapter how the *IS-LM* analysis has to be modified to take international trade and finance linkages into account. A first step is to discuss exchange rates and the balance of payments.

6-1 THE BALANCE OF PAYMENTS AND EXCHANGE RATES

The *balance of payments* is the record of the transactions of the residents of a country with the rest of the world. There are two main accounts in the balance of payments: the current account and the capital account.

The *current account* records trade in goods and services, as well as transfer payments. Services include freight, royalty payments, and interest payments. Services also include the category *net investment income,* which represents interest and profits on our assets abroad less the income foreigners earn on assets they own in the United States. Transfer payments consist of remittances, gifts, and grants. The *trade balance* simply records trade in goods. Adding trade in services and net transfers, we arrive at the current account balance. We talk of a current account *surplus* if exports exceed imports plus net transfers to foreigners, that is, if receipts from trade in goods and services and transfers exceed payments on this account.

The *capital account* records purchases and sales of assets, such as stocks, bonds, and land. There is a capital account surplus—also known as a net capital inflow—when our receipts from the sale of stocks, bonds, land, bank deposits, and other assets exceed our payments for our own purchases of foreign assets.

Surpluses and Deficits

The simple rule for balance of payments accounting is that any transaction that gives rise to a payment by a country's residents is a deficit item in that country's balance of payments. Thus, imports of cars, use of foreign shipping, gifts to foreigners, purchase of land in Spain, or making a deposit in a bank in Switzerland are all deficit items. Examples of surplus items, by contrast, would be U.S. sales of airplanes abroad, payments by foreigners for U.S. licenses to use American technology, pensions from abroad received by U.S. residents, and foreign purchases of General Motors stock.

The overall *balance of payments* surplus is the sum of the current and capital accounts surpluses. If both the current account and the capital account are in deficit, then the overall balance of payments is in deficit. When one account is in surplus and the other is in deficit to precisely the same extent, the overall balance of payments is zero—neither in surplus nor in deficit. We record these relationships as[1]

$$\text{Balance of payments surplus} = \text{current account surplus}$$
$$+ \text{capital account surplus} \qquad (1)$$

Table 6-1 presents the U.S. balance of payments accounts.[2] We show the accounts since the 1960s. In the 1960s the current account was in surplus, in the 1970s it was in a slight deficit, and so far in the 1980s it has been in a large deficit. The U.S. capital account was in deficit through the end of the 1970s. Equivalently, through the end of the 1970s there was a net capital *outflow,* meaning that U.S. residents purchased more assets abroad than foreigners bought in the United States. But the capital account deficit turned around in the 1980s. There has been a massive capital *inflow* as foreigners have on balance bought more U.S. assets than Americans have acquired foreign assets.

---

[1] In using equation (1), recall that a deficit is a negative surplus.

[2] We include in Table 6-1 the statistical discrepancies that arise from incomplete recording of actual trade in goods and services and assets. The data are reconciled by an entry called "errors and omissions," which are believed to arise largely from unreported capital flows.

TABLE 6-1

THE UNITED STATES BALANCE OF PAYMENTS (billions of dollars, annual averages)

	1960–1969	1970–1979	1980–1984	1985–1988
Current account	3.3	−0.2	−28.4	−136.1
Trade balance	3.6	−1.1	−52.1	−138.3
Capital account*	−4.6	−14.0	26.2	105.7
Balance of payments	−1.3	−14.2	−2.2	−30.4

* Including errors and omissions.

SOURCE: *Economic Report of the President,* various issues, and *Federal Reserve Bulletin,* May 1989.

Making International Payments

As already noted, any transaction that gives rise to a payment by U.S. residents to foreigners is a deficit item. An overall deficit in the balance of payments — the sum of the current and capital accounts — means, therefore, that U.S. residents are making more payments to foreigners than they are receiving from foreigners. Since foreigners want to be paid in their own currencies, the question of how these payments are to be made arises.

When the overall balance of payments is in deficit — when the sum of the current and capital accounts is negative — Americans have to pay more foreign currency to foreigners than is received. The Fed and foreign central banks provide the foreign currency to make payments to foreigners, and the net amount supplied is "official reserve transactions." Thus, official reserve transactions are equal to the overall balance of payments, the last row in Table 6-1.[3] When the U.S. balance of payments is in surplus, foreigners have to get the dollars with which to pay for the excess of their payments to the United States over their receipts from sales to the United States. The dollars are provided by the central banks in a manner we now explain.

Fixed Exchange Rates

We now examine in more detail the way in which central banks, through their official transactions, *finance,* or provide the means of paying for, balance of payments surpluses and deficits. At this point we distinguish between fixed and floating exchange rate systems.

In a *fixed exchange rate system,* foreign central banks stand ready to buy and sell

---

[3] The official presentation of balance of payments statistics as in Table 6-1 was stopped in 1976 after a review committee suggested that official reserve transactions are not a full measure of foreign exchange transactions by central banks. Nonetheless everyone but the government presents the data as in the table.

their currencies at a fixed price in terms of dollars. The major countries had fixed exchange rates against one another from the end of World War II until 1973.

In Germany, for example, the central bank, the Bundesbank, would buy or sell any amount of dollars in the 1960s at 4 deutsche marks (DM) per U.S. dollar. The French central bank, the Banque de France, stood ready to buy or sell any amount of dollars at 4.90 French francs (FF) per U.S. dollar. The fact that the central banks were prepared to buy or sell *any* amount of dollars at these fixed prices or exchange rates meant that market prices would indeed be equal to the fixed rates. Why? Because nobody who wanted to buy U.S. dollars would pay more than 4.90 francs per dollar when francs could be purchased at that price from the Banque de France. Conversely, nobody would part with dollars in exchange for francs for less than 4.90 francs per dollar if the Banque de France, through the commercial banking system, was prepared to buy dollars at that price.

In a fixed rate system, the central banks have to finance any balance of payments surplus or deficit that arises at the official exchange rate.[4] They do that simply by buying or selling all the foreign currency that is not supplied in private transactions. If the United States were running a deficit in the balance of payments vis-à-vis Germany, so that the demand for marks in exchange for dollars exceeded the supply of marks in exchange for dollars from Germans, the Bundesbank would buy the excess dollars, paying for them with marks.

Fixed exchange rates thus operate like any other price support scheme, such as those in agricultural markets. Given market demand and supply, the price fixer has to make up the excess demand or take up the excess supply. In order to be able to ensure that the price (exchange rate) stays fixed, it is obviously necessary to hold an inventory of foreign currencies, or foreign exchange, that can be provided in exchange for the domestic currency.

RESERVES

Foreign central banks held *reserves*—inventories of dollars and gold that could be sold for dollars—that they would sell in the market when there was an excess demand for dollars. Conversely, when there was an excess supply of dollars, they would buy up the dollars, as in our example of the U.S. balance of payments deficit vis-à-vis Germany.

INTERVENTION

Intervention is the buying or selling of foreign exchange by the central bank. What determines the amount of intervention that a central bank has to do in a fixed exchange

---

[4] We have so far avoided being specific on exactly which central bank did the intervening in the foreign exchange market in the fixed rate system. It is clear that if there was an excess supply of dollars and an excess demand for marks, either the Bundesbank could buy dollars in exchange for marks, or the Fed could sell marks in exchange for dollars. In practice, during the fixed rate period, each foreign central bank undertook to *peg* (fix) its exchange rate vis-à-vis the dollar, and most foreign exchange intervention was undertaken by the foreign central banks. The Fed was nonetheless involved in the management of the exchange rate system since it frequently made dollar loans to foreign central banks that were in danger of running out of dollars.

rate system? We already have the answer to that question. The balance of payments measures the amount of foreign exchange intervention needed from the central banks. So long as the central bank has the necessary reserves, it can continue to intervene in the foreign exchange markets to keep the exchange rate constant. However, if a country persistently runs deficits in the balance of payments, the central bank eventually will run out of reserves of foreign exchange and will be unable to continue its intervention.

Before that point is reached, the central bank is likely to decide that it can no longer maintain the exchange rate, and will devalue the currency. In 1967, for instance, the British devalued the pound from $2.80 per pound to $2.40 per pound. That meant it became cheaper for Americans and other foreigners to buy British pounds, and the devaluation thus affected the balance of payments by making British goods relatively cheaper.

Flexible Exchange Rates

We have seen that the central banks have to provide whatever amounts of foreign currency are needed to finance payments imbalances under fixed exchange rates. In *flexible rate systems*, by contrast, the central banks allow the exchange rate to adjust to equate the supply and demand for foreign currency. If the exchange rate of the dollar against the mark were 50 cents per mark, and German exports to the United States increased, thus increasing the demand for marks by Americans, the Bundesbank could simply stand aside and let the exchange rate adjust. In this particular case, the exchange rate could move from 50 cents per mark to a level such as 52 cents per mark, making German goods more expensive in terms of dollars and thus reducing the demand for them by Americans. We shall later in this chapter examine the way in which changes in exchange rates under floating rates affect the balance of payments. The terms *flexible rates* and *floating rates* are used interchangeably.

Floating, Clean and Dirty

In a system of *clean floating*, central banks stand aside completely and allow exchange rates to be freely determined in the foreign exchange markets. The central banks do not intervene in the foreign exchange markets in such a system, and official reserve transactions are, accordingly, zero. That means the balance of payments is zero in a system of clean floating: The exchange rate adjusts to make the current and capital accounts sum to zero.

In practice, the flexible rate system, in effect since 1973, has not been one of clean floating. Instead, the system has been one of *managed*, or *dirty, floating*. Under managed floating, central banks intervene to buy and sell foreign currencies in attempts to influence exchange rates. Official reserve transactions are, accordingly, not equal to zero under managed floating. The reasons for this central bank intervention under floating rates are discussed in Chapter 20.

Terminology

The language used with respect to exchange rates can be very confusing. In particular, the terms *depreciation* and *appreciation* and *devaluation* and *revaluation* recur in any discussion of international trade and finance.

Figure 6-1 shows the dollar-sterling exchange rate since 1960. We use the figure to clarify some points of terminology. The vertical axis shows the exchange rate measured as $U.S. per pound sterling. First note that we show two subperiods, the fixed rate period lasting through the 1960s until 1973 and the flexible rate regime.

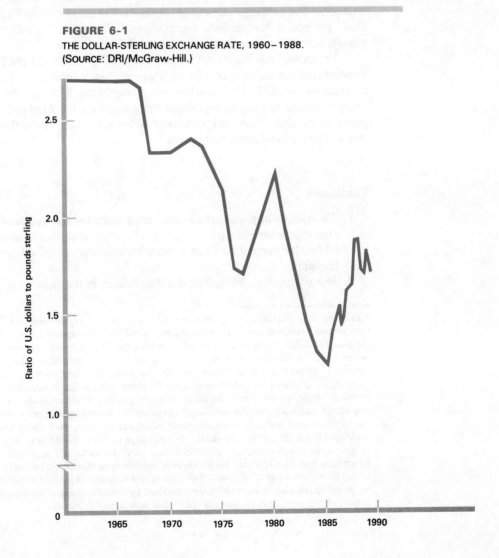

FIGURE 6-1
THE DOLLAR-STERLING EXCHANGE RATE, 1960–1988.
(SOURCE: DRI/McGraw-Hill.)

During the fixed rate period the dollar price of the pound remained constant for lengthy periods. It was constant, or pegged, at a given level by the Bank of England except for two adjustments. Until 1967 the exchange rate was $2.80 per pound sterling, but in that year sterling was devalued and the rate became $2.40 per pound. In 1971 sterling was revalued to $2.60 per pound.

A *devaluation* takes place when the price of foreign currencies under a fixed rate regime is increased by official action. A devaluation thus means that foreigners pay less for the devalued currency or that residents of the devaluing country pay more for foreign currencies. The opposite of a devaluation is a *revaluation*.

Changes in the price of foreign exchange under flexible exchange rates are referred to as *currency depreciation* or *appreciation*. A currency *depreciates* when, under floating rates, it becomes less expensive in terms of foreign currencies. For instance, if the exchange rate of the pound sterling changes from $1.50 per pound to $1.47 per pound, the pound is depreciating. By contrast, the currency *appreciates* when it becomes more expensive in terms of foreign money.

For example, in Figure 6-1 we see that in 1975–1976 and 1982–1985 sterling was depreciating, meaning that it took fewer and fewer dollars to buy a pound sterling. By contrast, in 1977–1980 sterling was appreciating. Although the terms devaluation/revaluation and depreciation/appreciation are used in fixed and flexible rate regimes, respectively, there is no economic difference. These terms describe the direction in which an exchange rate moves.[5]

Summary

1. The balance of payments accounts are a record of the transactions of the economy with other economies. The capital account describes transactions in assets, while the current account covers transactions in goods and services and transfers.

2. Any payment to foreigners is a deficit item in the balance of payments. Any

---

[5] An ambiguity in the way exchange rates are expressed sometimes causes confusion. The exchange rate between two currencies, say the pound sterling and the dollar, can be expressed in two ways, either as $1.60 per pound or 0.625 British pounds per dollar. Sterling (the British pound) depreciates when the pound becomes less valuable in terms of other currencies, for example, when the pound moves from $1.60 per pound to $1.50 per pound. Thus it would seem that the pound depreciates when the currency moves down. However, a depreciation from $1.60 per pound to $1.50 per pound is exactly equivalent to a shift from 0.625 pounds per dollar to 0.667 pounds per dollar — thus, we cannot unambiguously say that there is a depreciation when the exchange rate declines. In practice, there are national conventions about the way exchange rates are expressed, just as there is a convention in each country about which side of the road to drive on. In the United States the rule is "up is down." The exchange rate is expressed as so many dollars per unit of foreign currency, such as $1.50 per pound. In this case, when the exchange rate rises, the dollar depreciates, for example, from $1.50 per pound to $1.60 per pound — because the dollar is becoming less valuable. In the United Kingdom the rule is "up is up": the exchange rate is expressed as so many units of foreign currency per pound. In this case, when the exchange rate rises, the pound appreciates, for example, from $1.50 per pound to $1.60 per pound, because one pound now buys more U.S. money.

payment from foreigners is a surplus item. The balance of payments deficit (or surplus) is the sum of the deficits (or surpluses) on current and capital accounts.

3. Under fixed exchange rates, central banks stand ready to meet all demands for foreign currencies arising from balance of payments deficits or surpluses at a fixed price in terms of the domestic currency. They have to *finance* the excess demands for, or supplies of, foreign currency (that is, the balance of payments deficits or surpluses, respectively) at the pegged (fixed) exchange rate by running down, or adding to, their reserves of foreign currency.

4. Under flexible exchange rates, the demands for and supplies of foreign currency are equated through movements in exchange rates. Under clean floating, there is no central bank intervention and the balance of payments is zero. But central banks sometimes intervene in a floating rate system, engaging in so-called dirty floating.

6-2 EXCHANGE RATE MEASURES AND THE U.S. DOLLAR

Since 1973 the U.S. dollar has floated, more or less freely. Although there has been intervention for most of that period — except in the early 1980s — the dollar exchange rate has fluctuated substantially. Table 6-2 shows movements of the dollar relative to the yen and the deutsche mark (DM) over the period 1976 to 1986. The dollar depreciated sharply from 1976 to 1980, and then appreciated even more (against the DM) through 1985. In the first quarter of 1986 another sharp reversal set in, with the dollar depreciating rapidly against other currencies.

Table 6-2 shows several measures of exchange rates. The first two columns give the conventional measure, that is, the price of the foreign currency in terms of the dollar. For example, one DM cost 34 cents in 1985. These are also called *bilateral*

TABLE 6-2
NOMINAL AND REAL EXCHANGE RATES FOR THE U.S. DOLLAR

| | $/yen | $/DM | EFFECTIVE RATE INDEX, 1980 = 100 | |
			Nominal	Real
1976	0.00337	0.35	90	93
1980	0.00441	0.55	100	100
1985	0.00419	0.34	71	76
1987	0.00693	0.56	96	104
1989:1	0.00779	0.54	102	106

SOURCE: DRI/McGraw-Hill.

FIGURE 6-2
THE U.S. REAL AND NOMINAL EXCHANGE RATES, 1970–1988. (SOURCE: DRI/McGraw-Hill.)

nominal exchange rates. They are bilateral in the sense that they are exchange rates for one currency against another, and they are nominal because they specify the exchange rate in nominal terms, as so many dollars per DM or cents per yen.

Often we want to characterize the movement of the dollar relative to all other currencies in a single number rather than by looking at the separate exchange rates for the DM, the yen, the French franc, etc. That is, we want an *index* for the exchange rate against other currencies, just as we use a price index to show how the prices of goods in general have changed.

The third and fourth columns in Table 6-2 present indexes of the *multilateral or effective exchange rate.* The effective or multilateral rate represents the price of a representative basket of foreign currencies, each weighted by its importance to the United States in international trade. Thus the yen receives a large weight, as does the Canadian dollar, because large shares of our trade are with Japan and Canada. By contrast Germany, France, and Italy receive much smaller weights.

Figure 6-2 shows the effective dollar index with a base of 1980 = 100. The effective exchange rate index shows the very large appreciation of the dollar relative to the currencies of our trading partners in the 1980s — more than 40 percent between 1980 and 1985 — followed by a depreciation in the 1985 – 1988 period.

The effective exchange rate index measures the average nominal exchange rate. But to know whether our goods are becoming relatively cheaper or more expensive than foreign goods, we also have to take into account what happened to prices here and abroad. To do so, we look at the *real effective exchange rate,* or simply the *real exchange rate.*

The real exchange rate measures a country's competitiveness in international trade. It is given by the ratio of prices of goods abroad, measured in dollars, relative to prices of goods at home:

$$\text{Real exchange rate} = R = \frac{eP_f}{P} \qquad (2)$$

where P and P_f are the price levels here and abroad, respectively, and e is the dollar price of foreign exchange. Note that since P_f represents foreign prices, for example, prices measured in DM, and the exchange rate is measured as so many dollars per DM, the numerator expresses prices abroad measured in dollars; with the domestic price level, measured in this case in dollars, in the denominator, the real exchange rate expresses prices abroad relative to those at home.

A rise in the real exchange rate, or a real depreciation, means that foreign prices in dollars have increased relative to the prices of goods produced here. Goods abroad have become more expensive relative to goods at home, which other things equal, implies people are likely to switch some of their spending to goods at home. This is often described as an increase in the competitiveness of our products, as our goods become cheaper relative to foreign goods, both for us and for foreigners. Conversely a decline in R, or a real appreciation, means that our goods have become relatively more expensive or that we have lost competitiveness.

Figure 6-2 shows, in addition to the nominal effective exchange rate, the U.S. real exchange rate for the 1970s and 1980s. The measure reported here shows the dollar prices of our trading partners for manufactures relative to our own prices for manufactures, eP_f/P. There were very large losses in U.S. competitiveness in the 1980–1985 period. Note also how closely the nominal and real effective exchange rates move together. The reason is that movements in nominal exchange rates, not different rates of change in prices here and abroad, have been the main cause of changes in competitiveness. Inflation rates were not substantially different in the major industrialized countries, but exchange rates moved a lot.

6-3   TRADE IN GOODS, MARKET EQUILIBRIUM, AND THE BALANCE OF TRADE

We now study the effects of trade in goods on the level of income and the effects of various disturbances on both income and the trade balance — which, in this section, we use as shorthand for the current account. We also examine policy problems that arise when the balance of trade and the level of income require different corrective actions. We do not include the capital account at this stage, so that for the present the current account and the balance of payments are the same.

In this section we fit foreign trade into the *IS-LM* framework. We assume that the price level is given and that output that is demanded will be supplied. It is both conceptually and technically easy to relax the fixed price assumption, and we shall do so in Chapter 20. But because it is important to be clear on how the introduction of trade modifies the analysis of aggregate demand, we start from a familiar and basic level.

Domestic Spending and Spending on Domestic Goods

In this subsection we want to establish how foreign trade fits into the *IS* schedule. In an open economy, part of domestic output is sold to foreigners (exports), and part of spending by domestic residents falls on foreign goods (imports). We accordingly have to modify our analysis of aggregate demand.

The most important change is that domestic spending no longer determines domestic output. Instead, *spending on domestic goods* determines domestic output. Spending by domestic residents falls in part on domestic goods but also in part on imports. Part of the typical American's spending is for imported beer, for instance. Demand for domestic goods, by contrast, includes exports or foreign demand along with part of spending by domestic residents.

The effect of external transactions on the demand for domestic output was examined in Chapter 2. Recall the definitions:

$$\text{Spending by domestic residents} = A = C + I + G \tag{3}$$

$$\text{Spending on domestic goods} = A + NX = (C + I + G) + (X - Q) \\ = (C + I + G) + NX \tag{4}$$

where X is the level of exports, Q is imports, and NX is the trade (goods and services) surplus. The definition of spending by domestic residents $(C + I + G)$ remains that of the earlier chapters. Spending on domestic goods is total spending by domestic residents *less* their spending on imports *plus* foreign demand or exports. Since exports minus imports is the trade surplus, or net exports (NX), spending on domestic goods is spending by domestic residents plus the trade surplus.

With this clarification we can return to our model of income determination. We will assume that domestic spending depends on the interest rate and income, so that we can write

$$A = A(Y, i) \tag{5}$$

Further, we assume now that net exports depend on our income, which affects import spending; on foreign income Y_f, which affects foreign demand for our exports; and on the real exchange rate, R, defined above. A rise in R or a real depreciation improves our trade balance as demand shifts from goods produced abroad to those produced at home:[6]

$$NX = X(Y_f, R) - Q(Y, R) = NX(Y, Y_f, R) \tag{6}$$

---

[6] Note two points about net exports in equation (6). First, we measure net exports in terms of domestic output. To do so we must measure imports (Q) in terms of their value in our currency. Second, we *assume* that a real appreciation worsens the trade balance, and a real depreciation (a rise in R) improves the trade balance. This is a matter of assumption since there are opposing effects of changes in volume and in price. We return to this point in Chap. 20.

We can immediately state three important results:

- A rise in foreign income, other things being equal, improves the home country's trade balance and therefore raises aggregate demand.
- A real depreciation by the home country improves the trade balance and therefore increases aggregate demand.
- A rise in home income raises import spending and hence worsens the trade balance.

Figure 6-3 shows the net export schedule. The schedule is drawn for a given level of foreign income and a given real exchange rate. It is downward sloping, since imports rise with the level of home income and thus reduce net exports. At low levels of home income net exports are positive, since import spending is very low, but as income rises so does import spending, and hence net exports fall off and ultimately become negative. The schedule is steeper the greater the increase in import spending per dollar increase in income or the larger the *marginal propensity to import.*

An increase in foreign income shows up as an exogenous increase in exports and hence as an upward and rightward shift of the net export schedule. The same applies to a real depreciation. A real depreciation raises net exports at each level of income and

FIGURE 6-3

THE NET EXPORT SCHEDULE. Net exports are a declining function of the level of income. A rise in income raises imports and hence reduces net exports. The schedule is steeper the larger the marginal propensity to import. The schedule is drawn for a given level of foreign income, Y_f, and for a given real exchange rate, R.

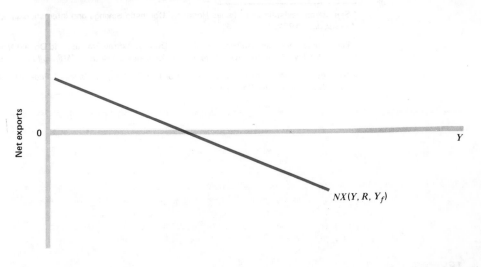

box 6-1

THE FELDSTEIN-HORIOKA PUZZLE

From the national income accounts identity stated at the end of Chapter 2, we have the important relationship involving national saving, investment, and the current account:

$$\text{Current account} = \text{saving} - \text{investment}$$

Note that saving here refers to the *national* saving rate, which is private saving less the budget deficit.

Thus when an economy can trade, its saving and investment rates (as a percentage of GNP) may differ. Accordingly, saving and investment may in principle move substantially independently of each other. Martin Feldstein and Charles Horioka have studied the relation between saving and investment for a cross section of twenty-three industrialized countries.[*] Their evidence, using averages for long periods of time, is shown in Figure 1. The data show that the higher is a country's saving rate, the higher the investment-GDP ratio. In the cross section, variations in the saving rate seem to be associated with variations in investment, not in the external balance. Thus despite the possibility that investment and saving move independently, in practice they are highly correlated.

Since Feldstein and Horioka first announced their finding there has been a substantial amount of research on the facts and on possible explanations.[†] The facts are for the most part not in question, and the search for an explanation is increasingly focused on how countries can finance persistent current account deficits.[‡] However, it is true that the national saving and investment rates in the United States have diverged considerably in the 1980s.

Whether changes in the national saving rate are reflected primarily in saving or the external balance is of importance for a very practical issue: If the U.S. budget deficit is corrected, will that eliminate the trade deficit? Feldstein-Horioka's evidence suggests no; their evidence leads us to believe that cutting the budget deficit will raise investment. But the 1980s data for the United States create some doubt about that strong conclusion. ∎

---

[*] See Martin Feldstein and Charles Horioka, "Domestic Savings and International Capital Flows," *Economic Journal*, June 1982.

[†] For a survey and assessment, see Michael Dooley, Jeffrey Frankel, and Donald Mathieson, "International Capital Mobility: What do Saving-Investment Correlations Tell Us?" *IMF Staff Papers*, September 1987.

[‡] See, too, the collection of essays "Studies on U.S. External Imbalances," Federal Reserve Bank of New York *Quarterly Review*, Winter-Spring 1989.

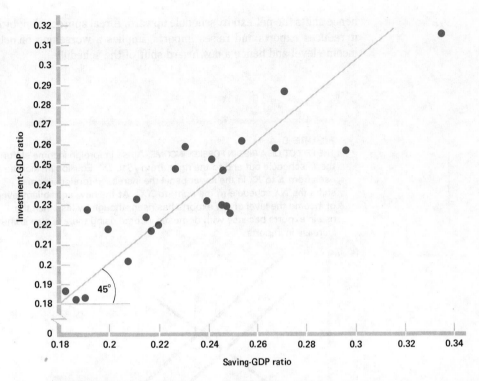

FIGURE 1
INVESTMENT AND SAVING, 1960–1986. Averages for twenty-three
industrialized countries. (SOURCE: DRI/McGraw-Hill.)

hence shifts the net export schedule upward. A real appreciation, by contrast, because it reduces exports and raises imports, implies a worsening of net exports at each income level and hence a downward shift of the schedule.

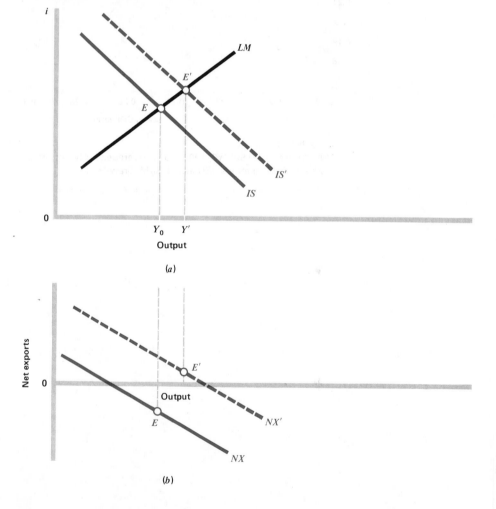

FIGURE 6-4

THE EFFECT OF A RISE IN FOREIGN INCOME. A rise in foreign income shifts the *IS* schedule out and to the right, from *IS* to *IS'*. Equilibrium income rises from *E* to *E'*. In the lower panel the increased foreign income shifts the *NX* schedule to the right, to *NX'*. At the new equilibrium level of income the level of net exports has risen, though by less than the rise in exports because with domestic income rising there is also some increase in imports.

Goods Market Equilibrium

The open economy *IS* curve now includes net exports as a component of aggregate demand. Thus we write

$$IS \text{ curve:} \qquad Y = A(Y, i) + NX(Y, Y_f, R) \qquad (7)$$

It is immediately clear from (7) that the equilibrium level of income will now depend on both foreign income and the real exchange rate. We will therefore have to ask how disturbances in foreign income, or real exchange rate changes, affect the equilibrium level of income.

Figure 6-4 shows the effects of an increase in foreign income. Income abroad rises, say because of a tax cut or increased government spending. As a result, foreign demand for our goods and net exports rise at each level of our income. This results in a rightward shift of the *IS* curve in Figure 6-4. The new equilibrium level of income is Y'. Thus a rise in foreign income unambiguously raises home income. The lower panel of Figure 6-4 shows the impact on net exports. The increased foreign income causes an upward shift of the *NX* schedule. At the new equilibrium level of income Y', net exports have increased.

In the same way we can show that a real depreciation by the home country shifts the *NX* schedule in the lower half of Figure 6-4 to the right. It thus shifts the *IS* schedule to the right and hence leads to a rise in equilibrium income and, moving back down to the lower half of the diagram, to an improvement in net exports.

Table 6-3 summarizes the effects of different disturbances on the equilibrium levels of income and net exports. Each of these examples can be worked out using the *IS* schedule in conjunction with the net export schedule.

Policy Dilemmas

Countries typically want their balance of payments to be close to balance. Otherwise the central bank is either losing reserves — which it cannot keep on doing — or gaining reserves, which it does not want to do forever. The goal of balance of payments

TABLE 6-3
EFFECTS OF DISTURBANCE ON INCOME AND NET EXPORTS

	Increase in home spending	Increase in foreign income	Real depreciation
Income	+	+	+
Net exports	−	+	+

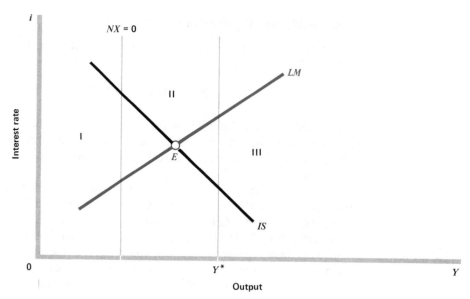

FIGURE 6-5

THE POLICY CONFLICT BETWEEN FULL EMPLOYMENT AND EXTERNAL
BALANCE. Along $NX = 0$ there is trade balance equilibrium, and at
output level Y^* there is full employment. In region I expansion in
demand eliminates unemployment without problems on the external
side. In region III demand restraint reduces overemployment and
eliminates the trade surplus. In region II there is a policy conflict: External
balance requires demand restraint while full employment requires
expansion.

equilibrium is called *external balance.*[7] In addition, countries want to maintain *internal balance,* or full employment. In this section and the next we discuss policy mixtures that will produce both internal and external balance.

Figure 6-5 shows possible conflicts between the objectives of external balance, defined for the moment as trade balance equilibrium, and full employment. The schedule $NX = 0$ shows balanced trade; there is only one level of income (given the real exchange rate and foreign income) at which imports equal exports. To the left there is a surplus — low income implies low imports and hence a surplus in the trade balance; conversely, to the right of $NX = 0$ there is a deficit. Full employment prevails at the level of output Y^* with unemployment to the left and overemployment to the right.

We show three regions corresponding to different combinations of internal and

---

[7] However, some governments do seem to want to run very large current account surpluses in order to be able to run capital account deficits that allow them to buy large amounts of foreign assets.

external balance. In region I there is unemployment and a surplus on the current account. Here there is no policy conflict: Monetary and/or fiscal expansion can take the economy to higher income levels without the risk that external constraints become binding. In region III there is also no conflict since the economy is overemployed and is experiencing a current account deficit. In this situation demand restraint through tight money or restrictive fiscal policy will help cure the deficit and reduce demand toward full employment.

However, there is a conflict in the middle range, region II, because an expansionary policy that aims for higher employment will increase the trade deficit.

In order to run a trade deficit, a country has to find some way of financing the deficit, that is, of paying for the excess of imports over exports. If financing is unavailable (as is the case for many developing countries today, especially in Africa and Latin America), then the trade balance sets the limit on any expansion. Policies that would shift the trade balance schedule, *NX* (in the lower half of Figure 6-4) out and to the right, for example, real depreciation, have to be used to reconcile the objective of full employment with the external constraint. Alternatively, if a country can borrow abroad, it can finance imports in excess of export earnings. In that case levels of income higher than those indicated by *NX* = 0 become possible.

Repercussion Effects

So far we have looked at the effects on the home country of disturbances such as a depreciation. We have not, however, taken account of the interdependence among economies. When we increase government spending, our income rises; part of the increase in income will be spent on imports, which means that income will rise abroad, too. The increase in foreign income will then raise foreign demand for our goods, which in turn adds to the domestic income expansion brought about by higher government spending, and so on.

These *repercussion effects* can be important in practice. When the United States expands, it tends, like a locomotive, to pull the rest of the world into an expansion. Likewise, if the rest of the world expands, we share in the expansion. To get an idea of the size of these interdependence effects, we look at estimates of international multipliers. Table 6-4 shows multipliers for an increase of one percentage point of GNP in government spending in various countries. The effect shown is on GNP in the second year after the increase in government spending.

First note that each country responds most to its own expansion. For instance, for the United States, an increase in its own level of government spending raises income much more than a foreign rise in spending. But foreign spending increases *do* spill over. A rise in government spending in Japan or in Germany will raise output in the United States and a U.S. rise in spending will have a sizable effect on Canada, a country from which we obtain a significant share of our total imports.

There is an asymmetry in the table: Why does an increase in government spending in the United States of 1 percent of GNP raise Japanese or German income more than a 1 percent increase in their spending raises income in the United States?

TABLE 6-4

INTERNATIONAL MULTIPLIERS (percentage increase in GNP due to increased government spending equal to 1 percent of GNP)

Effect on	INITIATING COUNTRY		
	U.S.	Japan	Germany
U.S.	1.7	0.1	0.1
Japan	1.3	1.3	0.1
Germany	0.4	0.2	1.3
Canada	1.0	0.1	0.0

SOURCE: H. Edison, J. Marquez, and R. Tryon, "The Structure and Properties of the Federal Reserve Board Multicountry Model," *Economic Modelling*, April 1987.

TABLE 6-5

IMPACT OF U.S. DEPRECIATION (percentage increase in GNP due to a 5 percent dollar depreciation)

Impact on	U.S./all	U.S./Japan	U.S./Germany
U.S.	0.3	0.1	0.2
Japan	−1.2	−1.1	−0.0
Germany	0.3	0.1	−0.7
Canada	−0.6	−0.0	−0.1

NOTE: The first column shows the impact of a 5 percent dollar depreciation against the currencies of Japan, Germany, Canada, and the United Kingdom. The second and third columns refer to a 5 percent depreciation of the dollar against the yen and the DM, respectively.

SOURCE: See Table 6-4.

The reason is that the United States has a much larger economy, so that a spending increase of 1 percent of U.S. income represents a much larger increase in world demand than does the same percentage increase in spending in Germany or Japan.

In Table 6-5 we show the impact of changes in real exchange rates on real GNP. The table reports the effect of a dollar depreciation of 5 percent against all other currencies (the first column) or against only the currencies of Japan and German (the second and third columns). The changes are those in the second year after the dollar depreciation. Note that dollar depreciation makes the United States more competitive and thus raises U.S. real GNP, as we assumed above. Thus for the United States, for example, a 5 percent real depreciation will raise output by 0.3 percentage points. But the effect abroad is the opposite. U.S. real depreciation draws demand away from the rest of the world and hence reduces income there. The table shows that a U.S. real depreciation will reduce output sizably in Japan, Canada, and Europe (Germany). Clearly then, real exchange rate exchanges are an important element in the determination of income and of international linkages.

6-4 CAPITAL MOBILITY

So far, we have been assuming that trade is confined to goods and services and does not include assets. Now we allow for trade in assets and see the effects of such trade on the equilibrium of the economy and its desired policy mix.

One of the striking facts about the international economy is the high degree of integration, or linkage, among financial, or capital, markets—the markets in which bonds and stocks are traded. The capital markets are very fully integrated among the main industrial countries. Yields on assets in New York and yields on comparable assets in Canada, or for that matter in Europe and Japan, move closely together. For example, if rates in New York rose relative to those in Canada, investors would turn to lending in New York, while borrowers would turn to Toronto. With lending up in New York and borrowing up in Toronto, yields would quickly fall into line.

In most industrial countries today there are no restrictions on holding assets abroad. U.S. residents, or residents in Germany or the United Kingdom, can hold their wealth either at home or abroad. They therefore will look for the highest return, adjusted for risk. This search for the highest (risk-adjusted) return will tend to equalize asset yields on comparable assets in all parts of the world. In the simplest world, in which exchange rates are fixed forever, taxes are the same everywhere, and foreign asset holders never face political risks (nationalization, restrictions on transfer of assets, default risk by foreign governments), we would expect all asset holders to simply pick the asset that has the highest return. That would force asset returns into strict equality everywhere in the world capital markets because no country could borrow for less. In reality, though, none of the three conditions is exactly met: There are tax differences, for example withholding taxes; there is the risk that exchange rates can change, perhaps significantly, and thus affect the payoff in dollars of a foreign investment; and finally, countries can put up obstacles to capital outflows or could simply find themselves unable to pay. For all these reasons interest rates are clearly not equal across countries.

It is interesting, however, to note that differentials, adjusted to eliminate the risk of exchange rate changes, tend to be quite small among major industrialized countries. Consider the case of the United States and Canada, shown in Figure 6-6. Because the interest rates are "covered," so that the exchange risk is eliminated, they should be exactly the same.[8] As can be seen clearly in the bottom part of the figure, they are not exactly the same. But the differential in fact is small, and the average of 0.5 percent reflects primarily tax differences. We take this evidence to support the view that capital is very highly mobile across borders, and we will ignore the minor residuals.

Our working assumption from now on is that capital is *perfectly* mobile. Capital is perfectly mobile internationally when investors can purchase assets in any country they choose, quickly, with low transactions costs, and in unlimited amounts. When capital is perfectly mobile, asset holders are willing and able to move large amounts of funds across borders in search of the highest return or lowest borrowing cost. Perfect capital mobility may be an overly strong assumption, but it has great analytical convenience and very powerful implications, as we shall now see.

The high degree of capital market integration that is reflected in Figure 6-6 suggests that any one country's interest rates cannot get too far out of line from those in the rest of the world without bringing about capital flows that tend to restore yields

---

[8] Cover, or protection, against the risk of exchange rate changes can be obtained by buying a futures contract, which promises (of course, at a cost) to pay a given amount of one currency in exchange for a specified amount of another currency at a given future date. There are in practice simpler ways of obtaining foreign exchange risk cover, but the essential mechanism is the same.

FIGURE 6-6
INTERNATIONAL INTEREST RATE LINKAGES, 1983 – 1988. (SOURCE:
DRI/McGraw-Hill.)

to the world level. As we have noted, if Canadian yields fell relative to U.S. yields, there would be a capital outflow from Canada because lenders would take their funds out of Canada and borrowers would try to raise funds in Canada. From the point of view of the balance of payments, this implies that a relative decline in interest rates — a decline in our rates relative to those abroad — will worsen the balance of payments because of the capital outflow resulting from lending abroad by U.S. residents.

The recognition that interest rates affect capital flows and the balance of payments has important implications for stabilization policy. First, because monetary and fiscal policies affect interest rates, the policies have an effect on the capital account and therefore on the balance of payments. The effects of monetary and fiscal policies on the balance of payments are *not* limited to the trade balance effects discussed above but extend to the capital account. The second implication is that the way in which monetary and fiscal policies work in affecting the domestic economy and the balance of payments changes when there are international capital flows. We will examine the monetary-fiscal policy mix that can be used to achieve internal and external balance, and we will see that capital flows can be used to *finance* the trade balance and thus help in achieving an overall balance of payments.

The Balance of Payments and Capital Flows

We introduce the role of capital flows within a framework in which we assume that the home country faces a given price of imports and a given export demand. In addition, we assume that the world rate of interest, i_f (i.e., the rate of interest in foreign capital markets), is given. Moreover, with perfect capital mobility, capital flows into the home country at an unlimited rate if our interest rate is above that abroad (from now on, until further notice, we assume that exchange risk is absent). Conversely, if our rate is below that abroad, capital outflows will be unlimited.

Next we look at the balance of payments. The balance of payments surplus, BP, is equal to the trade surplus, NX, plus the capital account surplus, CF:

$$BP = NX(Y, Y_f, R) + CF(i - i_f) \qquad (8)$$

In equation (8) we have shown the trade balance as a function of domestic and foreign income and the real exchange rate, and the capital account as depending on the *interest differential*.[9] An increase in income worsens the trade balance, and an increase in the interest rate above the world level draws capital inflows and thus improves the capital account. It follows that when income increases, even the tiniest increase in interest rates is enough to maintain an overall balance of payments equilibrium. The trade deficit would be financed by a capital inflow.

That idea is extremely important. Countries frequently face the following dilemma: Domestic output is low, and they want to expand, *but* the balance of payments is in difficulty and they do not believe they can run a larger balance of payments deficit. If the level of income increases, net exports will fall as domestic demand rises, thereby tending to worsen the balance of payments — which the country wants to avoid. The presence of interest-sensitive capital flows suggests that a country can undertake an expansionary domestic policy without necessarily running into balance of payments problems. The implication of perfect capital mobility is that interest rates would have to be raised only very slightly to obtain financing for the trade deficit.

A country can afford an increase in domestic income and in import spending, provided the increases are accompanied by an increase in interest rates so as to attract a capital inflow. But how can an expansion in domestic income be achieved at the same

---

[9] When capital mobility is perfect, the domestic and foreign interest rates cannot get out of line, so in equilibrium we will find that $i = i_f$; however we show the capital flows equation with i potentially not equal to i_f in order to demonstrate the forces at work — including potentially massive capital flows — that produce equilibrium.

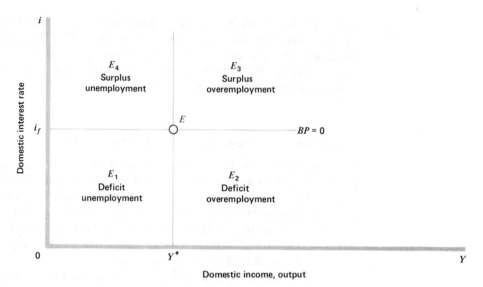

FIGURE 6-7

INTERNAL AND EXTERNAL BALANCE UNDER FIXED EXCHANGE RATES. Full employment is obtained at an output level Y^*. The internal balance schedule is therefore the vertical line at Y^*. Along $BP = 0$ the balance of payments is in equilibrium. Points above the BP schedule correspond to surpluses, and points below to deficits in the balance of payments. With perfect capital mobility the balance of payments can only be in equilibrium when home interest rates equal those abroad. Thus $BP = 0$ is flat at the level of world interest rates.

time as interest rates are increased, even very slightly? The answer is to use fiscal policy to increase aggregate demand to the full-employment level and monetary policy to get the right amount of capital flows.[10]

Internal and External Balance

We return now to the issue of internal and external balance, discussed previously using Figure 6-5. In Figure 6-7 we show the schedule $BP = 0$, derived from equation (8), along which we have balance of payments equilibrium. Our key assumption — perfect capital mobility — is reflected in the shape of the pictured schedule. Only at a level of interest rates equal to that of rates abroad can we have external balance; if domestic

---

[10] The idea of the policy mix for internal and external balance was suggested by Robert A. Mundell in his important paper, "The Appropriate Use of Monetary and Fiscal Policy under Fixed Exchange Rates," *IMF Staff Papers*, March 1962.

interest rates are higher, there is a vast capital account and overall surplus, and if they are below foreign rates, there is an unlimited deficit.

Thus $BP = 0$ must be flat at the level of world interest rates. Points above the $BP = 0$ schedule correspond to a surplus, and points below to a deficit. We have also drawn, in Figure 6-7, the full-employment output level, Y^*. Point E is the only point at which both internal and external balance are achieved. Point E_1, for example, corresponds to a case of unemployment and a balance of payments deficit. Point E_2, by contrast, is a case of deficit and overemployment.

We can talk about policy problems in terms of points in the four quadrants of Figure 6-7. Each such point would be an intersection of an IS and an LM curve, and the question is how to use monetary and fiscal policy — shifting the IS and LM curves — to get both internal and external balance. How the adjustment takes place depends critically on the exchange rate regime.

6-5 THE MUNDELL-FLEMING MODEL: PERFECT CAPITAL MOBILITY UNDER FIXED EXCHANGE RATES

We are now ready to extend the analysis of output determination to the open economy with perfect capital mobility. In this section we assume the exchange rate is fixed. In the next section we consider output determination with flexible exchange rates.

The analysis extending the standard IS-LM model to the open economy under perfect capital mobility has a special name, the *Mundell-Fleming model*. Robert Mundell, now a professor at Columbia University, and the late Marcus Fleming, who was a researcher at the International Monetary Fund, developed this analysis in the 1960s, well before flexible exchange rates came into operation.[11] Although later research has refined their analysis, the initial Mundell-Fleming formulation shown here remains essentially intact as a way of understanding how policies work under high capital mobility.

Under perfect capital mobility the slightest interest differential provokes infinite capital flows. It follows that in a situation of perfect capital mobility, central banks cannot conduct an independent monetary policy under fixed exchange rates. The

[11] Mundell's work on international macroeconomics has been extraordinarily important, and the adventurous student should certainly consult his two books: *International Economics* (New York: Macmillan, 1967) and *Monetary Theory* (Pacific Palisades, Calif.: Goodyear, 1971). See also Mundell, "Capital Mobility and Stabilization Policy under Fixed and Flexible Exchange Rates," *Canadian Journal of Economics*, November 1963, and Marcus Fleming "Domestic Financial Policies under Fixed and under Floating Exchange Rates," *IMF Staff Papers*, November 1962. An up-to-date discussion can be found in Jacob Frenkel and Michael Mussa, "Asset Markets, Exchange Rates and the Balance of Payments," in R. W. Jones and P. Kenen (eds.), *Handbook of International Economics*, vol. 2 (Amsterdam: North-Holland, 1985). Recent econometric model simulations in line with the Mundell-Fleming model can be found in R. Bryant et al. (eds.), *Empirical Macroeconomics for Interdependent Economies* (Washington, D.C.: Brookings Institution, 1988) and Pete Richardson, "The Structure and Simulation Properties of the OECD's Interlink Model," *OECD Economic Studies*, no. 10, Spring 1988.

reason is the following: Suppose a country wishes to raise interest rates. Monetary policy is tightened, and as a result interest rates rise. Immediately, portfolio holders worldwide see the higher rate and shift their wealth into the country with that rate. As a result of the huge capital inflow the balance of payments shows a gigantic surplus; the resulting pressure for currency appreciation forces the central bank to intervene, buying foreign money and selling domestic money in exchange. This intervention implies that the home money stock is increased. As a result the initial monetary contraction is undone. The process comes to an end when home interest rates have been pushed back down to the initial level.

The conclusion is: *Under fixed exchange rates and perfect capital mobility, a country cannot pursue an independent monetary policy. Interest rates cannot move out of line with those prevailing in the world market. Any attempt at independent monetary policy leads to capital flows and a need to intervene until interest rates are back in line with those in the world market.*

Table 6-6 shows the steps in the argument. Step 4—the pressure for appreciation—occurs because the existence of the capital inflow means that foreigners are trying to buy the domestic currency in exchange for their currency, thereby tending to raise the price of the domestic currency in terms of their currencies. The commitment to a fixed rate involves step 5. With the exchange rate tending to appreciate because foreigners are trying to buy the domestic currency, the central bank has to provide the domestic currency. Just as in an open market operation the central bank buys and sells bonds for money, so in intervention in the foreign exchange market the monetary authority buys and sells foreign money (yen, DM, or Canadian dollars) for domestic money. Thus the money supply is linked to the balance of payments. Surpluses imply *automatic* monetary expansion; deficits imply monetary contraction.

Monetary Expansion

It is worthwhile looking at this point in terms of the open economy *IS-LM* model. In Figure 6-8 we show the *IS* and *LM* schedules as well as the $BP = 0$ schedule which now, because of perfect capital mobility, is a horizontal line. Only at a level of interest rates equal to those abroad, $i = i_f$, can we have payments balance. Any slight increase in interest rates brings in infinite capital inflows, pressure for appreciation, intervention, and hence monetary expansion. Conversely, any tendency for interest rates to fall below the world level leads to capital outflows, pressure for exchange rate depreciation, intervention, and monetary contraction. Thus the *LM* schedule, rather than staying put, moves in response to the changing money supply.

Consider specifically a monetary expansion that starts from point *E*. The *LM* schedule shifts down and to the right, and the economy moves to point *E'*. But at *E'* there is a large payments deficit and hence pressure for the exchange rate to depreciate. The central bank must intervene, selling foreign exchange and buying home money. As a result, the *LM* schedule shifts back up and to the left. The process continues until the initial equilibrium at *E* is reestablished.

TABLE 6-6

PAYMENTS IMBALANCES, INTERVENTION, AND THE MONEY SUPPLY

1. Tightening of money
2. Increased interest rates
3. Capital inflow, payments surplus
4. Pressure for currency appreciation
5. Intervention by selling home money and buying foreign money
6. Monetary expansion due to intervention lowers interest rate
7. Back to initial interest rates and payments balance

FIGURE 6-8

MONETARY EXPANSION UNDER FIXED RATES AND PERFECT CAPITAL MOBILITY. Under perfect capital mobility the balance of payments can only be in equilibrium at the interest rate $i = i_f$. At even slightly higher rates there are massive capital inflows; at lower rates there are capital outflows. A monetary expansion that cuts interest rates to point E' causes downward pressure on the exchange rate. The monetary authorities must intervene, selling foreign exchange and buying domestic money until the LM schedule has shifted back to its initial position.

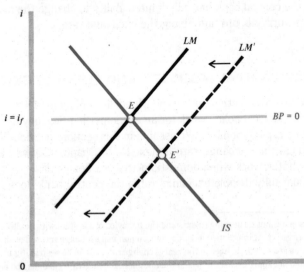

Indeed, with perfect capital mobility the economy never even gets to point E'. The response of capital flows is so large and rapid that the central bank is forced to reverse the initial expansion of the money stock as soon as it attempts it. Conversely, any attempt to contract the money stock would immediately lead to vast reserve losses, forcing an expansion of the money stock and a return to the initial equilibrium.

Fiscal Expansion

Fiscal expansion under fixed exchange rates with perfect capital mobility is, by contrast, extremely effective. We describe the effects in terms of the *IS-LM* model, but we do not draw the diagram, leaving that for one of the end-of-chapter problems.

With the money supply initially unchanged, a fiscal expansion moves the *IS* curve up and to the right, tending to increase both the interest rate and the level of output. The higher interest rate sets off a capital inflow that would lead the exchange rate to appreciate. To maintain the exchange rate, the central bank has to expand the money supply, thus increasing income further. Equilibrium is restored when the money supply has increased enough to drive the interest rate back to its original level, $i = i_f$.

The Endogenous Money Stock

Although the assumption of perfect capital mobility is extreme, it is a useful benchmark case that in the end is not too far from reality. The essential point is that *the commitment to maintain a fixed exchange rate makes the money stock endogenous* because the central bank has to provide the foreign exchange or domestic money that is demanded at the fixed exchange rate. Thus even when capital mobility is less than perfect, the central bank has only limited ability to change the money supply without having to worry about maintaining the exchange rate.

6-6 PERFECT CAPITAL MOBILITY AND FLEXIBLE EXCHANGE RATES

In this section we continue using the Mundell-Fleming model in order to explore how monetary and fiscal policy work for an economy that has fully flexible exchange rates and perfect capital mobility. We assume in this section that domestic prices are fixed, even though the exchange rate is flexible. In Chapter 20 we examine how flexible exchange rates work when domestic prices are flexible.[12]

Under fully flexible exchange rates the central bank does not intervene in the

---

[12] The reason it is not misleading to examine the behavior of a system with flexible exchange rates and fixed domestic prices is that in practice most changes in nominal exchange rates in economies with relatively low inflation rates are in fact changes in the real exchange rate, as can be seen in Figure 6-2. The analysis of this section would not apply in cases in which the nominal exchange rate changes and domestic prices rise in the same proportion so that the real exchange rate is unchanged.

market for foreign exchange. The exchange rate must adjust to clear the market so that the demand for and supply of foreign exchange balance. Without central bank intervention, therefore, the balance of payments must be equal to zero.

Under fully flexible exchange rates the absence of intervention implies a zero balance of payments. Any current account deficit must be financed by private capital inflows; a surplus, by capital outflows. Adjustments in the exchange rate ensure that the sum of the current and capital accounts is zero.

A second implication of fully flexible exchange rates is that the central bank can set the money supply at will. Since there is no obligation to intervene, there is no longer any link between the balance of payments and the money supply.

Perfect capital mobility implies that there is only one interest rate at which the balance of payments will balance:

$$i = i_f \qquad (9)$$

Only when the home interest rate is equal to that abroad will there not be infinite capital inflows or capital outflows.[13] Thus balance of payments equilibrium requires $i = i_f$. We show this in Figure 6-9 by the line $i = i_f$, which is a horizontal schedule at the level of the world interest rate, i_f. From equation (7) we remember that the real exchange rate is a determinant of aggregate demand and hence appears as a shift variable in the *IS* schedule. Given prices, P and P_f, a depreciation makes the home country more competitive, improves net exports, and hence shifts the *IS* schedule to the right. Conversely, a real appreciation means our goods become relatively more expensive, and hence the trade balance worsens and demand for domestic goods declines so that the *IS* schedule shifts to the left.

The arrows in Figure 6-9 link the movement of aggregate demand to the interest rate. If the home interest rate were higher than i_f, capital inflows would cause currency appreciation. At any point above the $i = i_f$ schedule, the exchange rate is appreciating, competitiveness is declining, and aggregate demand is falling. Thus the *IS* schedule will be shifting to the left. Conversely, any point below the $i = i_f$ schedule corresponds to depreciation, improving competitiveness, and increasing aggregate demand. The *IS* schedule will therefore be shifting to the right. We now see how various disturbances affect output and the exchange rate.

Adjustment to a Real Disturbance

We have now completed our model, represented by equations (7), (8), and (9), and can ask how the economy will adjust to disturbances. In particular, we want to know how various changes affect our level of output, the interest rate, and the exchange rate. The

---

[13] Equation (9) assumes that investors do not expect the exchange rate to change. Otherwise, nominal interest rates differ among countries by an amount that reflects expected changes in the exchange rate, in a way to be described in Chapter 20.

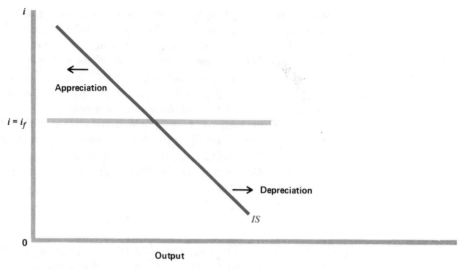

FIGURE 6-9

THE EFFECT OF EXCHANGE RATES ON AGGREGATE DEMAND. With perfect capital mobility and flexible rates, capital flows have a strong impact on demand. If home interest rates fall below i_f, there are capital outflows leading to exchange depreciation, a gain in competitiveness, and hence a rise in demand for domestic goods, shown by the rightward shift of the IS schedule. Conversely, if interest rates go above i_f, the capital inflows lead to appreciation, loss of competitiveness, and a decline in demand for domestic goods, shown by the leftward-shifting IS curve.

first change we look at is an exogenous rise in the world demand for our goods, or an increase in exports. The change in export demand is a real disturbance to the economy, or a disturbance that originates in the goods market.

Starting from an initial equilibrium at point E in Figure 6-10, we see that the increase in foreign demand implies an excess demand for our goods. At the initial interest rate, exchange rate, and output level, demand for our goods now exceeds the available supply. For goods market equilibrium at the initial interest rate and exchange rate, we require a higher level of output. Accordingly, the IS schedule shifts out and to the right, to IS'.

Now consider for a moment point E', at which the goods and money markets clear. Here output has increased to meet the increased demand. The rise in income has increased money demand and thus raised equilibrium interest rates. But is point E' an equilibrium? It is not, because the balance of payments is not in equilibrium. In fact, we would not reach point E' at all. The tendency for the economy to move in that direction, as we now show, will bring about an exchange rate appreciation that will take us all the way back to the initial equilibrium at E.

The Adjustment Process

Suppose, then, that the increase in foreign demand takes place and that, in response, there is a tendency for output and income to increase. The induced increase in money demand will raise interest rates and thus will bring us out of line with international interest rates. The resulting capital inflows immediately put pressure on the exchange rate. The capital inflow causes our currency to appreciate.

The exchange appreciation means, of course, that import prices fall and domestic

FIGURE 6-10

EFFECTS OF AN INCREASE IN THE DEMAND FOR EXPORTS. A rise in foreign demand for our goods, at the initial exchange rate and interest rate at point E, creates an excess demand for goods. The IS schedule shifts out to IS', and the new goods and money market equilibrium is at point E'. But at E' our interest rate exceeds that abroad. Capital will tend to flow into our country in response to the increased interest rate, and the resulting balance of payments surplus leads to currency appreciation. The appreciation means that we become less competitive. The IS schedule starts shifting back as a result of the appreciation, and the process continues until the initial equilibrium at E is reached. In the end, increased exports (or a fiscal expansion) do not change output. They simply lead to currency appreciation and thereby to an offsetting change in net exports.

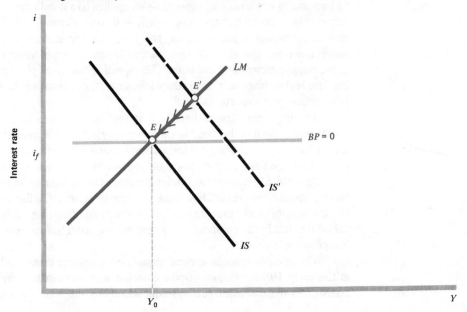

goods become relatively more expensive. Demand shifts away from domestic goods, and net exports decline. In terms of Figure 6-10, the appreciation implies that the *IS* schedule shifts back from *IS'* to the left. Next, we have to ask how far the exchange appreciation will go and to what extent it will dampen the expansionary effect of increased net exports.

The exchange rate will keep appreciating as long as our interest rate exceeds the world level. This implies that the exchange appreciation must continue until the *IS* schedule has shifted back all the way to its initial position. This adjustment is shown by the arrows along the LM schedule. Only when we return to point *E* will output and income have reached a level consistent with monetary equilibrium at the world rate of interest.

We have now shown that under conditions of perfect capital mobility, an expansion in exports has no lasting effect on equilibrium output. With perfect capital mobility the tendency for interest rates to rise, as a result of the increase in export demand, leads to currency appreciation and thus to a complete offset of the increase in exports. Once we return to point *E*, net exports are back to their initial level. The exchange rate has, of course, appreciated. Imports will increase as a consequence of the appreciation, and the initial expansion in exports is, in part, offset by the appreciation of our exchange rates.

Fiscal Policy

We can extend the usefulness of this analysis by recognizing that it is valid not only for an increase in exports. The same analysis applies to a fiscal expansion. A tax cut or an increase in government spending would lead to an expansion in demand in the same way as increased exports. Again, the tendency for interest rates to rise leads to appreciation and therefore to a fall in exports and increased imports. There is, accordingly, complete crowding out here. The crowding out takes place not, as in Chapter 5, because higher interest rates reduce investment, but because the exchange appreciation reduces net exports.

The important lesson here is that real disturbances to demand do not affect equilibrium output under flexible rates with perfect capital mobility. We can drive the lesson home by comparing a fiscal expansion under flexible rates with the results we derived for the fixed rate case. In the previous section, we showed that with a fixed exchange rate, fiscal expansion under conditions of capital mobility is highly effective in raising equilibrium output. For flexible rates, by contrast, a fiscal expansion does not change equilibrium output. Instead, it produces an offsetting exchange rate appreciation and a shift in the composition of domestic demand toward foreign goods and away from domestic goods.

This analysis helps in understanding developments in the United States economy in the early 1980s, when a fiscal expansion was accompanied by a current account deficit. Box 6-2 discusses this episode, which continues to affect the U.S. economy.

Adjustment to a Monetary Disturbance

We turn next to analysis of a monetary disturbance and show that under flexible exchange rates, an increase in the money stock leads to an increase in income and a depreciation of the exchange rate. The analysis uses Figure 6-11. We start from an initial position at point E and consider an increase in the nominal quantity of money, $\overline{M}$. Since prices are given, we have an increase in the real money stock, $\overline{M}/\overline{P}$. At E there will be an excess supply of real balances. To restore equilibrium, interest rates would have to be lower or income would have to be larger. Accordingly, the LM schedule shifts down and to the right to LM'.

We ask once again whether the economy is in equilibrium at point E'. At E',

---

FIGURE 6-11

EFFECTS OF AN INCREASE IN THE MONEY STOCK. A monetary expansion shifts the LM schedule to LM'. At point E' the goods and money markets clear, but our interest rate is below the world level. Therefore, capital will tend to flow out, the balance of payments goes into deficit, and the exchange rate depreciates. The depreciation means that we become more competitive. Net exports rise, and therefore the IS curve shifts out and to the right (not shown). The process continues until we reach point E''. Interest rates are again at the world level, and the depreciation has led to a higher level of income. Monetary policy thus works by increasing net exports.

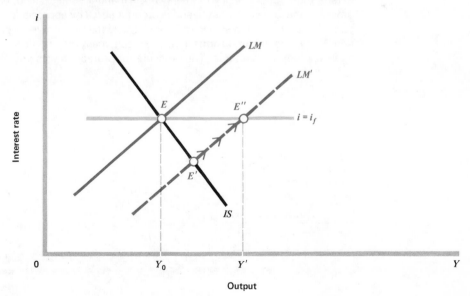

box 6-2

THE U.S. POLICY MIX, THE TWIN DEFICITS, AND THE DOLLAR IN THE 1980s

In the early 1980s the U.S. dollar, as we saw before, appreciated massively in world markets. A ready explanation is given by the behavior of fiscal policies in the United States and abroad. In the United States the budget shifted toward a large full-employment deficit. Abroad, by contrast, fiscal policies shifted toward restraint. The shift toward structural budget deficits in the United States brought with it trade deficits; far from being unrelated, these were *twin deficits*, a term coined by Martin Feldstein when he was President Reagan's chairman of the Council of Economic Advisers. There is no surprise about the effect of the combined deficits; indeed, the Mundell-Fleming model implies that, as a result, the U.S. dollar should have appreciated while the U.S. current account should have worsened. That is, of course, exactly what happened.

In addition, there was an increase in real interest rates worldwide, but particularly in the United States. This increase in the real interest rate was due to both the increase in the deficit in the United States and a tightening of monetary policy worldwide.

Table 1 shows the shifts in the full employment budget for the United States, Germany, and Japan. Figure 1 shows the impact of the fiscal policy changes on the real exchange rate and on the current account (measured as a percentage of GNP). The dollar appreciated strongly, and the external balance worsened steadily. It is interesting to note that the United States expanded strongly *despite* so large a deterioration in the external balance. The reason is that the deterioration in the current account only partly *crowded out* or offset the fiscal stimulus. The net effect of the fiscal expansion and the resulting deterioration in net exports was still an above-average recovery from the 1982 recession.

But the recovery was not shared equally by all sectors. In particular, the loss in external competitiveness was keenly felt in manufacturing. The openness of the economy, and the loss in competitiveness brought about by appreciation thus left manufacturing largely out of the strong recovery. The result was powerful pressure for protection. Many manufacturing firms and, as a result, many in Congress, called for protection against import competition. The pressure for protection was one of the reasons Con-

TABLE 1

CUMULATIVE CHANGE IN
FULL-EMPLOYMENT BUDGET
DEFICITS, 1980–1985
(percent of GNP)

U.S.	Germany	Japan
4.5	−4.2	−3.2

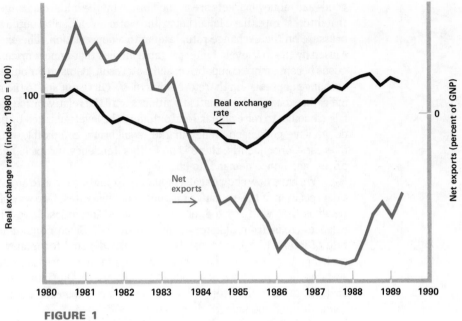

FIGURE 1

U.S. NET EXPORTS AND REAL EXCHANGE RATE, 1980–1989.

gress and the administration became more actively concerned about the need to correct the budget deficit and, with it, dollar overvaluation and excessive external deficits.

As of 1989, current account deficits were still running far above $100 billion per year. The United States was borrowing in world markets to finance its excess of spending over income. By the mid-1980s the United States had become a net debtor in world markets, and by the end of the decade U.S. net foreign liabilities amounted to about 15 percent of GNP. A discussion over whether deficits could be financed "forever" started, but for most of the decade financing seemed, if anything, to be easy for the United States to obtain, and hence there was little pressure to adjust the twin deficits.*

---

* For a discussion of the policy issues see the collection of papers "Studies in the U.S. External Imbalances," Federal Reserve Bank of New York *Quarterly Review,* Winter-Spring 1989, and Jeffrey Shafer, "What the U.S. Current Account Deficit of the 1980s Has Meant for Other OECD Countries," *OECD Economic Studies,* no.10, Spring 1988.

goods and money markets are in equilibrium (at the initial exchange rate), but it is clear that interest rates have fallen below the world level. Capital outflows will therefore put pressure on the exchange rate, leading to a depreciation. The exchange depreciation caused by the low level of interest rates implies that import prices increase, domestic goods become more competitive, and, as a result, demand for our output expands. The exchange depreciation therefore shifts the *IS* curve out and to the right. As the arrows indicate, exchange depreciation continues until the relative price of domestic goods has fallen enough to raise demand and output to the level indicated by point E''. Only at E'' do we have goods and money market equilibrium compatible with the world rate of interest. Consequently, there is no further tendency for exchange rates and relative prices, and hence demand, to change.[14]

We have now shown that a monetary expansion leads to an increase in output and a depreciation of the exchange rate under flexible rates. One way of thinking about this result is that with $\overline{P}$ fixed, an increase in $\overline{M}$ increases $\overline{M}/\overline{P}$. The demand for real balances (L) is, from Chapter 4, equal to $L(i, Y)$. Since i cannot differ from the world rate of interest, Y has to rise to equate the demand for money to the supply. The exchange depreciation raises net exports, and that increase in net exports, in turn, sustains the higher level of output and employment. One interesting implication of our analysis, then, is the proposition that monetary expansion improves the current account through the induced depreciation.

How do our results compare with those in a fixed exchange rate world? Under fixed rates, the monetary authorities cannot control the nominal money stock, and an attempt to expand money will merely lead to a reserve loss as the central bank attempts to restrain the tendency for the exchange rate to depreciate in response to declining interest rates. Under flexible rates, by contrast, the central bank does not intervene, and so the money stock increase is *not* reversed in the foreign exchange market. The depreciation and expansion in output actually do take place, given the assumed fixed prices. The fact that the central bank *can* control the money stock under flexible rates is one of the most important aspects of that exchange rate system.

Beggar-Thy-Neighbor Policy and Competitive Depreciation

We extend our analysis of the fixed price – variable employment model with a brief discussion of the international implications of exchange depreciation and changes in net exports. We showed that a monetary expansion in the home country leads to exchange depreciation, an increase in net exports, and therefore an increase in output and employment. But our increased net exports correspond to a deterioration in the trade balance abroad. The domestic depreciation shifts demand from foreign goods toward domestic goods. Abroad, output and employment decline. It is for this reason that a depreciation-induced change in the trade balance has been called a *beggar-thy-neighbor*

---

[14] In the problem set at the end of this chapter we ask you to show that the current account improves between E' and E'', even though the increased level of income increases imports.

policy — it is a way of exporting unemployment or of creating domestic employment at the expense of the rest of the world.

Recognition that exchange depreciation is mainly a way of shifting demand from one country to another, rather than changing the level of world demand, is important. It implies that exchange rate adjustment can be a useful policy when countries find themselves in different stages of a business cycle — for example, one in a boom (with overemployment) and the other in a recession. In that event, a depreciation by the country experiencing a recession would shift world demand in its direction and thus work to reduce divergences from full employment in each country.

By contrast, when countries' business cycles are highly synchronized, such as in the 1930s or in the aftermath of the oil shock of 1973, exchange rate movements will not contribute much toward worldwide full employment. The problem is that the level of total world spending is deficient or excessive, while exchange rate movements essentially affect only the allocation of a *given* world demand among countries.

Nevertheless, from the point of view of an individual country, exchange depreciation works to attract world demand and raise domestic output. If every country tried to depreciate to attract world demand, we would have *competitive depreciation* and a shifting around of world demand rather than an increase in the worldwide level of spending. And if everyone depreciated to roughly the same extent, we would end up with exchange rates about where they started. Coordinated monetary and/or fiscal policies rather than depreciations are needed to increase demand and output in each country.

6-7 SUMMARY

1. The balance of payments accounts are a record of the international transactions of the economy. The current account records trade in goods and services as well as transfer payments. The capital account records purchases and sales of assets. Any transaction that gives rise to a payment by a U.S. resident is a deficit item for the United States.
2. The overall balance of payments surplus is the sum of the current and capital accounts surpluses. If the overall balance is in deficit, we have to make more payments to foreigners than they make to us. The foreign currency for making these payments is supplied by central banks.
3. Under fixed exchange rates, the central bank holds constant the price of foreign currencies in terms of the domestic currency. It does this by buying and selling foreign exchange at the fixed exchange rate. For that purpose, it has to keep reserves of foreign currency.
4. Under floating or flexible exchange rates, the exchange rate may change from moment to moment. In a system of clean floating, the exchange rate is determined by supply and demand without central bank intervention. Under dirty floating, the central bank intervenes by buying and selling foreign exchange in an attempt to influence the exchange rate.

5. The introduction of trade in goods means that some of the demand for our output comes from abroad and that some spending by our residents is on foreign goods. The demand for our goods depends on the real exchange rate as well as the levels of income at home and abroad. A real depreciation or increase in foreign income increases net exports and shifts the *IS* curve out to the right. There is equilibrium in the goods market when the demand for domestically produced goods is equal to the output of those goods.

6. The introduction of capital flows points to the effects of monetary and fiscal policy on the balance of payments through interest rate effects on capital flows. An increase in the domestic interest rate relative to the world interest rate leads to a capital inflow that can finance a current account deficit.

7. A country facing the policy dilemma that it wants to expand output but cannot allow the balance of payments to deteriorate can handle that problem by combining restrictive monetary policy, so as to raise the interest rate and attract foreign capital, with fiscal expansion, so as to increase domestic employment.

8. When capital mobility is perfect, interest rates in the home country cannot diverge from those abroad. This has major implications for the effects of monetary and fiscal policy under fixed and floating exchange rates. These effects are summarized in Table 6-7.

9. Under fixed exchange rates and perfect capital mobility, monetary policy is powerless to affect output. Any attempt to reduce the domestic interest rate by increasing the money stock would lead to a huge outflow of capital, tending to cause a depreciation which the central bank would then have to offset by buying domestic money in exchange for foreign money. This reduces the domestic money stock until it returns to its original level. Under fixed exchange rates with capital mobility, the central bank cannot run an independent monetary policy.

10. Fiscal policy is highly effective under fixed exchange rates with complete capital mobility. A fiscal expansion tends to raise the interest rate, thereby leading the central bank to increase the money stock to maintain the exchange rate constant, reinforcing the expansionary fiscal effect.

TABLE 6-7

THE EFFECTS OF MONETARY AND FISCAL POLICY UNDER PERFECT CAPITAL MOBILITY

	Fixed rates	Flexible rates
Monetary expansion	No output change; reserve losses equal to money increase	Output expansion; trade balance improves; exchange depreciation
Fiscal expansion	Output expansion; trade balance worsens	No output change; reduced net exports; exchange appreciation

11. Under floating rates, monetary policy is highly effective and fiscal policy is ineffective in changing output. A monetary expansion leads to depreciation, increased exports, and increased output. Fiscal expansion, however, causes an appreciation and completely crowds out net exports.

12. If an economy with floating rates finds itself with unemployment, the central bank can intervene to depreciate the exchange rate and increase net exports and thus aggregate demand. Such policies are known as beggar-thy-neighbor policies because the increase in demand for domestic output comes at the expense of demand for foreign output.

KEY TERMS

Exchange rate
Current account
Capital account
Balance of payments
Fixed exchange rate
Floating exchange rate
Clean floating
Intervention
Dirty floating

Nominal and real exchange rate
Depreciation
Appreciation
Repercussion effects
Capital mobility
Internal and external balance
Mundell-Fleming model
Beggar-thy-neighbor policy

PROBLEMS

1. This problem formalizes some of the questions about income and trade balance determination in the open economy. (Before doing it, read the appendix to this chapter.) We assume, as a simplification, that the interest rate is given and equal to $i = i_0$. We assume aggregate spending by domestic residents is

$$A = \overline{A} + cY - bi$$

and net exports, NX, are given by

$$NX = X - Q$$

Import spending is given by

$$Q = \overline{Q} + mY$$

where $\overline{Q}$ is autonomous import spending. Exports are given and are equal to

$$X = \overline{X}$$

(a) What is the total demand for domestic goods? The balance of trade?
(b) What is the equilibrium level of income?

(c) What is the balance of trade at that equilibrium level of income?

(d) What is the effect of an increase in exports on the equilibrium level of income? What is the multiplier?

(e) What is the effect of increased exports on the trade balance?

2. Suppose that, in problem 1,

$$\bar{A} = 400 \quad c = 0.8 \quad b = 30 \quad i_0 = 5 \text{ (percent)} \quad \bar{Q} = 0 \quad m = 0.2 \quad X = 250$$

(a) Calculate the equilibrium level of income.

(b) Calculate the balance of trade.

(c) Calculate the open economy multiplier, that is, the effect of an increase in $\bar{A}$ on equilibrium output. (To answer this question, you may want to use the appendix to this chapter.)

(d) Assume there is a reduction in export demand of $\Delta X = 1$ (billion). By how much does income change? By how much does the trade balance worsen?

(e) How much does a one percentage point increase in the interest rate (from 5 percent to 6 percent) improve the trade balance? Explain why the trade balance improves when the interest rate rises.

(f) What policies can the country pursue to offset the impact of reduced exports on domestic income and employment as well as the trade balance?

3. It is sometimes said that a central bank is a necessary condition for a balance of payments deficit. What is the explanation for this argument?

4. Consider a country that is in a position of full employment and balanced trade. The exchange rate is fixed and capital is not mobile. Which of the following types of disturbance can be remedied with standard aggregate demand tools of stabilization? Indicate in each case the impact on external and internal balance as well as the appropriate policy response.

(a) A loss of export markets

(b) A reduction in saving and a corresponding increase in demand for domestic goods

(c) An increase in government spending

(d) A shift in demand from imports to domestic goods

(e) A reduction in imports with a corresponding increase in saving.

5. (a) Use the formula $1/(m + s)$ for the foreign trade multiplier (see the appendix) to discuss the impact on the trade balance of an increase in autonomous domestic spending.

(b) Comment on the proposition that the more open the economy, the smaller the domestic income expansion.

6. This question is concerned with the repercussion effects of a domestic expansion once we recognize that, as a consequence, output abroad will expand. Suppose that at home there is an increase in autonomous spending $\Delta \bar{A}$ that falls entirely on domestic goods. (Assume constant interest rates throughout this problem.)

(a) What is the resulting effect on income, disregarding repercussion effects? What is the impact on our imports? Denote the increase in imports by ΔQ.

(b) Using the result for the increase in imports, we now ask what happens abroad. Our increase in imports appears to foreign countries as an increase in their exports and therefore as an increase in demand for their goods. In response, their output expands. Assuming the foreign marginal propensity to save is s^* and the foreign propensity to import is m^*, by how much will a foreign country's income expand as a result of an increase in its exports?

(c) Now combine the pieces by writing the familiar equation for equilibrium in the domestic goods market: change in supply, ΔY, equals the total change in demand, $\Delta \overline{A} + \Delta X - m\Delta Y + (1 - s)\Delta Y$, or

$$\Delta Y = \frac{\Delta \overline{A} + \Delta X}{s + m}$$

Noting that our increase in exports, ΔX, is equal to foreigners' increase in imports, we can replace ΔX with the answer to part (b) above to obtain a general expression for the multiplier with repercussions.

(d) Substitute your answer to part (b) in the formula for the change in our exports, $\Delta X = m^* \Delta Y^*$.

(e) Calculate the complete change in our income, including repercussion effects. Now compare your result with the case in which repercussion effects are omitted. What difference do repercussion effects make? Is our income expansion larger or smaller with repercussion effects?

(f) Consider the trade balance effect of a domestic expansion with and without repercussion effects. Is the trade deficit larger or smaller once repercussion effects are taken into account?

7. Assume that capital is perfectly mobile, the price level is fixed, and the exchange rate is flexible. Now let the government increase purchases. Explain first why the equilibrium levels of output and the interest rate are unaffected. Then show whether the current account improves or worsens as a result of the increased government purchases of goods and services.

8. Assume that there is perfect mobility of capital. How does the imposition of a tariff affect the exchange rate, output, and the current account? (*Hint:* Given the exchange rate, the tariff reduces our demand for imports.)

9. Explain how and why monetary policy retains its effectiveness when there is perfect mobility of capital.

10. Show graphically how fiscal policy works with capital mobility and fixed exchange rates.

11. Was U.S. policy from 1980 to 1985 consistent with a beggar-thy-neighbor approach to trade policy?

APPENDIX

In this appendix we set out the open economy *IS-LM* model. We start by assuming a simple form for the net export equation:

$$NX = \overline{X} - mY + vR \qquad R = eP_f/P \tag{A1}$$

where $\overline{X}$ is a constant representing all other influences including the role of foreign income. Note that because the coefficient of the real exchange rate, v, is positive, a real depreciation or a rise in R improves the trade balance. The larger v is, the more responsive is the trade balance to the real exchange rate. Note, too, the influence of home income on the trade balance: A rise in income raises imports and hence worsens the trade balance. The coefficient m denotes the marginal propensity to import. It indicates the rise in imports per dollar increase in income.

With this formulation, equilibrium in the goods market becomes

IS curve:
$$Y = \overline{A} + NX = \overline{A} + cY - bi + \overline{X} - mY + vR \tag{A2}$$

or
$$Y = \frac{\overline{A} - bi + \overline{X} + vR}{1 - c + m} \tag{A2a}$$

Now note that the marginal propensity to consume, c, plus the marginal propensity to save, s, must be equal to unity: $1 = c + s$. Hence, substituting $1 - c = s$ into (A2a) we have

$$Y = \frac{\overline{A} - bi + \overline{X} + vR}{s + m} \tag{A2b}$$

We refer to the term $1/(s + m)$ as the simple open economy multiplier. It indicates the impact on home income, given interest rates, foreign income, and the real exchange rate, of an increase in domestic autonomous spending, $\Delta \overline{A}$. Equation (A2b) also shows the impact of real depreciation on home income: A rise in the real exchange rate, R, raises home income by $v/(s + m)$. The rise is larger the more responsive the trade balance is to the real exchange rate and the larger the simple open economy multiplier.

Consider next how the open economy model works under flexible exchange rates and perfect capital mobility. We simply add the *LM* schedule and the assumption $i = i_f$.

$$\overline{M}/\overline{P} = kY - hi_f \tag{A3}$$

In (A3) we have already made the substitution $i = i_f$.

Thus we can determine from (A3) that the equilibrium level of income is

$$Y = \left(\frac{1}{k} \frac{\overline{M}}{\overline{P}} + hi_f \right) \tag{A4}$$

The home real money supply and the world interest rate thus determine the equilibrium level of income. The exchange rate adjusts to clear the goods market. Equating equations (A2b) and (A4) allows us to solve for the equilibrium real exchange rate:

$$R = \frac{s + m}{kv} \frac{\overline{M}}{\overline{P}} + \frac{[(s + m)h + kb]i_f}{kv} - \frac{\overline{A} + \overline{X}}{v} \tag{A5}$$

Thus a fiscal expansion or a rise in $\overline{X}$ leads to real appreciation, while a monetary expansion leads to real depreciation.

DATA APPENDIX

In the following table, exports and imports in billions of constant 1982 dollars are given by $EX82$ and $IM82$ and in billions of current dollars by EX and IM. The current account, CA, is in billions of current dollars. The real exchange rate (R) is an index, with 1982 = 100.

	EX82	IM82	EX	IM	CA	R
1950	59.2	54.6	14.4	12.3	NA	NA
1951	72.0	57.4	19.8	15.3	NA	NA
1952	70.2	63.3	19.2	16.0	475	NA
1953	66.9	69.6	18.1	16.8	423	NA
1954	70.0	67.5	18.8	16.2	339	NA
1955	76.9	76.9	21.1	18.1	−440	NA
1956	87.9	83.6	25.2	19.9	585	NA
1957	94.9	87.9	28.2	20.9	605	NA
1958	82.4	92.8	24.4	21.1	−923	102.4
1959	83.8	101.9	25.0	23.5	−370	99.7
1960	98.4	102.4	29.9	24.0	−723	100.3
1961	100.7	103.4	31.8	23.9	−11	100.3
1962	106.9	114.4	33.8	26.2	314	100.0
1963	114.7	116.6	35.6	27.5	311	100.4
1964	128.8	122.9	40.5	29.6	−1,067	102.3
1965	132.0	134.7	43.0	33.2	−219	103.2
1966	138.4	152.1	46.6	39.1	226	102.5
1967	143.6	160.5	49.5	42.1	−1,102	102.1
1968	155.7	185.4	54.8	49.3	−1,183	100.7
1969	165.0	199.8	60.4	54.7	1,212	99.4
1970	178.3	208.3	68.9	60.5	1,985	101.0
1971	179.2	218.9	72.4	66.1	2,719	104.0
1972	195.2	244.6	81.4	78.2	508	110.3
1973	242.2	273.8	114.1	97.4	−2,419	117.2
1974	269.2	268.4	151.5	135.2	−7,481	116.7
1975	259.7	240.8	161.3	130.3	−3,417	117.0
1976	274.4	285.4	177.8	158.9	−1,683	113.0
1977	281.6	317.1	191.6	189.7	−209	116.2
1978	312.5	339.3	227.5	223.4	1,858	125.4
1979	356.6	353.1	291.2	272.5	−875	122.9
1980	389.0	332.0	351.0	318.9	7,520	121.6
1981	392.7	343.4	382.8	348.9	14,500	108.8
1982	362.0	335.6	361.9	335.6	8,041	100.0
1983	348.1	368.0	352.5	358.6	5,831	99.1
1984	371.8	455.8	383.5	442.4	2,608	93.8
1985	367.2	471.4	370.9	448.8	4,765	92.5
1986	378.4	515.9	378.4	482.8	158	112.8
1987	427.8	556.7	428.0	551.1	−4,913	126.0
1988	504.8	605.0	519.8	614.4	−26,089	131.6

SOURCE: DRI/McGraw-Hill and International Monetary Fund.

7

AGGREGATE SUPPLY AND DEMAND: AN INTRODUCTION

S o far, our analysis has assumed that the price level is fixed. We studied the impacts of changes in the money supply, or of taxes, or of government spending, assuming that whatever amount of goods was demanded would be supplied, *at the existing price level*.

To put the same point in different words, we have not yet analyzed *inflation*. But, of course, inflation is one of the major concerns of citizens, policy makers, and macroeconomists. The time has therefore come to bring the price level and the inflation rate — the rate of change of the price level — into the center of our analysis of the economy. We have to study the determination of both the level of output — on which we have concentrated thus far — and the price level.

Figure 7-1 shows the model of *aggregate demand and supply* that we shall use to study the joint determination of the price level and the level of output. The aggregate demand curve, *AD*, which is downward-sloping, is derived from the *IS-LM* model. We introduce and develop the aggregate demand curve in this chapter, and show why it slopes downward and what causes it to shift. The aggregate supply curve, *AS*, will also be introduced in this chapter and developed further in Chapter 13. The intersection of the *AD* and *AS* schedules at E determines the equilibrium level of output, Y_0, and the equilibrium price level, P_0. Shifts in either schedule cause the price level and the level of output to change.

The aggregate demand-supply model is the basic macroeconomic model for studying output and price level determination — just as, in microeconomics, demand and supply curves are the essential tools for studying output and price determination in a single market. But the aggregate demand and supply curves are not as simple as the

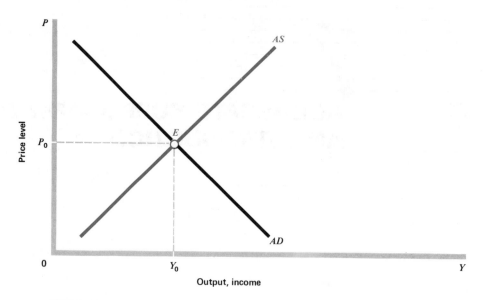

FIGURE 7-1

AGGREGATE SUPPLY AND DEMAND. The diagram shows the complete
model of aggregate demand and supply that is used to explain the joint
determination of the levels of output and prices. The aggregate demand
curve, *AD*, is based on the *IS-LM* model studied in earlier chapters. The
aggregate supply curve, *AS*, is developed in this chapter and Chapter
13. Their intersection at point *E* determines the level of output, Y_0, and
the price level, P_0.

microeconomic demand and supply curves. There is more going on in the background
of the aggregate curves than there is in that of the microeconomic curves.[1]

The aggregate demand-supply model can be used to identify major schools of
thought in macroeconomics: strict monetarists, who believe that the quantity of money
tightly governs the behavior of the price level, and old-fashioned Keynesians, who
believe that prices do not play a significant role in the short-run analysis of the business
cycle. Of course, these are extreme positions or near caricatures. But against these
polar extremes we can place in clear perspective the much more subtle and sophisticated views of modern Keynesians and modern monetarists. These distinctions and
their policy implications are the subject of much of macroeconomic discussion, and they
will occupy us throughout this book.

---

[1] The aggregate demand curve has sometimes been referred to as the *macroeconomic demand curve*, both
to emphasize that it is different from a regular demand curve in microeconomics and to distinguish it from the
aggregate demand schedule in Chap. 3. We stay with the same name *AD* here after warning that the present *AD* schedule represents a considerable extension of that in Chap. 3, since the schedule makes interest
rates endogenous along the curve.

7-1 INTRODUCING AGGREGATE DEMAND AND SUPPLY

Before we go deeply into the factors underlying the aggregate demand and supply curves, we show how the curves will be used. Suppose that the money supply is increased. What effects will that have on the price level and output? In particular, does an increase in the money supply cause the price level to rise, thus producing inflation? Or does the level of output rise, as it did in the analysis of earlier chapters? Or do both output and the price level rise?

Figure 7-2 shows that an increase in the money supply shifts the aggregate demand curve, AD, to the right, to AD'. We see later in this chapter why that should be so. The shift of the aggregate demand curve moves the equilibrium of the economy from E to E'. The price level rises from P_0 to P', and the level of output from Y_0 to Y'. Thus an increase in the money stock causes both the level of output and the price level to rise.

The Slope of the Aggregate Supply Curve

What determines how much the price level rises and how much output increases? Looking at Figure 7-3 a, we see that if the aggregate supply curve is relatively flat, a

FIGURE 7-2

THE EFFECTS OF AN INCREASE IN THE NOMINAL MONEY STOCK. An increase in the money stock shifts the aggregate demand curve from AD to AD'. The equilibrium moves from E to E', resulting in higher levels of both prices and output. Thus an increase in the money stock in part results in higher prices rather than entirely in higher output

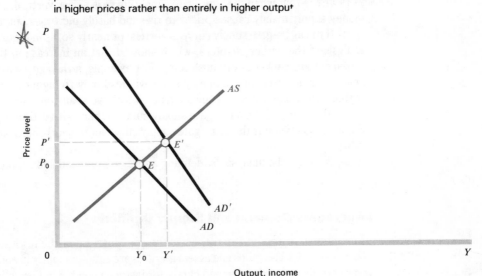

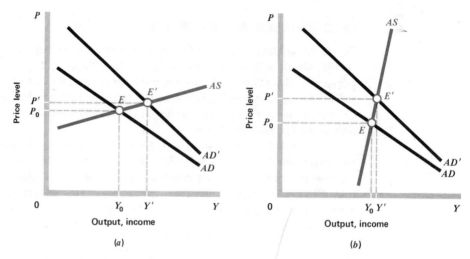

FIGURE 7-3

THE INTERACTION OF AGGREGATE SUPPLY AND DEMAND. The effects of a
shift in the aggregate demand curve from *AD* to *AD'* depend on the
slope of the aggregate supply curve. If the *AS* curve is relatively flat, as
in panel (*a*), the shift in the aggregate demand curve results mainly in an
increase in output. By contrast, in panel (*b*), the shift in the aggregate
demand curve results almost entirely in an increase in the price level and
very little in an increase in output.

shift in the *AD* curve raises output a lot and prices very little. By contrast, in Figure
7-3*b* we see that when the aggregate supply curve is nearly vertical, an increase in the
money supply mainly causes prices to rise and hardly increases output at all.

If the aggregate supply curve is vertical or nearly so, as in Figure 7-3*b*, then the
analysis of the earlier chapters, which showed that an increase in the money stock
raised output, could be very misleading. For example, if the aggregate supply curve is
vertical, an increase in the money stock will lead only to higher prices, not to more
output. Thus one of the key questions on which we shall concentrate is what determines the shape of the aggregate supply curve. When is it vertical or nearly so, as in
Figure 7-3*b*? When is the aggregate supply curve more nearly horizontal, as in Figure
7-3*a*?

We start the analysis by defining aggregate demand and supply.

Aggregate Demand and Supply Defined

The *aggregate demand curve* shows the combinations of the price level and level of
output at which the goods and assets markets are simultaneously in equilibrium. At any
point on the aggregate demand curve, for instance point *B* in Figure 7-4, we see that

for the given price level, P_B, the level of output at which the goods and assets markets are in equilibrium is Y_B.

We can already give a preliminary explanation of why the aggregate demand curve slopes downward. Suppose that the goods and assets markets are in equilibrium at a level of output like Y_B with given price level P_B. Now suppose the price level falls. With a given nominal stock of money, a fall in the price level creates an increase in the quantity of *real balances*. Recall that an increase in the quantity of real balances reduces interest rates, increases investment demand, and therefore increases aggregate spending. Accordingly, when the price level falls, the equilibrium level of spending rises; therefore the AD curve slopes down. We go into the details below.

We can also see, from the definition of the aggregate demand curve, why the analysis of the previous chapters is not at all wasted. The aggregate demand curve describes the joint equilibrium of the goods and assets markets. That is precisely what the *IS-LM* analysis describes. Thus the material we studied in earlier chapters is an essential part of the aggregate demand and supply model we shall use to analyze the simultaneous determination of the levels of output and prices.

FIGURE 7-4

AGGREGATE DEMAND AND SUPPLY CURVES DEFINED. At any point on the aggregate demand curve, such as point B, both the goods and assets markets are in equilibrium. This is the equilibrium given by the intersection of the *IS* and *LM* curves, as described in Chapter 4. For instance, with price level P_B, the level of output at which both goods and assets markets are in equilibrium is Y_B. The aggregate supply curve, AS, describes the relation between the price level and the amount of output firms wish to supply. For instance, at price level P_C, firms want to supply output Y_C.

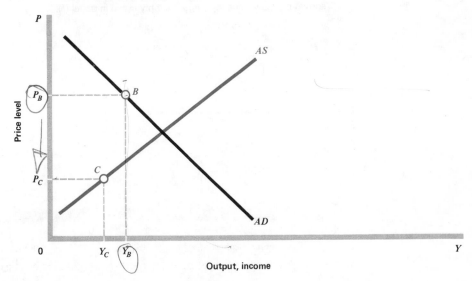

The *aggregate supply curve* describes the combinations of output and the price level at which firms are willing, at the given price level, to supply the given quantity of output. For instance, at point C in Figure 7-4, with price level P_C, firms are willing to supply output equal to Y_C. The amount of output firms are willing to supply depends on the prices they receive for their goods and the amounts they have to pay for labor and other factors of production. *Accordingly, the aggregate supply curve reflects conditions in the factor markets—especially the labor market—as well as the goods markets.*

7-2 AGGREGATE SUPPLY: TWO SPECIAL CASES

In this chapter we concentrate on two special cases in discussing aggregate supply. The first, the *Keynesian case* shown in Figure 7-5 *a*, is a horizontal aggregate supply curve. The *Keynesian aggregate supply curve* is horizontal, indicating that firms will supply whatever amount of goods is demanded at the existing price level.

The idea underlying the Keynesian aggregate supply curve is that because there

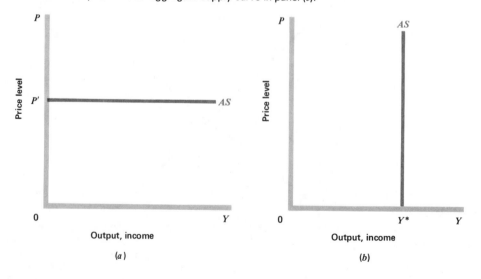

FIGURE 7-5

KEYNESIAN AND CLASSICAL SUPPLY FUNCTIONS. The Keynesian aggregate supply curve is horizontal, implying that any amount of output will be supplied at the existing price level. This is shown in panel (*a*), where the AS curve is horizontal at price level P'. The classical supply function is based on the assumption that there is always full employment of labor, and thus that output is always at the level corresponding to full employment of labor, Y^*, and *independent of the price level*. This is shown by the vertical aggregate supply curve in panel (*b*).

is unemployment, firms can obtain as much labor as they want at the current wage. Their average costs of production therefore are assumed not to change as their output levels change.[2] They are accordingly willing to supply as much as is demanded at the existing price level.

The Classical Supply Curve

Figure 7-5 *b* shows the opposite extreme, a vertical supply curve. In the *classical case,* the *aggregate supply curve* is vertical, indicating that the same amount of goods will be supplied whatever the price level.

The classical supply curve is based on the assumption that the labor market is always in equilibrium with full employment of the labor force. If the entire labor force is being employed, then output cannot be raised above its current level even if the price level rises. There is no more labor available to produce any extra output. Thus the aggregate supply curve will be vertical at a level of output corresponding to full employment of the labor force, Y^* in Figure 7-5 *b*.

The labor market equilibrium underlying the vertical schedule is assumed to be maintained by speedy adjustments of the nominal wage. For example, suppose that the economy is in equilibrium and the aggregate demand curve shifts to the right, as in Figure 7-2. At the existing price level, the quantity of goods demanded increases. Now firms try to obtain more labor. Each firm attempts to hire more labor, offering to pay higher wages if necessary. But there is no more labor available in the economy, and so firms are unable to obtain more workers. Instead, in competing against each other for workers, they merely bid up wages. Because wages are higher, the prices the firms charge for their output will also be higher. But output will be unchanged.[3]

The difference between the classical and Keynesian aggregate supply curves is that the classical supply curve is based on the belief that the labor market works smoothly, always maintaining full employment of the labor force. Movements in the wage are the mechanism through which full employment is maintained. The Keynesian aggregate supply curve is instead based on the assumption that the wage does not change much or at all when there is unemployment, and thus that unemployment can continue for some time.

These two cases — the classical, representing continuing labor market equilibrium, and the Keynesian, assuming wages do not adjust — are the two extremes. In

---

[2] The supply curve described here as Keynesian is not exactly the supply curve implied by Keynes himself in his classic *General Theory*. It is, however, the supply curve that is consistent with the use of the *IS-LM* model (as in Chap. 4), which was often used by Keynesians to describe the determination of output. There is often some difference between the views of Keynes in the *General Theory* and the simpler theories of some succeeding Keynesians. It is almost always the case that original sources are more subtle than the popular versions based on them.

[3] The adjustment described here assumes that there is a fixed supply of labor. However, *provided wages are fully flexible* the classical supply curve applies also when labor supply increases with the real wage. We will examine this case in Chap. 13.

Chapter 13 we develop the theory of aggregate supply and show why the aggregate supply curve is in practice positively sloped — lying between the Keynesian and classical cases.

7-3 THE AGGREGATE DEMAND SCHEDULE

The aggregate demand curve, or schedule, shows, for each price level, the level of output at which the goods and assets markets are simultaneously in equilibrium. At any given price level, we use the *IS-LM* model to determine the level of output at which the goods and assets markets are in equilibrium.

In the top panel of Figure 7-6 we show the *IS-LM* model. The position of the *IS* curve depends on fiscal policy. The *LM* schedule is drawn for a given nominal money stock, $\overline{M}$, and a given price level, P_0, and thus for a given real money stock $\overline{M}/P_0$. The equilibrium interest rate is i_0, and the equilibrium level of income and spending is Y_0.

A Change in the Price Level

Consider the effect of a fall in the price level from P_0 to P'. This reduction in the price level increases the real money stock from $\overline{M}/P_0$ to $\overline{M}/P'$. To clear the money market with an increased real money stock, either interest rates must fall, inducing the public to hold more cash balances, or output must rise, thus increasing the transactions demand for money.

Accordingly, the *LM* curve shifts downward and to the right, to *LM'*. The new equilibrium is shown at point E', where once again both the money market clears — because we are on the *LM* curve — and the goods market clears — because we are on the *IS* curve. The new equilibrium level of output is Y', corresponding to the lower price level P'. Thus a reduction in the price level, *given the nominal quantity of money,* results in an increase in equilibrium income and spending.

The derivation of the *AD* schedule can be seen in the lower panel of Figure 7-6. The economy is initially in equilibrium at points E in both panels. The equilibrium interest rate is i_0, the level of output is Y_0, and the corresponding price level is P_0. Now the price level drops to P'. In the upper panel, the equilibrium moves to E' as a result of the shift of the *LM* curve to *LM'*. Corresponding to point E' in the upper panel is point E' in the lower panel, at price level P' and the level of income and output Y'.

Thus both E and E' in the lower panel are points on the *AD* schedule. We could now consider all possible price levels and the corresponding levels of real balances. For each level of real balances there is a different *LM* curve in the upper panel. Corresponding to each *LM* curve is an equilibrium level of income, which would be recorded in the lower panel at the price level that results in the *LM* curve in the upper panel. Connecting all these points gives us a downward-sloping aggregate demand curve, *AD*, as shown in Figure 7-6.

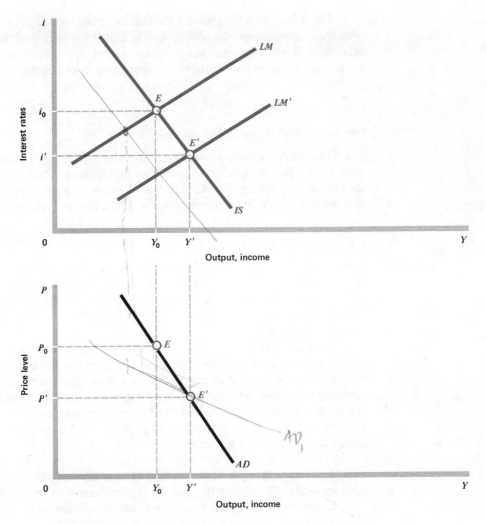

FIGURE 7-6

DERIVATION OF THE AGGREGATE DEMAND SCHEDULE. The upper panel
shows the *IS* schedule and the initial *LM* schedule drawn for the real
money stock, $\overline{M}/P_0$. Equilibrium is at point *E*. In the lower panel we
record that at a price level P_0 the equilibrium level of income and
spending is Y_0. This is shown by point *E*. At a lower level of prices,
say, P', the real money stock is $\overline{M}/P'$, and therefore the *LM* schedule
shifts to *LM'*. Equilibrium income now is at Y'. Again, in the lower
panel we show at point *E'* the combination of the price level, P', and
the corresponding equilibrium level of income and spending, Y'.
Considering different levels of prices and connecting the resulting
points such as *E* and *E'*, we derive the aggregate demand schedule,
AD. The schedule shows the equilibrium level of spending at each level
of prices, given the nominal money stock and fiscal policy.

The *AD* curve is downward-sloped because there is a definite relation between equilibrium spending and the price level: The higher the price level, the lower are real balances and hence the lower the equilibrium level of spending and output. Box 7-1 sets out this derivation of the aggregate demand curve more formally.

Properties of the *AD* Schedule

The *AD* schedule shows how the level of real spending changes with the level of prices, given fiscal policy, the quantity of money, and autonomous private spending. What are the precise properties of the *AD* schedule? We start with the slope, which tells us by how much real spending changes in response to a change in the level of prices.

THE SLOPE OF THE *AD* SCHEDULE

In Figure 7-6 we derived the *AD* schedule by considering the effect of changes in the price level, and hence in real balances, on the *LM* schedule and hence on equilibrium income and spending. The slope of the *AD* curve therefore reflects the extent to which a change in real balances changes the equilibrium level of spending, taking both assets and goods markets into account.

But we have already examined the effects of a change in the stock of real balances on the level of output that equilibrates the goods and assets markets. In Chapters 4 and 5 we showed the effect of an increase in the nominal stock of money on equilibrium spending and output, with the price level given. Now we ask, What is the effect of a change in real balances due to lower prices, given nominal money?

In discussing monetary policy in Chapters 4 and 5 we showed the following results using the *IS-LM* schedules:

- An increase in real balances leads to a larger increase in equilibrium income and spending, the smaller the interest responsiveness of money demand and the higher the interest responsiveness of investment demand.

- An increase in real balances leads to a larger increase in equilibrium income and spending, the larger the multiplier and the smaller the income response of money demand.

Because the slope of the AD curve is determined by the effect of a change in real balances on equilibrium spending and output, the same factors that determine the effects of a change in the stock of money on equilibrium output and spending also determine the slope of the AD curve. If a given change in real balances has a large impact on equilibrium spending, then the *AD* curve will be very flat — because a small change in the price level creates a large change in equilibrium spending. But if a given change in real balances has a small effect on equilibrium spending and output, then the *AD* curve will be steep: in that case it takes a large change in the price level to create a small change in spending and output.

Accordingly, we see that

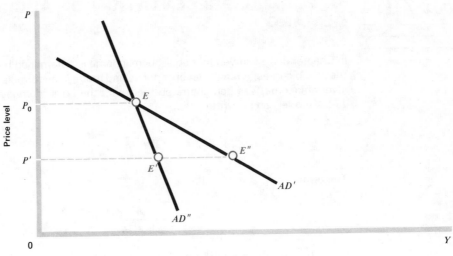

FIGURE 7-7

THE SLOPE OF THE AD SCHEDULE. The diagram shows two possible AD
schedules. Along AD'' a change in prices from P_0 to P' has a smaller
effect on spending than along AD'. The former corresponds to the case
in which changes in real balances have little impact on equilibrium
income and spending; the latter, to the case in which real balance
changes exert significant effects.

1. The AD curve is flatter (*a*) the smaller the interest responsiveness of the
   demand for money, and (*b*) the larger the interest responsiveness of investment
   demand.
2. The AD curve is flatter (*a*) the larger the multiplier, and (*b*) the smaller the
   income responsiveness of the demand for money.

To fix ideas further, it is useful to think for a moment about the AD schedule in
terms of the extreme classical and liquidity trap cases that we learned about in Chapter
4. In the classical case, in which money demand is entirely unresponsive to interest
rates and the LM curve is vertical, changes in real balances have a big effect on income
and spending. In Figure 7-7 that case corresponds to a very flat AD schedule, such as
AD', as we should expect based on point 1 *a* above. Conversely, in the liquidity trap
case, where the public is willing to hold any amount of real balances at unchanged
interest rates, a fall in prices and a rise in the real money stock have very little effect on
income and spending.[4] In Figure 7-7 that would correspond to an almost vertical AD

---

[4] The reason a reduction in prices increases output in this case is the *real balance effect:* With lower prices,
the value of real balances held by the public is higher, their wealth is accordingly higher, and therefore their
consumption spending and output are higher. The real balance effect is central to monetary theory as
developed in the classical treatise by Don Patinkin, *Money, Interest, and Prices* (New York: Harper &
Row, 1965).

box 7-1

A FORMAL PRESENTATION OF AGGREGATE DEMAND

In Chapter 5 we showed that equilibrium income is determined by the intersection of the *IS-LM* curves, *given* the level of prices and money and formulas for the equilibrium level of income. We demonstrated there that the equilibrium level of income in the *IS-LM* model can be written as

$$Y = \gamma \overline{A} + \beta \frac{\overline{M}}{P}$$

(B1)

The terms

$$\gamma = \frac{\overline{\alpha}h}{h + k\overline{\alpha}b} \qquad \beta = \gamma \frac{b}{h}$$

are constants that depend on all the parameters. These "multipliers" represent a convenient shorthand notation for all the channels through which the impact of changes in autonomous spending or real balances affect equilibrium income. We remember that γ is interpreted as the government spending multiplier when interest rates are endogenous. The coefficient β is the multiplier for changes in the *real* money stock.

The key point in understanding the *AD* curve is to recognize that it is nothing more than the intersections of *IS-LM* curves for different price levels—which is how we derived it in Figure 7-6. Accordingly equation (B1) is the equation that identifies the *AD* schedule. (B1) shows the equilibrium price level associated with each level of prices, *given* exogenous spending, $\overline{A}$, and the *nominal* quantity of money, $\overline{M}$. We can focus more explicitly on the price level by simply solving (B1) for the price level. Rearranging the terms of the resulting equation we have

$$P = \beta \frac{\overline{M}}{Y - \gamma \overline{A}}$$

(B2)

In this convenient form we immediately recognize that the *AD* schedule is drawn for a given level of nominal money and exogenous spending $\overline{A}$. We also note that, given output and exogenous spending, prices are proportionate to the money stock. Thus changes in $\overline{M}$ translate into equiproportionate changes in P. We return to this point later in discussing monetarism.

This handy formula for the *AD* schedule makes it easier to consider the factors that determine the position of the *AD* curve. ∎

curve, as suggested again by point 1*a* above. A vertical *AD* curve means that the planned level of spending is unresponsive to the price level.

You should now experiment with alternative *IS* and *LM* schedules to see how the effects of a change in the price level depend on the slopes of the *IS* and *LM* curves and the factors underlying those slopes. In doing so you will confirm the points summarized above and implied by the equations in Box 7-1. In problem 4 at the end of the chapter, we ask you to demonstrate these links.

THE EFFECT OF A FISCAL EXPANSION

We noted above that the same factors that determine the positions of the *IS* and *LM* schedules also determine the position of the *AD* curve. We now show how changes in fiscal and monetary policy shift the *AD* curve, starting with a fiscal expansion.

In the upper panel of Figure 7-8 the initial *LM* and *IS* schedules correspond to a given nominal quantity of money and the price level P_0. Equilibrium is obtained at point *E*, and there is a corresponding point on the *AD* schedule in the lower panel.

Now the government increases the level of spending, say on defense. As a consequence, the *IS* schedule shifts outward and to the right. At the initial price level there is a new equilibrium at point *E'* with higher interest rates and a higher level of income and spending. Thus at the initial level of prices, P_0, equilibrium income and spending are now higher. We show this by plotting point *E'* in the lower panel. Point *E'* is a point on the new schedule *AD'* reflecting the effect of higher government spending.

Of course, we could have started with any other point on the original *AD* curve, and we would then have shown in the lower panel how the rise in government spending leads to a higher equilibrium level of output at each price level. In that way we trace out the entire *AD'* schedule, which lies to the right of *AD*.

In fact, we can say more: At each level of prices, and hence of real balances, the *AD* schedule shifts to the right by an amount indicated by the fiscal policy multiplier developed in Chapter 5. As we saw there, a fiscal expansion leads to a higher level of income and spending, the larger the interest responsiveness of money demand, the smaller the interest responsiveness of aggregate demand, and the larger the marginal propensity to consume.

Thus if the fiscal policy multiplier derived in Chapter 5 was, for example, 1.5, then a $1 (billion) increase in government spending would increase equilibrium income and spending by $1.5 (billion), at the given price level. In response to any change in government spending, the *AD* schedule would shift to the right by 1.5 times the increase in $\overline{G}$.[5]

THE EFFECT OF A MONETARY EXPANSION ON THE *AD* SCHEDULE

An increase in the nominal money stock implies a higher real money stock at each level of prices. In the assets markets interest rates decline to induce the public to hold higher real balances. That decline in interest rates, in turn, stimulates aggregate

---

[5] In Chap. 5 and Box 7-1 we show that the fiscal policy multiplier is given by the expression $\gamma = h\overline{\alpha}/(h + kb\overline{\alpha})$, where *h* is the interest responsiveness of money demand, $\overline{\alpha}$ the simple Keynesian multiplier, *k* the income response of money demand, and *b* the interest response of investment demand.

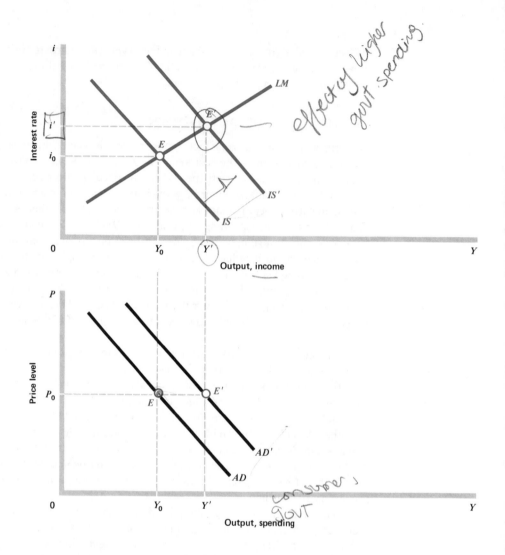

(handwritten: effect of higher govt spending)

(handwritten near lower panel: consumer ↓ govt)

FIGURE 7-8

THE EFFECT OF A FISCAL EXPANSION ON THE *AD* SCHEDULE. A fiscal expansion, such as an increase in government spending, shifts the *IS* curve in the upper panel to *IS'*. At any given price level, such as P_0, the equilibrium in the upper panel shifts to E', with higher level of output Y' and higher interest rate i'. Point E' in the lower panel is on the new aggregate demand schedule, *AD'*, corresponding to price level P_0. We could similarly trace the effect of increased government spending on the equilibrium level of output and spending in the lower panel for every price level, and thus show that the *AD* curve shifts out to *AD'* when fiscal policy is expansionary.

demand and thus raises the equilibrium level of income and spending. In Figure 7-9 we show that an increase in the nominal money stock shifts the AD schedule up and to the right.

The extent to which an increase in nominal money shifts the AD schedule to the right depends on the monetary policy multiplier. If the monetary policy multiplier is large, say because money demand is not very interest-elastic and goods demand is, the AD schedule will shift a lot. Conversely, if the LM schedule is nearly flat, in which case monetary policy in ineffective, the AD schedule will shift very little.

We can also ask about the *upward* shift of the schedule. Here an interesting and important point emerges. Recall that what matters for equilibrium income and spending is the *real* money supply, $\overline{M}/P$. If an increase in nominal money is matched by an equiproportionate increase in prices, $\overline{M}/P$ is unchanged, and hence interest rates, aggregate demand, and equilibrium income and spending will remain unchanged. This gives us the clue to the vertical shift of the AD schedule.

An increase in the nominal money stock shifts the AD schedule up exactly in proportion to the increase in nominal money. Thus if, starting at point E in the lower panel of Figure 7-9, we have a 10 percent increase in $\overline{M}$, real spending will be unchanged only if prices also rise by 10 percent, thus leaving real balances unchanged. Therefore the AD schedule shifts upward by 10 percent. At point K in Figure 7-9, *real* balances are the same as at E, and therefore interest rates and equilibrium income and spending are the same as at E.

We have now completed the derivation of the aggregate demand schedule. The important points to recall are that the AD schedule is shifted to the right both by increases in the money stock and by expansionary fiscal policy. In the remainder of this chapter we show how to use this tool to discuss the effects of monetary and fiscal policy *on both the level of output and the price level* under alternative assumptions about the supply side.

7-4 MONETARY AND FISCAL POLICY UNDER ALTERNATIVE SUPPLY ASSUMPTIONS

In Figure 7-2 we showed how the aggregate supply and demand curves together determine the equilibrium level of income and prices in the economy. Now that we have shown how the aggregate demand curve is derived and how it is shifted by policy changes, we use the aggregate demand and supply model to study the effects of monetary and fiscal policy in the two extreme supply cases — Keynesian and classical.

We should expect that the conclusions we reach in the Keynesian supply case are precisely the same as those reached in Chapters 4 and 5. In those chapters, in developing the $IS\text{-}LM$ model, we assumed that whatever amount of goods was demanded would be supplied at the existing price level. And of course, as Figure 7-5a shows, the Keynesian supply curve implies that any amount of goods demanded will be supplied at the existing price level.

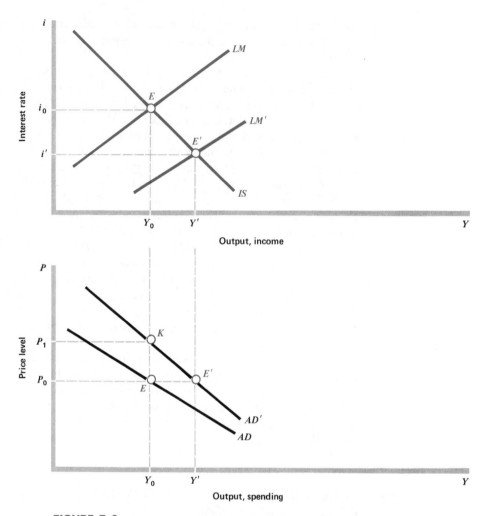

FIGURE 7-9

THE EFFECTS OF AN INCREASE IN THE MONEY STOCK ON THE *AD* SCHEDULE.
An increase in the money stock shifts the *LM* curve to *LM'* in the upper
panel. The equilibrium level of income rises from Y_0 to Y' at the initial
price level, P_0. Correspondingly, the *AD* curve moves out to the right, to
AD', with point E' in the lower panel corresponding to E' in the upper
panel. The *AD* curve shifts up in exactly the same proportion as the
increase in the money stock. For instance, at point K the price level, P_1,
is higher than P_0 in the same proportion that the money supply has
risen. Real balances at K on *AD'* are therefore the same as at E on *AD*.

The Keynesian Case

In Figure 7-10 we combine the aggregate demand schedule with the Keynesian aggregate supply schedule. The initial equilibrium is at point E, where AS and AD intersect. At that point the goods and assets markets are in equilibrium.

Consider now a fiscal expansion. As we have already seen, increased government spending, or a cut in tax rates, shifts the AD schedule out and to the right from AD to AD'. The new equilibrium is at point E', where output has increased. Because firms are willing to supply *any* amount of output at the level of prices P_0, there is no effect on prices. The only effect of higher government spending in Figure 7-10 is to increase output and employment. In addition, as we know from the *IS-LM* model that lies behind the AD schedule, the fiscal expansion will raise equilibrium interest rates.

We leave it to you to show that, in the Keynesian case, an increase in the nominal quantity of money likewise leads to an expansion in equilibrium output. With a horizontal AS schedule there is again no impact on prices. The magnitude of the output expansion then depends, in this Keynesian case, only on the monetary policy multiplier that determines the extent of the horizontal shift of the AD schedule.

Thus, as we expected, all our conclusions about the effects of policy changes in the Keynesian supply case are those of the simple *IS-LM* model.

FIGURE 7-10
A FISCAL EXPANSION: THE KEYNESIAN CASE. In the Keynesian case, with output in perfectly elastic supply at a given price level, a fiscal expansion increases equilibrium income from Y to Y'. This is exactly the result already derived with the IS and LM schedules.

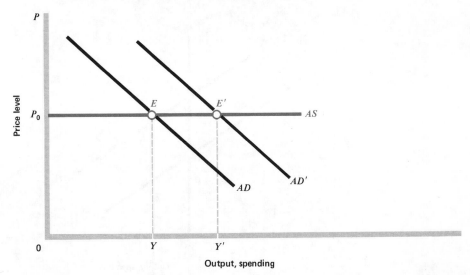

The Classical Case: Fiscal Policy

In the classical case the aggregate supply schedule is vertical at the full-employment level of output. Firms will supply the level of output Y^* whatever the price level. Under this supply assumption we obtain results very different from those reached using the Keynesian model. Now the price level is not given but, rather, depends on the interaction of supply and demand.

In Figure 7-11 we study the effect of a fiscal expansion under classical supply assumptions. The aggregate supply schedule is AS, with equilibrium initially at point E. Note that at point E there is full employment because, by assumption, firms supply the full-employment level of output at any level of prices.

The fiscal expansion shifts the aggregate demand schedule from AD to AD'. At the initial level of prices, P_0, spending in the economy rises to point E'. At price level P_0 the demand for goods has risen. But firms cannot obtain the labor to produce more output, and output supply cannot respond to the increased demand. As firms try to hire

FIGURE 7-11

A FISCAL EXPANSION: THE CLASSICAL CASE. The supply of output is perfectly inelastic at the full-employment level of output, Y^*. A fiscal expansion raises equilibrium spending, at the initial price level P_0, from E to E'. But now there is excess demand because firms are unwilling to supply that much output. Prices increase, and that reduces real balances until we reach point E''. At E'' government spending is higher, but the higher price level means lower real balances, higher interest rates, and hence reduced private spending. At E'' increased government spending has crowded out an equal amount of private spending.

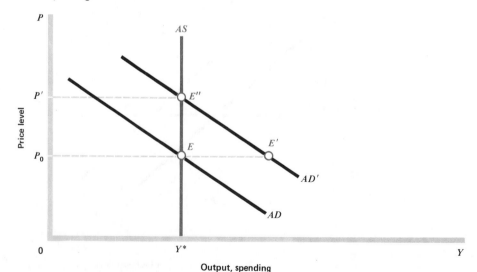

more workers, they only bid up wages and their costs of production, and therefore they charge higher prices for their output. The increase in the demand for goods therefore leads only to higher prices, and not to higher output.

The increase in prices reduces the real money stock and leads to an increase in interest rates and a reduction in spending. The economy moves up the AD' schedule until prices have risen enough, and real balances have fallen enough, to raise interest rates and reduce spending to a level consistent with full-employment output. That is the case at price level P'. At point E'' aggregate demand, at the higher level of government spending, is once again equal to aggregate supply.

Crowding Out Again

Note what has happened in Figure 7-11: Output is unchanged at the full-employment level, Y^*, but government spending is higher. That must imply less spending by the private sector. There is thus *full,* or complete, *crowding out.* Recall that crowding out occurs when an increase in government spending results in less spending by the private sector. Typically, as we showed in Chapter 5, government spending crowds out investment. In the case shown in Figure 7-11, with a classical supply curve, every dollar increase in real government spending is offset by a dollar reduction in private spending, so that crowding out is complete.

We thus reach the following important result: *In the classical case increased real government spending leads to full crowding out.* We now explain the mechanism through which crowding out occurs.

Figure 7-12 shows the *IS-LM* diagram, but augmented by the line Y^* at the full-employment level of output. The initial equilibrium is at point E, at which the money market clears and planned spending equals output. The fiscal expansion shifts the *IS* schedule to *IS'*. At an unchanged price level, and assuming firms were to meet the increase in demand by expanding production, we would move to point E'. But that is not possible under classical supply assumptions. Faced with an excess demand for goods, firms end up raising prices rather than output.[6] The price increase, in turn, reduces real balances and therefore shifts the *LM* schedule up. Prices will increase until the excess demand has been eliminated. That means the *LM* schedule shifts up and to the left until we reach a new equilibrium at point E''.

At E'' the goods market clears at the full-employment level of output. Interest rates have increased compared with the initial equilibrium at E, and that increase in interest rates has reduced private spending to make room for increased government purchases. Note that the money market is also in equilibrium. Output and income are the same as at point E. The higher interest rate reduces the demand for real balances, matching the decline in the real money stock.

Note that we have now seen two mechanisms that produce full crowding out. In

---

[6] We say "end up" because the increased demand for goods will lead firms to try to hire more labor, bidding up the nominal wage, which in turn leads to an increase in prices.

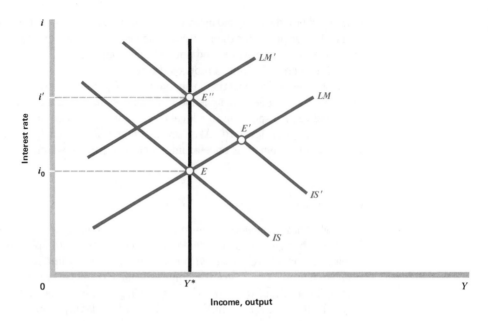

FIGURE 7-12

CROWDING OUT IN THE CLASSICAL CASE. A fiscal expansion in the classical case leads to full crowding out. The fiscal expansion shifts the *IS* schedule to *IS'*. At the initial price level the economy would move to point *E'*, but there is excess demand since firms supply only *Y**. Prices increase, shifting the *LM* schedule up and to the left until *LM'* is reached. The new equilibrium is at point *E"*, at which interest rates have risen enough to displace an amount of private spending equal to the increase in government demand.

Chapter 5, crowding out is complete if the *LM* curve is vertical. In that case, crowding out occurs because money demand is interest-inelastic. In this chapter, full crowding out occurs because aggregate supply limits total output. In brief, in Chapter 5 crowding out is a demand phenomenon; here it is a supply phenomenon.

We summarize in Table 7-1 the effects of a fiscal expansion in the cases of classical and Keynesian supply conditions. In each case we show what happens to output, interest rates, and the price level.

The table reinforces our understanding of the two models; in one case only prices adjust; in the other case, only output. These models are clearly extremes, and we would expect that often adjustment in both output and prices occurs. That is the adjustment process we study in Chapter 13. We shall see there that the Keynesian case comes close to describing the short-run effects of a fiscal expansion, while the classical case more accurately predicts what happens in the long run after all adjustments have taken place.

TABLE 7-1
THE EFFECTS OF A FISCAL EXPANSION

Aggregate supply	Output	Interest rate	Prices
Keynesian	+	+	0
Classical	0	+	+

Monetary Expansion under Classical Conditions

We have already seen the impact of monetary policy under Keynesian supply conditions: With prices given, a rise in the nominal money stock is a rise in the real money stock. Equilibrium interest rates decline as a consequence, and output rises. Consider now the adjustments that occur in response to a monetary expansion when the aggregate supply curve is vertical and the price level is no longer fixed.

In Figure 7-13 we study an expansion in the nominal money stock under classical supply conditions. The initial full-employment equilibrium is at point E, where the AD and AS schedules intersect. Now the nominal money stock is increased, and accordingly, the aggregate demand schedule shifts up and to the right to AD'. If prices were fixed, the economy would move to E', the Keynesian equilibrium. But now output is in fixed supply. The increase in aggregate demand leads to an excess demand for goods. Firms that attempt to expand, hiring more workers, bid up wages and costs. Prices increase in response, which means real balances fall back toward their initial level. In fact prices keep rising until the excess demand for goods disappears. Thus they must increase until the economy reaches point E'', where AS intersects the new aggregate demand schedule, AD'. Only when aggregate demand is again equal to full-employment supply does the goods market clear and the pressure for prices to rise disappear.

Consider now the adjustment that takes place in moving from E to E''. There is no change in output, only a change in the price level. Note, moreover, that prices rise in exactly the same proportion as the nominal quantity of money.[7] This we know because we saw earlier that in response to an increase in nominal money the AD schedule shifts upward in the same proportion as the increase in money. Thus at point E'' the real money stock, $\overline{M}/P$, is back to its initial level. At E'' both nominal money and the price level have changed in the same proportion, leaving real money and hence interest rates and aggregate demand unchanged. We thus have an important implication of the classical model: *Under classical supply conditions an increase in nominal money raises the price level in the same proportion, but leaves interest rates and real output unchanged.*

---

[7] In problem 7 we ask you to use the IS and LM curves to show how the change in the money supply works. To answer the problem you have to use Fig. 7-9 along with the fact that the LM schedule shifts as the price level changes.

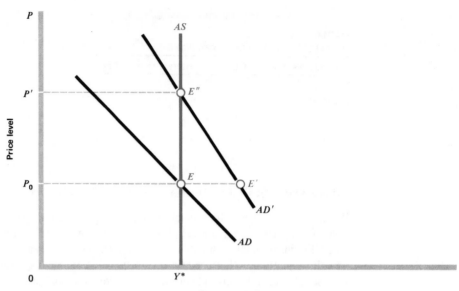

FIGURE 7-13

THE EFFECT OF A MONETARY EXPANSION UNDER CLASSICAL SUPPLY
ASSUMPTIONS. Starting from the full-employment equilibrium at point E,
an increase in the nominal money stock shifts the aggregate demand
schedule to AD'. At the initial price level there is now an excess
demand for goods. Prices increase, and thus the real money stock
declines toward its initial level. Price increases continue until the
economy reaches point E''. Here the *real* money stock has returned to
its initial level, and with output unchanged, interest rates are again at
their initial level. Thus a monetary expansion affects only prices, not
output or interest rates.

TABLE 7-2
THE EFFECTS OF AN INCREASE IN THE NOMINAL MONEY STOCK

Aggregate supply	Output	Interest rate	Prices	Real balances
Keynesian	+	−	0	+
Classical	0	0	+	0

In Table 7-2 we summarize the effects of an increase in the nominal money stock under Keynesian and classical supply conditions. Once again we look at the effects on output, prices, and interest rates. In addition we show the effect on real balances, $\overline{M/P}$. The table brings out the fact that under classical supply conditions, none of the *real* variables, such as output, interest rates, or real balances, is affected by a change in the nominal money stock. Only the price level changes.

7-5 THE QUANTITY THEORY AND THE NEUTRALITY OF MONEY

The classical model of supply, in combination with the *IS-LM* model describing the demand side of the economy, has extremely strong implications. Because, by assumption, output is maintained at the full-employment level by full wage and price flexibility, monetary and fiscal policy do not affect output. Fiscal policy affects interest rates and the *distribution* of spending between the government and the private sector and between consumption and investment. Monetary policy affects only the price level.

These implications about the effects of monetary policy on output are consistent with the *quantity theory of money.* The quantity theory of money in its strongest form asserts that the price level is proportional to the stock of money. For instance, in the case of the classical supply curve, an increase in the quantity of money produces, in equilibrium, a proportional increase in the price level. In this case, money is *neutral.*

The Neutrality of Money

Money is *neutral* when changes in the money stock lead only to changes in the price level, with no real variables (output, employment, and interest rates) changing. For instance, money is neutral in the second row of Table 7-2, where in response to a change in the money stock, only the price level changes, with output, interest rates, and real balances remaining unchanged.

We saw above that the classical supply curve has the powerful and important implication that fiscal policy cannot affect output. The neutrality of money likewise has strong policy implications. For instance, if money were neutral, there would be an easy way to reduce the inflation rate if we ever wanted to do that. All we would have to do would be to reduce the rate at which the money stock is growing.

In practice, it is very difficult to change the inflation rate without producing a recession, as in the 1979–1983 period in the United States. When a lower growth rate of money leads first to unemployment, and only later to lower inflation, as it did in the recession in 1982, then we know that money is not neutral. Changes in the quantity of money then have real effects — monetary policy affects the level of output. This means that the aggregate supply curve cannot be vertical in the short run. In the next section, and in Chapter 13, we develop theories showing why in the short run the aggregate supply curve is quite flat, whereas over longer periods it is more nearly vertical.

box 7-2

THE QUANTITY THEORY OF MONEY

Irving Fisher (1867–1947) and Milton Friedman (born 1912) are two of the foremost monetary economists in the United States in this century. Both strongly advocated the quantity theory of money as the right model of price level determination.
Fisher wrote in 1920:*

> In recent popular discussions a great variety of reasons have been assigned for the "high cost of living," *e.g.*, "profiteering"; speculation; hoarding; the middleman; the tariff; cold storage; longer hauls on railroads; marketing by telephone; the free delivery system; the individual package; the enforcement of sanitary laws; the tuberculin testing of cattle; the destruction of tainted meat; sanitary milk; the elimination of renovated butter and of "rots" and "spots" in eggs; food adulteration; advertising; unscientific management; extravagance; higher standards of living; the increasing cost of government; the increasing cost of old-age pensions, and of better pauper institutions, hospitals, insane asylums, reformatories, jails and other public institutions; I shall not discuss in detail this list of alleged explanations. While some of them are important factors in raising particular prices, none of them has been important in raising the *general* scale of prices.

> The ups and downs of prices roughly correspond with the ups and downs of the money supply. Throughout all history this has been so. For this general broad fact the evidence is sufficient even where we lack the index numbers by which to make accurate measurements. Whenever there have been rapid outpourings from mines, following discoveries of the precious metals used for money, prices have risen with corresponding rapidity. This was observed in the sixteenth century, after great quantities of the precious metals had been brought to Europe from the New World, and again in the nineteenth century, after the Californian and Australian gold mining of the fifties; and, still again, in the same century after the South African, Alaskan, and Cripple Creek mining of the nineties. Likewise when other causes than mining, such as paper money issues, produce violent changes in the quantity or quality of money, violent changes in the price level usually follow.

The Modern Quantity Theory: Monetarism

The strict quantity theory asserts that the price level is proportional to the quantity of money. Although the quantity theory is centuries, and perhaps millennia, old, few have believed in the strict quantity theory. That is, few have believed that the price level is strictly proportional to the money stock, or that money is the *only* factor affecting the price level. Rather, quantity theorists argued and argue that the money stock is, in practice, the single most important factor producing inflation.

Box 7-2 presents quotations from Irving Fisher (1867–1947), widely thought to be the greatest American economist of his time, and from Milton Friedman, the leading exponent of the quantity theory and the importance of money in the modern era. The two differ in emphasis: The quotation from Fisher comes close to asserting that *only* changes in the quantity of money affect the price level; Friedman is clearer in arguing that other factors can affect the price level, but that these other factors are of secondary importance.

Friedman wrote:†

Since men first began to write systematically about economic matters they have devoted special attention to the wide movements in the general level of prices that have intermittently occurred. Two alternative explanations have usually been offered. One has attributed the changes in prices to changes in the quantity of money. The other has attributed the changes in prices to war or to profiteers or to rises in wages or to some other special circumstance of the particular time and place and has regarded any accompanying change in the quantity of money as a common consequence of the same special circumstance. The first explanation has generally been referred to as the quantity theory of money, although that designation conceals the variety of forms the explanation has taken, the different levels of sophistication on which it has been developed, and the wide range of the claims that have been made for its applicability.

In its most rigid and unqualified form the quantity theory asserts strict proportionality between the quantity of what is regarded as money and the level of prices. Hardly anyone has held the theory in that form, although statements capable of being so interpreted have often been made in the heat of argument or for expository simplicity. Virtually every quantity theorist has recognized that changes in the quantity of money that correspond to changes in the volume of trade or of output have no tendency to produce changes in prices. Nearly as many have recognized also that changes in the willingness of the community to hold money can occur for a variety of reasons and can introduce disparities between changes in the quantity of money per unit of trade or of output and changes in prices. What quantity theorists have held in common is the belief that these qualifications are of secondary importance for substantial changes in either prices or the quantity of money, so that the one will not in fact occur without the other. ∎

---

* Irving Fisher, *Stabilizing the Dollar* (New York: Macmillan, 1920), pp. 10–11 and 29.

† Milton Friedman, "Money: The Quantity Theory," in *The International Encyclopedia of the Social Sciences,* vol. X, 1968, pp. 432–447.

Friedman is the recognized intellectual leader of an influential group of economists, called *monetarists,* who emphasize the role of money and monetary policy in affecting the behavior of output and prices. Leading monetarists include the late Karl Brunner of the University of Rochester, Allan Meltzer of Carnegie-Mellon University, William Poole of Brown University, Anna Schwartz of the National Bureau of Economic Research and Hunter College, and Robert Barro of Harvard University. Another prominent monetarist is Beryl Sprinkel, chairman of the Council of Economic Advisers in the second Reagan administration (1985–1989), whose views are strongly reflected in the emphasis on monetary policy in the 1986 report of the Council of Economic Advisers.

Modern quantity theorists, as well as Irving Fisher, disagree also with the strict quantity theory in not believing that the supply curve is vertical in the short run. Monetarists such as Friedman argue that a reduction in the money stock does in practice *first* reduce the level of output, and only later have an effect on prices.

Thus Friedman and other monetarists make an important distinction between the short- and long-run effects of changes in money.[8] They argue that in the long run money is more or less neutral. Changes in the money stock, after they have worked their way through the economy, have no real effects and only change prices: the quantity theory and the neutrality of money are, from this long-run perspective, not just theoretical possibilities, but instead a reasonable description of the way the world works. But in the short run, they argue, monetary policy and changes in the money stock can and do have important real effects.

There is more to monetarism than the argument that money is the most important determinant of macroeconomic performance, but we leave the evidence on this and the other tenets of monetarism for further discussion in Chapters 13 and 18.

*7-6 THE MARKET-CLEARING APPROACH: THE LUCAS SUPPLY CURVE

We have so far looked only at extreme cases of aggregate supply: a vertical supply curve called the "classical case" and a flat schedule representing the "Keynesian case." In Chapters 13 and 14 we develop in detail the dynamics of aggregate supply, and we will see there that these two extreme cases are both useful, not necessarily representing different worlds but, rather, different phases of the adjustment process. The Keynesian case represents short-run supply behavior and the classical case gives a good idea of how the economy behaves when all adjustments have taken place.

That view shifts the central question to a new issue: Why does it take time for the economy to adjust to a disturbance? There are two basic answers. One is that wages and prices are sticky in the short run: it takes time for wages and prices to change in response to increases in the quantity of labor and goods demanded at their existing levels. That answer in its extreme form underlies the Keynesian theory of supply, and also underlies more sophisticated new or modern Keynesian theories that will be developed in Chapters 13 and 14.

There is, however, another, extremely interesting approach, which we introduce in this section[9] and which will also be developed later. The argument is that wages and prices are sticky in the short run as a result of *information problems*: The argument is that wages and prices, while fully flexible, adjust only partially because households have

---

[8] For a recent statement of the monetarist position see Milton Friedman, "The Quantity Theory of Money," in *The New Palgrave Dictionary of Economics* (New York: Stockton, 1987) and, by the same author, "Monetary History, Not Dogma," *Wall Street Journal*, February 1987, and "Whither Inflation," *Wall Street Journal*, July 1989. See, too, William Dewald, "Monetarism Is Dead: Long Live the Quantity Theory of Money," Federal Reserve Bank of St. Louis *Review*, July/August, 1988. The collection by James Dorn and Anna Schwartz, *The Search for Stable Money* (Chicago: University of Chicago Press, 1987) contains an interesting collection of essays in a monetarist persuasion. In Irving Fisher's writings, which long precede modern monetarism, he too drew a distinction between the short-run effect of a change in the money stock — which he argued was not neutral — and the long-run effect, which he argued was neutral.

[9] The asterisk at the beginning of this section indicates that the material in this section is somewhat more difficult than average, certainly at this stage of the book. It can be omitted without loss of continuity; it can also be read rather than worked through at this stage, as an introduction to an alternative and more microeconomics-based way of thinking about aggregate supply.

only partial information. It simply takes time for households and firms to figure out what exactly is happening in their economic environment, and to recognize that wages and prices should change. Once they do, they adjust fully to the new environment. This latter approach, which has become known as the *rational expectations equilibrium*, has powerful implications for the role of money in the economy:[10] The rational expectations – equilibrium view asserts that changes in money affect economic activity only as long, and only to the extent, that they are unexpected. In short, only *unexpected money matters*. We now briefly introduce this important view.

A frequent assumption made in this approach is that some people do not know the aggregate price level but do know the absolute (dollar) price at which they can buy and sell. For instance, at a given moment of time, a worker knows that the going wage rate is $12 per hour but does not know all prices in the economy and hence the aggregate price level, and thus does not know the real wage (the nominal wage divided by the price level, equal to the amount of goods the wage will buy). Since it is the real wage, not the absolute wage, that determines whether and how many hours she wants to work, the worker has somehow to estimate the aggregate price level.

With these assumptions it is possible to explain why changes in the stock of money affect real output. Assume that labor supply depends on the *real* wage, w. In Figure 7-14 we show the upward-sloping labor supply curve, N_s. We show in addition the downward-sloping labor demand curve, N_d, which implies that firms demand more labor the lower the real wage.[11] If both firms and workers have full information, the real wage will adjust to the level w^*, at which there is full employment of labor at the level N^*; corresponding to labor employment of N^*, output is at its full employment level, Y^*.

We call w^* the *full-employment real wage*. Next we assume that workers and firms do not have the same information about the actual aggregate price level at the time that they decide how much work is to be done. Suppose that beforehand both firms and workers expected the price level to be P^e. Figure 7-15 shows the *nominal* wage, W, on the vertical axis, and labor supply and demand curves. Labor supply curve N_s^* corresponds to the supply curve when workers think the actual price level is P^e. Labor demand curve N_d^* shows the labor demand curve when firms, also, believe the actual price level is P^e. If each is correct, the level of employment will be N^*, at wage rate W^*, corresponding to the equilibrium real wage $w^*(= W^*/P^e)$ in Figure 7-14.

Now suppose that at any given time the firms know the *actual* price level, P, whereas workers are not informed about the actual price level, and believe it is P^e. Suppose in particular that the actual price level, P, exceeds the expected price level,

---

[10] Robert E. Lucas, Jr., of the University of Chicago is the intellectual founder of this approach. See his famous article, "Some International Evidence on Output-Inflation Tradeoffs," *American Economic Review*, June 1973, for an example of the approach. For advanced expositions see Steven Sheffrin, *Rational Expectations* (New York: Cambridge University Press, 1983) and Kevin Hoover, *The Classical Macroeconomics* (Oxford, U.K.: Basil Blackwell, 1988).

[11] The labor demand curve slopes down because firms increase their profits by supplying more goods when the real wage declines; equivalently, given the nominal wage, firms will want to supply more output if prices are higher. We explain the derivation of the labor demand curve more formally in Chapter 13.

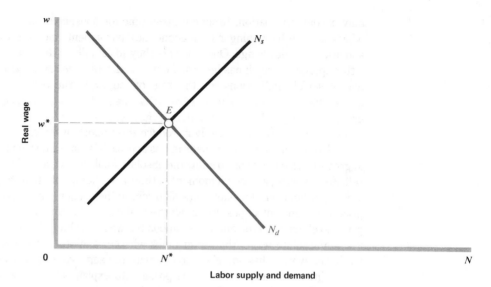

FIGURE 7-14

LABOR MARKET EQUILIBRIUM. The equilibrium real wage is determined by the intersection of an upward-sloping supply curve of labor, N_s^*, and a downward-sloping demand curve for labor, N_d^*. The full-employment equilibrium is at E, with equilibrium real wage w^* and equilibrium quantity of labor N^*. Corresponding to the full employment of labor, N^*, is the full-employment level of output, Y^*.

P^e. Here comes the crucial point: At any given nominal wage, firms now demand more labor than they would have if the actual price level were P^e. Why? Because at the actual price level, P, and any given nominal wage, say W_0, the *real* wage (W_0/P) is lower than it would be at the same nominal wage and P^e [i.e., with $P > P^e$, $(W_0/P) < (W_0/P^e)$]. In Figure 7-15 N_d' shows the labor demand curve of firms when they know the price level is P (which is greater than P^e).

As a result of the shift in the labor demand curve to N_d', the nominal wage rises from W^* to W'. Most important, the level of employment rises from N^* to N'. *Thus as a result of the imperfect information of the workers, a rise in the price level leads to an increase in the level of employment, and therefore of output.* We could similarly show that if the actual price level is below the predicted level, the demand-for-labor curve would shift to the left, the nominal wage and employment would fall, and accordingly output would fall.

We want to explore in a bit more detail the mechanism that causes an increase in the price level to raise output in Figure 7-15. The key assumption is the difference in information between firms and workers. When the price level rises, workers do not know that. All they can see is that the nominal wage they are being offered has risen. Therefore they think the real wage is higher, and they are willing to work more. Thus

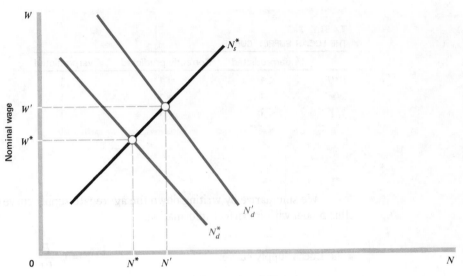

W

Nominal wage

Labor supply and demand

FIGURE 7-15

THE EFFECT OF AN INCREASE IN THE PRICE LEVEL. The labor supply and demand curves are now shown as functions of the *nominal* wage, which is on the vertical axis. Their position thus depends on the price level expected by firms (the labor demand curve) and workers (labor supply), respectively. With the price level equal to and expected to be P_0^e, the equilibrium nominal wage is W^*, and employment is N^*. When the price level increases, but workers do not know that, the labor demand curve shifts to N_d' but the supply curve stays put. The nominal wage and output both rise, to W' and N', respectively. Workers willingly supply more labor in the mistaken belief that their real wage has risen. Firms willingly employ more workers in the correct belief that the real wage has fallen.

at point E' in Figure 7-15, there is a difference of views between firms and workers on what the real wage is. Firms know that at E' the real wage is lower than w^* in Figure 7-14; workers by contrast believe the real wage is higher than w^*. Without that difference in views, the increase in the price level would not have increased output.[12]

---

[12] Shouldn't workers refuse to work any more than N^* when there is an increase in the demand for their services? After all, they know the firms are better informed than they are, and should suspect they will end up with a lower real wage than w^*. This would be true if the demand in a given market were affected only by increases in aggregate demand or the aggregate price level. However, so long as there are also relative shifts in demand, so that a worker in a given market *may* be facing a relative increase in the demand for her or his services, workers will respond to increases in the wages they are offered — on the basis that the increase in demand may be a result of a relative shift in demand. This is worked out in detail in the article by Lucas cited in footnote 10.

TABLE 7-3
THE LUCAS SUPPLY CURVE

	Underpredicted	Correctly predicted	Overpredicted
P^e/P	< 1	$= 1$	> 1
w/w^*	> 1	$= 1$	< 1
Y/Y^*	< 1	$= 1$	> 1

We summarize by writing down the aggregate supply curve that emerges from this model with imperfect information:

The Lucas supply curve:
$$Y = \psi \, \frac{P}{P^e} \tag{1}$$

where output increases with P/P^e through the mechanism described in Figure 7-15. The aggregate supply curve is named the *Lucas supply curve* because it was advanced in pioneering work by Robert Lucas of the University of Chicago.[13] The Lucas supply curve shows that the amount of output firms are willing to supply increases as the ratio of the actual to the expected price level increases.[14]

Table 7-3 shows how the actual real wage, employment and output are related to P/P^e. To give an example, if price predictions are too high, so that the actual price level is below the expected price level (first column), then the actual real wage turns out to be too high for full employment and the level of output will be below the full-employment level. The Lucas supply curve, which corresponds to part of Table 7-3, is shown in Figure 7-16. For instance at point B, P is greater than P^e, the actual real wage will be lower than w^*, and output will be above Y^*.

Adding the Demand Side

The next step is to close the model by talking about how the expected price level is determined. In Box 7-1 we developed an equation for the equilibrium price level along the AD demand schedule:

---

[13] See the reference in footnote 10.

[14] The particular justification for the Lucas supply function offered in Figure 7-15 was developed by Milton Friedman in "The Role of Monetary Policy," *American Economic Review*, March 1968. Lucas's contribution was to develop the microeconomic foundations for the incomplete information approach and show that they resulted in a supply equation of the form of equation (1). For the Lucas supply curve to take the form of equation (1), it is not necessary that firms know the aggregate price level while workers do not. Rather, the assumption is that firms have a more accurate estimate of the price level than workers.

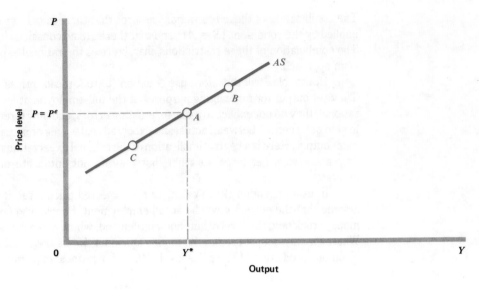

FIGURE 7-16

THE LUCAS SUPPLY CURVE. The AS curve represents equation (1) and is drawn for a given expected price level, P^e. If the actual price level is equal to the expected price level, that is, $P = P^e$, the amount of output supplied is Y^*. If prices are higher, and hence real wages are lower, firms supply more output than Y^*, and conversely if prices are lower.

Aggregate demand:
$$P = \frac{\beta \overline{M}}{Y - \gamma \overline{A}}$$
(2)

We turn now to the *rational expectations* aspect of this approach. How are firms and workers to form expectations of the price level? The rational expectations approach assumes people use all relevant information in forming expectations of economic variables. In particular, we assume that workers and firms will think through the economic mechanisms underlying the determination of the expected price level. How should they figure that out?

Households and firms expect that full employment will prevail. To determine that level of output, they need to figure out the expected price level. At the expected price level

- There are no expectational errors, $P = P^e$, and output is expected to be at the full-employment level, Y^*.

- The price level must be such as to equate aggregate demand and supply, that is, $AS = AD$.

The combination of these restrictions assures that there is market clearing, which is implied by the condition $AS = AD$, and that there are no conscious forecasting errors. The combination of these restrictions characterizes the rational expectations equilibrium approach.

Households will therefore use equation (2) to forecast prices, *setting $Y = Y^*$*. They set output for forecasting purposes at the full-employment level because, being rational, they do not expect to make forecasting errors, and only forecasting errors can lead to divergences between actual and expected real wages or actual and full-employment output. Here is a central implication of the rational expectations approach: people may not always get forecasts right, but they do not anticipate making *systematic* errors.

In using equation (2) to calculate the expected price level, it is not enough to assume that the economy will be at full employment. People also need to predict the money stock (and the level of autonomous demand, which we shall assume they know). Whatever way people predict the money stock, let M^e be the expected money stock. Then our prediction of the price level, P^e, under rational expectations, is

$$P^e = \frac{\beta M^e}{Y^* - \gamma \overline{A}} \qquad (3)$$

Note how price prediction now revolves around predicting the money stock.

We are now ready to see the implications of the Lucas supply curve approach, namely, the distinction between anticipated and unanticipated changes in the money supply. In Figure 7-17 we show aggregate supply and demand curves. The aggregate demand curves are familiar from earlier figures. The aggregate supply curve is based on equation (1), the Lucas supply curve. The position of the aggregate supply curve depends on the expected price level.

Consider Figure 7-17 a. The AS curve is the aggregate supply curve for a given initial expected price level P_0^e. Now suppose the money supply is increased and that the increase was expected. We are thus dealing with an *anticipated* increase in the money stock. The aggregate demand curve certainly shifts up in proportion to the increase in the money stock. But at output level Y^*, so does the aggregate supply curve: as equation (3) shows, at Y^*, P^e increases in the same proportion as the expected increase in money stock.

Accordingly the new equilibrium of the economy is at E', with a price level, P, equal to P_1^e, corresponding to the higher money stock, and unchanged output. Underlying this result are adjustments in the labor market: both firms and workers knew that the money stock and aggregate demand were going to increase in the proportion P_1^e/P_0^e, and accordingly the nominal wage went up in that same proportion.[15] Thus with anticipated increases in money there are no *real* effects (just as in the classical case before!); money, nominal wages, prices — actual and expected — all increase in the same proportion.

---

[15] You may want to use a figure like Figure 7-15 to make sure that you understand why the nominal wage rises in the same proportion as the price level is expected to rise when both firms and workers have the same expectations.

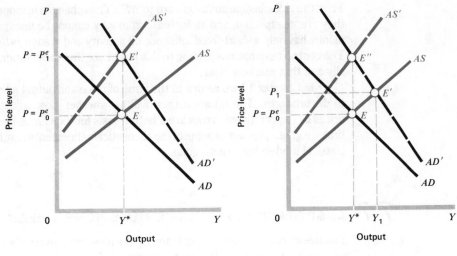

(a) Anticipated money

(b) Unanticipated money

FIGURE 7-17

EXPECTED AND UNEXPECTED INCREASES IN MONEY. (*a*) An anticipated
increase in money is fully reflected in expected prices and hence in the
supply curve. With an anticipated increase in money *both* the *AS* and *AD*
schedules shift upward in the same proportion at output level Y^*.
Hence, at the new equilibrium, at E', output remains at the level Y^*.
Thus anticipated money increases have no *real* effects. (*b*) An
unanticipated increase in money is not reflected in expected prices.
Therefore initially only the *AD* schedule shifts. The short-run equilibrium
is at E' with output higher. But because prices exceed expected prices,
expectations will now be revised upward, the *AS* schedule will shift,
and the economy will move to E''. Unexpected money increases
therefore have real effects, but they will be transitory.

Consider next the case of *un*anticipated money. Now, because there is no change
in the price level expected by workers, we have the situation illustrated in Figure
7-17 *b*. The increase in the money stock causes the aggregate demand curve to move to
AD', as in Figure 7-17 *b*. But because the workers did not expect the price level to rise,
the aggregate supply curve, *AS*, does not shift. As a result we move to a new equilibrium at point E'. Here actual prices have increased above expected prices, that is,
$P > P_0^e$, and as a result output has increased. Thus unanticipated (by the workers)
monetary expansion leads to an increase in output.

But note immediately that under rational expectations this state of affairs, point
E', cannot last for long. Prices are above expectations, and households and firms will
revise their forecasts. For example, if households and firms expect the increase in the
money stock to be maintained, they revise their price expectations upward, to P_1^e.

Then the *AS* schedule shifts upward to *AS'*. Thus changes in money matter only while they are unexpected, and an increase in money cannot be unexpected forever. Thus money has only a short-lived influence on activity and is soon *fully* reflected in prices. The central assumptions leading to this result are that expectations are formed rationally and that markets clear.

In Chapter 13 we return to the issue of price and output adjustment in response to disturbances. The question then will be whether slow adjustment of wages and prices or expectational errors are a better basis for explaining the facts. In the meantime we give a preview of some of the theoretical refinements that Keynesian and other classical models have undergone.

7-7   AGGREGATE SUPPLY: THE QUESTIONS AHEAD

The theory of aggregate supply is among the most controversial and the least settled of any in macroeconomics. Here is the difficulty. From the viewpoint of logic and simplicity, the classical theory of supply — that the labor market clears all the time and that output is always at the full-employment level — is compelling. After all, if output is below the full-employment level, there are some workers who want to work but cannot find a job. Surely they could find a job by offering to work at a lower real wage. Much of microeconomics suggests that markets are mostly in equilibrium (quantity demanded is equal to quantity supplied) and, if not, are at least moving that way. So economists have a professional bias in favor of equilibrium.

But the facts do not support the classical theory of supply.

- Output is not always at the full-employment level. The unemployment rate varies, and is sometimes very high; sometimes there are many people wanting work who cannot find it, and therefore the quantity of labor supplied exceeds the quantity demanded.

- Further, if output is always at the full-employment level, then changes in the money stock affect only prices and not output: Money is neutral. But changes in monetary policy in fact frequently appear not to be neutral. Sharp reductions in money growth, for instance, when governments try to reduce inflation, almost always cause recessions. And increases in money growth often appear to cause rapid growth of real output.

Indeed, the broad facts come closer to supporting the Keynesian aggregate supply curve than the classical view. Increases in aggregate demand caused, for instance, by expansionary fiscal or monetary policy in the short run raise real output much more than prices.

However, the assumption that prices are completely fixed, which underlies the Keynesian supply function, is bothersome. When prices are fixed and markets do not clear, people can benefit from changing prices. The unemployed would be willing to work at a wage below that earned by the currently employed. Employers should be happy to employ labor at a lower wage. Why do not employers and the unemployed get together, agree on a lower wage, and get rid of the unemployment? In other words, why does the labor market not move quickly to equilibrium?

In a nutshell, the difficulty facing the theory of aggregate supply is that logic and simple microeconomic theory lead us to believe we should be in a classical world, but the real world appears not to be classical. The challenge for macroeconomics is to explain the real world.

There are three leading approaches to explaining the short-run stickiness of wages and prices, the short-run nonneutrality of money, and the varying and often persistently high rates of unemployment that exist in the real world. We give the flavor of the arguments here and take them up more systematically in Chapters 13, 14, and 18.

Modern Keynesian Approaches

The original Keynesian approach was to assume that the wage is fixed.[16] Modern Keynesian theories argue that the wage and price levels are very slow to change, rather than being fixed. The aggregate supply curve is viewed as being close to flat in the short run and close to vertical in the long run. Attention focuses mainly on wages and the adjustment process to explain why adjustment is not immediate or at least very fast.

CONTRACTS

Wages are slow to change because they are fixed in long-term contracts. These contracts may be explicit, as with the 3-year union contracts that are found in the United States. Or they may be implicit, an unwritten agreement between firm and employee that the wage will remain fixed for a period of a year and will not be cut.

If wages (and prices) are adjusted at different times for different firms and industries, then the economywide average wage and the aggregate price level adjust only slowly to policy changes or other changes. This is so because the averages are made up of many wages or many prices and only a small number of them will be adjusted at any one time.

COORDINATION

The nonneutrality of money can be accounted for by the difficulty of coordinating wage and price changes when wages and prices are not all adjusted simultaneously. When the quantity of money is changed, the extent to which any individual should change his or

---

[16] In the *General Theory of Employment, Interest and Money* (London: Macmillan, 1936) Keynes assumed for most of the book that the nominal wage was fixed. But he also argued that flexible wages would not succeed in stabilizing output and employment and that the active use of fiscal policy was a preferable means of maintaining full employment.

her own price or wage depends on how much others change their prices. If everyone else changes prices in proportion to the change in the money supply, then the last remaining firm would do the same. But if no one else or only a few firms do, then the firm raising its price in proportion to an increase in the money stock will lose customers because its price is out of line with the prices of others. Because all the firms in an economy cannot get together to coordinate, they will raise prices slowly as the effects of the change in money are felt through increased demand for their goods at the existing prices.

EFFICIENCY WAGES

Another strand of modern Keynesian supply theory, efficiency wage theory, focuses on the wage as a means of motivating labor.[17] The amount of effort workers make on the job is related to how well the job pays relative to alternatives. Firms may want to pay employees wages above the market-clearing wage to ensure that they work hard in order not to lose their "good" jobs. By the same token, firms are reluctant to cut wages because that affects worker morale and output. This theory does not explain why the average *nominal* wage is slow to change, but it does help explain the existence of unemployment.

These are not the only recent models that seek to explain aggregate supply along broadly Keynesian lines in which markets may not always clear. Aggregate supply is an area of intensive research. There is not as yet a dominant, completely persuasive microeconomic explanation of the positively sloped aggregate supply curve, but there are many suggestive theories. We will examine the main explanations of upward sloping, but not vertical, supply curves in Chapter 13.

New Classical Approaches

The modern Keynesian approaches are willing to assume that markets do not clear. New classical approaches, by contrast, assume that markets clear. We have already developed one of the new classical approaches, the rational expectations equilibrium approach that is used to generate the Lucas supply function.

This approach is sometimes called the imperfect information market-clearing approach. As already sketched in the previous section, it does not assert that people make *stupid* mistakes in deciding how much to work and produce. Rather people do their best to understand the situation in which they find themselves but lack the full information to make the correct decision. Under some conditions, this leads to an upward-sloping aggregate supply function, as seen in Figures 7-16 and 7-17.

---

[17] See, for example, George Akerlof and Janet Yellen (eds.), *Efficiency Wage Models of the Labor Market* (New York: Cambridge University Press, 1986), and Assar Lindbeck and Dennis J. Snower, *The Insider-Outsider Theory of Employment and Unemployment* (Cambridge: MIT Press, 1989).

SEARCH

The imperfect information – market-clearing approach can also be used to explain unemployment. Suppose that workers who become unemployed search for a new job, staying unemployed until they find a suitable job at the right real wage. Suppose further that they do not know the aggregate price level exactly. Now suppose that the money supply increases, that the aggregate price level goes up (though less than proportionately), and that firms raise the wages they are willing to pay.

Workers are unaware that the price level is up. They find higher wages when they look for a job, think that the real wage is higher, and take the job. The unemployment rate falls as a result of the increase in the money stock. What might look like a Keynesian effect of an increase in the money stock on unemployment is instead explained by imperfect information: The real wage is lower than the worker thought it was when taking the job.

Real Business Cycles and the Role of Money

A third approach, real business cycle theory — which really developed out of the imperfect information – market-clearing approach — starts from the market-clearing view by assuming that markets are always in equilibrium. Its distinctive feature is the argument that changes in the money stock play no serious role in the business cycle.[18] Real business cycle theorists recognize that output fluctuates over time, but argue that the fluctuations are a result of *real* shocks to the economy.

Real shocks are taken as coming mainly from the supply side of the economy. Changes in the weather or the price of oil or new methods of production affect the level of output. On the demand side, changes in government spending can also affect the level of output. But real business cycle theory by definition does not give a causal role to changes in the money stock in affecting output. Rather, the argument is that the quantity of money adjusts itself to the level of output. Thus real business cycle theorists argue that changes in output cause changes in the quantity of money rather than the other way around. The explanation is that when the level of output rises, people demand more real balances, and the banks can generally respond by creating more money.

---

[18] Carl Walsh, "New View of the Business Cycle: Has the Past Emphasis on Money Been Misplaced?" *Business Review,* Federal Reserve Bank of Philadelphia, January /February 1986, and Carl Walsh and Peter Hartley, "Financial Intermediation, Monetary Policy, and Equilibrium Business Cycles," Federal Reserve Bank of San Francisco *Review,* Fall 1988, provide an excellent introduction to the topic. Much more advanced treatments are given in Hoover, *The Classical Macroeconomics*; in the collection of essays in Robert Barro (ed.), *Modern Business Cycle Theory* (Cambridge: Harvard University Press, 1989); and in Bruce Greenwald and Joseph Stiglitz, "Examining Alternative Macroeconomic Theories," *Brookings Papers on Economic Activity*, 1, 1988. Our Chap. 18 studies modern business cycle theory in more detail.

A Look Ahead

We will not evaluate the different approaches here, but we keep returning to them in subsequent chapters, especially Chapter 18 where we discuss the interactions of events and ideas in macroeconomics.

In Chapter 13 we develop a theory of aggregate supply that produces a positively sloped aggregate supply curve that is relatively flat in the short run while vertical in the long run. We base the theory largely on the modern Keynesian approach, but combine that with the emphasis on expectations that comes from the rational expectations approach to macroeconomics and aggregate supply, which we developed in the previous section.

7-8 SUMMARY

1. The aggregate supply and demand model is used to show the determination of the equilibrium levels of *both* output and prices.
2. The aggregate supply schedule, *AS,* shows at each level of prices the quantity of real output firms are willing to supply.
3. The Keynesian supply schedule is horizontal, implying that firms supply as much goods as are demanded at the existing price level. The classical supply schedule is vertical. It would apply in an economy that has full price and wage flexibility. In such a frictionless economy, employment and output are always at the full-employment level.
4. The aggregate demand schedule, *AD,* shows at each price level the level of output at which the goods and assets markets are in equilibrium. This is the quantity of output demanded at each price level. Along the *AD* schedule fiscal policy is given, as is the nominal quantity of money. The *AD* schedule is derived using the *IS-LM* model.
5. Moving down and along the *AD* schedule, lower prices raise the real value of the money stock. Equilibrium interest rates fall, and that increases aggregate demand and equilibrium spending.
6. A fiscal expansion or an increase in the nominal quantity of money shifts the *AD* schedule outward and to the right.
7. Under Keynesian supply conditions, with prices fixed, both monetary and fiscal expansion raise equilibrium output. A monetary expansion lowers interest rates, while a fiscal expansion raises them.
8. Under classical supply conditions a fiscal expansion has no effect on output. But a fiscal expansion raises prices, lowers real balances, and increases equilibrium interest rates. That is, under classical supply conditions there is full crowding out. Private spending declines by exactly the increase in government demand.
9. A monetary expansion, under classical supply conditions, raises prices in the same proportion as the rise in nominal money. All real variables — specifically, output and interest rates — remain unchanged. When changes in the money stock have no real effects, money is said to be *neutral.*

10. The strict quantity theory of money states that prices move in proportion to the nominal money stock. Modern quantity theorists or monetarists accept the view that there is no exact link between money and prices, but argue that changes in the money stock are, in practice, the most important single determinant of changes in the price level.

*11. The rational expectations equilibrium approach to aggregate supply assumes that wages and prices are flexible but that workers and firms have different information about the aggregate price level. The Lucas supply function then implies that the position of the aggregate supply curve depends on the expected price level. Using the rational expectations approach, an expected increase in the money stock is fully neutral: The price level rises in proportion to the increase in the money stock, and output does not change. However, an unanticipated increase in the money supply is not neutral: The price level rises less than proportionately, and real output rises.

KEY TERMS

Aggregate supply curve
Aggregate demand curve
Keynesian aggregate supply curve
Classical aggregate supply curve
Efficiency wage theory
Full crowding out
Quantity theory of money

Neutrality of money
Monetarism
Market-clearing approach
Lucas supply curve
Rational expectations equilibrium approach
Rational expectations

PROBLEMS

1. Define the aggregate demand and supply curves.

2. Explain why the classical supply curve is vertical and explain the mechanisms that ensure continued full employment of labor in the classical case.

3. Discuss, using the *IS-LM* model, what happens to interest rates as prices change along a given *AD* schedule.

4. Show graphically that the *AD* curve is steeper the larger the interest responsiveness of the demand for money and the smaller the multiplier.

5. Suppose full-employment output increases from Y^* to $Y^{*'}$. What does the quantity theory predict will happen to the price level?

6. In goods market equilibrium in a closed economy, $S + T = I + G$. Use this equation to explain why, in the classical case, a fiscal expansion must lead to full crowding out.

7. Show, using *IS* and *LM* curves, why money is neutral in the classical supply case. (Refer to footnote 7 for hints.)

8. Suppose the government reduces the personal income tax rate from t to t'.
   (a) What is the effect on the *AD* schedule?

(b) What is the effect on the equilibrium interest rate?

(c) What happens to investment?

9. Suppose there is a decline in the demand for money. At each output level and interest rate the public now wants to hold lower real balances.

(a) In the Keynesian case, what happens to equilibrium output and to prices?

(b) In the classical case, what is the effect on output and on prices?

10. Repeat question 9, using the quantity theory of money to explain the effect of the money demand shift on prices.

11. Suppose the government undertakes a balanced budget increase in spending. Government spending rises from G to G', and there is an accompanying increase in tax rates so that at the initial level of output the budget remains balanced.

(a) Show the effect on the AD schedule.

(b) Discuss the effect of the balanced budget policy on output and interest rates in the Keynesian case.

(c) Discuss the effect in the classical case.

12. (a) Define the strict quantity theory.

(b) Define monetarism.

(c) What type of statistical evidence would you need to collect in order to support or refute the major argument of monetarism presented in this chapter?

13. Explain the basic difficulty facing the theory of aggregate supply.

*14. Show the impact on output and the price level of

(a) A fully anticipated increase in autonomous aggregate demand.

(b) An increase in autonomous demand that was not anticipated.

(c) Using diagrams like those in Figures 7-14 and 7-15, explain the economic mechanisms that account for the different answers to parts (a) and (b) of this question.

---

* An asterisk denotes a more difficult problem.

part two

8

CONSUMPTION AND SAVING

*T*he *IS-LM* model provides a comprehensive framework for understanding the interactions of the main macroeconomic variables that determine aggregate demand. Now we retrace our steps to present a more detailed and sophisticated treatment of the key relationships in the *IS-LM* model. The present chapter deals with the consumption function and with saving. Since consumption purchases account for more than 60 percent of aggregate demand, this is the natural place to begin. The following three chapters flesh out the behavior of investment, money demand, and money supply, and thus move us to a more realistic and reliable understanding of the working of the economy.

We are interested in consumption, though, for reasons that go beyond its importance as a share of aggregate demand. That part of a household's disposable income that is not consumed is saved and is available to finance investment.[1] The United States has the lowest household saving rates of all the major developed countries, as can be seen in Table 8-1. Many who are concerned that the United States is falling behind other countries economically attribute both its slow growth relative to countries such as Japan and its large current account deficit to its low saving rate. To understand consumption and saving we have to go beyond the simple consumption function of earlier chapters so as to try to understand why consumption varies over the business cycle and why saving rates differ among nations.[2]

---

[1] Recall, though, from the end of Chap. 3 that saving is equal to investment plus the government budget deficit plus the current account surplus. Thus saving finances not only investment, but also the government budget deficit and the acquisition of assets from foreigners.

[2] We see in Sec. 8-4 that there is a difference between household saving rates and *national* saving rates because both the government and the business sectors save (or maybe dissave) and thus contribute to national saving.

TABLE 8-1

HOUSEHOLD SAVING
RATES, 1985–1987
(percent of
disposable income)

United States	4.3
Japan	16.4
Germany	12.0
France	13.6
United Kingdom	7.4
Italy	24.0
Canada	12.1

SOURCE: *OECD Economic Outlook*, December 1988.

FIGURE 8-1

THE CONSUMPTION-INCOME RELATION, 1948–1988. There is a close
relationship in practice between consumption spending and disposable
income. Consumption spending rises on average by nearly 92 cents for
every extra dollar of disposable income. The solid line is the fitted
regression line that summarizes the relationship shown by the points
for the individual years.

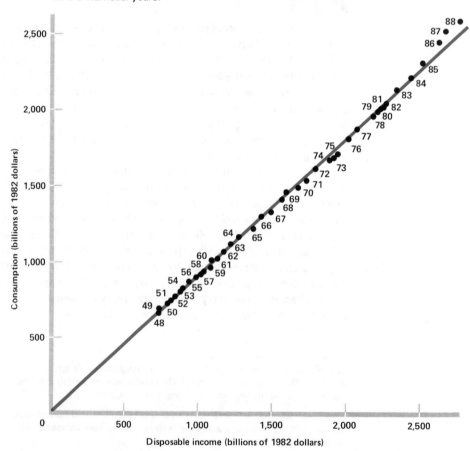

Our starting point in examining consumption behavior is the consumption function we have been using in previous chapters. Thus far we have assumed that consumption (C) is proportional to disposable income (YD):[3]

$$C = cYD \qquad 1 > c > 0 \tag{1}$$

We have already seen in the figure in Box 3-1 that the facts broadly support the relationship described by equation (1). Figure 8-1 reproduces the Box 3-1 figure, which shows a very close link between consumption and disposable income. To find numerical estimates of the relationship, we "fit" a regression line to the observations. The regression line is fitted to the data using the method of least squares, which produces the linear equation that best characterizes the relation between consumption and disposable income contained in the data.[4]

The estimated regression line is shown in Figure 8-1 as the solid line and is reported in equation (2). The estimate of the marginal propensity to consume is 0.917:

$$C = 0.917\ YD \qquad \text{(annual data, 1948–1988)} \tag{2}$$

As a first approximation equation (2) provides a reasonable summary of consumption behavior.[5] The next step is to ask whether equation (2) can be improved upon, and if so, to determine how.

Figure 8-2 shows the actual average propensity to consume, C/YD, in each year, compared with the average of 0.917 implied by the regression result in equation (2). The actual propensity to consume jumps around a good deal, and stays above or below the historical average ratio of 0.917 for years at a time, for example, from 1970 to 1976. The differences are not all trivial. For example, in 1973 the actual propensity to

---

[3] Recall from Chap. 3 that the simple consumption function (1) is sometimes written including a constant term, as

$$C = C' + cYD$$

where $C' > 0$ is constant. However in practice the value of C' is indistinguishable from zero, and we therefore omit it.

[4] The line drawn in Fig. 8-1 is the line represented by equation (2). That line is calculated by minimizing the sum of the squares of the vertical distances of the points in Fig. 8-1 from the line, and it provides a good description of the general relationship between the two variables. Those familiar with the method should note that we have corrected for serial correlation in calculating equation (2). For further details on the fitting of such lines, called least-squares regression lines, see Robert S. Pindyck and Daniel L. Rubinfeld, *Econometric Models and Economic Forecasts,* 2d ed. (New York: McGraw-Hill, 1981); 3d ed. forthcoming.

[5] Equation (2) shows the average propensity to consume as 0.917, implying an average propensity to save of 0.083 ($= 1 - 0.917$) or 8.3 percent. Yet Table 8-1 shows the household saving rate in the United States as averaging 4.3 percent between 1985 and 1987. There are two reasons for the difference. First, the propensity to consume was about 2 percentage points above its long-run average in the years 1985–1987. Second, part of household disposable income (in recent years between 2.5 percent and 3 percent) is used to pay interest; this part counts as neither consumption nor saving (since it represents interest payments on past consumption spending). This means that in the data it is not true that the sum of the propensity to consume and the propensity to save is unity.

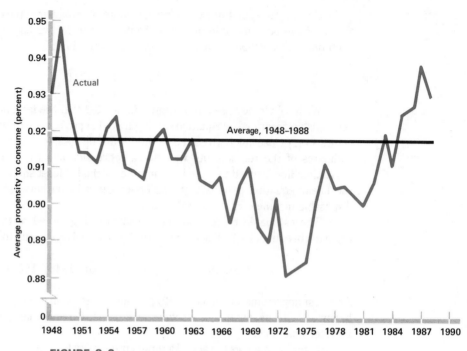

FIGURE 8-2

THE ACTUAL AND PREDICTED AVERAGE PROPENSITY TO CONSUME, 1948–1988. The average propensity to consume implied by equation (2), 0.917, is shown by the black "Predicted" line. The actual average propensity to consume fluctuates around the value of 0.917. (SOURCE: DRI/McGraw-Hill.)

consume was only 0.882. In 1987 by contrast the average propensity to consume was 0.938. The difference of 0.021 in 1987 translates into an error in predicting consumption of about $67 billion or nearly 1.5 percent of GNP. Errors of that size strongly suggest that the simplest consumption function can be improved upon.

We develop the two basic modern theories of consumption in the remainder of this chapter. They are the *life-cycle* theory, associated primarily with Franco Modigliani of MIT, the 1985 Nobel prizewinner in economic science,[6] and the *permanent income* theory, associated primarily with Milton Friedman of the University of Chicago, the 1976 winner of the Nobel Prize in economics. These theories are quite similar. Like much of good macroeconomics, they have in common a careful attention to microeconomic foundations. The life-cycle theory in particular starts from an indi-

---

[6] Modigliani developed the life-cycle theory together with Richard Brumberg, who died tragically young, and Albert Ando of the University of Pennsylvania. Modigliani's Nobel Prize lecture, "Life Cycle, Individual Thrift, and the Wealth of Nations," appears in the June 1986 *American Economic Review*.

vidual's lifetime consumption planning, and develops from that a macroeconomic theory of consumption and saving.

Box 8-1 describes an empirical puzzle about the simple consumption function that was historically important in leading to the new theories of the consumption function.[7]

8-1 THE LIFE-CYCLE THEORY OF CONSUMPTION AND SAVING

The consumption function (1) is based on the simple notion that individuals' consumption behavior in a given period is related to their income in that period. The *life-cycle hypothesis* views individuals, instead, as planning their consumption and saving behavior over long periods with the intention of allocating their consumption in the best possible way over their entire lifetimes.

The life-cycle hypothesis views savings as resulting mainly from individuals' desires to provide for consumption in old age. As we shall see, the theory points to a number of unexpected factors affecting the saving rate of the economy; for instance, the age structure of the population is, in principle, an important determinant of consumption and saving behavior.

savings: provide Coin old age

To anticipate the main results of this section, we state here that we will derive a consumption function of the form

$$C = aWR + cYL$$ (3)

where *WR* is real wealth, *a* is the marginal propensity to consume out of wealth, *YL* is *labor income*, and *c* is the marginal propensity to consume out of labor income. Labor income is the income that is earned by labor, as opposed to the income earned by other factors of production, such as the rent earned by land or the profits earned by capital.

In developing the life-cycle hypothesis of saving and consumption, we show what determines the marginal propensities *a* and *c* in equation (3), why wealth should affect consumption, and how the life-cycle hypothesis helps explain the Kuznets puzzle described in Box 8-1.

Consider a person who expects to live for *NL* years, work and earn income for *WL* years, and be in retirement for (*NL* − *WL*) years. The individual's year 1 is the first year of work. We shall, in what follows, ignore any uncertainty about either life expectancy or the length of working life. We shall assume, too, that no interest is earned on savings, so that current saving translates dollar for dollar into future con-

---

[7] The theories of the consumption function developed hereafter are also useful for explaining another empirical puzzle. In *cross-sectional* studies of the relationship between consumption and income — studies in which the consumption of a sample of families is related to their income — the marginal propensity to consume out of disposable income also appears to be lower than the average propensity to consume, with the average propensity to consume falling as the level of income rises. If you are interested in the reconciliation of this evidence with the long-run evidence of Kuznets, you should look at the ingenious explanation advanced by Milton Friedman through the permanent-income hypothesis. Follow up the reference given in footnote 12.

box 8-1

AN HISTORICAL CONSUMPTION FUNCTION PUZZLE

The puzzle consists of two types of evidence that made their appearance in the late 1940s and that were apparently in conflict. The first type of evidence came from estimates of the standard consumption function, equation (1), using annual data for the 1929–1941 period. (No earlier data were available then.) The estimated equation (in 1972 dollars) is

$$C = 47.6 + 0.73\,YD \qquad \text{(annual data, 1929–1941)} \qquad \text{(B1)}$$

This equation implies that the average propensity to consume falls as the level of income rises. It also shows a low marginal propensity to consume. If we used this equation to predict the 1988 average propensity to consume, the estimate would be 0.77, which is far from the actual ratio of 0.93.

The second piece of evidence was the finding by Nobel Prize winner Simon

TABLE 1
THE KUZNETS FINDING

	1869–1898	1884–1913	1904–1933
Average propensity to consume	0.867	0.867	0.879

SOURCE: Simon Kuznets, *National Income, A Summary of Findings* (New York: National Bureau of Economic Research, 1946), table 16.

sumption possibilities. With these assumptions, we can approach the saving or consumption decision with two questions. First, what are the individual's lifetime consumption possibilities? Second, how will the individual choose to distribute his or her consumption over a lifetime?

Consider now the consumption possibilities. For the moment we ignore property income (income from assets) and focus attention on labor income, YL. Income, YL, and consumption, C, are measured in real terms. Given WL years of working life, *lifetime income* (from labor) is $(YL \times WL)$, income per working year times the number of working years. Consumption over someone's lifetime cannot exceed this lifetime income unless that person is born with wealth, which we initially assume is not the case. Accordingly, we have determined the first part of the consumer's problem in finding the limit of lifetime consumption.

We assume the individual will want to distribute consumption over his or her lifetime so that he or she has a flat or even flow of consumption. Rather than consume a lot in one period and very little in another, the preferred profile is to consume exactly

$C \leq \tfrac{1}{2} * W\text{ife}$

Kuznets (1901–1985), using averages of data over long periods—10 and 30 years—that there was near proportionality between consumption and income.* The average propensity to consume that he found for three overlapping 30-year periods is shown in Table 1. The Kuznets results suggest, using long-term averages, that there is little variation in the ratio of consumption to income and, in particular, that there is no tendency for the average propensity to decline as disposable income rises. Proportionality, though with a higher average propensity to consume, is found also in the consumption function (2) fitted with post-World War II data.

There is clearly a conflict between the implications of the consumption function in equation (B1) and Kuznets's findings. The Kuznets results suggest that the average propensity to consume is constant over long periods, whereas equation (B1) suggests it falls as income rises. It is also clear that the consumption function estimated above on the basis of the prewar data is inconsistent with the same function estimated on the basis of postwar data, that is, with the estimate in equation (2).

The puzzle of the discrepancy was well known by the time the alternative theories we outline in this chapter were developed. In resolving the puzzle, both theories draw on the notion that consumption is related to a broader income measure than just current income. The broader measures go under the names of *lifetime income* and *permanent income*. These concepts have in common the recognition that consumption spending is maintained relatively constant in the face of fluctuations of current income. Consumption spending is not geared to what we earn today, but to what we earn on average. The important question obviously is what "average" means in this context. This is analyzed in the theories developed in this chapter. ■

* Simon Kuznets, *National Product Since 1869 and National Income, A Summary of Findings* (New York: National Bureau of Economic Research, 1946).

equal amounts in each period.[8] Clearly, this assumption implies that consumption is geared not to *current* income (zero during retirement), but rather to *lifetime income*.

Lifetime consumption equals lifetime income. This means that the planned level of consumption, C, which is the same in every period, times the number of years of life, NL, equals lifetime income:

$$C_L = (WL * YL) + W$$

[8] Why? The basic reason is the notion of diminishing marginal utility of consumption. Consider two alternative consumption plans. One involves an equal amount of consumption in each of two periods; the other involves consuming all in one period and none in the other. The principle of diminishing marginal utility of consumption implies that in the latter case, we would be better off by transferring some consumption from the period of plenty toward that of starvation. The loss in utility in the period of plenty is *more* than compensated for by the gain in utility in the period of scarcity. And there is a gain to be made by transferring consumption so long as there is any difference in consumption between the two periods. The principle of diminishing marginal utility of consumption conforms well with the observation that most people choose stable life styles—not, in general, saving furiously in one period to have a big bust in the next but, rather, consuming at about the same level every period.

$$C \times NL = YL \times WL \tag{4}$$

Dividing through by NL, we have planned consumption per year, C, which is proportional to labor income:

$$C = \frac{WL}{NL} \times YL \tag{5}$$

each year of working life

The factor of proportionality in equation (5) is WL/NL, the fraction of lifetime spent working. Accordingly, equation (5) states that in each year of working life a fraction of labor income is consumed, where that fraction is equal to the proportion of working life in total life.

NUMERICAL EXAMPLE: Suppose a person starts working at age 20, plans to work till 65, and will die at 80. The working life, WL, is thus 45 years (= 65 − 20) and the number of years of life, NL, is 60 years (= 80 − 20). Annual labor income, YL, is $30,000. Then

$$\text{Lifetime income} = YL \times WL$$
$$= \$30,000 \times 45 = \$1,350,000$$

This person will receive a total of $1,350,000 over a working lifetime.

The lifetime income, $1,350,000, has to be spread over the 60 years of life. The consumer wants to spread it evenly, and so

$$C = \frac{\$1,350,000}{60} = \$22,500 = \frac{WL}{NL} \times YL$$
$$= \frac{45}{60} \times 30,000$$

In this example, 0.75 of labor income is consumed each year the person works. Why is the propensity to consume out of labor income in this example equal to 0.75? Because that is the fraction of lifetime that the person works.

Saving and Dissaving

The counterpart of equation (5) is the saving function. Remembering that saving is equal to income less consumption, we have

$$S \equiv YL - C = YL \times \frac{NL - WL}{NL} \tag{6}$$

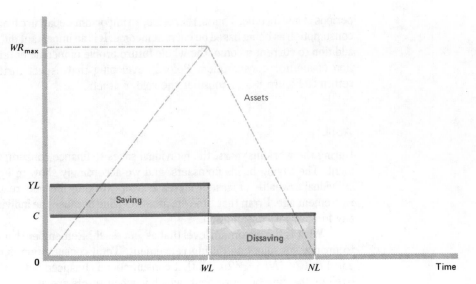

FIGURE 8-3

LIFETIME INCOME, CONSUMPTION, SAVINGS, AND WEALTH IN THE LIFE-CYCLE MODEL. During the working life, lasting WL years, the individual saves, building up assets. At the end of the working life, the individual begins to live off these assets, dissaving for the next ($NL \times WL$) years, till the end of life. Consumption is constant at level C throughout the lifetime. All assets have been used up at the end of life.

Equation (6) states that saving during the period in which the individual works is equal to a fraction of labor income, with that fraction being equal to the proportion of life spent in retirement.

Figure 8-3 shows the lifetime pattern of consumption, saving, and *dissaving*.[9] Over the whole lifetime, there is an even flow of consumption at the rate of C, amounting in total to $C \times NL$. That consumption spending is financed during working life out of current income. During retirement the consumption is financed by drawing down the savings that have been accumulated during working life. Therefore the shaded areas ($YL - C$) $\times$ WL and $C \times (NL - WL)$ are equal, or equivalently, saving during working years finances dissaving during retirement.

The important idea of the life-cycle theory of consumption is apparent from Figure 8-3. It is that consumption plans are made so as to achieve a smooth or even level of consumption by saving during periods of high income and dissaving during

---

[9] Figure 8-3 was developed by Franco Modigliani in "The Life Cycle Hypothesis of Saving, the Demand for Wealth and the Supply of Capital," *Social Research*, vol. 33, no. 2, 1966.

periods of low income. This is, therefore, an important departure from the treatment of consumption as being based on current income. It is an important difference because, in addition to current income, the whole future profile of income enters into the calculation of lifetime consumption. Before developing that aspect further, however, we return to Figure 8-3 to consider the role of assets.

ASSETS

During the working years, the individual saves to finance consumption during retirement. The saving builds up assets, and we accordingly show in Figure 8-3 how the individual's wealth or assets increase over working life and reach a maximum at retirement age. From that time on, assets decline because the individual sells assets to pay for current consumption.

What is the maximum level that assets reach? Remember that assets are built up to finance consumption during retirement. Total consumption during retirement is equal to $C \times (NL - WL)$. All that consumption is financed out of the assets accumulated by the date of retirement, which is when assets are at their peak.

Denote the maximum level of assets by WR_{max}. Then,

$$WR_{max} = C \times (NL - WL)$$

For instance, in the numerical example above, where C was \$15,000 and $(NL - WL)$ was equal to 15, the individual would have \$15,000 $\times$ 15 = \$225,000 saved at the date of retirement. Equivalently, the person has worked for 45 years, saving \$5,000 each year, thus accumulating \$225,000 at age 65.

This simple case gives the spirit of the life-cycle theory of consumption and saving. People do not want to consume over their lifetimes at precisely the same times and in the same amounts as they earn income. Thus they save and dissave so as to consume their lifetime incomes in the pattern they want. Typically, the theory argues, they will save while working, and then use the savings to finance spending in their retirement years.

$$S = YL + WR - C$$

SAVING

The life-cycle theory of consumption is also of course a theory of life-cycle saving. In its simplest version, as in Figure 8-3, the theory implies that individuals save for their retirement while working. But there is a more general theory of saving implied by the life-cycle theory. Namely, individuals aim to have smooth patterns of consumption over their lifetimes. Their income patterns may not be so smooth: they may go to school at one stage, or retire at another, or take a year off to find themselves at the age of 40. *The life-cycle theory of saving predicts that people save a lot when their income is high relative to lifetime average income, and dissave when their income is low relative to the lifetime average.*

Introducing Wealth

The next step is to extend this model by allowing for initial assets, that is, by assuming the individual was born into wealth.[10] We can draw on the previous insight that the consumer will spread any existing resources to achieve an even lifetime consumption profile. The individual who has assets in addition to labor income will plan to use these assets to add to lifetime consumption. A person who is at some point T in life, with a stock of wealth, WR, and with labor income accruing for another $(WL - T)$ years at the rate of YL, and with a life expectancy of $(NL - T)$ years to go, will behave as follows. The person's lifetime consumption possibilities are

$$C \times (NL - T) = WR + (WL - T) \times YL \qquad (7)$$

where we have included wealth, WR, along with lifetime labor income as a source of finance for lifetime consumption. From equation (7), consumption in each period is equal to

$$C = aWR + cYL \qquad a \equiv \frac{1}{NL - T} \qquad c \equiv \frac{WL - T}{NL - T} \qquad WL > T \qquad (8)$$

where the coefficients a and c are, respectively, the marginal propensities to consume out of wealth and out of labor income.

In the numerical example above we considered a person starting to work at age 20 who will retire at 65 and die at 80. Thus, $WL = (65 - 20) = 45$; and $NL = (80 - 20) = 60$. We also assumed $YL = 20,000$.

Now suppose the person is 40 years old. Accordingly $T = 20$, meaning that the person is in the twentieth year of working life. We can calculate the propensity to consume out of wealth, a, and the propensity to consume out of income, c, from equation (8). For this person, at age 40 (i.e., for $T = 20$):

$$a = \frac{1}{NL - T} = \frac{1}{60 - 20} = 0.025$$

$$c = \frac{WL - T}{NL - T} = \frac{45 - 20}{60 - 20} = 0.625$$

Suppose now that the individual's wealth is $200,000. Then from the consumption function, equation (8), we find:

$$C = (0.025 \times 200,000) + (0.625 \times 20,000) = 17,500$$

---

[10] The individual may receive wealth early in life through gifts or bequests. In the fully developed life-cycle model, the individual, in calculating lifetime consumption, has also to take account of any bequests he or she may want to leave. We discuss the role of bequests in Box 8-2.

Note that the consumption level here is higher than in the previous example. That is because this individual has more wealth at age 40 than he or she would have if all this wealth came from saving out of labor income. (That amount would be $100,000, since the individual in the previous example saved $5,000 per year, and at $T = 20$, has been working 20 years.) We can conclude that we are dealing here with someone who started out working life with inherited wealth.

Thus, in our model of individual lifetime consumption, we have derived a consumption function like equation (3), in which both wealth and labor income affect the individual's consumption decisions. It is important to recognize from equation (8) that the marginal propensities are related to the individual's position in the life cycle. The closer a person is to the end of lifetime, the higher the marginal propensity to consume out of wealth. Thus, someone with 2 more years of life will consume half his or her remaining wealth in each of the remaining 2 years. The marginal propensity to consume out of labor income is related both to the remaining number of years during which income will be earned, $WL - T$, and to the number of years over which these earnings are spread, $NL - T$. It is quite clear from equation (8) that an increase in either wealth or labor income will raise consumption expenditures. It is apparent, too, that lengthening working life relative to retirement will raise consumption because it increases lifetime income and reduces the length of the period of dissaving. The most basic point, however, is that equation (8) shows both (lifetime) income and wealth as determinants of consumption spending.

To summarize where we have come so far, we note that in this particular form of the life-cycle model:

1. Consumption is constant over the consumer's lifetime.
2. Consumption spending is financed by lifetime income plus initial wealth.
3. During each year a fraction, $1/(NL - T)$, of wealth will be consumed, where $NL - T$ is the individual's life expectancy.
4. Current consumption spending depends on current wealth and lifetime income.

Extensions

The model as outlined makes very strong simplifying assumptions. It can be extended to remove most of the strong assumptions without affecting the underlying result of equation (8), namely, that consumption is related to both labor income and wealth.

First, it is necessary to take account of the possibility that savings earn interest, so that a dollar not consumed today will provide more than a dollar's consumption tomorrow. Second, the analysis has to be extended to allow for the fact that individuals are uncertain of the length of their lifetimes and, also, that they sometimes want to leave bequests to their heirs. In the latter case, they would not plan to consume all their resources over their own lifetimes. Similarly, the model has to be extended to take account of the composition of the family over time, so that some consumption is provided for children before they begin to work. These extensions are important and have interesting implications for the behavior of consumption, but — as stated above — they do not change the basic result contained in equation (8).

A final extension is very important. In practice, one never knows exactly what one's lifetime labor income will be, and lifetime consumption plans have to be made on the basis of predictions of future labor income. This, of course, raises the issue of how income is to be predicted. We do not pursue the issue here, but leave it to the next section on permanent income, which is an estimate of lifetime income. However, *expected* lifetime labor income would be related to *current* disposable labor income, leading to a form of the consumption function like equation (3), perhaps with other variables also included.

Indeed, it is useful to think of the life-cycle and permanent-income theories as being fundamentally the same, with the life-cycle theory developing most carefully the implications of the model for the role of wealth and other variables in the consumption function, and the permanent-income theory concentrating on the best way to predict lifetime income.

Aggregate Consumption and Saving

The theory outlined so far is strictly a microeconomic theory about consumption and saving by individuals over the course of their lifetimes. How does it relate to aggregate consumption, which is, after all, the focus of macroeconomic interest in consumption? Imagine an economy in which population and the GNP were constant through time. Each individual in that economy would go through the life cycle of saving and dissaving outlined in Figure 8-3. The economy as a whole, though, would not be saving. At any one time, the saving of working people would be exactly matched by the dissaving of retired people. However, if the population were growing, there would be more young people than old, thus more saving in total than dissaving, and there would be net saving in the economy. Thus, aggregate consumption depends in part on the age distribution of the population. It also depends on such characteristics of the economy as the average age of retirement and the presence or absence of a social security program. These surprising implications of the theory indicate the richness of the approach.

Some economists argue that these demographic factors help account for the fact that, as seen in Table 8-1, household saving rates in Japan are much higher than those in the United States. One possible reason is that the proportion of retired people is lower in Japan than in the United States. Because the percentage of the elderly in the Japanese population is rising rapidly, some economists expect the Japanese saving rate will start falling before the end of the century.[11]

---

[11] See OECD, *The Ageing Population* (Paris: 1988).

box 8-2 THE LIFE-CYCLE HYPOTHESIS, CONSUMPTION
BY THE ELDERLY, AND BEQUESTS

Although the life-cycle hypothesis remains the leading microeconomic theory of consumption behavior, recent empirical evidence raises questions about the particular
form of the theory developed in this chapter. In the form of the theory developed by
Modigliani, the assumption is that people save mainly for retirement and draw down
their savings during that period.

There is some evidence contesting the assumed motive for saving and the implication that people draw down their savings when old. Laurence Kotlikoff and Lawrence
Summers* have made calculations suggesting that most saving is done to provide
bequests rather than to provide for consumption when old. Of course, the savings are
there for the old to use in retirement, but, they argue, the amount of wealth in the
economy is far too large for people to have been saving only for their retirement.
Rather, they conclude, people are saving mainly to pass wealth on to their descen-
dants.

A detailed examination of the consumption propensities of the elderly by Sheldon Danziger, Jacques van der Gaag, Eugene Smolensky, and Michael Taussig† contains the remarkable conclusion that the elderly save a higher proportion of their in-

---

* "The Role of Intergenerational Transfers in Aggregate Capital Accumulation," *Journal of Political Economy,*
August 1981.

† "The Life Cycle Hypothesis and the Consumption Behavior of the Elderly," *Journal of Post-Keynesian Economics,* Winter 1982–1983.

Implications

We return to equation (3) to emphasize again the role of wealth. Note from equation (3)
that with an increase in wealth, the ratio of consumption to disposable income would
rise. This has a bearing on the puzzle described in Box 8-1. On the basis of equation
(B1), the average propensity to consume seems to decline with income but, on the basis
of Kuznets's findings, remain constant over long periods.

If we divide through in equation (8) by YD, we obtain

$$\frac{C}{YD} = a\,\frac{WR}{YD} + c\,\frac{YL}{YD} \tag{9}$$

Now, if the ratio of wealth to disposable income and the ratio of disposable labor income
to total disposable income are constant, then equation (9) shows that the ratio of
consumption to disposable income will be constant. However, if the ratio of wealth to

comes than the young. This fact is inconsistent with the simple form of the life-cycle hypothesis set out in the chapter.

How might this evidence be reconciled with existing theories? First, the facts are not yet definitive. Franco Modigliani has taken strong issue with the detailed calculations that underlie the Kotlikoff-Summers claim.‡ In Japan, where similar results have been found,§ the elderly typically move in and pool their wealth with their children. They are thus probably drawing down wealth during their retirement, but their wealth cannot be distinguished from that of the children, who are saving.

If the basic evidence that the elderly who remain on their own accumulate wealth holds up, an explanation will have to take into account their increasing fears of being left alone without financial help from family, and with possibly large medical expenses, as they get older. The need for wealth may increase with age if complete insurance against medical expenses is not available—as it is not.

Whether people save for their own lifetimes, or also save to pass wealth on to their children—including transfers that take place during the parents' lifetime, such as paying for college education—does not affect the fact that wealth belongs in the consumption function, as in equation (3). But as Section 8-4 shows, the question of the goals of saving has potentially important implications for the effects of fiscal policy on the economy. ■

‡ "The Role of Intergenerational Transfers and Life Cycle Saving in the Accumulation of Wealth," *Journal of Economic Perspectives*, vol. 2, Spring 1988. See also the discussion of this article by Laurence Kotlikoff that follows.

§ See Albert Ando and Arthur Kennickell, "How Much (or Little) Life Cycle Saving Is There in Micro Data?" in Rudiger Dornbusch, Stanley Fischer, and John Bossons (eds.), *Macroeconomics and Finance: Essays in Honor of Franco Modigliani* (Cambridge: MIT Press, 1986).

disposable income is changing, the average propensity to consume will also be changing.

This suggests, as an explanation of the Kuznets puzzle, the possibility that the ratio of wealth to disposable income is roughly constant over long periods and that it varies considerably in the short run. This also helps explain the fluctuations in the average propensity to consume, which are shown in Figure 8-2, as resulting from short-run changes in the wealth-income ratio.

The life-cycle hypothesis also provides a channel for the stock market to affect consumption behavior. The value of stocks held by the public is part of wealth and is included in WR in equation (8). When the value of stocks is high—when the stock market is booming—WR is high and tends to increase consumption, and the reverse occurs when the stock market is depressed.

We continue now to the permanent-income theory of consumption, bearing in mind that we have not yet discussed the determinants of expected lifetime labor income in equation (9) in any detail, and recalling that the two theories should be thought of as complementary rather than competing.

box 8-3 **CONSUMPTION AND THE 1987 STOCK MARKET CRASH**

On October 19, 1987, when the New York stock market crashed (other stock markets all around the world suffered similar huge falls that day or the next), with stocks losing over 20 percent of their value in a single day, economists used a consumption function like (9) to estimate the likely effect of the crash on the level of consumption. Stocks lost over $500 billion in value on October 19, 1987. Figure 1 shows an index of household real net worth. In the fourth quarter of 1987 this index fell by 4 percent.

The coefficient of real wealth, a, in equation (9) is typically estimated to be about 0.045. Accordingly, the stock market crash would have reduced consumption by about $25 billion, or just over 0.5 percent of GNP at the time. This is a sizable fall, whose effects on GNP could, however, be overcome through an expansionary monetary policy.

Table 1 shows the behavior of the household saving rate in the quarters around the stock market crash, which took place near the beginning of the fourth quarter of 1987. The crash was followed by an increase in the saving rate of about two percentage points. This would imply a decrease in consumption of about $66 billion at an annual rate (disposable personal income was $3.3 trillion in 1987:4). Thus the stock market crash was followed by a bigger decline in consumption than can be accounted for by the wealth term in the consumption function.

There are at least two possible reasons for this. First, the stock market crash made people much more uncertain about the future of the economy, and increased uncertainty usually leads to more saving. And second, the estimates of the impact of changes in wealth on consumption are in any case not exact. The important point is that the experience confirms the link between consumption and wealth. ∎

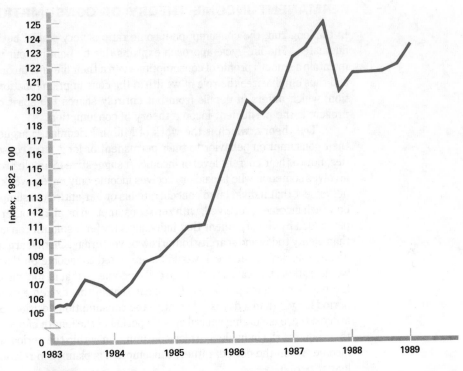

FIGURE 1

HOUSEHOLD REAL NET WORTH, 1983–1989. (SOURCE: DRI/McGraw-Hill.)

TABLE 1

THE U.S. HOUSEHOLD SAVING RATE, 1987:1–1988:3 (percent of disposable income)

1987:1	1987:2	1987:3	1987:4	1988:1	1988:2	1988:3
4.2	2.2	2.3	4.3	4.4	3.7	4.2

SOURCE: *Economic Report of the President*, 1989.

8-2 PERMANENT-INCOME THEORY OF CONSUMPTION

In the long run, the consumption-income ratio is very stable, but in the short run, it fluctuates. The life-cycle approach explains this by pointing out that people want to maintain a smooth profile of consumption even if their lifetime income profile is uneven, and thus emphasizes the role of wealth in the consumption function. Another explanation, which differs in details from but entirely shares the spirit of the life-cycle approach, is the permanent-income theory of consumption.

The theory, which is the work of Milton Friedman,[12] argues that people gear their consumption behavior to their permanent or long-term consumption opportunities, not to their current level of income. A suggestive example provided by Friedman involves someone who is paid or receives income only once a week, on Fridays. We do not expect that individual to concentrate his or her entire consumption on the one day on which income is received, with zero consumption on all the other days. Again we are persuaded by the argument that individuals prefer a smooth consumption flow rather than plenty today and scarcity tomorrow or yesterday. On that argument, consumption on any one day of the week would be unrelated to income on that particular day but would, rather, be geared to average daily income — that is, income per week divided by the number of days per week. It is clear that in this extreme example, income for a period longer than a day is relevant to the consumption decision. Similarly, Friedman argues, there is nothing special about a period of the length of one quarter or one year that requires the individual to plan consumption within the period solely on the basis of income within the period; rather, consumption is planned in relation to income over a longer period.

The idea of consumption spending that is geared to long-term or average or permanent income is appealing and essentially is the same as the life-cycle theory. It leaves two further questions. The first concerns the precise relationship between current consumption and permanent income. The second question is how to make the concept of permanent income operational, that is, how to measure it.

In its simplest form the permanent-income hypothesis of consumption behavior argues that consumption is proportional to permanent income:

$$C = cYP \tag{10}$$

where YP is permanent (disposable) income. From equation (10), consumption varies in the same proportion as permanent income. A 5 percent increase in permanent income raises consumption by 5 percent. Since permanent income should be related to long-run average income, this feature of the consumption function is clearly in line with the observed long-run constancy of the consumption-income ratio.

---

[12] Milton Friedman, *A Theory of the Consumption Function* (Princeton, N.J.: Princeton University Press, 1957).

Estimating Permanent Income

The next problem is how to think of and measure permanent income. We define permanent income as follows:[13] *Permanent income* is the steady rate of consumption a person could maintain for the rest of his or her life, given the present level of wealth and income earned now and in the future.

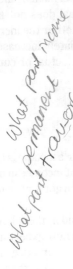

To think about the measurement of permanent income, imagine someone trying to figure out what his or her permanent income is. The person has a current level of income and has formed some idea of the level of consumption he or she can maintain for the rest of life. Now income goes up. The person has to decide whether that income increase represents a permanent increase or merely a *transitory* change, one that will not persist. In any particular case, the individual may know whether the increase is permanent or transitory. A government official who is promoted one grade will know that the increase in income is likely to be maintained, and a worker who has exceptionally high overtime in a given year will likely regard that year's increased income as transitory. But in general, a person is not so certain about what part of any change in income is likely to be maintained and is therefore permanent, and what part is not likely to be maintained and is therefore transitory. Transitory income is assumed not to have any substantial effect on consumption.

The question of how to infer what part of an increase in income is permanent is typically resolved in a pragmatic way by assuming that permanent income is related to the behavior of current and past incomes. To give a simple example, we might estimate permanent income as being equal to last year's income plus some fraction of the change in income from last year to this year:

$$YP = Y_{-1} + \theta(Y - Y_{-1}) \qquad 0 < \theta < 1$$
$$= \theta Y + (1 - \theta)Y_{-1} \tag{11}$$

where θ is a fraction and Y_{-1} is last year's income. The second line in equation (11) shows permanent income as a *weighted average* of current and past income. The second formulation is, of course, equivalent to that in the first line.

To understand equation (11), assume we had a value of $\theta = 0.6$, that this year's income was $Y = \$25,000$, and that last year's income was $Y_{-1} = \$24,000$. The value of permanent income would be $YP = \$24,600 \ (= 0.6 \times \$25,000 + 0.4 \times \$24,000)$. Thus, permanent income is an average of the two income levels. Whether it is closer to this year's or last year's income depends on the weight, θ, given to current income. Clearly, in the extreme, with $\theta = 1$, permanent income is equal to current income.

Some special features of equation (11) deserve comment. First, if $Y = Y_{-1}$, that is, if this year's income is equal to last year's, then permanent income is equal to the

---

[13] There is no standard definition of permanent income in Friedman's exposition of his theory. The definition given above is similar to average lifetime income. But it is not quite the same, because it effectively converts wealth into income in defining permanent income. Those with no labor income and only wealth are defined as having permanent income equal to the amount they could consume each year by using up wealth at a steady rate over the remainder of their lives.

income earned this year and last year. This guarantees that an individual who had always earned the same income would expect to earn that income in the future. Second, note that if income rises this year compared with last year, then permanent income rises by *less* than current income. The reason is that the individual does not know whether the rise in income this year is permanent. Not knowing whether the increase in income will be maintained or not, the individual does not immediately increase the expected or permanent income measure by the full amount of the actual or current increase in income.

Rational Expectations and Permanent Income

An estimate of permanent income that uses only current and last year's income is likely to be an oversimplification. Friedman forms the estimate by looking at incomes in many earlier periods, as well as current income, but with weights that are larger for the more recent, as compared with the more distant, incomes.[14]

The rational expectations approach, discussed in Chapter 7 and in the following section, emphasizes that there is no simple theory that would tell us how expectations are or should be formed without looking at how income changes in practice. If, in practice, changes in income are typically permanent or long-run changes, then consumers who see a given change in their income will believe that it is mostly permanent. Such consumers would have a high θ, as in equation (11). Consumers whose income is usually very variable will, however, not pay much attention to current changes in income in forming an estimate of permanent income. Such consumers will have low values of θ.[15]

At the same time, any sensible theory of expectations, including rational expectations, would emphasize that a formula like (11), based on the behavior of income in the past, cannot include all the factors that influence a person's beliefs about future income. The discovery of a vast amount of oil in a country, for instance, would raise the permanent incomes of the inhabitants of the country as soon as it was announced, even though a (mechanical) formula like equation (11), based on past levels of income, would not reflect such a change.

Permanent Income and the Dynamics of Consumption

Using equations (10) and (11), we can now rewrite the consumption function:

$$C = cYP = c\theta Y + c(1 - \theta)Y_{-1} \tag{12}$$

---

[14] Friedman also adjusts permanent income by taking into account the growth of income over time.

[15] Recall that although we restricted our measure of permanent income to a 2-year average, there is no reason why the average should not be taken over longer periods. If current income is unstable, an appropriate measure of permanent income may well be an average over 5 or more years, perhaps adjusted for the fact that income is on average growing over time.

The marginal propensity to consume out of *current* income is then just $c\theta$, which is clearly less than the long-run average propensity to consume, c. Hence, the permanent-income hypothesis implies that there is a difference between the short-run marginal propensity to consume and the long-run marginal (equal to the average) propensity to consume.

The reason for the lower short-run marginal propensity to consume is that when current income rises, the individual is not sure that the increase in income will be maintained over the longer period on which consumption plans are based. Accordingly, the person does not fully adjust consumption spending to the higher level that would be appropriate if the increase in income were permanent. However, if the increase turns out to be permanent, that is, if next period's income is the same as this period's, then the person will (next year) fully adjust consumption spending to the higher level of income. Note, though, that the adjustment here is completed in 2 years only because we have assumed, in equation (11), that permanent income is an average of 2 years' income. Depending on how expectations of permanent income are formed, the adjustment could be much slower. Or, if the consumer knew that this year's increase in income was permanent, he or she would increase consumption more rapidly than indicated by equation (12).[16]

The argument is illustrated in Figure 8-4. Here we show the long-run consumption function as a straight line through the origin with slope c, which is the constant average and marginal propensity to consume out of permanent income. The lower flat consumption function is a short-run consumption function drawn for a given history of income which is reflected in the intercept $c(1 - \theta)Y_0$. Assume that we start out in long-run equilibrium with actual and permanent income equal to Y_0 and consumption therefore equal to cY_0, as is shown at the intersection, point E, of the long-run and short-run consumption functions. Assume next that income increases to the level Y'. In the short run, which means during the current period, we revise our estimate of permanent income upward by θ times the increase in income and consume a fraction, c, of that increase in permanent income. Accordingly, consumption moves up along the short-run consumption function to point E'.

Note immediately that in the short run the ratio of consumption to income declines as we move from point E to E'. Going one period ahead and assuming that the increase in income persists, so that income remains at Y', we get a shift in the consumption function. The consumption function shifts upward because, as of the given higher level of income, the estimate of permanent income is now revised upward to Y'. Accordingly, consumers want to spend a fraction of c of their new estimate of permanent income, Y'. The new consumption point is E'', at which the ratio of consumption to income is back to the long-run level. The example makes clear that in the short run,

---

[16] There is another reason consumption may adjust relatively slowly even to changes in permanent income: the consumer may take time to purchase consumer durables. For instance, someone whose permanent income has doubled will at some point end up in a more luxurious house, but will take some time to buy such a house and the furnishings that go with it. Here, as in much of economic life, there are two reasons for slow adjustment to changes: expectations change slowly, and there are lags in adjusting to changed circumstances.

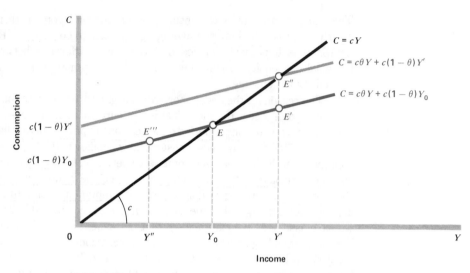

FIGURE 8-4

THE EFFECTS ON CONSUMPTION OF A SUSTAINED INCREASE IN INCOME. The short-run consumption functions, shown in color, have a marginal propensity to consume of $c\theta$. The position of the short-run consumption function depends on the level of income in the previous period. The long-run consumption function is shown by the black line and has average and marginal propensity to consume equal to c. When the level of income rises from Y_0 to Y', consumption rises only to E' in the short run because consumers are not sure the change in income is permanent. But with income remaining at Y', the short-run consumption function shifts up and consumption rises to point E'', as consumers realize their permanent income has changed.

an increase in income causes a decline in the average propensity to consume because people do not anticipate that the increase in income will persist or be permanent. Once they observe that the increase in income does persist, however, they fully adjust consumption to match their higher permanent income.

Like the life-cycle hypothesis, the permanent-income hypothesis has some unexpected and interesting implications. For instance, we noted above that an individual whose income is very unstable would have a low value of θ, whereas one whose income is more stable would have a higher value of θ. Looking at equation (12), this means that the short-run marginal propensity to consume of someone whose income is very variable will be relatively low because the short-run marginal propensity to consume is $c\theta$. Friedman showed that this implication is borne out by the facts. Farmers, for instance, have very variable incomes and a low marginal propensity to consume out of current income.

The Life-Cycle and Permanent-Income Hypotheses

To conclude this section, it is worth briefly considering again the relationship between the life-cycle and permanent-income hypotheses. The two hypotheses are not mutually exclusive. The life-cycle hypothesis pays more attention to the motives for saving than the permanent-income hypothesis does, and provides convincing reasons to include wealth as well as income in the consumption function. The permanent-income hypothesis, on the other hand, pays more careful attention to the way in which individuals form expectations about their future incomes than the original life-cycle hypothesis does. Recall that current labor income entered into the life-cycle consumption function to reflect expectations of future income. The more detailed analysis of the determinants of expected future income that is provided by the permanent-income hypothesis can be, and has been, included in the life-cycle consumption function.

Indeed, modern theories of the consumption function combine the expectations formation emphasized by the permanent-income approach with the emphasis on wealth and demographic variables suggested by the life-cycle approach. A simplified version of a modern consumption function would be

$$C = aWR + b\theta YD + b(1 - \theta)YD_{-1} \tag{13}$$

where YD in equation (13) would be disposable labor income. Equation (13) combines the main features that are emphasized by modern consumption theory.[17] It also shows the role of wealth, which is an important influence on consumption spending.

We end this section by repeating a warning. An equation like (13) performs quite well on average in predicting consumption. But it is always important to remember the underlying theory when using it. Equation (13) embodies the estimate of permanent income implied by equation (11). If we have knowledge about some particular change in income — for example, that it is transitory — then we should use that knowledge in predicting consumption. For instance, as we shall see, a temporary 1-year tax increase that reduced current disposable income would reduce current consumption by much less than a tax increase of the same size that was known to be permanent, even though equation (13) does not show that.

8-3 RATIONAL EXPECTATIONS, EXCESS SENSITIVITY, AND LIQUIDITY CONSTRAINTS

One of the most fascinating areas of research in modern consumption theory concerns the question of whether consumption responds excessively to changes in current

---

[17] To fix these ideas, you should draw a graph of equation (13) with consumption on the vertical axis and current disposable labor income on the horizontal axis. What is the intercept? How does the diagram differ from Fig. 8-4? Show the effects of (1) a transitory increase in income, (2) a sustained increase in income, and (3) an increase in wealth.

income. Modern research in this area, originating with work by Robert Hall of Stanford University and Marjorie Flavin of the University of Virginia, focuses on the combined implications of rational expectations and the life-cycle–permanent-income theory of consumption.[18]

In the previous section we noted that if expectations are rational, consumers' estimates of their permanent incomes should be consistent with the way income actually changes in the real world. When current income increases, it is usually impossible to be certain whether this increase represents a transitory or a permanent rise in income. But the consumer can use experience to determine what is the expected relationship between changes in current and in permanent income. For example historically a $1 increase in current income might typically have represented a 25-cent increase in permanent income, with the remaining 75 cents being transitory. Let θ be the fraction of a dollar increase in current income that represents the permanent increase. Then the consumption function in (10) together with this extra information about the current–permanent-income relation will yield a propensity to consume out of current income equal to $c\theta$. Thus if $c = 0.9$ and $\theta = 0.25$ the marginal propensity to consume out of current income should be 0.225, as implied by equation (12).

The researcher determines the value of θ, the proportion of a current change in income that is permanent, by examining the past behavior of income.[19] The next step is to see whether consumption reacts to the change in income by the right amount, $c\theta$, implied by the combined rational expectations–permanent-income theory. The striking finding, for instance in Flavin's 1981 paper referred to above, is that consumption *systematically* responds too much to current income, or is excessively sensitive. When income rises, consumption goes up by more than $c\theta$, and when income falls, consumption goes down by more than $c\theta$.[20]

On the assumption, still, that the permanent-income hypothesis serves as a correct framework of consumption behavior, there are two possible explanations for this overreaction. The first is that households do not correctly understand how changes in income are to be divided between those that are permanent and those that are transitory. This shortcoming is called a failure of the rational expectations hypothesis; it implies that households have not done their homework and are not forecasting in the best possible way and using all available information about how income behaves. For

---

[18] See Robert E. Hall, "Stochastic Implications of the Life Cycle-Permanent Income Hypothesis: Theory and Evidence," *Journal of Political Economy*, vol. 86, December 1978; and Marjorie Flavin, "The Adjustment of Consumption to Changing Expectations about Future Income," *Journal of Political Economy*, vol. 89, October 1981.

[19] Income changes over time in a more complicated way than is implied by equation (11), but that does not affect the principle that the test figures out how *estimated* permanent income should change with current income, and then sees whether changes in consumption are in accord with that estimate.

[20] More recently, Angus Deaton of Princeton University has argued that consumption may be too *insensitive* to changes in income or, as he puts it, excessively smooth. (See, for instance, his paper, "Life-cycle models of consumption: Is the evidence consistent with the theory?" in Truman Bewley (ed.), *Advances in Econometrics, Fifth World Congress*, vol. 2 (New York: Cambridge University Press, 1987). The issue turns on the nature of the behavior of income, with Deaton essentially arguing that changes in income tend to be more permanent than other researchers have believed. The issue is as yet unsettled.

simplicity, we can call this the *myopia hypothesis,* where myopia means shortsightedness. The alternative hypothesis is that while households in fact understand how income changes are divided between those that are permanent and those that are transitory, they fail to adjust to these changes properly because of liquidity constraints.

Excess Sensitivity, Liquidity Constraints, and Myopia

A liquidity constraint exists when a consumer cannot borrow to sustain current consumption in the expectation of higher future income. Students in particular should appreciate the possibility that liquidity constraints exist. Most students can look forward to a much higher income in the future than they receive as students. The life-cycle theory says they should be consuming on the basis of their lifetime incomes, which means they should be spending much more than they earn. To do that, they would have to borrow. They can borrow to some extent, through student loan plans. But it is entirely possible that they cannot borrow enough to support consumption at its permanent level.

Such students are liquidity-constrained. When they leave college and take jobs, their incomes will rise, and their consumption will rise, too. According to the life-cycle theory, consumption should not rise much when income rises, so long as the increase was expected. In fact, because of the liquidity constraint, consumption will rise a lot when income rises. Thus consumption will be more closely related to *current* income than is implied by the theory.

Or consider a household that suffers a decline in current income and that believes the decline is transitory because in the past, on average, falls in income have been mostly transitory. The household would therefore maintain consumption substantially unchanged, dissaving today. If there are no assets to run down to finance the excess of consumption over income, the household would borrow today, repaying the loan when income rises again as expected. Here imperfect capital markets come in. If the household cannot borrow because nobody wants to lend against uncertain (though likely) future income, then it faces liquidity constraints and for that reason is forced to consume according to current rather than permanent income. Consumption will then fall substantially along with current income — an overreaction, in terms of the permanent-income theory, that occurs because of the impossibility of borrowing.

How serious are these liquidity constraints in fact? There is substantial evidence that liquidity constraints help account for the excess sensitivity of consumption to income, and separate evidence that low-income households are indeed liquidity-constrained.[21] When liquidity constraints are present, consumption behaves more like the simple Keynesian consumption function equation (2) than life-cycle theory implies.

---

[21] For instance, Marjorie Flavin, "Excess Sensitivity of Consumption to Current Income: Liquidity Constraints or Myopia?" *Canadian Journal of Economics,* vol. 18, February 1985; Fumio Hayashi, "The Effect of Liquidity Constraints on Consumption: A Cross-Sectional Analysis," *Quarterly Journal of Economics,* vol. 100, February 1985; and Stephen P. Zeldes, "Consumption and Liquidity Constraints: An Empirical Investigation," *Journal of Political Economy,* vol. 97, April 1989.

The strength of liquidity constraints will depend on economic conditions. Suppose the government initiates a tax cut. If we are in a period of deep recession during which many households have already run down their assets, the tax cut will translate into a large increase in spending: Liquidity-constrained household members, by definition, are spending less than they would like and hence will spend every extra penny they can lay their hands on. By contrast a tax cut that occurs in a period of prosperity will have much less of an impact because few households are in a liquidity-constrained position in which they spend, at the margin, all of an extra dollar of income.

The alternative explanation for the sensitivity of consumption to current income, that consumers are myopic, is hard to distinguish in practice from the liquidity constraints hypothesis. For instance, David Wilcox of the Federal Reserve Board of Governors[22] has shown that the announcement that social security benefits will be increased (which always happens at least 6 weeks before the change) does not lead to a change in consumption *until the benefit increases are actually paid.* Once the increased benefits are paid, recipients certainly do adjust spending — primarily on durables. This could be either because recipients do not have the assets to enable them to adjust spending before they receive higher payments (liquidity constraints), or because they fail to pay attention to the announcements (myopia), or perhaps because they do not believe the announcements.

Summary

There is by now substantial evidence that U.S. consumers do not in practice act fully as life-cycle – permanent-income consumers. Rather, they are a mixture of life-cycle – permanent-income consumers and simple Keynesian consumers of the type represented by equations (1) and (2). Indeed, in recent empirical work, it has been estimated that about half of U.S. consumption is accounted for by people who act as life-cycle – permanent-income consumers, and the other half by people who essentially consume all their current income.[23] There is little doubt that this is in part due to the existence of liquidity constraints; myopia and perhaps other factors are also likely to contribute to some real world departures from the life-cycle – permanent-income hypotheses.

8-4 FURTHER ASPECTS OF CONSUMPTION BEHAVIOR

In this section we briefly review three topics in consumption, starting with international comparisons of saving behavior.

---

[22] David W. Wilcox, "Social Security Benefits, Consumption Expenditure, and the Life Cycle Hypothesis," *Journal of Political Economy,* vol. 97, April 1989.

[23] John Campbell and N. Gregory Mankiw, "Consumption, Income, and Interest Rates: Reinterpreting the Time Series Evidence," *NBER Macroeconomics Annual,* 1989.

TABLE 8-2

INTERNATIONAL COMPARISONS OF SAVING RATES,
1981–1987 (percent)

	U.S.	Japan	Germany	U.K.	Italy	Canada
Net national saving*	3.9	20.2	10.7	6.2	7.5	9.4
Gross national saving†	16.3	31.1	21.8	17.5	15.6	20.3
Gross private saving†	18.7	26.8	20.0	18.4	21.7	22.5
Government saving†	−2.4	4.3	1.8	−0.9‡	−6.0	−2.2

* As percentage of NNP.

† As percentage of GNP.

‡ Adjusted to account for apparent discrepancy in original data.

SOURCE: OECD, *Historical Statistics.*

International Differences in Saving Rates

Consumers in the United States save a lower proportion of their disposable income than consumers in other developed countries, as we saw in Table 8-1. A more detailed set of saving rates is presented in Table 8-2.

The most commonly quoted comparison of saving rates internationally is that in Table 8-1, which shows household saving rates as a percentage of disposable income. The comparisons in Table 8-2 are, however, more relevant to the concern over economic growth, which is related to total saving as a share of GNP rather than to household saving as a share of disposable income.

The comparison of gross private saving rates in Table 8-2 does not show such dramatic differences among saving rates as those seen in Table 8-1. The U.S. *private sector* (including corporations) saves only slightly less than the private sectors of Germany and Italy. Arithmetically the difference between the data given in Table 8-1 for household saving and those in Table 8-2 for gross private sector saving are accounted for by the difference between household and corporate saving rates. Evidently corporations in the United States save relatively more than those in Germany and Italy.[24] Corporations save when they use part of their profits to reinvest in the business rather than paying the money out to their shareholders.

Government saving increases national saving, and government dissaving (budget deficits) reduces national saving. A good part of the difference among national saving

---

[24] A major question that has been examined in the literature is whether households "pierce the corporate veil" when businesses that they own undertake saving, and save correspondingly less themselves. There is some evidence to this effect for the United States, in the fact that the sum of corporate and household savings has been reasonably stable. This is known as *Denison's law,* after Edward Denison of the Brookings Institution. See Paul David and Jon Scadding, "Private Savings: Ultrarationality, Aggregation, and 'Denison's Law,'" *Journal of Political Economy,* vol. 82, March/April 1974.

rates is accounted for by differences in government saving rates. Thus for the period 1981–1987 the Japanese government sector saved 6.7 percent of GNP more than the U.S. government sector. The Italian government ran such large budget deficits that it used up a large part of the available (and comparatively large) private sector saving, which was therefore not available to finance investment.

The difference between net and gross national saving rates (the first two rows of the table) arises from the depreciation of the capital stock. The data show that depreciation in the United States is a larger share of the capital stock than in the other major industrialized countries. However, it is widely suspected that data on depreciation are highly unsatisfactory, and economists are therefore generally reluctant to put much weight on *net* saving rates.

However suspect the data may be, there is no question that there is an enormous difference between the national saving rates (whether gross or net) in Japan and the United States. The United States is among the lowest gross savers in the group and is far and away the lowest net saver. The concern over this low saving rate is really a concern over the low growth rate of the United States — and the high-saving countries in Table 8-2 are indeed the rapidly growing countries.

While demographic factors appear to account for some of the differences in national saving rates, there has not yet been a satisfactory explanation that accounts for most of the differences. This is a major challenge for consumption theory. Some economists will in the end argue that there may simply be differences in national attitudes toward saving, but most hope to find economic explanations for those underlying attitudes.

Some differences among national saving rates appear to be due to differences in government saving rates, but as we shall see below, there is even a question as to whether the private sector might not systematically offset the impact of changes in government saving.

Consumption, Saving, and Interest Rates

What can be done about a low saving rate? One suggestion is to make saving more worthwhile for the saver. Anyone who saves receives a return in the form of interest or of dividends and capital gains (an increase in the price) on stocks. It seems, then, that the natural way to raise saving is to raise the return available to savers. Think of someone saving and receiving an interest rate of 5 percent each year for each dollar saved. Surely an increase in the rate to, say, 10 percent would make that person save more. This thinking has at times influenced tax policy in the United States. For instance, the interest received on savings in individual retirement accounts is exempt from the payment of taxes. This means the return received by the saver is raised compared with what it would be if the return were taxed.

But should we really expect an increase in the interest rate to increase savings? It is true that when the interest rate rises, saving is made more attractive. But it is also made less necessary. Consider someone who has decided to save an amount which will ensure that $10,000 per year will be available for retirement. Suppose the interest rate is now 5 percent, and the person is saving $1,000 per year. Now let the interest rate rise to 10 percent. With such a high interest rate, the individual needs to save less now to provide the given $10,000 per year during retirement. It may be possible to provide the same retirement income by saving only about $650 a year. Thus an increase in the interest rate might reduce saving.

What do the facts show? Does saving rise when the interest rate increases because every dollar of saving generates a higher return? Or does saving fall because there is less need to save to provide a given level of future income? The answers from the data are ambiguous. Many researchers have examined this question, but few have found strong positive effects of interest rate increases on saving. Typically, research suggests the effects are small and certainly hard to find.[25]

Tax Cuts, the Barro-Ricardo Hypothesis, and Saving

The Reagan administration cut personal income tax rates by 30 percent in 1981–1983 on the argument that increased incentives to save and invest would enhance the productive capacity of the U.S. economy. But the question of crowding out was raised. Would so large a tax cut not mean that consumption spending and interest rates would rise and thus crowd out investment? Advocates of the tax cuts argued that on the contrary the tax cuts would be saved and there was no risk of crowding out. Indeed, higher interest rates would lead to more saving.

We already reviewed above the view that interest rates affect saving and found that there is no evidence to support the existence of a strong effect of interest rates on saving. We have not explicitly discussed the argument that tax cuts might be saved rather than spent. In fact, the analysis of *temporary* tax cuts suggests those are primarily saved rather than consumed. But there was no suggestion in 1981 that the tax cuts were expected to be only temporary or transitory.

The debate about tax cuts centers around an argument originally noted and rejected by David Ricardo in the nineteenth century, but revived and supported in 1974 by Robert Barro of Harvard University.[26] Here is the argument: Suppose the budget is balanced initially, and the government cuts taxes. There will be a budget deficit, financed by borrowing. The debt that is issued today must be retired next year or in some future year, along with the interest that it carries. To repay the debt the government will have to raise taxes in the future. Thus a tax cut today means a tax

---

[25] The best-known study finding positive interest rate effects is that by Michael Boskin, who was appointed chairman of the Council of Economic Advisers in 1989. See his "Taxation, Saving, and the Rate of Interest," *Journal of Political Economy*, part 2, April 1978. For more typical results, see Gerald A. Carlino, "Interest Rate Effects and Intertemporal Consumption," *Journal of Monetary Economics*, March 1982. Campbell and Mankiw, referred to above, also find very little effect of the interest rate on saving.

[26] "Are Government Bonds Net Wealth?" *Journal of Political Economy*, vol. 82, November/December 1974. Theory and evidence on this topic are extensively analyzed in Douglas Bernheim, "Richardian Equivalence: An Evaluation of Theory and Evidence," *NBER Macroeconomics Annual*, 1987, and Lawrence Kotlikoff, *What Determines Saving?* (Cambridge: MIT Press, 1989).

increase in the future. Hence changes in taxes should have no effect on consumption because *permanent* income is really unaffected by this intertemporal jiggling of tax rates.

But if permanent income is unaffected by the tax cut, then consumption should be unaffected. When taxes are cut today, households save the tax cut so that they can pay the higher taxes tomorrow. We review this theory in more detail in Chapter 16, which deals with the government budget, but we can already run a preliminary check on the argument by studying saving behavior in the early 1980s, when taxes were cut substantially.

On the Barro-Ricardo theory, the tax cuts should have been saved, and the household saving rate should have risen. Figure 8-5 shows the household saving rate to

FIGURE 8-5

THE PERSONAL SAVING RATE, 1979–1988. The diagram shows personal saving as a percentage of disposable income. Despite tax cuts starting in 1981, the personal saving rate did not increase as the Barro-Ricardo hypothesis suggests it should have. (SOURCE: DRI/McGraw-Hill.)

be lower in 1985 than it was in 1980. How can we interpret the behavior of the saving rate? Liquidity constraints already noted above are one element in the explanation. Another is that households may not in fact behave exactly in the way prescribed by the Barro-Ricardo hypothesis. They see themselves as recipients of present tax cuts, but (perhaps rationally) they do not see themselves but rather future generations (in whose well-being they are not especially interested) as paying the future taxes.[27] A third possibility is that the Barro-Ricardo view is correct and that national saving did not fall despite the decline in government and household saving, because corporations increased their saving. In fact, though, the national saving rate did fall over this period.

The evidence thus suggests that tax cuts *do* have an effect on consumption and saving, quite likely as a result of liquidity constraints.[28] This suggests that the differences in government saving rates seen in Table 8-2 do have an effect on national saving rates.

8-5 CONSUMPTION AND THE *IS-LM* FRAMEWORK

In this section we discuss briefly how the more sophisticated theories of consumption we have developed in this chapter affect the *IS-LM* analysis of Chapters 4 and 5. We focus on two implications. The first is that consumption is a function of wealth and not, as we assumed previously, of income only. The second is that the response of consumption to various changes — for instance, in autonomous spending — may take time, as individuals gradually adjust their estimates of permanent income.

Wealth in the Consumption Function

The life-cycle hypothesis and estimated consumption functions of a form like equation (13) show that the rate of consumption depends on the level of wealth as well as on disposable income. This means that the position of the *IS* curve, representing equilibrium in the goods market, depends on the level of wealth.

Figure 8-6 shows how an increase in the level of wealth affects equilibrium output and the interest rate. The economy is initially in equilibrium at point *E*. There is then an increase in wealth: perhaps the stock market has gone up because everyone is optimistic that the economy is recovering from a recession. The higher wealth raises consumption spending, and the *IS* curve thus shifts up to *IS'*. The new equilibrium is at *E'*.

---

[27] We noted above that whether individuals save for their children affects fiscal policy. If parents are concerned enough about their children, they will regard future taxes to be paid by their children as equivalent to taxes on themselves, and the Ricardian view then is more likely to be true. Thus the discussion in Box 8-2 of the importance of bequests also has implications for the effectiveness of fiscal policy in affecting aggregate demand.

[28] Evidence on the effects of tax cuts on consumption has been examined by James Poterba, "Are Consumers Forward Looking? Evidence from Fiscal Experiments," *American Economic Review, Papers and Proceedings,* vol. 78, May 1988. Poterba concludes that tax cuts do increase consumption.

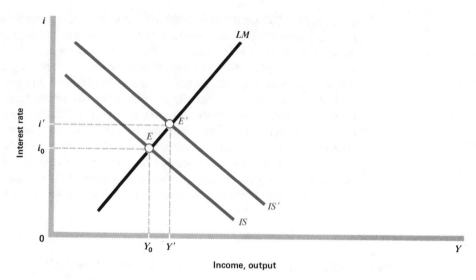

FIGURE 8-6

THE EFFECTS OF A SHIFT IN WEALTH. An increase in wealth shifts the consumption function, raising consumption demand at any level of income. Accordingly, the *IS* curve shifts to *IS'*, the level of output rises from Y_0 to Y', and the interest rate rises from i_0 to i'.

At E', the interest rate and level of output are higher than at E. Thus an increase in wealth raises equilibrium output. Since the increase in wealth was assumed to result from expectations that the economy was recovering from a recession, we see that the expectation is partly self-fulfilling. A self-fulfilling prophecy is one which, purely as a result of being made, produces the prophesied result.

The Dynamics of Adjustment

In Section 8-3 and Figure 8-4, we examined the dynamic response of consumption spending to a shift in disposable income. Now we want to embody that dynamic adjustment in a full *IS-LM* model. The slow adjustment of consumption to a given change in disposable income will mean that income itself adjusts slowly to any given shift in autonomous spending that is not at first recognized as permanent, as we now show.

We assume here that people do not know whether the shift in autonomous demand is permanent or transitory. Rather, the only way they can figure that out is by seeing whether the change in demand persists or goes away. Figure 8-7 illustrates the effects of a permanent shift in autonomous demand, the nature of which (permanent or transitory) is not known to consumers.

Suppose that the economy is initially in equilibrium at point E. Now there is a shift in autonomous investment demand. In the long run, such a shift will move the IS curve to IS'. The extent of the shift is determined by the *long-run* multiplier $1/(1-c)$, where c is the long-run propensity to consume. When expectations of income have fully adjusted, the economy will be at position E', with output level Y' and interest rate i'.

But in the short run the marginal propensity to consume is not c, but only $c\theta$. Thus the short-run multiplier is only $1/(1-c\theta)$. In the short run, the IS curve shifts only to IS''. Thus the immediate effect of the shift in investment demand is to raise income to Y'' and the interest rate to i''.

Next period, the IS curve shifts again. It does not shift all the way to IS' though. Consumers have adjusted their estimate of permanent income upward, but they have not yet adjusted it all the way to Y', because income last period was only Y'' and not Y'. (To keep the diagram simple, we do not show the IS curve for the second or later periods.) Income and the interest rate will rise above Y'' and i'', but still fall short of Y' and i'.

FIGURE 8-7

THE DYNAMICS OF ADJUSTMENT TO A SHIFT IN INVESTMENT DEMAND.
Autonomous investment demand rises by amount ΔI, but it is not known whether the shift is permanent or transitory. It is in fact permanent, so that the IS curve will eventually be at IS', shifted to the right by an amount $\Delta I/(1-c)$, where $1/(1-c)$ is the long-run multiplier. But in the first period, the IS curve shifts only to IS'', by amount $\Delta I/(1-c\theta)$, which is determined by the short-run consumption function and multiplier. Over time, the economy moves gradually from E'' to E', as individuals come to recognize that the shift in investment demand is permanent.

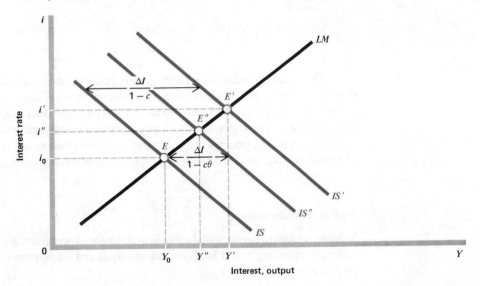

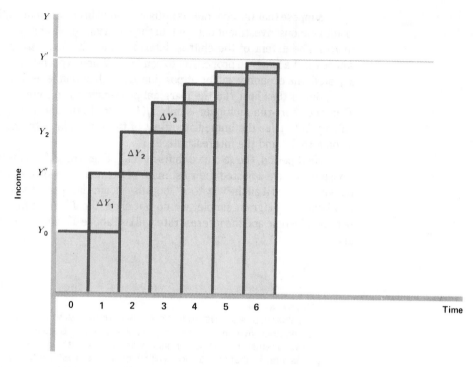

FIGURE 8-8

THE INCOME ADJUSTMENT PROCESS. The figure shows the *dynamic multiplier* of investment spending on income. This is how a given change in autonomous investment spending affects the level of output over time. Income rises in the first period from Y_0 to Y''. Then in subsequent periods it continues to rise toward its long-run equilibrium level, Y'.

This process continues, with the consumption function gradually shifting up over time, as people come to realize that their permanent incomes have risen. A single shock to autonomous demand therefore produces a slow, or *distributed lag*, effect on output. Figure 8-8 shows how income adjusts gradually to its new equilibrium level. The time pattern of changes in income caused by the increase in investment demand is called the *dynamic multiplier* of income with respect to autonomous investment.

Policy Implications

Suppose we have a permanent decline in investment expenditure. As we have seen, the decline in spending would lead to a fall in output and employment, occurring over a period of time.

Suppose the government wants to offset the reduction in aggregate demand by using tax cuts to keep income at the full-employment level. Since consumption adjusts only gradually to the changes in income resulting from both the initial fall in investment and tax cuts, the policy maker who wants to stabilize output *over time* will have to know about the adjustment pattern of consumption so as not to overreact. The problems may be further complicated by the fact that frequently the policy maker, too, reacts only with a lag to changed circumstances.

In the short run, consumption does not respond fully to changes in income. Therefore, it takes a relatively large tax cut to obtain a given change in consumption with which to offset the decline in investment. Over time, though, consumption adjusts to the change in disposable income, and the tax cut that was initially just sufficient to offset reduced investment now turns out to be too generous. The compensating policy must therefore be one of a tax cut that is *front-loaded* and gradually phased down to the long-run level. The difference between the short-run and the long-run tax cuts is determined by the relative size of the short-run and long-run tax multipliers.

Indeed, the observant reader will recall that we assumed consumers had no special knowledge about the nature of the changes in income they experienced as a result both of the initial change in investment and of subsequent tax adjustments. Remarkably enough, if consumers knew that the investment shift was permanent, and if they could be persuaded that the change in government policy was permanent, a one-time reduction in taxes, calculated using the long-run multiplier implied by the consumption function, would precisely stabilize income. For, in that case, the response to the fall in investment would recognize the permanent nature of the change, implying that the long-run multiplier is relevant; and the response to the tax change would also recognize the permanent nature of the change. Consumption would adjust immediately, rather than gradually.

The conclusion of this section is that policy making, and understanding the behavior of the economy, cannot be successful unless careful attention is paid to expectations formation — bearing in mind that expectations depend in part on how the policy makers are perceived to be acting. This is the message of rational expectations, to which we return in Chapters 14 and 18.

8-6 SUMMARY

1. The simple Keynesian consumption function

$$C = 0.917 \ YD \qquad (2)$$

accounts well for observed consumption behavior. The equation suggests that out of an additional dollar of disposable income, nearly 92 cents is spent on consumption. The consumption function implies that the ratio of consumption to income, C/YD, is constant and independent of the level of income.

2. Early empirical work on consumption showed that the average propensity to

consume declined with the level of income. Postwar studies, by contrast, find a relatively constant average propensity to consume of about 0.92.

3. The evidence is reconciled by a reconsideration of consumption theory. Individuals want to maintain relatively smooth consumption profiles over their lifetime. Their consumption behavior is geared to their long-term consumption opportunities — permanent income or lifetime income plus wealth. With such a view, current income is only one of the determinants of consumption spending. Wealth and expected income play a role, too. A consumption function that represents this idea is

$$C = aWR + b\theta YD + b(1 - \theta)YD_{-1} \qquad (13)$$

which allows for the role of real wealth, WR, current disposable income, YD, and lagged disposable income, YD_{-1}.

4. The life-cycle hypothesis suggests that the propensities of an individual to consume out of disposable income and out of wealth depend on the person's age. It implies that saving is high (low) when income is high (low) relative to lifetime average income. It also suggests that aggregate saving depends on the growth rate of the economy and on such variables as the age distribution of the population.

5. The permanent-income hypothesis emphasizes the formation of expectations of future income. It implies that the propensity to consume out of permanent income is higher than the propensity to consume out of transitory income.

6. Both theories do well, in combination, in explaining aggregate consumption behavior. But there are still some consumption puzzles, including the excess sensitivity of consumption to current income and the fact that the elderly do not appear to draw down their savings as they age. In addition, differences in national saving rates have not been well explained.

7. The excess sensitivity of consumption to current income may be caused by liquidity constraints that prevent individuals from borrowing enough to maintain smooth consumption patterns. It could also be accounted for by myopia about future income prospects.

8. The rate of consumption, and thus of saving, could in principle be affected by the interest rate. But the evidence for the most part shows little effect of interest rates on saving.

9. The Barro-Ricardo hypothesis implies that cuts in tax rates that produce deficits will not affect consumption. The evidence seems to show that tax cuts do, however, affect consumption.

10. Lagged adjustment of consumption to income results in a gradual adjustment of the level of income in the economy to changes in autonomous spending and other economic changes. An increase in autonomous spending raises income. But the adjustment process is spread out over time because the rising level of income raises consumption only gradually. This adjustment process is described by dynamic multipliers that show by how much income changes in each period following a change in autonomous spending (or other exogenous variables).

KEY TERMS

Life-cycle hypothesis
Dissaving
Permanent income
Rational expectations
Liquidity constraints

Myopia
Dynamic multiplier
Excess sensitivity
Barro-Ricardo hypothesis

PROBLEMS

1. What is the significance of the ratio of consumption to GNP in terms of the level of economic activity? Would you expect it to be higher or lower than normal during a recession (or depression)? Do you think the ratio would be higher in developed or developing countries? Why?

The Life-Cycle Hypothesis

2. The text implies that the ratio of consumption to accumulated savings declines over time until retirement.
   (a) Why? What assumption about consumption behavior leads to this result?
   (b) What happens to this ratio after retirement?

3. (a) Suppose you earn just as much as your neighbor but are in much better health and expect to live longer than she does. Would you consume more or less than she does? Why? Derive your answer from equation (5).
   (b) According to the life-cycle hypothesis, what would be the effect of the Social Security system on your average propensity to consume out of (disposable) income?
   (c) How would equation (8) be modified for an individual who expects to receive $X per year of retirement benefits? Verify your result in problem 3b.

4. Give an intuitive interpretation of the marginal propensity to consume out of wealth and income at time T in the individual's lifetime in equation (8).

5. In equation (5), consumption in each year of working life is given by

$$C = \frac{WL}{NL} \times YL \tag{5}$$

In equation (8), consumption is given as

$$C = aWR + cYL \qquad a \equiv \frac{1}{NL - T} \qquad c \equiv \frac{WL - T}{NL - T} \tag{8}$$

Show that equations (5) and (8) are consistent for an individual who started life with zero wealth and has been saving for T years. [*Hint:* First calculate the individual's wealth after T years of saving at rate $YL - C$. Then calculate the level of consumption implied by equation (8) when wealth is at the level you have computed.]

Permanent-Income Hypothesis

6. In terms of the permanent-income hypothesis, would you consume more of your Christmas bonus if (a) you knew there was a bonus every year; (b) this was the only year such bonuses were given out?

7. Suppose that permanent income is calculated as the average of income over the past 5 years; that is,

$$YP = \frac{1}{5}(Y + Y_{-1} + Y_{-2} + Y_{-3} + Y_{-4})$$

Suppose, further, that consumption is given by $C = 0.9\,YP$.
   (a) If you have earned $10,000 per year for the past 10 years, what is your permanent income?
   (b) Suppose next year (period $t + 1$) you earn $15,000. What is your new YP?
   (c) What is your consumption this year and next year?
   (d) What is your short-run marginal propensity to consume (MPC)? Long-run MPC?
   (e) Assuming you continue to earn $15,000 starting in period $t + 1$, graph the value of your permanent income in each period, using the above equation.

8. Explain why good gamblers (and thieves) might be expected to live very well even in years when they don't do well at all.

9. The graph (below) shows the lifetime earnings profile of a person who lives for four periods and earns incomes of $30, $60, and $90 in the first three periods of the life cycle. There are no earnings during retirement. Assume that the interest rate is 0.
   (a) You are asked to determine the level of consumption, compatible with the budget constraint, for someone who wants an even consumption profile throughout the life cycle. Indicate in which periods the person saves and dissaves and in what amounts.
   (b) Assume now that, contrary to 9a, there is no possibility of borrowing. The credit markets are closed to the individual. Under this assumption, what is the flow of con-

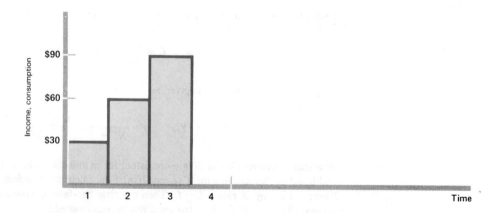

sumption the individual will pick over the life cycle? In providing an answer, continue to assume that if possible, an even flow of consumption is preferred. (*Note:* You are assuming here that there are liquidity constraints.)

(c) Assume next that the person described in 9b receives an increase in wealth, or nonlabor income. The increase in wealth is equal to $13. How will that wealth be allocated over the life cycle with and without access to the credit market? How would your answer differ if the increase in wealth were $23?

(d) Relate your answer to the problem of excess sensitivity of consumption to current income.

10. Consider the consumption function in equation (13). Assume autonomous investment spending is constant, as is government spending. The economy is close to full employment and the government wishes to maintain aggregate demand precisely constant. In these circumstances, assume there is an increase in real wealth of $10 billion. What change in income taxes will maintain the equilibrium level of income constant in the present period? What change is required to maintain income constant in the long run?

11. Equation (13) shows consumption as a function of wealth and current and lagged disposable income. To reconcile that consumption function with the formation of permanent-income expectations, you are asked to use equation (11) and the consumption function

$$C = 0.045 \ WR + 0.55 \ YD + 0.17 \ YD_{-1}$$

to determine the magnitude of θ and $(1 - \theta)$ that is implied by equation (13).

12. (a) Explain why the interest rate might affect saving.

(b) Why does this relation matter?

Adjustment and Dynamics

13. Here is a challenge to your ability to develop diagrams. You are asked to show short-run and long-run income determination in the 45° diagram of Chapter 3. Assume that investment demand is totally autonomous and does not respond to the interest rate. Thus, you do not need to use the full *IS-LM* model.

(a) Draw the short-run and long-run consumption functions and the aggregate demand schedule, with $I = \bar{I}$.

(b) Show the initial full equilibrium.

(c) Show the short-run and long-run effects of increased investment on equilibrium income.

DATA APPENDIX

This following table shows U.S. data in 1982 dollars for disposable income (YD), total consumption (C), consumption of durable goods (CD), household net worth (WR), the average personal saving rate (S/YD), and the average propensity to consume (C/YD).

DATA FOR CONSUMPTION STUDIES (dollars in billions)

Year	YD	C	CD	WR	S/YD	C/YD
1948	$ 733.1	$ 681.8	$ 61.7	NA	5.9%	93.0%
1949	733.2	695.4	67.8	NA	3.9	94.8
1950	791.8	733.2	80.7	NA	6.1	92.6
1951	819.0	748.7	74.7	NA	7.3	91.4
1952	844.3	771.4	73.0	NA	7.3	91.4
1953	880.0	802.5	80.2	$ 3,893.2	7.2	91.2
1954	894.0	822.7	81.5	4,257.8	6.3	92.0
1955	944.5	873.8	96.9	4,548.7	5.7	92.5
1956	989.4	899.8	92.8	4,716.9	7.2	90.9
1957	1,012.1	919.7	92.4	4,632.1	7.2	90.9
1958	1,028.8	932.9	86.9	5,082.1	7.5	90.7
1959	1,067.2	979.4	96.9	5,201.7	6.3	91.8
1960	1,091.1	1,005.1	98.0	5,247.0	5.8	92.1
1961	1,123.2	1,025.2	93.6	5,642.1	6.7	91.3
1962	1,170.2	1,069.0	103.0	5,520.3	6.5	91.4
1963	1,207.3	1,108.4	111.8	5,803.6	5.9	91.8
1964	1,291.0	1,170.6	120.8	6,119.9	7.0	90.7
1965	1,365.7	1,236.4	134.6	6,427.2	7.0	90.5
1966	1,431.3	1,298.9	144.4	6,414.9	6.8	90.8
1967	1,493.2	1,337.7	146.2	6,956.8	8.0	89.6
1968	1,551.3	1,405.9	161.6	7,430.4	7.0	90.6
1969	1,599.8	1,456.7	167.8	7,209.0	6.4	91.1
1970	1,668.1	1,492.0	162.5	7,191.8	8.1	89.4
1971	1,728.4	1,538.8	178.3	7,545.6	8.5	89.0
1972	1,797.4	1,621.9	200.4	8,041.3	7.3	90.2
1973	1,916.3	1,689.6	220.3	7,824.3	9.4	88.2
1974	1,896.6	1,674.0	204.9	7,429.5	9.3	88.3
1975	1,931.7	1,711.9	205.6	7,760.2	9.2	88.6
1976	2,001.0	1,803.9	232.3	8,328.0	7.6	90.2
1977	2,066.6	1,883.8	254.0	8,628.3	6.6	91.2
1978	2,167.4	1,961.0	267.4	9,097.9	7.1	90.5
1979	2,212.6	2,004.4	266.5	9,494.9	6.8	90.6
1980	2,214.3	2,000.4	245.9	9,822.5	7.1	90.3
1981	2,248.6	2,024.2	250.8	9,898.0	7.5	90.0
1982	2,261.5	2,050.7	252.7	9,836.3	6.8	90.7
1983	2,331.9	2,146.0	283.1	10,252.9	5.4	92.0
1984	2,469.8	2,249.3	323.1	10,436.3	6.1	91.1
1985	2,542.8	2,354.8	355.1	10,902.9	4.4	92.6
1986	2,640.9	2,455.2	385.0	11,481.5	4.0	93.0
1987	2,686.3	2,521.0	391.0	11,517.0	3.2	93.9
1988	2,788.3	2,592.2	409.7	11,695.4	4.2	93.0

NA = not available.
SOURCE: DRI/McGraw-Hill.

9

INVESTMENT SPENDING

Consumption spending in the United States is on average about 62 percent of GNP and thus accounts for most of aggregate demand. Investment spending is typically less than 20 percent of GNP in the United States. However, because investment spending fluctuates much more than consumption, the former is of particular interest in understanding business cycle fluctuations. Investment is also important as it is one of the prime determinants of an economy's long-run growth and productivity performance. Some other major industrial countries, including Japan and Germany, not only have higher saving rates than the United States, but also invest a higher share of their GNP.[1] Anyone concerned with the long-term growth of the economy worries that the United States invests such a small share of GNP and would like to find policies to encourage investment.

Figure 9-1 shows investment (and its main components) as a share of GNP in the period since World War II. In every recession or shortly before it, the share of investment in GNP falls sharply, and then investment begins to recover as the recovery gets under way. The cyclical relationships shown in Figure 9-1 extend much further back in history. For instance, in the great depression, gross investment fell to less than 4 percent of GNP in both 1932 and 1933. Understanding investment, then, will go a long way toward helping us understand the business cycle.

The importance of fluctuations in investment relative to other components of GNP can be seen in Table 9-1, which shows how the components of aggregate demand changed in the most recent recession, that of 1981–1982, and in the subsequent recovery through the end of 1985. From the third quarter of 1981 to the fourth quarter of 1982, consumption and government spending increased despite the recession.

---

[1] The Feldstein-Horioka finding, discussed in Chap. 8, that a nation's saving and investment ratios typically move closely together, implies that the high-saving countries are likely also to be high-investment countries.

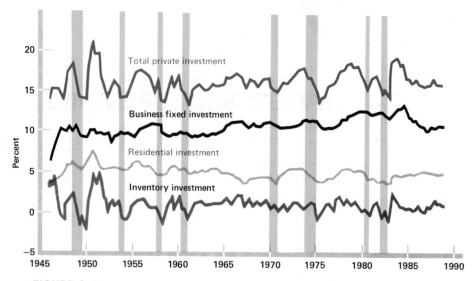

FIGURE 9-1

COMPONENTS OF INVESTMENT SPENDING AS A PERCENTAGE OF GNP,
1947–1989. Shaded bars mark periods of recession. (SOURCE: DRI/
McGraw-Hill.)

TABLE 9-1

REAL GNP AND ITS COMPONENTS IN RECESSION AND RECOVERY (billions of 1982 dollars)

	Change from 1981:3 to 1982:4	Change from 1982:4 to 1985:4
GNP	−105.3	503.1
Consumption	47.2	308.1
Government	29.9	92.6
Investment	−151.9	239.2
Net exports	−30.4	−136.8

SOURCE: DRI/McGraw-Hill.

(Recall from Chapter 8 that consumption is affected by permanent or lifetime disposable income and not only by current GNP.) But GNP nevertheless fell sharply, mostly because gross investment spending declined by more than total GNP.

In the subsequent recovery, investment boomed. The fluctuations in investment between 1981 and 1985 far exceed the fluctuations in consumption — and it is these relatively large fluctuations in investment that lead to a focus on investment in studying the business cycle.

In this chapter we continue our in-depth analysis of the components of aggregate demand. We provide a foundation for the essential component of the simple investment function of Chapter 4 — that investment demand is reduced by increases in the interest rate — and, also, go beyond that investment function by discussing the roles of output, financial constraints, and taxes in determining investment. We also examine how investment spending can be affected by policy. High interest rates, caused by restrictive monetary policy and expansive fiscal policy, reduce investment spending; policies that reduce interest rates and provide tax incentives for investment can increase investment spending.

One simple relationship is vital to the understanding of investment. Investment is spending devoted to increasing or maintaining the stock of capital. The stock of capital consists of the factories, machines, offices, and other durable products used in the process of production. The capital stock also includes residential housing as well as inventories. Investment is spending that adds to these components of capital stock.

Recall the distinction drawn in Chapter 2 between *gross* and *net investment.* Gross investment represents total additions to the capital stock. Net investment subtracts depreciation — the reduction in the capital stock, equal to about 11 percent of GNP, that occurs each period through wear and tear and the simple ravages of time — from gross investment. Net investment thus measures the increase in the capital stock in a given period of time.

In this chapter we disaggregate investment spending into three categories, as shown in Figure 9-1. The first is *business fixed investment,* consisting of business firms' spending on durable machinery, equipment, and structures such as factories. Business fixed investment accounts for most of investment. The second category is *residential investment,* consisting largely of investment in housing. And the third is *inventory investment.* As can be seen in Figure 9-1, inventory investment on average accounts for only a small share of GNP — indeed, sometimes it is negative, as firms reduce their inventories — but it fluctuates a great deal.

In the remainder of this chapter we develop theories and discuss evidence about the determinants of the rate of investment in each of the three major categories shown in Figure 9-1. We will develop what look like different models to explain each of the categories of investment spending. However, the theories are essentially similar, sharing a common view of the interaction between a desired capital stock and the rate at which the economy adjusts toward that desired stock.

9-1 INVENTORY INVESTMENT

Inventories consist of raw materials, goods in the process of production, and completed goods held by firms in anticipation of the products' sale. The ratio of inventories to annual final sales in the United States has been in the range of 23 to 35 percent over the past 25 years. That is, on average, firms hold inventories that constitute about 3 to 4 months' worth of their final sales.

Inventories are held for several interrelated reasons.

- Sellers hold inventories to meet future demand for goods because goods cannot be instantly manufactured or obtained from the manufacturer to meet demand.

- Inventories are also held because it is less costly for a firm to order goods less frequently in large quantities than to order small quantities frequently — just as the average householder finds it useful to keep several days' supplies on hand in the house so as not to have to visit the supermarket daily.

- Producers may hold inventories as a way of smoothing their production. It is costly to keep changing the level of output on a production line, and producers therefore may produce at a relatively steady rate even when demand fluctuates, building up inventories when demand is low and drawing them down when demand is high.[2]

- Some inventories are held as an unavoidable part of the production process; there is an inventory of meat and sawdust inside the sausage machine during the manufacture of sausage, for example.

Firms have a desired ratio of inventories to final sales that depends on economic variables. The smaller the cost of ordering new goods and the greater the speed with which such goods arrive, the smaller the inventory-sales ratio. The more uncertainty about the demand for the firms' goods, given the expected level of sales, the higher the inventory-sales ratio. The inventory-sales ratio may also depend on the level of sales, with the ratio falling with sales because there is relatively less uncertainty about sales as sales increase.

Finally, there is the *interest rate*. Since firms carry inventories over time, the firms must tie up resources in order to buy and hold the inventories. There is an interest cost involved in such inventory holding, and the desired inventory-sales ratio should be expected to fall with increases in the interest rate.

Anticipated versus Unanticipated Inventory Investment

The most interesting aspect of inventory investment lies in the distinction between anticipated (desired) and unanticipated (undesired) investment. Inventory investment could be high in two circumstances. First, if sales are unexpectedly low, firms would find unsold inventories accumulating on their shelves; that constitutes unanticipated inventory investment. This is the type of inventory investment discussed in Chapter 3. Second, inventory investment could be high because firms plan to restore depleted

---

[2] This reason for holding inventories, the so-called *production-smoothing* model of inventory behavior, has been the focus of much recent research. Although most evidence has been against the production-smoothing model (see, for instance, Jeffrey A. Miron and Stephen P. Zeldes, "Seasonality, Cost Shocks, and the Production Smoothing Model of Inventories," *Econometrica*, July 1988), there is some evidence suggesting that the data, rather than the theory, may be at fault. See Ray C. Fair, "The Production Smoothing Model is Alive and Well," NBER Working Paper 2877 (Cambridge, Mass.: National Bureau of Economic Research, February 1989).

inventories. The two circumstances obviously have very different implications for the behavior of aggregate demand. Unanticipated inventory investment is a result of unexpectedly low aggregate demand. On the other hand, planned inventory investment can be a response to recent, unexpectedly high aggregate demand; that is, rapid accumulation of inventories could be associated with either rapidly declining aggregate demand or rapidly increasing aggregate demand.

Inventories in the Business Cycle

Inventory investment fluctuates substantially in the business cycle — proportionately more than any other component of aggregate demand. In every post-World War II recession in the United States there has been a decline in inventory investment — the rate at which firms add to their inventories — between peak and trough. Column 2 of Table 9-2 gives the data on the change in the rate of inventory investment during postwar recessions. At the end of every recession, firms have been reducing their inventories, meaning that inventory investment has been negative in the final quarter of every recession. (This information is not shown in Table 9-2 but may be seen in Figure 9-1.)

Column 3 of the table calculates how much less GNP grew in fact between peak and trough than it would have grown had GNP kept on growing at a trend rate of 3.2 percent per annum. That is a rough measure of the fall in output during the recession. Typically 20 to 40 percent or more of that decline is directly attributable to a decline in inventory investment. The last column of Table 9-2 gives an indication that the change

TABLE 9-2
INVENTORY DECUMULATION IN RECESSIONS (cols. 1 to 3 in billions of 1982 dollars)

RECESSION		Change in real GNP (1)	Change in rate of inventory investment (2)	Change in real GNP relative to trend* (3)	Cols. (2)/(3), percent
Peak	Trough				
1948:4	1949:4	−22.2	−28.3	−58.7	48.2
1953:2	1954:2	−43.7	−18.4	−90.5	20.3
1957:3	1958:1	−55.4	−22.5	−80.5	28.0
1960:2	1961:1	+4.5	−14.4	−35.8	40.2
1969:4	1970:4	−9.7	−20.9	−88.2	23.7
1973:4	1975:1	−120.1	−78.1	−232.4	33.6
1980:1	1980:3	−74.3	−33.6	−126.2	26.6
1981:3	1982:4	−105.3	−95.0	−238.0	39.9

* Change in real GNP relative to trend is calculated by assuming GNP would have continued to grow at a quarterly rate of 0.8 percent from the peak level of income.

Source: DRI/McGraw-Hill.

in inventory investment typically plays a significant role in the decline in GNP during a recession.

The role of inventories in the business cycle is a result of a combination of unanticipated and anticipated inventory change. Figure 9-2 illustrates the combination using data from the most recent recessions, at the start of the 1980s. The behavior of sales and output for the 1981–1982 recession was typical. Before the recession began, GNP increased rapidly, recovering from the previous recession. That meant firms were running down their inventories. From the beginning of 1981 firms began to accumulate inventories, as output exceeded their sales. Firms were probably anticipating high sales in the future and decided to build up their stocks of goods for future sale. Thus there was *intended* inventory accumulation.

FIGURE 9-2
SALES AND OUTPUT IN RECESSION AND RECOVERY, 1979–1983. Shaded bars mark periods of recession. (SOURCE: DRI/McGraw-Hill.)

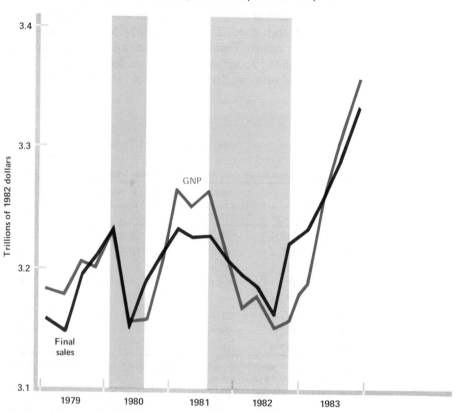

Final sales turned down at the beginning of 1981, but GNP stayed high until the third quarter. Then firms realized their inventories were too high and cut production to get them back in line. In the first quarter of 1982, firms had cut output way back and finally were successfully and *intentionally* reducing their inventories; hence, sales exceed output.

The behavior seen in the 1981–1982 recession explains much of the role of inventories in recessions. Before the recession there is a reduction in aggregate demand, reflected in a slowdown in sales. But output does not respond much, and inventories build up unintentionally. Then firms decide to get rid of their inventories, reducing production and planning to sell out of inventories; this is *intended* inventory reduction. In almost all post-World War II recessions there has been a stage at which output falls quite sharply as firms intentionally cut back production to get inventories back in line. And this cutback accentuates the recession.

Note that the behavior of inventories reflects the adjustment mechanism for output that we discussed in Chapter 3. When there is a fall in aggregate demand, firms unanticipatedly accumulate inventories. They cut back production in order to get output back in line with demand. As we noted in the footnotes in Chapter 3, though, in the process of reducing production to cut back inventories, firms may cause a larger reduction in GNP than would have happened had inventories not been unintentionally accumulated. This is known as the *inventory cycle*.

To understand the inventory cycle, consider the case of a hypothetical automobile dealer who sells, say, thirty cars per month, and holds an average of 1 month's sales — namely, thirty cars — in inventory. As long as sales stay steady at thirty cars per month, the dealer will be ordering thirty cars per month from the factory. Now suppose sales drop to twenty-five cars per month, and it takes the dealer 2 months to respond to the change. During those 2 months inventories will have climbed to forty cars. In the future the dealer will want an inventory of only twenty-five cars on hand. Thus when responding to the fall in demand, the dealer cuts the order from the factory from thirty cars to ten in the third month, to get the inventory back to 1 month's sales. After the desired inventory-sales ratio has been restored, the order will be twenty-five cars per month. We see in this extreme case how the drop in demand of five cars, instead of leading to a simple drop in car output of five cars per month, causes a drop in output of twenty cars in 1 month, followed by the longer-run drop in output of five cars per month.

The 1980 recession is one exception to the standard pattern of inventory behavior during a recession. As can be seen from Figure 9-2, in that recession there were only small movements in inventories. Sales and output basically moved together, and there was no pattern of an inventory cycle. This helps account for the brevity of the recession.

If inventories could be kept more closely in line with sales, or aggregate demand, fluctuations in inventory investment and in GNP would be reduced. As business methods are improving all the time, the hope is often expressed that new methods of management will enable firms to keep tighter control over their inventories and thus that the prospects for steadier growth can be improved.

9-2 BUSINESS FIXED INVESTMENT: THE NEOCLASSICAL APPROACH

The machinery, equipment, and structures used in the production of goods and services constitute the *stock* of business fixed capital. Our analysis of business fixed investment in this section proceeds in two stages. First, we ask how much capital firms would like to use, given the costs and returns of using capital and the level of output they expect to produce. That is, we ask what determines the *desired capital stock.* The desired capital stock is the capital stock that firms would like to have in the long run, abstracting from the delays they face in adjusting their use of capital. However, because it takes time to order new machines, build factories, and install the machines, firms cannot instantly adjust the stock of capital used in production. Second, therefore, we discuss the rate at which firms adjust from their existing capital stock toward the desired level over the course of time. The rate of adjustment determines how much firms spend on adding to the capital stock in each period; that is, the adjustment rate determines the rate of investment.

The Desired Capital Stock: Overview

Firms use capital, along with labor, to produce goods and services for sale. The goal is, of course, to maximize profits. In deciding how much capital to use in production, firms have to balance the contribution that more capital makes to their revenues against the cost of using more capital. The *marginal product of capital* is the increase in output produced by using one more unit of capital in production. The *rental (user) cost of capital* is the cost of using one more unit of capital in production.

To derive the rental cost of capital, we think of the firm as financing the purchase of the capital (whether the firm produces the capital itself or buys it from some other firm) by borrowing at an interest cost, *i.* In order to obtain the services of an extra unit of capital, in each period the firm must pay the interest cost, *i,* for each dollar of capital that it buys. Thus the basic measure of the rental cost of capital is the interest rate.[3] Later we shall go into more detail about the rental cost of capital, but for the meantime we shall think of the interest rate as determining the rental cost.

In deciding how much capital they would like to use in production, firms compare the value of the marginal product of capital with the user, or rental cost, of capital. The value of the marginal product of capital is the increase in the *value* of output obtained by using one more unit of capital. For a competitive firm, the value of the marginal product of capital is equal to the price of output times the marginal product of capital. So long as the value of the marginal product of capital is above the rental cost, it pays the firm to add to its capital stock. Thus the firm will keep investing until the value of the output produced by adding one more unit of capital is equal to the cost of using that capital — the rental cost of capital. In equilibrium, we must have

---

[3] Even if the firm finances the investment out of profits it has made in the past — retained earnings — it should still think of the interest rate as the basic cost of using the new capital, since the firm could otherwise have lent out those funds and earned interest on them, or paid them out as dividends to shareholders.

$$\text{Value of marginal product of capital} = \text{rental cost of capital} \qquad (1)$$

To give content to this relationship, we have to specify what determines the productivity of capital and what determines the user (rental) cost of capital. The marginal product of capital is examined next, and then we turn to the rental cost of the capital.

The Marginal Productivity of Capital

To understand the marginal productivity of capital, it is important to note that firms can substitute capital for labor in the production of output. Different combinations of capital and labor can be used to produce a given level of output. If labor is relatively cheap, the firm will want to use relatively more labor; and if capital is relatively cheap, the firm will want to use relatively more capital.

The general relationship among the desired capital stock (K^*), the rental cost of capital (rc), and the level of output is given by

$$K^* = g(rc, Y) \qquad (2)$$

Equation (2) indicates that the desired capital stock depends on the rental cost of capital and the level of output. The lower the rental cost of capital, the larger the desired capital stock. And the greater the level of output, the larger the desired capital stock.[4]

The relationship shown in equation (2) says that firms want to have more capital on hand if they have to produce more output, and that they want to have more capital the cheaper it is to use capital. We now explain in more detail the factors underlying equation (2).

As the firm combines progressively more capital with relatively less labor in the production of a *given* amount of output, the marginal product of capital declines. This relation is shown in the downward-sloping schedules in Figure 9-3. Those schedules show how the marginal product of capital falls as more capital is used in producing a given level of output. The schedule YY_1 is drawn for a level of output Y_1. The schedule YY_2 is drawn for the higher output level, Y_2. The marginal product of capital, given the capital stock, say K_0, is higher on schedule YY_2 than on YY_1. That is because more labor is being used in combination with the given amount of capital, K_0, to produce level of output Y_2 than to produce Y_1.

Figure 9-3 shows the marginal product of capital in relation to the level of output and the amount of capital being used to produce that output. Figure 9-4 is a similar diagram that shows the desired capital stock as related to the rental cost of capital and the level of output. Given the level of output, say Y_1, the firm will want to use more capital the lower the rental cost of capital because at low rental costs of capital, the firm can afford to use capital even when its marginal productivity is quite low. If the rental

---

[4] In writing equation (2), we assume that the real wage paid to labor is given and does not change as the rental cost of capital changes. In general, the rental cost of capital *relative to* the real wage determines the desired capital stock, given Y. (See footnote 6 for an example.)

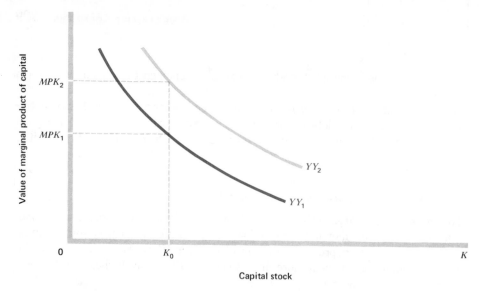

FIGURE 9-3

THE MARGINAL PRODUCT OF CAPITAL IN RELATION TO THE LEVEL OF
OUTPUT AND THE CAPITAL STOCK. The marginal product of capital
decreases as relatively more capital is used in producing any given level
of output. Thus the schedules YY_1 and YY_2 are downward-sloping. The
higher the level of output, for any given capital input, the higher the
marginal product of capital. Thus schedule YY_2, with output level Y_2
greater than Y_1, is above schedule YY_1.

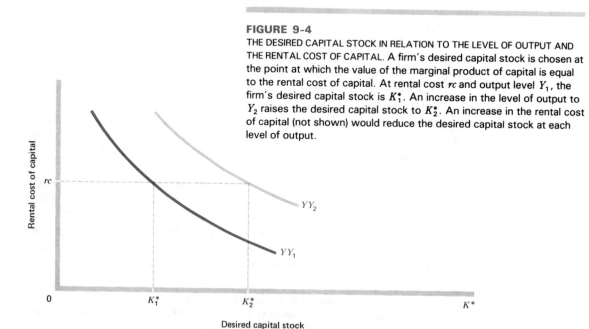

FIGURE 9-4

THE DESIRED CAPITAL STOCK IN RELATION TO THE LEVEL OF OUTPUT AND
THE RENTAL COST OF CAPITAL. A firm's desired capital stock is chosen at
the point at which the value of the marginal product of capital is equal
to the rental cost of capital. At rental cost rc and output level Y_1, the
firm's desired capital stock is K_1^*. An increase in the level of output to
Y_2 raises the desired capital stock to K_2^*. An increase in the rental cost
of capital (not shown) would reduce the desired capital stock at each
level of output.

310

cost of capital is high, the firm will be willing to use capital only if its marginal productivity is high—which means that the firm will not want to use very much capital and will instead substitute labor for capital. In producing a higher level of output, say Y_2, the firm will use both more capital and more labor, given the rental cost of capital. Therefore, at higher levels of output, the desired capital stock is higher.

THE COBB-DOUGLAS PRODUCTION FUNCTION

While equation (2) provides the general relationship determining the desired capital stock, a particular form of the equation, based on the *Cobb-Douglas production function*,[5] is frequently used in studies of investment behavior. The particular equation that is used is[6]

$$K^* = \frac{\gamma Y}{rc} \tag{3}$$

where γ is a constant. In this case, the desired capital stock varies in proportion to output. Given output, the desired capital stock varies inversely with the rental cost of capital.

ESTIMATING THE RETURN TO CAPITAL

The value of the marginal product of capital is the increase in the value of output that is obtained by increasing the capital stock by one unit. If the capital stock were increased by $1 today, the marginal product of capital would be the increase in the real value of output in subsequent years. An estimate of this return to capital is shown in Table 9-3.

---

[5] The Cobb-Douglas production function is written in the form

$$Y = N^{1-\gamma}K^\gamma \qquad 1 > \gamma > 0$$

where N is the amount of labor used. This production function is particularly popular because it is easy to handle and, also, because it appears to fit the facts of U.S. economic experience reasonably well. The coefficient γ of equation (3) is the same as the γ of the production function. The reader trained in calculus will want to show that g is the share of capital in total income, on the assumption that factors are paid their marginal products.

[6] We draw attention here to a subtle point: Equation (3) gives the marginal product of capital (*MPK*) when the *input of labor* is held fixed, while in Figs. 9-3 and 9-4 we work with the *MPK* when labor is being adjusted so that *output* is kept fixed. The desired stock that corresponds to Figs. 9-3 and 9-4 is

$$K^* = \left[\frac{\gamma w}{(1-\gamma)rc} \right]^{1-\gamma} Y \tag{3a}$$

where w is the real wage.

Equation (3a), like equation (3), implies that desired capital is proportional to Y and varies inversely with the rental cost of capital. We use equation (3) rather than equation (3a) in the text because the former is the form that has been used in empirical studies. Note, however, that we should certainly expect the implication of equation (3a), that a higher wage rate increases K^* to hold in practice.

TABLE 9-3

RETURN TO CAPITAL (percent per annum)

	1952–1959	1960–1969	1970–1979	1980–1983	1984–1987
Average annual return	9.7	10.4	7.8	6.1	7.7

SOURCE: Lawrence Summers, "What is the Social Return to Capital Investment," 1989 (typescript).

The annual numbers on which Table 9-3 is based are typically in the 6 to 12 percent range, meaning that $1 of capital generates a return of 6 to 12 cents per year. The number varies from year to year and, according to the table, has been falling, particularly since the 1960s. The return to capital is lower in recessions.[7]

Table 9-3 suggests that a $1 increase in the capital stock would generate a return of about 8 to 9 cents or more in the form of increased output. There are many who argue that such a real rate of return is well worth having, and that one of the keys to reviving growth in the United States is to find ways to increase investment and thus the capital stock.

Expected Output

In determining the desired capital stock, we have to specify the relevant time period for which the decision on the capital stock applies. In this section we are discussing the capital stock that the firm desires to hold in order to produce at some future time. For some investments the future time at which the output will be produced is a matter of months or only weeks. For other investments — such as power stations — the future time at which the output will be produced is years away.

This suggests that the notion of permanent income (in this case, permanent output) introduced in Chapter 8 is relevant to investment as well as consumption. For longer-lived investments, the firm's capital demand is governed primarily by its views on the level of output it will be producing on average in the future. The firm's long-run

---

[7] An alternative estimate of the marginal product of capital can be obtained using the fact that the share of output received by capital is about 0.20. The share of capital in output, in turn, is equal to the marginal product of capital times the capital stock, divided by the level of output:

$$\text{Share of capital} = MPK \times \frac{K}{Y}$$

With the capital-output ratio (K/Y) in manufacturing at about 2 and the share of capital at 20 percent, we obtain

$$MPK = \frac{0.20}{2.0} = 10\%$$

This estimate of 10 percent is in the same ballpark as the numbers in Table 9-3.

demand for business fixed capital, which depends on the normal or permanent level of output, is thus relatively independent of the current level of output and depends on *expectations* of future output levels. However, it is affected by current output to the extent that current output affects expectations of permanent output.[8]

The Desired Capital Stock: Summary

It is worthwhile stepping back for a moment to summarize the main results so far:

1. The firm's demand for capital — the desired capital stock, K^* — depends on the rental cost of capital, rc, and the expected level of output.
2. Firms balance the costs and benefits of using capital. The lower the rental cost of capital, the higher the optimal level of capital relative to output. This relation reflects the lower marginal productivity of capital when it is used relatively intensively.
3. The higher the level of output, the larger the desired capital stock. The firm plans its capital stock in relation to expected future or permanent output. Current output affects capital demand to the extent that it affects expectations about future output.

The Rental Cost of Capital Again

As a first approximation, we identified the rental cost of capital, rc, with the interest rate, on the argument that firms would have to borrow to finance their use of capital. Now we go into more detail on the cost per period of using capital.

To use capital for a single period, say a year, the firm can be thought of as buying the capital with borrowed funds and paying the interest on the borrowing. At the end of the year, the firm will still have some of the capital left. But the capital is likely to have depreciated over the course of the year. We shall assume that the firm intends to continue using the remaining capital in production in future years and that its depreciation simply represents the using up of the capital in the process of production — physical wear and tear. We now examine the rental cost, taking into account interest costs and depreciation. Later we will show that taxes also affect the rental cost of capital.

Leaving aside taxes, the rental cost of using capital consists of interest and depreciation costs. We assume that the rate of depreciation is a constant, equal to d, implying that a fixed proportion, d, of the capital is used up per period.[9] The rental cost,

---

[8] The role of permanent income in investment has been emphasized by Robert Eisner. Much of his work is summarized in his *Factors in Business Investment* (Cambridge, Mass.: Ballinger, 1978).

[9] Why is depreciation considered as a cost? The firm continues using the capital and therefore has to devote expenditures to maintaining the productive efficiency of the capital, thus offsetting wear and tear. We are assuming that, per dollar of capital, d dollars per period are required to maintain productive efficiency.

or user cost, of capital per dollar's worth of capital, *rc*, is therefore

$$rc = \text{interest rate} + d \tag{4}$$

The Real Rate of Interest

We have now to take a careful look at the interest rate term in equation (4). The distinction between the *real* and *nominal* interest rates, described in Box 5-1, is essential here. As described there, the real interest rate is the nominal (stated) rate of interest minus the rate of inflation.

It is the *expected real* rate of interest that should enter the calculation of the rental cost of capital. Why? The firm is borrowing in order to produce goods for sale in the future. On average, across all firms, it is reasonable to believe that the prices of the goods the firms sell will be rising along with the general price level. Thus the value of what the firm will be producing in the future will be rising with the price level, but the nominal amount of interest it has to pay back on account of its borrowings does not rise with the price level. The real value of the debt it has incurred by borrowing will be falling over time, as a result of inflation, and the firm should take that reduction in the real value of its outstanding debts into account in deciding how much capital to employ.

Accordingly, we can be more precise in the way we write equation (4) for the rental cost of capital. We write the rental cost of capital, taking account of expected inflation at the rate π^e, as

$$rc \equiv r + d \equiv i - \pi^e + d \tag{5}$$

where r is the real interest rate, i the nominal interest rate, and

$$r \equiv i - \pi^e \tag{6}$$

Equation (6) states that the real rate of interest is the nominal interest rate minus the expected rate of inflation.[10]

To reiterate, it is important to note that the interest rate relevant to the firm's demand for capital is the *real* rate, and not the nominal rate. This makes it clear that the nominal rate of interest is not a good guide to the rental cost of capital. If the rate of inflation is zero and is expected to be zero and the nominal interest rate is 5 percent, then the real interest rate is 5 percent. By contrast, if the nominal interest rate is 10 percent and the inflation rate is 10 percent, the real interest rate is zero. Other things equal, the desired capital stock in this example would tend to be higher with the

---

[10] Accordingly the real interest rate in equation (6) is the *expected* real rate. At the end of the period, when the rate of inflation is known, we can also state what the *actual*, or realized, real rate of interest for the period was—namely, the nominal interest rate, i, minus the actual rate of inflation.

nominal interest rate of 10 percent than with the nominal rate of 5 percent because those rates correspond to real rates of zero and 5 percent, respectively. As you have no doubt deduced, and as we shall show, investment spending tends to be higher when the rental cost of capital is lower. But because of the distinction between real and nominal interest rates, that is *not* the same as saying that investment tends to be higher when the nominal rate of interest is lower.

Taxes and the Rental Cost as Capital

The rental cost of capital is affected by taxes as well as by the interest rate and depreciation. The two main tax variables to consider are the corporate income tax and the investment tax credit. The corporate income tax is an essentially proportional tax on profits,[11] whereby the firm pays a proportion, say t, of its profits in taxes. The investment tax credit was in place for most of the period 1962–1986 but was discontinued in 1986. It allowed firms to deduct from their taxes a certain fraction, say τ, of their investment expenditures in each year. Thus a firm spending $1 million for investment purposes in a given year could deduct 10 percent of the $1 million, or $100,000, from the taxes it would otherwise have to pay the federal government.

We want to know what effects the corporate income tax and the investment tax credit have on the rental cost of capital. The easier case is the investment tax credit. The investment tax credit reduces the price of a capital good to the firm by the ratio τ, since the Treasury returns to the firm a proportion, τ, of the cost of each capital good. The investment tax credit therefore reduces the rental cost of capital.

To a first approximation, the corporate income tax, surprisingly, has no effect on the desired stock of capital. In the presence of the corporate income tax, the firm will want to equate the *after-tax* value of the marginal product of capital with the *after-tax* rental cost of capital in order to ensure that the marginal contribution of the capital to profits is equal to the marginal cost of using it.

Let us focus on the interest component of the rental cost. The basic point is that interest cost is treated as a deduction from revenues in the calculation of the corporation's taxes. Suppose there were no corporate income tax, no inflation, no depreciation, and an interest rate of 10 percent. The desired capital stock would be that level of the capital stock, say, K_0^*, such that the marginal product of capital was 10 percent. Now suppose that the corporate income tax rises to 34 percent and the interest rate remains constant. At the capital stock K_0^*, the after-tax marginal product of capital is now 6.6 percent (since 34 percent of the profits are paid in taxes). But if the interest rate stays at 10 percent and the firm gets to deduct 34 percent of its interest payments from taxes, the after-tax cost of capital will be 6.6 percent too. In that case, the desired capital stock is unaffected by the rate of corporate taxation.

However, there are complexities in the tax laws, which we do not go into here, that make the total effect of the corporate income tax on the desired capital stock

---

[11] The 1986 Tax Reform Act cut the top corporate tax rate from 46 percent to 34 percent.

ambiguous. The ambiguities arise when the special tax treatment of depreciation,[12] of inflation, and of investment financing other than through borrowing is taken into account.[13]

In brief: The investment tax credit reduces the rental cost of capital and increases the desired stock of capital. The corporate income tax has ambiguous effects on the desired stock of capital.

The Stock Market and the Cost of Capital

We have, so far, assumed that the firm finances its investment by borrowing. But a firm can also finance investment by selling shares, or equity. That way it raises the financing it needs to pay for the investment. The people buying the shares expect to earn a return from dividends and/or, if the firm is successful, from the increase in the market value of their shares, that is, *capital gains.*

When the stock market is high, a company can raise a lot of money by selling relatively few shares. When stock prices are low, the firm has to sell more shares to raise a given amount of money. The owners of the firm, the existing shareholders, will be more willing for the firm to sell shares to raise new money if they have to sell few shares to do so. If many shares have to be sold, the current shareholders will own a smaller share of the company in the future. Thus we expect corporations to be more willing to sell equity to finance investment when the stock market is high than when it is low.

In estimating the rental cost of capital, economists sometimes assume that the investment project will be financed by a mixture of borrowing and equity. The cost of equity capital is frequently measured by the ratio of the firm's dividends to the price of its stock.[14] Then, obviously, the higher the price of the stock, the lower the cost of equity capital, and the lower the overall cost of capital.[15] That is why a booming stock market is good for investment.

---

[12] The Internal Revenue Service counts depreciation as a business expense, but these allowances follow complicated rules and are not generally equal to the depreciation that the capital stock actually undergoes.

[13] As we describe below, some investment is financed through the sale of equity. Part of the return to equity holders typically takes the form of dividend payments. However, dividends are not treated as a deduction from profits in the calculation of corporate income taxes. Thus the basic argument presented in the case of interest payments, that the corporate income tax does not affect the desired capital stock, would not apply for equity-financed investment.

[14] An alternative measure is the ratio of the firm's *earnings* (some of which are not paid out to shareholders) to the price of its stock. However, neither measure is really correct, for the cost of equity capital is the amount the investment is expected to yield *in the future* to the people who buy it now.

[15] An alternative approach to the firm's investment decision, Tobin's *q* theory of investment, focuses on the stock market as the primary source of funds. The basic approach is outlined in James Tobin, "A General Equilibrium Approach to Monetary Theory," *Journal of Money, Credit and Banking,* February 1969. For an empirical implementation, see Lawrence H. Summers, "Taxation and Corporate Investment: A *q*-Theory Approach," *Brookings Papers on Economic Activity,* 1981. In Sec. 9-4, we outline the *q* theory in discussing housing investment.

Summary and Effects of Fiscal and Monetary Policy on the Desired Capital Stock

We summarize using equation (2), which states that the desired capital stock increases when the expected level of output rises and when the rental cost of capital falls.

The rental cost of capital falls when the real interest rate and the rate of depreciation fall. It likewise falls when the investment tax credit rises. Changes in the rate of corporate taxation have ambiguous effects on the desired capital stock.

The major significance of these results is their implication that monetary and fiscal policy affect the desired capital stock. Fiscal policy exerts an effect through both the corporate tax rate, t, and the investment tax credit, τ. Both these instruments are used to affect capital demand and thus investment spending.

Fiscal policy affects capital demand by its overall effects on the position of the *IS* curve, as discussed in Chapter 5. A high-tax – low government-spending policy keeps the real interest rate low and encourages the demand for capital. (At this point you may want to refer to Figure 5-6.) A low-tax – high government-spending policy that produces large deficits raises the real interest rate and discourages the demand for capital.

Monetary policy affects capital demand by affecting the market interest rate.[16] A lowering of the nominal interest rate by the Federal Reserve System (given the expected inflation rate), as reflected in a downward shift in the *LM* curve, will induce firms to desire more capital. This expansion in capital demand, in turn, will affect investment spending, as we shall now see.

From Desired Capital Stock to Investment

Equation (2) specifies the desired capital stock. The actual capital stock will often differ from the capital stock firms would like to have. At what speed do firms change their capital stocks in order to move toward the desired capital stock? In particular, is there any reason why firms do not attempt to move to their desired capital stocks immediately?

Since it takes time to plan and complete an investment project, and because attempts to invest quickly are likely to be more expensive than gradual adjustments of the capital stock, it is unlikely that firms would attempt to adjust their capital stocks to the long-run desired level instantaneously. Very rapid adjustment of the capital stock would require crash programs by the firm that would distract management from its routine tasks and interfere with ongoing production. Thus, firms generally plan to adjust their capital stocks gradually over a period of time rather than immediately.

---

[16] We should note that the Federal Reserve System is able to affect *nominal* interest rates directly by its sales and purchases of bonds. Its ability to control *real* interest rates is more limited.

Capital Stock Adjustment

There are a number of hypotheses about the speed at which firms plan to adjust their capital stock over time; we single out the *gradual adjustment hypothesis*, or *flexible accelerator model*, here.[17] The basic notion behind the gradual adjustment hypothesis is that the larger the gap between the existing capital stock and the desired capital stock, the more rapid a firm's rate of investment. The hypothesis is that the firm plans to close a fraction, λ, of the gap between the desired and actual capital stocks each period. Denote the capital stock at the end of the last period by K_{-1}. The gap between the desired and actual capital stocks is $(K^* - K_{-1})$. The firm plans to add to last period's capital stock (K_{-1}) a fraction (λ) of the gap $(K^* - K_{-1})$ so that the actual capital stock at the end of the current period (K) will be

$$K = K_{-1} + \lambda(K^* - K_{-1}) \tag{7}$$

Equation (7) states that the firm plans to have the capital stock at the end of the period, K, be such that a fraction, λ, of the gap (between the desired capital stock, K^*, and the capital stock, K_{-1}, that existed at the end of last period) is closed. To increase the capital stock from K_{-1} to the level of K indicated by equation (7), the firm has to achieve an amount of net investment, $I \equiv K - K_{-1}$, indicated by equation (7). We can therefore write net investment as

$$I = \lambda(K^* - K_{-1}) \tag{8}$$

which is the gradual adjustment formulation of net investment. Notice that equation (8) implies that investment is larger the larger the gap between actual and desired capital stocks.[18] With a zero gap, net investment is zero.

In Figure 9-5 we show the adjustment process of capital in a circumstance in which the initial capital stock is K_1 and the given desired capital stock is K^*. The assumed speed of adjustment is $\lambda = 0.5$. Starting from K_1, one-half the discrepancy between target capital and current actual capital is made up in every period. First-period net investment is therefore $0.5(K^* - K_1)$. In the second period, investment will be less because the previous period's investment reduces the gap. Investment continues until the actual capital stock reaches the level of target capital. The speed with which this process allows actual capital to reach target capital is determined by λ. The larger λ is, the faster the gap is reduced.

In equation (8), we have reached our goal of deriving an investment function that shows current investment spending determined by the desired stock of capital, K^*, and the actual stock of capital, K_{-1}. According to equation (8), any factor that increases the

---

[17] The term *flexible accelerator* is used because the model is a generalized form of the older *accelerator* model of investment, in which investment is proportional to the change in the level of GNP. The original accelerator model is examined in Sec. 9-3.

[18] Gross investment, as opposed to the net investment described in equation (8), includes, in addition, depreciation. Thus, gross investment is $I + dK_{-1}$, where d is again the rate of depreciation.

desired stock increases the rate of investment. Therefore, an increase in expected output, a reduction in the real interest rate, or an increase in the investment tax credit will each increase the rate of investment. We thus have derived a quite complete theory of business fixed investment that includes many of the factors we should expect to affect the rate of investment. And the theory of investment embodied in equation (8) also contains aspects of *dynamic behavior*—that is, behavior that depends on values of economic variables in periods other than the current period.

There are two sources of dynamic behavior in equation (8). The first arises from expectations. The K^* term depends on the firm's estimate of future or permanent output. To the extent that the firm forms its estimates of permanent output as a weighted average of past output levels, there will be lags in the adjustment of the level of permanent output to the actual level of output. In turn, investment will therefore also adjust slowly to a change in the level of output. The second source of dynamic behavior arises from adjustment lags. Firms plan to close only a proportion of the gap between the actual and desired capital stocks each period, as shown in Figure 9-5. The adjustment lags produce a lagged response of investment to changes in the variables that affect the desired capital stock.

FIGURE 9-5

THE GRADUAL ADJUSTMENT OF THE CAPITAL STOCK. The desired capital stock is K^*, and the current capital stock is K_1. The firm plans to close half the gap between the actual and the desired capital stock each period ($\lambda = 0.5$). Thus, in period 1 the firm moves to K_2, with (net) investment equal to $K_2 - K_1$, which in turn is equal to one-half of $K^* - K_1$. In each subsequent period the firm closes half the gap between the capital stock at the beginning of the period and the desired capital stock, K^*.

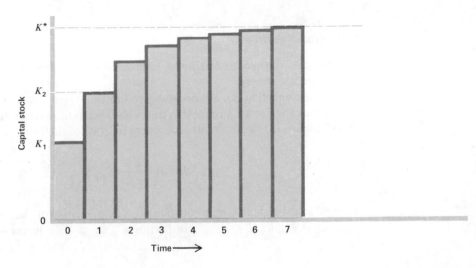

The Timing of Investment and the Investment Tax Credit

The flexible accelerator model provides a useful summary of the dynamics of investment. But it does not sufficiently emphasize the *timing* of investment. Because investment is undertaken for the long run and often requires several years to complete, there is flexibility in the dates on which the actual investment is undertaken. For example, suppose a firm wanted to have some machinery in place within 3 years. Suppose that it knew the investment tax credit would be raised substantially a year from now. Then the firm might be wise to delay the investment for a year and to make or acquire the machinery at a faster rate during the next 2 years, receiving the higher investment tax credit as the reward for waiting the extra year. Similarly, if a firm anticipated that the cost of borrowing next year would be much lower than this year, it might wait a year to undertake its investment project.

The flexibility in the timing of investment leads to an interesting contrast between the effects of the investment tax credit and the income tax on investment and consumption, respectively. We saw in Chapter 8 that a *permanent* change in the income tax has a much larger effect on consumption than a *transitory* change. However, the rate of investment *during the period* that a *temporary* investment tax credit is in effect would be higher than the rate of investment that would occur over the same period during which a *permanent* credit of the same magnitude was in effect. Why? If firms know the investment tax credit is temporary, they will advance the timing of their planned investments in order to take advantage of the higher credit during the current period. If there is a permanent change in the investment tax credit, then the desired capital stock will rise and there will on that account be more investment, but there will not be a bunching of investment.

It is for this reason that temporary changes in the investment tax credit have been suggested as a highly effective countercyclical policy measure. However, this is not a simple policy tool, as expectations about the timing and duration of the credit might conceivably worsen the instability of investment.

Empirical Results

How well does the neoclassical model, summarized in equation (8), do in explaining the behavior of investment?

To use equation (8), it is necessary to substitute some specific equation for K^*, the desired capital stock. Frequently, the Cobb-Douglas form is chosen. Using equation (3) in equation (8) yields a (net) investment function of the form

$$I = \lambda\left(\frac{\gamma Y}{rc} - K_{-1}\right) \tag{9}$$

The rental cost of capital, rc, in equation (9), is as in equation (5), but adjusted for taxes.

Early empirical evidence, in particular that of Dale Jorgenson and his asso-

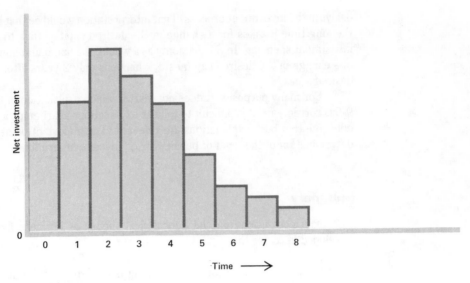

FIGURE 9-6

EFFECTS OF AN INCREASE IN OUTPUT IN PERIOD ZERO ON NET INVESTMENT
IN SUBSEQUENT PERIODS.

ciates,[19] showed that an investment function including the variables in equation (9) provided a reasonable explanation of the behavior of business fixed investment. However, the form shown in equation (9) could be improved upon by allowing more scope for investment to respond slowly to changes in output. The empirical evidence suggests that the adjustment of investment to output takes the bell-shaped form in Figure 9-6, rather than the shape seen in Figure 9-5. The major impact of a change in output on actual investment occurs with a 2-period (year) lag. The impact in the first year is less than the impact 2 years later.

There are two, not mutually exclusive, explanations for the behavior shown in Figure 9-6, corresponding to the two sources of dynamic behavior in equation (8) that we discussed above. The first possibility is that the lag pattern of Figure 9-6 reflects the way in which expectations about future output, and thus the long-run desired capital stock, are formed. In that view, only a sustained increase in output will persuade firms that the capital stock should be increased in the long run. Figure 9-6 would then imply that it takes about 2 years for changes in the variables that determine the desired capital stock to have a major impact on expectations.

The second explanation relies less on expectations and more on the physical

---

[19] See Dale W. Jorgenson, "Econometric Studies of Investment Behavior: A Survey," *Journal of Economic Literature*, December 1971.

delays in the investment process. That interpretation would be that Figure 9-6 reflects the long time it takes for a change in the desired capital stock to be translated into investment spending. In the economy as a whole, the maximum impact on investment of a change in the desired capital stock happens only 2 years after the change in the desired stock.

For many purposes, it does not matter which explanation of the form of Figure 9-6 is correct, and it is difficult to tell the explanations apart empirically. It is undoubtedly true that both explanations are relevent. The important point is that lags in the determination of the level of business fixed investment are long.

Summary

The main conclusions on the neoclassical theory of business fixed investment as developed here are that

1. Over time, net investment spending is governed by the discrepancy between actual and desired capital.
2. Desired capital depends on the rental cost of capital and the expected level of output. Capital demand rises with expected output and the investment tax credit, and declines with an increase in *real* interest rates. This last point both justifies and modifies (by distinguishing real from nominal interest rates) the standard investment demand functions, in which investment is negatively related to the interest rate.
3. Monetary and fiscal policies affect investment via the desired capital stock, although with long lags.
4. The empirical evidence is broadly consistent with the neoclassical theory, but certainly leaves room for improvement.

9-3 BUSINESS FIXED INVESTMENT: ALTERNATIVE APPROACHES

In this section we briefly discuss the way a firm approaches its investment decisions and also describe approaches to business fixed investment other than the neoclassical theory.

The Business Investment Decision: The View from the Trenches

Businesspeople making investment decisions typically use *discounted cash flow analysis*. The principles of discounting are described in the appendix to this chapter. Consider a businessperson deciding whether to build and equip a new factory. The first step is to figure out how much it will cost to get the factory into working order and how much revenue the factory will bring in each year after it starts operation.

For simplicity we consider a very short-lived project, one that costs $100 in the

TABLE 9-4

DISCOUNTED CASH FLOW ANALYSIS AND PRESENT VALUE (dollars)

	Year 1	Year 2	Year 3	Present discounted value
Cash or revenue	−100	+50	+80	
Present value of $1	1	1/1.12 = 0.893	$(1/1.12^2)$ = 0.797	
Present value of costs or revenue	−100	50 × 0.893 = 44.65	80 × 0.797 = 63.76	(−100 + 44.65 + 63.76) = 8.41

first year to set up and that then generates $50 in revenue (after paying for labor and raw materials) in the second year and a further $80 in the third year. By the end of the third year the factory has disintegrated.

The manager wants to know whether to undertake such a project. Discounted cash flow analysis says that the revenues received in later years should be *discounted* to the present in order to calculate their present value. As the appendix on discounting shows, if the interest rate is 10 percent, $110 a year from now is worth the same as $100 now. Why? Because if $100 were lent out today at 10 percent, a year from now the lender would end up with $110. Thus to calculate the value of the investment project, the businessperson calculates its present discounted value at the interest rate at which the business can borrow. If the present value is positive, then the project is undertaken.

Suppose that the relevant interest rate is 12 percent.[20] The calculation of the present discounted value of the investment project is shown in Table 9-4. The $50 received in year 2 is worth only $44.65 today: $1 a year from now is worth $1/1.12 = 0.893 today, and so $50 a year from now is worth $44.65. The present value of the $80 received in year 3 is calculated similarly. The table shows that the present value of the net revenue received from the project is positive ($8.41) and thus that the firm should undertake the project.

Note that if the interest rate had been much higher — say, 18 percent — the decision would have been *not* to undertake the investment. We thus see how the interest rate affects the investment decision of the typical firm. The higher the interest rate, the less likely the firm will be to undertake any given investment project.

Each firm has at any time an array of possible investment projects and estimates of the costs and the revenues from those projects. Depending on the level of the interest rate, the firm will want to undertake some of the projects and not undertake others. Taking all firms in the economy together and adding their investment demands, we obtain the total demand for investment in the economy at each interest rate.

---

[20] The interest rate here is nominal because we are calculating the present value of dollars to be received in the future.

This approach to the investment decision, which, of course, can be applied to investment projects of any duration and complexity, seems far from the description of Section 9-2 in terms of a desired capital stock and rate of adjustment.

Actually, the two approaches are quite consistent. First, we should think of the desired capital stock as being the stock of capital that will be in place when the firms have their factories and new equipment online. Second, the adjustment speed tells us how rapidly firms on average succeed in installing that capital.

We started with the formulation in terms of the desired capital stock because the framework provides a very clear way of including the different factors that affect investment. For instance, it is easy to see how expectations of future output and taxes affect investment.

But because the two approaches are consistent, the same factors could be included using discounted cash flow analysis. The effects of expectations of future output can be analyzed using the discounted cash flow approach by asking what determines the firms' projections of their future revenues (corresponding to the $50 in year 2 and $80 in year 3 in the example above); expected demand for their goods and their output must be relevant. Similarly, taxes can be embodied by analyzing how taxes affect the amount of after-tax revenue the firm has left in each future year; for example, the investment tax credit reduces the amount the firm has to lay out in the early years when it is actually building the project because the Treasury provides a refund of part of the cost of the project through taxes.

Finally, the firm makes decisions about the speed of adjustment by considering the cash flows associated with building the project at different speeds. If the project can be built more rapidly, the firm will decide on the speed with which it wants the project brought online by considering the present discounted costs and revenues associated with speeding it up.

The Accelerator Model of Investment

The *accelerator model of investment* asserts that the rate of investment is proportional to the *change* in the economy's output. To derive the accelerator model of investment, assume that there is complete adjustment of the capital stock to its desired level within one period (that is, that $\lambda = 1$), so that $K = K^*$; that there is no depreciation, so that $d = 0$; and that the desired capital-output ratio is a constant, independent of the rental cost of capital:

$$K^* = vY \tag{10}$$

In equation (10), v is a constant equal to the desired capital-to-output ratio. Substituting equation (10) into equation (8), setting $\lambda = 1$, and noting that (when $\lambda = 1$), $K_{-1} = K^*_{-1}$, we obtain

$$I = v(Y - Y_{-1}) \tag{11}$$

which is precisely the accelerator model of investment.

The accelerator model creates the potential for investment spending to fluctuate a good deal. If investment spending is proportional to the *change* in GNP, then when the economy is in a recovery, investment spending is positive, and when the economy is in a recession, investment will be negative.[21] Thus the accelerator model predicts that investment will fluctuate considerably, as Figure 9-1 shows it does.

Cost of Capital Effects, Credit Rationing, and Internal Sources of Finance

The neoclassical model of investment assumes that the cost of capital affects the desired capital stock in just the same way as expected output does. This can be seen in equation (9), which relates investment to the ratio of output to the rental cost of capital (*Y*/*rc*). One issue is whether the rental cost of capital in fact matters as much for investment as the neoclassical model implies.

Some research suggests that the (somewhat expanded) accelerator model of equation (10), which ignores the costs of capital, does about as good a job of explaining investment behavior as the neoclassical model.[22] The more general accelerator model is expanded in empirical work to make the rate of investment depend not only on the change in income this period but also on the change in income in earlier periods. In empirical applications this simple accelerator model therefore differs from the neoclassical model mainly in that the former omits the cost of capital.

There are also findings that the rental cost of capital does affect investment.[23] It is clear from the conflicting findings that the evidence is not strong enough to decide the precise relative roles of the cost of capital and expectations of future output. No doubt both are major determinants of investment spending. Certainly theory suggests that the rental cost of capital should play an important role in affecting investment. But there are reasons and evidence to question whether it is the only financial variable that affects investment.

CREDIT RATIONING AND INTERNAL SOURCES OF FUNDS

Table 9-5 shows the sources of manufacturing firms' funding in the United States during the period 1970–1984. The predominance of retained earnings as a source of financing stands out. Firms of all sizes rely mostly on reinvested profits for finance;

---

[21] The accelerator is not in practice a complete model of investment, for gross investment spending cannot be negative.

[22] Peter K. Clark, "Investment in the 1970's: Theory, Performance and Predictions," *Brookings Papers on Economic Activity*, 1979:1.

[23] For example, Martin Feldstein, "Inflation, Tax Rules and Investments: Some Econometric Evidence," *Econometrica*, July 1982, and Ben Bernanke, "The Determinants of Investment: Another Look," *American Economic Review*, Papers and Proceedings, May 1983.

TABLE 9-5

SOURCES OF FUNDS, U.S. MANUFACTURING FIRMS, 1970–1984

Firm size	SOURCE OF FUNDS,* % OF TOTAL				% of long-term debt from banks	Average retention ratio, %
	Short-term bank debt	Long-term bank debt	Other long-term debt	Retained earnings		
All firms	0.6	8.4	19.9	71.1	29.6	60
Asset class						
Under $10 million	5.1	12.8	6.2	75.9	67.3	79
Over $1 billion	−0.6	4.8	27.9	67.9	14.7	52

* Equity financing is excluded, but is very small. Minus sign indicates firm has net assets (rather than liabilities) in this category.

SOURCE: Steven M. Fazzari, R. Glenn Hubbard, and Bruce C. Petersen, "Financing Constraints and Corporate Investment," *Brookings Papers on Economic Activity*, 1988:1.

they use outside funding from banks, the bond markets, and equity[24] only to a limited extent. The last column of the table shows the average percentage of their earnings that firms retain rather than paying out to their owners (the stockholders): the ratio is above 50 percent for firms of all sizes, and is relatively most important for the smallest firms.

What do these facts mean for the investment decision? They suggest that there is a close link between the earnings of firms and the state of their *balance sheets*, the assets and liabilities that they have available. And if firms cannot readily obtain funding from outside sources when they need it, then the amount of assets they have on hand will affect their ability to invest. This would mean that the state of a firm's balance sheet and not just the cost of capital is a financial determinant of investment decisions.

Box 9-1 describes the important phenomenon of *credit rationing*, which occurs when individuals cannot borrow even though they are willing to do so at the existing interest rates. There are good reasons for credit rationing to occur, all stemming from the fact that the lender faces the risk that the borrower will not repay, for instance because the borrower goes bankrupt. These arguments suggest that credit rationing is more likely for small firms without an established reputation than for large firms with a track record. The fact that the retention ratio in Table 9-5 declines with firm size is consistent with this implication. The data in Table 9-5, as well as the experience of those who want to borrow, are consistent with the assumption that firms' are rationed in their access to funding.

Under such conditions, firms' investment decisions will be affected not only by

---

[24] Equity funding is excluded from the table, but independent evidence, noted in the article by Fazzari, Hubbard, and Petersen (cited in Table 9-5) shows that it provides very little financing for firms, especially small ones. The data in the table tend to underemphasize the importance of retained earnings for financing because depreciation allowances are not included in earnings but are used to finance new gross investment.

box 9-1

CREDIT RATIONING

In the *IS-LM* model, interest rates are the only channel of transmission between financial markets and aggregate demand. Credit rationing is an important additional channel of transmission of monetary policy.[*] Credit rationing takes place when lenders limit the amount individuals can borrow, even though the borrowers are willing to pay the going interest rate on their loans.

When banks relax the limits on borrowing by their customers, investment spending by firms and spending on consumer durables by households increases and hence demand and output increase. Conversely, when banks tighten credit constraints, spending falls off because households and firms cannot finance their spending.

Credit rationing can occur for two different reasons. First, a lender often cannot tell whether a particular customer (or the project the customer is financing) is good or bad. A bad customer will default on the loan and not repay it. Given the risk of default, the obvious answer seems to be to raise the interest rate.

However, raising interest rates works the wrong way: honest or conservative customers are deterred from borrowing because they realize their investments are not profitable at higher interest rates. But customers who are reckless or dishonest will borrow because they do not in any case expect to pay the interest if the project turns out badly. Even if lenders screen their customers carefully, the lenders cannot altogether escape this moral hazard problem of finding themselves lending to many borrowers who have no intention of repaying. The answer is to limit the amount lent to any one customer. Most customers get broadly the same interest rate (with some adjustments), but the amount of credit they are allowed is rationed both according to the kind of security the customer can offer and to the prospects of the economy that the bank perceives.

When times are good, banks lend cheerfully because they believe that the average customer will not default. When the economy turns down, credit rationing intensifies because banks feel that their loans become less safe — and this may happen even though interest rates decline.

These shifts in credit rationing are reinforced when lenders see a change in monetary policy. If they perceive that the Fed is shifting to restraint and higher interest rates so as to cool down the economy, they help it along by tightening credit. Conversely, if they believe policy is expansionary, they ease credit, both via lower interest rates and via expanded credit rations. Credit rationing thus is another channel for monetary policy.

A second type of credit rationing can occur when the central bank imposes credit limits on commercial banks and other lenders. Banks are then not allowed to expand their loans during a given period by more than, say, 5 percent, or even less. Such a credit limit can put an abrupt end to a boom. A striking example occurred in the United States in early 1980. Concerned with the risk of double-digit inflation, the Fed clamped on credit controls. In no time the economy fell into a recession, with output falling at an annual rate of 9 percent.

Credit controls thus are an emergency brake for the central bank. They work, but they do so in a very blunt way. For that reason their use is very infrequent and remains reserved for occasions when dramatic, fast effects are desired. ∎

---

[*] An early and important reference to credit rationing is Dwight Jaffee and Robert Russell, "Imperfect Information, Uncertainty and Credit Rationing," *Quarterly Journal of Economics*, November 1966. The recent literature on credit rationing is surveyed by Linda Allen, "The Credit Rationing Phenomenon: A Survey of the Literature," Salomon Brothers Center, New York University, 1987.

the interest rate, but also by the amount of funds they have succeeded in retaining out of past earnings and by their current profits.[25] There is indeed evidence that the rate of investment is affected by the volume of retained earnings and by profits.

The existence of credit rationing modifies the neoclassical theory of investment by pointing to the state of a firm's balance sheet as a potentially important determinant of the rate of investment. As described in Box 9-1, it also suggests that monetary policy can affect investment and the economy by controlling credit as well as by changing interest rates.

Why Does Investment Fluctuate?

The facts with which we started this chapter show that investment fluctuates much more than consumption spending. The accelerator model provides one explanation of these fluctuations. There are two other basic explanations: the uncertain basis for expectations and the flexibility of the timing of investment.

UNCERTAIN EXPECTATIONS

Keynes, in the *General Theory,* emphasized the uncertain basis on which investment decisions are made. In his words, ". . . we have to admit that our basis of knowledge for estimating the yield ten years hence of a railway, a copper mine, a textile factory, the goodwill of a patent medicine . . . amounts to little and sometimes to nothing. . . ."[26] Thus, he argued, investment decisions are very much affected by how optimistic or pessimistic the investors feel.

The term "animal spirits" is sometimes used to describe the optimism or pessimism of investors; the term indicates that there may be no good basis for the expectations on which investors base their decisions. If there is no good basis for the expectations, then they could change easily — and the volume of investment along with the expectations.

THE TIMING OF INVESTMENT DECISIONS

The second possible reason for fluctuations in investment is that investment decisions can be delayed if the project will take a long time to come online. Suppose a firm has an investment project it would like to undertake, but the economy is currently in a

---

[25] This is not to say that the cost of capital does not affect the investment decision, for (as noted in footnote 3) firms that retain earnings still have to consider the alternative of investing their funds in financial assets rather than plant and equipment. Rather, the point is that other financial variables affect the investment decision as well.

[26] J. M. Keynes, *The General Theory of Employment, Interest and Money* (London: Macmillan, 1936), pp. 149–150.

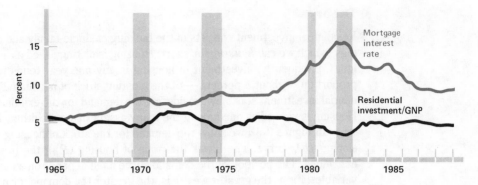

FIGURE 9-7
HOUSING INVESTMENT AND THE MORTGAGE INTEREST RATE, 1965–1988.
Mortgage rate is for new houses. Shaded bars mark periods of
recession. (SOURCE: DRI/McGraw-Hill.)

recession and the firm is not sure when the recession will end. Further, at the current
time it cannot even usefully employ all the capital it already has. Such a firm might
choose to wait until the prospects for the economy look better — when the recovery
gets under way — before deciding to start the investment project.

Either or both of those factors could help account for the substantial fluctuations
that are seen in business investment spending. Indeed, they may also explain the
success of the accelerator theory of investment, for if firms wait for a recovery to get
under way before investing, their investment will be closely related to the change in
GNP.

9-4 RESIDENTIAL INVESTMENT

We study residential investment separately from business fixed investment both to
introduce a slightly different model of investment[27] and because residential investment
shows large cyclical fluctuations, as can be seen in Figure 9-7.

Figure 9-7 shows residential investment spending as a percentage of GNP for the
1965–1988 period, together with the nominal mortgage interest rate. Residential
investment declines in all recessions. Thus in 1969–1970, 1973–1975, 1980, and
1981–1982, there are dips in residential investment. The same is true for the 1966–
1967 minirecession.

---

[27] We relate the model of this section to the model of investment behavior of Sec. 9-3 in the concluding
section of this chapter.

Theory

Residential investment consists of the building of single-family and multifamily dwellings, which we call *housing* for short. Housing is distinguished as an asset by its long life. Consequently, investment in housing in any one year tends to be a very small proportion—about 3 percent—of the existing stock of housing. The theory of residential investment starts by considering the demand for the existing *stock* of housing. Housing is viewed as one among the many assets that a wealthholder can own.

In Figure 9-8*a* we show the demand for the stock of housing in the downward-sloping DD_0 curve. The lower the price of housing (P_H), the greater the quantity demanded. The position of the demand curve itself depends on a number of economic variables: First, the greater wealth is, the greater the demand for housing. The more wealthy individuals are, the more housing they desire to own. Thus an increase in wealth would shift the demand curve from DD_0 to DD_1. Second, the demand for housing as an asset depends on the real return available on other assets. If returns on other forms of holding wealth—such as bonds—are low, then housing looks like a relatively attractive form in which to hold wealth. The lower the return on other assets, the greater the demand for housing. A reduction in the return on other assets, such as bonds or common stock, shifts the demand curve from DD_0 to DD_1.

FIGURE 9-8
THE HOUSING MARKET: DETERMINATION OF THE ASSET PRICE OF HOUSING AND THE RATE OF HOUSING INVESTMENT. The supply of and demand for the stock of housing determine the asset price of housing (P_H^0) in panel (*a*). The rate of housing investment (Q_H^0) is determined by the flow supply of housing at price P_H^0 in panel (*b*).

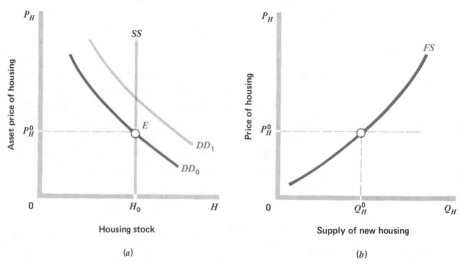

(*a*) (*b*)

Third, the demand for the housing stock depends on the net real return obtained by owning housing. The gross return — before taking costs into account — consists either of rent, if the housing is rented out, or of the implicit return that the homeowner receives by living in the home plus capital gains arising from increases in the value of the housing. In turn, the costs of owning the housing consist of interest costs, typically the mortgage interest rate, plus any real estate taxes, and depreciation. These costs are deducted from the gross return and, after tax adjustments, constitute the net return. An increase in the net return on housing, caused, for example, by a reduction in the mortgage interest rate, makes housing a more attractive form in which to hold wealth and shifts the demand curve for housing from DD_0 to DD_1.

The price of housing is determined by the interaction of this demand with the stock supply of housing. At any time the stock supply is fixed — there is a given stock of housing that cannot be adjusted quickly in response to price changes. The supply curve of the stock of housing is the SS curve of Figure 9-8a. The equilibrium *asset price of housing, P_H^0*, is determined by the intersection of the supply and demand curves. The asset price of housing is the price of a typical house or apartment. At any one time, the market for the stock of housing determines the asset price of housing.

THE RATE OF INVESTMENT

We now consider the determinants of the rate of investment in housing, and for that purpose turn to Figure 9-8b. The FS curve represents the supply of new housing as a function of the price of housing. This curve is the same as the regular supply curve of any industry. The supply curve shows the amount of a good that suppliers want to sell at each price. In this case, the good being supplied is new housing. The position of the FS curve is affected by the costs of factors of production used in the construction industry and by technological factors affecting the cost of building.

The FS curve is sometimes called the flow supply curve, since it represents the *flow* of new housing into the market in a given time period. In contrast, the *stock* supply curve, SS, represents the total amount of housing in the market at a moment of time.

Given the price of housing established in the asset market, P_H^0, building contractors supply the amount of new housing, Q_H^0, for sale at that price. The higher the asset price, the greater the supply of new housing. Thus, the supply of new housing is nothing other than gross investment in housing — total additions to the housing stock. Figure 9-8 thus represents our basic theory of the determinants of housing investment.

Any factor affecting the demand for the existing stock of housing will affect the asset price of housing, P_H, and thus the rate of investment in housing. Similarly, any factor shifting the flow supply curve, FS, will affect the rate of investment. We have already investigated the major factors shifting the DD demand curve for housing, but will briefly repeat that analysis.

Suppose the interest rate — the rate that potential homeowners can obtain by investing elsewhere — rises. Then the asset demand for housing falls and the price of housing falls; that, in turn, induces a decline in the rate of production of new housing, or a decline in housing investment. Or suppose that the mortgage interest rate rises: once

box 9-2

INVESTMENT IN THE 1980s; THE 1982–1985 BOOM AND AFTER

We saw in Table 9-1 that increased investment accounted for over half the increase in GNP during the 3 years following the trough of the last recession, in 1982. Investment typically grows fast during recovery, but the recovery after 1982 was nonetheless exceptional: While GNP grew no faster in the first 2 years of the recovery than it normally does, business fixed investment grew twice as fast as normal during those 2 years.

Table 1 shows an estimate of the real rate of interest along with the ratio of business fixed investment to GNP and the real (adjusted for inflation) Standard & Poor's index of stock prices. The real interest rate rose sharply in the early eighties: indeed, interest rates were at record post-World War II levels during this period. The high real

TABLE 1

INVESTMENT AND INTEREST RATES, 1976–1988 (percent)

	$(I/Y)_N$	Real bond rate	Stock price index	$(I/Y)_R$
1976–1979	11.1	0.2	142.9	11.3
1980	11.8	3.8	138.6	11.9
1981	12.1	6.7	136.2	12.2
1982	11.6	6.8	119.7	11.6
1983	10.5	6.1	154.5	11.0
1984	11.0	7.8	148.4	12.1
1985	11.0	7.5	168.5	12.5
1986	10.2	5.7	207.5	11.6
1987	9.9	6.1	243.7	11.6
1988	10.0	6.3	218.4	12.2

SOURCE: *Economic Report of the President*, 1989, and *Survey of Current Business*, May 1989. First column is ratio of nominal nonresidential fixed investment spending to nominal GNP. Second column is Moody's Aaa corporate bond rate for the given year, minus the average inflation rate (of the GNP deflator) over the past 3 years, the current year, and the next 2 years. Third column is the Standard & Poor's composite stock market index divided by the GNP deflator (and multiplied by 100). Last column is the ratio of *real* investment spending to *real* GNP.

again there is a fall in the asset price of housing and a reduction in the rate of construction.

Because the existing stock of housing is so large relative to the rate of investment in housing, we can ignore the effects of the current supply of new housing on the price of housing in the short run. However, over time, as the new construction increases the

interest rates should have been expected to produce sluggish, not booming, investment. What happened?

In a careful study, Barry Bosworth of the Brookings Institution concludes that the rental cost of capital did not increase between 1982 and 1984 even though the real interest rate rose substantially.* Four factors affected the rental cost of capital:

1. One, which we did not discuss in the text, is the purchase price of capital goods. The prices of capital goods fell sharply during the 1982–1984 period. Prices of computers in particular fell. This made investment cheaper for firms to carry out.
2. Tax treatment of investment—changes in depreciation allowances and the investment tax credit—was made substantially more favorable in the 1981 and 1982 tax bills.
3. The stock market boomed, making equity financing cheaper.
4. Real interest rates rose sharply, making debt financing more expensive.

The contrast between the first and fourth columns of the table brings out sharply the effects of the fall in the price of investment goods. Measured in nominal terms, using current prices, the share of business fixed investment in GNP in 1985 was at practically the same level as in 1980; but measured in constant prices, there was an increase of a full 1.3 percent of GNP in the share of business fixed investment in GNP between 1980 and 1985. The stock market boom that started in 1983 and the rise in real interest rates are also clearly visible in the table.

The net effect, Bosworth concludes, is that the rental cost of capital did not increase over this period, and indeed fell for many types of investment. But that is not sufficient to account for an investment boom—only for the fact that there was not an investment slump. Indeed, Bosworth points out that a large share of the investment boom was in business purchases of computers and automobiles, neither of which benefited from improved tax treatment.

So what caused the investment boom? Expectations of a booming economy or animal spirits may both have played a part. So, too, may subtleties in the tax law that made debt financing less expensive than the simple increase in the real interest rate implies.

After 1985 the share of nominal investment in nominal GNP fell back to a level well below that of 1980–1981. But because the prices of investment goods, particularly computers, continued to decline, the share of real investment in real GNP was the same in 1988 as in 1981, despite continued high real interest rates. The booming stock market probably helped, too. ◼

---

* Taxes and the Investment Recovery," *Brookings Papers on Economic Activity*, 1985:1.

housing stock it shifts the *SS* curve of panel (*a*) to the right. The long-run equilibrium in the housing industry would be reached, in an economy in which there was no increase in population or wealth over time, when the housing stock became constant. Constancy of the housing stock requires gross investment to be equal to depreciation, or net investment to be equal to zero. The asset price of housing would have to be at the level at which the rate of construction was just equal to the rate of depreciation of the existing stock of housing in long-run equilibrium. If population or income and wealth were growing at a constant rate, the long-run equilibrium would be one in which the rate of construction was just sufficient to cover depreciation and the steadily growing stock demand. In an economy subjected to continual, nonsteady changes, that long-run equilibrium is not necessarily ever reached.

Minor qualifications to the basic theoretical structure arise chiefly because new housing cannot be constructed immediately in response to changes in P_H; rather, it takes a short time for that response to occur. Thus, the supply of new housing responds, not to the actual price of housing today, but to the price expected to prevail when the construction is completed. However, the lags are quite short; it takes less than a year to build a typical house. Another qualification stems from that same construction delay. Since builders have to incur expenses before they sell their output, they need financing over the construction period. They are frequently financed at the mortgage interest rate by the thrift institutions, that is, savings and loan associations and mutual savings banks. Hence, the position of the flow supply curve is affected by the mortgage interest rate as well as the amount of lending undertaken by the thrift institutions.[28]

THE q THEORY OF INVESTMENT

We sidestep for a moment to note that the model of the housing market that emphasizes the asset market and the rate of addition to the stock can similarly be used to analyze business fixed investment. Indeed, an increasingly used view of business fixed investment is the q theory, which focuses on the stock market (see footnote 15). It can be cast in terms very similar to those of the housing model. At any one moment all the shares in the economy are in inelastic supply, just like the housing stock. Stock market investors place a value on those shares, with the price of shares in the stock market corresponding to P_H in Figure 9-8.

The price of a share in a company is the price of a claim on the capital in the company. The managers of the company can then be thought of as responding to the price of the stock by producing more new capital — that is, investing — when the price of shares is high and producing less new capital or not investing at all when the price of shares is low.

What is q? It is an estimate of the value the stock market places on a firm's assets relative to the cost of producing those assets. When the ratio is high, firms will want to produce more assets, so that investment will be rapid. Similarly, P_H can be thought of as the price of an existing house relative to the cost of building a new one. When that ratio is high, there will be lots of building.

---

[28] The theory of housing investment of this section is outlined in J. R. Kearl "Inflation, Mortgages, and Housing," *Journal of Political Economy*, October 1979. See, too, James Poterba, "Tax Subsidies to Owner-Occupied Housing: An Asset-Market Approach," *Quarterly Journal of Economics*, November 1984.

TABLE 9-6

MONTHLY PAYMENTS ON MORTGAGES

Interest rate, %	5	10	15
Monthly payment, $	292	454	640

NOTE: The assumed mortgage is a loan for $50,000, paid back over 25 years, with equal monthly payments throughout the 25 years.

Monetary Policy and Housing Investment

Monetary policy has powerful effects on housing investment. Part of the reason is that most houses are purchased with the aid of mortgage financing. Since the 1930s, a mortgage has typically been a debt instrument of very long maturity, 20 to 30 years, with a fixed rate and with monthly nominal repayments that remain fixed for the 20 to 30 years to maturity.[29]

Monetary policy has powerful effects on housing investment because the demand for housing is sensitive to the interest rate. There is sensitivity to both the *real* and *nominal* interest rates. The reason for this sensitivity can be seen in Table 9-6, which shows the monthly payment that has to be made by someone borrowing $50,000 through a conventional mortgage at different interest rates. All these interest rates have existed at some time during the last 25 years: 5 percent at the beginning of the sixties, 10 percent at the end of the seventies and in 1989, and 15 percent in 1981 and 1982.

The monthly repayment by the borrower approximately doubles when the interest rate doubles. Thus an essential component of the cost of owning a home rises almost proportionately with the interest rate. It is therefore not surprising that the demand for housing is very sensitive to the interest rate.

The above statements have to be qualified. In the first place, there are substantial tax advantages to the homeowner who finances through a mortgage, because the interest payments can be deducted from income before calculating taxes. Second, of course, we should be concerned with the *real* and not the nominal interest cost of owning a house — and certainly much of the rise of the mortgage interest rate is a result of increases in the expected rate of inflation.

But the *nominal* interest rate also affects the homeowner. The reason has to do with the form of the mortgage. The conventional mortgage makes the borrower pay a fixed amount each month over the lifetime of the mortgage. Even if the interest rate rises only because the expected rate of inflation has risen — and thus the real rate is constant — the payments that have to be made *today* by a borrower go up. But the

---

[29] So-called ARMs (adjustable rate mortgages) became increasingly popular in the 1980s. As the name suggests, the interest rate on such mortgages is adjusted in accordance with some reference rate, such as the 1-year Treasury bill rate. Both fixed rate mortgages and ARMs are now used to finance housing.

inflation has not yet happened. Thus the real payments made today by a borrower rise when the *nominal* interest rate rises, even if the real rate does not rise.[30] Given the higher real monthly payments when the *nominal* interest rate rises, we should expect the nominal interest rate also to affect housing demand. And the data shown in Figure 9-6 are quite consistent with the view that the nominal interest rate affects housing demand.

Disintermediation, Mortgage Availability, and Regulation Q

Before 1978 monetary policy affected housing demand through a channel known as *disintermediation.* Mortgage financing is provided mostly by savings and loan institutions. These institutions have assets (mortgages) that have very long lives. Up to 1978 they obtained the funds they loaned out mainly from depositors, who made savings deposits in the institutions. The depositors had the right to remove their funds immediately, sometimes on payment of a penalty, or within a short time at no charge.

At that time the Fed controlled the interest rates that savings and loans (and banks and other financial institutions) could pay to their depositors.[31] The control was exercised through Regulation Q. Reg Q, as it was called, in effect set the interest rate maximum to be paid on deposits by savings and loans at 5.5 percent. The financial institutions were generally in favor of Reg Q, since it limited the amount they had to pay to, in effect, borrow (that is, attract depositors).

The savings and loans in particular were concerned that the rate of interest they paid depositors should not rise. This was because the S&Ls had made long-term loans (mortgages) at low interest rates. Thus they knew that they would for a long time be earning only 5 or 6 percent on the loans they had made. They could not afford to pay out more than 5 percent to their depositors.

But when market interest rates started rising, depositors limited to 5.5 percent at the financial institutions went elsewhere with their money. This is the process of *disintermediation.* As the depositors withdrew their deposits, for instance, buying Treasury bills instead, the savings and loans had nothing left to loan. There were no mortgages available; however, the interest rate that the savings and loans were quoting (this was the rate they would charge if they could find the money to lend) was not especially high.

With housing loans unavailable, there was a *credit crunch.* The first serious crunch took place in 1966–1967. (Note the dip in residential investment in Figure 9-1 even though there is no evident increase in the mortgage rate.) Disintermediation happened again in 1969–1970 and in the 1973–1975 recession. But then the savings

---

[30] How can the real payments rise if the real interest rate stays the same? The explanation is that today's real payments rise, but the real present value of future payments falls: the repayment stream tilts toward the present.

[31] These controls were phased out between 1980 and 1986 under the terms of the 1980 Depository Institutions Decontrol and Monetary Control Act.

and loans invented new ways of borrowing, and since then, monetary policy has affected housing investment directly through interest rates, rather than through the roundabout route of disintermediation.

What about the problem that the savings and loans, borrowing by paying high interest rates to depositors, would be paying out more than they were earning on the loans they had made? This was a very real problem in the late seventies and early eighties. Several savings and loan institutions failed (went bankrupt) and were bought out by other financial institutions.[32]

As a result of the removal of controls on interest rates, monetary policy now affects housing investment through interest rates, but not through disintermediation. Indeed, this is one reason the interest rate in the late seventies and early eighties went so high: The Fed wanted to reduce aggregate demand and had to do so through the direct route of putting pressure on rates and not through the indirect route of disintermediation.

9-5 CONCLUDING REMARKS

We have presented several different models to explain the different categories of investment behavior in this chapter. Nonetheless, there is a basic common element in the models: the interaction of the demand for the stock of capital with investment. In each case we started by examining the determinants of the desired stock — capital or housing. The discussion of inventory investment started by examining the determinants of the desired inventory-sales ratio. Then, in each case, we went on to analyze or describe the determinants of the rate per year of that type of investment.

We come now to the question of why there is a difference between the theoretical models used to explain the level of business fixed investment and that of residential investment. The fundamental difference arises because of the low degree of standardization of the capital goods involved in business fixed investment and the associated question of the extent, or even existence, of a good market for used capital goods. Much of business fixed investment is in capital goods that are specifically designed for a given firm and are not of much use to other firms. It is, accordingly, difficult to establish a market price for the stock of that type of capital, and the theory used in discussing residential investment would be difficult to apply in those cases. Although housing, too, varies a good deal, it is, nonetheless, possible to talk of a price of housing. Further, used

---

[32] At the end of the eighties it became increasingly recognized that there were massive bankruptcies in the savings and loan (S&L) industry. Estimates of the cost of saving the failed institutions ranged from $150 billion to $300 billion. These failures were not primarily the result of a gap between the rate at which the S&Ls borrowed and the rate at which they lent, but rather a result of bad loans and excessive risk taking by many owners of S&Ls, particularly in the early part of the decade. The failures were concentrated in parts of the country where the real estate market had deteriorated sharply, especially Texas. But there is also no doubt that in many cases S&L owners behaved recklessly and sometimes illegally. They were able to behave this way in large part because their depositors were insured by the federal government and therefore did not need to ask themselves how sound the institutions in which they were placing their funds were.

housing is a very good substitute for new housing, whereas that is less often true for many capital goods.

Looking both back and ahead, recall that although investment is important as a component of aggregate demand, it is also — by adding to a country's productive capacity — a key to aggregate supply, especially in the long run. We turn to the supply-side aspect of investment in Chapter 19.

9-6 SUMMARY

1. Investment constitutes less than 20 percent of aggregate demand in the United States, but fluctuations in investment account for a large share of business cycle movements in GNP. We analyze investment in three categories: business fixed investment, residential investment, and inventory investment.
2. Investment is spending that adds to the capital stock.
3. Inventory investment fluctuates proportionately more than any other class of investment. Firms have a desired inventory-to-sales ratio. That may get out of line if sales are unexpectedly high or low, and then firms change their production levels to adjust inventories. For instance, when aggregate demand falls at the beginning of a recession, inventories build up. Then when firms cut back production, output falls even more than did aggregate demand. This is the inventory cycle.
4. The neoclassical theory of business fixed investment sees the rate of investment being determined by the speed with which firms adjust their capital stocks toward their desired levels. The desired capital stock is larger the more output the firm expects to produce and the smaller the rental or user cost of capital. Since investment is undertaken for *future* production, it is expected future (permanent) output that determines the desired capital stock.
5. The real interest rate is the nominal (stated) interest rate minus the inflation rate.
6. The rental cost of capital is higher the higher the real interest rate, the lower the price of the firm's stock, and the higher the rate of depreciation of capital. Taxes also affect the rental cost of capital, in particular through the investment tax credit. The investment tax credit is, in effect, a government subsidy for investment.
7. In practice, firms decide how much to invest using discounted cash flow analysis. This analysis gives answers that are consistent with those of the neoclassical approach.
8. The accelerator model of investment is a special case of the gradual adjustment model of investment. It predicts that investment demand is proportional to the *change* in GNP.
9. Because credit is rationed, firms' investment decisions are affected also by the state of their balance sheets, and thus by the amount of earnings they have retained.
10. Empirical results show that business fixed investment responds with long lags to

changes in output. The accelerator model, which does not take into account changes in the rental cost of capital, does almost as good a job of explaining investment as the more sophisticated neoclassical model.

11. The theory of housing investment starts from the demand for the *stock* of housing. Demand is affected by wealth, the interest rates available on alternative investments, and the mortgage rate. Increases in wealth increase the stock demand for housing; increases in either the interest rate on alternative assets or the mortgage rate reduce the stock demand. The price of housing is determined by the interaction of the stock demand and the given stock supply of housing available at any given time. The rate of housing investment is determined by the rate at which builders supply housing at the going price.

12. Under current conditions housing investment is affected by monetary policy because housing demand is sensitive to the interest rate (real and nominal), and in the past it was also affected by disintermediation.

13. We now summarize the common elements of the different models. First, aggregate investment is the sum of the different types of investment spending. Thus any variable that affects any of the categories of investment analyzed also affects aggregate investment. Second, monetary and fiscal policy both affect investment, particularly business fixed investment and housing investment. The effects take place through changes in real (and nominal in the case of housing) interest rates and through tax incentives for investment. Third, there are substantial lags in the adjustment of investment spending to changes in output and other determinants of investment. This is true particularly for business fixed investment; there are also lags in the relation between GNP and inventory investment. Such lags are likely to increase fluctuations in GNP.

KEY TERMS

Investment	Cobb-Douglas production function
Business fixed investment	Real interest rate
Residential investment	Gradual adjustment hypothesis
Inventory investment	Discounted cash flow analysis
Inventory cycle	Accelerator model of investment
Desired capital stock	Credit rationing
Marginal product of capital	Present discounted value
Rental (user) cost of capital	q theory

PROBLEMS

1. (a) Explain how final sales and output can differ.
   (b) Point out in Figure 9-2 periods of planned and unplanned inventory investment and drawing down.
   (c) During a period of slow but steady growth, how would you expect final sales and output to be related? Explain. Draw a hypothetical figure like Figure 9-2 for such a period.

2. At the end of 1988 and the beginning of 1989, the inventory-to-sales ratio, although very low, was beginning to rise. Business cycle forecasters argued that this was a worrying sign (among other signs, including a rising dollar and higher interest rates) and that there could be a recession later in 1989. Explain why this would be a recessionary signal, and check the data to see whether there was a recession or slowdown in 1989.

3. We have seen in Chapters 8 and 9 that *permanent* income and output, rather than current income and output, determine consumption and investment.
    (a) How does this affect the *IS-LM* model built in Chapter 4? (Refer to Figure 8-4.)
    (b) What are the policy implications of the use of "permanent" measures?

4. In Chapter 4 it was assumed that investment rises during periods of low interest rates. That, however, was not the case during the 1930s, when investment and interest rates were both very low. Explain how this can occur. What would have been appropriate fiscal policy in such a case?

5. According to the description of business fixed investment in this chapter, how would you expect a firm's investment decisions to be affected by a sudden increase in demand for its product? What factors would determine the speed of its reaction?

6. Describe how a car rental agency would calculate the rate at which it rents cars, and relate your description to equation (5).

7. It is often suggested that investment spending is dominated by animal spirits — the optimism or pessimism of investors. Is this argument at all consistent with the analysis of Sections 9-2 and 9-3?

8. Here are the cash flows for an investment project:

Year 1	Year 2	Year 3
-200	100	120

Should the firm undertake this project:
    (a) If the interest rate is 5 percent?
    (b) If the interest rate is 10 percent?

9. Is there any relation between the neoclassical theory of investment and the way firms make their investment decisions in practice?

10. (a) Give at least two reasons why higher profits may increase the rate of investment.
    (b) Explain why lenders may ration the quantity of credit rather than merely charge higher interest rates to more risky borrowers.

11. Explain how the two panels of Figure 9-8 react together over time. What would happen if the demand for housing stock (*DD*) shifts upward and to the right over time?

12. Using Figure 9-8, trace carefully the step-by-step effects on the housing market of an increase in interest rates. Explain each shift and its long-run and short-run effects.

13. (a) Explain why the housing market usually prospers when (real) mortgage rates are low.
    (b) In some states, usury laws prohibit (nominal) mortgage rates in excess of a legal maximum. Explain how this could lead to an exception to the conclusion in part a of this problem.
    (c) Could that happen in the absence of inflation? Explain.

14. Suppose that an explicitly temporary tax credit is enacted. The tax credit is at the rate of 10 percent and lasts only 1 year.
    (a) What is the effect of this tax measure on investment in the long run (say, after 4 or 5 years)?
    (b) What is the effect in the current year and the following year?
    (c) How will your answers under parts a and b of this problem differ if the tax credit is permanent?

*15. For this question use the Cobb-Douglas production function and the corresponding desired capital stock given by equation (3). Assume that

$$v = 0.3, \; Y = \$2.5 \text{ trillion, and } rc = 0.15$$

   (a) Calculate the desired capital stock, K^*.
   (b) Now suppose that Y is expected to rise to $3 trillion. What is the corresponding desired capital stock?
   (c) Suppose that the capital stock was at its desired level before the change in income was expected. Suppose further that $\lambda = 0.4$ in the gradual adjustment model of investment. What will the rate of investment be in the first year after expected income changes? In the second year?
   (d) Does your answer in part c refer to gross or net investment?

APPENDIX: INTEREST RATES, PRESENT VALUES, AND DISCOUNTING

In this appendix we deal with the relationships among bond coupons, interest rates and yields, and the prices of bonds. In doing so, we shall introduce the very useful concept of present discounted value (*PDV*).

Section 1

We start with the case of a perpetual bond, or perpetuity. Such bonds have been issued in a number of countries, including the United Kingdom where they are called Consols. The Consol is a promise by the British government to pay a fixed amount to the holder of the bond every year and forever. Let us denote the promised payment per Consol by Q_c, the *coupon*.[33]

The *yield* on a bond is the return per dollar that the holder of the bond receives. The yield on a savings account paying 5 percent interest per year is obviously just 5 percent. Someone paying $25 for a Consol that has a coupon of $2.50 obtains a yield of 10 percent [($2.50/25) × 100 percent].

The yield on a Consol and its price are related in a simple way. Let us denote the price of

---

* An asterisk denotes a more difficult problem.

[33] The *coupon rate* is the coupon divided by the face value of the bond, which is literally the value printed on the face of the bond. Bonds do not necessarily sell for their face value, though customarily the face value is close to the value at which the bonds are sold when they first come on the market.

the Consol by P_c and the coupon (as before) by Q_c. Then, as the above example suggests, the yield, i, is just

$$i = \frac{Q_c}{P_c} \tag{A1}$$

which says that the yield on a perpetuity is the coupon divided by the price.

Alternatively, we can switch equation (A1) around to

$$P_c = \frac{Q_c}{i} \tag{A2}$$

which says that the price is the coupon divided by the yield. So, given the coupon and the yield, we can derive the price, or given the coupon and the price, we can derive the yield.

None of this is a theory of the determination of the yield or the price of a perpetuity. It merely points out the relationship between price and yield. Our theory of the determination of the yield on bonds is presented in Chapter 4. The interest rate in Chapter 4 corresponds to the yield on bonds, and we tend to talk interchangeably of interest rates and yields.

We shall return to the Consol at the end of this appendix.

Section 2

Now we move on to a short-term bond. Let us consider a bond that was sold by a borrower for $100 and on which the borrower promises to pay $108 after 1 year. This is a 1-year bond. The yield on the bond to the person who bought it for $100 is 8 percent. For every $1 lent, the lender obtains both the $1 principal and 8 cents extra at the end of the year.

Next we ask a slightly different question. How much would a promise to pay $1 at the end of the year be worth? If $108 at the end of the year is worth $100 today, then $1 at the end of the year must be worth $100/108, or 92.6 cents, today. That is the value today of $1 in 1 year's time. In other words, it is the present discounted value of $1 in 1 year's time. It is the present value because it is what would be paid today for the promise of money in 1 year's time, and it is discounted because the value today is less than the promised payment in a year's time.

Denoting the 1-year yield or interest rate by i, we can write the present discounted value of a promised payment of Q_1 1 year from now as

$$PDV = \frac{Q_1}{1 + i} \tag{A3}$$

Let us return to our 1-year bond and suppose that the day after the original borrower obtained the money, the yield on 1-year bonds rises. How much would anyone *now* be willing to pay for the promise to receive $108 after 1 year? The answer must be given by the general formula (A3). That means that the price of the 1-year bond will fall when the interest rate or yield on such bonds rises. Once again, we see that the price of the bond and the yield are inversely related, given the promised payments to be made on the bond.

As before, we can reverse the formula for the price in order to find the yield on the bond, given its price and the promised payment Q_1. Note that the price, P, is equal to the present discounted value, so we can write

$$1 + i = \frac{Q_1}{P} \tag{A4}$$

Section 3

Next we consider a 2-year bond. Such a bond would typically promise to make a payment of interest, which we shall denote Q_1, at the end of the first year, and then a payment of interest and principal (usually the amount borrowed), Q_2, at the end of the second year. Given the yield, i, on the bond, how do we compute its *PDV*, which will be equal to its price?

We start by asking first what the bond will be worth 1 year from now. At that stage, it will be a 1-year bond, promising to pay the amount Q_2 in 1 year's time, and yielding i. Its value 1 year from now will accordingly be given by equation (A3), except that Q_1 in equation (A3) is replaced by Q_2. Let us denote the value of the bond 1 year from now by PDV_1, and note that

$$PDV_1 = \frac{Q_2}{1 + i} \tag{A5}$$

To complete computing the *PDV* of the 2-year bond, we can now treat it as a 1-year bond that promises to pay Q_1 in interest 1 year from now and, also, to pay PDV_1 1 year from now, since it can be sold at that stage for that amount. Hence, the *PDV* of the bond, equal to its price, is

$$PDV = \frac{Q_1}{1 + i} + \frac{PDV_1}{1 + i} \tag{A6}$$

or

$$PDV = \frac{Q_1}{1 + i} + \frac{Q_2}{(1 + i)^2} \tag{A6\textit{a}}$$

As previously, given the promised payments Q_1 and Q_2, the price of the bond will fall if the yield rises, and vice versa.

It is now less simple to reverse the equation for the price of the bond to find the yield than it was before; that is because from equation (A6), we obtain a quadratic equation for the yield, which has two solutions.

Section 4

We have now provided the outline of the argument whereby the present discounted value of *any* promised stream of payments for any number of years can be computed. Suppose that a bond, or any other asset, promises to pay amounts $Q_1, Q_2, Q_3, \ldots, Q_n$ in future years 1, 2, 3, $\ldots$, *n*. By pursuing the type of argument given in Section 3, it is possible to show that the *PDV* of such a payments stream will be

$$PDV = \frac{Q_1}{1 + i} + \frac{Q_2}{(1 + i)^2} + \frac{Q_3}{(1 + i)^3} + \cdots + \frac{Q_n}{(1 + i)^n} \qquad (A7)$$

As usual, the price of a bond with a specified payments stream will be inversely related to its yield.

Section 5

The formula (A7) is the general formula for calculating the present discounted value of any stream of payments. Indeed, the payments may also be negative. Thus in calculating the *PDV* of an investment project, we expect the first few payments, for example, Q_1 and Q_2, to be negative. Those are the periods in which the firm is spending to build the factory or buy machinery. Then in later years the Q_i become positive as the factory starts generating revenues.

Firms undertaking discounted cash flow analysis are calculating present values using a formula such as (A7).

Section 6

Finally, we return to the Consol. The Consol promises to pay the amount Q_c forever. Applying the formula, we can compute the present value of the Consol by

$$PDV = Q_c \left[\frac{1}{(1 + i)} + \frac{1}{(1 + i)^2} + \frac{1}{(1 + i)^3} + \cdots + \frac{1}{(1 + i)^n} + \cdots \right] \qquad (A8)$$

The contents of the parentheses on the right-hand side are an infinite series, the sum of which can be calculated as $1/i$. Thus,

$$PDV = \frac{Q_c}{i} \qquad (A9)$$

This section casts a slightly different light on the commonsense discussion in Section 1 of this appendix. Equations (A8) and (A9) show that the Consol's price is equal to the *PDV* of the future coupon payments.

10

THE DEMAND FOR MONEY

*M*oney is a means of payment or medium of exchange. In the United States, the basic measure of the money stock is currency plus checkable deposits, or *M*1. This is the money that people keep in order to make payments for their purchases. *M*1 in the United States was about $800 billion in the middle of 1989. With a population of 248 million, this means that average (*M*1) money holdings per person were above $3,200. Changes in the financial system in the last two decades have made it more and more difficult to distinguish money from closely related assets, and accordingly other definitions of the money stock are used increasingly. The most common of these is the broader monetary aggregate, *M*2, which includes interest-bearing deposits; this was $3,000 billion in mid-1989, or about $12,000 per capita.

We start discussing money demand with a review of the concept of the demand for *real balances*. One of the essentials of money demand is that individuals are interested in the purchasing power of their money holdings — the value of their cash balances in terms of the goods the cash will buy. They are not concerned with their *nominal* money holdings, that is, the number of dollar bills they hold. Two implications follow:

1. *Real* money demand is unchanged when the price level increases, and *all* real variables, such as the interest rate, real income, and real wealth, remain unchanged.
2. *Nominal* money demand increases in proportion to the increase in the price level, given the constancy of the real variables just specified.[1]

---

[1] Be sure you understand that statements (1) and (2) say the same thing in slightly different ways.

We have a special name for behavior that is not affected by changes in the price level, all real variables remaining unchanged. An individual is free from *money illusion* if a change in the level of prices, holding all real variables constant, leaves the person's real behavior, including real money demand, unchanged. By contrast, an individual whose real behavior is affected by a change in the price level, all real variables remaining unchanged, is said to suffer from money illusion.

Empirical evidence supports the theoretical argument that the demand for money is a demand for real balances — or that the demand for nominal balances, holding real variables constant, is proportional to the price level.

In Chapter 4, we assumed that the demand for money increases with the level of real income and decreases with the nominal interest rate. Recall that the response of the demand for money to interest rates is important in determining the effectiveness of fiscal policy. Changes in fiscal variables, such as tax rates or government spending, affect aggregate demand if the demand for money changes when the interest rate changes — if the demand for money is interest-elastic. If the demand for money does not react at all to changes in the interest rate, increases in government spending totally *crowd out* private spending and leave the level of income unaffected.

The demand for money has been studied very intensively at both the theoretical and empirical levels. There is by now almost total agreement that the demand should, as a theoretical matter, increase as the level of real income rises and decrease as the nominal interest rate rises. Much empirical work bears out these two properties of the demand-for-money function.

However, the money demand function has been a problem for the last 15 years. Until 1973, empirical work showed a very *stable* simple demand-for-money function, with real balances demanded increasing with the level of income and decreasing with interest rates. But then from about 1974 on, the demand-for-money function seemed to shift several times. Through the early 1980s the shifts generally showed lower real balances being demanded at given levels of income and interest rates than before. However, in the 1980s there have been shifts in the demand for $M1$ in the opposite direction, in which the quantity of real balances demanded has increased at given levels of income and interest rates. Explaining these shifts in money demand, or money demand instability, has been a major, though so far not very successful, area for research. Many of the problems are undoubtedly due to a series of changes in the financial system that we discuss below.

Even as the demand for $M1$ has become unstable, it appears that $M2$ demand, which includes a broader range of assets toward which demand shifted in the course of financial deregulation, *is* stable. Because of this stability $M2$ is currently the focal point of monetary policy.

10-1 COMPONENTS OF THE MONEY STOCK

In the U.S. economy there is a vast variety of financial assets, from currency to complicated claims on corporations. Which part of these assets is called money? There are four main monetary aggregates: currency, $M1$, $M2$, and $M3$. Box 10-1 describes the components of the different measures of money. Table 10-1 shows the definitions of the different money stock measures. The left-hand column of the table lists various claims held by households or firms, and the three right-hand columns show which particular claim belongs to which particular monetary aggregate.

TABLE 10-1
MONETARY AGGREGATES

Item	M1	M2	M3
Currency in circulation*	x	x	x
Traveler's checks	x	x	x
At commercial banks			
Demand deposits	x	x	x
NOW (negotiable order of withdrawal) accounts	x	x	x
ATS (automatic transfer service) accounts	x	x	x
At thrift institutions			
Demand deposits (at mutual savings banks)	x	x	x
NOW accounts	x	x	x
ATS accounts	x	x	x
Credit union share draft balances	x	x	x
At commercial banks			
Overnight RPs (repurchase agreements)		x	x
Small time deposits (less than $100,000)		x	x
Savings deposits		x	x
At thrift institutions			
Savings deposits (at mutual savings banks and S&Ls)		x	x
Small time deposits (less than $100,000)		x	x
Other			
Overnight Eurodollar deposits†		x	x
Money market mutual fund shares		x	x
At commercial banks			
Large time deposits [$100,000 or more, including large negotiable CDs (certificates of deposit)]			x
Term RPs			x
At thrift institutions			
Large time deposits ($100,000 or more, including large negotiable CDs)			x
Term RPs			x
Total outstanding as of December 1988, $ billions	790	3,069	3,919

* The stock of currency in circulation was $211 billion.

† Deposits of nonbank U.S. residents at Caribbean branches of Federal Reserve System member banks.

SOURCE: Federal Reserve Bank of Dallas and *Federal Reserve Bulletin.*

box 10-1

COMPONENTS OF THE MONETARY AGGREGATES

We briefly describe here the components of the monetary aggregates.

1. *Currency:* Consists of coins and notes in circulation.
2. *Demand deposits:* Non-interest-bearing checking accounts at commercial banks, excluding deposits of other banks, the government, and foreign governments.
3. *Traveler's checks:* The total comprises only those checks issued by nonbanks (such as American Express). Traveler's checks issued by banks are included in demand deposits.
4. *Other checkable deposits:* Interest-earning checking accounts, including NOW and ATS accounts. ATS stands for automatic transfers from savings accounts. With ATS a deposit holder keeps assets in a savings account, and the bank transfers them automatically to the checking account when a payment has to be made.

$$M1 = (1) + (2) + (3) + (4)$$

5. *Overnight repurchase agreements* (RPs): Borrowing by a bank from a nonbank customer. The bank sells a security (for example, a Treasury bill) to the customer today and promises to buy it back at a fixed price tomorrow. That way the bank gets to use the amount borrowed for a day.
6. *Overnight Eurodollars:* Deposits that pay interest and mature the next day, held in Caribbean branches of U.S. banks.
7. *Money market mutual fund shares:* Interest-earning checkable deposits in mutual funds that invest in short-term assets. Some MMMF shares are held by institutions; these are excluded from $M2$ but included in $M3$.
8. *Money market deposit accounts:* MMMFs run by banks, with the advantage that they are insured up to $100,000. Introduced at the end of 1982 to allow the banks to compete with MMMFs.

$M1$ comprises those claims that can be used *directly, instantly,* and *without restrictions* for third-party payments. These claims are *liquid.* An asset is liquid if it can immediately, conveniently, and cheaply be used for making payments. $M1$ corresponds most closely to the traditional definition of money as the means of payment. $M2$ includes, in addition, claims that are not instantly liquid — withdrawal of time deposits, for example, may require notice to the depository institution; money market mutual funds may set a minimum on the size of checks drawn on an account. But with these qualifications, the claims also fall into a broader category of money. Finally, in $M3$ we include items that most people never see, namely, large negotiable deposits and repurchase agreements. These are held primarily by corporations, but also by wealthy individuals. Their attraction is their combination of liquidity and yield.

We concentrate first on $M1$ because it is the definition of the money supply that

9. *Savings deposits:* Deposits at banks and other thrift institutions that are not trans-ferrable by check, often recorded in a separate passbook kept by the depositor.
10. *Small time deposits:* Interest-bearing deposits with a specific maturity date. Be-fore that date they can be used only if a penalty is paid. "Small" means less than $100,000.

$$M2 = M1 + (5) + (6) + (7) + (8) + (9) + (10)$$

11. *Large-denomination time deposits:* Interest-earning deposits of more than $100,000 denomination. The total excludes amounts held by MMMFs or MMDAs (and some other institutions) to make sure the same asset is not counted twice in the monetary aggregates.
12. *Term repurchase agreements:* These are RPs sold by thrift institutions, typically for longer than overnight.

$$M3 = M2 + (11) + (12) + \text{MMMFs held by institutions}$$

13. *Other Eurodollar deposits:* Longer-term (than overnight) Eurodollars.
14. *Savings bonds:* U.S. government bonds, typically sold to the small saver.
15. *Banker's acceptances:* These are orders to pay a specific amount at a specific time that are obligations of banks. They arise largely in international trade.
16. *Commercial paper:* Short-term liabilities of corporations.
17. *Short-term Treasury securities:* Securities issued by the U.S. Treasury that have less than 12 months to maturity.

$$L = M3 + (13) + (14) + (15) + (16) + (17) \qquad \blacksquare$$

SOURCE: See *Federal Reserve Bulletin,* which reports the data and definition in each monthly issue. For further discussion see Daniel J. Larkins, "The Monetary Aggregates: An Introduction to Definitional Issues," *Survey of Current Business,* January 1983; *Handbook of Securities of the United States Government and Federal Agencies,* First Boston Corporation; Data Resources, Inc.

corresponds most closely to the role of money as a *medium of exchange.* Payments can be made directly with coin and notes and also, for most transactions, with a check. To make a payment using a passbook savings account, it is generally necessary first to transfer money out of the savings account into a checking account and then to write the check. That is why savings and similar accounts are not included in the basic definition of the money supply.

Currency consists of notes and coin in circulation; notes predominate. Checkable deposits are, as the name suggests, deposits against which checks can be written. They are held in commercial banks and thrift institutions. The financial institutions referred to as thrifts are savings and loan associations, mutual savings banks, and credit unions. Before 1980, only demand deposits at commercial banks were included in what was *then* called M1. However, because there is no obvious difference in the economic function served by checkable deposits at commercial banks and other thrift institutions, the definition of $M1$ was expanded in 1980. Now $M1$ includes other checkable deposits, such as NOW accounts.[2]

Information on the distribution of the ownership of demand deposits is available,[3] but there are no systematic records of the ownership of currency. About a third of demand deposits are held by consumers, with businesses holding most of the rest.

A 1984 survey of cash holdings of U.S. households, undertaken for the Federal Reserve System, showed that the average amount of currency held per person surveyed then was about $100.[4] At that time, total currency outstanding divided by population was $675. Thus the vast majority of the currency outstanding is not held by U.S. households — or at least they do not admit to holding it. Some currency is held by legitimate businesses, but large amounts must be held to finance illegal activities, particularly drug-related ones, or are held outside the United States. In many foreign countries $100 bills are regularly used to conduct large, and frequently illegal, transactions.

Although the money supply concepts have often been revised, the present definition of $M1$ still does not correspond exactly to the role of money as a means of making payments. For instance, there is a question of whether credit cards should be regarded as a means of making payment. If so — and the argument is certainly persuasive — we should probably count the amounts that people are allowed to charge by using their credit cards as part of the money stock.

Historically, there have often been changes in the type of assets that could be used as means of payment and, simultaneously, disagreements about what constitutes money in those circumstances. When checks first began to be widely used in England, early in the nineteenth century, there was a disagreement over whether demand deposits should be regarded as part of the money stock. Now that point is not disputed. We can expect there to be continuing changes in the financial structure over the years, with consequent changes in the definitions of the various money supply concepts.

M2 and Other Monetary Aggregates

There is a wide variety of ways of holding assets, and thus there are many substitutes that individuals might hold instead of the assets that make up $M1$. All the assets described in Box 10-1 are to some extent substitutes for one another. The Fed therefore publishes data for wider definitions of the money supply than $M1$. The wider definitions, from $M2$ to $M3$ to L (liquid assets), are for aggregates that are seen as increasingly less liquid substitutes for $M1$.

$M2$ adds to $M1$ assets that are close to being usable as a medium of exchange.

---

[2] A NOW account is an interest-bearing checking account.

[3] The data, available each quarter, are published in the *Federal Reserve Bulletin*.

[4] "The Use of Cash and Transaction Accounts by American Families," *Federal Reserve Bulletin*, February 1986.

The largest part of *M*2 consists of savings and small (less than $100,000) time deposits at banks and thrift institutions. These can be used almost without difficulty for making payments. In the case of a savings deposit, the bank has to be notified to transfer funds from the savings deposit to a checking account; for time deposits, it is in principle necessary to wait until the time deposit matures, or else to pay an interest penalty.

The second largest category of assets in *M*2 consists of money market mutual funds and deposit accounts. A money market mutual fund (MMMF) is one that invests its assets in short-term interest-bearing securities, such as certificates of deposit (CDs)[5] and Treasury bills. MMMFs pay interest and permit the owner of the account to write checks (typically the checks have to be for more than $500) against the account. Money market deposit accounts (MMDAs) are MMMFs held in commercial banks. A limited number of checks can be written against MMDAs each month. Obviously MMDAs and MMMFs are close to being checkable deposits — only the limits on the size and number of checks that can be written against these accounts keep them out of *M*1.

Until 1987, *M*1 was the most closely watched money stock, mainly because it seems to come closest to the theoretical definition of money as a medium of exchange. But, as we shall see below, the demand for *M*1 has been quite unstable in this decade, and many economists, including those on the Federal Reserve Board, now pay more attention to the behavior of *M*2 than that of *M*1. Until 1987 the Fed set target growth rates for both *M*1 and *M*2 (as well as broader measures of assets), but it stopped specifying an *M*1 target in 1987. The fact that the Fed had to shift its attention away from *M*1 and toward *M*2, and the fact that there are broader definitions of the money supply, such as *M*3, reflect the difficulty of defining *uniquely* a set of assets used as the medium of exchange when other assets are very close substitutes.

To some extent the cutoff between money and other assets is arbitrary. Why are negotiable certificates of deposit part of *M*3 but not the equally negotiable Treasury bills or CDs of large corporations. Two further aggregates are regularly reported by the Federal Reserve: liquid assets and debt. They amounted, respectively, to $4,689 billion and $8,992 billion in December 1988. The former includes in addition to *M*3 all short-term debt instruments of the government and the private sector. The aggregate "debt" is the most comprehensive measure, including the entire debt of the nonfinancial sector. Neither the liquid assets nor the debt aggregates are regarded as monetary aggregates.

Financial Innovation

It is worth discussing briefly the reasons for changes in money supply definitions. The definitional changes followed financial innovations that changed the nature of the assets that banks and thrifts issued. For instance, thrifts, which pay interest on deposits and had been forbidden to have checkable accounts, invented NOW accounts as a way of

---

[5] CDs are liabilities of the banks that can be bought and sold in the open market like other securities. Typically they come in large denominations of $100,000 or more.

getting around the prohibition. A NOW, a negotiable order of withdrawal, looks and smells like a check, but was not, legally speaking, a check. Banks were trying to compete with one another and with thrifts by finding ways of paying interest on demand deposits, again something they were forbidden from doing. As ways were found around the prohibitions, deposits formerly called savings deposits, such as NOW accounts, in fact became demand deposits, and eventually the definitions changed. Similarly, money market mutual funds were invented only in 1973. Until 1982, banks were not allowed to issue money market deposit accounts, but as soon as they were permitted to do so, there was a rapid inflow of such deposits to banks: MMDA deposits rose from zero in November 1982 to $320 billion in March 1983.

In summary, there is no unique set of assets that will always constitute the money supply. In recent years the focus has shifted from the relatively narrow $M1$ definition to the broader $M2$. Perhaps $M2$ is a better real world approximation to the concept of the medium of exchange because, for example, checks (to be sure, in limited numbers) can be written against MMDAs each month. And there are even arguments for using a less broad definition than $M1$ — for example, should $1,000 bills, which are not easily used to buy groceries, be included? And over the course of time, the particular assets that serve as a medium of exchange, or means of payment, will certainly change further.

10-2 THE FUNCTIONS OF MONEY

Money is so widely used that we rarely step back to think how remarkable a device it is. It is impossible to imagine a modern economy operating without the use of money or something very much like it. In a mythical barter economy in which there is no money, every transaction has to involve an exchange of goods (and/or services) on both sides of the transaction. The examples of the difficulties of barter are endless. The economist wanting a haircut would have to find a barber wanting to listen to a lecture on economics; the actor wanting a suit would have to find a tailor wanting to watch movies; and so on. Without a medium of exchange, modern economies could not operate.

Money, as a medium of exchange, makes it unnecessary for there to be a "double coincidence of wants" in exchanges. By the double coincidence, we have in mind the above examples. The wants of two individuals would have to be identically matched for the exchange to take place. For instance, the man selling movie tickets would have to find a buyer whose goods he wanted to buy (the suit), while, at the same time, the woman selling suits would have to find a buyer whose goods she wanted to buy (the movie tickets).

There are four traditional functions of money, of which the medium of exchange is the first.[6] The other three are store of value, unit of account, and standard of deferred payment. These stand on a different footing from the medium-of-exchange function.

A *store of value* is an asset that maintains value over time. Thus, an individual

---

[6] For the classic statement of the functions of money, see W. S. Jevons, *Money and the Mechanism of Exchange* (London: Routledge, Kegan, Paul, 1910).

holding a store of value can use that asset to make purchases at a future date. If an asset were not a store of value, then it would not be used as a medium of exchange. Imagine trying to use ice cream as money in the absence of refrigerators. There would hardly ever be a good reason for anyone to give up goods for money (ice cream) if the money were sure to melt within the next few minutes. And if the sellers were unwilling to accept the ice cream in exchange for their goods, then the ice cream would not be a medium of exchange. But there are many stores of value other than money—such as bonds, stocks, and houses.

The *unit of account* is the unit in which prices are quoted and books kept. **Prices are quoted in dollars and cents, and dollars and cents are the units in which the money stock is measured. Usually, the money unit is also the unit of account, but that is not essential. In the German hyperinflation of 1922–1923, dollars were the unit of account for some firms, whereas the mark was the medium of exchange.**

Finally, as a *standard of deferred payment,* money units are used in long-term transactions, such as loans. The amount that has to be paid back in 5 or 10 years is specified in dollars and cents. Dollars and cents are acting as the standard of deferred payment. Once again, though, it is not essential that the standard of deferred payment be the money unit. For example, the final payment of a loan may be related to the behavior of the price level, rather than being fixed in dollars and cents. This is known as an indexed loan.

The last two of the four functions of money are, accordingly, functions that money *usually* performs, but not functions that it *necessarily* performs. And the store-of-value function is one that many assets perform.

There are fascinating descriptions of different types of money that have existed in the past which we do not have room to review here.[7] But there is one final point we want to emphasize. *Money is whatever is generally accepted in exchange.* However magnificently a piece of paper may be engraved, it will not be money if it is not accepted in payment. And however unusual the material of which it is made, anything that is generally accepted in payment is money. The only reason money is accepted in payment is that the recipient believes that the money can be spent at a later time. There is thus an inherent circularity in the acceptance of money. Money is accepted in payment because it is believed that it will also be accepted in payment by others.

10-3 THE DEMAND FOR MONEY: THEORY

In this section we review the three major motives underlying the demand for money. In doing so, we will concentrate on the effects of changes in income and changes in the interest rate on money demand.

The three theories we are about to review correspond to Keynes's famous three motives for holding money:[8]

---

[7] See Paul Einzig, *Primitive Money* (New York: Pergamon, 1966).

[8] J. M. Keynes, *The General Theory of Employment, Interest and Money* (New York: Macmillan, 1936), chap. 13.

- The transactions motive, which is the demand for money arising from the use of money in making regular payments;

- The precautionary motive, which is the demand for money to meet unforeseen contingencies; and

- The speculative motive, which arises from uncertainties about the money value of other assets that an individual can hold. In discussing the transactions and precautionary motives, we are mainly discussing $M1$, whereas the speculative motive refers more to $M2$ or $M3$, as we shall see.

Although we examine the demand for money by looking at the three motives for holding it, we cannot separate a particular person's money holdings, say, $500, into three neat piles of, say, $200, $200, and $100, each being held from a different motive. Money being held to satisfy one motive is always available for another use. The person holding unusually large balances for speculative reasons also has those balances available to meet an unexpected emergency, so that they serve, too, as precautionary balances. All three motives influence an individual's holdings of money, and as we shall see, each leads to the prediction that the demand for money should fall as the interest rate on other assets increases.

This final point is worth emphasizing. Money ($M1$, that is currency and some checkable deposits) generally earns no interest or less interest than other assets. Anyone holding money is giving up interest that could be earned by holding some other asset, such as a savings deposit or a bond. The higher the interest loss from holding a dollar of money, the less money we expect the individual to hold. The demand for money will thus be higher, the greater the interest rate on money itself if interest is paid on demand deposits, and will be lower, the higher the interest rate on alternative assets. In practice, we can measure the cost of holding money as the difference between the interest rate paid on money (perhaps zero) and the interest rate paid on the most nearly comparable other asset, such as a savings deposit or, for corporations, a certificate of deposit or commercial paper. The interest rate on money is referred to as the *own* rate of interest, and the *opportunity cost* of holding money is equal to the difference between the yield on other assets and the own rate.

The Transactions Demand

The transactions demand for money arises from the use of money in making regular payments for goods and services. In the course of each month, an individual makes a variety of payments for such items as rent or a mortgage, groceries, the newspaper, and other purchases. In this section we examine how much money an individual would hold to finance these purchases.

In analyzing the transactions demand, we are concerned with a tradeoff between the amount of interest an individual forgoes by holding money and the costs and inconveniences of holding a small amount of money. To make the problem concrete, consider someone who is paid, say, $1,800 (after taxes) each month. Assume the person spends the $1,800 evenly over the course of the month, at the rate of $60 per day. Now at one extreme, the individual could simply leave the $1,800 in cash (whether in currency or as demand deposits) and spend it at the rate of $60 per day. Alternatively, on the first day of the month the individual could take the $60 to spend that day and put the remaining $1,740 in a daily-interest savings account. Then every morning the person could go to the bank to withdraw that day's $60 from the savings account. By the end of the month the depositor would have earned interest on the money retained each day in the savings account. That would be the *benefit* of keeping the money holdings down as low as $60 at the beginning of each day. The *cost* of keeping money holdings down is simply the cost and inconvenience of the trips to the bank to withdraw the daily $60. To decide on how much money to hold for transactions purposes, the individual has to weigh the costs of holding small balances in hand against the interest advantage of doing so.

We now study the tradeoff in more detail and derive a formula for the demand for money. Suppose the nominal monthly income of the individual is Y_N.[9] We make the simplifying assumption that Y_N is paid into the person's savings account, rather than the checking account, each month. The money is spent at a steady rate over the course of the month. To spend it, the individual has to get it out of the savings account and into cash, which may be currency or a checking account. If left in the savings account, the deposit earns interest at a rate of i per month. It earns zero interest as cash. The cost to the individual of making a transfer between cash and the savings account (which we henceforth call bonds for convenience) is $tc. That cost may be the individual's time, or it may be a cost explicitly paid to someone else to make the transfer. For convenience we refer to it as a broker's fee.

THE INVENTORY APPROACH

The approach we are describing is known as the *inventory-theoretic approach*.[10] You should think of this inventory-theoretic approach as applying equally well, with small changes in terminology and assumptions, to firms and households.

The individual has to decide how many transactions to make between bonds and cash each month. If just one transaction is made, transferring Y_N into cash at the beginning of the month, the cash balance over the course of the month will be as shown

---

[9] As a reminder, nominal income, Y_N, is defined as real income, Y, times the price level, P: $Y_N = P \times Y$.

[10] The approach was originally developed to determine the inventories of goods a firm should have on hand. In that context, the amount Y_N would be the monthly sales of the good, tc the cost of ordering the good, and i the interest rate for carrying the inventory. The analogy between money as an inventory of purchasing power, standing ready to buy goods, and an inventory of goods, standing ready to be bought by customers, is quite close. The inventory-theoretical approach to the demand for money is associated with the names of William Baumol and James Tobin: William Baumol, "The Transactions Demand for Cash: An Inventory Theoretic Approach," *Quarterly Journal of Economics*, November 1952; and James Tobin, "The Interest Elasticity of Transactions Demand for Cash," *Review of Economics and Statistics*, August 1956. The most famous result of Baumol's and Tobin's work is the *square-root law* of the demand for money, which is presented later in equation (4).

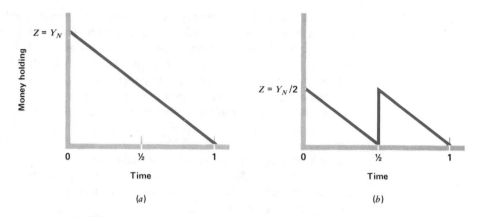

FIGURE 10-1

THE AMOUNT OF CASH HELD DURING THE MONTH RELATED TO THE NUMBER OF WITHDRAWALS. Panel (*a*) shows the pattern of money holding during the month when the individual makes just one transaction from the savings account to cash during the month. At the beginning of the month the individual transfers the entire amount to be spent, Y_N, into cash, and then spends it evenly over the month. Panel (*b*) shows the pattern of money holding when there are two transactions, one at the beginning of the month and one in the middle of the month. In panel (*a*), average cash holdings for the month are $Y_N/2$; in panel (*b*) they are $Y_N/4$.

in Figure 10-1 *a*. It starts at Y_N, is spent evenly over the month, and is down to zero by the end of the month, at which time a new payment is received by the individual and transferred into the person's checking account. If he or she makes two withdrawals from the savings account, then the first, $Y_N/2$, is transferred into cash at the beginning of the month, resulting in a cash balance that is run down to zero in the middle of the month, at which time another $Y_N/2$ is transferred into cash and spent evenly over the rest of the month.[11] Figure 10-1*b* shows the individual's cash holdings in that case.

We shall denote the size of a cash withdrawal from the bond portfolio (savings account) by Z, and the number of withdrawals from the bond portfolio by n. Thus, n is the number of times the individual adds to his or her cash balance during the month. If the individual makes n equal-sized withdrawals during the month, transferring funds from the savings account to the checking account, then the size of each transfer is Y_N/n, since a total of Y_N has to be transferred from the savings account into cash. For example, if Y_N is $1,800 and n, the number of transactions, is 3, then Z, the amount transferred to cash each time, is $600. Accordingly, we can write

---

[11] With simple interest being paid on the savings account, the individual's transactions between bonds and cash should be evenly spaced over the month. We leave the proof of that for the case in which there are two transactions to problem 13.

$$nZ = Y_N \qquad (1)$$

Suppose that the amount, Z, is transferred from bonds to cash at each withdrawal. What then is the *average* cash balance over the course of the month? We want to find the size of the average cash balance in order to measure the interest that is lost as a result of holding cash; if that amount were not held as cash, it could be held as interest-earning bonds. In Figure 10-1 *a*, the average cash balance held during the month is $Y_N/2 = Z/2$, since the cash balance starts at Y_N and runs down in a straight line to zero.[12] In the case of Figure 10-1 *b*, the average cash balance for the first half of the month is $Y_N/4 = Z/2$, and the average cash balance for the second half of the month is also $Z/2$. Thus, the average cash balance for the entire month is $Y_N/4 = Z/2$. Similarly, if three withdrawals were made, the average cash balance would be $Y_N/6 = Z/2$. In general, the average cash balance is $Z/2$, as you might want to confirm by drawing diagrams similar to Figure 10-1 for $n = 3$ or other values of n.

The interest cost of holding money is the interest rate times the average cash balance, or $iZ/2$. From equation (1), that means the total interest cost is $iY_N/2n$. The other component of the cost of managing the portfolio is the brokerage cost, or the cost in terms of the individual's time and inconvenience in managing his or her money. That cost is just the number of withdrawals made, n, times the cost of each withdrawal, tc, and is thus equal to $n \times tc$. The total cost of managing the portfolio is the interest cost plus the total brokerage cost:

$$\text{Total cost} = (n \times tc) + \frac{iY_N}{2n} \qquad (2)$$

Equation (2) shows formally that the brokerage cost ($n \times tc$) increases as the number of withdrawals (transactions between bonds and money) rises, and that the interest cost decreases as the number of withdrawals increases. It thus emphasizes the tradeoff faced in managing money, and suggests that there is an optimal number of withdrawals the individual should make to minimize the total cost of holding money to meet transactions requirements for buying goods.

To derive that optimal point, we want to find the point at which the benefit of carrying out another withdrawal is less than, or just equal to, the cost of making another transaction between bonds and money. If the benefit of making another transaction is greater than the cost, then another withdrawal should be made, and the original point could not have been optimal. The cost of making another transaction is always equal to tc. In Figure 10-2, we show the cost of making a further transaction by the marginal cost curve, MC, which is horizontal at the level tc. The financial benefit from making another transaction is represented by the MB (marginal benefit) curve in Figure 10-2, which represents the interest *saved* by making another withdrawal and thus having a smaller cash balance on average during the month.

---

[12] The average cash balance is the average of the amount of cash the individual holds at each moment during the month. For instance, if the balance held is $400 for 3 days and zero for the rest of the month, the average cash balance would be $40, or one-tenth (3 days divided by 30 days) of the month times $400.

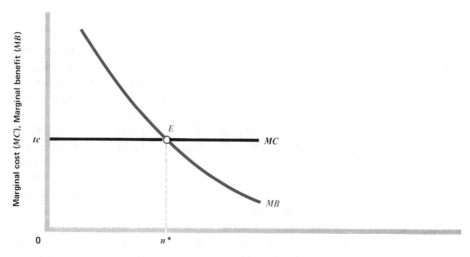

FIGURE 10-2

OPTIMAL CASH MANAGEMENT DETERMINING THE OPTIMAL NUMBER OF
WITHDRAWALS. The marginal cost of making another transaction is the
constant amount, tc, as shown by the MC curve. The marginal benefit
(MB) of making another transaction is the amount of interest saved by
holding smaller money balances. The marginal benefit decreases as the
number of withdrawals from the savings account increases. Point E is
the point at which the cost of managing money holdings is minimized.
Corresponding to point E is n^*, the optimal number of withdrawals to
make from the savings account into money.

The more transactions between money and bonds an individual makes, the lower
is the total interest cost. But the reduction of the interest cost that is obtained by
making more transactions falls off rapidly as the number of withdrawals increases.
There is a substantial saving in interest costs by making two withdrawals rather than
one, but very little saving in interest costs by making thirty-one transactions rather
than thirty.

This suggests that the marginal benefit of making more withdrawals decreases as
the number of withdrawals becomes large. The MB curve in Figure 10-2 is, accordingly, downward-sloping.[13]

In Figure 10-2, the optimal number of transactions is given by n^*, the number at

---

[13] Two points about Fig. 10-2: First, note that we have, for convenience, drawn the curves as continuous,
even though you will recognize that it is possible to make only an integral number of transactions, and not, for
example, 1.6 or 7.24 transactions. Second, if you can use the calculus, try to derive the equation of the
marginal benefit curve from the component of costs in equation (2) that is due to interest lost.

which the marginal benefit in terms of interest saved is equal to the marginal cost of making a transaction. Given the number of transactions and the individual's income, we also know the average cash balance, M, using the relationship between average money holdings and the size of each transfer, which we derived earlier:

$$M = \frac{Z}{2} = \frac{Y_N}{2n} \tag{3}$$

⌐⁷ PROPERTIES OF MONEY DEMAND

From Figure 10-2 we can see two important results. First, suppose the brokerage cost rises. That shifts the MC curve up, decreases the number of withdrawals (n), and therefore [from equation (3), where M is inversely related to n] *increases* the average holding of money. Second, an increase in the interest rate shifts up the MB curve, therefore increasing n, and thus [again, from equation (3)] reducing the holding of money: when the interest rate is higher, the individual is willing to make more trips to the bank to earn the higher interest now available. Figure 10-2 thus shows one of the key results we wanted to establish — that the demand for money is inversely related to the interest rate.

In the case of an increase in income, Figure 10-2 is unfortunately less useful. An increase in income shifts up the MB curve and increases the number of transactions. But from equation (3), we see that an increase in the number of transactions accompanying an increase in income does not necessarily imply that the demand for money rises, since it seems that n could increase proportionately more than Y_N. However, more complete algebraic analysis of the individual's optimal behavior will show that the demand for money in this model rises when income rises.

The famous *square-root formula* for money demand, developed by William Baumol and James Tobin,[14] makes the results of the graphical analysis of Figure 10-2 more precise and, also, resolves the ambiguity about the effects of income on the demand for money. The formula gives the demand for money that is obtained as a result of minimizing the total costs in equation (2) with respect to the number of withdrawals and then using equation (3) to derive the cash balance.[15] The formula is

$$M^* = \sqrt{\frac{tc \times Y_N}{2i}} \tag{4}$$

Equation (4) shows that the transactions demand for money increases with the brokerage fee, or the cost of transacting, and with the level of income. The demand for money decreases with the interest rate.

---

[14] See the references in footnote 10.

[15] If you can handle calculus, try to derive equation (4) by minimizing the total cost with respect to n in equation (2).

MONEY DEMAND ELASTICITIES

Equation (4) also shows that an increase in income raises the demand for money proportionately less than the increase in income itself. To put the same point somewhat differently, the ratio of income to money, Y_N/M, rises with the level of income. A person with a higher level of income holds proportionately less money. This point is sometimes put in different words by saying that there are *economies of scale* in cash management.

Yet another way of saying the same thing is that the income elasticity of the demand for money is less than 1 [it is equal to 1/2 in equation (4)]. The income elasticity measures the percentage change in the demand for money due to a 1 percent change in income.[16] Similarly, equation (4) implies that the elasticity of the demand for money with respect to the brokerage fee is 1/2, and the elasticity with respect to the interest rate is $-1/2$.

What accounts for the fact that people can somehow manage with less cash per dollar of spending as income increases? The reason is that cash management is more effective at high levels of income because the average cost per dollar of transaction is lower with large-size transactions. In turn, the lower average cost of transactions results from the fixed brokerage fee per transaction: It costs as much to transfer $10 as $10 million, so the average cost per dollar transferred is lower for large transfers.

However, in the case of households, we should recognize that the "brokerage cost" (tc, the cost of making withdrawals from a savings account) is in part the cost of time and the nuisance of having to go to the bank. Since the cost of time to individuals is likely to be higher the higher their income, tc may rise with Y_N. In that case, an increase in income would result in an increase in the demand for money by more than the income elasticity of 1/2 indicates, because tc goes up together with Y_N.

THE DEMAND FOR REAL BALANCES

We started this chapter by emphasizing that the demand for money is a demand for real balances. It is worth confirming that the inventory theory of the demand for money implies that the demand for real balances does not change when all prices double (or increase in any other proportion). When all prices double, both Y_N and tc in equation (4) double, that is, both nominal income and the nominal brokerage fee double. Accordingly, the demand for nominal balances doubles, so that the demand for real balances is

---

[16] The income elasticity of demand is

$$\frac{\dfrac{\Delta(M/P)}{M/P}}{\dfrac{\Delta Y}{Y}}$$

Similarly, the interest elasticity is

$$\frac{\dfrac{\Delta(M/P)}{M/P}}{\dfrac{\Delta i}{i}}$$

unchanged. The square-root formula does not imply any money illusion in the demand for money. Thus we should be careful when saying that the income elasticity of demand for money implied by equation (4) is 1/2. The elasticity of the demand for *real* balances with respect to *real* income is 1/2. But if income rises only because all prices (including *tc*) rise, then the demand for *nominal* balances rises proportionately.

INTEGER CONSTRAINTS

So far we have ignored the important constraint that it is possible to make only an integral number of transactions, such as 1, 2, 3, etc., and that it is not possible to make 1.25 or 3.57 transactions. However, when we take account of this constraint, we shall see that it implies that many people do not make more than the essential one transaction between money and bonds within the period in which they are paid.[17]

Consider our previous example of the person who received $1,800 per month. Suppose, realistically, that the interest rate per month on savings deposits is 0.5 percent. The individual cannot avoid making one initial transaction, since income initially arrives in the savings account. The next question is whether it pays to make a second transaction. That is, does it pay to keep half the monthly income for half a month in the savings account and make a second withdrawal after half a month? With an interest rate of 0.5 percent per month, interest for half a month would be 0.25 percent. Half the income would amount to $900, and the interest earnings would, therefore, be $900 × 0.0025 = $2.25.

Now if the brokerage fee exceeds $2.25, the individual will not bother to make more than one transaction. And $2.25 is not an outrageous cost in terms of the time and nuisance of making a transfer from the savings to the checking account. Thus, for many individuals whose monthly net pay is below $1,800, we do not expect formula (4) to hold exactly. Their cash balance would instead simply be half their income. They would make one transfer into cash at the beginning of the month; Figure 10-1*a* would describe their money holdings. For such individuals, the income elasticity of the demand for money is 1, since their demand for money goes up precisely in proportion with their income. The interest elasticity is zero so long as they make only one transaction.

The very strong restrictions on the income and interest elasticities of the demand for money of equation (4) are not valid when the integer constraints are taken into account. Instead, the income elasticity is an average of the elasticities of different people, some of whom make only one transaction from bonds to money, and the income elasticity is therefore between 1/2 and 1. Similarly, the interest elasticity is also an average of the elasticities across different individuals, ranging between −1/2 and zero.[18] Because firms deal with larger amounts of money, they are likely to make a

---

[17] If we had assumed that individuals were paid in cash, it would turn out that many people would not make any transactions at all between money and bonds in managing their transactions balances.

[18] See Robert J. Barro, "Integer Constraints and Aggregation in an Inventory Model of Money Demand," *Journal of Finance*, 1976.

large number of transactions between money and bonds, and their income and interest elasticities of the demand for money are therefore likely to be close to the 1/2 and −1/2 predicted by equation (4).

THE PAYMENT PERIOD

Once the integer constraints are taken into account, it can also be seen that the transactions demand for money depends on the frequency with which individuals are paid (the payment period). If one examines the square-root formula, equation (4), the demand for money does not seem to depend on how often a person is paid, since an increase in the payments period increases both Y_N and i in the same proportion. Thus the demand for money appears unaffected by the length of the period. However, consider a person who makes only one transaction from bonds to money at the beginning of each month. The person's money demand is $Y_N/2$. If such a person were paid weekly, his or her demand for money would be only one-quarter of the demand with monthly payments. Thus we should expect the demand for money to increase with the length of the payment period.

SUMMARY

The inventory-theoretic approach to the demand for money gives a precise formula for the transactions demand for money: The income elasticity of the demand for money is 1/2, and the interest elasticity is −1/2. When integer constraints are taken into account, the limits on the income elasticity of demand are between 1/2 and 1, and the limits on the interest elasticity are between −1/2 and zero. We have outlined the approach in terms of an individual's demand for money, but a similar approach is relevant for firms.

Some of the assumptions made in deriving the square-root formula are very restrictive. People do not spend their money evenly over the course of the month, and they do not know exactly what their payments will be. Their checks are not paid into savings accounts, and so on. It turns out, though, that the major results we have derived are not greatly affected by the use of more realistic assumptions. There is thus good reason to expect the demand for money to increase with the level of income and to decrease as the interest rate on other assets (or, generally, the cost of holding money) increases.

The Precautionary Motive

In discussing the transactions demand for money, we focused on transactions costs and ignored uncertainty. In this section, we concentrate on the demand for money that arises because people are uncertain about the payments they might want, or have, to make.[19] Suppose, realistically, that an individual did not know precisely what payments

---

[19] See Edward H. Whalen, "A Rationalization of the Precautionary Demand for Cash," *Quarterly Journal of Economics*, May 1966.

he or she would be receiving in the next few weeks and what payments would have to be made. The person might decide to have a hot fudge sundae, or need to take a cab in the rain, or have to pay for a prescription. If the individual did not have money with which to pay, he or she would incur a loss. The loss could be missing a fine meal, or missing an appointment, or having to come back the next day to pay for the prescription. For concreteness, we shall denote the loss incurred as a result of being short of cash by $q. The loss clearly varies from situation to situation, but as usual we simplify.

The more money an individual holds, the less likely he or she is to incur the costs of illiquidity (that is, not having money immediately available). But the more money the person holds, the more interest he or she is giving up. We are back to a tradeoff situation similar to that examined in relation to the transactions demand. Somewhere between holding so little money for precautionary purposes that it will almost certainly be necessary to forgo some purchase (or to borrow in a hurry) and holding so much money that there is little chance of not being able to make any payment that might be necessary, there must be an optimal amount of precautionary balances to hold. That optimal amount will involve the balancing of interest costs against the advantages of not being caught illiquid.

Once more, we write down the total costs of holding an amount of money, M.[20] This time we are dealing with expected costs, since it is not certain what the need for money will be. We denote the probability that the individual is illiquid during the month by $p(M, \sigma)$. The function $p(M, \sigma)$ indicates that the probability of the person's being illiquid at some time during the month depends on the level of money balances, M, being held and the degree of uncertainty, σ, about the net payments that will be made during the month. The probability of illiquidity is lower the higher is M, and higher the higher the degree of uncertainty, σ. The *expected cost* of illiquidity is $p(M, \sigma)q$—the probability of illiquidity times the cost of being illiquid. The interest cost associated with holding a cash balance of M is just iM. Thus, we have

$$\text{Expected costs} = iM + p(M, \sigma)q \qquad (5)$$

To determine the optimal amount of money to hold, we compare the marginal costs of increasing money holding by $1 with the expected marginal benefit of doing so. The marginal cost is again the interest forgone, or i. That is shown by the MC curve in Figure 10-3. The marginal benefit of increasing money holding arises from the lower expected costs of illiquidity. Increasing precautionary balances from zero has a large marginal benefit, since that takes care of small, unexpected disbursements that are quite likely to occur. As we increase cash balances further, we continue to reduce the probability of illiquidity, but at a decreasing rate. We start to hold cash to insure against quite unlikely events. Thus, the marginal benefit of additional cash is a decreasing function of the level of cash holdings—more cash on hand is better than less, but at a diminishing rate. The marginal benefit of increasing cash holdings is shown by the MB curve in Figure 10-3.

The optimal level of the precautionary demand for money is reached where the

---

[20] This paragraph contains technical material that is optional and can easily be skipped.

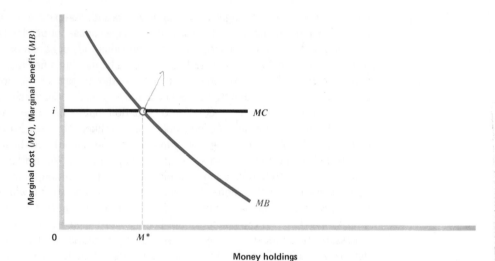

FIGURE 10-3

THE PRECAUTIONARY DEMAND FOR MONEY. The *MC* schedule shows the marginal cost of holding an extra dollar of money; holding an extra dollar means losing interest, and so the *MC* curve is horizontal at a level equal to the interest rate (or, more generally, the difference between the interest rate on money and alternative assets). The marginal benefit (*MB*) of holding an extra dollar is that the consumer is less likely to be short of money when it is needed. The marginal benefit declines with the amount of money held. The optimal amount of money to hold is shown by *M**, at which marginal cost is equal to marginal benefit.

two curves intersect. That level of money is shown as *M** in Figure 10-3. Now we can use Figure 10-3 to examine the determinants of the optimal level of the precautionary demand. It is apparent that precautionary balances will be larger when the interest rate is lower. A reduction in the interest rate shifts the *MC* curve down and increases *M**. The lower cost of holding money makes it profitable to insure more heavily against the costs of illiquidity. An increase in uncertainty leads to increased money holdings because it shifts up the *MB* curve. With more uncertainty about the flow of spending, there is more scope for unforseen payments and thus a greater danger of illiquidity. It therefore pays to insure more heavily by holding larger cash balances. Finally, the lower the costs of illiquidity, *q*, the lower the money demand. A reduction in *q* moves the *MB* curve down. Indeed, if there were no cost to illiquidity, no one would bother to hold money. There would be no penalty for not having it, while holding it would mean a loss of interest.

The model of precautionary demand can be applied to goods other than money. It is a broad theory that applies to any commodity inventory that is held as insurance against contingencies. For instance, cars carry spare tires. You can work out circumstances under which one would want to have more than one spare tire in a car, and even circumstances in which zero would be the optimal number. The idea of the precautionary demand for money or for goods is quite general. So, too, are the determinants of the precautionary demand: the alternative cost in terms of interest forgone, the cost of illiquidity, and the degree of uncertainty that determines the probability of illiquidity.

The Speculative Demand for Money

The transactions demand and the precautionary demand for money emphasize the medium-of-exchange function of money, for each refers to the need to have money on hand to make payments. Each theory is more relevant to the $M1$ definition of money than any other, though the precautionary demand could certainly explain part of the holding of savings accounts and other relatively liquid assets that are part of $M2$. Now we move over to the store-of-value function of money and concentrate on the role of money in the investment portfolio of an individual.

An individual who has wealth has to hold that wealth in specific assets. Those assets make up a *portfolio*. One would think an investor would want to hold the asset that provides the highest returns. However, given that the return on most assets is uncertain, it is unwise to hold the entire portfolio in a single *risky asset*. You may have the hottest tip that a certain stock will surely double within the next 2 years, but you would be wise to recognize that hot tips are far from infallible and that you could lose a lot of money in that stock as well as make money. A prudent, risk-averse investor does not put all his or her eggs in one basket. Uncertainty about the returns on risky assets leads to a diversified portfolio strategy.

As part of that diversified portfolio, the typical investor will want to hold some amount of a safe asset as insurance against capital losses on assets whose prices change in an uncertain manner. The safe asset would be held precisely because it is safe, even though it pays a lower expected return than risky assets. Money is a safe asset in that its nominal value is known with certainty.[21] In a famous article, James Tobin argued that money would be held as the safe asset in the portfolios of investors.[22] The title of the article, "Liquidity Preference as Behavior towards Risk," explains the essential notion. In this framework, the demand for money — the safest asset — depends on the expected yields as well as on the riskiness of the yields on other assets. The riskiness of the returns on other assets is measured by the variability of the returns. Using reasonable assumptions, Tobin shows that an increase in the expected return on other assets — an increase in the opportunity cost of holding money (that is, the return lost by holding money) — lowers money demand. By contrast, an increase in the riskiness of the returns on other assets increases money demand.

---

[21] Of course, when the rate of inflation is uncertain, the real value of money is also uncertain, and money is no longer a safe asset. Even so, the uncertainties about the values of equity are so much larger than the uncertainties about the rate of inflation that money can be treated as a relatively safe asset.

[22] James Tobin, "Liquidity Preference as Behavior toward Risk," *Review of Economic Studies*, February 1958.

An investor's aversion to risk certainly generates a demand for a safe asset. The question we want to consider is whether that safe asset is money. That is, we want to ask whether considerations of portfolio behavior do generate a demand for money. The relevant considerations in the portfolio are the returns on and risks of assets. From the viewpoint of the yield and risks of holding money, it is clear that time or savings deposits or MMDAs have the same risks as currency or checkable deposits. However, the former generally pay a higher yield. The risks in both cases are the risks arising from uncertainty about inflation. Given that the risks are the same, and with the yields on time and savings deposits higher than on currency and demand deposits, portfolio diversification explains the demand for assets such as time and savings deposits better than the demand for $M1$. But even so, there are certainly transaction motives for holding assets like MMDAs, and thus income and the opportunity cost of holding these assets should help explain the amounts households or firms hold.

The implications of the speculative, or risk-diversifying, demand for money are similar to those of the transactions and precautionary demands. An increase in the interest rate on nonmoney assets, such as long-term bond yields or equity yields, will reduce the demand for $M2$. An increase in the rate paid on time deposits will increase the demand for time deposits, perhaps even at the cost of the demand for $M1$, as people take advantage of the higher yields they can earn on their investment portfolios to increase the size of those portfolios.

One final point on speculative demand. Many individuals with relatively small amounts of wealth will indeed hold part of that wealth in savings accounts in order to diversify their portfolios. But bigger investors are sometimes able to purchase other securities which pay higher interest and also have fixed (that is, risk-free) nominal values. Large CDs (in excess of $100,000) may be an example of such assets, as may be Treasury bills. For such individuals or groups, the demand for a safe asset is not a demand for money.

10-4 EMPIRICAL EVIDENCE

This section examines the empirical evidence — the studies made using actual data — on the demand for money. We know that the *interest elasticity* of the demand for money plays an important role in determining the effectiveness of monetary and fiscal policies. We showed in Section 10-3 that there are good theoretical reasons for believing the demand for real balances should depend on the interest rate. The empirical evidence supports that view. Empirical studies have established that the demand for money is responsive to the interest rate. An increase in the interest rate reduces the demand for money.

The theory of money demand also predicts that the demand for money should depend on the level of income. The response of the demand for money to the level of income, as measured by the *income elasticity* of money demand, is also important from a policy viewpoint. As we shall see below, the income elasticity of money demand provides a guide to the Fed as to how fast to increase the money supply in order to support a given rate of growth of GNP without changing the interest rate.

Lagged Adjustment

The empirical work on the demand for money has introduced one complication that we did not study in the theoretical section — that the demand for money adjusts to changes in income and interest rates *with a lag*. When the level of income or the interest rate changes, there is first only a small change in the demand for money. Then, over the course of time, the change in the demand for money increases, slowly building up to its full long-run change. Reasons for this lag are not yet certain. The two usual possibilities exist in this case, too. The lags may arise because there are costs of adjusting money holdings or may arise because money holders' expectations are slow to adjust. If people believe that a given change in the interest rate is temporary, they may be unwilling to make a major change in their money holdings. As time passes and it becomes clearer that the change is not transitory, they are willing to make a larger adjustment.

Empirical Results for $M1$ Demand

The standard $M1$ demand-for-money function until the mid-1970s was that estimated by Stephen Goldfeld of Princeton University in a comprehensive 1973 study.[23] Goldfeld studied the demand for $M1$ using quarterly postwar data and, of course, the 1973 definition of $M1$. Table 10-2 summarizes the major conclusions from that early empirical work. The table shows the elasticities of the demand for real balances with respect to real income, Y (real GNP), and interest rates. Goldfeld uses the interest rates on time deposits, i_{TD}, and on commercial paper, i_{CP}. Commercial paper represents short-term borrowing by corporations. The interest rate on commercial paper is relevant to the demand for money because commercial paper is an asset that is very liquid for corporations that hold it instead of money for short periods of time.

According to Goldfeld's results, in the short run (one quarter), the elasticity of demand with respect to real income is 0.19. This means that a 1 percent increase in real income raises money demand by 0.19 percent, which is considerably less than proportionately. The table shows that the elasticity of money demand with respect to interest rates is negative: An increase in interest rates reduces money demand. The short-run interest elasticities are quite small. An increase in the rate on time deposits from 4 percent to 5 percent, that is, a 25 percent increase ($5/4 = 1.25$), reduces the demand for money by only 1.12 percent ($= 0.045 \times 25$ percent). An increase in the rate on commercial paper from 4 to 5 percent would reduce money demand by only 0.47 percent.

The long-run elasticities exceed the short-run elasticities by a factor of more than 3, as Table 10-2 shows. The long-run real income elasticity is 0.68, meaning that in the long run the increase in real money demand occurring as a result of a given increase in real income is only 68 percent as large as the proportional increase in

---

[23] Stephen M. Goldfeld, "The Demand for Money Revisited," *Brookings Papers on Economic Activity,* 1973:3. A review of other early work on the demand for money is contained in the very readable book by David Laidler, *The Demand for Money: Theories and Evidence,* 2d ed. (New York: Dun-Donnelley, 1977).

TABLE 10-2

ELASTICITIES OF REAL *M*1 MONEY DEMAND

	Y	i_{TD}	i_{CP}
Short run	0.19	−0.045	−0.019
Long run	0.68	−0.160	−0.067

SOURCE: S. Goldfeld, "The Demand for Money Revisited," *Brooking Papers on Economic Activity,* 1973:3.

TABLE 10-3

DYNAMIC PATTERNS OF ELASTICITIES OF MONEY DEMAND WITH RESPECT TO REAL INCOME AND INTEREST RATES

Quarters elapsed	Y	i_{TD}	i_{CP}
1	0.19	−0.045	−0.019
2	0.33	−0.077	−0.033
3	0.43	−0.100	−0.042
4	0.50	−0.117	−0.049
8	0.63	−0.148	−0.062
Long run	0.68	−0.160	−0.067

SOURCE: S. Goldfeld, "The Demand for Money Revisited," *Brooking Papers on Economic Activity*, 1973:3.

income. Real money demand thus rises less than proportionately to the rise in real income. The long-run interest elasticities sum to a little over 0.2, meaning that an increase in *both* i_{TD} and i_{CP} from 4 percent to 5 percent would reduce the demand for money by less than 6 percent.

How long is the long run? That is, how long does it take the demand for money to adjust from the short-run elasticities of Table 10-2 to the long-run elasticities shown in the table? Actually, it takes forever for the full long-run position to be reached. Table 10-3, however, shows the elasticities of the demand for real balances in response to changes in the level of income and interest rates after 1, 2, 3, 4, and 8 quarters. Three-fourths of the adjustment is completed within the first year, and over 90 percent of the adjustment is completed within the first 2 years.

In summary, we have so far described four essential properties of money demand as estimated by Goldfeld:

- The demand for real money balances responds negatively to the rate of interest. An increase in interest rates reduces the demand for money.

- The demand for money increases with the level of real income. However, the income elasticity of money demand is less than 1, so that money demand increases less than proportionately with income.

- The short-run responsiveness of money demand to changes in interest rates and income is considerably less than the long-run response. The long-run elasticities are estimated to be over 3 times the size of the short-run elasticities.

- The demand for nominal money balances is proportional to the price level. There is no money illusion; in other words, the demand for money is a demand for *real* balances.

*M*1 Money Demand Instability

Until 1973 the demand for real money balances was considered one of the best understood and most highly stable equations in the U.S. macroeconomy. Since then, the demand-for-money function (*M*1) appears to have been shifting — the "missing money" — and it has not yet settled down to the extent that there is agreement on the empirically correct form of the money demand function — though there is nearly general agreement on the fact that money demand is affected primarily by income and interest rates.

Most research on money demand in the last 15 years has tried to explain these money demand shifts.[24] There are several explanations for the missing money episode. The most plausible, and most widely accepted is that the financial innovations of the mid- and late 1970s led to changes in money demand. For example, in 1975 it became possible to make transfers between accounts by telephone instruction rather than by actually going to the bank. This reduced the brokerage cost, *tc*, and reduced the demand for *M*1. Similarly, during this period corporations were for the first time allowed to own savings deposits, leading them to reduce holdings of *M*1. In addition, the invention of money market mutual funds (see Section 10-1) reduced the demand for money.

An associated explanation argued that there were permanent shifts in money demand associated with the very high interest rates of 1973–1974 and 1978–1982. The argument here is that when interest rates became very high, firms undertook studies of how to economize on money, developing new methods of *cash management*. These are sophisticated methods that firms can use in order to reduce the amount of money held in the normal course of business. Among these methods are "sweep accounts," whereby the bank undertakes to monitor the account and automatically invest any excess balances in short-term financial assets.

It was argued by those studying the missing money episode that the adoption of these new methods would cause a permanent reduction in the demand for money even after interest rates had fallen from their record levels, because once the firm had figured out the new methods of managing its cash, it continued to use them. Of course, we now know that the demand for money started rising by more than the Goldfeld equation would imply after interest rates declined in 1982. There is as yet no fully satisfactory explanation for this change.

One possibility is that with interest now being paid on about one-third of *M*1, the interest elasticity of *M*1 demand may have changed. Another is that when interest rates declined from their extremely high levels, some of the causes of the missing money, for instance, the increased efficiency of money management, did reverse themselves.

Another possibility is that the Goldfeld demand function is not the correct

[24] A careful and comprehensive examination of money demand estimates is presented in Stephen M. Goldfeld and Daniel E. Sichel, "The Demand for Money," Princeton University, 1988 (mimeographed). Other recent papers include Robert Rasche, "M1-Velocity and Money-Demand Functions: Do Stable Relationships Exist?" in Karl Brunner and Allan H. Meltzer (eds.), *Carnegie-Rochester Conference Series on Public Policy*, vol. 27, Autumn 1987, and William Poole, "Monetary Policy Lessons of Recent Inflation and Disinflation," *Journal of Economic Perspectives*, Summer 1988.

empirical form. Alternative forms of the money demand function include long-term interest rates and rates of return on equity, on the grounds that all assets, including long-term bonds and stocks, are substitutes for money. Some estimated money demand functions include wealth as a determinant of money demand, on the grounds that money is part of the portfolio, as we discussed in examining the speculative demand for money. Some researchers argue that the income elasticity of the demand for money should be unity (rather than the long-run value of 0.68 estimated in the original Goldfeld paper), and show that money demand functions with that property behave, in some respects, better than the original Goldfeld model.[25] However, none of the estimated functions succeeds in explaining both the episode of the missing money and the episode of the returning money.

Despite all these difficulties, it does remain possible to estimate demand functions for $M1$ that take account of, but do not explain, the apparent shifts in money demand in the mid-1970s and early 1980s. This work still finds that the demand for money is positively related to income and negatively related to interest rates.

$M2$ Money Demand

Even as the demand for $M1$ exhibits instability, the demand for $M2$ shows (for the moment!) stability.[26] We would expect real money demand to depend positively on the own rate of interest on $M2$ (a weighted average of the interest rates paid on various kinds of deposits) and negatively on the alternative cost of holding $M2$. The alternative cost can be measured by the rate on money market instruments such as Treasury bills. We also expect real $M2$ money demand to depend positively on the level of income.

These hypotheses are, indeed, confirmed by the empirical evidence. An estimate with quarterly data for the period 1961 to 1988 yields the elasticities shown in Table 10-4.

The table confirms that the elasticity with respect to the own rate is positive and the elasticity with respect to the commercial paper rate is negative. The short-run elasticities are smaller than the long-run elasticities, and the own-rate elasticity is less than the elasticity with respect to the commercial paper rate. The latter property implies that an equiproportionate increase in the own rate and the commercial paper rate will reduce the demand for $M2$. Thus even though a large share of $M2$ is interest-bearing, an (equiproportionate) increase in the level of all interest rates reduces $M2$.

The income elasticity of $M2$ is clearly positive and is approximately equal to unity. This implies that, other things equal, the ratio of real balances to real GNP will remain constant over time. We return to this property below.

[25] The paper by Rasche cited in footnote 24 carefully evaluates these and related possibilities. Rasche also shows that it is possible to find money demand functions that fit the data quite well, provided that account is taken of shifts in 1975 and 1982.

[26] See the discussion in D. Small and R. Porter, "Understanding the Behavior of M2 and V2," *Federal Reserve Bulletin*, April 1989, and J. Wenninger "Money Demand—Some Long Run Properties," Federal Reserve Bank of New York *Quarterly Review*, Spring 1988.

box 10-2

MONEY DEMAND AND HIGH INFLATION

The demand for real balances depends on the alternative cost of holding money. That cost is normally measured by the yield on alternative assets, say Treasury bills, commercial paper, or money market funds. But there is another margin of substitution. Rather than holding their wealth in financial assets, households or firms can also hold real assets: stocks of food or houses or machinery. This margin of substitution is particularly important in countries in which inflation is very high and capital markets do not function well. In that case it is quite possible that the return on holding goods can even be higher than that on financial assets.

Consider a household deciding.whether to hold $100 in currency or a demand deposit or to hold it in the form of groceries on the shelf. The advantage of holding groceries is that, unlike money, they maintain their real value. Rather than having the purchasing power of money balances eroded by inflation, the household gets rid of money, buying goods and thus avoiding a loss.

This "flight out of money" occurs systematically when inflation rates become high. In a famous study of hyperinflations (defined in the study as inflation rates of more than 50 percent *per month*), Phillip Cagan of Columbia University found large changes in real balances taking place as inflation increased.* In the most famous hyperinflation, that in Germany in 1922–1923, the quantity of real balances at the height of the hyperinflation had fallen to one-twentieth of its preinflation level. The increased cost of holding money leads to a reduction in real money demand and with it to changes in the public's payments habits as everybody tries to pass on money like a hot potato. We shall see more on this in Chapter 16, in which we study money and inflation.

In well-developed capital markets, interest rates will reflect expectations of inflation, and hence it will not make much difference whether we measure the alternative cost of holding money by interest rates or inflation rates. But when capital markets are not free because interest rates are regulated or have ceilings, it is often appropriate to use inflation, not interest, rates as the measure of the alternative cost. Franco Modigliani has offered the following rule of thumb: The right measure of the opportunity cost of holding money is the higher of the two, interest rates or inflation. ∎

---

* Phillip Cagan, "The Monetary Dynamics of Hyperinflation," in Milton Friedman (ed.), *Studies in the Quantity Theory of Money* (Chicago: University of Chicago Press, 1956).

TABLE 10-4
ELASTICITIES OF *M2* MONEY DEMAND, 1961–1988

	Own rate	Commercial paper rate	Income
Short run	0.023	−0.039	0.136
Long run	0.176	−0.293	1.030

SOURCE: From equations estimated by the authors and based on results in D. Small and R. Porter, "Understanding the Behavior of *M2* and *V2*," *Federal Reserve Bulletin*, April 1989.

10-5 THE INCOME VELOCITY OF MONEY AND THE QUANTITY THEORY

The *income velocity of money* is the number of times the stock of money is turned over per year in financing the annual flow of income. It is equal to the ratio of GNP to the money stock. Thus in 1988 GNP was about $4,860 billion, the money stock ($M1$) averaged $775 billion, and velocity was therefore 6.27. The average dollar of money balances financed $6.27 of spending on final goods and services, or the public held an average of just under $0.16 of $M1$ per dollar of income. While we usually calculate velocity for the economy as a whole, we can also calculate it for an individual. For someone who earns $20,000 per year and has average money balances during the year of $2,000, the income velocity of money holdings is 10.[27]

Income velocity (from now on we shall refer to velocity rather than income velocity) is defined as

$$V \equiv \frac{Y_N}{M} \qquad (6)$$

that is, the ratio of nominal income to the nominal money stock. An alternative way of writing equation (6) recognizes that Y_N (nominal GNP) is equal to the price level, P, times real income, Y. Thus

$$M \times V = P \times Y \qquad (7)$$

The Quantity Theory

Equation (7) is the famous *quantity equation,* linking the product of the price level and the level of output to the money stock. The quantity equation became the (classical) *quantity theory of money* when it was argued that both V, the income velocity of money, and Y, the level of output, were fixed. Real output was taken to be fixed because the economy was at full employment, and velocity was assumed not to change much. Neither of these assumptions holds in fact, but it is, nonetheless, interesting to see where they lead. *If both V and Y are fixed, then it follows that the price level is proportional to the money stock.* Thus the classical quantity theory was a theory of inflation. The classical quantity theory is the proposition that the price level is proportional to the money stock:

---

[27] Why do we say income velocity and not plain velocity? There is another concept, transactions velocity, which is the ratio of *total transactions* to money balances. Total transactions far exceed GNP for two reasons. First, many transactions involving the sale and purchase of assets do not contribute to GNP. Second, a particular item in final output typically generates total spending on it that exceeds the contribution of that item to GNP. For instance, 1 dollar's worth of wheat generates transactions as it leaves the farm, as it is sold by the miller, as it leaves the baker for the supermarket, and then as it is sold to the household. One dollar's worth of wheat may involve several dollars of transactions before it is sold for the last time. Transactions velocity is thus higher than income velocity.

$$P = \frac{V \times M}{Y} \qquad (7a)$$

The classical quantity theory applies in the *classical case* supply function examined in Chapter 7.[28] Recall that in that case, with a vertical aggregate supply function, changes in the quantity of money result in changes in the price level, with the level of output remaining at its full-employment level. When the aggregate supply function is not vertical, increases in the quantity of money increase both the price level and output, and the price level is therefore not proportional to the quantity of money. Of course, if velocity is constant, *nominal GNP* (the price level times output) is proportional to the money stock.

Velocity and Policy

Velocity is a useful concept in economic policy making. We see how to use it by rewriting (6) as

$$Y_N \equiv V \times M \qquad (6a)$$

Given the nominal money stock and velocity, we know the level of nominal GNP. Thus if we can predict the level of velocity, we can predict the level of nominal income, given the money stock.

Further, *if* velocity were constant, changing the money supply would result in proportionate changes in nominal income. Any policies, including fiscal policies, that did not affect the money stock would not affect the level of income. You will probably now recognize that we have previously discussed a case of constant velocity. In Chapter 5, we discussed the effectiveness of fiscal policy when the demand for money is not a function of the interest rate and the *LM* curve is therefore vertical. That vertical *LM* curve is the same as the assumption of constant velocity.

Velocity and the Demand for Money

The discussion of constant velocity is closely related to the behavior of the demand for money. Indeed, the notion of velocity is important largely because it is a convenient way of talking about money demand.

We now examine the relationship between velocity and the demand for money. Let the demand for real balances be written $L(i, Y)$, consistent with Chapter 4. Recall that Y is real income. When the supply of money is equal to the demand for money, we have

---

[28] For more on the quantity theory, see Chap. 7.

$$\frac{M}{P} = L(i, Y) \tag{8}$$

or $M = P \times L(i, Y)$. Now we can substitute for M, the nominal money supply, in equation (6) to obtain

$$V = \frac{Y_N}{P \times L(i, Y)} = \frac{Y}{L(i, Y)} \tag{6b}$$

where we have recognized that $Y_N/P = Y$ is the level of real income. Income velocity is the ratio of the level of real income to the demand for real balances.

From equation (6b) we note that velocity is a function of real income and the interest rate. An increase in the interest rate reduces the demand for real balances and therefore increases velocity: when the cost of holding money increases, money holders make their money do more work and thus turn it over more often.

The way in which changes in real income affect velocity depends on the income elasticity of the demand for money. If the income elasticity of the demand for real balances were 1, then the demand for real balances would change in the same proportion as income. In that case, changes in real income would not affect velocity. Suppose that real income increased by 10 percent. The numerator, Y, in equation (6b) would increase by 10 percent, as would the denominator, and velocity would be unchanged. However, we have seen that the income elasticity of the demand for money ($M1$) is probably less than 1. That means that velocity *increases* with increases in real income. For example, suppose that real income rose by 10 percent and the demand for real balances increased only by 6.8 percent ($= 0.68 \times 10$ percent), as Goldfeld's results suggest. Then the numerator of equation (6b) would increase by more than the denominator, and velocity would rise. By contrast, for the $M2$ equation shown in Table 10-4, the income elasticity is approximately unity. In this case changes in real income leave the velocity of $M2$ unchanged.

The empirical work reviewed in Section 10-4 makes it clear that the demand for money and, therefore, also velocity do react systematically to changes in interest rates and the level of real income. The empirical evidence therefore decisively refutes the view that velocity is unaffected by changes in interest rates and that fiscal policy is, accordingly, incapable of affecting the level of nominal income. In terms of equation (6b), and using the analysis of Chapter 4, expansionary fiscal policy can be thought of as working by increasing interest rates, thereby increasing velocity, and thus making it possible for a given stock of money to support a higher level of nominal GNP.

Velocity in Practice

The empirical evidence we reviewed in Section 10-4 is useful in interpreting the behavior of velocity. Figure 10-4 shows a very striking change in the behavior of $M1$ velocity. From 1960 to approximately 1980, velocity steadily increases at an average rate of roughly 3 percent per year. Indeed, that increase is even more marked over

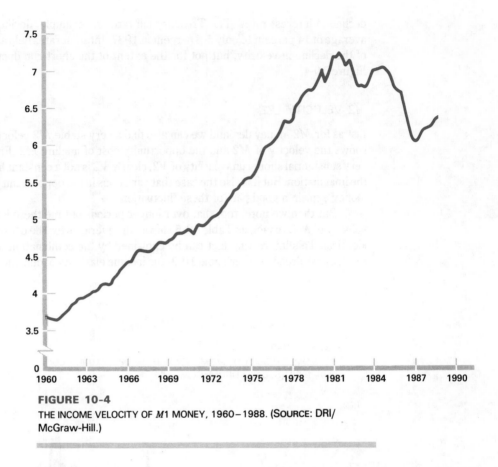

FIGURE 10-4

THE INCOME VELOCITY OF $M1$ MONEY, 1960–1988. (SOURCE: DRI/
McGraw-Hill.)

longer periods: In the midfifties velocity was about 3, whereas by 1980 it was well
above 6. Then in 1981 the pattern changes, and velocity turns around, apparently
reversing the trend of the previous two decades—and, also, displaying much bigger
fluctuations than before.

$M1$ VELOCITY

The pattern of $M1$ velocity ($V1$) can in principle be explained by the same factors that
explain the demand for money—as equation (6*b*) shows. It is possible to argue that
velocity was rising over the period 1960–1980 because income was rising (since the
income elasticity of demand is less than 1) and because interest rates were rising. But it
has not been easy to account for the behavior of $M1$ velocity since 1980, as our earlier
discussion of the demand for money in this period suggests.

   Why has $M1$ velocity both fallen on average in the 1980s and fluctuated so much
within those years? One ready explanation for the overall decline in velocity is the

decline in interest rates. The Treasury bill rate, for example, declined from a 1981 average of 14 percent to only 5.8 percent in 1987. Interest rates help account for some of the decline in velocity, but not for the extent of the short-run fluctuations seen in Figure 10-4.

*M*2 VELOCITY (*V*2)

Just as for *M*2 money demand we can also find a very stable *M*2 velocity. Figure 10-5 shows the velocity of *M*2 and the opportunity cost of holding *M*2. First we note the very substantial short-run volatility of *V*2; clearly *V*2 is not a constant by any stretch of the imagination. But it is also the case that variations in the oppportunity cost of holding money explain a good part of these fluctuations.

But then we note, too, that over longer periods of time there is no trend in the velocity of *M*2. In fact, as Table 10-5 shows, the averages for the decades are virtually identical. This interesting fact can be explained by the combination of three factors. First, as we already saw in Table 10-3, the income elasticity of demand for *M*2 is about

FIGURE 10-5
THE INCOME VELOCITY OF *M*2 MONEY AND THE OPPORTUNITY COST, 1960–1988. (SOURCE: DRI/McGraw-Hill.)

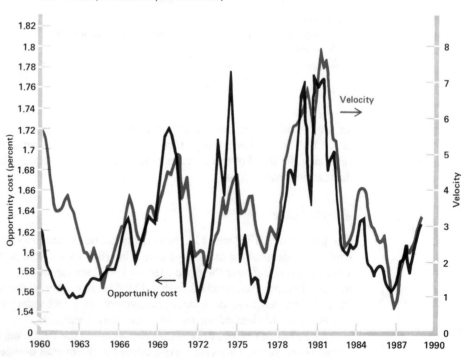

TABLE 10-5
THE VELOCITY OF *M*2 (period averages)

	1960–1969	1970–1979	1980–1988
Velocity	1.63	1.65	1.65
Own rate	2.32	4.06	6.61
Commercial paper rate	4.54	7.16	9.75
Opportunity cost	2.22	3.10	3.14

SOURCE: DRI/McGraw-Hill.

unity, which implies that income growth does not affect velocity. Second, interest rates on money market instruments have risen from the 1960s to the 1980s, but so has the own rate of interest on *M*2. As a result the opportunity cost of holding *M*2 has changed very little. Third, even though the opportunity cost has risen from 2 to 3 percent, the elasticity of demand with respect to the opportunity cost is exceedingly small. As a result there is an increase in velocity, but it is almost negligible.

The relative constancy of *M*2 velocity over longer time intervals thus is not puzzling. But what are the implications for policy? With a constant (over long averages) velocity there is a direct link between nominal income and the quantity of nominal *M*2. Thus the Federal Reserve could determine the path of nominal income by setting the path of *M*2. We return to this issue in Chapter 11 when we discuss monetary policy. But we conclude with a word of caution. Often (some say always) when a stable relationship is discovered and starts to be used, it breaks down. This pattern is referred to as *Goodhart's law*, so named by Charles Goodhart of the London School of Economics, who drew attention to this fact. Certainly the disappearance of a stable *M*1 money demand equation was an instance of Goodhart's law and the same might well happen to the stability of *V*2.

10-6 SUMMARY

1. The demand for money is a demand for real balances. It is the purchasing power, not the number, of their dollar bills that matters to holders of money.
2. The money supply, *M*1, is made up of currency and checkable deposits. A broader measure, *M*2, includes savings and time deposits at depository institutions as well as some other interest-bearing assets.
3. The chief characteristic of money is that it serves as a means of payment.
4. There are two broad reasons why people hold money and thus forgo interest that they could earn by holding alternative assets. These reasons are transactions costs and uncertainty.
5. Transactions costs are an essential aspect of money demand. If it were costless to move (instantaneously) in and out of interest-bearing assets, nobody would hold

money. Optimal cash management would involve transfers from other assets (bonds or saving deposits) just before outlays, and it would involve immediate conversion into interest-bearing form of any cash receipts. The existence of transactions costs — brokerage costs, fees, and time costs — makes it optimal to hold some money.

6. The inventory-theoretic approach shows that an individual will hold a stock of real balances that varies inversely with the interest rate but increases with the level of real income and the cost of transactions. According to the inventory approach, the income elasticity of money demand is less than unity, implying that there are economies of scale.

7. Transactions costs in combination with uncertainty about payments and receipts give rise to a precautionary demand for money. Money holdings provide insurance against illiquidity. Optimal money holdings are higher the higher the variability of net disbursements and the higher the cost of illiquidity. Since holding money implies forgoing interest, optimal money holdings will vary inversely with the rate of interest.

8. Portfolio diversification involves the tradeoff between risk and return. Saving deposits form part of an optimal portfolio because they are less risky than other assets — their nominal value is constant. Saving deposits dominate currency or demand deposits, which are also safe nominal assets, because they bear interest. Thus the speculative portfolio demand for money is a demand for saving or time deposits or similar assets, such as MMMF shares.

9. The empirical evidence provides support for a negative interest elasticity of money demand and a positive income elasticity. Because of lags, short-run elasticities are much smaller than long-run elasticities. Estimates for periods up to 1973 are that the long-run income elasticity of $M1$ demand is about 0.7, and the long-run interest elasticity is about -0.2.

10. Over the decade 1970–1980 the demand for money shifted; less money ($M1$) was demanded than should have been demanded according to the standard demand-for-money equation. The reduction in money demand was a result of both the introduction of new assets and improvements in cash management methods.

11. There is a stable demand function for $M2$. The demand has a unit income elasticity, a positive elasticity with respect to the own rate and a negative elasticity with respect to the commercial paper rate.

12. The income velocity of money is defined as the ratio of income to money or the rate of turnover of money. Since the 1950s, velocity has doubled to a level in excess of 6.

13. Given an income elasticity of the demand for $M1$ money of less than unity, and a negative interest elasticity of demand, an increase in real income raises velocity, as does an increase in the rate of interest. At higher levels of income or at higher interest rates, there is a lower demand for money in relation to income. Higher interest rates lead people to economize on cash balances.

14. The velocity of $M2$ is roughly constant over long periods of time. The constancy

is a reflection of small changes in the opportunity cost of holding money and of a unit income elasticity.

15. Inflation implies that money loses purchasing power, and inflation thus creates a cost of holding money. The higher the rate of inflation, the lower the amount of real balances that will be held. Hyperinflations provide striking support for this prediction. Under conditions of very high expected inflation, money demand falls dramatically relative to income. Velocity rises as people use less money in relation to income.

KEY TERMS

Real balances
Money illusion
$M1$
$M2$
Liquid
Medium of exchange
Store of value
Unit of account
Standard of deferred payments
Transactions demand

Inventory-theoretic approach
Square-root formula
Precautionary demand
Speculative demand
Income velocity of money
Quantity equation
Quantity theory of money
Goodhart's law
Hyperinflation

PROBLEMS

1. To what extent would it be possible to design a society in which there was no money? What would the problems be? Could currency at least be eliminated? How? (Lest all this seems too unworldly, you should know that some people are beginning to talk of a "cashless economy" in the next century.)

2. Evaluate the effects of the following changes on the demand for $M1$ and $M2$. Which of the functions of money do they relate to?
   (a) "Instant cash" machines that allow 24-hour withdrawals from savings accounts at banks
   (b) The employment of more tellers at your bank
   (c) An increase in inflationary expectations
   (d) Widespread acceptance of credit cards
   (e) Fear of an imminent collapse of the government
   (f) A rise in the interest rate on time deposits

3. (a) Do you think credit card credit limits should be counted in the money stock?
   (b) Should MMDAs be part of $M1$?

4. (a) Determine the optimal strategy for cash management for the person who earns $1,600 per month, can earn 0.5 percent interest per month in a savings account, and has a transaction cost of $1.
   (b) What is the individual's average cash balance?

(c) Suppose income rises to $1,800. By what percentage does the individual's demand for money change? (Pay attention to the integer constraints.)

5. Discuss the various factors that go into an individual's decision regarding how many traveler's checks to take on a vacation.

6. In the text, we said that the transactions demand-for-money model can also be applied to firms. Suppose a firm sells steadily during the month and has to pay its workers at the end of the month. Explain then how it would determine its money holdings.

7. In the text we argued that the demand for money fell when corporations received permission to hold savings accounts.
(a) For which demand-for-money concept is this true? For which is it false?
(b) Explain why this change would have been more important for small firms than for large ones.

8. Explain why the demand-for-money function shifted during the seventies and early eighties.

9. (a) Is V high or low relative to trend during recessions? Why?
(b) How can the Fed influence velocity?

10. This chapter emphasizes that the demand for money is a demand for real balances. Thus the demand for nominal balances rises with the price level. At the same time, inflation causes the real demand to fall. Explain how these two assertions can both be correct.

11. "Muggers favor deflation." Comment.

12. Explain why the income velocity of $M2$, unlike that of $M2$, behaved well in the 1980s.

*13. The assumption was made in the text that, in the transactions demand for cash model, it is optimal to space transactions evenly throughout the month. Prove this as follows in the case where $n = 2$. Since one transaction must be made immediately, the only question is when to make the second one. For simplicity, call the beginning of the month $t = 0$ and the end of the month $t = 1$. Then consider a transaction strategy that performs the second transaction at the time t. If income is Y_N, then this will require moving tY_N into cash now and $(1 - t)Y_N$ at time t. Calculate the total cost incurred under this strategy, and try various values of t to see which is optimal. (If you are familiar with calculus, prove that $t = 1/2$ minimizes total cost.)

*14. For those students familiar with calculus, derive equation (4) from equation (2) by minimizing total costs with respect to n.

---

* An asterisk denotes a more difficult problem.

DATA APPENDIX

In the following table, PGNP is the GNP deflator, set at 1.00 in 1982; OWN is the own rate of return on *M2*; and COMM is the commercial paper rate.

	M1	M2	PGNP	V1	V2	OWN	COMM
1960	141.933	310.967	0.309	3.673	1.694	1.393	3.733
1961	146.033	333.400	0.313	3.731	1.644	1.550	2.811
1962	148.667	359.967	0.319	3.922	1.640	2.100	3.124
1963	154.633	391.100	0.324	4.019	1.599	2.238	3.430
1964	161.433	422.100	0.329	4.144	1.586	2.342	3.849
1965	168.533	456.067	0.338	4.312	1.593	2.505	4.281
1966	173.233	477.867	0.350	4.514	1.638	2.670	5.481
1967	184.300	521.367	0.360	4.593	1.622	2.720	5.032
1968	197.833	562.200	0.377	4.694	1.638	2.793	5.842
1969	205.467	586.800	0.398	4.784	1.665	2.853	7.831
1970	215.800	622.733	0.420	4.855	1.684	3.130	7.714
1971	230.233	706.667	0.444	4.940	1.632	3.163	5.045
1972	249.600	797.100	0.465	5.071	1.594	3.248	4.663
1973	263.967	854.633	0.496	5.300	1.626	4.023	8.203
1974	273.500	904.700	0.540	5.469	1.661	4.485	10.015
1975	286.900	1,014.267	0.593	5.677	1.648	3.858	6.250
1976	304.400	1,149.500	0.630	5.997	1.627	3.938	5.236
1977	329.467	1,278.400	0.673	6.217	1.613	4.138	5.547
1978	356.467	1,380.500	0.722	6.492	1.679	4.658	7.942
1979	384.067	1,493.733	0.786	6.725	1.729	5.930	10.970
1980	412.700	1,627.367	0.857	6.899	1.743	7.080	12.658
1981	434.367	1,778.133	0.939	7.181	1.780	8.978	15.325
1982	471.900	1,939.400	1.000	6.990	1.690	7.965	11.892
1983	520.100	2,174.800	1.038	6.768	1.615	6.575	8.878
1984	547.667	2,342.600	1.077	7.005	1.657	7.413	10.097
1985	613.567	2,550.967	1.110	6.843	1.619	6.165	7.954
1986	709.500	2,788.300	1.140	6.370	1.579	5.160	6.495
1987	754.700	2,905.767	1.177	6.081	1.581	4.865	6.812
1988	787.467	3,056.900	1.217	6.268	1.616	5.300	7.656

SOURCE: DRI/McGraw-Hill and Board of Governors of the Federal Reserve.

THE FED, MONEY, AND CREDIT

*I*n the basic versions of the *IS-LM* and the aggregate supply-demand models, we described monetary policy as the choice of the quantity of money, *M*, or the nominal interest rate, *i*. In this chapter we extend the analysis of monetary policy and the assets markets. First we set out how the Fed affects the money supply and interest rates. Then we show that monetary policy does not work exclusively through interest rates, but also by affecting the availability of credit in the economy. Credit consists of loans, short- and long-term, to firms, households, and the government.

We start this chapter with a brief discussion of the mechanics of money supply determination. Then we go on to discuss monetary policy: both how the Fed conducts monetary policy and controversies about how it should conduct monetary policy. In particular, we ask whether the Fed should aim to affect the money supply, or the interest rate, or the quantity of credit — some or all of them.

11-1 MONEY STOCK DETERMINATION: THE COMPONENTS

We ignore here the distinction between various kinds of deposits (and thus the distinction between $M1$ and $M2$) and consider the money supply process as if there were only a uniform class of deposits, D. Using that simplification, we define money as deposits plus currency (CU):

$$M \equiv CU + D \tag{1}$$

Starting from equation (1), we begin to develop the details of the process by which the money stock is determined. Both the public and the depository institutions (which we shall refer to simply as banks[1]) have an influence on the determination of the money supply. The public has a role because its demand for currency affects the currency component, *CU*, and its demand for deposits affects the deposit component, *D*. The banks have a role because deposits, *D*, are a liability of the banks, that is, a debt the banks owe their customers. We know too that the Fed has a part (the most important) in determining the money supply. The interactions among the actions of the public, the banks, and the Fed determine the money supply.

We shall summarize the behavior of the public, the banks, and the Fed in the money supply process by three variables: the *currency-deposit ratio*, the *reserve ratio*, and the *stock of high-powered money*.

The Currency-Deposit Ratio

The currency-deposit ratio is determined primarily by the behavior of the public, which decides in what proportion to hold currency and deposits. In 1988 (using the data appendix at the end of the chapter) the currency-deposit ratio (*cu*) was 0.073.

The currency-deposit ratio is determined primarily by the payment habits of the public. It is affected by the convenience and accessibility of banks; for instance, if it is easy to obtain cash from a cash machine, individuals will on average carry less cash with them because the costs of running out are lower. The currency-deposit ratio increases when the ratio of consumption to GNP increases, since currency demand is more closely linked to consumption than to GNP, while deposit demand is more closely linked to GNP. The ratio has a strong seasonal pattern, being highest around Christmas.

For the remainder of the chapter we shall treat the currency-deposit ratio as independent of interest rates and constant.[2] It is possible, though, that with interest paid on demand deposits, the currency-deposit ratio is negatively related to the interest rate.

The Reserve-Deposit Ratio

Bank reserves consist of notes and coin held by the banks and deposits the banks hold at the Fed. The banks hold reserves to meet (1) the demands of their customers for cash and (2) payments their customers make by checks that are deposited in other banks.

Banks have to keep reserves in the form of notes and coin because they are

---

[1] Recall that nonbank depository institutions include savings and loan associations, savings banks, and credit unions.

[2] This assumption is convenient but not accurate. In fact the currency-deposit ratio rose fairly steadily from 1960 to the early 1980s, and then began to decline quite rapidly from 1984 on. See Albert E. Burger, "The Puzzling Growth of the Monetary Aggregates in the 1980s," Federal Reserve Bank of St. Louis *Review*, September/October 1988.

TABLE 11-1

BANK BALANCE SHEET

Assets	Liabilities
Reserves	Deposits
Bank credit	
Loans	
Investments	
Less	
Borrowing from Fed	
Borrowing in the Fed funds market (net)	

obliged to provide currency to customers who want it.[3] They keep accounts at the Fed mainly to make payments among themselves. Thus, when my bank has to make a payment to your bank because I paid you with a check drawn on my bank account, my bank makes the payment by transferring money from its account at the Fed to your bank's account at the Fed. Banks can also use their deposits at the Fed to obtain cash; the Fed sends the cash over in an armored truck on request.[4]

We denote by *re* the ratio of bank reserves to deposits, or the reserve-deposit ratio. The reserve ratio is less than 1, since banks hold assets other than reserves, such as loans they make to the public and securities, in their portfolios. Table 11-1 presents a simplified bank balance sheet. Banks in 1988 held $60.4 billion of reserves. With deposits of $2,804.2 billion, the reserve-deposit ratio, *re*, was 0.0215.

DETERMINANTS OF THE RESERVE-DEPOSIT RATIO

The reserve-deposit ratio is determined by two sets of considerations. First, the banking system is subject to Fed regulation in the form of *minimum reserve requirements*. The reserve requirements vary by type of deposit and also by bank size: requirements against time deposits are lower than those against demand deposits, and are lower for smaller banks than for larger banks.[5] The reserve requirements are imposed partly for reasons of safety, to make sure that the banks have a cushion of safe

---

[3] For an overview of the economics of financial intermediation, which we do not deal with here, see James Tobin, "Financial Intermediaries," *The New Palgrave Dictionary of Economics*, 1987.

[4] Depository institutions in 1988 held about 40 percent of their reserves in currency as vault cash and 60 percent as reserve balances at the Federal Reserve.

[5] Data on reserve requirements are printed in the monthly *Federal Reserve Bulletin*. For instance, in early 1989, large banks (with deposits exceeding $41.5 million) had to hold reserves equal to 12 percent of their demand deposits, and small banks had to hold reserves equal to only 3 percent of their demand deposits. The requirements and the definition of a large bank change from time to time.

assets to draw on when depositors want to be paid, and partly because they give the Fed a way of controlling the money supply, as we shall see below.[6]

Second, banks may want to hold *excess reserves* beyond the level of required reserves. In deciding how much excess reserves to hold, a bank's economic problem is very similar to the problem of an individual in deciding on a precautionary demand for money. As noted above, banks hold reserves to meet demands on them for cash or payments to other banks.[7] If a bank cannot meet those demands, it has to borrow either from the Fed or from other banks that happen to have spare reserves.

The *discount rate* is the interest rate charged by the Fed to banks that borrow from it to meet temporary needs for reserves. While the discount rate is the explicit cost of Fed borrowing, there may also be an implicit cost, since the Fed will make known its disapproval of the imprudent behavior of a bank that is frequently short of reserves.[8]

The cost of borrowing from other banks is the *federal funds rate*. Federal funds are simply reserves that some banks have in excess and others need. The federal funds rate varies with the overall availability of reserves to the banking system, and can be affected by the Fed. Thus banks that are short of reserves face a cost of borrowing to meet their reserve requirements; that cost is affected by the Fed either directly through the discount rate or indirectly through the federal funds rate.

There is also a cost to a bank in holding reserves. Reserves do not earn interest. By holding smaller reserves, a bank is able to invest in interest-earning assets (this can be seen in Table 11-1) and increase its profits. By reducing its reserves, the bank is able to increase its loans or investments on which it earns interest. There is thus a tradeoff of the sort examined in Chapter 10 in discussing the precautionary demand for money. The more reserves a bank holds, the less likely it is to have to incur the costs of borrowing. But the more reserves it holds, the more interest it forgoes.

The bank's choice of reserve ratio therefore depends on three factors in addition to the required reserve ratio. The first is the uncertainty of its net deposit flow. The more variable the inflows and outflows of cash a bank experiences, the more reserves it will want to hold. The second is the cost of borrowing when the bank runs short of re-

---

[6] Reserve requirements usually constitute a tax on banks or their depositors. This is because reserves pay no interest to the banks. To the extent that the banks have to hold assets that pay no interest, they can pay less interest to their depositors. As we shall see below, governments can help finance their budget deficits by imposing high reserve requirements. Frequently reserve requirements are very high in countries where governments have large deficits and high inflation.

[7] Many banks, particularly small ones, hold deposits at other banks to facilitate transactions of this sort. These *interbank deposits* serve the same function as reserves but are not included in our measure of reserves. They are excluded from the definitions of the money stock.

[8] The Fed does lend to banks for extended periods, but at a rate much above the discount rate. Again, details can be found in the *Federal Reserve Bulletin;* for instance, at the beginning of 1989 the discount rate was 6.5 percent, while the cost of borrowing for more than thirty days was 9.65 percent. At one time the discount rate had considerable importance as a signal of the Fed's intentions with regard to the behavior of interest rates. More recently, the Fed has tended to use discount policy passively, letting the discount rate adjust gradually as the general level of interest rates changes.

serves. We shall take the discount rate, i_D, to be the cost of borrowing. The third factor is the interest forgone by holding reserves, which we shall take as the market interest rate, i. We can therefore write the bank's reserve-deposit ratio, re, as a function of the market interest rate, the discount rate, the required reserve ratio r_R, and σ:

$$re = r(i, i_D, r_R, \sigma) \tag{2}$$

where σ indicates the uncertainty characteristics of the bank's deposit inflows and outflows.

How does each of the factors in equation (2) affect the reserve-deposit ratio? An increase in the market interest rate on earning assets decreases the reserve ratio, since the rate increase makes reserves more costly to hold. An increase in the discount rate increases the ratio by raising the cost of running short of reserves.[9] And an increase in the required reserve ratio increases the actual reserve ratio. We thus see that the reserve ratio is a function of market interest rates. This implies that the supply of money itself is also a function of market interest rates, as we shall see below.

DEPOSIT INSURANCE AND BANK RUNS

Excess reserves in the last 10 years have averaged less than 1 percent of total reserves. Indeed, in the entire postwar period, they have been small compared with levels reached in the 1930s. The 1930s were a period of great economic uncertainty, during which there were many bank failures; that is, banks were unable to meet the demands of their depositors for cash. If you have a deposit in a failed bank, you cannot "get your money out."

In the 1930s, it became necessary for banks to hold large reserves. The reason is that a bank that holds relatively few reserves, with most of its assets in loans or securities, cannot quickly meet its depositors' demands for currency. A bank that holds low reserves is exposed to the risk that a run by depositors — an attempt to convert their deposits into currency — will drive the bank into default. But it is precisely when depositors are afraid that a bank is in danger of defaulting that they are likely to attempt to withdraw their money from the bank before it is too late. That is to say, a run on a bank may occur precisely because its depositors believe that a run on the bank is likely to occur.[10]

---

[9] The precise behavior of excess reserves depends on how the Fed is conducting monetary policy. One possible method is for the Fed to allow banks to borrow as much as they want to meet the required reserve ratio, r_R. If banks hold exactly to that ratio, there are never any excess reserves, so excess reserves are unaffected by the discount rate. In that case, an increase in the discount rate would not affect excess reserves (which would remain at zero), nor the reserve ratio (which would remain equal to r_R). More generally, we should expect the relationship stated in the text, in which the reserve ratio declines with increases in the discount rate.

[10] The notion of self-justifying runs on banks has both intuitive appeal and historical support. It has only recently been formalized, in an ingenious but very difficult article by Douglas Diamond and Philip Dybvig, "Bank Runs, Deposit Insurance and Liquidity," *Journal of Political Economy,* June 1983.

In a general atmosphere of instability, such as prevailed in the 1930s, it therefore becomes important for banks to demonstrate their ability to meet cash withdrawals by holding large reserves, that is, by holding excess reserves. Only by being in a position to meet large cash demands can the banks avoid having their depositors actually make those demands. The massive bank failures of the 1930s, as a consequence of runs on banks, gave rise to an important institutional reform, the creation of the *Federal Deposit Insurance Corporation* (FDIC). That institution insures bank deposits, so that depositors get paid even if a bank fails. Bank failure, although far less dramatic today than in the early 1930s, does remain a factor. Table 11-2 shows data for failures of banks insured by the FDIC.

In form, the FDIC operates like an insurance company. Banks pay premiums to insure their deposits. In principle, insurance applies only for up to $100,000 on an account. In fact, the FDIC is more than a private insurance company. When banks fail, the FDIC usually steps in to arrange the sale of the bank and to ensure that all depositors do not lose, not only those with small accounts. Further, the FDIC itself is too small to pay out all deposits if there should be a massive run on many banks. It remains effective though because there is little doubt that the U.S. government would intervene to support the FDIC if the latter's own funds began to run short (see Box 11-1).

There are three main reasons why excess reserves are now so small. First, bank deposits are insured, mainly through the FDIC. Individual depositors now know that their deposit will ultimately be paid back. The threat of runs on banks is accordingly much reduced, and banks do not have to hold large reserves to guard against runs. Second, the development of financial markets and communication has reduced the cost to banks of managing their balance sheets in such a way as to keep excess reserves small. Third, the relatively high level of interest rates makes it costly for banks to hold idle reserves rather than interest-earning assets.

TABLE 11-2

NUMBER AND DEPOSITS OF FDIC-INSURED BANKS CLOSED BECAUSE OF FINANCIAL DIFFICULTIES (annual averages)

	Number of closed banks	Deposits at closed banks, $ millions	Percent of total deposits at insured banks
1934–1939	52.5	49.0	0.1
1940–1949	10.0	23.5	0.02
1950–1959	3.1	10.5	0.005
1960–1969	4.4	28.5	0.008
1970–1979	7.6	513.0	0.06
1980–1983	27.5	4,848.0	0.32
1984–1987	130.2	6,937.3	0.34

SOURCE: Federal Reserve Bank of Minneapolis, *A Case for Reforming Federal Deposit Insurance.* *1988 Annual Report.*

box 11-1

DEPOSIT INSURANCE AND THE SAVINGS AND LOAN DEBACLE

Deposits in federally chartered savings and loan associations (S&Ls) are insured by FSLIC (pronounced "fizz-lick"), the Federal Savings and Loan Insurance Corporation. Like the FDIC, FSLIC finances itself by charging premiums on the deposits it insures.

As the 1980s drew to a close, it was clear that FSLIC had spectacularly run out of funds. In early 1989 a bailout plan was announced: The Federal government would borrow—by some estimates as much as $100 billion—to provide FSLIC with the resources to deal with bankrupt S&Ls.

What happened? From the great depression until 1980, the interest rates depository institutions could pay on their deposits were controlled. As market interest rates rose in the late 1970s, the S&Ls started losing deposits, which moved off toward MMMFs. The S&Ls were thus supporters of the gradual deregulation of interest rates permitted by the important Depository Institutions Deregulation and Monetary Control Act of 1980.

After deregulation, S&Ls competed for deposits by raising the interest rates on their deposits. Depositors, protected by deposit insurance, went for the highest interest rates, and so any sufficiently aggressive insured S&L could obtain funds to lend. S&Ls that raised funds aggressively also invested them aggressively. Many S&Ls, especially in Texas and the southwest, made loans mainly for real estate. As the real estate market in those areas collapsed, the value of the assets held by the S&Ls also collapsed, and they went bankrupt.

FSLIC had to step in to protect the depositors. Typically, FSLIC arranged for some other institution, such as a more sound S&L or a businessperson, to take over the failed S&L, and provided funds to ensure that the reorganized S&L would be profitable. Between 1980 and early 1989 over a third of the more than 4,000 savings and loans in the United States were recognized to be insolvent and were either liquidated or merged with other institutions.

The expensive lesson in this episode is that interest rate deregulation in the presence of deposit insurance has to be handled very carefully. The deposits were insured, so depositors had no need to consider the safety of the institutions in which they were placing their assets. Reckless competition for deposits could thus take place. Of course, the dangers should have been foreseen by FSLIC, which should also have monitored the investments the S&Ls were making with the deposits they received.

Although there have been many failures of banks insured by the FDIC, the scale is far smaller than that of FSLIC. This success is generally attributed to more careful regulation of bank portfolios by the FDIC. ■

High-Powered Money

High-powered money (or the monetary base) consists of currency (notes and coin) and banks' deposits at the Fed. Part of the currency is held by the public. The remaining currency (around 10 percent) is held by banks as part of their reserves. The notes that constitute most of the outstanding stock of currency are issued by the Fed,[11] and the reserves held by member banks as Fed deposits are a liability of the Fed, that is, a debt of the Fed to the member banks.

11-2 THE MONEY MULTIPLIER

In this section we develop a simple approach to money stock determination, using as the key variables the currency-deposit ratio, the reserve-deposit ratio, and high-powered money. The approach is organized around the supply of and demand for high-powered money. The Fed can control the *supply* of high-powered money. The total *demand* for high-powered money comes from the public, who want to use it as currency, and the banks, which need it as reserves. Because the public has a preferred ratio of currency to deposits and because the banks have a desired ratio of reserves to deposits, we can calculate the total money stock that can be supported by any given stock of high-powered money.

Before going into details, we want to think briefly about the relationship between the money stock and the stock of high-powered money (Figure 11-1). At the top of the figure we show the stock of high-powered money. At the bottom we show the stock of money. They are related by the *money multiplier.* The money multiplier is the ratio of the stock of money to the stock of high-powered money.

The money multiplier is larger than 1. It is clear from the diagram that the multiplier is larger the larger are deposits as a fraction of the money stock. That is true because currency uses up one dollar of high-powered money per dollar of money. Deposits, by contrast, use up only amount *re* of high-powered money (in reserves) per dollar of money stock. For instance, if the reserve ratio, *re*, is 10 percent, every dollar of the money stock in the form of deposits uses up only 10 cents of high-powered money.

The precise relationship among the money stock, M, the stock of high-powered money, H, the reserve-deposit ratio, *re*, and the currency-deposit ratio, *cu*, is derived in the appendix to this chapter. Here we present the resulting expression for the money supply expressed in terms of its principal determinants, *re, cu,* and H:[12,13]

---

[11] Coins are minted by the Treasury and sold to the Fed by the Treasury. This detail complicates the bookkeeping but is of no real importance to the process of money supply determination.

[12] See the appendix for the key equations.

[13] Using the actual values for 1988 (see the Data Appendix) we have as ratios to $M2$ deposits: $cu = 0.073$ and $re = 0.022$; $H = 265.7$. Thus we obtain $M2 = [(1 + 0.073)/(0.073 + 0.022)] \times 265.7 = 3,001$.

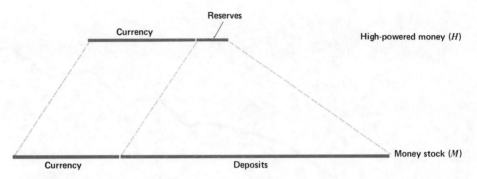

FIGURE 11-1
THE MONEY MULTIPLIER. The money multiplier is the ratio of the money
stock (the base of the diagram) to high-powered money. The multiplier
is larger than 1. It is larger the smaller the ratio of currency to deposits
and the smaller the ratio of reserves to deposits.

$$M = \frac{1 + cu}{re + cu} \, H \equiv mm \times H \tag{3}$$

where *mm* is the money multiplier given by

$$mm \equiv \frac{1 + cu}{re + cu} \tag{4}$$

It is thus clear that

- *The money multiplier is larger the smaller the reserve ratio,* re.
- In addition, *the money multiplier is larger the smaller the currency deposit ratio,* cu. That is because the smaller is *cu*, the smaller the proportion of the high-powered money stock that is being used as currency (which translates high-powered money only one for one into money) and the larger the proportion that is available to be reserves (which translates much more than one for one into money).

The Multiplier in Practice

Since the Fed controls *H*, it would be able to control the money stock, *M, exactly* if the multiplier were constant or fully predictable. Actual data for the money multipliers for

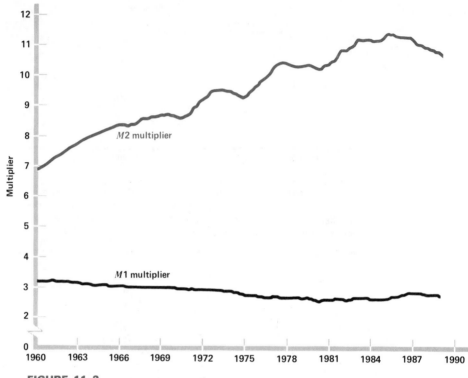

FIGURE 11-2

THE *M*1 AND *M*2 MONEY MULTIPLIERS, 1969–1989. (SOURCE: DRI/ McGraw-Hill.)

*M*1 and *M*2 are shown in Figure 11-2. It is clear that the money multiplier is neither constant nor exactly predictable.[14] This means that the Fed cannot exactly determine the money stock in any period by setting the base at a specific level. Even small, unexpected variations in the multiplier can, for a given stock of high-powered money, bring about significant changes in the money supply.

We next examine more closely the process by which the Fed determines *H*. We then turn to the question of how the Fed conducts monetary policy in practice and to an examination of the role of credit in the economy.

---

[14] A sophisticated method of predicting the money multiplier is presented in James M. Johannes and Robert H. Rasche, "Predicting the Money Multiplier," *Journal of Monetary Economics,* July 1979. See also, by the same authors, *Controlling the Growth of the Monetary Aggregates* (Kluwer, 1987).

TABLE 11-3
SIMPLIFIED FORM OF THE FED BALANCE SHEET, SHOWING SOURCES AND USES OF HIGH-POWERED MONEY, MARCH 1989 (billions of dollars)*

Assets (sources)			Liabilities (uses)		
Gold and foreign exchange		$ 16.4	Currency		$229.6
			Held by the public	$202.4	
			Vault cash	27.2	
Federal reserve credit		246.7	Bank deposits at the Fed		39.3
Loans and discounts	$ 2.1		Other deposits		9.0
Government securities	247.5		Treasury	8.7	
Net other credit	(2.9)		Foreign and other	0.3	
Plus			Capital		4.2
Net other assets		18.0			
Monetary base (sources)		$281.1	Monetary base (uses)		$281.1

SOURCE: *Federal Reserve Bulletin,* June 1989.

11-3 CONTROLLING THE STOCK OF HIGH-POWERED MONEY

Table 11-3 shows a highly simplified form of the Fed's balance sheet, designed to illustrate the sources of the monetary base — the way the Fed creates high-powered money — and the uses of, or demand for, the base. The Fed's main assets appear on the left-hand side and its liabilities appear on the right.[15]

The reason to focus on the Federal Reserve balance sheet is to see how operations by the Fed affect the stock of high-powered money outstanding. High-powered money is created when the Fed acquires assets and pays for these assets by creating liabilities. The two main classes of liabilities, or *uses* of the base, are currency and member bank deposits.

An Open Market Purchase

The method by which the Fed most often changes the stock of high-powered money is an open market operation. We examine the mechanics of an open market *purchase,* an operation in which the Fed buys, say $1 million of government bonds from a private individual. An open market purchase *increases* the monetary base.

---

[15] We have simplified the balance sheet by lumping together a number of assets in the entry "Net other assets." More detail on the Fed's balance sheet and the monetary base can be obtained by examining the tables in the *Federal Reserve Bulletin.*

TABLE 11-4

EFFECTS OF AN OPEN MARKET PURCHASE ON THE FED BALANCE SHEET (millions of dollars)

Assets		Liabilities	
Government securities	+1	Currency	0
All other assets	0	Bank deposits at Fed	+1
Monetary base (sources)	+1	Monetary base (uses)	+1

The accounting for the Fed's purchase is shown in Table 11-4. The Fed's ownership of government securities rises by $1 million, which is reflected in the "Government securities" entry on the assets side of the balance sheet. How does the Fed pay for the bond? It writes a check on itself. In return for the bond, the seller receives a check instructing the Fed to pay (the seller) $1 million. The seller takes the check to his or her bank, which credits the depositor with the $1 million and then deposits the check at the Fed. That bank has an account at the Fed; the account is credited with $1 million, and the "Bank deposits at Fed" entry on the "Liabilities" side of the balance sheet rises by $1 million. The commercial bank has just increased its reserves by $1 million, which are held in the first instance as a deposit at the Fed.[16]

The only unexpected part of the story of the open market purchase is that the Fed can make payments by creating deposits in its own books for the seller. The payment is made by giving the eventual owner of the check a deposit at the Fed. That deposit can be used to make payments to other banks, or it can be exchanged for currency. Just as the ordinary deposit holder at a bank can obtain currency in exchange for deposits, the bank deposit holder at the Fed can acquire currency in exchange for its deposits. When the Fed pays for the bond with a deposit at the Fed, it creates high-powered money with a stroke of the pen. The Fed can create high-powered money at will merely by buying assets, such as government bonds, and paying for them with its liabilities.

The Fed Balance Sheet

We return now to the balance sheet and start by examining the assets. As we have just seen, the purchase of assets generates high-powered money. The gold and foreign exchange that the Fed owns were acquired in the past, when the Fed paid for them by

---

[16] In problem 2 we ask you to trace through the effects of an open market sale that reduces *H*.

writing checks on itself. There is, accordingly, almost no difference between the way in which an open market purchase of gold affects the balance sheet and the way in which an open market purchase of bonds affects the balance sheet.[17]

Foreign Exchange and the Base

Table 11-3 shows the effects of Fed purchases of foreign exchange on the monetary base. The Fed sometimes buys or sells foreign currencies in an attempt to affect exchange rates. These purchases and sales of foreign exchange — *foreign exchange market intervention* — affect the base. Note from the balance sheet that if the central bank buys gold or foreign exchange, there is a corresponding increase in high-powered money, as the Fed pays with its own liabilities for the gold or foreign exchange that is purchased. The first point to note, then, is the direct impact of foreign exchange market operations on the base.[18]

The second point concerns *sterilization*. By that term we denote attempts by the Fed to neutralize the effects of its intervention in the foreign exchange market on the base. For instance, if the Fed sells foreign exchange (thereby reducing the monetary base when purchasers of foreign exchange pay the Fed), it at the same time makes an open market purchase of bonds (thereby restoring the base to its original level). The net effect, therefore, is to leave the base unchanged but to change the portfolio composition of the Fed's balance sheet. There will be an increase in the gold and foreign exchange entry and an offsetting reduction in Federal Reserve credit and thus no change in high-powered money.

Loans and Discounts

The Fed's role as a lender is reflected by the "Loans and discounts" item in Table 11-3. The Fed provides high-powered money to banks that need it by lending to them (crediting their account at the Fed) against the collateral of government securities. The rate that the Fed charges for the loans is called the *discount rate*. The willingness of banks to borrow from the Fed is affected by the rate the Fed charges, and the discount rate accordingly influences the volume of borrowing. Since borrowed reserves are also part of high-powered money, the Fed's discount rate has some effect on the monetary base.

---

[17] The Fed's 1989 holdings of gold were about $11 billion, valued at $42 an ounce. The market value of the gold is much higher, since the market price of gold is far above $42 per ounce. In problem 5, you are asked to show how the balance sheet would be affected if the Fed decided to value its gold at the free market price. For that purpose you will have to adjust the item "Net other assets" appropriately.

[18] Details of this impact may be complicated by the fact, which we do not pursue, that the Fed and the Treasury usually collaborate in foreign exchange intervention.

box 11-2 **THE FED AS LENDER OF LAST RESORT**

An important function assigned to central banks is to act as lender of last resort. When financial panic threatens the collapse of the financial system, swift action by the Fed can restore confidence and avoid a systemwide run on financial intermediaries, a freezing of credit lines, or, worse, a calling in of loans. The Fed does act in this role whenever major financial institutions go under or when, as in the case of the October 1987 stock market collapse, there is a serious risk of instability.

The need for a lender of last resort emerges from the following consideration. The credit system is by its very nature *illiquid*, though not *insolvent*—various debtors can in principle repay their loans, but cannot do so on demand. But many liabilities, for example, bank deposits or large CDs of banks and corporations, have very short maturities. If all creditors presented themselves to ask for redemption, many of the debtors would not be able to pay and would have to default. But imagine that a major financial institution, say First Bank of Nowhere (First for short) has payment difficulties. The propagation of the crisis stems from the fact that other financial institutions may well have lent to First and will be eager to recover their money before other creditors can lay their hands on any liquid assets. The other creditors magnify the bank run. Yet other financial institutions are aware that *some* institutions have lent to First, cannot recover their loans, and are therefore vulnerable themselves, as are their creditors in turn. There arises a general uncertainty as to who lent to whom and who is in trouble because someone (or many) in the many layers of credit and intermediation cannot meet redemption demands. As a result *all* credit freezes; nobody wants to lend to anyone because everyone is afraid to be pulled into the default. But if nobody wants to lend, short-term credit lines cannot be rolled over, and many institutions become illiquid. The process deteriorates in a 1930s-style financial collapse as assets are liquidated to recover liquidity.

The Fed enters in such a situation by *isolating* the center of the storm, guaranteeing the assets of the individual financial institution (beyond the guarantees of the FDIC). The guarantee assures everybody that third parties will not suffer losses and hence not become a risk. Thus the lender-of-last-resort function amounts to avoiding the spillover effects to the credit market of individual payment difficulties. But the function also comes into its own when there is a marketwide problem. Walter Bagehot (1826–1877) in his famous 1873 book, *Lombard Street*, gave the classic prescription: "*During crisis discount freely!*"

Milton Friedman and Anna Schwartz, in their *A Monetary History of the United States*, blamed the Fed for not responding to the systemwide problems induced by the

The Treasury and the Fed

The balance sheet of Table 11-3 conceals one important item in the "Net other assets" entry. Among those net assets are deposits that the Treasury holds at the Fed. (Actually, Treasury deposits are Fed *liabilities*, which are negative net assets.) The Treasury makes almost all its payments for the purchases of goods and services and repays maturing government debt out of its accounts at the Fed. That has the interesting implication that Treasury purchases affect the stock of high-powered money.

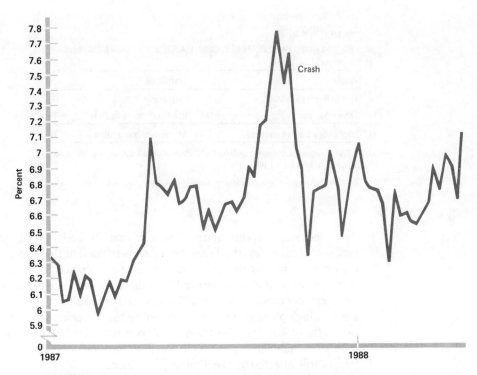

FIGURE 1

THE CRASH AND THE FEDERAL FUNDS RATE, 1987–1988. Friday quotations of the Federal Funds rate, percent per year. (SOURCE: DRI/McGraw-Hill.)

stock market crash of 1929, thus violating Bagehot's prescription. But during the stock market crash of 1987, the lesson had been learned. Fed chairman Alan Greenspan did not hesitate. He announced that the Fed stood behind the banking system. The Fed immediately reduced interest rates, as shown in Figure 1, providing the much needed liquidity that would help stem the risk of a credit collapse. ∎

For instance, suppose the Treasury, to buy weapons, makes a payment of $1 billion out of its Fed account by writing a check on that account. Such a check would look much like any other check, except that it would instruct the Fed, rather than a commercial bank, to pay $1 billion to the bearer of the check. The seller of the weapons deposits the check in a commercial bank, which, in turn, presents it to the Fed. The Fed then credits the commercial bank account at the Fed for $1 billion. Member bank deposits have risen. We show these changes in the balance sheet in Table 11-5.

TABLE 11-5

FED BALANCE SHEET: EFFECT OF TREASURY PAYMENT (billions of dollars)

Assets		Liabilities	
Net other assets*	+1	Currency	0
Other assets	0	Bank account at Fed	+1
Monetary base (sources)	+1	Monetary base (uses)	+1

* The Treasury's payment *reduces* Fed liabilities by $1 billion, therefore *increasing* assets by $1 billion.

Because payments by the Treasury from its Fed accounts affect the stock of high-powered money, the Treasury attempts to prevent those accounts from fluctuating excessively. For that purpose, it also keeps accounts at commercial banks, the so-called *tax and loan accounts*. When the Treasury receives tax payments, it typically deposits them in commercial banks, rather than the Fed, so as not to affect the stock of high-powered money; then, before the Treasury has to make a payment, it moves the money from the commercial bank to the Fed. If the payment is made fairly soon after the money is moved to the Fed, the stock of high-powered money is only temporarily affected by the Treasury purchase.

Financing Federal Deficits

The relationship between the Fed and the Treasury is also important in understanding the financing of government budget deficits. In some countries the central bank automatically finances the Treasury and, in fact, is subordinated to the Treasury. In the United States, by contrast, the Federal Reserve responds to Congress and the Fed's ability to exercise policy independence is assured by its organization.[19] Such deficits can be financed by the Treasury's borrowing from the public. In that case, the Treasury sells bonds to the public. The public pays for the bonds with checks, which are deposited in a tax and loan account. This, accordingly, does not affect the stock of high-powered money. When the Treasury makes its payments, it moves the money in and out of its Fed account, leaving the monetary base unchanged. Thus, Treasury deficit financing through borrowing from the public has only a temporary effect on the monetary base, and has no effect on the base after the Treasury has used the borrowed funds to make the payments for which the funds were raised.

Alternatively, the Treasury can finance its deficit by borrowing from the Fed. It

[19] See Sayre Ellen Dykes "The Establishment and Evolution of the Federal Reserve Board: 1913–1923," *Federal Reserve Bulletin*, April 1989, and the special issue on the seventy-fifth anniversary of the Fed in the Federal Reserve Bank of New York *Quarterly Review*, Spring 1989.

is simplest to think of the Treasury's selling a bond to the Fed instead of to the public. When the bond is sold, the Fed's holdings of government securities increase, and simultaneously the asset "Net other assets" falls because Treasury deposits, a liability of the Fed, have risen. But then when the Treasury uses the borrowed money to make a payment, the stock of high-powered money rises, just as in Table 11-5. Accordingly, when a budget deficit is financed by the Treasury borrowing from the Fed, the stock of high-powered money is increased.

We sometimes talk of central bank financing of government deficits as financing through the printing of money. It is not necessarily true that the deficit is literally financed by the central bank through the printing of money, but it is true that central bank financing increases the stock of high-powered money, which comes to much the same thing.

The Fed is not legally obliged to finance government deficits by buying bonds. Thus it still retains its ability to control the stock of high-powered money even when the Treasury is running a budget deficit.

Summary

1. The main point of this section is that the Fed controls the stock of high-powered money primarily through open market operations.
2. The Fed has some influence over the stock of high-powered money through the indirect route of changing the discount rate and thereby affecting the volume of member bank borrowing.
3. Treasury financing of its budget deficits through borrowing from the public leaves the stock of high-powered money unaffected, whereas Treasury financing by borrowing from the Fed increases the monetary base.

11-4 THE MULTIPLIER AND THE ADJUSTMENT PROCESS

We now develop the economics of the money multiplier by showing how the interactions of the banks and the public produce a multiple expansion of the money stock. We sketch the argument here and refer to the appendix for the basic equations.

The monetary expansion following an open market operation involves adjustments by banks and the public. When the Fed buys securities from the public, the monetary base is increased. To start with, the increase in the base shows up as an increase in bank reserves. This is because the Fed pays for the securities by writing a check on itself, which the seller of the securities deposits in his or her bank account. The bank in turn will present the check for collection to the Fed and will be credited with an increase in its reserve position at the Fed.

At this stage the public has an increase in deposits without an increase in currency. That means the currency-deposit ratio is out of line — it is too low. The public will therefore convert deposits into currency, thus reducing bank reserves and deposits.

More important in the story is the fact that the bank in which the original check was deposited now has a reserve ratio that is too high. Its reserves and deposits have gone up by the same amount. Therefore, its ratio of reserves to deposits has risen. To reduce the ratio of reserves to deposits, it chooses to expand its loans.

When the bank makes a loan, the person receiving the loan gets a bank deposit. At this stage, when the bank makes a loan, *the money supply has risen by more than the amount of the open market operation.* The person who sold the security to the Fed has increased his or her holdings of money — some in currency and some in deposits — by the value of the bonds sold. The person receiving the loan has a new bank deposit — and thus the process has already generated a multiple expansion of the money stock.

In the subsequent adjustment, part of the increase in high-powered money finds its way into the public's holdings of currency, and part serves as the basis for an expansion of credit by the banking system. Bank loans and purchases of securities are described as *bank credit.* It is the existence of bank credit that makes the money stock larger than the stock of high-powered money. If banks did not extend credit (that is, did not make loans or buy securities), the entire multiple expansion process would never get off the ground, and we would have $M = H$.

When banks make loans, they do so by crediting the deposits of their loan customers with the loan. Since deposits are part of the money supply, banks therefore create money whenever they make loans. The expansion of loans, and hence money, continues until the banking system has increased loans to the point at which the reserve-deposit ratio has fallen to the desired level and the public again has achieved its desired currency-deposit ratio. The money multiplier summarizes the total expansion of money created by a dollar increase in the monetary base.

11-5 THE MONEY SUPPLY FUNCTION AND THE INSTRUMENTS OF MONETARY CONTROL

We have now completed our in-depth examination of the variables in formula (4) for the determinants of the money supply: the currency-deposit ratio (cu), the reserve-deposit ratio (re), and the stock of high-powered money (H). We now return to equation (4) to summarize the discussion by writing a *money supply function* that takes account of the behavior of the banking system and the public:

$$M = \frac{1 + cu}{re + cu} H$$
$$= mm(i,\ i_D,\ r_R,\ cu,\ \sigma)H \tag{5}$$

In equation (5) we have written the money multiplier, *mm*, as a function of interest rates, the discount rate, required reserves, the currency-deposit ratio, and the variability of deposit flows.

Given the stock of high-powered money, the supply of money increases with the money multiplier, *mm.* The multiplier, in turn, increases with the level of market interest rates and decreases with the discount rate, the required reserve ratio, and the currency-deposit ratio. We refer to equation (5) as a supply *function* because it describes the behavior that determines the money supply, given H. Note that the Fed affects the money supply through three routes: H, controlled primarily through open market operations; the discount rate, i_D; and the required reserve ratio, r_R. Of these three *instruments of monetary control,* open market operations are the most frequently used.[20]

Why can the Fed not control the money stock exactly? The reasons emerge by looking at the money multiplier formula in equation (5). We have assumed cu is constant — but, in fact, the public does not keep an exactly constant ratio of currency to deposits, and the Fed does not know in advance exactly what the value of cu will be. Similarly, the reserve ratio, re, varies, both because deposits move among banks with different reserve ratios and because banks change the amount of excess reserves they want to hold.

In brief, the Fed cannot control the money stock exactly because the money multiplier is not constant, nor is it fully predictable.

11-6 EQUILIBRIUM IN THE MONEY MARKET

We can now combine the money supply function in equation (5) with the money demand function developed in Chapter 10 to study money market equilibrium. For that purpose we will assume that the price level is given at the level P_0. Furthermore, for the purposes of this section, we will take the level of real income as given, that is, $Y = Y_0$. With both the price level and level of income fixed, money demand depends only on the interest rate, while the money market equilibrium will determine the equilibrium interest rate and quantity of money for given P_0 and Y_0.

The equilibrium condition in the money market is that the real money supply, M/P, equals the demand for real balances, or

$$\frac{M}{P} = L(i, Y) \tag{6}$$

Substituting expression (5) for M in the money market equilibrium condition (6), and noting that $P = P_0$ and $Y = Y_0$ by assumption, we obtain

$$mm(i, i_D, r_R, cu, \sigma)\frac{H}{P_0} = L(i, Y_0) \tag{7}$$

---

[20] Until 1986 there was a fourth instrument of monetary control. Through its Regulation Q, the Fed controlled the interest rates paid on deposits. By changing the permissible interest rates, the Fed could affect the currency deposit ratio, cu, and thus affect the multiplier. Regulation Q was phased out between 1980 and 1986, leaving the Fed with three major instruments of monetary control.

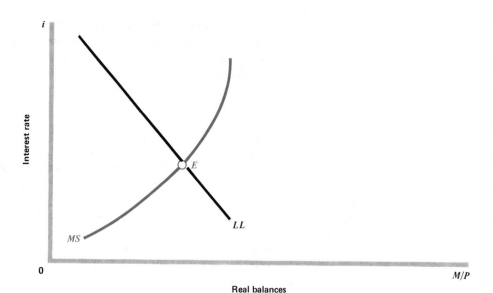

FIGURE 11-3

EQUILIBRIUM IN THE MONEY MARKET. The downward-sloping curve is the demand for money. The quantity of money demanded is greater the lower the interest rate. The upward-sloping curve is the money supply function. This slopes up because, given the quantity of high-powered money, banks reduce their demand for excess reserves when the interest rate rises. Thus the reserve ratio is lower and the money multiplier higher at higher interest rates. The equilibrium interest rate and stock of money are determined at the intersection point, E.

We now have the money market equilibrium condition in terms of interest rates and the other variables affecting the supply of, and demand for, money.

In Figure 11-3 we show the real money demand function (LL) as a downward-sloping schedule, drawn for a given level of real income. The real money supply function (MS), given i_D, r_R, cu, σ, and P_0, is upward-sloping and is drawn for a given stock of high-powered money, H. The positive slope of MS reflects the fact that at higher interest rates banks prefer to hold fewer reserves, so that the money multiplier is higher.[21] The equilibrium money supply and interest rate are jointly determined at point E.

---

[21] At sufficiently high interest rates, the money supply schedule becomes vertical. This is because excess reserves become zero at very high interest rates and the banks cannot squeeze out any more loans on the basis of the reserves they have.

Figure 11-4 shows the effects of an open market purchase on interest rates, given the price level and the level of income. An increase of ΔH in the monetary base shifts the MS curve to the right to MS', increasing the money stock and reducing the interest rate. Because the interest rate falls, the money multiplier declines as a result of the increase in H. But despite the decline in the interest rate, the money stock unquestionably increases.

In Figure 11-4, we, in effect, look at the effects of a change in the stock of high-powered money on the LM curve. Figure 11-5 shows the IS and LM curves. The LM curve represents the combinations of income levels and the interest rate at which the money market is in equilibrium. What happens to the LM curve when the stock of high-powered money is increased? In Figure 11-4 we saw that for any given level of income, Y_0, an increase in H reduces the equilibrium interest rate. That means that the LM curve in Figure 11-5 shifts down to LM' when H increases. The equilibrium shifts from E to E', with output rising and the interest rate falling. Thus our analysis

FIGURE 11-4

THE EFFECTS OF AN INCREASE IN HIGH-POWERED MONEY. From the initial equilibrium at E, an increase in high-powered money shifts the money supply schedule to MS'. The new equilibrium is at E'. The money stock rises, and the equilibrium interest rate declines.

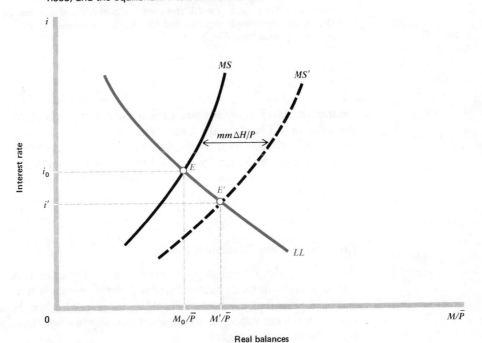

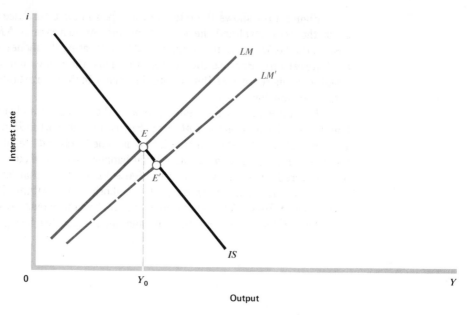

FIGURE 11-5

THE EFFECTS OF AN INCREASE IN THE STOCK OF HIGH-POWERED MONEY. For any given level of output, an increase in the stock of high-powered money reduces the interest rate at which the money market is in equilibrium. That means the *LM* curve shifts down when *H* is increased. The equilibrium interest rate falls and the level of output rises as the economy moves from *E* to *E'*.

confirms that the Fed, by increasing the stock of high-powered money, can reduce the interest rate and increase the level of income.

This is basically what we concluded in Chapter 4, except that there we assumed the Fed controlled the money supply directly. Now we know the Fed does not have such direct control but can, nonetheless, shift the *LM* curve and affect output and the interest rate.

Changes in the Discount Rate

We can also analyze the effects of an increase in the discount rate on the position of the *LM* curve and thus on the interest rate and output. We know from our analysis of the demand for reserves that banks will hold higher reserves when the discount rate rises because it is more expensive to run short of reserves when the cost of borrowing to cover the shortage is higher.

An increase in the discount rate therefore reduces the money multiplier. Figure

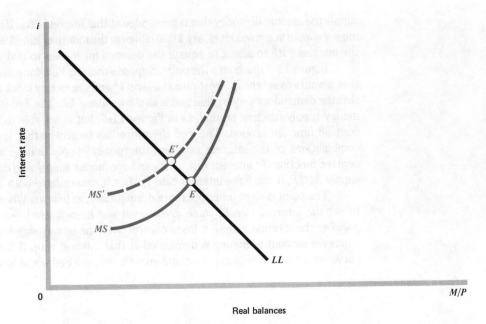

FIGURE 11-6

THE EFFECTS OF AN INCREASE IN THE DISCOUNT RATE. An increase in the discount rate increases the amount of reserves that banks want to hold at each level of market interest rates, i. Thus the money multiplier is reduced, and the money supply function shifts from MS to MS'. Accordingly, the market interest rate rises, and the quantity of real balances falls. Increasing the discount rate is a contractionary monetary policy.

11-6 shows in terms of the money market, at a given level of income, that the money supply curve shifts up to MS'. The interest rate rises at the given level of income. In terms of the IS-LM analysis, the LM curve would therefore move to the left (we do not show this here, but ask you to do so in problem 12), the interest rate would rise, and output would fall. Thus an increase in the discount rate is a contractionary monetary policy.

11-7 CONTROL OF THE MONEY STOCK AND CONTROL OF THE INTEREST RATE

We make a simple but important point in this section: The Fed cannot simultaneously set both the interest rate and the stock of money at any given target levels that it may choose. If the Fed wants to achieve a given interest rate target, say 8 percent, it has to supply the amount of money that is demanded at that interest rate. If it wants to set the money supply at a given level, say $950 billion in the month of June 1991, it has to allow the interest rate to adjust to equate the demand for money to that supply of money.

Figure 11-7 illustrates the point. Suppose that the Fed, for some reason, decides that it wants to set the interest rate at a level i^* and the money stock at a level M^*, but that the demand-for-money function is as shown along LL. The Fed is able to move the money supply function around, as in Figure 11-5, but is not able to move the money demand function around. The Fed therefore has to accept that it can set only the combinations of the interest rate and the money supply that lie along the money demand function. At interest rate i^*, it can have money supply $M_0/\overline{P}$. At target money supply $M^*/\overline{P}$, it can have interest rate i_0. But it cannot have both $M^*/\overline{P}$ and i^*.

The point is sometimes put more dramatically, as follows. When the Fed decides to set the interest rate at some given level and keep it fixed — a policy known as *pegging* the interest rate — it loses control over the money supply. It has to supply whatever amount of money is demanded at that interest rate. If the money demand curve were to shift, because of income growth, say, the Fed would have to increase the

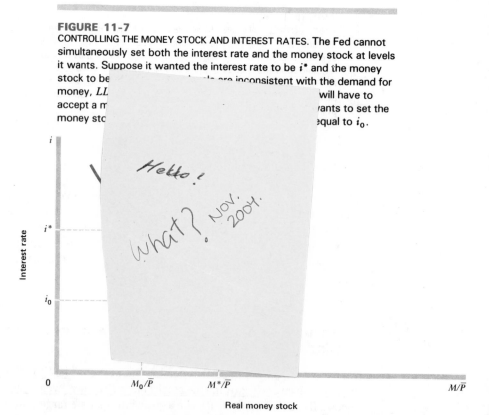

FIGURE 11-7
CONTROLLING THE MONEY STOCK AND INTEREST RATES. The Fed cannot simultaneously set both the interest rate and the money stock at levels it wants. Suppose it wanted the interest rate to be i^* and the money stock to be ⟨...⟩ are inconsistent with the demand for money, LL ⟨...⟩ will have to accept a m⟨...⟩ants to set the money sto⟨...⟩ equal to i_0.

stock of high-powered money to increase the money supply to the new, higher level demanded at the pegged interest rate.

As an operational matter, the Fed in its day-to-day operations can more easily control interest rates exactly than it can control the money stock exactly. The Fed buys and sells government securities through its *open market desk* in the New York Fed every day. If the Fed wanted to raise the price of government securities (lower the interest rate), it would have to buy the securities at the price it wanted. If it wanted to reduce prices of government securities (raise the interest rate), it would sell a sufficient amount of securities from its large portfolio. Thus, on a day-to-day basis, the Fed can determine the federal funds rate quite accurately at the level it chooses.[22]

However, the Fed cannot determine the money supply precisely on a day-to-day basis. For one thing, there is a lag in obtaining data on the money stock. Some time must pass before reasonably good money supply data for a given date become available. That would not affect the Fed's ability to control the money stock if the money multiplier were constant, for then the Fed would be able to deduce, from the behavior of the monetary base, what the money stock was. But as we have seen earlier, the multiplier is not constant. It varies as a result of changes in the currency-deposit and reserve-deposit ratios.

These are *technical* reasons why the Fed cannot control the money supply exactly in the sense that the Fed cannot hit the target stock of money exactly even if it wants to. But over a slightly longer period, the Fed can determine the money supply fairly accurately. As data on the behavior of the money stock and the money multiplier become available, the Fed can make midcourse corrections to its setting of the base. For example, if the Fed were aiming for monetary growth of 5 percent over a given period, it might start the base growing at 5 percent. If it found halfway into the period that the multiplier had been falling, and the money stock therefore growing by less than 5 percent, the Fed would step up the growth rate of the base to compensate.

The main reasons the Fed does not hit its money growth targets are not technical, but rather have to do with its having both interest rate *and* money stock targets, and as we have seen in this section, it cannot hit them both at the same time.

11-8 MONEY STOCK AND INTEREST RATE TARGETS

Over the period since the 1950s, the emphasis the Fed has placed on controlling the interest rate versus controlling the money supply has changed. Initially the emphasis was almost entirely on interest rates[23] — indeed, it was not until 1959 that the Fed even began to publish money stock data. Until 1982 there was a more or less steadily increasing emphasis on monetary targets. Since 1982 the emphasis has shifted back

---

[22] For a description of techniques of monetary control, see Daniel Thornton, "The Borrowed-Reserves Operating Procedure: Theory and Evidence," Federal Reserve Bank of St. Louis *Review,* January/February 1988.

[23] And also on bank credit, a topic to which we return below.

—though only part of the way—toward interest rates and toward a more eclectic approach to monetary policy.[24]

In this section we discuss the issues involved in the choice between interest rate and money stock targets.

Making Monetary Policy

Monetary policy is made by the Fed's Open Market Committee (FOMC), which meets eight times a year and also holds frequent consultations between meetings. At these meetings the Fed issues a *monetary policy directive* to the open market desk in New York, describing the type of monetary policy it wants.[25]

In recent years, the directive has instructed the open market desk to conduct open market operations to produce money stock growth within given target ranges. The target ranges since 1976, for M_1 and M_2, are given in Table 11-6. The Fed specifies, in addition, target ranges for $M3$ and, since 1982, for total nonfinancial debt in the economy. This latter total is the amount of lending to spending units in the economy. In addition, the committee specifies a range within which it expects interest rates to be during the period until the next meeting. If interest rates threaten to move outside the range, the committee members will typically consult (on the telephone) and decide whether to change the instructions to the open market desk.

Two features stand out in Table 11-6. First, comparison of actual money growth rates with target ranges makes it hard to believe the Fed treated the target ranges for M_1 very seriously: in 8 of the 11 years shown the Fed exceeded the target ranges for M_1. The record for M_2 is better, but even in that case there is a persistent tendency for the actual growth rate to be at the top end of or above the target range. The second feature is that in 1987 the Fed stopped specifying targets for M_1. That is because the velocity of M_1 became very unstable. We now examine the implications for the conduct of monetary policy of instability in the demand for money.

Interest Rate or Money Targets?

There are two levels on which the discussion of interest rate versus money targets proceeds. The first is at the technical level of the open market desk. The question here is whether a given target level of the money stock can be attained more accurately by holding the interest rate fixed or by fixing H. The second level is that of the economy as

---

[24] For the recent history, see Ann-Marie Meulendyke, "A Review of Federal Reserve Policy Targets and Operating Guides in Recent Decades," Federal Reserve Bank of New York *Quarterly Review,* Autumn 1988. See also Michelle R. Garfinkel, "The FOMC in 1988: Uncertainty's Effects on Monetary Policy," Federal Reserve Bank of St. Louis *Review,* March/April 1989.

[25] A summary of the FOMC's discussions and the directive are published in the *Federal Reserve Bulletin.* You may find it useful to read one of these reports, to see if you can interpret the Fed's arguments.

TABLE 11-6

TARGET AND ACTUAL GROWTH RATES OF MONEY*

Period	M1		M2	
	Target range	Actual	Target range	Actual
1976	4.5–7.5	5.8	7.5–10.5	10.9
1977	4.5–6.5	7.9	7–10	9.8
1978	4–6.5	7.2	6.5–9	8.7
1979	1.5–4.5	7.7	5–8	8.2
1980	4–6.5	7.4	6–9	9.0
1981	3.5–6	5.2	6–9	9.3
1982	2.5–5.5	8.7	6–9	9.1
1983	4–8	10.2	7–10	12.1
1984	4–8	5.3	6–9	7.7
1985	4–7	12.0	6–9	8.9
1986	3–8	15.6	6–9	9.3
1987		6.4	5.5–8.5	4.2
1988		4.3	4–8	5.3
1989			3–7	

* Money definitions are those in effect at the time targets were set. Rates are for a 1-year period ending in the fourth quarter of the specified year.

SOURCE: Various issues of the *Federal Reserve Bulletin*.

a whole. The question here is whether the Fed makes the economy more stable by aiming for a particular money stock or for a particular interest rate. The analyses for evaluating these questions are similar. In the text we present the second issue, leaving the first to be examined in problem 15 at the end of this chapter.

We assume that the Fed's aim is for the economy to reach a particular level of output. The question is whether the Fed can do that more accurately by targeting the money stock or by fixing interest rates. We should think of the analysis as applying to a reasonably short period such as 3 to 9 months.[26]

Figure 11-8 starts with the *IS* and *LM* curves. Recall that the *LM* curve shows combinations of the interest rate and output at which the money market is in equilibrium. The *LM* curve labeled *LM(M)* is the *LM* curve that exists when the Fed fixes the money stock. The *LM* curve labeled *LM(i)* describes money market equilibrium when the Fed fixes the interest rate. It is horizontal at the chosen level of the interest rate, *i**.

---

[26] The analysis we are presenting here is based on William Poole, "Optimal Choice of Monetary Policy Instruments in a Simple Stochastic Macro Model," *Quarterly Journal of Economics*, May 1970.

The problem for policy is that the IS and LM curves shift in ways that cannot be predicted. When they shift, output ends up at a level different from the target level. In Figure 11-8 a we show two alternative positions for the IS curve: IS_1 and IS_2. We assume that the Fed does not know in advance which IS curve will obtain: the position depends, for instance, on investment demand, which is difficult to predict. The Fed's aim is to have income come out as close as possible to the target level, Y^*.

In Figure 11-8 a we see that the level of output stays closer to Y^* if the LM curve is $LM(M)$. In that case the level of output will be Y_1 if the IS curve is IS_1 and Y_2 if the IS curve is IS_2. If policy had kept the interest rate constant, we would in each case have a level of income that is further from Y^*: Y_1' instead of Y_1, and Y_2' instead of Y_2.

Thus we have our first conclusion: If output deviates from its equilibrium level

FIGURE 11-8

MONEY AND INTEREST RATE TARGETS. In panel (a), the IS curve shifts. If the Fed targets the money stock, the LM curve is shown by $LM(M)$. $LM(i)$ is the LM curve when the interest rate is held constant. The aim of policy is to hit output level Y^*. If the LM curve is $LM(M)$, the output levels will be either Y_1 or Y_2, depending on where the IS curve turns out to be. In the case of an interest rate target, the corresponding levels of output are Y_1' and Y_2', both further from the desired level of output, Y^*. Thus, monetary targeting leads to more stable output behavior. In panel (b) it is the LM curve that is shifting, because of shifts in the demand for money. With LM shifting and the IS curve stable, output will be at the target level Y^* if the interest rate is held constant at i^*, but will be at either Y_1 or Y_2 if the money stock is held constant. Therefore, the Fed should target the interest rate if the demand-for-money function is unstable.

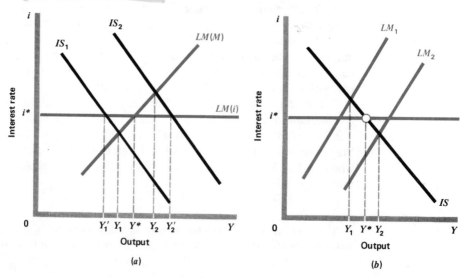

(a)

(b)

mainly because the *IS* curve shifts about, then output is stabilized by keeping the money stock constant. The Fed should, in this case, have monetary targets.

We can see from Figure 11-8*a* why it is more stabilizing to keep *M* rather than *i* constant. When the *IS* curve shifts to the right and the *LM*(*M*) curve applies, the interest rate rises, thereby reducing investment demand and moderating the effect of the shift. But if the *LM*(*i*) curve applies, there is no resistance from monetary policy to the effects of the *IS* shift. Monetary policy is thus automatically stabilizing in Figure 11-8*a* when the *IS* curve shifts and the money stock is held constant.

In Figure 11-8*b* we assume that the *IS* curve is stable. Now the uncertainty about the effects of monetary policy results from shifts in the *LM* curve. Assuming that the Fed can fix the money stock, the *LM* curve shifts because the money demand function shifts. The Fed does not know when it sets the money stock what the interest rate will be. The *LM* curve could end up being either LM_1 or LM_2. Alternatively the Fed could simply fix the interest rate at level $i*$. That would ensure that the level of output is $Y*$.

If the Fed were to fix the money stock, output could be either Y_1 or Y_2. If it fixes the interest rate, output will be $Y*$. Thus we have our second conclusion: If output deviates from its equilibrium level mainly because the demand-for-money function shifts about, then the Fed should operate monetary policy by fixing the interest rate. That way it automatically neutralizes the effects of the shifts in money demand. In this case the Fed should have interest rate targets.

It is important to note that the argument discusses Fed targeting over short periods. The Fed should readjust its targets in light of the changing behavior of the economy. The Fed is *not* to be thought of as announcing or desiring that the interest rate will be, say, 8 percent forever. Rather, the target interest rate might be 5 percent at the bottom of a recession and 15 percent when the economy is overheating. Similarly, the money growth targets could also be adjusted in response to the state of the economy.

The Poole analysis can also be used to explain why the Fed stopped specifying M_1 targets from 1987 on, while continuing to target M_2 (and M_3 and total nonfinancial debt). The increasing instability of the demand for M_1 limited its usefulness as a monetary target. Indeed, the increasing instability of demand for all the monetary aggregates has led the Fed to place less weight on monetary targets in the period since 1982 than it did between 1979 and 1982 (see Box 11-3).

THE SHORT RUN AND THE LONG RUN

The Poole analysis describes well the reasons why the Fed might choose either the money stock or the interest rate as a target at which to aim over a period of less than a year. In particular, at a time when money demand is shifting a lot — as it did in the seventies and eighties — the Fed should pay attention to the behavior of interest rates. The reason is that when money demand is shifting, it is hard to evaluate the meaning of money stock data.

Suppose the Fed is aiming for nominal GNP to increase by 8 percent per year, and has decided that achieving that target requires money growth of 8 percent. Suppose the money stock is growing at 8 percent. However, nominal GNP is increasing

box 11-3 **THE MONETARY POLICY EPISODE OF 1979–1982**

In October 1979 the Fed announced a major change in monetary policy: It would henceforth stay close to its target path for the money stock and allow interest rates to fluctuate more than in the past. The change was made at a time of high inflation (the consumer price index — CPI — inflation rate over 1979 was more than 13 percent).

The Fed, under the chairmanship of Paul Volcker, made the change as part of its program to fight inflation. It wanted to get the inflation rate down, and it wanted everyone to understand that it was committed to doing so, even if that meant interest rates had to reach very high levels.

The change in monetary policy was evident in the increase in the ranges the Fed presented for target levels of the interest rate. Up to the end of 1979, the Fed had specified a narrow range of about 0.5 percent within which the interest rate (the federal funds rate) would be allowed to move. And the rate was kept reasonably close to the target range. After the reform the range increased to 5 percent, and large swings in interest rates indeed occurred. Thus the announced change in monetary policy operating procedures was certainly followed by much larger interest rate fluctuations than before.

But the change did not lead to more stable monetary growth. Figure 1 shows graphically what can also be seen in Table 11-6: The Fed came no closer to hitting its money targets after 1979 than it did before. Note also that the Fed typically went above its target range for the money stock.

In the fall of 1982 the Fed announced that it was increasing its money targets for the year above the level that had been announced at the end of 1981. Similarly, in the middle of 1985 the money target for 1985 was increased. On both occasions the reason was an apparent shift in the demand function for money, a reduction in velocity. In the fall of 1982 the economy was in a deep recession, which the Fed feared would get worse unless the growth rate of money were sharply increased to offset the apparent decline in velocity. In 1985 the Fed feared that the recovery would be aborted because of the unexpected decline in velocity, and it pumped up money growth accordingly.

In both cases the Fed seems to have done the right thing. Further monetary restraint in the fall of 1982 would have worsened the recession. Instead, the rapid money growth aided a vigorous recovery. In the middle of 1985 the economy was growing slowly, a recession was possible, and the Fed acted. GNP growth for the remainder of the year was moderate, and there was no resurgence of inflation as critics of the Fed had predicted. ·

by only 4 percent and the economy is in a recession. That could easily happen because the demand for money has been shifting, increasing the quantity demanded at any given interest rate. How could the Fed tell things are going wrong? By looking at interest rates. If there has been a shift in money demand, increasing the quantity demanded at any interest rate, the interest rate will rise. If the Fed were paying attention to the behavior of the interest rate, it would automatically adjust the money stock to account for that shift in money demand. That is why interest rate targets are useful.

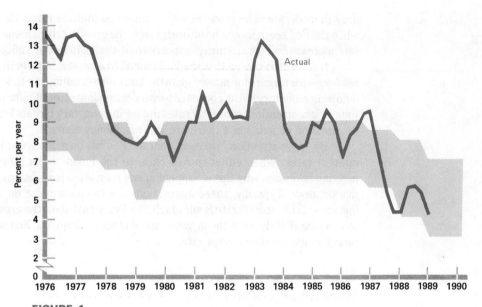

FIGURE 1

TARGET AND ACTUAL MONEY STOCK (*M*2), 1979–1989. The band shows
the target zone for *M*2 growth rates. The actual growth rate of *M*2
(over 4 quarters) occasionally passes outside the range. (SOURCE:
DRI/McGraw-Hill and various issues of the *Federal Reserve Bulletin*.)

The Fed's willingness since 1982 to give up its money targets when circumstances warrant suggests that the 1979 change in monetary policy lasted only 3 years. During that period the Fed succeeded in creating the recession that brought the inflation rate down from around 12 percent per year to the present 3 to 4 percent. With inflation lower, the Fed felt able to reduce the emphasis on money growth. In the late 1980s, the Fed's target ranges for the money stock do little other than describe what the Fed will be doing until it seems reasonable to change policy.   ■

But monetarist proponents of money stock targeting have another argument in favor of targeting the money stock. They might concede that in the short run the Fed may do better targeting interest rates. But, they say, a policy of targeting interest rates can over long periods lead to big trouble by steadily raising the growth rate of money. They point, rightly, to the fact that changes in monetary policy take a long time to affect the economy. They argue that increases in the money stock lead eventually to inflation and that the only way to avoid inflation in the long run is by keeping money growth moderate. The problem with focusing on interest rates, they suggest, is that while the Fed keeps its eye on interest rates, the growth rate of money and the inflation rate increase.[27] This argument appears to fit the facts of the 1960s and 1970s well.

It is for that reason that the Fed moved to a two-track targeting system and has set *long-run* targets for money growth. Thus it has continually to worry whether it is following monetary paths consistent with desired low rates of inflation.[28] At the same time it pays attention to interest rates in case its monetary targets lead in the short run to recession or inflation if there are shifts in money demand.

By "pays attention" we mean that the Fed has target ranges for both money and interest rates. When either moves close to the limits of the range, the Fed has a meeting to discuss why this is happening and then gives fresh instructions to the open market desk. Typically, these instructions are to compromise on both targets. For instance, if the interest rate is very high, the Fed would allow the growth rate of money to increase slightly. Or if the growth rate of money is high, the Fed would increase the target range for the interest rate.

Monetarism and the Fed

Since the 1960s the Fed has been criticized by monetarists, who argue that it should conduct monetary policy by targeting the money stock (typically either M_1 or M_2). The monetarist criticism seemed to be having an impact as the Fed adopted monetary targets in the 1970s and then in 1979 announced that it was giving them greater weight. Even so the monetarist critics were not impressed, describing the Fed's use of monetary targets as "rhetorical camouflage,"[29] a perfectly reasonable comment.

Their criticisms of the Fed's monetary policy take place at several levels. First, as noted above, monetarists argue that the Fed's propensity to try to stabilize interest rates tends to make it follow inflationary policies. Whether that criticism is justified in the 1980s is unclear. Certainly the inflation rate in the long expansion from 1982 to 1989 stayed low even as the economy in 1989 reached the lowest unemployment rate in 15 years.

In reply to the analysis that shows the interest rate as a good guide for monetary policy when money demand is unstable, critics of the Fed argue that velocity changes are infrequent. The instability of the demand for M_1 in the 1980s makes this claim less

---

[27] Another argument for money targeting arises from the distinction between real and nominal interest rates. The nominal interest rate can rise because inflation is expected. If the Fed fights this increase in the nominal rate by increasing the money stock, it is only feeding the inflation. We examine this argument in more detail in Chap. 14.

[28] A comprehensive discussion of monetary policy and the Fed's operating procedures, generally critical of monetary targeting, is presented in Ralph C. Bryant, *Controlling Money. The Federal Reserve and Its Critics* (Washington, D.C.: The Brookings Institution, 1983). See also Bennett T. McCallum, "On Consequences and Criticisms of Monetary Targeting," *Journal of Money, Credit and Banking,* November 1985, part 2, and the subsequent comments and discussion.

[29] Milton Friedman, "The Fed Hasn't Changed Its Ways," *Wall Street Journal,* August 20, 1985.

plausible, though of course that instability results in part from deregulation of interest rates. Monetarists such as Allan Meltzer of Carnegie-Mellon argue now that the Fed should target the growth rate of M_2. Further, they contend, money demand would be more stable if the Fed followed steady policies.

At a second level, monetarist critics argue that the Fed's operating procedures — the procedures by which it attempts to control the money stock — are technically defective.[30] Changes would enable it to hit its targets more accurately, if it wanted to.

There is a more basic monetarist criticism. It argues that the Fed should simply attempt to keep the growth rate of money constant, quarter by quarter and year by year, rather than change its targets frequently. The argument is that policy that reacts to the way the economy is behaving ends up causing more instability rather than less.

Within this overall criticism, a particular complaint about the Fed's targeting procedure has received considerable attention.

BASE DRIFT AND THE FAN

The criticism is that the Fed's money targeting procedures provide no long-run assurance of what the money supply will be. The argument can be seen in Figure 11-9. The key point is that the Fed sets its target range for a given year on the basis of where the money stock is at the end of the previous year.

Suppose the starting point for 1990 is *A*, with a target range of 4 to 7 percent money growth over the next year. The figure shows values of the money stock consistent with the target range by the shaded, fan-shaped area *ABC*. One year later the Fed is at *B*, the top of its range. At that point the Fed will announce its targets for 1991, *starting from point B*. Now there is a new fan-shaped target area, *BDE*, also shaded. Continuing, we see that the procedure of starting from wherever the money stock is at the end of the year allows the money stock to wander very far from a path of growing at the rate of 5.5 percent per year, which presumably is the target that the Fed intends when it announces a range of 4 to 7 percent. In effect, the fan keeps fanning.

The alternative preferred by critics of the Fed's procedure is that the Fed should announce a target *band* around a growth path of, say, 5.5 percent. That band is shown in Figure 11-9 by the dashed lines. The money stock will always be within say, 1.5 percent of the target path of 5.5 percent growth under the band procedure. The difference between the fan and the band procedures is that under the band, the Fed commits itself each year to try to come back to the original target path by correcting the deviation of the previous year. Under the fan approach, past misses are ignored, and the target is reset each year.

The process followed by the Fed allows *base drift*. The base is not the monetary base, but rather the baseline to which the money stock target is reset. Under the band, the base stays fixed. Under the fan, the base shifts, or drifts.[31]

---

[30] Meulendyke, referred to above, provides a brief review of these procedures.

[31] For more on base drift, see Alfred Broaddus and Marvin Goodfriend, "Base Drift and Longer Run Growth of M1: Experience from a Decade of Monetary Targeting," Federal Reserve Bank of Richmond *Economic Review,* November/December 1984.

Which is the better procedure? That depends on the reason the Fed missed the target in the first place. If it was responding to shifts in velocity, the choice depends on the nature of shocks to velocity. If velocity shocks are transitory, then fanning allows nominal GNP to wander over time from its target path. If shocks to velocity are permanent, then fanning is better because it keeps nominal GNP closer to its target level over time. In practice some velocity shocks will be permanent—for instance, those associated with changes in regulations—and some transitory. So there is no hard and fast rule for whether a particular velocity change should be incorporated into the target money stock.

Our own views in this area are that rigid commitment to monetary targets is unwise in light of shifts in the money demand function and that the Fed should target interest rates as well as the stock of money. We note also that on a year-to-year basis (excepting the period of deregulation in 1981–1983) the Fed has maintained quite stable growth of M_2—not much different from that of other leading countries, such as Japan and Germany. The Fed thus does not let money growth get out of hand. If the growth rate is very high for a short time, the growth rate will typically later be reduced to compensate for the high growth and bring the money stock closer to target.

FIGURE 11-9

THE FAN VERSUS THE BAND IN MONEY TARGETING, OR BASE DRIFT. The Fed's target range for 1990, starting from *A*, is shown by the fan *ABC*. At the end of the year the money stock is *B*. The Fed then announces a new target range, which implies the fan *BDE*. The alternative is to fix a band around a target path for the money stock, as shown by the dashed lines. That way the money stock cannot wander far from its original target path.

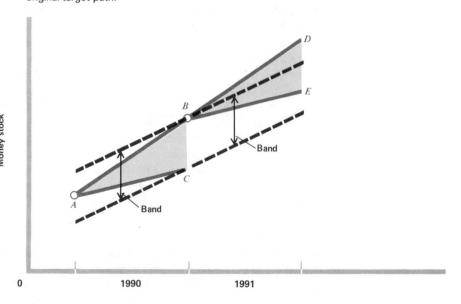

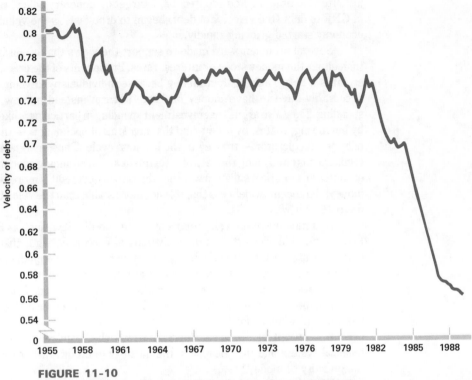

FIGURE 11-10
THE RATIO OF GNP TO PRIVATE DEBT, 1956–1989. (SOURCE: DRI/McGraw-Hill.)

11-9 MONEY, CREDIT, AND INTEREST RATES

The Fed targets not only M_2 and M_3, but also the increase in total debt of the nonfinancial sectors, that is, the debt of the government, households, and firms other than financial firms. The debt of the government, households, and firms is equal to the credit (lending) that has been extended to them. Thus the Fed can also be described as having credit targets.

Why? In the first instance, this is a very old approach of the Fed, which had credit targets already in the 1950s. The Fed returned to them in 1982 in part because of econometric evidence by Benjamin Friedman[32] showing that there was a tighter link between the volume of debt in the economy and GNP than between money and nominal GNP. As shown in Figure 11-10, the velocity of debt was remarkably stable up to 1983,

---

[32] "The Roles of Money and Credit in Macroeconomic Analysis," in James Tobin (ed.), *Macroeconomics, Prices, and Quantities* (Washington, D.C.: The Brookings Institution, 1983).

just after the time the Fed adopted it as a target of monetary policy. But then the ratio of GNP to debt (the velocity of debt) began to drop fast, as the volume of debt in the economy started growing rapidly.[33]

Several arguments are made to support the views that credit is a better target than either the money stock or interest rates. Proponents of the credit view argue that credit is a better target than money because individuals who want to spend do not necessarily have to have money on hand, but can instead borrow to finance their spending. They also argue that investment spending in particular is likely to be financed by borrowing, that is, by credit, and that investment spending is — through the multiplier and accelerator — the key to the business cycle. Thus, maintaining control over credit means controlling the rate of investment and maintaining economic stability. It is of course an empirical question whether the velocity of credit is more stable than that of money: the recent evidence is that it is not more stable than the velocity of M_2, though up to 1982 it was.

At a fundamental level, proponents of the credit view, such as Ben Bernanke of Princeton and Mark Gertler of the University of Wisconsin, argue that investment and output are significantly affected by the extent of financial intermediation — the volume of lending and borrowing through financial institutions — in the economy. Financial intermediation occurs when financial institutions channel funds from savers to investors, as depository institutions do when they lend funds deposited with them to borrowers who want to invest. Bernanke's research suggests that a large part of the decline in output in the great depression was the result of the breakdown of the financial system and the collapse in the quantity of credit, rather than the decline in the quantity of money.[34]

The view that credit is a better target than interest rates results from the phenomenon of *credit rationing,* already discussed in Chapter 9. Credit is rationed when individuals who want to borrow at a given interest rate are not able to borrow as much as they want. Credit is rationed because lenders fear that borrowers who are willing to borrow may nonetheless not be able to repay. But if credit is rationed at a given interest rate, then that interest rate does not fully describe the impact of monetary policy on investment and aggregate demand. The Fed should rather, argue proponents of the credit view, focus directly on the volume of credit to see what impact

---

[33] This is another example of the operation of Goodhart's law, which is due to Charles Goodhart of the London School of Economics. The law, a cousin of Murphy's law, states that the behavior of any variable will change as soon as it becomes a target of economic policy.

[34] Ben Bernanke, "Non-Monetary Effects of the Financial Crisis in the Propagation of the Great Depression," *American Economic Review,* June 1983. See, too, Ben Friedman, "Monetary Policy Without Quantity Variables," *American Economic Review,* May 1988; Karl Brunner and Allan Meltzer, "Money and Credit in the Transmission Process," *American Economic Review,* May 1988; Joseph Stiglitz, "Money, Credit and Business Fluctuations," NBER Working Paper 2823, (Cambridge, Mass.: National Bureau of Economic Research, January 1989); Mark Gertler, "Financial Structure and Aggregate Economic Activity: An Overview," *Journal of Money, Credit and Banking,* August 1988, part 2; and Mark Gertler and R. Glenn Hubbard, "Financial Factors in Business Fluctuations," in Federal Reserve Bank of Kansas, *Financial Market Volatility,* 1989.

monetary policy is having on demand. Box 9-1 explained credit rationing in more detail.

What do these arguments imply for the importance of credit and for monetary policy? First, there is no question that a well-functioning financial system is important for the efficient allocation of investment in the economy and that a collapse of the financial system, and thus of credit, can indeed severely reduce investment and GNP. Second, credit rationing does take place, and the extent of credit rationing varies with the lenders' views of economic prospects. Thus, the volume of credit is likely to contain relevant information about the impact of monetary policy on the economy. Third, in practice the velocity of credit has not recently been stable. Fourth, the Fed does not directly control the quantity of credit, since the overall volume of lending and borrowing in the economy is not under its direct control. These conflicting considerations suggest we need to take a closer look at the notion of targets of monetary policy.

11-10 WHICH TARGETS FOR THE FED?

The Fed sets target ranges for M_2, M_3, and debt growth, as well as ranges for interest rates. It typically fails to hit most of the targets. Why would it need so many targets? should it have fewer or only one? and if so which?[35]

There are three points to note before we get down to the details:

1. A key distinction is between *ultimate targets* of policy and *intermediate targets*. Ultimate targets are variables such as the inflation rate and the unemployment rate (or real output) whose behavior matters. The interest rate or the rate of growth of money or debt or credit are intermediate targets of policy — targets the Fed aims at only so that it can hit the ultimate targets more accurately. The discount rate, open market operations, and reserve requirements are the instruments the Fed has with which to hit the targets.
2. It is also essential to know how often the targets are reset. If the intermediate target is reset frequently, such as every month, it does not much matter what intermediate target is being used, provided the ultimate targets — for example, inflation and unemployment — are given. That is because the intermediate target can be reset as needed to be consistent with the ultimate targets. But if the intermediate targets are held constant for a long period, then the choice of target matters. For instance, if the Fed were to commit itself to 5.5 percent money growth over a period of several years, it would have to be sure that the velocity of money was not going to change unpredictably; otherwise, the actual level of GNP would be far different from the targeted level.
3. In an ideal world, there would be no need for targeting. If the Fed had the right ultimate goals in mind and knew how the economy worked, it would do whatever was needed to keep the economy as close to its ultimate targets as possible.

[35] See Edward Kane, "Selecting Monetary Targets in a Changing Financial Environment," in Federal Reserve Bank of Kansas, *Monetary Policy Issues in the 1980s,* 1983.

box 11-4 CHANGING FED TARGETS AND MONEY STOCK ANNOUNCEMENTS

On Thursdays at 4 P.M. the Fed announces the amount of the money supply. From 1979, when the Fed announced its change in monetary policy, until sometime in the mid-1980s, the announcements would have immediate effects — within minutes or even seconds — on interest rates, the stock market, commodity prices, and exchange rates. When the money stock was unexpectedly high, short-term interest rates increased; when the money stock was unexpectedly low, interest rates fell. In recent years, and especially since Paul Volcker was replaced as chairperson of the Federal Reserve Board by Alan Greenspan, the financial markets have paid more attention to announcements of the U.S. balance of trade, inflation data, and the unemployment rate.

Why did markets react to money supply announcements, and why now do they pay more attention to other variables? The markets reacted to money supply announcements during the period when the Fed was believed to be paying serious attention to its monetary targets. They react now to other variables because the markets believe the Fed will react to those variables more than to money stock announcements.

Consider first the money stock announcements. The point of departure is a distinction between expected and unexpected announcements. Let M be the actual announcement and M' the market's expectations, or guess, of what the announcement would turn out to be. The difference between these two is called the *unanticipated increase in the money supply*, or simply *news;* thus $(M - M')$ = news. Researchers can actually measure news because there are weekly survey data on the market's expectations, M', which, in combination with the actual announcement, M, yield a series for news.

Whenever the money supply announcement would come out large relative to the expected money supply, interest rates would increase, the dollar would strengthen, and stock prices would fall. Note in particular the apparent reversal of the normal relationship between the money stock and interest rates. Increases in the money stock *reduce* interest rates according to the *IS-LM* model. Yet the announcement that the money stock was high would *increase* the interest rate.

Several theories were advanced to explain this phenomenon. Each relies on the fact that markets look forward and are trying to predict the state of the money market — in particular, interest rates — over the coming weeks and months. We develop two of those theories.

So what is the point of targeting? Intermediate targets give the Fed something concrete and specific to aim for in the next year. That has the advantage of enabling the Fed itself to know where it wants to go. The targets also help the private sector know what to expect for the future. If the Fed announces and will stick to its targets, firms and consumers have a better idea of what monetary policy will be. Of course, since the private sector is interested in future levels of prices and output rather than future monetary policy, it would not help the private sector much to know about future

The first hypothesis focuses on the Fed. If the Fed follows a target path for money and it turns out that money was unexpectedly high relative to that path, the market will assume that the Fed will try to pull money growth back down to the target path in the period ahead. The announcement of high $(M - M')$ therefore conveys the news that the Fed will tighten monetary policy, reducing the supply of money. This implies that future interest rates will be higher. Anyone who had expected to borrow will immediately rush to do so before rates rise. And, of course, the rush will raise rates instantly. This explanation would be expected to have particular force when the Fed sticks very tightly to targets for monetary aggregates, as for example in the period 1979–1982.

The second argument draws on a tight and rapid link between changes in the money supply and inflation: Unanticipatedly high money leads the market to revise upward its estimate of inflation. At going interest rates it becomes more profitable to borrow and hold goods or stocks that are expected to appreciate. The increased borrowing in turn pushes up interest rates immediately.

Empirical research* focused on three issues. First, is it *only* the news that explains changes in interest rates or asset prices, or does the anticipated part of the announcement also have an effect? The evidence suggests that both the news and the expected change in money affects interest rates. Second, the research results tended to support the first hypothesis rather than the second; that is, it did not support the view that interest rates rose because of concern over future inflation.

In addition, the research examined whether the response of interest rates and asset prices in news changed as Fed policy changed. That third question appears to be settled by virtue of the fact that the markets have lost interest in the money supply announcement and now focus on other macroeconomic data. The markets do that because they know the Fed will respond to the trade balance, the inflation rate, and the rate of unemployment. A greater trade deficit, higher inflation, and lower unemployment all tend to make the Fed tighten monetary policy and raise interest rates. With the Fed paying more attention to the behavior of the ultimate targets of monetary policy than it did in the early 1980s, there is less reason to respond to the intermediate targets than there used to be. ■

---

* A good summary of this research is presented in R. Sheehan, "Weekly Money Supply Announcements: New Information and Its Effects," Federal Reserve Bank of St. Louis *Review*, August/September 1985. See, too, the comment by B. Falk and P. Orazem and the reply by B. Cornell in *American Economic Review*, June 1985; and G. Dwyer and R. Hafer, "Interest Rates and Economic Announcements," Federal Reserve Bank of St. Louis *Review*, March/April 1989.

monetary policy unless that policy increased the predictability of future output and prices.

Another benefit of specifying targets for monetary policy is that the Fed can then be held *accountable* for its actions. It has a job to do. By announcing targets the Fed makes it possible for outsiders to discuss whether it is aiming in the right direction. In addition, the targets make it possible to judge whether the Fed succeeds in its aims.

The ideal intermediate target is a variable that the Fed can control exactly and that at the same time has an exact relationship with the ultimate targets of policy. For instance, if the ultimate target could be expressed as some particular level of nominal GNP, and if the money multiplier and velocity were both constant, the Fed could hit its ultimate target by having the money base as its intermediate target.

In practice, life is not so simple. Rather, in choosing intermediate targets, the Fed has to trade off between those targets it can control exactly and those targets that are most closely related to its ultimate targets.

Sometimes proposed, at one extreme, is *monetary base targeting*. The Fed can essentially control the monetary base exactly. If that were the intermediate target, the Fed would have no trouble hitting the bull's eye. Further, it could certainly be held accountable for not hitting the target, since it could not plausibly blame factors beyond its control for any failures.

The problem with monetary base targeting is that the Fed might be hitting the bull's eye on the money base target while completely missing the ultimate targets of policy. Unpredictable changes in the money multiplier and in velocity break the tight link between the money base and nominal GNP.

Nominal GNP targeting is at the other end of the tradeoff. In this scheme the Fed would announce a target path for nominal GNP—for instance, that it wants nominal GNP to grow by 10 percent—and then set the money stock to try to achieve that goal. By targeting nominal GNP growth, the Fed would be aiming at both inflation and real output goals. Relative to money stock targeting, nominal GNP targeting implies that the Fed automatically adjusts money targets for velocity shifts.

In addition, nominal GNP targeting builds in an automatic policy tradeoff between inflation and output. If inflation turns out high, the nominal income growth target implies that the Fed will be aiming for a lower level of output growth than it otherwise would have.[36] Nominal GNP targeting is close to the ultimate targets but far from what the Fed controls directly. It would not be plausible to blame the Fed if nominal GNP does not hit the target—fiscal policy or supply shocks could be just as responsible as monetary policy. Thus those who believe the main problem in monetary policy is controlling the Fed typically argue for monetary base or money stock rules. Those who believe the Fed can be trusted to do the right thing tend to prefer nominal GNP targeting.

Beyond the issue of trusting the Fed lie questions of whether the economy would be more stable if over periods of a year or so nominal GNP growth were held constant or if money base growth or interest rates were held constant. There are no simple answers at this stage: the answer depends on what shocks are likely to hit the economy, as the Poole analysis above illustrates.

To start with, we had asked why the Fed has so many targets and which it should

---

[36] See Stephen McNees, "Prospective Nominal GNP Targeting: An Alternative Framework for Monetary Policy," Federal Reserve Bank of New England, *New England Economic Review,* September/October 1987. John B. Taylor provides a technical discussion of nominal income targeting in "What Would Nominal GNP Targeting Do to the Business Cycle," in Karl Brunner and Allan H. Meltzer (eds.), *Understanding Monetary Regimes,* Carnegie-Rochester Conference Series on Public Policy, vol. 22 (Amsterdam: North-Holland, 1985).

have. Critics of the Fed argue that by having many targets, the Fed gives itself flexibility to vary monetary policy. With so many targets, it is likely to hit one of them—and can then claim success. Equally plausibly, it may have many targets because the relationship between each intermediate money target and the ultimate targets is uncertain. By having many targets, the Fed in effect reduces the risk of making a big mistake.

Which target should the Fed have? The goals of targeting can be achieved if the Fed announces money stock targets and, also, interest rate targets for the next year and explains why those targets are consistent with the ultimate targets of policy. Similarly, by announcing a debt target the Fed is stating that it believes the growth rate of debt conveys some information about the behavior of output—even though the Fed cannot directly control the level of debt.

What does the Fed actually do? At present its policies are eclectic. It pays attention to many macroeconomic variables, being willing to adjust monetary policy as new information comes in. It specifies money and debt targets, but it does not stick to them closely. It is behaving more as it did in the 1950s and 1960s than in the 1970s and early 1980s. So far it has been very successful. But critics fear that an eclectic monetary policy is one that can go anywhere, and that without firm, simple guidelines for policy, the Fed will go astray.[37]

11-11 SUMMARY

1. The stock of money is determined by the Fed through its control of the monetary base (high-powered money); the public, through its preferred currency-deposit ratio; and the banks, through their preferred reserve holding behavior.
2. The money stock is larger than the stock of high-powered money because part of the money stock consists of bank deposits, against which the banks hold less than 1 dollar of reserves per dollar of deposits.
3. The money multiplier is the ratio of the money stock to high-powered money. It is larger the smaller the reserve-deposit ratio and the smaller the currency-deposit ratio.
4. The Fed creates high-powered money when it buys assets (for example, Treasury bills, gold, foreign exchange) by creating liabilities on its balance sheet. Purchases of these assets by the Fed increase banks' reserves held at the Fed and lead, through the multiplier process, to an increase in the money stock which is larger than the increase in high-powered money.
5. The money multiplier builds up through an adjustment process in which banks make loans (or buy securities) because deposits have increased their reserves above desired levels.

---

[37] This fear is expressed by William Poole in "Monetary Policy Lessons of Recent Inflation and Disinflation," *Journal of Economic Perspectives,* Summer 1988. See also the article by Benjamin Friedman in the same issue, and the interesting interchange between the two scholars on the lessons of monetary policy in the 1980s.

6. The Fed has three basic policy instruments: open market operations, the discount rate, and required reserves for depository institutions.

7. Because the desired reserve-deposit ratio of banks decreases as the interest rate rises, the supply-of-money function is interest-elastic.

8. The Fed cannot control both the interest rate and the money stock exactly. It can only choose combinations of the interest rate and money stock that are consistent with the demand-for-money function.

9. The Fed operates monetary policy by specifying target ranges for both the money stock and the interest rate. In order to hit its target level of output, the Fed should concentrate on its money targets if the *IS* curve is unstable or shifts about a good deal. It should concentrate on interest rate targets if the money demand function is the major source of instability in the economy.

10. In 1979 the Fed announced a major change in monetary policy whereby it would stick closely to money targets and allow interest rates to fluctuate more. Over the next 3 years interest rates indeed fluctuated more than before, but money growth did not hit targets more accurately. Since the fall of 1982 the Fed has again been paying less attention to money targets, adjusting them as it believes appropriate in the light of shifts in money demand and conditions in the economy.

11. The Fed targets not only M_2 and M_3 and interest rates, but also total nonfinancial debt, or the volume of credit, in the economy. The velocity of debt was more stable than that of money through 1983, but has changed sharply recently.

12. Because of credit rationing, the volume of credit is likely to convey additional information about future levels of spending, particularly investment spending, than is conveyed by interest rates. Credit targets therefore can make sense. However, the relation between credit and nominal GNP became very unstable in the 1980s.

13. In choosing targets for monetary policy, the Fed faces a tradeoff between targets that it can hit exactly but that may be far from the ultimate targets of policy, and targets that are closer to ultimate targets but are more difficult to hit. Critics of the Fed argue that in addition the Fed should chose targets on which it can be held accountable for its actions — this suggests the Fed's selecting intermediate targets that it can hit quite accurately.

KEY TERMS

Currency-deposit ratio	Multiple expansion of money stock
Reserve-deposit ratio	Money supply function
High-powered money (monetary base)	Money stock and interest rate targets
Money multiplier	Intermediate targets
Discount rate	Ultimate targets
Excess reserves	Base drift
FDIC	Fan versus band
Lender of last resort	Credit

PROBLEMS

1. Use Figure 11-1 to discuss how (a) an increase in the currency-deposit ratio and (b) an increase in the reserve-deposit ratio affect the money stock, given the monetary base.

2. Show how an open market sale affects the Fed's balance sheet and also the balance sheet of the commercial bank of the purchaser of the bond sold by the Fed.

3. When the Fed buys or sells gold or foreign exchange, it automatically offsets, or sterilizes, the impact of these operations on the monetary base by compensating open market operations. Show the effects on the Fed balance sheet of a purchase of gold and a corresponding sterilization through an open market operation.

4. How much do bank loans and security purchases increase when the Fed increases the monetary base by $1? Give the answer in terms of cu and re.

5. Explain how the Fed's balance sheet would be affected if it valued gold at the market price.

6. A proposal for "100 percent banking" involves a reserve-deposit ratio of unity. Such a scheme has been proposed for the United States in order to enhance the Fed's control over the money supply.
   (a) Indicate why such a scheme would help monetary control.
   (b) Indicate what bank balance sheets look like under this scheme.
   (c) Under 100 percent money, how would banking remain profitable?

7. Discuss the impact of credit cards on the money multiplier.

8. Use Figures 11-4 and 11-5 to show the effect of an increase in required reserves on (a) the equilibrium money supply, (b) interest rates, and (c) the equilibrium level of income.

9. The Federal Deposit Insurance Corporation insures commercial bank deposits against bank default. Discuss the implications of that deposit scheme for the money multiplier.

10. Assume required reserves were zero. Would banks hold any reserves?

11. Under what circumstances should the Fed conduct monetary policy by targeting mainly (a) interest rates or (b) the money stock?

12. (a) Why does the Fed not stick more closely to its target paths for money?
    (b) Should the Fed use a fan or a band approach to monetary targeting?

13. Show the effect of a discount rate increase on (a) the money supply and (b) income and interest rates.

14. The Fed's target for monetary policy should be to produce constant growth of real GNP at a rate of 3.5 percent per year. Discuss.

15. This lengthy problem asks you to analyze the following question: Suppose the Fed has already decided that it wants to target the money stock: Will the Fed come closer to the target by setting the interest rate at a given level, or will it do better by fixing H? You should think of this analysis as applying to a very short horizon of a few weeks—about the period between meetings of the Open Market Committee.
    The analysis should use a diagram like Figure 11-4, and then apply an analysis similar to that of Figure 11-8. The result of such an analysis involves the relative stability of money demand and the money multiplier. Show that:
    (a) If the demand-for-money function is stable, then fixing interest rates ensures that the Fed will come closer to hitting the target money stock.

(b) If the demand-for-money function is relatively unstable (compared to the money multiplier), then the Fed should target H if it wants to hit its target level of the money stock more closely.

(Your results imply that the Fed may want to target an interest rate in the short run *in order to hit the target money stock more closely.* More generally, this analysis suggests again why the Fed should pay attention to the behavior of both interest rates and the money stock. Shifts in money demand may reveal themselves first in movements in interest rates—and if the Fed wants to stabilize the economy, it should respond to shifts in money demand.)

APPENDIX: THE MONEY STOCK AND THE MONEY MULTIPLIER

We derive the equilibrium money stock and the multiplier by looking at the demand for and supply of money and high-powered money. Consider, first, equilibrium between the supply of money and the demand for money, which, in turn, equals deposits plus currency:

$$M = D + CU \equiv (1 + cu)D \tag{A1}$$

where we have substituted for $CU = cu \times D$, denoting the public's desired ratio of currency to deposits, cu.

Equilibrium between the supply of high-powered money and the demand for high-powered money, which equals reserves plus currency, implies

$$H = RE + CU \equiv (re + cu)D \tag{A2}$$

Again we have expressed the demand side in terms of the desired ratio of currency to deposits and of the banks' desired reserve-deposit ratio, re. When (A1) and (A2) both hold, we are in monetary equilibrium because people hold their money balances in the preferred ratio and banks hold just the right ratio of reserves to deposits.

Dividing (A2) by (A1) yields an expression for the money multiplier (mm):

$$\frac{M}{H} \equiv mm = \frac{1 + cu}{re + cu} \tag{A3}$$

The money multiplier thus depends on the cu and re ratios. We can also use (A3), multiplying both sides by H, to obtain the money supply in terms of the principal determinants mm and H:

$$M = mm \times H \tag{A4}$$

In writing (A4) we remember that mm is dependent on the currency-deposit preferences of the public and the reserve-deposit preferences of banks. It thus takes into account preferences about the composition of balance sheets.

DATA APPENDIX

This appendix reports annual data, in current dollars, for currency, reserves, the monetary base (high-powered money), all deposits included in *M2*, and the Federal Funds rate.

DATA FOR THE MONEY SUPPLY PROCESS

Year	Currency	Reserves	Base	Deposits	Fed funds
1960	28.775	14.541	43.316	275.550	3.216
1961	28.875	14.917	43.793	295.992	1.956
1962	29.867	15.261	45.128	320.275	2.682
1963	31.292	15.553	46.844	348.367	3.178
1964	33.133	15.993	49.126	376.233	3.497
1965	34.900	16.586	51.486	407.600	4.072
1966	37.117	17.005	54.122	434.292	5.112
1967	39.025	17.773	56.798	464.667	4.219
1968	41.542	18.877	60.418	503.842	5.658
1969	44.375	19.465	63.840	534.750	8.207
1970	47.233	20.117	67.350	555.942	7.181
1971	50.558	21.686	72.244	625.817	4.662
1972	54.033	23.182	77.215	706.892	4.431
1973	58.608	25.011	83.619	777.650	8.728
1974	64.075	26.309	90.384	823.133	10.503
1975	70.092	26.743	96.835	899.992	5.824
1976	76.633	27.029	103.662	1,019.058	5.046
1977	83.592	28.112	111.704	1,150.833	5.538
1978	91.867	29.873	121.740	1,247.767	7.931
1979	100.917	30.264	131.180	1,349.433	11.194
1980	110.367	32.048	142.415	1,456.367	13.356
1981	118.942	34.650	153.592	1,595.350	16.378
1982	127.767	35.990	163.757	1,746.533	12.258
1983	140.067	38.706	178.772	1,968.683	9.087
1984	152.017	40.791	192.808	2,124.467	10.225
1985	162.350	45.494	207.844	2,318.242	8.101
1986	174.417	52.514	226.930	2,512.525	6.805
1987	188.775	58.984	247.759	2,674.467	6.657
1988	205.258	60.435	265.693	2,804.183	7.568

12

STABILIZATION POLICY: PROSPECTS AND PROBLEMS

Figure 12-1, which shows the unemployment rate over the period 1926–1988, gives the clear impression that stabilization policy has left something to be desired. Standing out is the disaster of the great-depression decade of the thirties, when the unemployment rate peaked at almost 25 percent of the labor force. But unemployment has sometimes been high even in the post-World War II period, as in the 1973–1975 and 1981–1982 recessions.

The historical record forcefully raises the question of why the economy has not done better. The preceding chapters have laid out a clear body of theory that seems to show exactly the measures that can be used to maintain full employment. High unemployment, or a large GNP gap, can be reduced by expansionary monetary or fiscal policies. Similarly, a boom and inflation can be contained by restrictive monetary or fiscal policies.

The policies needed to prevent the fluctuations in unemployment seen in Figure 12-1 accordingly appear to be simple. The policy maker knows the full-employment level of output. If there is unemployment, a policy maker can use a model, such as the *IS-LM* model, to calculate the level of government spending or taxes needed to get income to the full-employment level. But if it is all so simple, how did the fluctuations in Figure 12-1 occur?

The answer must be that policy making is far from simple. Part of the difficulty arises from the possible *conflict between the maintenance of full employment and the target of low inflation.* Because expansionary fiscal or monetary policy raises both output and prices, policy to reduce unemployment may increase inflation. We pursue that problem, which can be understood using the aggregate supply-demand analysis of Chapter 7, in more detail in Chapters 14 and 15.

In this chapter we discuss both the optimistic prospects for stabilization policy and problems in the execution of policy. The Keynesian approach to stabilization policy

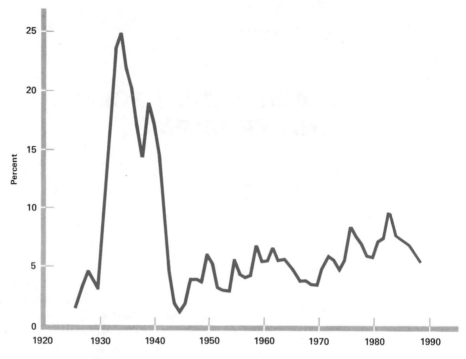

FIGURE 12-1

THE CIVILIAN UNEMPLOYMENT RATE IN THE UNITED STATES, 1926–1988. (SOURCE: DRI/McGraw-Hill and Bureau of the Census, *Historical Statistics of the United States,* 1976.)

developed out of the great depression. We set the scene by describing the events of the great depression and the New Economics that it spawned, with its emphasis on the potential for active policy, particularly fiscal policy, to help stabilize the economy.

Then we turn to technical problems in policy making, which imply that policy cannot be expected to keep the economy always close to full employment with low inflation. We begin by briefly discussing the types of disturbances that cause the economy to move away from the full-employment level of output in the first place and then describe *econometric models,* models of the economy with specific numerical values for parameters and multipliers, that can be used to assist policy making. The bulk of the chapter is taken up by a discussion of three factors that in large measure account for the failure of policy continually to achieve its targets. The three *handicaps of policy making are:*

- Lags in the effects of policy
- The role of expectations in determining private sector responses to policy
- Uncertainty about the effects of policy

In a nutshell, we will argue that a policy maker who (1) observes a disturbance, (2) does not know whether it is permanent or not, and (3) takes time to develop a policy that (4) takes still more time to affect behavior and (5) has uncertain effects on aggregate demand is very poorly equipped to do a perfect job of stabilizing the economy.

12-1 THE GREAT DEPRESSION

The great depression of the 1930s is the event that shaped both many institutions in the economy, including the Fed, and modern macroeconomics. The essential facts about the depression are shown in Figure 12-2 and in Table 12-1. Between 1929 and 1933, GNP fell by nearly 30 percent. Over the same period, the unemployment rate rose from 3 to 25 percent. For the 10 years 1931 to 1940, the unemployment rate

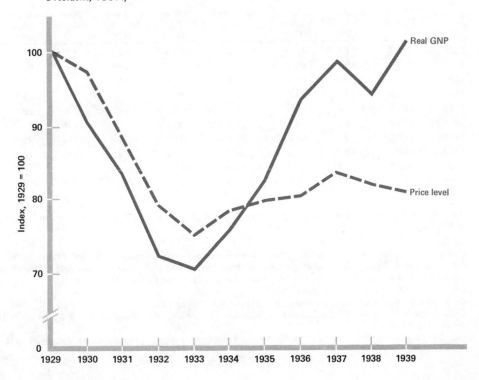

FIGURE 12-2
OUTPUT AND PRICES IN THE GREAT DEPRESSION, 1929–1939. (SOURCE: U.S. Department of Commerce, *The National Income and Product Accounts of the United States*, 1929–1974, and *Economic Report of the President*, 1957.)

averaged 18.8 percent, ranging between a low of 14.3 percent in 1937 and a high of 24.9 percent in 1933. By contrast, the post-World War II high, reached in 1982, was under 11 percent. Investment collapsed in the great depression; indeed, net investment was negative from 1931 to 1935. The consumer price index fell nearly 25 percent from 1929 to 1933; the stock market fell 80 percent between September 1929 and March 1933. From 1933 to 1937, real GNP grew fast, at an annual rate of nearly 9 percent, but even that did not get the unemployment rate down to normal levels. Then, in 1937–1938 there was a major recession within the depression, pushing the unemployment rate back up to nearly 20 percent. In the second half of the decade, short-term interest rates, such as the commercial paper rate, were near zero.

Facts such as those in Table 12-1 raise a host of questions. The two most important are, Why did this happen? and Could it have been prevented? Underlying these questions is one that many economists are asked whenever the economy is in recession—and that they ask themselves in their bad moments, such as on October 19, 1987, when the stock market suffered its biggest ever 1-day loss: Could it happen again?

TABLE 12-1

ECONOMIC STATISTICS OF THE GREAT DEPRESSION

Year	GNP, 1972 $ billion (1)	I/GNP, % (2)	G, 1972 $ billion (3)	Unemploy-ment rate, % (4)	CPI, 1929 = 100 (5)	Commer-cial paper rate, % (6)	AAA rate, % (7)	Stock market index (8)	M1, 1929 = 100 (9)	Full-employ-ment surplus Y*, % (10)
1929	314.7	17.8	40.9	3.2	100.0	5.9	4.7	83.1	100.0	−0.8
1930	285.2	13.5	44.6	8.7	97.4	3.6	4.6	67.2	96.2	−1.4
1931	263.3	9.0	46.2	15.9	88.7	2.6	4.6	43.6	89.4	−3.1
1932	226.8	3.5	44.0	23.6	79.7	2.7	5.0	22.1	78.0	−0.9
1933	222.1	3.8	42.8	24.9	75.4	1.7	4.5	28.6	73.5	1.6
1934	239.4	5.5	48.7	21.7	78.0	1.0	4.0	31.4	81.4	0.2
1935	260.8	9.2	49.8	20.1	80.1	0.8	3.6	33.9	96.6	−0.1
1936	296.1	10.9	58.5	16.9	80.9	0.8	3.2	49.4	110.6	−1.1
1937	309.8	12.8	56.3	14.3	83.3	0.9	3.3	49.2	114.8	1.8
1938	297.1	8.1	61.3	19.0	82.3	0.8	3.2	36.7	115.9	0.6
1939	319.7	10.5	63.8	17.2	81.0	0.6	3.0	38.5	127.3	−0.1

NOTE: Stock market index is Standard & Poor's composite index, which includes 500 stocks; September 1929 = 100. Y^* denotes full-employment output.

SOURCE:

Cols. 1, 2, 3: U.S. Department of Commerce, *The National Income and Product Accounts of the United States*, 1929–1974.

Col. 4: Revised Bureau of Labor Statistics data taken from Michael Darby, "Three-and-a-Half Million Employees Have Been Mislaid: Or, an Explanation of Unemployment, 1934–1941," *Journal of Political Economy*, February 1976.

Cols. 5, 6, 7: *Economic Report of the President*, 1957.

Col. 8: Standard & Poor's Statistical Service, *Security Price Index Record*, 1978.

Col. 9: Milton Friedman and Anna J. Schwartz, *A Monetary History of the United States, 1867-1960* (Princeton, N.J.: Princeton University Press, 1963), table A1, col. 7.

Col. 10: E. Cary Brown, "Fiscal Policy in the Thirties: A Reappraisal," *American Economic Review*, December 1956, table 1, cols. 3, 5, and 19.

The depression and the stock market crash of October 1929 are popularly thought of as almost the same thing. In fact, the economy started turning down before the stock market crash. The peak of the business cycle is estimated to have been in August 1929, whereas the stock market peaked in September 1929. The Standard & Poor's composite stock price index, calculated using September 1929 as the base period, fell from 100 in September to 66 in November. It rose again through March 1930, but then the collapse continued until the index fell to 15 in June 1932.

By early 1931, the economy was suffering from a very severe depression, but not one that was out of the range of the experience of the previous century.[1] It was in the period from early 1931 until Franklin Roosevelt became President in March 1933 that the depression became "great."

Economic Policy

What was economic policy during this period? The money stock fell from 1929 to 1930, and then fell rapidly in 1931 and 1932 and continued falling through April 1933. At the same time, the composition of the money stock changed. In March 1931 the currency-demand deposit ratio was 18.5 percent; 2 years later, it was 40.7 percent.

The fall in the money stock was in part the result of large-scale bank failures. Banks failed because they did not have the reserves with which to meet customers' cash withdrawals, and in failing they destroyed deposits and hence reduced the money stock. But the failures went further in reducing the money stock, because they led to a loss of confidence on the part of depositors and hence to an even higher desired currency-deposit ratio. Furthermore, banks that had not yet failed adjusted to the possibility of a run by holding increased reserves relative to deposits. The rise in the currency-deposit ratio and the reserve-deposit ratio reduced the money multiplier and hence sharply contracted the money stock.

The Fed took very few steps to offset the fall in the money supply; for a few months in 1932 it did undertake a program of open market purchases, but otherwise it seemed to acquiesce in bank closings and certainly failed to understand that the central bank should act vigorously in a crisis to prevent the collapse of the financial system.[2]

Fiscal policy, too, was not vigorous. The natural impulse of politicians then was to balance the budget in times of trouble, and much rhetoric was devoted to that proposition. The presidential candidates campaigned on balanced budget platforms in 1932. In fact, as Table 12-2 shows, the federal government ran large deficits, particularly for that time, averaging 2.6 percent of GNP from 1931 to 1933 and even more later.

---

[1] The classic work by Milton Friedman and Anna J. Schwartz, *A Monetary History of the United States, 1867–1960* (Princeton, N.J.: Princeton University Press, 1963), gives a very detailed account of the great depression, comparing it with other recessions and emphasizing the role of the Fed. For a more general economic history of the period, see Robert A. Gordon, *Economic Instability: The American Record* (New York: Harper & Row, 1974), chap. 3.

[2] Friedman and Schwartz speculate on the reasons for the Fed's inaction; the whodunit or who didn't do it on pp. 407–419 of their book (cited in footnote 1) is fascinating.

TABLE 12-2
GOVERNMENT SPENDING AND REVENUE (percent)

| Year | TOTAL GOVERNMENT[a] | | FEDERAL GOVERNMENT | | Total government: full employment surplus/Y^{*}[b] |
	Expenditure/ GNP	Actual surplus/ GNP	Expenditure/ GNP	Actual surplus/ GNP	
1929	10.0	1.0	2.5	1.2	−0.8
1930	12.3	−0.3	3.1	0.3	−1.4
1931	16.4	−3.8	5.5	−2.8	−3.1
1932	18.3	−3.1	5.5	−2.6	−0.9
1933	19.2	−2.5	7.2	−2.3	1.6
1934	19.8	−3.7	9.8	−4.4	0.2
1935	18.6	−2.8	9.0	−3.6	−0.1
1936	19.5	−3.8	10.5	−4.4	−1.1
1937	16.6	0.3	8.2	0.4	1.8
1938	19.8	−2.1	10.2	−2.5	0.6
1939	19.4	−2.4	9.8	−2.4	−0.1

[a] Including federal, state, and local.

[b] Y^{*} = potential output.

SOURCE:
Cols. 1, 2, 3, 4: Economic Report of the President, 1972, tables B1 and B70.
Col. 5: E. Cary Brown, "Fiscal Policy in the Thirties: A Reappraisal," *American Economic Review,* December 1956, table 1, cols. 3, 5, and 19.

(These actual deficits are lower as a percentage of GNP than those in the mid-1980s.) The belief in budget balancing was more than rhetoric, however, for state and local governments raised taxes to match their expenditures,[3] as did the federal government, particularly in 1932 and 1933. President Roosevelt tried seriously to balance the budget — he was no Keynesian. The full-employment surplus shows fiscal policy (combined state, local, and federal) as most expansionary in 1931, and moving to a more contractionary level from 1932 to 1934. In fact, the full-employment surplus was positive in 1933 and 1934, despite the actual deficits.[4] Of course, the concept of the full-employment surplus had not yet been invented in the 1930s.

Economic activity recovered in the period from 1933 to 1937, with fiscal policy becoming more expansionary and the money stock growing rapidly. The growth of the money stock was based on an inflow of gold from Europe. This provided high-powered

---

[3] You can calculate the surplus of state and local governments as a percentage of GNP by subtracting the fourth column in Table 12-2 from the second column.

[4] Note that in this chapter, unlike Chap. 3 and elsewhere in the book, the full-employment deficit includes federal, state, and local governments.

money for the monetary system. It was in the 1930s that the Fed acquired most of its current holdings of gold.[5]

Institutional Change

The period from 1933 to 1937 also saw substantial legislative and administrative action — the *New Deal* — from the Roosevelt administration. The Fed was reorganized, and the Federal Deposit Insurance Corporation (FDIC) was established.

A number of regulatory agencies were also created, most notably the Securities and Exchange Commission, which regulates the securities industry. Its purpose was to prevent speculative excesses that were thought to be largely responsible for the stock market crash. The Social Security Administration was set up so that the elderly would not have to rely on their own savings to ensure themselves a minimally adequate standard of living in retirement. The Roosevelt administration also believed that the route to recovery lay in increasing wages and prices, so it encouraged trade unionization, as well as price-raising and price-fixing schemes by business, through the National Recovery Administration.

International Aspects

Another important aspect of the depression deserves mention: It was virtually world-wide. To some extent, this was the result of the collapse of the international financial system.[6] It resulted, too, from the mutual adoption by many countries (including the United States) of high-tariff policies, which were intended to keep out foreign goods in order to protect domestic producers. And, of course, if each country keeps out foreign goods, the volume of world trade declines, providing a contractionary influence on the world economy.

The experience of the 1930s varied internationally. Sweden began an expansionary policy in the early 1930s and reduced its unemployment relatively fast in the second half of the decade. Britain's economy suffered high unemployment in both the 1920s and the 1930s. Germany grew rapidly after Hitler came to power and expanded government spending. China escaped the recession until after 1931, essentially because it had a floating exchange rate. As always, there is much to be learned from the exceptions.

In 1939, real GNP in the United States rose above its 1929 level for the first time in the decade. But it was not until 1942, after the United States formally entered World War II, that the unemployment rate finally fell below 5 percent.

---

[5] For details of the way in which the Fed acquired the gold, see Friedman and Schwartz, *A Monetary History of the United States*, p. 506.

[6] This aspect of the depression is emphasized by Charles Kindleberger, *The World in Depression, 1929–1939* (Berkeley: University of California Press, 1986), and Gottfried Haberler, *The World Economy, Money and the Great Depression* (Washington, D.C.: American Enterprise Institute, 1976).

12-2 THE GREAT DEPRESSION: THE ISSUES AND IDEAS

In Section 12-1 we asked what caused the great depression, whether it could have been avoided, and whether it could happen again. The question of what caused the depression seems purely academic, but it is much more than that. The depression was the greatest economic crisis the western world had experienced.

The classical economics of the time had no well-developed theory that would explain persistent unemployment nor any policy prescriptions to solve the problem. Many economists of the time did, in fact, recommend government spending as a way of reducing unemployment, but they had no macroeconomic theory by which to justify their recommendations.

Keynes wrote his great work, *The General Theory of Employment, Interest and Money*, in the 1930s, after Britain had suffered during the 1920s from a decade of double-digit unemployment and while the United States was in the depths of its depression. He was fully aware of the seriousness of the issues. As Don Patinkin of the Hebrew University puts it:[7]

> . . . the period was one of fear and darkness as the Western world struggled with the greatest depression that it had known. . . . [T]here was a definite feeling that by attempting to achieve a scientific understanding of the phenomenon of mass unemployment, one was not only making an intellectual contribution, but was also dealing with a critical problem that endangered the very existence of Western civilization.

Keynesian theory explained what had happened, what could have been done to prevent the depression, and what could be done to prevent future depressions. The explanation soon became accepted by most macroeconomists, in the process described as the Keynesian revolution. The Keynesian revolution did not have much impact on economic policy making in the United States until the 1960s, but it affected macroeconomics much earlier than that, setting the foundation for post-World War II macroeconomics — inspiring both Keynesian models and the alternative approaches that were developed as a result of difficulties with the Keynesian approach.[8]

The Keynesian Explanation

The essence of the Keynesian explanation of the great depression is based on the simple aggregate demand model developed in Chapter 3. Growth in the 1920s, in this view, was based on the mass production of the automobile and radio and was fueled by a

---

[7] In "The Process of Writing *The General Theory:* A Critical Survey," in Don Patinkin and J. Clark Leith (eds.), *Keynes, Cambridge and the General Theory* (Toronto: University of Toronto Press, 1978), p. 3. For a short biography of Keynes, see D. E. Moggridge, *John Maynard Keynes* (New York: Penguin Books, 1976).

[8] These include the rational expectations equilibrium approach, introduced in Chap. 7, and monetarism, which is discussed later in this chapter.

housing boom. The collapse of growth in the 1930s resulted from the drying up of investment opportunities and a downward shift in investment demand. The collapse of investment, shown in Table 12-1, fits in with this picture. Some researchers also believe there was a downward shift in the consumption function in 1930.[9] Poor fiscal policy, as reflected in the perverse behavior of the full-employment surplus from 1931 to 1933, shares the blame, particularly for making the depression worse.

What does this view have to say about the monetary collapse? The Fed argued in the 1930s that there was little it could have done to prevent the depression, because interest rates were already as low as they could possibly go. A variety of sayings of the type, "You can lead a horse to water but you can't make it drink," were used to explain that further reductions in interest rates would have had no effect if there was no demand for investment. Investment demand was thought to be very unresponsive to the rate of interest — implying a very steep *IS* curve. At the same time, the *LM* curve was believed to be quite flat, though not necessarily reaching the extreme of a liquidity trap. In this situation, as we saw in Chapter 4, monetary expansion would be relatively ineffective in stimulating demand and output.

It was also widely believed that the experience of the depression showed that the private economy was inherently unstable in that it could self-depress with no difficulty if left alone. The experience of the 1930s was, implicitly or explicitly, the basis for the belief that an active stabilization policy was needed to maintain good economic performance.

The Keynesian model not only offered an explanation of what had happened, but also suggested policy measures that could have been taken to prevent the depression, and that could be used to prevent future depressions. Vigorous use of countercyclical fiscal policy was the preferred method for reducing cyclical fluctuations. If a recession ever showed signs of deteriorating into a depression, the cure would be to cut taxes and increase government spending. And those policies would, too, have prevented the depression from being as deep as it was.

There is nothing in the *IS-LM* model developed in Chapter 4 that suggests that fiscal policy is more useful than monetary policy for stabilization of the economy. Nonetheless, it is true that until the 1950s, Keynesians tended to give more emphasis to fiscal than to monetary policy.

The Monetarist Challenge

The Keynesian emphasis on fiscal policy, and its downplaying of the role of money, was increasingly challenged by Milton Friedman and his coworkers during the 1950s.[10] During this period Friedman was developing much of the analysis and evidence that provided the basis for monetarism, which we describe in detail in Chapter 18. The main

---

[9] Peter Temin, *Did Monetary Forces Cause the Great Depression?* (New York: Norton, 1976).

[10] See, in particular, Milton Friedman (ed.), *Studies in the Quantity Theory of Money* (Chicago: University of Chicago Press, 1956).

thrust was a heavy emphasis on the role of monetary policy in determining the behavior of both output and prices.

If monetary policy was to be given an important role, though, it was necessary to dispose of the view that monetary policy had been tried in the great depression and had failed. In other words, the view that "You can lead a horse to the water, etc.," had to be challenged.

The view that monetary policy in the thirties had been impotent was attacked in 1963 by Friedman and Schwartz in their *Monetary History.* They argued that the depression, far from showing that money does not matter, "is in fact a tragic testimonial to the importance of monetary factors."[11] They argued, with skill and style, that the failure of the Fed to prevent bank failures and the decline of the money stock from the end of 1930 to 1933 was largely responsible for the recession's being as serious as it was. This monetary view, in turn, came close to being accepted as the orthodox explanation of the depression.[12]

Synthesis

Both the Keynesian and the monetarist explanations of the great depression fit the facts, and both provide answers to the question of why it happened, and how to prevent it from happening again. Both inept fiscal and inept monetary policies made the great depression severe. If there had been prompt, strong, expansive monetary and fiscal policy, the economy would have suffered a recession but not the trauma it did.

On the question of whether it could happen again, there is agreement that it could not, except, of course, in the event of truly perverse policies. But these are less likely now than they were then. For one thing, we have history to help us avoid its repetition. Taxes would not again be raised in the middle of a depression, nor would attempts be made to balance the budget. The Fed would seek actively to keep the money supply from falling. In addition, the government now has a much larger role in the economy than it did then. The higher level of government spending, which is relatively slow to change, and automatic stabilizers, including the income tax,[13] unemployment insurance, and Social Security, give the economy more stability than it had then.[14]

One example was seen immediately after the worldwide October 19, 1987, stock market crash. Conscious of the history of the great depression, the Fed announced that

---

[11] Friedman and Schwartz, *A Monetary History of the United States,* p. 300.

[12] Ben Bernanke, in "Nonmonetary Effects of the Financial Crisis in the Propagation of the Great Depression," *American Economic Review,* June 1983, takes issue with the monetary view, arguing instead that the destruction of the financial system made it difficult for borrowers to obtain funds needed for investment. However, there is no conflict between that argument and the view that more decisive monetary policy by the Fed in 1930 and 1931 would have mitigated the depression.

[13] Recall from Chap. 3 that a proportional income tax reduces the multiplier.

[14] See Martin Baily, "Stabilization Policy and Private Economic Behavior," *Brookings Papers on Economic Activity,* 1978: 1.

it would lend as needed to prevent financial collapse, and immediately undertook open market operations, driving down the interest rate sharply as it undertook expansionary monetary policy. The Fed's actions, and those of other major central banks, helped to contain the panic and prevented it from affecting output.

There is no inherent conflict between the Keynesian and monetarist explanations of the great depression. The *IS-LM* model, augmented by the supply-side analysis of wage and price adjustment in Chapter 7, easily combines both explanations. Why, then, has there been controversy over the causes of the great depression? The reason is that the 1930s are seen as the period that set the stage for massive government intervention in the economy. Those opposed to an active role for government have to explain away the debacle of the economy in the 1930s. If the depression occurred because of, and not despite, the government (particularly the Fed), the case for an active government role in economic stabilization is weakened. Further, the 1930s are a period in which the economy behaved in such an extreme way that competing theories have to be subjected to the test of whether they can explain that period. Those are the main reasons the dispute over the causes of the great depression continues more than 60 years after it began.[15]

12-3 THE NEW ECONOMICS

Keynesian economics was rapidly accepted by most macroeconomists, but it affected policy less rapidly. The budget was used as a countercyclical policy tool in Britain in the entire post-World War II period. In the United States, the Employment Act of 1946 imposed on the government the obligation to follow policies that would produce high employment. Nonetheless, it was not until the Kennedy administration in the early 1960s that an administration began to follow avowedly Keynesian policies.

The approach was described as the *New Economics*. The analytical approach consists basically of the tools we have outlined in Chapters 3 through 11. The philosophy characterizing that approach to economics is a mix of activism and optimism. It is well characterized by an excerpt from the 1962 *Economic Report of the President* (page 68):[16]

---

[15] Among the relevant contributions is Michael Darby, "Three-and-a-Half Million U.S. Employees Have Been Mislaid: Or, an Explanation of Unemployment, 1934–1941," *Journal of Political Economy,* February 1976. Darby argues that unemployment is mismeasured after 1933 because those on government work relief programs are counted as unemployed. Adjusted for those individuals, the unemployment rate falls rapidly from 20.6 percent in 1933 to below 10 percent in 1936. See also Thomas Mayer, "Money and the Great Depression: A Critique of Professor Temin's Thesis," *Explorations in Economic History,* April 1978, and Karl Brunner (ed.), *The Great Depression Revisited* (Boston: Martinus Nijhoff, 1981).

[16] President Kennedy's Council of Economic Advisers was served by many distinguished economists, among them three who later won the Nobel prize: James Tobin of Yale, Kenneth Arrow of Stanford, and Robert Solow of MIT. A fourth Nobel prizewinner, Paul Samuelson, served as an unofficial adviser.

Insufficient demand means unemployment, idle capacity, and lost production. Excessive demand means inflation — general increases in prices and money incomes, bringing forth little or no gains in output and real income. The objective of stabilization policies is to minimize these deviations, i.e., to keep over-all demand in step with the basic production potential of the economy.

Stabilization does not mean a mere leveling off of peaks and troughs in production and employment. It does not mean trying to hold over-all demand for goods and services stable. It means minimizing deviations from a rising trend, not from an unchanging average. In a growing economy, demand must grow in order to maintain full employment of labor and full utilization of capacity at stable prices. The economy is not performing satisfactorily unless it is almost continuously setting new records of production, income, and employment. . . .

The contrast between economic policy in the 1930s and in the 1960s is marked. In the 1960s, policy makers came into a not very difficult economic situation with

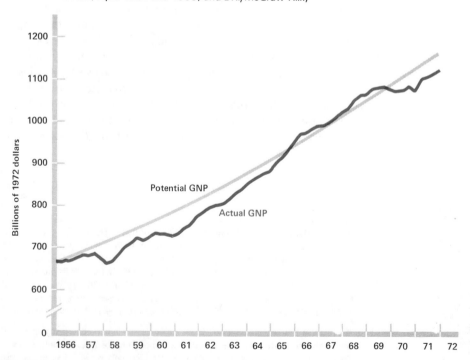

FIGURE 12-3
ACTUAL AND POTENTIAL GNP, 1956–1971. (SOURCE: *Survey of Current Business*, April 1982 and 1983, and DRI/McGraw-Hill.)

well-thought-out theories and policies to apply. Those policies were based on the Keynesian analysis that developed in the 1930s and on the experience of that decade. In the 1930s, policy fumbled, and badly, for some way to get the economy moving again. The Roosevelt administration did run budget deficits, but most unwillingly, and it had no concept of the full-employment surplus; the Kennedy-Johnson administration, by contrast, planned a tax cut in 1963–1964 when the budget was in deficit, and sold the policy to a skeptical Congress.

The New Economics emphasized the goal of reattaining full employment after the high unemployment levels of the late 1950s. We briefly review the basic analytical concepts of the New Economics before concluding this section by discussing what was new in the New Economics.

Potential Output and the GNP Gap

To focus attention on the target of full employment and for use as an operating guide to policy, the *Council of Economic Advisers* (CEA), and particularly the late Arthur Okun, developed and stressed the concept of potential output. Potential output or full-employment output, introduced in Chapter 1, measures the level of real GNP the economy can produce with full employment. The full-employment rate of unemployment used in defining potential output in the 1960s was about 4 percent, below the rates of 5 to 6 percent used more recently. Figure 12-3 shows potential output for the 1956–1971 period.

Along with the concept and measurement of potential output went the notion of the GNP gap. The gap is the difference between actual and potential real output. For the years 1961–1965, actual GNP was below its potential level, and the GNP gap was therefore positive. At the beginning of 1961, the GNP gap was more than 7 percent of GNP. A gap of that magnitude clearly called for expansionary monetary or fiscal policy to raise aggregate demand to a level closer to the economy's potential.

Although the notions of potential output and the GNP gap seem very simple, they dramatize the costs of unemployment in easily understood terms of output lost due to unemployment.

The Full-Employment Budget Surplus

The full-employment budget surplus was discussed in Chapter 3, and we will therefore be brief here. The concept is important and useful because it directs attention away from the actual budget, which is a misleading indicator of fiscal policy, toward the full-employment surplus — a more relevant, although still imperfect, indicator of policy.

The New Economists planned to use fiscal policy as the instrument with which to close the GNP gap. It was important for them to get across to Congress and the public the idea of the full-employment surplus because the federal budget was in actual deficit.

Any proposals to increase spending or cut taxes would certainly imply a larger deficit. Congress could then be relied upon to look with great suspicion on any policy that might increase the budget deficit. By focusing attention on the full-employment budget, the New Economists succeeded in shifting attention away from the state of the actual budget to concern with how the budget would look at full employment — which had the side benefit of focusing attention on the full-employment issue itself.

Growth

The New Economics emphasized economic growth in two ways. First, there was the need for aggregate demand to grow in order to achieve full employment. In that respect, growth was a matter of achieving full employment and maintaining it. Second, there was an emphasis on achieving a high rate of growth of potential output itself. The emphasis was on investment spending to encourage growth in productive potential. To that end the administration introduced an investment tax credit in 1962.

The Behavior of Money Wages

The New Economics emphasized the behavior of money wages in affecting the rate of inflation. This is in accord with the aggregate demand-supply analysis of Chapter 7 and with the more sophisticated analysis to follow in Chapter 14.

Early in the Kennedy-Johnson years, in 1962, the CEA set up *guideposts*[17] for the behavior of money wages. The basic guidepost was that money wages should not grow faster than the average rate at which labor productivity was increasing in the economy. Labor productivity is the ratio of output to labor input.

When productivity is growing, less labor is being used to produce the same amount of goods. Thus if wages are growing as fast as productivity, the labor costs of producing a good are constant. Assuming, as the New Economics did, that prices are set as a markup on labor costs, prices would not rise if wages were rising no faster than productivity.[18]

---

[17] For an interesting, and sometimes amusing, discussion of the guideposts, see George P. Shultz (an economist who later became famous in other contexts) and Robert Z. Aliber (eds.), *Guidelines* (Chicago: The University of Chicago Press, 1966).

[18] This argument also implies that more rapid investment — which contributes to productivity increases — can help reduce inflation from the supply side. This argument was also advanced in the early 1980s by supply-side economists. While it is correct, it is important to get the orders of magnitude right. Given the growth rate of money, an increase in the growth rate of output results in a lower rate of inflation because the demand for real balances grows faster when output grows faster. A one-percentage-point increase in the rate of output growth would, via the quantity theory, tend to reduce the inflation rate by 1 percent. Such an increase in productivity growth would be very large by historical standards, and very important for long-run standards of living (see Chap. 19), but a one-percentage-point reduction in the inflation rate is not very large.

What Was New?

What was new about the New Economics? Intellectually, the approach to stabilization policy along the lines of fiscal activism, potential output objectives, and emphasis on the full-employment budget was not new, and was, indeed, mainline professional macroeconomics. But the activism the CEA displayed was new.

The active use of fiscal policy met much resistance in the political process at the time. Herbert Stein, himself chairperson of the CEA under President Nixon, reviews the progress toward the major policy measure of the early 1960s, the 1964 tax cut, in his book *The Fiscal Revolution in America*.[19] He shows how both the Kennedy administration and the Congress had to get accustomed to the idea that, during recession, a move toward an increased budget deficit was not a step toward fiscal irresponsibility.

Thus, what was new about the New Economics was not the analysis, which was standard macroeconomics, but rather the active and successful use of that analysis in the operation of fiscal policy.

The New Economics and the Economy

The most ambitious and successful policy action of the Kennedy-Johnson administration was the tax cut of 1964, which we analyzed in Chapter 5. The tax cut kept the economy growing rapidly through the mid-1960s, thus reducing the unemployment rate. At the same time, as Figure 12-4 shows, the inflation rate stayed below 3 percent per year.

Through the middle of the 1960s, the economy was behaving as well as it ever has. Productivity growth was high, output was growing fast, unemployment was falling, and the inflation rate was low. It is little wonder that there was considerable optimism about the possibilities of the New Economics.

In the late 1960s things began to go wrong. Part of the problem was political. Government spending for the Vietnam war was rising rapidly, but President Johnson feared that a tax increase would make the war more unpopular. In 1966 and 1967, it was left to monetary policy to fight the increasing expansionary pressure of fiscal policy. Only in 1968 was the Johnson administration willing to ask Congress for a tax increase to try to contain the expansionary pressure of military spending.

The decision was made to go for a transitory tax increase. The contractionary effect of the tax increase was overestimated, so that by the end of the Johnson administration at the beginning of 1969, the inflation rate was up to more than 5 percent. To be sure, the unemployment rate was below 4 percent, and the economy was still in its longest expansion on record: there was no recession between 1961 and 1969.[20]

---

[19] Chicago: University of Chicago Press, 1969.

[20] At the time of writing, the recovery that started in November 1982 has a chance of becoming the longest on record. It will achieve that status if there is no recession before September 1991.

FIGURE 12-4
INFLATION AND UNEMPLOYMENT, 1961–1970. (SOURCE: DRI/McGraw-Hill.)

The record of the 1960s is one of full employment, expansion, and rising inflation. Keynesian economics, or the New Economics, received the popular credit for the expansion of the mid-1960s following the tax cut. Similarly, it received the blame for the rising inflation, even though many of the economic advisers to the President were urging a tax increase as early as 1966.

The apparent failure of the activist New Economics reopened the question of whether active monetary and fiscal policy could be used successfully to control the economy. We turn now to examine the general principles and problems of stabilization policy.

12-4 ECONOMIC DISTURBANCES

Before identifying the obstacles in the way of successful policy making, we briefly discuss economic disturbances in terms of their sources, persistence, and importance for policy. Economic disturbances are shifts in aggregate demand or aggregate supply, or shifts in money demand or money supply, that cause output, interest rates, or prices to diverge from their target paths.

We return to the *IS-LM* model as the framework for the discussion of economic disturbances in this chapter. In Figure 12-5 we show the *IS* and *LM* schedules and also the full-employment level of output, Y^*. The economy is initially at full employment at point E. What disturbances might cause the economy to move away from full employment? Obviously, anything that shifts the *IS* and/or *LM* curves would disturb the economy and move it away from E.

In terms of overall economic impact, the major disturbances to the economy — the forces moving the *IS* and *LM* curves — have typically been wars. The effects of the increases in government spending associated with World War II, the Korean war, and the Vietnam war can be seen in Figure 12-1 in the very low unemployment rates in those periods. Of these, World War II had the largest impact on the economy. At the height of the war, in 1944, federal government spending exceeded 40 percent of GNP.

FIGURE 12-5

AN AGGREGATE DEMAND DISTURBANCE. The economy is initially in equilibrium at point E, with level of output Y^*. An increase in government spending (for example, for defense) shifts the *IS* curve to *IS'*. This disturbance tends to raise the level of output above the full-employment level. Monetary and/or fiscal policy, or even rationing, may be used to try to keep the level of demand in check, shifting the *IS'* curve back to *IS* and/or shifting the *LM* curve up and to the left.

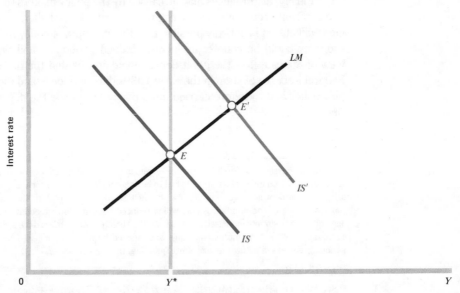

As shown in Figure 12-5, the increase in government spending would shift the *IS* schedule upward. The aggregate demand curve in Chapter 7 shifts to the right, with both output and prices increasing. To free resources needed for war, the government will both raise taxes and perhaps run a tight monetary policy. But this is not usually enough to prevent wartime inflations.[21]

Changes in government spending or tax policies not connected with wars, such as increased spending on social programs that is not financed by taxes, may also constitute economic disturbances.

Other economic disturbances that lead to changes in aggregate demand originate in the private sector. If consumers decide to consume more out of their disposable income at any given level of income, the *IS* curve of Figure 12-5 shifts upward. If there is no economic explanation for the shift in the consumption function, we describe the shift as a disturbance. Similarly, if investment spending increases for no apparent economic reason, then we attribute the increase to an unexplained change in the optimism of investors about the returns from investment, or an increase in their *animal spirits*.[22] Some shifts in the investment function are caused by new inventions that require large amounts of investment for their successful marketing, such as the development of the railroads in the nineteenth century and the spread of the automobile in the 1920s. Similarly, shifts in the demand for money constitute a possible source of private sector economic disturbances.

Among other disturbances are increases in exports, caused by changes in foreigners' demand for our goods, which tend to increase the level of income. Changes in supply conditions, such as the oil price increases of 1973–1974 and 1979–1980 and the oil price decrease of 1985–1986, will affect the level of income. In addition, the behavior of wages may constitute a source of economic disturbances.

Finally, disturbances may be caused by the policy makers themselves. There are two different arguments concerning this important possibility. First, since policy making is difficult, it is entirely possible that the attempts of policy makers to stabilize the economy could be counterproductive. Indeed, Friedman and Schwartz's influential view of the causes of the great depression[23] argues that the officials in charge of the Federal Reserve System in the early 1930s did not understand the workings of monetary policy and therefore carried out a policy that made the depression worse rather than better.

---

[21] Often *rationing* is used to limit private demand in wartime. For instance, in World War II, a system was set up under which investment projects had to be licensed. That system served to reduce the overall rate of private investment and also to direct investment toward areas helpful for the war effort. There was also some rationing of consumption goods, which reduced consumption expenditure as some of the rationed demand spilled over into increased saving rather than being diverted toward the purchase of goods. Thus, the aggregate level of consumption spending was reduced by using rationing to reduce the consumption of various goods essential for the war effort (gasoline, tires, meat, shoes, etc.).

[22] See Chap. 9.

[23] See Milton Friedman and Anna J. Schwartz, *The Great Contraction* (Princeton, N.J.: Princeton University Press, 1965).

The second argument that policy makers themselves may be responsible for economic disturbances arises from the relationship between election results and economic conditions. It appears that incumbents tend to be reelected when economic conditions, primarily the unemployment rate, are improving in the year before the election. Accordingly, it is tempting for incumbents to try to improve economic conditions in the period before the election; their efforts may involve tax reductions or increases in government spending — at the least, governments tend not to raise taxes in election years. It is now quite common to talk of the *political business cycle.* The political business cycle consists of economic fluctuations produced by economic policies designed to help win elections.[24]

We proceed next to discuss econometric models and the factors that make the task of policy makers far more difficult than an overly literal interpretation of the simple *IS-LM* model in Figure 12-5 might suggest.

12-5 ECONOMETRIC MODELS FOR POLICY MAKING AND FORECASTING

Consider a government faced with a recession. It has to decide whether to react, and if so, what policies to change. It could cut taxes or raise government spending and/or it could use expansionary monetary policy. But it has to know not only what policies to change — what medicines to use — but also the right doses. If government spending should be increased by $50 billion, it will not do much good to increase it by $5 billion. But if it should be increased by only $5 billion, an increase in government spending of $50 billion will push the economy well beyond the point of full employment and create inflationary pressures.

In other words, policy makers have to know the *multipliers* associated with monetary and fiscal policy. To calculate these multipliers, they typically rely on *econometric models.* An econometric model is an equation or a set of equations with numerical values for parameters, based on the past behavior of the economy, describing the behavior of some specific sectors of the economy or the economy as a whole.

Figure 12-6 shows estimates of the effects of monetary policy in the DRI (Data Resources, Inc.) model. The monetary policy change permanently increases the amount of unborrowed reserves held by the banks by $1 billion in period zero. The figure shows the resultant changes in GNP in subsequent periods, measured as a percent of GNP. There is very little change in GNP in period 1, but then the effect builds up, reaching a peak after 2 years.[25]

Figure 12-6 presents a *dynamic multiplier,* with the effects of monetary policy

---

[24] For a discussion of the political business cycle which is also interesting as a creative application of the (mathematical) theory of games to economics and politics, see "Alberto Alesina and Howard Rosenthal, "Partisan Cycles in Congressional Elections and the Macroeconomy," NBER Working Paper #2706, Sept. 1988. For evidence on the impact of economic conditions on voting, see, for example, Ray Fair, "The Effect of Economic Events on Votes for President: 1984 Update," *Political Behavior,* 1988.

[25] This pattern is strikingly similar to that seen in Fig. 9-6.

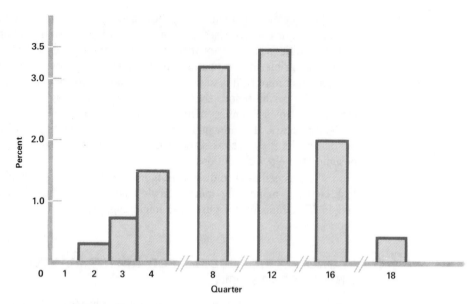

FIGURE 12-6

MONETARY POLICY MULTIPLIER FROM THE DRI MODEL. The figure shows
the dynamic multiplier for a one-time increase of 3 percent in the
nominal stock of M_1, to occur during the first four quarters. For each
quarter the figure shows the increase in the level of real output relative
to the path the economy would otherwise have taken. Thus for the
eighth quarter, for example, the 3 percent increase in money implies a
rise of real GNP of 3.2 percent. By the eighteenth quarter, output is
nearly back to its normal path. (SOURCE: DRI/McGraw-Hill.)

on real GNP first building up and then dying away.[26] The monetary policy multiplier in
Figure 12-6 seems to be exactly what is needed for policy making. We thus want to look
more closely at econometric models.

Econometric models that describe the entire economy are, as we should expect,
called *macroeconometric models*.[27] Macroeconometric models differ enormously in
size. The smallest model may be a single equation that estimates how the level of real
GNP depends on the money stock and fiscal policy variables. By contrast, the WEFA
(Wharton Econometric Forecasting Associates, Inc.) model attempts to predict 10,000
variables, among them the level of GNP, the inflation rate, interest rates, and prices
and output levels in particular industries.

---

[26] Dynamic multipliers were defined in Chap. 8.

[27] We do not describe the statistical methods of estimating such models. For an introduction to these
methods, see Robert S. Pindyck and Daniel L. Rubinfeld, *Econometric Models and Economic Forecasts*, 2d
ed. (New York: McGraw-Hill, 1981).

The Big Models

Many econometric models are owned by corporations, which sell the forecasts and analyses produced by the models. The best-known large commercial macroeconometric models are the DRI and the WEFA models. Customers receive the forecasts of the model for the behavior of the economy over the next few quarters and years.[28] These forecasts are based on assumptions about future economic policy and also about such important factors as future oil prices.

Macroeconometric models are also used by the government. The Federal Reserve Board in Washington uses a model it originally helped develop, now called the MPS [MIT-(University of) Pennsylvania – Social Science Research Council (SSRC)] model, to predict the effects of different policy choices. The Department of Commerce maintains and uses the BEA (Bureau of Economic Analysis) model.

The models mentioned rely on an extended *IS-LM* framework for the modeling of aggregate demand. They estimate equations for the components of aggregate demand, consumption, different categories of investment, exports, and state and local government spending. The consumption function, for instance, would be similar to the sophisticated consumption function we discussed in Chapter 8. In modeling the financial markets, the models typically include a money demand function similar to that which we presented in Chapter 10. They may also include a money supply *function* like that of Chapter 11, relating the stock of money to the supply of high-powered money. In brief, we can think of the aggregate demand side of most of the larger econometric models as attempts to describe statistically the extended *IS-LM* framework outlined in Chapters 4 and 5 and developed in Chapters 8 through 11.

There are, in addition, many smaller models with much less detail. Among these is the St. Louis model, produced by the St. Louis Federal Reserve Bank, which starts from an equation that links the behavior of nominal GNP to monetary and fiscal policy. It thus leaves out the details of the ways in which policy affects the economy and looks only at the final effects of policy. Four additional equations allow the model to predict the level of real as well as nominal GNP (and thus the GNP deflator and the inflation rate) and also to predict interest rates.

The aggregate supply side of the models typically builds on a Phillips curve linking wage changes to unemployment and on markup pricing, relating prices to wages.

Forecast Accuracy

How accurate are the models? There are many different models, none of them predicting exactly the same set of variables, and none of them predicting better than all the other models on all occasions. There is thus no simple answer to the question of how well econometric models in general predict.[29]

---

[28] They also typically obtain access to computer programs and data associated with the models.

[29] See Stephen McNees, "How Accurate are Macroeconomic Forecasts," *New England Economic Review*, July/August 1988. McNees's results indicate that macroeconometric forecasts have improved over time.

TABLE 12-3
ECONOMETRIC FORECASTS*

Year	REAL GNP, % CHANGE			INFLATION RATE (GNP DEFLATOR), %		
	Actual	Predicted	Error	Actual	Predicted	Error
1980	−0.3	−0.8	−0.5	9.8	8.2	−1.6
1981	0.9	2.4	0.5	8.9	9.1	0.2
1982	−1.2	2.8	5.3	4.5	7.1	2.6
1983	3.5	2.5	−1.1	3.8	5.1	1.3
1984	6.5	5.2	−1.6	4.1	4.7	0.6
1985	3.4	3.3	−0.1	3.0	4.1	1.1
1986	2.8	2.9	0.1	2.7	3.6	0.9
Average error, 1971–1986:		1.5				1.5
CEA forecast for 1989:†						
	?	3.5	?	?	3.7	?

* These are the median forecasts for those collected in each year. For further explanation of the variables in this table, see footnote 30.

† The reader is to supply the actual values for 1989; see problem 9a.

SOURCE: Federal Reserve Bank of Richmond, *Business Forecasts*, various years. CEA forecast from *Economic Report of the President*, 1989, fourth quarter 1988 to fourth quarter, 1989.

Table 12-3 gives some idea of the accuracy of forecasts. In November and December each year until the end of 1985 the Federal Reserve Bank of Richmond collected forecasts for the next year from a large number of different forecasters, several of which use econometric models. At the end of 1985, for instance, the Richmond Fed collected 43 forecasts. Table 12-3 shows the median forecasts for the growth rate of real GNP and the inflation rate collected over the period 1980–1986. We also show the average error made by the median forecasts over the period 1971–1986.[30]

In addition we present in Table 12-3 the forecasts of the Council of Economic Advisers for the growth of output and the GNP deflator from the fourth quarter of 1988 to the fourth quarter of 1989. Since the final data for 1989 will be available only after this book is published, you will have to fill in for yourself in the table how well or badly the President's economic advisers did in forecasting 1989 macroeconomic performance.

---

[30] Two definitions are needed. First, the *median forecast* for each variable is the middle forecast when the forecasts are lined up in order. Second, the average error in Table 12-3 is the *average absolute error*—the average difference between the forecast and the actual value of the variable, whether positive or negative. For instance, if there are three forecasts, with errors of −3, −1, and 5, the average absolute error is 3 [= (3 + 1 + 5)/3].

It is quite clear from Table 12-3 that econometric forecasting is not perfect. A particularly big error was made in 1982. Forecasters did not expect a recession and overpredicted both output and inflation. But typically the forecasters do not make such large errors. For the other years shown, real GNP was generally about 1 percent from the predicted level.

Why do the forecasters make mistakes? One reason is that unexpected events happen over the next year; for instance, economic policy may be different from that which the forecasters expected when they made their predictions, or the price of oil may rise or fall unexpectedly. But this is not the only reason. A second reason is that the models themselves are not accurate. That is, even when the actual values of government spending, the money stock, the price of oil, etc., are fed into a model, it does not respond with the actual values of real GNP, or the inflation rate, or the unemployment rate. Why? Because we do not know accurately how the economy works.[31]

With this description of econometric models as background, we are ready to discuss the three handicaps of policy making: lags, expectations, and uncertainty about the effects of policy.

12-6 LAGS IN THE EFFECTS OF POLICY

Suppose that the economy is at full employment and has been affected by an aggregate demand disturbance that reduces the equilibrium level of income below full employment. Suppose further that there was no advance warning of this disturbance and that, consequently, no policy actions were taken in anticipation of its occurrence. Policy makers now have to decide *whether to respond at all* and *how* to respond to the disturbance.

The first concern — and the first difficulty — should be over the permanence of the disturbance and its subsequent effects. Suppose the disturbance is only transitory, such as a one-period reduction in consumption spending. When the disturbance is transitory, so that consumption rapidly reverts to its initial level, the best policy may be to do nothing at all. Provided suppliers or producers do not mistakenly interpret the decrease in demand as permanent but, rather, perceive it as transitory, they will absorb it by production and inventory changes rather than by capacity adjustments. The disturbance will affect income in this period but will have very little permanent effect. Since today's policy actions take time to have an effect, today's actions would be hitting an economy that would otherwise have been close to full employment, and would tend to move the economy *away* from the full-employment level. Thus, if a disturbance is temporary and it has no long-lived effects and policy operates with a lag, then the best policy is to do nothing.

Figure 12-7 illustrates the main issue. Assume that an aggregate demand disturbance reduces output below potential, starting at time t_0. Without active policy inter-

---

[31] Indeed, one of the most useful pieces of statistical information that comes with econometric model estimates is a measure of the confidence that can be attached to estimates of parameters and also multipliers.

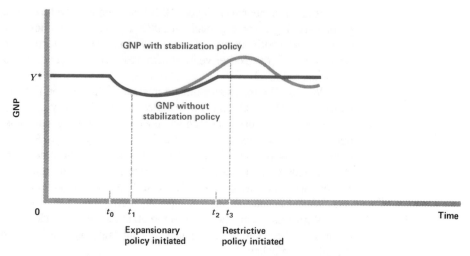

FIGURE 12-7

LAGS AND DESTABILIZING POLICY. A disturbance at time t_0 reduces output below the full-employment level. It takes until t_1 before policy responds, and there is a further lag until the policy starts working. By the time the full effects of the policy are evident, output would already have returned to the full-employment level even without action. But because a policy action has been taken, output now rises *above* the full-employment level and then fluctuates around Y^*. The lags in policy thus have made policy a source of fluctuations in output that would not otherwise have happened.

vention output declines for a while but then recovers and reaches the full-employment level again at time t_2. Consider next the path of GNP under an active stabilization policy, but one that works with the disadvantage of lags. Thus, expansionary policy might be initiated at time t_1 and start taking effect some time after. Output now tends to recover faster as a consequence of the expansion and, because of poor dosage and/or timing, actually overshoots the full-employment level. By time t_3, restrictive policy is initiated, and some time after, output starts turning down toward full employment and may well continue cycling for a while. If this is an accurate description of the potency or scope of stabilization policy, then one has to ask whether it is worth trying to stabilize output or whether the effect of stabilization policy is, in fact, to make things worse. Stabilization policy may actually *destabilize* the economy.

One of the main difficulties of policy making is in establishing whether or not a disturbance is temporary. It was clear enough in the case of World War II that a high level of defense expenditures would be required for some years. However, in the case of the Arab oil embargo of 1973–1974, it was not at all clear how long the embargo would last or whether the high prices for oil that were established in late 1973 would persist. At the time, there were many who argued that the oil cartel would not survive and that oil prices would soon fall—that is, that the disturbance was temporary. "Soon" turned out to be 12 years. Let us suppose, however, that it is known that the disturbance will have effects that will last for several quarters and that the level of income will, without intervention, be below the full-employment level for some time. What lags do policy makers encounter?

We now consider the steps required before action can be taken after a disturbance has occurred, and then the process by which that policy action affects the economy. There are delays, or lags, at every stage. It is customary and useful to divide the lags into an *inside lag*, which is the time period it takes to undertake a policy action—such as a tax cut or an increase in the money supply—and an *outside lag*, which describes the timing of the effects of the policy action on the economy. The inside lag, in turn, is divided into recognition, decision, and action lags.

The Recognition Lag

The *recognition lag* is the period that elapses between the time a disturbance occurs and the time the policy makers recognize that action is required. This lag could, in principle, be *negative* if the disturbance could be predicted and appropriate policy actions considered *before* it even occurs. For example, we know that seasonal factors affect behavior. Thus it is known that at Christmas the demand for currency is high. Rather than allow this to exert a restrictive effect on the money supply, the Fed will accommodate this seasonal demand by an expansion in high-powered money.

In other cases the recognition lag has been positive, so that some time has elapsed between the disturbance and the recognition that active policy was required. This was true, for example, of the 1974–1975 recession. The unemployment rate started increasing very rapidly in the third, and particularly in the fourth, quarter of 1974. It is now clear that expansionary action was required no later than September 1974. Yet, in October 1974, the administration was still calling for a tax *increase* to reduce aggregate demand and inflation. Only in January did the President call for a tax reduction.

Solow and Kareken have studied the history of policy making and have found that on average the recognition lag is about 5 months.[32] The lag was found to be somewhat shorter when the required policy was expansionary and somewhat longer when restrictive policy was required. The speed with which tax cuts follow sharp increases in unemployment was clearly evident in both 1975 and 1980.

---

[32] See John Kareken and Robert Solow, "Lags in Monetary Policy," in *Stabilization Policies,* prepared for the Commission on Money and Credit (Englewood Cliffs, N.J.: Prentice-Hall, 1963). See, too, the review of the evidence in Thomas Mayer, *Monetary Policy in the United States* (New York: Random House, 1968), chap. 6, and Michael J. Hamburger, "The Lag in the Effect of Monetary Policy: A Survey of the Recent Literature," Federal Reserve Bank of New York *Monthly Review,* December 1971. This question has not, so far as we know, been reexamined recently.

The Decision and Action Lags

The recognition lag is the same for monetary and fiscal policy. The Federal Reserve Board, the Treasury, and the Council of Economic Advisers are in constant contact with one another and share their predictions about the future course of the economy. By contrast, for the *decision lag*— the delay between the recognition of the need for action and the policy decision— there is a difference between monetary and fiscal policy. The Federal Reserve System's Open Market Committee meets frequently to discuss and decide on policy. Thus, once the need for a policy action has been recognized, the decision lag for monetary policy is short. Further, the *action lag*— the lag between the policy decision and its implementation— for monetary policy is also short. The major monetary policy actions, we have seen, are open market operations and changes in the discount rate. These policy actions can be undertaken almost as soon as a decision has been made. Thus, under the existing arrangements of the Federal Reserve System, the decision lag for monetary policy is short and the action lag practically zero.

However, fiscal policy actions are less rapid. Once the need for a fiscal policy action has been recognized, the administration has to prepare legislation for that action. Next, the legislation has to be considered and approved by both houses of Congress before the policy change can be made. That may be a lengthy process. Even after the legislation has been approved, the policy change has still to be put into effect. If the fiscal policy takes the form of a change in tax rates, it may be some time before the change in tax rates begins to be reflected in paychecks — that is, there may be an action lag. On occasion, though, as in early 1975 when taxes were reduced, the fiscal decision lag may be short; in 1975 it was about 2 months.

The lengthy legislative process for fiscal policy in the United States led in the past to repeated suggestions that the President be granted the authority to undertake certain fiscal actions without legislation. One proposal was that the President should be allowed to vary tax rates by limited amounts in either direction without first obtaining specific authorization from Congress but subject to congressional veto. This proposal would reduce the decision lag. Whether such a change is desirable from the economic viewpoint depends, obviously, on whether the President would, on average, make changes in tax rates that tend to offset disturbances to the economy. Do remember, though, the political business cycle. The proposal is no longer on the policy agenda; indeed, the U.S. experience with fiscal policy in the 1980s, in which political resistance to tax increases has been extremely strong, suggests that fiscal policy cannot at present be thought of as an anticyclical policy tool in the United States.

Built-in Stabilizers

The existence of the inside lag in policy making focuses attention on the built-in or automatic stabilizers that we discussed in Chapter 3. One of the major benefits of automatic stabilizers is that their inside lag is zero. The most important automatic stabilizer is the income tax. It stabilizes the economy by reducing the multiplier effects of any disturbance to aggregate demand. The multiplier for the effects of changes in autonomous spending on GNP is inversely related to the income tax rate. Similarly, unemployment compensation is another automatic stabilizer. When workers become unemployed and reduce their consumption, that reduction in consumption demand tends to have multiplier effects on output. Those multiplier effects are reduced when a worker receives unemployment compensation because disposable income is reduced by less than the loss in earnings.

Figure 12-8 shows the practical importance of automatic stabilizers (and active fiscal policy) in the U.S. economy. The figure shows personal disposable income as a percentage of GNP. Personal disposable income, as you will remember from Chapter 2, is the income that actually accrues to households after all taxes and inclusive of all transfers. The figure brings out the fact that during periods of a high GNP gap — the early 1960s, the 1969 – 1971, 1974 – 1975, and 1981 – 1982 periods — personal dis-

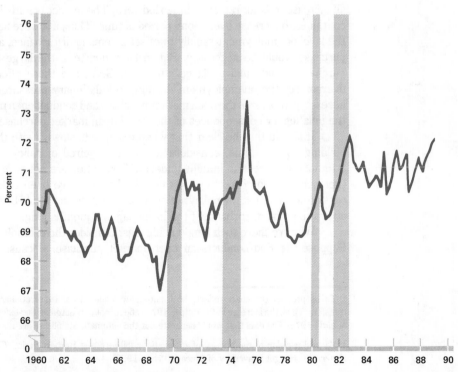

FIGURE 12-8
AUTOMATIC STABILIZERS: THE RATIO OF PERSONAL DISPOSABLE INCOME
TO GNP, 1960–1989. Shaded bars mark periods of recession. (SOURCE:
DRI/McGraw-Hill.)

posable income rises relative to GNP. In those periods, transfer payments rise and the growth in income tax collection slows down.[33]

Although built-in stabilizers have desirable effects, they cannot be carried too far without also affecting the overall performance of the economy. The multiplier could be reduced to 1 by increasing the tax rate to 100 percent, and that would appear to be a stabilizing influence on the economy. But with 100 percent marginal tax rates, the desire to work, and consequently the level of GNP, would be reduced. Thus there are limits on the extent to which automatic stabilizers are desirable.[34] Nonetheless, automatic stabilizers play an important role in the economy; it has been argued that the absence of significant unemployment compensation in the 1930s was one of the major factors that made the great depression so severe, and that the existence of the stabilizers alone makes the recurrence of such a deep depression unlikely.

The Outside Lag

The inside lag of policy is a discrete lag in which policy can have no effect on the economy until it is implemented. The outside lag is generally a distributed lag: once the policy action has been taken, its effects on the economy are spread over time. There is usually a small immediate effect of a policy action, but other effects occur later.

The idea that policy operates on aggregate demand and income with a distributed lag was already shown in Figure 12-6. There we showed the effects of a once-and-for-all increase in bank reserves in period zero. The impact is initially very small, and it continues to increase over a long period of time. Thus, if it were necessary to increase the level of employment rapidly to offset a demand disturbance, a large open market purchase would be necessary. But in later quarters, the large initial open market purchase would build up large effects on GNP, and those effects would probably overcorrect the unemployment, leading to inflationary pressures. It would then be necessary to reverse the open market purchase and conduct open market sales to avoid the inflationary consequences of the initial open market purchase.

It should thus be clear that when policy acts slowly, with the impacts of policy building up over time, considerable skill is required of policy makers if their own attempts to correct an initially undesirable situation are not to lead to problems that themselves need correcting. Recall also that we have been talking here about the outside lag, and that the policy action we are considering would be taken only 6 months after the initial disturbance if the inside lag is 6 months long.

Why are there such long outside lags? Consider the example of monetary policy. Suppose the Fed conducts an open market purchase. Because aggregate demand

---

[33] To be precise, the chart reflects both automatic stabilizers and discretionary changes in taxes and transfers. Thus, the increase in the ratio in 1975 reflects not only automatic transfers but also the tax rebate of early 1975. The data that would separate out the automatic stabilizers are not conveniently available.

[34] For a discussion of the history of automatic stabilizers, see Herbert Stein, *The Fiscal Revolution in America* (Chicago: University of Chicago Press, 1969).

depends heavily on lagged values of income, interest rates, and other economic variables, the open market purchase initially has effects mainly on interest rates and not on income. The interest rates, in turn, affect investment with a lag, and also affect consumption by affecting the value of wealth.[35] Then when aggregate demand is affected by the initial open market purchase, the increase in aggregate demand itself produces lagged effects on subsequent aggregate demand through the fact that both consumption and investment depend on past values of income. So the effects of an initial open market purchase will be spread through time, as in Figure 12-6.

Monetary versus Fiscal Policy Lags

The discussion of the previous paragraph suggests that fiscal policy and certainly changes in government spending, which act directly on aggregate demand, may affect income more rapidly than monetary policy. This is indeed the case. However, while fiscal policy has a shorter outside lag, it has a considerably longer inside lag. Thus, while the active use of fiscal policy seems attractive because of the short outside lag, that advantage is more than offset by a potentially long inside lag.

Our analysis of lags indicates clearly one difficulty in undertaking stabilizing short-term policy actions: It takes time to set the policies in action, and then the policies themselves take time to affect the economy. But that is not the only difficulty. Further difficulties, considered in Sections 12-7 and 12-8, arise from uncertainty about the exact timing and magnitude of the effects of policy.

12-7 THE ROLE OF EXPECTATIONS

We have discussed the two basic sources of lags in economic behavior in earlier chapters. The first source is the cost of rapid adjustment. For example, in Chapter 9 we showed how the costs of adjusting the actual capital stock to the desired capital stock lead to lags in the investment function. The second source of lags is expectations. In this section we focus on expectations, their formation, and the results they have on policy and its effectiveness.

While it is undoubtedly true that the past behavior of a variable influences expectations about its future behavior, it is also true that consumers and investors will sometimes use more information than is contained in the past behavior of a variable when trying to predict its future behavior.

Consider, for example, forecasts of permanent income—long-run average income. In Chapter 8, as in Friedman's original work on the consumption function, permanent income is estimated as an average of income in the recent past. But, as we

---

[35] Recall that in Chap. 8 we discussed the life-cycle model of consumption demand, in which consumption is affected by the level of wealth. Part of wealth is the value of stock market assets, which rises when the long-term interest rate falls. Thus, interest rates affect consumption through a wealth effect.

noted there, individuals take more information into account in forming expectations than just past levels of income. As emphasized by the rational expectations approach, individuals take all economically relevant information into account in forming expectations. Someone who discovers an oil well in his backyard today does not base his estimate of expected income on what he earned last year. Or, suppose that you have been estimating the expected rate of inflation as an average of past rates of inflation at a time when the inflation rate is high, but then a new government is elected on a strictly anti-inflationary platform. You would lower your estimate of the inflation rate; that is, you would use more information in predicting it than is contained solely in its past behavior.

It is, in general, very difficult to incorporate all relevant information that is used by economic agents within a simple econometric model. That means that there will inevitably be errors in what the models predict for the consequences of various policy actions, meaning, in turn, that it is difficult to control the economy precisely.

Expectations and Policy

It is particularly important to consider the effects of a given policy action itself on expectations, since it is possible that a new type of policy will affect the way in which expectations are formed.[36] Suppose that the Federal Reserve System announced that from now on its policy would be aimed *solely* at maintaining price stability, and that in response to any price level increase it would reduce the money supply (and vice versa). If people believed the announcement, they would not base expectations of inflation on the past behavior of the inflation rate.

While correct expectations mechanisms must therefore use information about policy responses to disturbances, such care is difficult to apply in practice. Most expectations mechanisms embodied in econometric models of the U.S. economy and used for the assessment of policies assume that expectations affecting consumption and investment spending are based entirely on past values.

Econometric Policy Evaluation Critique

The preceding example of the effects of a change in policy on expectations is part of a wider *econometric policy evaluation critique* formulated by Robert E. Lucas of the University of Chicago, who is the intellectual leader of the rational expectations approach to macroeconomics.[37] Lucas argues that existing macroeconometric models cannot be used to study the effects of policy changes *because the way private agents*

---

[36] The interactions of policy and expectations have been the focus of the rational expectations approach to macroeconomics, introduced in Chap. 7, and to be pursued in greater detail in Chap. 18. For an early statement, see Thomas J. Sargent and Neil Wallace, "Rational Expectations and the Theory of Economic Policy," *Journal of Monetary Economics,* April 1976.

[37] See "Econometric Policy Evaluation: A Critique," in R. E. Lucas, Jr., *Studies in Business Cycle Theory* (Cambridge, Mass.: MIT Press, 1981).

(firms and consumers) respond to changes in income and prices depends on the types of policy being followed.

Lucas argues that problems of this sort are pervasive in macroeconometric models. He does not argue that it will never be possible to use econometric models to study policy — only that existing models cannot be used for that purpose.

Accordingly, the Lucas critique is not one that rules out the use of econometric models. It suggests rather that very careful modeling of the responses of consumers and firms to changes in income and prices, and particularly to changes in policy, is necessary.

Summary

This section has made two important points about the role of expectations in explaining the difficulties of policy making. First, the general point is that the difficulties of modeling the way in which expectations are formed will inevitably lead to errors in economists' forecasts of the effects of particular policy actions on the economy. The second point, a particular one, is that expectations themselves are likely to be affected by policy measures, and that failure to take account of the effects of policy on expectations will lead to mistaken predictions of the effects of those policies.

12-8 UNCERTAINTY AND ECONOMIC POLICY

So far in this chapter we have described the disturbances that affect the economy, econometric models that are used in policy making, the difficulties of making policy decisions when there are long lags in the effects of policy, and the problem of modeling expectations. We can summarize most of the implied problems for policy making by saying that it is impossible to predict the effects of any given policy action exactly.

How should a policy maker react in the face of these uncertainties? We distinguish between uncertainty about the correct model of the economy and uncertainty about the precise values of the parameters or coefficients within a given model of the economy, even though the distinction is not watertight.

First, there is considerable disagreement and therefore uncertainty about the correct model of the economy, as evidenced by the large number of macroeconometric models. Reasonable economists can and do differ about what theory and empirical evidence suggest are the correct behavioral functions of the economy. Generally, each economist will have reasons for favoring one particular form and will use that form. But, being reasonable, the economist will recognize that the particular formulation being used may not be the correct one, and will thus regard its predictions as subject to a margin of error. In turn, policy makers will know that there are different predictions about the effects of a given policy, and will want to consider the range of predictions that are being made in deciding on policy.

Second, as we noted in Section 12-5, even within the context of a given model there is uncertainty about the values of parameters and multipliers. The statistical evidence does allow us to say something about the likely range of parameters or

box 12-1

POLICY MAKING UNDER UNCERTAINTY: 1980

In October 1979, in response to the high and rising inflation, the Fed changed its policies with the intention of keeping money growth under control in order to fight inflation. (This change was discussed in Chapter 11.)

At the beginning of 1980 the inflation news was all bad, as Table 1 shows. From month to month the inflation rate was at an annual rate of about 18 percent. Much of this increase was due to higher oil prices, but the Fed and the administration, nonetheless, were deeply concerned over rising prices. Although a recession had been expected, and would reduce inflation if it happened, the unemployment rate hardly increased in early 1980. At the same time, the demand for loans in the economy was very high; firms and consumers were doing a lot of borrowing despite record high interest rates, which suggested that the demand for investment and consumer durables would be high — thus also suggesting that there would not be a recession.

Although interest rates were at record highs, monetary growth data presented a mixed picture. This was a period when the money stock measures were being redefined. $M1$ (there were then two versions) was growing reasonably slowly, while $M2$ was growing more rapidly. Thus, judging from interest rates, monetary policy was restrictive, while judging from money growth, it was uncertain what was happening.

In March the administration acted. Worried by the continuing inflation and continuing high level of borrowing, the President announced a program of credit controls. Limits were placed on the amount of loans banks could make, and other steps were taken to reduce the growth of assets that were close substitutes for money, such as money market mutual funds. The growth rate of money ($M1$) had already started falling in March and was negative also for the next 2 months. Interest rates came down sharply in May and June.

The second quarter of 1980 saw the sharpest decline in GNP in a single quarter in the post-World War II period. The unemployment rate increased sharply from March to April and from April to May. The recession that had been widely expected was now

multipliers,[38] so that we can at least get some idea of the type of errors that could result from a particular policy action.

Uncertainty about the size of the effects that will result from any particular policy action is known as *multiplier uncertainty*. For instance, our best estimate of the multiplier of an increase in government spending might be 1.2. If GNP has to be increased by $60 billion, we would increase government spending by $50 billion. But the statistical evidence might be better interpreted as saying only that we can be quite confident that the multiplier is between 0.9 and 1.5. In that case, when we increase government spending by $50 billion, we expect GNP to rise by some amount between $45 and $75 billion.

---

[38] We are discussing here confidence intervals about estimates of parameters; see Pindyck and Rubinfeld, *Econometric Models and Economic Forecasts*, for further discussion. This is the point made in footnote 31.

TABLE 1
ECONOMIC DATA, JANUARY–JUNE 1980* (percent)

Month	Inflation rate (CPI), per annum	Civilian unemployment rate	Money growth rate ($M1$), per annum	Money growth rate ($M2$), per annum	Treasury bill rate
January	18.7	6.2	5.4	7.3	12.0
February	17.8	6.2	10.4	10.0	12.8
March	18.7	6.3	−0.3	5.1	15.5
April	14.4	6.9	−13.2	−2.4	14.0
May	12.5	7.6	−1.2	9.9	9.2
June	14.1	7.5	15.6	19.7	7.0

* Inflation and money growth rates are one-month changes at annual rates.
SOURCE: *Economic Report of the President*, 1981.

fully visible. Indeed, the National Bureau of Economic Research later decided that the recession had begun in January 1980. Thus the credit controls were put in place after the recession had begun.

Most likely the credit controls were overkill. The economy was already into a recession when they were imposed. But policy makers and outside observers did not know that then. And the signs in early 1980 were, indeed, very mixed. The problem of policy making is that it cannot be done with the benefit of hindsight. But with the benefit of hindsight we can see that the policy makers in March 1980 were wrong about the current economic situation and the likelihood of recession. Such uncertainties about both the current situation and the future are certain to occur, and to complicate the policy-making task. ∎

What is optimal behavior in the face of such multiplier uncertainty? The more precisely policy makers are informed about the relevant parameters, the more activist the policy can afford to be. Conversely, if there is a considerable range of error in the estimate of the relevant parameters — in our example, the multiplier — then policy should be more modest. With poor information, very active policy runs a large danger of introducing unnecessary fluctuations in the economy (see Box 12-1).

12-9 ACTIVIST POLICY

We started this chapter by asking why there are any fluctuations in the American economy when the policy measures needed to iron out those fluctuations seem to be so simple. The list of difficulties in the way of successful policy making that we have outlined may have raised a different question: Why should one believe that policy can do anything to reduce fluctuations in the economy?

Indeed, considerations of the sort spelled out in the previous four sections have led Milton Friedman and others to argue that there should be no use of active counter-cyclical monetary policy and that monetary policy should be confined to making the money supply grow at a constant rate. The precise value of the constant rate of growth of money, Friedman suggests, is less important than the fact that monetary growth should be constant and that policy should *not* respond to disturbances. At various times, he has suggested growth rates for money of 2 or 4 or 5 percent. As Friedman has expressed it, "By setting itself a steady course and keeping to it, the monetary authority could make a major contribution to promoting economic stability. By making that course one of steady but moderate growth in the quantity of money, it would make a major contribution to avoidance of either inflation or deflation of prices."[39] Friedman thus advocates a simple monetary rule in which the Fed does not respond to the condition of the economy. Policies that respond to the current or predicted state of the economy are called *activist policies.*

In discussing the desirability of activist monetary and fiscal policy, we want to distinguish between policy actions taken in response to major disturbances to the economy and *fine tuning,* in which policy variables are continually adjusted in response to small disturbances in the economy. We see no case for arguing that monetary and fiscal policy should not be used actively in the face of major disturbances to the economy. Most of the considerations of the previous sections of this chapter indicate some uncertainty about the effects of policy, but there are still clearly definable circumstances in which there can be no doubt that the appropriate policy is expansionary or contractionary. An administration coming to power in 1933 should not have worried about the uncertainties associated with expansionary policy that we have outlined. The economy does not move from 25 percent unemployment to full employment in a short time (precisely because of those same lags that make policy difficult). Thus, expansionary measures, such as a rapid growth of the money supply, or increased government expenditures, or tax reductions, or all three, would have been appropriate policy since there was no chance they would have an impact only after the economy was at full employment. Similarly, contractionary policies for private demand are called for in wartime. In the fall of 1982, with unemployment rising above 10 percent and the inflation rate falling, expansionary monetary policy was clearly appropriate, and was implemented. In the event of large disturbances in the future, activist monetary and/or fiscal policy should once again be used.[40]

Fine tuning presents more complicated issues. In the case of fiscal policy, the long inside lags make discretionary fine tuning virtually impossible, though automatic stabilizers are in fact fine tuning all the time. But with monetary policy decisions being made frequently, fine tuning of monetary policy is indeed possible. The question then is whether a small increase in the unemployment rate should lead to a small increase in

---

[39] Milton Friedman, "The Role of Monetary Policy," *American Economic Review,* March 1968. See also his book, *A Program for Monetary Stability* (New York: Fordham University Press, 1959).

[40] Interestingly, in the article cited in the preceding footnote, Friedman argues for the use of active policy in the face of major disturbances.

the growth rate of money, or whether policy should not respond until the increase in unemployment becomes large, say more than 1.0 percent.

The problem is that the disturbance that caused the increase in unemployment may be either transitory or permanent. If it is transitory, nothing should be done. If it is permanent, policy should react to a small disturbance in a small way. Given uncertainty over the nature of the disturbance, the technically correct response is a small one, between the zero that is appropriate for a transitory shock and the full response that would be appropriate for a permanent disturbance. Accordingly we believe that fine tuning is appropriate provided that policy responses are always kept small in response to small disturbances.

However, we should emphasize that the argument for fine tuning is a controversial one. The major argument against it is that in practice policy makers do not behave as suggested — making only small adjustments in response to small disturbances. Rather, it is argued, they tend to try to do too much if allowed to do anything. Instead of merely trying to offset disturbances, policy makers attempt to keep the economy always at full employment and therefore undertake inappropriately large policy actions in response to small disturbances.

The major lesson of the previous sections is not that policy is impossible, but that policy that is too ambitious in trying to keep the economy always at full employment (with zero inflation) is impossible. The lesson is to proceed with extreme caution, always bearing in mind the possibility that policy itself may be destabilizing. We see no reason why the Federal Reserve System should try to keep the money supply always growing at the same rate; we believe, on the contrary, that the stability of the economy would be improved by the Fed's following a careful countercyclical policy. Similarly, if fiscal policy were not subject to a long inside lag, we would believe it possible for cautiously used active fiscal policy to be stabilizing.

The successful record of the economy since 1982, when the Fed abandoned a policy that was ostensibly guided by a wish to keep money supply growth constant in favor of a more active and discretionary policy, has led many who were critical of activist policy to reassess their views.

Rules versus Discretion

Finally, in this chapter, we want to discuss the issue of "rules versus discretion." The issue is whether the monetary authority and also the fiscal authority should conduct policy in accordance with a preannounced rule that describes precisely how their policy variables will be determined in all future situations, or whether they should be allowed to use their discretion in determining the values of the policy variables at different times.

One example is the constant growth rate rule, say at 4 percent, for monetary policy. The rule is that no matter what happens, the money supply will be kept growing at 4 percent. Another example would be a rule stating that the money supply growth rate will be increased by 2 percent per year for every 1 percent unemployment in excess of, say 5 percent. Algebraically, such a rule would be expressed as

$$\frac{\Delta M}{M} = 4.0 + 2(u - 5.0) \tag{1}$$

where the growth rate of money $\Delta M/M$ is an annual percentage rate, and u is the percentage unemployment rate.

The activist monetary rule of equation (1) is shown in Figure 12-9. On the horizontal axis, we show the unemployment rate, and on the vertical axis, the growth rate of the money stock. At 5 percent unemployment, monetary growth is 4 percent. If unemployment rises above 5 percent, monetary growth is *automatically* increased. Thus, with 7 percent unemployment, monetary growth would be 8 percent, using equation (1). Conversely, if unemployment dropped below 5 percent, monetary growth would be lowered below 4 percent. The rule therefore gears the amount of monetary stimulus to an indicator of the business cycle. By linking monetary growth to the unemployment rate, an activist, anticyclical monetary policy is achieved, but this is done without any discretion.

The issue of rules versus discretion has been clouded by the fact that most proponents of rules have been nonactivists, whose preferred monetary rule is a constant growth rate rule. Consequently, the argument has tended to center on whether

FIGURE 12-9

AN ACTIVIST MONETARY RULE. The figure describes an activist monetary rule. The growth rate of money is high when the unemployment rate is high and is low when unemployment is low. That way monetary policy is expansionary in times of recession and contractionary in a boom.

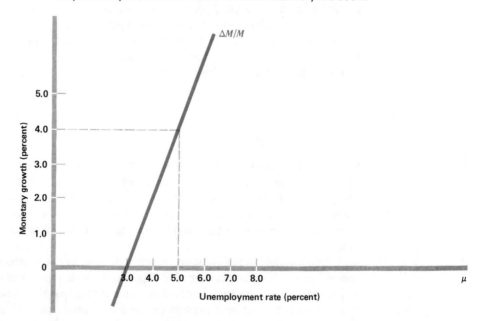

box 12-2

DYNAMIC INCONSISTENCY AND RULES VERSUS DISCRETION

In the last decade economists have developed an intriguing argument in favor of rules rather than discretion. The argument is that policy makers who have discretion will in the end not act consistently, even though it would be better for the economy in the long run if they were consistent.*

How can that be? Here is a noneconomic example. By threatening to punish their children, parents can generally make the children behave better. So long as the children behave well, all is well. But when a child misbehaves, the parent has a problem, since punishing the child is unpleasant for both parent and child. One solution is not to punish but to threaten to punish next time. But if there was no punishment this time, there is unlikely to be punishment next time either, and the threat loses its beneficial effect. The dynamically consistent parent will use punishment each time the child misbehaves, thereby producing better behavior in the long run despite its short-run cost.

What does this have to do with economics? Suppose the inflation rate has risen because of a supply shock. The Fed is considering whether or not to accommodate it by expanding the money supply. If the Fed accommodates, prices will rise more now, but there will be less unemployment. So that seems like a good thing to do. This is the equivalent of not punishing the misbehaving child. But—warn those in favor of rules who worry about dynamic consistency—if the Fed accommodates every inflationary pressure because it fears unemployment, people will soon come to expect it to do that, and they will build an allowance for expected inflation into the wages they set. The Fed will lose whatever reputation it had as an inflation fighter, and the economy will develop an inflationary bias, with the inflation rate creeping up over time.

Much better, says the dynamic consistency approach, that the Fed should have a rule that prevents it from making responses that are right from the short-run viewpoint but wrong from the long-run perspective. Those who, nonetheless, favor discretion for the Fed emphasize the importance of preserving flexibility for monetary policy. To the dynamic inconsistency argument, they counter that as long as the Fed is aware that having a good reputation helps it keep the inflation rate low, it will take any loss of reputation into account when it decides how to respond to particular shocks, and thus will not be dynamically inconsistent. ∎

---

* The basic reference is Finn Kydland and Edward Prescott, "Rules Rather than Discretion; The Inconsistency of Optimal Plans," *Journal of Political Economy*, June 1977. This is very difficult reading. See also V. V. Chari, "Time Consistency and Optimal Policy Design," Federal Reserve Bank of Minneapolis *Quarterly Review*, Fall 1988.

---

activist policy is desirable or not. The fundamental point to recognize is that we can design *activist rules*. We can design rules that have countercyclical features without at the same time leaving any discretion about their actions to policy makers. The point is made by equation (1), which is an activist rule because it expands money supply when unemployment is high and reduces it when unemployment is low. The equation leaves no room for policy discretion and in this respect is a rule (see Box 12-2).

Given that both the economy and our knowledge of it are changing over time, there is no economic case for stating permanent policy rules that would tie the hands of the monetary and fiscal authorities permanently. Two practical issues then arise in the rules-versus-discretion debate. The first is where the authority to change the rule is located. At one extreme, the growth rate of money could be prescribed by the Constitution. At the other it is left to the Fed or the "Fisc" (the equivalent fiscal policy-making body). In each case policy can be changed, but changing the Constitution takes longer than it takes the Fed to change its policy. In the tradeoff between certainty about future policy and flexibility of policy, activists place a premium on flexibility, and those in favor of rules that are difficult to change place a premium on the fact that the Fed has often made mistakes in the past. Because the financial system responds very quickly to shocks and is so interconnected, we believe it essential that the Fed have considerable discretion and thus flexibility to respond to disturbances. But that is far from a universal judgment.

The second issue is whether the policy makers should announce in advance the policies they will be following for the foreseeable future. Such announcements are in principle desirable because they aid private individuals to forecast future policy. In fact, as we described in Chapter 11, the chairperson of the Fed has been required to announce to Congress the Fed's monetary targets. In practice, however, these announcements have not been a great help because the Fed does not stick to its targets. If the Fed is able to keep output close to potential and inflation low by departing from announced policy, then it helps private individuals forecast the variables in which they are really interested — their future incomes and, in the case of firms, the demand for their goods — rather than those, like the money supply, that they need know only as an intermediate step in forecasting.

12-10 SUMMARY

1. Despite the apparent simplicity of policies needed to maintain continuous full employment, the historical record of the behavior of unemployment, shown in Figure 12-1, implies that successful stabilization policy is difficult to carry out.
2. The great depression shaped both modern macroeconomics and many of the economy's institutions. The extremely high unemployment and the length of the depression led to the view that the private economy was unstable and that government intervention was needed to maintain high employment levels.
3. Keynesian economics succeeded because it seemed to explain the causes of the great depression — a collapse of investment demand — and because it pointed to expansionary fiscal policy as a means of preventing future depressions.
4. Keynesian views did not much affect economic policy making in the United States until the New Economics of the Kennedy-Johnson administration. The greatest success of the New Economics was the tax cut of 1964. The New Economics is perceived by the public as having been responsible for increasing inflation during the 1960s. As confidence in the New Economics declined, its emphasis on active stabilization policy was reexamined.

5. The potential need for stabilizing policy actions arises from economic disturbances. Some of these disturbances, such as changes in money demand, consumption spending, or investment demand, arise from within the private sector. Others, such as wars, may arise for noneconomic reasons.

6. Inappropriate economic policy may also tend to move the economy away from full employment. Policy may be inappropriate because policy makers make mistakes or because policy is manipulated for political reasons, leading to the political business cycle.

7. Policy makers work with econometric models in predicting the effects of their policy actions. Econometric models are typically statistical descriptions of the types of model we have worked with in earlier chapters. The models do not forecast with perfect accuracy, partly because they cannot forecast policy and disturbances such as changes in the price of oil. But, in addition, their forecasts are inaccurate because we do not have accurate knowledge of the workings of the economy.

8. The three key difficulties of stabilization policy are that (*a*) policy works with lags; (*b*) the outcome of policy depends very much on private sector expectations, which are difficult to predict and which may react to policy; and (*c*) there is uncertainty about both the structure of the economy and shocks that hit the economy.

9. There are clearly occasions on which active monetary and fiscal policy actions should be taken to stabilize the economy. These are situations in which the economy has been affected by major disturbances.

10. Fine tuning — continuous attempts to stabilize the economy in the face of small disturbances — is more controversial. If fine tuning is undertaken, it calls for small policy responses in an attempt to moderate the economy's fluctuations, rather than to remove them entirely. A very active policy in response to small disturbances is likely to destabilize the economy.

11. In the rules-versus-discretion debate, it is important to recognize that activist rules are possible. The two important issues in the debate are how difficult it should be to change policy, and whether policy should be announced as far ahead as possible. There is a tradeoff between the certainty about future policy that comes from rules, and the flexibility of the policy makers in responding to shocks.

KEY TERMS

New Deal
New Economics
Economic disturbances
Political business cycle
Econometric models
Macroeconometric models
Inside lag
Recognition lag
Decision lag

Action lag
Outside lag
Multiplier uncertainty
Activist policy
Policy rule
Fine tuning
Rules versus discretion
Dynamic inconsistency

PROBLEMS

1. It is sometimes said that the great depression would have been a severe recession if it had stopped in 1931, but would not have been the calamity it was.
   (a) From Table 12-1 calculate the rate at which GNP was falling from 1929 to 1931.
   (b) How does that rate compare with the rate at which real GNP fell during the 1981–1982 recession?
   (c) Do you agree with the first sentence in this question? Explain.

2. Using Table 12-2, explain why concentration on the actual budget deficit might have given a misleading impression of fiscal policy at some stages between 1929 and 1933.

3. In Table 12-1 examine the behavior of the short-term (commercial paper) interest rate and the growth rate of money. Explain why a Keynesian might have thought monetary policy was expansionary during the great depression, while a monetarist would argue that monetary policy was, on the contrary, contractionary.

4. Suppose that GNP is $40 billion below its potential level. It is expected that next-period GNP will be $20 billion below potential, and that two periods from now it will be back at its potential level. You are told that the multiplier for government spending is 2 and that the effects of the increased government spending are immediate. What policy actions can be taken to put GNP back on target each period?

5. The basic facts about the path of GNP are as above. But there is now a one-period outside lag for government spending. Decisions to spend today are translated into actual spending only tomorrow. The multiplier for government spending is still 2 in the period that the spending takes place.
   (a) What is the best that can be done to keep GNP as close to target as possible each period?
   (b) Compare the path of GNP in this question with the path in problem 4 after policy actions have been taken.

6. Life has become yet more complicated. Government spending works with a distributed lag. Now when $1 billion is spent today, GNP increases by $1 billion this period and $1.5 billion next period.
   (a) What happens to the path of GNP if government spending rises enough this period to put GNP back to its potential level this period?
   (b) Suppose fiscal policy actions are taken to put GNP at its potential level this period. What fiscal policy will be needed to put GNP on target next period?
   (c) Explain why the government has to be so active in keeping GNP on target in this case.

7. Suppose that you knew that the multiplier for government spending was between 1 and 2.5, but that its effects ended in the period in which spending was increased. How would you run fiscal policy if GNP would, without policy, behave as in problem 4?

8. Explain why monetary policy works with a distributed lag, as in Figure 12-6.

9. (a) Check the *Economic Report of the President* for 1990 or some other publication (for example, *Survey of Current Business* or *Economic Indicators*) to see how accurate the typical forecast in Table 12-3 was for 1989.
   (b) Explain why econometric forecasts are not totally accurate.

10. Evaluate the argument that monetary policy should be determined by a rule rather than discretion. How about fiscal policy?

11. Evaluate the arguments for a constant growth rate rule for money.

part three

13

AGGREGATE SUPPLY: WAGES, PRICES, AND EMPLOYMENT

*I*n this chapter and the next we develop the aggregate supply side of the economy, which was introduced in Chapter 7. We show the links between wages, prices, and employment, and the adjustment process to disturbances in aggregate demand—monetary or fiscal policy changes or autonomous changes in spending. The development of the aggregate supply side of the economy also allows us to study how the economy adjusts to *supply shocks,* such as the increases in oil prices in 1973–1974 and 1979–1980 or the decline in oil prices in 1985–1986.

The supply side of the economy is an essential part of the *dynamics* of prices (inflation) and output, that is, of the adjustment of prices and output over time when the economy is hit by a disturbance. Investing the time needed to study aggregate supply is worthwhile because the theory is essential in understanding inflation and, in particular, the policy dilemma that comes from the existence of a short-run tradeoff between inflation and unemployment.

The theory of aggregate supply is one of the least settled areas in macroeconomics. The difficulty, already noted at the end of Chapter 7, arises from the contrast between an idealized world, in which output is always at the full-employment level, and the real world, in which the labor market in particular seems to adjust slowly to changes in aggregate demand. We start with the frictionless neoclassical model of the labor market to illustrate how the labor market would work in an idealized model. Then, in Section 13-2, we present the Phillips curve, which shows the basic fact that wages adjust slowly to changes in aggregate demand. This fact is explained in terms of wage-setting behavior in Section 13-3. In Sections 13-4 and 13-5 we develop a theory of aggregate supply that is consistent with and accounts for the behavior of wages seen in the Phillips curve. We use that theory in Section 13-6 to study the response of the economy to supply shocks.

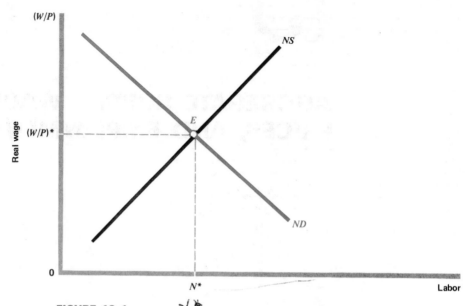

FIGURE 13-1

LABOR MARKET EQUILIBRIUM AND FULL EMPLOYMENT. The labor supply
curve, *NS*, shows the quantity of labor supplied increasing with the real
wage. Along *ND* a reduction in the real wage causes an increase in the
quantity of labor demanded. The labor market is in equilibrium at point *E*.

13-1 THE FRICTIONLESS NEOCLASSICAL MODEL OF THE LABOR MARKET

We have already shown, in Chapter 7, the vertical aggregate supply curve of the
classical case, which exists when the labor market clears continuously and immediately
in response to shocks. In this section we derive this classical aggregate supply curve
starting from microeconomic foundations.

Figure 13-1 presents a microeconomic analysis of the labor market.[1] There is a
downward-sloping demand curve for labor, *ND*. The curve shows that the quantity of
labor demanded is greater the lower is the hourly real wage. The real wage is the ratio
of the wage rate to the price level, or the amount of goods that can be bought with an
hour of work. Also shown is an upward-sloping supply curve of labor, *NS*, indicating
that workers want to supply more hours of work the higher the real wage.

The full derivation of the demand curve for labor in Figure 13-1 is presented in
the appendix to this chapter. The demand curve slopes downward because it is assumed that the marginal productivity of labor decreases as more labor is employed.

---

[1] Figure 13-1 is the same as Figure 7-14.

Firms are competitive and are therefore willing to pay a real wage equal to the value of the marginal product of labor. There is a fixed amount of capital. As more labor is added, each new worker has less machinery with which to produce than the previous workers, and therefore the amount the new worker adds to output (the marginal product of labor) is lower than the amount added by the previous workers. The marginal productivity of labor is thus declining, and the demand curve slopes downward.

The supply curve of labor is shown as upward-sloping because typically as the wage rises, more workers come into the labor force seeking work. But the aggregate supply curve could be vertical (or completely inelastic) if the amount of labor supplied is insensitive to the real wage.[2]

The labor supply and demand curves intersect at point E, with a corresponding level of labor input or employment, N^*, and an equilibrium real wage, $(W/P)^*$. N^* is the *full-employment level of employment*. In this idealized, frictionless neoclassical model, everyone is working precisely as much as he or she wants to at the real wage, $(W/P)^*$, at point E. And firms are hiring precisely the amount of labor they want at the real wage, $(W/P)^*$, at point E. There is always full employment in the frictionless neoclassical world.

Corresponding to the full-employment level of employment, N^*, is the full-employment level of output, Y^*. That is the level of output that is produced using the existing amounts of other factors (the capital stock, land, and raw materials) and the full-employment amount of labor, N^*.[3]

A Change in the Quantity of Money

In Figure 13-2 we show the labor supply and demand curves with the *nominal* wage on the vertical axis. The price level is assumed to be at a given level, say P_0. With a constant price level, a change in the nominal wage is also a change in the real wage, and the labor supply and demand curves thus look exactly as they do in Figure 13-1. The equilibrium nominal wage is W_0.

Now suppose there is an increase in aggregate demand, say because the Fed increases the quantity of money. At the existing price and wage levels the real money

---

[2] If you have studied microeconomics, you have probably seen the "backward-bending" labor supply curve, which is negatively sloped at high wages. That occurs because when the wage rises, individuals can both work less and earn more income. They may choose to respond to higher wages by working less. Although the labor supply curve may well bend backward in the long run (we work fewer hours than our grandparents did and have much higher wages than they had) the supply curve of labor *for the economy* in the short run of a few years is positively sloped. That is because as the wage rises, people who were not working decide it is worthwhile to take a job rather than work at home, and they enter the labor force. Further, people already on the job may, in the short run, want to work longer hours when the real wage rises.

[3] In our description here, technology and the stock of capital are given. But these can change and, as a result, the full-employment level of output will change, too. For example, an increase in the capital stock will raise full-employment output, as does an improvement in technology.

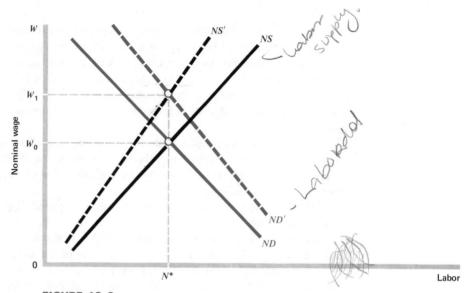

FIGURE 13-2

THE EFFECT OF A CHANGE IN THE PRICE LEVEL ON THE LABOR MARKET.
Labor supply and demand curves *NS* and *ND* are shown for a constant
price level. An increase in the price level shifts both curves upward in
the same proportion, to *NS'* and *ND'*, respectively. The equilibrium level
of employment, *N**, is unaffected by the change in the price level.

stock, M/P, is higher and interest rates are lower. Hence more goods will be de-
manded. Suppose that the increase in the demand for goods raises the price level above
P_0. Then the labor demand and supply curves in Figure 13-2 will shift up to *ND'* and
NS', respectively.

The two curves shift upward by exactly the same proportion since, at each level
of the nominal wage, the real wage is now lower in the same proportion as the price
level has risen. When the two curves shift upward by the same proportion, they
intersect at the same level of employment, *N**. Thus the level of employment will
remain at *N** despite the increase in the price level. The nominal wage rises in Figure
13-2 to the level W_1, but the real wage remains unchanged. Indeed, any increase in the
price level will simply shift both curves by the same vertical distance, leaving the level
of employment unaffected. Only when the price level has risen in the same proportion
as the money stock will the economy be back in equilibrium with the same real
balances, the same real wage, and the same level of employment. Money is neutral in
this frictionless neoclassical world, as we saw in Chapter 7.[4]

---

[4] The analysis underlying Figure 13-2 also explains why the aggregate supply curve in Chapter 7 is vertical in
the classical case. We have just shown in this case that an increase in the price level leads to no change in the
level of employment (and therefore of output), but only a change in the nominal wage. Output supplied
therefore is constant, regardless of the price level, as in the case of the classical supply curve.

Frictional Unemployment and the Natural Rate of Unemployment

Taken literally, the frictionless neoclassical model implies that there is no unemployment. But by including frictions, the theory can account for some unemployment of labor. The frictions occur because the labor market is always in a state of flux. Some people are retiring from their jobs, other people are looking for jobs for the first time, some firms are expanding and are hiring new workers, others have lost business and have to reduce employment, firing workers.

Because it takes time for an individual to find the right new job, there will always be some *frictional* unemployment as people search for jobs. Frictional unemployment is the unemployment that exists as a result of individuals' shifting between jobs and looking for new jobs.

There is some amount of frictional employment associated with the full-employment level of employment, N^*, and full-employment level of output, Y^*. That amount of unemployment is called the *natural rate.* The natural rate of unemployment is the rate of unemployment arising from labor market frictions that exist when the labor market is in equilibrium.

We do not go into the determinants and estimates of the natural rate of unemployment here, reserving that for Chapter 15. We merely note that the natural rate has been estimated at different times at 4 to 7 percent of the labor force.

The important point is that the existence of some unemployment is not necessarily inconsistent with the neoclassical model of the labor market in which the economy is always at the full-employment level of output.

13-2 WAGES, PRICES, AND OUTPUT: THE FACTS

Two major implications of the neoclassical theory of the labor market are at odds with the facts. First, the rate of unemployment fluctuates far more than is consistent with the view that all unemployment is frictional. Figure 13-3 shows the unemployment rate for the period since 1959. It cannot be that the 10 percent unemployment rate in 1982 is equal to the natural rate, much less that the 25 percent unemployment rate in 1933 seen in Figure 12-1 can have been equal to the natural rate. Thus it cannot be that the labor market is always in equilibrium at the full-employment level of employment.

The Phillips Curve

The second fact that is inconsistent with the neoclassical theory is that there appears to be a systematic relationship between the rate of change of wages and the level of demand. In 1958 A. W. Phillips, then a professor at the London School of Economics, published a comprehensive study of wage behavior in the United Kingdom for the years 1861–1957.[5] The main finding is summarized in Figure 13-4, reproduced from his

---

[5] A. W. Phillips, "The Relation between Unemployment and the Rate of Change of Money Wages in the United Kingdom, 1861–1957," *Economica,* November 1958.

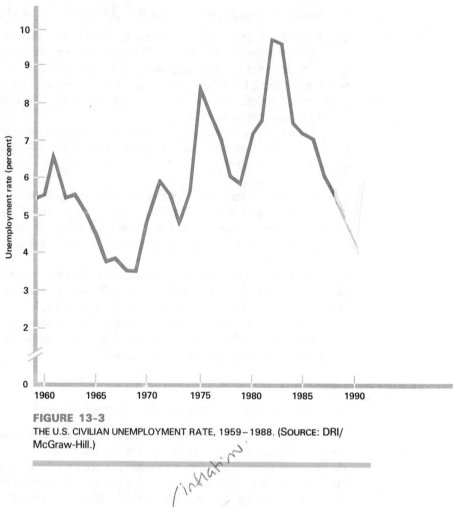

FIGURE 13-3
THE U.S. CIVILIAN UNEMPLOYMENT RATE, 1959–1988. (SOURCE: DRI/
McGraw-Hill.)

article: The Phillips curve is an inverse relationship between the rate of unemployment
and the rate of increase in money wages. The higher the rate of unemployment, the
lower is the rate of wage inflation. In other words, there is a tradeoff between wage
inflation and unemployment.

The Phillips curve shows that the rate of wage inflation decreases with the
unemployment rate. Letting W be the wage this period, and W_{-1} the wage last
period, the rate of wage inflation, g_w, is defined as

$$g_w = \frac{W - W_{-1}}{W_{-1}} \tag{1}$$

With u^* representing the natural rate of unemployment we can write the simple
Phillips curve as

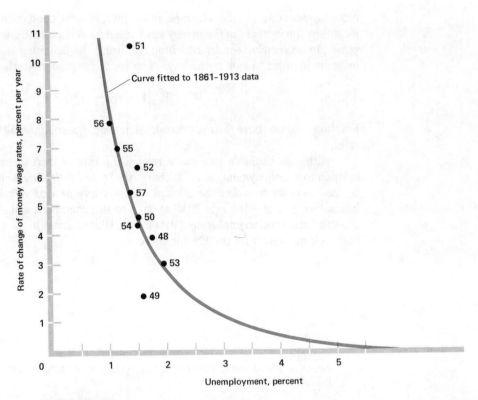

FIGURE 13-4
THE ORIGINAL PHILLIPS CURVE FOR THE UNITED KINGDOM. (SOURCE: A. W.
Phillips, "The Relation between Unemployment and the Rate of Change
of Money Wages in the United Kingdom, 1861–1957," *Economica*,
November 1958.)

$$g_w = -\epsilon(u - u^*) \tag{2}$$

where ϵ measures the responsiveness of wages to unemployment. This equation states
that wages are falling when the unemployment rate exceeds the natural rate, that is,
when $u > u^*$, and rising when unemployment is below the natural rate.

The Phillips curve implies that wages and prices adjust slowly to changes in
aggregate demand. Why? Suppose the economy is in equilibrium with prices stable and
unemployment at the natural rate. Now there is an increase in the money stock of, say,
10 percent. Prices and wages both have to rise by 10 percent for the economy to get
back to equilibrium. But the Phillips curve shows that for wages to rise by an extra 10
percent, the unemployment rate will have to fall. That will cause the rate of wage
increase to go up. Wages will start rising, prices too will rise, and eventually the

economy will return to the full-employment level of output and unemployment. In the meantime the increase in the money stock caused a reduction in unemployment. This point can be readily seen by rewriting (2), using the definition of the rate of wage inflation, in order to look at the level of wages today relative to the past level:

$$W = W_{-1}[1 - \epsilon(u - u^*)] \qquad (2a)$$

For wages to rise above their previous level, unemployment must fall below the natural rate.

Although Phillips's own curve relates the rate of increase of wages or wage inflation to unemployment, as in (2) above, the term *Phillips curve* gradually came to be used to describe either the original Phillips curve *or* a curve relating the rate of increase of *prices*—the rate of inflation—to the unemployment rate. Figure 13-5 shows inflation and unemployment data for the United States in the 1960s that appear entirely consistent with the Phillips curve.

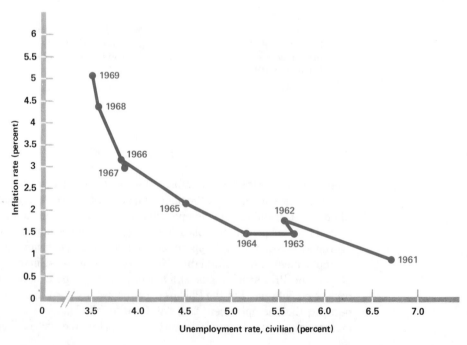

FIGURE 13-5
INFLATION AND UNEMPLOYMENT, UNITED STATES, 1961–1969. (SOURCE: DRI/McGraw-Hill.)

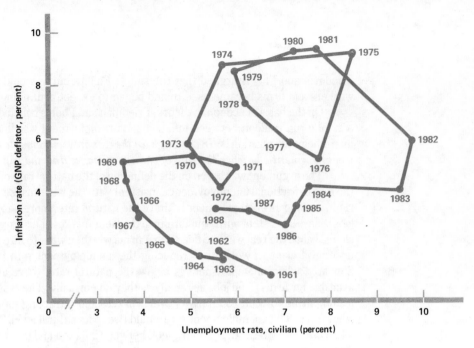

FIGURE 13-6
INFLATION AND UNEMPLOYMENT, UNITED STATES, 1961–1988. (SOURCE: DRI/McGraw-Hill.)

The Policy Tradeoff

The Phillips curve rapidly became a cornerstone of macroeconomic policy analysis. It suggested that policy makers could choose different combinations of unemployment and rates of inflation. For instance, they could have low unemployment as long as they put up with high inflation — say the situation in the late 1960s in Figure 13-5. Or they could maintain low inflation by having high unemployment, as in the early 1960s.

But that simple Phillips curve relationship has not held up well since the 1960s, either in Britain or in the United States. Figure 13-6 shows the behavior of inflation and unemployment in the United States over the entire period since 1960. The data for the 1970s and 1980s do not fit the simple Phillips curve story.

The Friedman-Phelps Amendment

Remarkably, the death of the simple Phillips curve was predicted in the late 1960s by Milton Friedman, then of the University of Chicago, and Edmund Phelps of Columbia.[6]

---

[6] Milton Friedman, "The Role of Monetary Policy," *American Economic Review,* March 1968, and Edmund S. Phelps, "Phillips Curves, Expectations of Inflation, and Optimal Unemployment Over Time," *Economica,* 1967.

Friedman and Phelps argued that the simple Phillips curve would shift over time as workers and firms became used to and began to expect continuing inflation.

On the basis of economic theory, Friedman and Phelps concluded that the notion of a long-run tradeoff between inflation and unemployment was illusory.[7] The Friedman-Phelps proposition is: *In the long run the economy will move to the natural rate of unemployment whatever the rate of change of wages and the inflation rate.*

The argument was based on the definition of the natural rate of unemployment as the rate of frictional unemployment consistent with the labor market's being in equilibrium. As long as unemployment is above the natural rate, more people are looking for jobs than is consistent with equilibrium in the labor market. This excess unemployment should cause the real wage to fall, so that firms will then want to hire more workers and fewer will want to work, thus reducing the unemployment rate to its natural rate. Similarly, when unemployment is below the natural rate, there are too few people available for firms to fill jobs as rapidly as they do normally. The real wage should rise, leading firms to want to employ fewer workers and attracting more people into the labor force. The unemployment rate would rise to its natural level. Thus, they argued, while there may be a short-run tradeoff between inflation and unemployment, there is no long-run tradeoff.

Empirical Evidence

Modern empirical analysis broadly supports the Friedman-Phelps view.[8] In the short run an increase in the money stock affects primarily output and has little effect on inflation or prices or wages. Over longer periods of years, the impact of an increase in money is almost entirely reflected in prices and wages and very little in output. This point is brought out by looking at the estimates of the impact of a monetary expansion in the DRI macroeconometric model for the U.S. economy. Figure 13-7 shows the impact of a 0.5 percent monetary expansion on output and on the price level for the subsequent 16 quarters or 4 years.[9]

The bars show the percentage difference in output and prices relative to what they would have been in the absence of a monetary expansion. To start with, output expands with practically no impact on prices. Gradually the output expansion builds up and prices, too, start increasing. Only after a year does output start falling back as price

---

[7] Remember that at the time they were writing, the facts appeared to support the Phillips curve as a long-run tradeoff — after all, Phillips's own data covered a period of nearly a century.

[8] For a comprehensive review of both theory and evidence, see Palle S. Andersen, "Inflation and Output: A Review of the Wage-Price Mechanism," Bank for International Settlements, Basle, Switzerland, 1989.

[9] The experiment is a 0.5 percent increase in the monetary base. See Data Resources, *U.S. Review,* August 1987. See, too, M. Akhtar and E. Harris, "Monetary Policy Influence of the Economy — An Empirical Analysis," Federal Reserve Bank of New York *Quarterly Review,* Winter 1987, and J. Chouraqui, M. Driscoll, and M. Straus-Kahn, *The Effects of Monetary Policy on the Real Sector: An Overview of Empirical Evidence for Selected OECD Countries,* OECD Working Paper 51, April 1988.

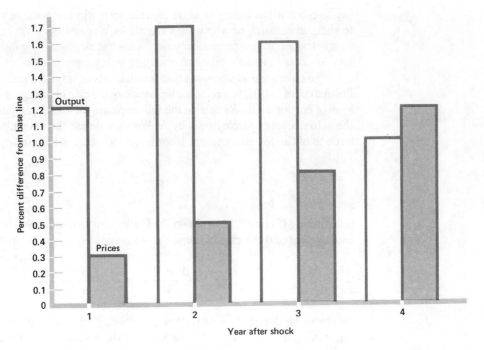

FIGURE 13-7
THE IMPACT OF A CHANGE IN THE MONEY STOCK ON THE PRICE LEVEL AND
OUTPUT. (SOURCE: Data Resources, *U.S. Review*, April 1983.)

increases build up and bring real balances back down. But even after 16 quarters or 4
years, output is still above its initial level and prices have not yet risen by a full
percentage point. In the long run the model has neoclassical properties, but it is
apparent that quite a long time passes before the economy gets there. The exact time
shape of response may vary from one model to another. Some will have more rapid
price responses and less protracted increases in output, and others will show even
longer lags in the adjustment of prices. But virtually all models and studies of the
economy agree that the adjustment takes years, not weeks.

We explain these results in the next section.

13-3 WHY ARE WAGES STICKY?

The assumption that wages are slow to adjust to shifts in demand is essential to our
derivation of an aggregate supply curve that produces a gradual rather than an instantaneous adjustment of the economy to disturbances. With gradual adjustment of wages,
a monetary or fiscal expansion has an extended effect on output and employment. The

key question in the theory of aggregate supply is why the nominal wage adjusts slowly to shifts in demand, or why wages are *sticky.* Wages are sticky, or wage adjustment sluggish, when wages move slowly over time, rather than being fully and immediately flexible, so as to assure full employment at every point in time.

To clarify the assumptions that we make about wage stickiness, we translate the Phillips curve in (2) into a relationship between the rate of change of wages, g_w, and the level of employment. We denote the full-employment level of employment by N^*, and the actual level of employment by N. We then define the unemployment rate as the fraction of the full-employment labor force, N^*, that is not employed.[10]

$$u = \frac{N^* - N}{N^*} \tag{3}$$

Substituting (3) into (2), we obtain the Phillips curve relationship between the level of employment and the rate of change in wages:[11]

$$g_w = \frac{W - W_{-1}}{W_{-1}} = -\epsilon \left(\frac{N^* - N}{N^*} \right) \tag{2b}$$

or, rewriting the equation, we show the Phillips curve as a relationship between the wage this period, the wage last period, and the actual level of employment:

$$W = W_{-1} \left[1 + \epsilon \left(\frac{N - N^*}{N^*} \right) \right] \tag{4}$$

Equation (4), the wage-employment relation, *WN*, is shown in Figure 13-8. The wage this period is equal to the wage that prevailed last period (say, last quarter), but with an adjustment for the level of employment. At full employment ($N = N^*$), this period's wage is equal to last period's. If employment is above the full-employment level, the wage increases above last period's wage. If employment is below the full-employment level, the wage this period falls below last period's wage. The extent to

---

[10] Two related points should be noted: (*a*) With a positively sloped labor supply curve, the full-employment level of the labor force depends on the real wage. We mean by N^* the equilibrium level of N when the labor market is in the neoclassical equilibrium shown in Fig. 13-1, adjusted for frictional unemployment. (*b*) Equation (3) implies that the unemployment rate is zero at full employment, when $N = N^*$. In fact, there is positive frictional unemployment even when the economy is at full employment. We are implicitly defining the unemployment rate in equation (3) relative to the natural rate of unemployment. Thus when u in equation (3) is positive (or negative), the actual rate of unemployment exceeds (or is less than) the natural rate. Actual unemployment can be below the natural rate because people are working overtime.

[11] We note here that the Friedman-Phelps amendment to the Phillips curve adds the expected rate of inflation to the right-hand side of equation (2). We work with this *expectations-augmented* Phillips curve in the next chapter, but do not introduce it yet in order to develop the exposition of wage-price and output dynamics step by step.

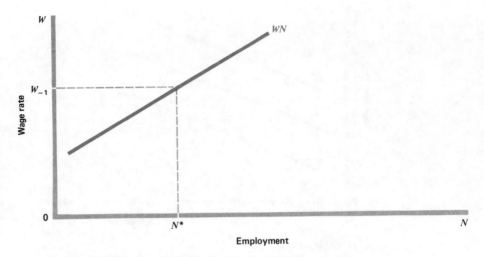

FIGURE 13-8
THE WAGE-EMPLOYMENT RELATION. Within a period, the wage increases
with the level of employment, as shown by *WN*. If employment is at its
neoclassical equilibrium level, N^*, the wage level in this period is equal
to the wage last period.

which the wage responds to employment depends on the parameter ϵ. If ϵ is large,
unemployment has large effects on the wage and the *WN* line is steep.

The Phillips curve relationship in (4) also implies that the *WN* relationship
shifts over time, as in Figure 13-9. If there is overemployment this period, the *WN*
curve will shift upward next period to *WN'*. If there is less than full employment this
period, the *WN* curve will shift downward next period to *WN''*. Thus, changes in
aggregate demand that alter the rate of unemployment this period will have effects on
wages in subsequent periods. In other words, the adjustment to a change in employment is dynamic, that is, it takes place over time.

The central element in any explanation of wage stickiness is the fact that the
labor market involves long-term relations between firms and workers. Most of the
labor force expects to continue in its current job for some time. Working conditions,
including the wage, are renegotiated periodically, but not frequently. That is because it
is costly to negotiate frequently if the wage is set by negotiation and costly to obtain
information about alternative wages if the wage is supposed to be set by market
conditions. Typically, firms and workers reconsider wages and adjust them once a
year.[12]

---

[12] The frequency with which wages (and prices) are reset depends on the stability of the level of output and
prices in the economy. In extreme conditions, such as hyperinflations, wages might be reset daily or weekly.
The need to reset prices and wages frequently is indeed seen as one of the costs of high and unstable rates of
inflation.

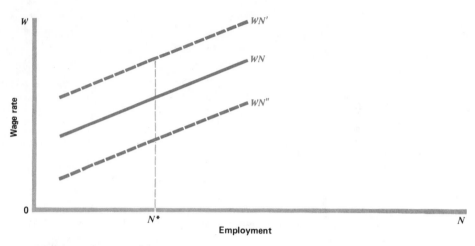

FIGURE 13-9

THE SHIFTING WAGE-EMPLOYMENT RELATION. The *WN* curve shifts over time if employment differs from the full-employment level, *N**. If *N* exceeds *N** this period, the *WN* curve will shift upward to *WN'* next period.

Wages are usually set in nominal terms in economies with low rates of inflation.[13] Thus the agreement is that the firm will pay the worker so many dollars per hour or per month for the next quarter or year. Some formal union labor contracts last 2 or 3 years and may fix nominal wages for the period of the contract. Frequently union contracts include separate wage rates for overtime hours, which implies that the wage rate paid by firms is higher the more hours are worked. That is one reason the *WN* curve in Figure 13-8 is positively sloped.

At any moment of time, firms and workers will have agreed, explicitly or implicitly, on the wage schedule that is to be paid to currently employed workers. There will be some base wage that corresponds to a given number of hours of work per week and depends on the type of job, with perhaps a higher wage for overtime. The firm then sets the level of employment each period. If demand is high, employment will be high, as will the nominal wage.

Now consider how wages adjust when the demand for labor shifts and firms increase the hours of work. In the short run, wages rise along the *WN* curve. With demand up, workers will press for an increase in the base wage at the next labor negotiation. However, it will take some time before all wages are renegotiated. Further, not all wages are negotiated simultaneously. Rather, wage-setting dates are

---

[13] In economies with high inflation, wages are likely to be *indexed* to the price level, that is, adjusted for changes in prices. Even in the United States, some long-term labor contracts contain indexing clauses under which the wage is increased to compensate for past price increases. The indexing clauses typically adjust wages once a quarter (or once a year) to compensate for price increases in the past quarter (or year).

staggered, that is, they overlap.[14] Assume that wages for half the labor force are set in January and the other half in July. Suppose the money stock went up in September. In the first instance, prices will be slow to adjust because no wage is adjusted until three months after the change in the money stock. Second, when the time comes to renegotiate half the contracts, in January, both the firms and the workers negotiating know that other wages will not change for the next 6 months.

Workers do not adjust their base wage all the way to the level that will take the economy to the long-run equilibrium because, if they did, their wages would be very high relative to other wages for the next 6 months. Firms will prefer to employ workers whose wages have not yet risen; there is thus a danger of unemployment to the January wage-setting workers if the renegotiated wages go too high. They are therefore adjusted only partway toward equilibrium.

Then in July, when the time comes to reset the other half of the wages, those too are not driven all the way to the equilibrium level because the January wages will then be relatively lower. So the July wages will go above the January wages, but still only part way to the full-employment equilibrium base wage.

This process keeps on going, with the supply curve rising from period to period as wages leapfrog each other, while first one wage and then another is renegotiated. The position of the aggregate supply curve in any period will depend on where it was last period because each unit renegotiating wages has to consider the level of its wage relative to the wages that are not being reset. And the level of the wages that are not being reset is reflected in last period's wage rate. That is why there is a W_{-1} term on the right-hand side of the Phillips curve equation (4).

During the adjustment process, firms will also be resetting prices as wages (and thus firms' costs) change. The process of wage and price adjustment continues until the economy is back at the full-employment equilibrium with the same real balances. The real-world adjustment process is more complicated than the January-July example because wages are not reset quite as regularly as that and, also, because not only wage but also price adjustments have to be taken into account.[15] But the January-July example gives the essence of the adjustment process.

This account of slow wage and price adjustment raises at least two serious questions. The first is why firms and workers do not adjust wages more frequently when clearly understandable disturbances affect the economy. If they did, then perhaps they could adjust wages so as to maintain full employment. Recent research emphasizes that the comparatively small costs of resetting wages and prices can keep adjustment processes from operating fast.[16] Further, the problems of coordinating wage and

---

[14] The adjustment process we present here is based on John Taylor, "Aggregate Dynamics and Staggered Contracts," *Journal of Political Economy,* February 1980.

[15] For an interesting study of the frequency of price adjustments (for newspapers) see Stephen G. Cecchetti, "Staggered Contracts and the Frequency of Price Adjustment," *Quarterly Journal of Economics,* Supplement, 1985.

[16] These theories are at the frontier of research. For the flavor of the argument, see N. Gregory Mankiw, "Small Menu Costs and Large Business Cycles: A Macroeconomic Model of Monopoly," *Quarterly Journal of Economics,* May 1985. A comprehensive but difficult review is presented in Julio Rotemberg, "The New Keynesian Microfoundations," *NBER Macroeconomics Annual,* 1987.

price adjustments so that wages and prices move back rapidly to equilibrium are formidable in a large economy in which there are many different forces affecting supply and demand in individual markets.

The second is why firms and unemployed workers do not get together when there is a high unemployment, with the firms giving jobs to the unemployed at wages below those their current workers receive. The main reason, discussed in the *efficiency wage theory* approach noted at the end of Chapter 7, is that such practices are probably bad for the morale and therefore the productivity of those in the labor force who are on the job. There was in fact a limited introduction of such practices in the United States after the 1982 recession, in the so-called *two-tier* wage system. In this system veterans are on one wage schedule and new employees on a much lower schedule. But — and that is precisely the point of this section — the introduction of the two-tier system did not happen immediately as unemployment developed but, rather, took place slowly over a period of years. That pattern is consistent with the sluggish adjustment of wages.

To summarize, the combination of the assumptions that wages are preset for a period of time and wage adjustments are staggered generates the type of gradual wage and output adjustment we observe in the real world. That accounts for the dynamics. The upward-sloping aggregate supply curve, to which we now turn, is accounted for by overtime wages for some workers and by the fact that wages in those contracts that are renegotiated within the period (such as a quarter) do respond to market conditions.

13-4 THE AGGREGATE SUPPLY CURVE

We derive the aggregate supply curve in four steps. First, we relate output to employment. Second, we relate the prices firms charge to their costs. Third, we use the Phillips curve relationship between wages and employment. Then we put the three components together to derive an upward-sloping aggregate supply curve, a relationship between the price level and output, of the type shown in Figure 7-1.

The Production Function

The production function links the level of employment of labor to the level of output. The simplest production function is one in which output is proportional to the input of labor:

$$Y = aN \tag{5}$$

Here Y is the level of output produced, and N is the amount of labor input or employment (measured in hours of work, for example). The coefficient a is called the input coefficient, or *labor productivity*. Labor productivity is the ratio of output to labor input, Y/N, that is, the amount of output produced per unit of labor employed. For instance, if *a* is equal to 3, then one unit of labor (1 hour of work) will produce three units of output.

The assumption in equation (5) is that the productivity of labor is constant. In fact labor productivity changes over time. It tends to grow over long periods, as workers become better trained, educated, and equipped with more capital. It also changes systematically during the business cycle. Productivity tends to begin to fall before the start of a recession and then to start recovering either during the recession or at the beginning of the recovery. This productivity behavior is explained in Box 13-1.

We simplify by assuming that labor productivity is constant. In the neoclassical model in Section 13-1, labor productivity declines as output rises. This does not appear to be the case in practice, as Figure 1 in Box 13-1 shows. That is one reason the neoclassical analysis is not an accurate description of the behavior of wages and prices over the business cycle.[17]

Costs and Prices

The second step in developing the theory of supply is to link firms' prices to their costs. Labor costs are the main component of total costs. The guiding principle here is that a firm will supply output at a price that at least covers its costs. Of course, firms would like to charge far more than cost, but competition from existing firms and firms that might enter to capture some of the profits prevent prices from getting far out of line with costs.

We assume that firms base price on the labor cost of production. Since each unit of labor produces *a* units of output, the labor cost of production per unit is W/a. For instance, if the wage is $15 per hour and *a* is 3, then the labor cost is $5 per unit. The ratio W/a is often called the *unit labor cost.*

Firms set price as a *markup, z,* on labor costs:

$$P = \frac{(1 + z)W}{a} \qquad (6)$$

The markup over labor costs covers the cost of other factors of production that firms use, such as capital and raw materials, and includes an allowance for the firms' normal

---

[17] A major reason is that the assumption of neoclassical analysis that capital remains fully employed throughout is not correct. Note from the appendix to this chapter that the diminished marginal product of labor follows from the assumption that, because the capital stock is fixed in the short run, each succeeding worker has less capital with which to work. However, the use of capital also varies over the cycle, with capital being unemployed in recessions and heavily employed during booms. For instance, factories may run on three shifts a day during booms, using the capital all the time, and only one shift a day during recessions. Data on the use of capital, so-called capacity utilization data, are imperfect, but suggest that, if anything, the ratios of capital in use to labor may be higher during booms than during recessions. In that case neoclassical theory would not predict that the marginal productivity of labor is lower in booms, as it does in Fig. 13-1.

box 13-1 = THE CYCLICAL BEHAVIOR OF PRODUCTIVITY

In developing the sticky wage macroeconomic model we made a strong assumption about the link between output and employment, namely, $Y = aN$. According to our assumption, labor productivity, Y/N, is equal to a constant, a. This contrasts with the assumption made in the frictionless neoclassical model that labor productivity is high when output is low, and vice versa.

That assumption is readily testable by looking at the data for labor productivity or output per worker, Y/N. The data are shown in Figure 1. It is immediately clear that productivity varies over time — it grows over time, as we shall see in Chapter 19 — but it also moves cyclically.

The figure shows that when or shortly before the economy moves into a recession, productivity declines, while productivity begins to grow again some time after the recession starts. Thus productivity is, if anything, higher when output is high than when output is low.

How do we explain these facts, and what implications do they have for our model? Firms maintain long-term relations with their labor force. An aspect of that long-term relation is that during recessions firms are slow to dismiss personnel, especially highly specialized workers whom the firm does not want to risk losing permanently. This applies also to managers, because even if the firm produces only half the normal level of output, it is difficult to reduce management by half.

Thus employment tends to fluctuate *less* than output or production. During a recession output falls, but employment falls relatively less. Hence productivity — the ratio of output to employment — falls. Conversely, in a recovery production rises, but because the firm has kept on or *hoarded* a lot of the work force, employment increases less. Thus productivity rises in a recovery.

The effects we have just described are reinforced by the fact that the firm bases its hiring and firing on expectations about future production. A firm will hire more workers and incur the expense of increasing employment only if there is an expectation that production and output will be higher for some time. Otherwise, paying overtime to the existing labor force would be a cheaper solution. Conversely, a firm will lay off or dismiss workers only if it believes the decline in demand will last some time. Here then is another source of discrepancy between current employment and current production. Current production may be low but employment high because firms believe the decline in demand is only transitory.

profits. If competition in the industry is less than perfect, then the markup will also include an element of monopoly profit.[18]

---

[18] Students who have taken microeconomics will realize that in competitive industries price is assumed to be determined by the market, rather than set by firms. That is quite consistent with equation (6), for if the industry were competitive, z would cover only the costs of other factors of production and normal profits, and the price would thus be equal to the competitive price. Equation (6) is slightly more general, because it allows also for price setting by firms in industries that are less fully competitive.

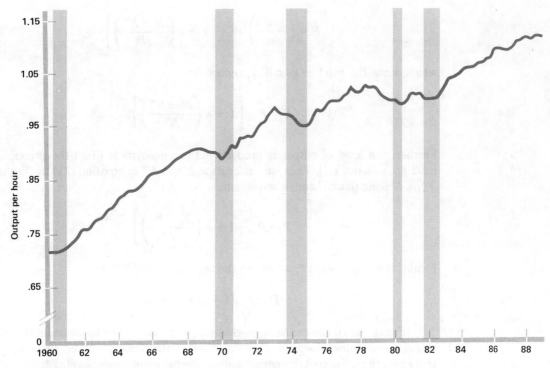

FIGURE 1

THE PRODUCTIVITY OF LABOR, 1960–1988. Shaded bars mark periods of
recession. (SOURCE: DRI/McGraw-Hill.)

By assuming a tight link between output and employment, our model thus simplifies the complex relationships between a firm's production decisions and its employment decisions. For purposes of understanding aggregate supply, the simplification is
justifiable, since output and employment do, in practice, move in the same direction,
even if not exactly in lockstep. ∎

Employment and Wages and the Aggregate Supply Curve

The three components of the aggregate supply curve are the production function (5),
the price-cost relation (6), and the Phillips curve (4). The price level is proportional to
the wage [from equation (6)]. But today's wage is linked through the Phillips curve (4)
to the level of employment and to past wages. We can use that wage equation and
replace the wage in (6) to obtain a link between the level of employment and the price
level:

$$P = \left(\frac{1+z}{a}\right) W_{-1} \left[1 + \epsilon \left(\frac{N - N^*}{N^*}\right)\right] \tag{7}$$

which, since $P_{-1} = [(1 + z)/a] W_{-1}$, reduces to

$$P = P_{-1} \left[1 + \epsilon \left(\frac{N - N^*}{N^*}\right)\right] \tag{7a}$$

Further, the level of output is proportional to employment [from the production function, equation (5)]. Thus we can replace N and N^* in equation (7 a) by Y/a and Y^*/a. Making those changes, we obtain

$$P = P_{-1} \left[1 + \epsilon \left(\frac{Y - Y^*}{Y^*}\right)\right]$$

Finally, defining $\lambda \equiv \epsilon/Y^*$, we obtain the *aggregate supply curve*

$$P = P_{-1}[1 + \lambda(Y - Y^*)] \tag{8}$$

Figure 13-10 shows the aggregate supply curve implied by equation (8). The supply curve is upward-sloping. Like the *WN* curve on which it is based, the *AS* curve shifts over time. If output this period is above the full-employment level, Y^*, then next period the *AS* curve will shift up to *AS'*. If output this period is below the full-employment level, the *AS* curve next period will shift down to *AS"*. Thus the properties of the *AS* curve are those of the *WN* curve. This results from two assumptions: that the markup is fixed at z, and that output is proportional to employment.

The *AS* curve is the aggregate supply curve under conditions in which wages are less than fully flexible. Prices increase with the level of output because increased output implies increased employment, reduced unemployment, and therefore increased labor costs. The fact that prices rise with output is entirely a reflection of the adjustments in the labor market, in which higher employment increases wages.[19] Firms pass on these wage increases by raising prices, and for that reason prices rise with the level of output.

---

[19] Note an important implication of markup pricing in (6). Because firms are assumed to maintain a constant markup of price over cost, the *real wage* does not change with the level of employment in the theory developed in this chapter. Because different theories of aggregate supply have different implications about the cyclical behavior of real wages, that behavior has been studied intensively. For instance, some theories suggest that the level of employment is determined by the neoclassical demand curve, *ND*, in Fig. 13-1. In that case the real wage would be high in recessions and low in booms. Empirical evidence shows, however, that wages and employment are essentially independent over the cycle. For a study based on data from twelve countries that reaches that conclusion, see P. T. Geary and J. Kennan, "The Employment – Real Wage Relationship: An International Study," *Journal of Political Economy*, August 1982. It is because the data show no clear pattern that we assume in our theoretical development that the real wage is independent of the level of employment.

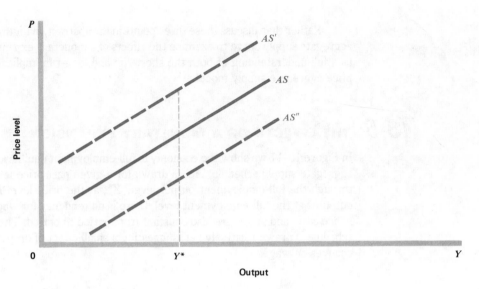

FIGURE 13-10

THE AGGREGATE SUPPLY CURVE. The aggregate supply curve, *AS*, is derived from the *WN* curve, with the added assumptions that output is proportional to employment and that prices are set as a markup on labor costs. The *AS* curve, too, shifts over time, depending on the level of the output. For instance, if output this period is above the full-employment level, *Y**, the *AS* curve will shift upward to *AS'* next period.

Properties of the Aggregate Supply Curve

We have now provided a derivation of the aggregate supply schedule, *AS*, used in Chapter 7 and can, with the help of (8), explore its properties more closely. We emphasize three points:

1. The aggregate supply schedule is flatter the smaller the impact of output and employment changes on current wages. If wages respond very little to changes in unemployment, then the *AS* schedule in Figure 13-10 will be very flat. The coefficient λ in equation (8) captures this employment-wage–change linkage.
2. The position of the aggregate supply schedule depends on the past level of prices. The schedule passes through the full-employment level of output, *Y**, at $P = P_{-1}$. For higher output levels there is overemployment, and hence prices today are higher than those last period. Conversely, when unemployment is high, prices today will be below those last period.
3. The aggregate supply schedule shifts over time. If output is maintained above the full-employment level, *Y**, then over time wages continue to rise and the wage increases are passed on as increased prices.

Rather than discuss these three points in the abstract, in Figure 13-11 we use the aggregate supply curve to examine the effects of a monetary expansion. This will give us a full understanding of both the short-run and long-run implications of the wage-price aggregate supply model.

13-5 THE EFFECTS OF A MONETARY EXPANSION

In Figure 13-11 we show the economy in full-employment equilibrium at point E. The aggregate supply schedule, AS, is drawn for a given past price level, P_{-1}. It passes through the full-employment output level, Y^*, at the price level P_{-1} because when output is at the full-employment level, there is no tendency for wages to change, and hence costs and prices are also constant from period to period. The aggregate supply schedule is drawn relatively flat, suggesting a small effect of output and employment changes on wages.

FIGURE 13-11

THE SHORT-RUN EFFECT OF AN INCREASE IN THE MONEY STOCK. The initial equilibrium at E is disturbed by an increase in the money stock that shifts the aggregate demand curve from AD to AD'. Short-run equilibrium is at E', at which both the price level and output have increased. Prices are higher because the output expansion has caused an increase in wages, which is passed on into prices. The AS schedule is drawn quite flat, reflecting the assumption that wages are quite sticky.

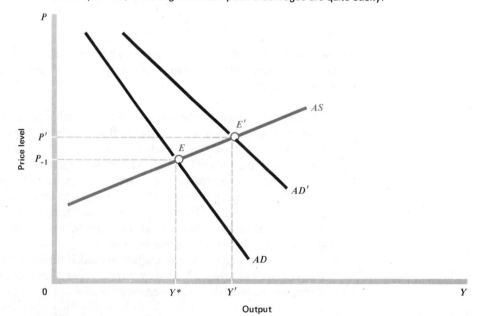

Short-Run Effects

Suppose now that the nominal money stock is increased. At each price level real balances are higher, interest rates are lower, and hence the demand for output rises. The AD schedule shifts upward and to the right, to AD'. At the initial price level, $P = P_{-1}$, there is now an excess demand for goods. Firms find that their inventories are running down and accordingly hire more labor and raise output until the economy reaches E', the short-run equilibrium point. Note that at E' both output and prices have risen. A monetary expansion has led to a short-run increase in output. The rise in prices is due to the increase in labor costs as production and employment rise.

Compare now the short-run result with the Keynesian and classical models of Chapter 7 and the neoclassical model of this chapter. Our new equilibrium at E' has a feature of each: Output is higher, and prices have risen. Whether we are more nearly in the classical or Keynesian situation depends entirely on the slope of the aggregate supply schedule, that is, on the coefficient, λ, that translates employment changes into wage changes.

Medium-Term Adjustment

The short-run equilibrium at point E' is not the end of the story. At E' output is above normal. Therefore, as equation (7) indicates, prices *will keep on rising*. Consider now in Figure 13-12 what happens in the second period. Once we are in the second period, looking back, the price in the preceding period was P' at point E'. Therefore, the second-period supply curve passes through the full-employment output level at a price equal to P'. We show this by shifting the aggregate supply schedule up to AS', reflecting the increase in wages that has taken place since last period in response to the high level of employment.

With the new aggregate supply schedule, AS', and with the aggregate demand schedule unchanged at the higher level AD', the new equilibrium is at E''. Comparing E' and E'', we note that output now has fallen compared with the first period and prices have risen further. The increase in wages has been passed on by firms as an upward shift of the AS schedule, and the resulting price increase reduces real balances, raises interest rates, and lowers equilibrium income and spending. Thus, starting in the second period, we enter a phase of the adjustment process in which the initial expansion begins to be reversed. We continue this process by looking at the long-term adjustment.

Long-Term Adjustment

As long as output is above normal, employment is above normal, and therefore wages are rising. Because wages are rising, firms experience cost increases, and these are passed on, at each output level, as an upward shift of the aggregate supply schedule. As long as the short- and medium-term equilibrium positions of the economy (points E', E'', etc.) lie to the right of Y^*, the AS schedule is shifting upward and to the left. As a

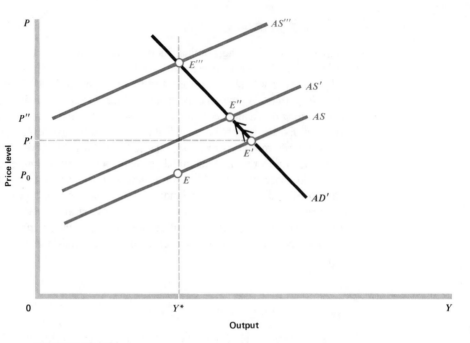

FIGURE 13-12

THE LONGER-TERM EFFECTS OF AN INCREASE IN THE MONEY STOCK. The increase in the money stock led to a short-run equilibrium at E'. But because output is above the full-employment level, wages are rising and the AS curve is shifting upward. In the next period the AS curve shifts to AS', leading to equilibrium in that period at E'', with a higher price level than in the previous period, but lower output. The adjustment from E to E' reflects cost pressures that arise in an overemployed economy. Prices continue to rise and output to fall until the economy reaches equilibrium at E''', with aggregate supply curve AS''', at which point prices have risen in the same proportion as the money stock and output is back at Y^*.

result, output will be declining toward the full-employment level and prices will keep rising. This adjustment is shown in Figure 13-12.

Figure 13-12 shows that the upward-shifting AS schedule gives us a series of equilibrium positions on the AD schedule, starting with E' and moving up toward E'''. During the entire adjustment process, output is above the full-employment level, and prices are rising. The AS curve keeps shifting up, until the aggregate supply curve, AS''' intersects the aggregate demand curve at E''', at which point the economy has returned to full employment.

At E''', prices have risen in the same proportion as the nominal money stock, and so the real money stock, M/P, is again at the initial level. When real balances and therefore interest rates are again at the initial level, so are aggregate demand, output, and employment. In the long run, once wages and prices have had time to adjust fully, the model has the same predictions as the classical case of Chapter 7 and Section 13-1. *The difference is only in the adjustment process.* In the classical case a monetary expansion leads immediately to an equiproportionate rise in prices with no real expansion. Here, *both* output and prices rise in the short and medium term, and only in the long run do we reach the classical case. By assumption, though, the real wage remains constant in the adjustment process. In the short run the predictions of our model more closely resemble the Keynesian case of Chapter 7, and the more slowly that wages adjust to changes in employment, the greater the resemblance.

Because the adjustments of wages and prices are, in fact, slow, the short- and medium-term adjustments are an important aspect of macroeconomics.

13-6   SUPPLY SHOCKS

From the 1930s to the late 1960s, it was generally assumed that movements in output and prices in the economy were caused by shifts in the aggregate demand curve — by changes in monetary and fiscal policy (including wars as fiscal expansions) and investment demand. But the macroeconomic story of the 1970s was largely a story of *supply shocks.*

A supply shock is a disturbance to the economy whose first impact is to shift the aggregate supply curve. The two major supply shocks in the 1970s were the increases in the price of oil in 1973–1974 and 1979–1980. Figure 13-13 shows the real price of oil, which is defined there as the world crude oil price deflated by the U.S. GNP deflator and expressed as an index, with the first quarter of 1981 — the highest level attained over the period — as 100. The first OPEC shock, which produced a quadrupling of the

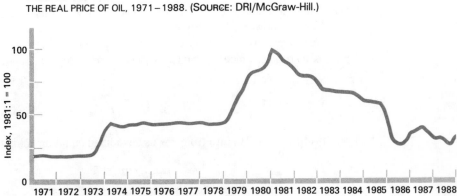

FIGURE 13-13
THE REAL PRICE OF OIL, 1971–1988. (SOURCE: DRI/McGraw-Hill.)

real price of oil between 1971 and 1974, helped push the economy into the 1973–1975 recession, up to then the worst recession of the post-World War II period. And the second OPEC price increase, which doubled the price of oil, sharply accelerated the inflation rate. The high inflation led in 1980–1982 to a tough monetary policy to fight the inflation, with the result that the economy went into even deeper recession than in 1973–1975.

These two oil-price-shock–related recessions leave no doubt that supply shocks matter. But the second shock left the oil price so high that some OPEC producers exceeded their production quotas, and many new producers came into the market; in mid-1986, and again at the end of 1988, the real price of oil was at almost its end-1973 level. The oil price decline in the mid-1980s was a favorable oil price shock.

We start examining the effects of supply shocks by incorporating prices of materials into the aggregate supply curve.

Incorporating Materials Prices in the Analysis

In equation (6) labor costs (and the markup) were the only determinants of output prices. Materials such as energy or copper or cotton were not explicitly included. But clearly the manufacturing sector does use these inputs, and their prices, too, have an impact on the prices of final goods.

We incorporate materials prices in our analysis by modifying the price equation to include not only labor costs and the markup, but also *materials prices,* which we denote by P_m:

$$P = \frac{W(1+z)}{a} + \theta P_m \tag{9}$$

In (9) the term θ denotes the materials requirement per unit of output, and hence θP_m is the component of unit costs that comes from materials inputs.

The wage rate, we recall, increases with the level of output. Hence from equation (9) we still get an upward-sloping supply curve. Further, any increase in the price of materials will increase the price level at a given W. Thus an increase in P_m shifts the AS curve upward, as in Figure 13-14.

Alternatively, we can write the price equation in terms of the *relative* or *real* price of materials, which we denote by the lowercase p_m. The relative price is given by

$$p_m = \frac{P_m}{P} \tag{10}$$

Substituting from (10) into (9) gives us a modified equation linking wages and prices:

$$P = \frac{1+z}{1-\theta p_m} \frac{W}{a} \qquad 1 > \theta p_m \tag{11}$$

Equation (11) shows that for given wages, profit margins, and labor productivity, an increase in the real price of materials will increase prices simply because it raises costs. The impact of a change in real materials prices, therefore, is to shift the aggregate supply schedule upward at each level of output, as in Figure 13-14.

An Adverse Supply Shock

An *adverse supply shock* is one that shifts the aggregate supply curve up. Figure 13-14 shows the effects of such a shock—an increase in the price of oil—reflecting an increase in p_m in equation (11). The AS curve shifts upward to AS', and the equilibrium of the economy moves from E to E'. The immediate effect of the supply shock

FIGURE 13-14

AN ADVERSE SUPPLY SHOCK. An increase in the real price of oil shifts the aggregate supply schedule upward and to the left because the cost of production is now higher at each level of output. Because wages do not adjust enough in the short run, the economy moves into an unemployment equilibrium at E'. Prices are higher and output is lower because of the reduction in real balances. Over time, wages decline because of unemployment and the economy returns to the initial equilibrium at E. Accommodating monetary or fiscal policies could shift the AD schedule to AD', reducing the unemployment effects of the supply shock but increasing its inflationary impact.

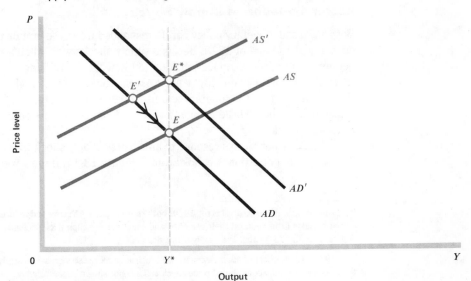

is thus to raise the price level and reduce the level of output. An adverse supply shock is doubly unfortunate: it causes *higher* prices and *lower* output.

There are two points to note about the impact of the supply shock. First, the shock shifts the *AS* curve upward because each unit of output now costs firms more to produce. Second, we are assuming that the supply shock does not affect the level of potential output, which remains at Y^*.[20]

What happens after the shock has hit? In Figure 13-14, the economy moves from E' back to E. The unemployment at E' forces wages and thus the price level down. The adjustment is slow because wages are slow to adjust. The adjustment takes place along the *AD* curve, with wages falling until E is reached.

At E the economy is back at full employment, with the price level the same as it was before the shock. But the nominal wage rate is lower than it was before the shock, because the unemployment in the meantime has forced the wage down. Thus the *real* wage, too, is lower than it was before the shock: the adverse supply shock reduces the real wage.

1973–1975

Table 13-1 shows data for the 1973–1975 oil price increase.[21] From 1973 to 1974 the oil price increased by 23 percent more than other prices and then increased further in 1975. The GNP deflator increased rapidly in both 1974 and 1975. Real GNP fell, as we should expect from Figure 13-14. And the real wage fell in both years.

Thus the analysis presented in Figure 13-14 describes well the economy's responses to the first OPEC shock.

Accommodation of Supply Shocks

Both fiscal and monetary policy barely responded when the first oil price shock hit the economy at the end of 1973. Because supply shocks were then a new phenomenon, neither economists nor policy makers knew what, if anything, could be done about them. But when the unemployment rate went above the then high level of 8 percent at the end of 1974, both monetary and fiscal policy turned stimulatory in 1975–1976. These policies helped the economy recover from the recession more rapidly than it otherwise would have.

But why not always respond to an adverse supply shock with stimulatory policy? To answer that question, we look again at Figure 13-14. If the government had, at the

---

[20] The increase in the price of oil in the 1970s both shifted up the *AS* curve and reduced the level of potential output because firms reduced their use of oil and could not use capital as efficiently as before. But we are assuming in Fig. 13-14 that the supply shock does not affect Y^*.

[21] In 1973–1974, prices of other raw materials, such as copper, also increased sharply. These increases had the same type of impact as the oil price shock and are not shown separately.

TABLE 13-1
THE 1973–1975 OIL PRICE SHOCK

	1974	1975
Real fuel price, 1973 = 100	122.6	138.8
GNP deflator, 1973 = 100	108.8	118.9
Real GNP growth, % per year	−0.6	−1.2
Real wage change,* % per year	−2.8	−0.8

* The real wage is adjusted hourly earnings in the private nonagricultural sector.
SOURCE: *Economic Report of the President*, 1983.

TABLE 13-2
GROWTH AND INFLATION OF INDUSTRIALIZED COUNTRIES*
(percent annum)

	1986	1987	1988	1989
Real GNP growth	2.7	3.4	4.1	3.3
Inflation (GNP deflator)	3.1	3.2	3.6	4.5

* Data are for the seven largest OECD economies: the United States, Japan, Germany, France, Italy, the United Kingdom, and Canada.
SOURCE: OECD.

time of the oil price increase, increased aggregate demand enough, the economy could have moved to E^* rather than E'. Prices would have risen by the full extent of the upward shift in the aggregate supply curve. Money wages would have remained unchanged, and the economy would have stayed at full employment. Of course, the real wage would have been lower, but in the end it is lower anyway.

The monetary and fiscal policies that shift the AD curve to AD' in Figure 13-14 are known as *accommodating* policies. There has been a disturbance that requires a fall in the real wage. Policy is adjusted to make possible, or accommodate, that fall in the real wage *at the existing nominal wage.*

So the question now is why accommodating policies were not undertaken in 1973–1975. The answer is that there is a tradeoff between the inflationary impact of a supply shock and its recessionary effects. The more accommodation there is, the greater the inflationary impact of the shock and the smaller the unemployment impact. The policy mix actually chosen resulted in an intermediate position—some inflation (quite a lot) and some unemployment.

The Effects of a Favorable Oil Shock

The short-run analysis presented in Figure 13-14 shows an adverse supply shock increasing the price level and decreasing GNP, and also decreasing the real wage. A favorable oil price shock should reduce the price level, increase GNP, and raise the real wage. In the mid-1980s the relevant shock was a favorable one.

Although it is difficult to disentangle the timing of the impact of the lower oil prices in 1986, it is quite likely that the oil price decline helped increase and maintain rapid low-inflation growth in the industrialized economies in 1987 and 1988. Table 13-2 shows the growth rate of real GNP and inflation for the seven largest nonsocialist economies (taken together) between 1986 and 1989. The combination of increased growth and low inflation is at least in part a result of the decline of oil prices in 1986.

13-7 EXPECTATIONS, CONTRACTS, AND AGGREGATE SUPPLY

We indicated at the beginning of this chapter that the theory of aggregate supply is as yet unsettled. While there are several competing theories, most have the same aim — which can be described as showing why the aggregate supply curve slopes up in the short run but is vertical in the long run.[22] We have in this chapter ascribed the positive slope of the short-run aggregate supply schedule to the pressure on wages that occurs as output rises and to the slow process of adjustment of wages. Thus wage stickiness is the fundamental cause for non-neoclassical behavior in the model of this chapter.

The Rational Expectations Equilibrium Approach

In Chapter 7 we presented an alternative explanation for a positively sloped short-run aggregate supply curve: in the *rational expectations equilibrium approach*, the positive slope of the aggregate supply curve occurs because workers and firms have different information about the aggregate price level. That section was marked with an asterisk, but it should now be read.

The rational expectations equilibrium approach starts from exactly the same point as the frictionless neoclassical model: in the labor market. But as a result of the imperfect information assumption, it too produces a positively sloped supply curve. This approach implies that unanticipated changes in the money stock (or in fiscal policy) have a positive impact on output and the price level, while anticipated changes in monetary or fiscal policy affect only prices. While the early evidence for these propositions was quite favorable, later evidence has been less supportive.[23]

The Contracting Approach

Between the rational expectations equilibrium approach and the approach developed in this chapter is an explicit *contracting approach* that is identified with the new Keynesian approach to macroeconomics. The contracting approach also starts from the labor market and the frictionless neoclassical model of Section 13-1, but assumes that the wage is fixed by contract at the beginning of a period (say a year) while prices of goods may change within the period.

---

[22] The one exception is real business cycle theory (briefly described at the end of Chap. 7), which argues that monetary phenomena are of no importance.

[23] For the early evidence see Robert J. Barro, "Unanticipated Money, Output, and the Price Level in the United States," *Journal of Political Economy*, August 1978; two technically difficult articles that did not support the theory are John Boschen and Herschel Grossman, "Tests of Equilibrium Macroeconomics with Contemporaneous Monetary Data," *Journal of Monetary Economics*, Novermber 1982, and Frederic Mishkin, "Does Anticipated Monetary Policy Matter? An Econometric Investigation," *Journal of Political Economy*, February 1982.

The assumption is that both firms and workers set the wage at the level that they expect will produce equilibrium in the labor market. Thus in terms of Figure 13-1, they set a nominal wage, W_n, which they hope will correspond to a real wage, $(W/P)^*$, that is, the equilibrium real wage. Let P^e be the expected price level. Then the workers and firms will agree to set the wage at that level which is expected to make the real wage equal to $(W/P)^*$. This means that

$$(W_n/P^e) = (W/P)^*$$

Assuming for convenience that $(W/P)^*$ is equal to 1, then the nominal wage is set such that

$$W_n = P^e \tag{12}$$

Once the wage has been set, firms will produce for the market, taking the cost of labor as given. Because of the assumed diminishing marginal productivity of labor, firms will want to supply more output the lower the real wage they face — or, since the nominal wage is fixed by contract, the higher the price level. Accordingly, there is in the short run a positively sloped aggregate supply curve:

$$
\begin{aligned}
Y &= f(P/W_n) \\
&= f(P/P^e)
\end{aligned}
\tag{13}
$$

Note that, remarkably, this very different approach reaches exactly the same aggregate supply curve as the Lucas supply curve in Chapter 7. Combined with the rational expectations assumption of Chapter 7, this approach, too, implies that unanticipated changes in the money stock have real effects on output while anticipated changes do not. This simple form of the contracting approach is therefore also rejected by the evidence cited in footnote 23.

The contracting approach does, however, provide for an increased possibility of slow adjustment of prices when it is recognized that contracts are not all signed for only one period, and that they are not all renegotiated at the same time. Under those conditions, there can be room for the supply curve to shift slowly over time, as old contracts are renegotiated, and there is room for anticipated monetary policy changes to affect output for several years so long as there are some contracts in the economy with a longer life than that.

The Cyclical Behavior of the Real Wage

Both the Lucas supply curve and the contracting approach rely on the diminishing productivity of labor to generate a positively sloped aggregate supply curve. They both imply, also, that the real wage should decline when expansions in aggregate demand produce an increase in output (because the reason output rises is that firms want to supply more when the real wage is lower). The evidence on the cyclical behavior of the real wage is not very clear, but it certainly does not show that the real wage is consistently lower when output is higher, or, in other words, that the real wage is countercyclical.[24]

That is one reason to prefer an approach to aggregate supply such as that in the bulk of this chapter, in which the real wage is assumed constant.[25] However, the Friedman-Phelps amendment to the Phillips curve, the rational expectations equilibrium approach, and the more explicit contracting approach discussed in this section all point to the need to embody expectations of inflation in our theory of aggregate supply. That is done in the next chapter.

13-8 SUMMARY

This chapter has covered a lot of hard ground. The major point to be established was that output variations along the short-run aggregate supply schedule are accompanied by only moderate price changes. In the short run, the price level varies little with the level of output. Over time, however, wages, costs, and prices will keep rising if output is above normal and keep falling if output is below normal.

We summarize the contents of the chapter as follows:

1. With wages and prices freely flexible, the equilibrium level of employment is determined in the labor market. The labor market is continuously in equilibrium at the full-employment level of employment. Aggregate supply would therefore be the amount of output produced by that amount of labor. Given that the labor market is always in equilibrium, the aggregate supply curve is vertical at the full-employment level of output.
2. The frictions that exist in real world labor markets as workers enter the labor market and look for jobs, or shift between jobs, mean that there is always some frictional unemployment. The amount of frictional unemployment that exists at the full-employment level of unemployment is the *natural rate* of unemployment.
3. The labor market does not adjust quickly to disturbances. Rather the adjustment process takes time. The Phillips curve shows that nominal wages change slowly in accordance with the level of employment. Wages tend to rise when employment is high and fall when employment is low.
4. We assume that the productivity of labor is constant over the business cycle and that prices are based on costs of production. Thus when wages rise because the level of employment is high, prices are increased too.

---

[24] See Robert Barsky and Gary Solon, "Real Wages Over the Business Cycle," NBER Working Paper #2888, March 1989, for evidence that the real wage is basically procyclical.

[25] The contracting approach can be made consistent with the assumption that the real wage is constant, as can be seen, for instance, in the paper by John Taylor referred to in footnote 14.

5. The Phillips curve, together with the assumptions that output is proportional to employment and that price is proportional to costs, implies an upward-sloping aggregate supply curve that shifts over time. A shift in the aggregate demand curve increases the price level and output. The increase in output and employment increases wages somewhat in the current period.

6. The full impact of changes in aggregate demand on prices occurs only over the course of time. High levels of employment generate increases in wages that feed into higher prices. As wages adjust, the aggregate supply curve shifts until the economy returns to equilibrium.

7. The aggregate supply curve is derived from the underlying assumptions that wages (and prices) are not adjusted continuously and that they are not all adjusted together. The positive slope of the aggregate supply curve is a result of some wages being adjusted in response to market conditions and of previously agreed overtime rates coming into effect as employment changes. The slow movement of the supply curve over time is a result of the slow and uncoordinated process by which wages and prices are adjusted.

8. Materials prices, along with wages, are a determinant of costs and prices. Changes in materials prices are passed on as changes in prices and, therefore, as changes in real wages. Materials price changes have been an important source of aggregate supply shocks.

9. Supply shocks, such as a materials price increase, pose a difficult problem for macroeconomic policy. They can be accommodated through an expansionary aggregate demand policy, with the effect of increased prices but stable output. Alternatively, they can be offset, so that prices remain stable because of deflationary aggregate demand policy, but then output falls.

10. Among alternative approaches to aggregate supply, both the rational expectations equilibrium approach and the formal contracting approach to aggregate supply imply a positively sloped short-run aggregate supply curve. However, some other implications of the simplest forms of these approaches—namely, that unanticipated changes in monetary or fiscal policy affect both output and the price level, while anticipated policy changes affect only prices and the implied cyclical behavior of the real wage—have not been confirmed. These approaches, though, point to the need to embody expectations in the theory of aggregate supply, a step we are about to take.

KEY TERMS

Frictionless neoclassical model
Frictional unemployment
Natural rate of unemployment
Phillips curve
Labor productivity
Unit labor cost
Markup

Sticky wages
Supply shock
Accommodation of supply shocks
Rational expectations equilibrium
    approach
Contracting approach

PROBLEMS

1. In the frictionless neoclassical model, assume that labor becomes more productive, with the labor demand curve shifting upward and to the right.
   (a) What is the effect of this change on the full-employment levels of employment and output?
   (b) What is the effect on the full-employment real wage?
   (c) How would your answers to (a) and (b) be affected if the labor supply curve were vertical?

2. What is the effect of an increase in the productivity of labor on the equilibrium price level in the frictionless neoclassical model? (Recall from Chapter 7 the type of aggregate supply curve implied in this case.)

3. Using Figures 13-11 and 13-12, analyze the effects of a reduction in the money stock on the price level and on output when the aggregate supply curve is positively sloped and wages adjust slowly over time.

4. In problem 3, what happens to the level of real balances as a result of the reduction in the nominal money stock?

5. Suppose that the productivity of labor rises, that is, that coefficient a in equation (1) increases. What are the short- and long-run impacts on prices, output, and the real wage? Compare your answer here with the answers to problems 1 and 2 above.

6. Discuss the short-run and long-run adjustments to an increase in government spending, using diagrams similar to Figures 13-11 and 13-12.

7. Suppose the economy is in a recession. How can monetary and fiscal policies speed up the recovery? What would happen in the absence of these policies?

8. The government increases income taxes. What are the effects on output, prices, and interest rates (a) in the short run and (b) in the long run?

9. Discuss why wages move only sluggishly.

10. Use the aggregate supply and demand framework to show the effect of a decline in the real price of materials. Show the effects (a) in the short run and (b) in the long run.

11. Suppose a policy could be found to shift the AS curve down.
    (a) What are the effects?
    (b) Why do you think there is great interest in such policies? [In Chapter 14 we discuss TIPs (tax-based incentive programs) that are intended to shift the AS schedule down.]

12. Suppose that an increase in materials prices is accompanied by a fall in the level of potential output. There is no change in monetary or fiscal policy, and so the AD curve does not shift.
    (a) What is the long-run effect of the disturbance on prices and output? Compare the effect with the case in the text in which potential output does not fall.
    (b) Assume that the upward shift of the AS schedule leads initially to a decline in output below the new potential level. Then show the adjustment process by which output and prices reach the new long-run equilibrium.

13. (a) Explain why the short-run aggregate supply curve slopes up in both the rational expectations equilibrium and the contracting approaches. (For a full understanding you may have to draw on the material in the appendix that follows.)
    (b) Explain why anticipated changes in the money stock would have no effect on output in these models.

APPENDIX: THE NEOCLASSICAL MODEL OF THE LABOR MARKET

The frictionless classical model is an idealized case in which wages and prices are *fully* flexible, there are no costs either to workers in finding jobs or to firms in increasing or reducing their labor force, and firms behave competitively and expect to sell all they produce at prevailing prices. That case both serves as a benchmark for the discussion of more realistic cases and also allows us to introduce such useful concepts as the production function and the demand for labor. Throughout, we assume that labor is the only *variable* factor of production in the short run and that the capital stock is given.

The Production Function

A production function provides a relation between the quantity of factor inputs, such as the amount of labor used, and the maximum quantity of output that can be produced using those inputs. The relation reflects only technical efficiency. In equation (A1) we write the production function

$$Y = F(N, \ldots) \tag{A1}$$

where Y denotes real output, N is labor input, and the dots denote other cooperating factors (capital, for example) that are in short-run fixed supply. The production function is shown in Figure 13-A1. The production function exhibits *diminishing returns* to labor, which means that the increase in output resulting from the employment of one more unit of labor declines as the amount of labor used increases.

Diminishing returns are shown in the production function by its shape, which is neither a straight line through the origin (constant returns) nor an upward-curving line (increasing returns). Diminishing returns are explained by the fact that as employment increases and other inputs remain constant, each laborer on the job has fewer machines with which to work and therefore becomes less productive. Thus, increases in the amount of labor progressively reduce the addition to output that further employment can bring. An increase in the labor force will always raise output, but progressively less so as employment expands. The marginal contribution of increased employment is indicated by the slope of the production function, $\Delta Y / \Delta N$. It is readily seen that the slope flattens out as we increase employment, thus showing that increasing employment makes a diminishing, but still positive, contribution to output.

Labor Demand

From the production function we proceed to the demand for labor. We are asking how much labor a firm would want to hire. The rule of thumb is to hire additional labor and expand production as long as doing so increases profits. A firm will hire additional workers as long as they will bring in more in revenue than they cost in wages.

The contribution to output of additional labor is called the *marginal product of labor*. It is equal, in Figure 13-A1, to the slope of the production function. The marginal product, as we have seen, is both positive — additional labor is productive — and diminishing, which means that additional employment becomes progressively less productive. *A firm will employ additional labor as long as the marginal product of labor* (MPN) *exceeds the cost of additional labor.* The cost of additional labor is given by the real wage, that is, the nominal wage divided by the price

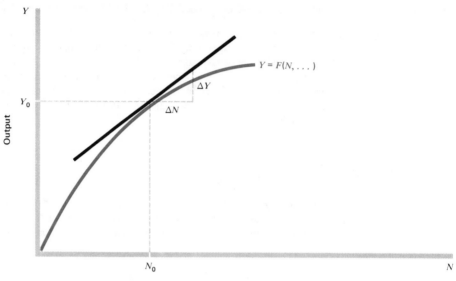

FIGURE 13-A1

THE PRODUCTION FUNCTION AND THE MARGINAL PRODUCT OF LABOR. The production function links the amount of output produced to the level of labor input, given other factors of production, such as capital. The schedule shows diminishing returns. Successive increases in labor yield less and less extra output. The marginal product of labor is shown by the slope of the production function, $\Delta Y/\Delta N$, that is, the increase in output per unit increase in employment. The flattening of the slope shows that the marginal product of labor is declining.

level. The real wage measures the amount of real output the firm has to pay each worker. Since hiring one more worker results in an output increase of MPN and a cost to the firm of the real wage, firms will hire additional labor if the MPN exceeds the real wage. This point is formalized in Figure 13-A2, which looks at the labor market.

The downward-sloping schedule in Figure 13-A2 is the demand for labor schedule, which is the MPN schedule; firms hire labor up to the point at which the MPN is equal to the real wage. The MPN schedule shows the contribution to output of additional employment. It follows from our reasoning that the MPN is positive but that additional employment reduces it, so that the MPN schedule is negatively sloped.

Now consider a firm that currently employs a labor force, N_1, and assume that the real wage is $(W/P)_0$, where W is the money wage and P is the price of output. At employment level N_1, in Figure 13-A2, the firm is clearly employing too much labor, since the real wage exceeds the MPN at that level of employment. What would happen if the firm were to reduce employment by one unit? The reduction in employment would decrease output by the amount of the MPN, and therefore reduce revenue to the firm. On the other side of the calculation, we have the reduction in the wage bill. For a unit reduction in employment, the wage bill would fall at the rate

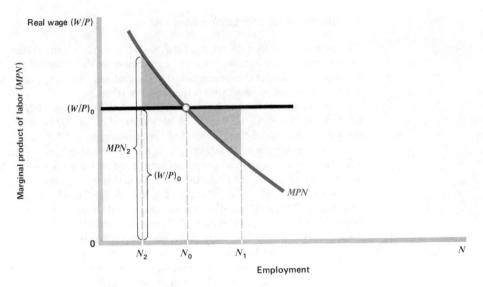

FIGURE 13-A2

THE OPTIMAL EMPLOYMENT CHOICE FOR A GIVEN REAL WAGE. The marginal product of labor, *MPN*, is a declining function of the level of employment because of diminishing returns. Given a real wage $(W/P)_0$, the optimal employment choice is N_0. At N_1, the marginal product of labor is less than the real wage, so that the firm would save by reducing employment. Conversely, at N_2 the marginal product exceeds the real wage, so that the firm would gain by hiring additional workers.

of the real wage $(W/P)_0$. The net benefit of a reduction in the employment level is thus equal to the vertical excess of the real wage over the *MPN* in Figure 13-A2. It is apparent that at a level of employment N_1, the excess is quite sizable, and it pays the firm to reduce the employment level. Indeed, it pays to reduce employment until the firm gets to point N_0. Only at that point does the cost of additional labor — the real wage — exactly balance the benefit in the form of increased output.

The same argument applies to employment level N_2. Here employment is insufficient because the contribution to output of additional employment, MPN_2, exceeds the cost of additional employment, and it therefore pays to expand the level of employment. It is readily seen that with real wage $(W/P)_0$, the firm's profits are maximized when employment is N_0. In general, given *any* real wage, the firm's demand for labor is shown by the *MPN* curve.

The firm's optimal employment position is formalized in equation (A2). At the optimal employment level the marginal product of labor (which is a declining function of employment), $MPN(N)$, is equal to the real wage:

$$MPN(N) = \frac{W}{P}$$

(A2)

Equilibrium in the Labor Market

We have now developed the relation between output and employment (the production function) and the optimal employment choice for a given real wage that is implied by the demand for labor. It remains to consider the determination of the real wage as part of labor market equilibrium. What we have not yet dealt with is the supply of labor.

We assume that labor supply increases with the real wage (W/P). In Figure 13-A3 the labor supply curve, NS, intersects the labor demand curve, MPN, at E. The equilibrium real wage is $(W/P)_0$, and the equilibrium level of employment is N^*.

How would the labor market get to that equilibrium? Suppose that the real wage fell whenever there was an excess supply of labor and that it rose whenever there was an excess demand. In terms of Figure 13-A3 this would mean that the real wage would decline whenever it was above $(W/P)_0$. At $(W/P)_1$, for example, labor demand is only N_1 and thus falls short of the labor supply. This would put downward pressure on the real wage, causing the real wage to fall and making it profitable to expand employment. Exactly the reverse argument holds for real wages lower than $(W/P)_0$, where there is an excess demand for labor.

From Figure 13-A3 we see that adjustment of the real wage would bring the labor market into full-employment equilibrium at real wage $(W/P)_0$ and employment level N^*. Figure 13-A4 summarizes the complete equilibrium in the labor market and the corresponding level of *full-employment output*, Y^*, which is the level of output associated with employment equal to the given labor supply.

FIGURE 13-A3

EQUILIBRIUM IN THE LABOR MARKET. The labor supply curve is *NS*. The demand for labor is the marginal product schedule, *MPN*. Labor market equilibrium obtains at real wage $(W/P)_0$. At that real wage the demand for labor equals the quantity of labor supplied. At a lower real wage there is an excess demand for labor; at a higher real wage there is an excess supply or unemployment.

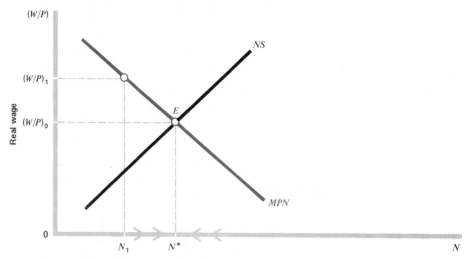

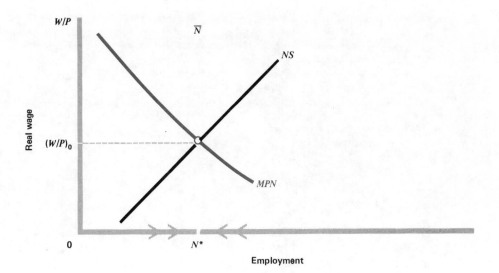

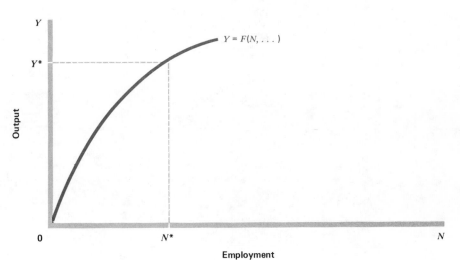

FIGURE 13-A4

EQUILIBRIUM IN THE LABOR MARKET AND FULL-EMPLOYMENT OUTPUT. The upper panel repeats the labor market equilibrium depicted in Figure 13-A3. The lower panel shows the production function. The equilibrium employment level, N^*, which is also the full-employment level, leads to output Y^*, which is the full-employment level of output.

INFLATION AND UNEMPLOYMENT

The 1981–1982 recession was a painful experience for many. . . . The protracted recession was an unexpected and unwanted part of the economy's transition to lower inflation.

Economic Report of the President, 1985

Like the 1970s the 1980s were a difficult period for the economies of the world. The move to slower monetary growth reduced inflation rates in the major industrialized nations, but it caused one of the most severe downturns of the postwar period.

Economic Report of the President, 1989

From the late 1950s through the end of the 1970s the inflation rate in the United States increased in every successive business cycle. During a recession, inflation would fall below its previous trend, but in the following recovery it would rise again and, before long, exceed its past level. Figure 14-1 shows that pattern of an ever-increasing inflation rate from just above 2 percent in the early 1950s to about 10 percent in 1979–1980. In late 1979 the Fed made a dramatic decision: monetary policy was to be changed decisively to stop inflation from rising and to force it back down to the level of the 1950s.

The decision was dramatic because there was little disagreement among economists of widely different macroeconomic persuasions that the move toward tight money would cause a recession along with a reduction in the inflation rate. The claim in the 1985 *Economic Report of the President* that the recession was an unexpected part of the disinflationary process is simply not accurate — and it appears not to be shared even by the 1989 *Economic Report*.

There was indeed a sharp disinflation in 1982, as Figure 14-2 shows. There was also a major recession, with the economy reaching the highest level of unemployment since the end of the great depression, 10.3 percent, at the end of 1982. Figure 14-2 also shows the rapid improvement in economic performance that came after the recession, as unemployment fell but inflation did not increase. Through 1989 the U.S. economy succeeded in maintaining a low average rate of inflation — not as low as that of the 1950s, but well below that of the 1970s — while continuing strong growth. But in 1989 the inflation rate showed signs of rising to the 5 percent range, and the Fed was once again faced with the tough question of how far to go in fighting inflation, knowing that the tighter its monetary policy to control inflation, the greater the risk that it would bring on a recession.

In this chapter we address the problem of inflation and unemployment, extending the analysis of Chapter 13 that focused on the determinants of the price level, to examine the inflation rate. We develop the short- and long-run aggregate supply curves, emphasizing the role of inflationary expectations in shifting the supply curve, and we extend the aggregate demand curve to take account of ongoing inflation.

A key question is: Why is it apparently inevitable that inflation stabilization should bring about unemployment and recession? The distinction between the short- and long-run aggregate supply curves is essential here. In the short run, inflation cannot be reduced without creating a recession; in the long run, though, there is no tradeoff between inflation and unemployment.

We develop the analysis of the determination of output and inflation in Sections 14-1 to 14-6. This material includes the analysis of adjustments to changes in money

FIGURE 14-1

CYCLICAL AVERAGE INFLATION RATES. Inflation rate is GNP deflator; averages are peak to peak; last cycle is from 1981 : 3 to 1989 : 1. (Source: DRI.)

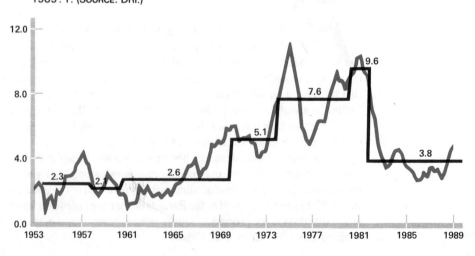

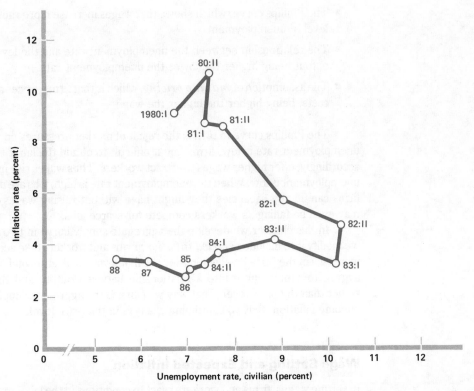

FIGURE 14-2
INFLATION AND UNEMPLOYMENT, 1980–1988. (SOURCE: DRI/McGraw-Hill.)

growth and to fiscal policy changes. The chapter concludes with an important application of the dynamic model, the examination of alternative strategies for reducing inflation.

14-1 INFLATION, EXPECTATIONS, AND THE AGGREGATE SUPPLY CURVE

The aggregate supply curve in Chapter 13 shows the price level at which firms are willing to produce and sell different levels of output. The aggregate supply curve is

$$P = P_{-1}[1 + \lambda(Y - Y^*)] \tag{1}$$

where P is the price level, Y the level of output, and Y^* the full-employment level of output.

Recall now that the aggregate supply curve builds on three foundations:

- The Phillips curve, which shows that wages increase more rapidly the lower the level of unemployment

- The relationship between the unemployment rate and the level of output, with output being higher the lower the unemployment rate

- The assumption of *markup pricing*, which is that firms' prices are based on labor costs, being higher the higher the wage

The Phillips curve in turn is the result of market pressures on wages. When the unemployment rate is low, firms find it difficult to obtain the labor they demand and, accordingly, offer higher wages to attract workers. Thus wages rise more rapidly when unemployment is low. When the unemployment rate is high, jobs are difficult to find and firms can fill any vacancies they might have without raising wages — indeed, wages may even be falling as workers compete for scarce jobs.

In this chapter we develop the aggregate supply curve in two directions. First, we modify it to include *expected inflation;* firms and workers take account of expected increases in the price level when they are fixing wages. And second, we transform the aggregate supply curve into a relationship between output and the *inflation rate* rather than the price level. That way we can use the aggregate supply curve to model ongoing inflation, that is, continuing changes in the price level.

Wage Setting and Expected Inflation

In setting wages, firms and workers react to conditions in the labor market. Thus when output and employment are high, wages tend to rise fast. When output and employment are low, wages do not rise fast and may even fall. The *wage*-Phillips curve introduced in Chapter 13 summarizes the link between wage inflation and the output gap. With the notation $g_w = (W - W_{-1})/W_{-1}$ for the rate of wage inflation, the wage-Phillips curve is

$$g_w = \lambda(Y - Y^*) \tag{2}$$

which states that the rate of wage increase is larger the higher the level of output.

Friedman and Phelps pointed out[1] one major flaw in the wage-Phillips curve as described in equation (2): It ignores the effects of expected inflation on wage setting. Workers are interested in *real* wages (the amount of goods they can buy with their wages) not *nominal* wages (the dollar value of wages).

It is clear that workers, who are concerned with the real wage they receive, will want the nominal wage to fully reflect the inflation they expect during the period between the time the wage is fixed and the time the wage is actually paid. In other

---

[1] See footnote 6 in Chap. 13. In addition, we continue for the most part to omit from the aggregate supply curve changes in the prices of factors of production other than labor, such as raw materials.

words, quite independent of the effects of the level of employment on wage bargaining, workers will want compensation for expected inflation.

But what about the other side? Why do firms agree to raise wages more rapidly when they expect higher prices? The reason is that they can afford to pay higher nominal wages if they will be able to sell their goods at higher prices. And if all prices are rising, each firm can expect to be able to sell its output for a higher price because the prices of competing goods are increasing. Indeed, when wages and prices are rising at the same rate, both firms and workers are in essentially the same position as they would be if there were no inflation and the real wage were constant.

When inflation is expected, the wage-Phillips curve becomes

$$g_w = \pi^e + \lambda(Y - Y^*) \tag{3}$$

Here π^e is the expected inflation rate. Equation (3) is called the *expectations-augmented* wage-Phillips curve; that is, it is the original Phillips curve augmented or adjusted to take account of expected inflation. At any given level of output, wages rise more the higher the expected rate of inflation: indeed, the assumption is that nominal wages rise 1 percent faster for each extra 1 percent of expected inflation.

The Aggregate Supply Curve

The next step is to transform the expectations-augmented wage-Phillips curve into a relationship between the inflation rate and the level of output, which depends on the expected rate of inflation. Once again we assume that firms maintain a constant markup of prices over wages. But that implies that the rate of increase of prices will be equal to the rate of increase in wages. Denote the rate of increase of prices or the rate of inflation as $\pi = (P - P_{-1})/P_{-1}$. With this notation the statement that inflation is equal to the rate of wage increase becomes

$$\pi = g_w \tag{4}$$

Substituting the rate of wage increase [equation (3)] into (4) yields the *dynamic aggregate supply curve:*

$$\pi = \pi^e + \lambda(Y - Y^*) \tag{5}$$

Equation (5) is one of the two building blocks of a model of the inflation process. It is the *expectations-augmented aggregate supply curve,* which we use in the remainder of this chapter to study the behavior of output and inflation. The fundamental difference between that curve [equation (5)] and the aggregate supply curve of equation (8) in Chapter 13 is the inclusion of the expected inflation rate. In addition, because equation (5) deals with the inflation rate rather than the price level, it is a convenient form of the supply curve for studying ongoing inflation.

14-2 SHORT- AND LONG-RUN AGGREGATE SUPPLY CURVES

Expectations-augmented short-run aggregate supply curves are shown in Figure 14-3. There is an aggregate supply curve corresponding to each expected rate of inflation. For example, on SAS the expected inflation rate is 5 percent, as can be seen from the fact that when $Y = Y^*$, at point A on SAS, the inflation rate on the vertical axis is 5 percent. [Note from equation (5) that when $Y = Y^*$, $\pi = \pi^e$.] The short-run aggregate supply curve shows the relationship between the inflation rate and the level of output when the expected rate of inflation is held constant. The curves are called short run because it is assumed that the expected rate of inflation is constant (or at least does not change much) in the short run of a few months or as much as a year.

Given the expected inflation rate, the short-run aggregate supply curve shows the inflation rate rising with the level of output: The higher the level of output, the higher the rate of inflation. This is a reflection of the effect of higher output levels on the rate of increase of wages and, through higher wages, on the rate of increase of prices.

The higher the expected inflation rate, the higher the aggregate supply curve. Thus on SAS', the expected inflation rate is 10 percent. And for any expected inflation

FIGURE 14-3

THE SHORT-RUN AGGREGATE SUPPLY CURVE. The expected inflation rate is constant on a short-run aggregate supply curve: it is 5 percent on SAS, 10 percent on SAS'. Each short-run aggregate supply curve is shown quite flat, reflecting the fact that, in the short run, it takes a large change in output to generate a given change in inflation.

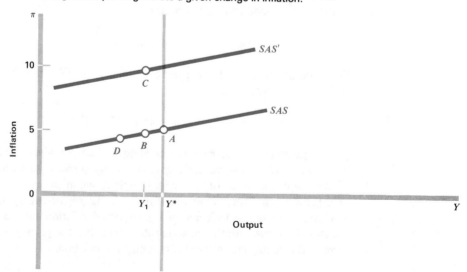

rate, there is a corresponding short-run aggregate supply curve, parallel to *SAS* and *SAS'*, with the vertical distance between any two short-run supply curves equal to the difference in expected inflation rates between them.

On each short-run aggregate supply curve there is a tradeoff between inflation and output. To reduce the inflation rate it is necessary to reduce the level of output, producing a recession, forcing the rate of wage increase down through unemployment, and thus achieving a lower inflation rate.

We show the short-run aggregate supply curves in Figure 14-3 as quite flat, reflecting the evidence that in the short run — up to a year or even two — it takes a large recession to bring about a substantial reduction in the inflation rate. That was the choice made, for example, in the United States in 1982 and 1983 when the inflation rate was reduced.

Changes in the Expected Inflation Rate

Each aggregate supply curve is drawn for a given expected rate of inflation. As the expected rate of inflation changes, the economy moves from one short-run aggregate supply curve to another. That means that the combination of the level of output and inflation rate that occurs depends on the expected inflation rate. For instance, the level of output of Y_1 in Figure 14-3 would be consistent with a low inflation rate at point *B* on *SAS* and a higher inflation rate at point *C* on *SAS'*.

Changes in the expected rate of inflation help explain why the simple Phillips curve relationship seen in Figure 13-5 for 1961–1969 seemed to break down later (as seen in Figure 13-6). Through the end of the 1960s, there was relatively little awareness of inflation, and the economy was basically moving along an *SAS* curve. When at the end of the 1960s, people in the United States began to expect inflation to continue, the short-run aggregate supply curve began to shift, generating higher inflation at each given output level. The Friedman-Phelps analysis thus can explain why the simple Phillips curve of the sixties seemed to break down in the seventies — and recall that their analysis was made before the Phillips curve began to shift.

The conclusion of this section is the most important practical lesson macroeconomists and economic policy makers learned in the last 20 years. *The short-run aggregate supply curve shifts with the expected rate of inflation. The inflation rate corresponding to any given level of output therefore changes over time as the expected inflation rate changes. The higher the expected inflation rate, the higher the inflation rate corresponding to a given level of output.* That is why it is possible for the inflation rate and the unemployment rate to increase together, or for the inflation rate to rise while the level of output falls.

The Vertical Long-Run Aggregate Supply Curve

On each short-run aggregate supply curve, the expected inflation rate is constant and, except at points such as *A*, at which $Y = Y^*$, will turn out to be different from the actual inflation rate. For instance, at point D on SAS in Figure 14-3 the expected inflation rate is 5 percent, but the actual inflation rate is only 4 percent.

If the inflation rate remains constant for any long period, firms and workers will expect that rate to continue, and the expected inflation rate will become equal to the actual rate. The assumption that $\pi = \pi^e$ distinguishes the *long-run* from the short-run aggregate supply curve. The long-run aggregate supply curve describes the relationship between inflation and output when actual and expected inflation are equal.

With the actual and expected inflation rates equal (that is, $\pi = \pi^e$), the aggregate supply curve (5) shows that

$$Y = Y^* \tag{6}$$

The long-run aggregate supply curve, LAS, in Figure 14-4 is a vertical line joining points on short-run aggregate supply curves at which the actual and expected inflation rates are equal.

The meaning of the vertical long-run aggregate supply curve is that *in the long-run the level of output is independent of the inflation rate.* Note the important contrast between the short and the long run: In the short run, with a given expected

FIGURE 14-4

SHORT- AND LONG-RUN AGGREGATE SUPPLY CURVES. The long-run aggregate supply curve *(LAS)* joins points on short-run aggregate supply curves *(SAS)* at which expected inflation is equal to actual inflation. The long-run curve is thus the vertical line *LAS*, at level of output Y^*.

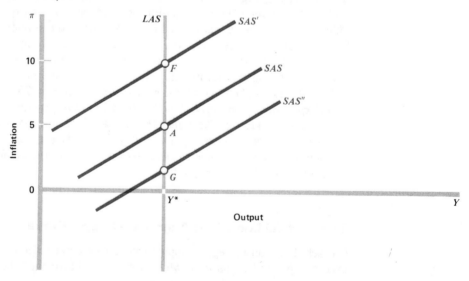

rate of inflation, higher inflation rates are accompanied by higher output; in the long run, with the expected rate of inflation equal to the actual rate, the level of output is independent of the inflation rate.

14-3 THE ROLE OF EXPECTED INFLATION

Many of the controversies in macroeconomics are connected with the inclusion of expected inflation in the aggregate supply function. We therefore expand the discussion of the expectations-augmented Phillips curve in this section. There are three key questions. First, what exactly is the process by which expected inflation comes to be reflected in wages? Second, is it clearly *expected* inflation rather than compensation for *past* inflation that shifts the short-run aggregate supply curve? And third, what determines expected inflation?

Wage Adjustment

Wages are generally set before the work is done. Further, these are typically nominal, or dollar, wages. In some cases, particularly where there are union contracts, wages will be set for as long as 3 years ahead. In other cases, wages are adjusted once a year in an annual salary review.

It is in the adjustment of these wages that expected inflation makes its way into the wage. Wages will adjust both because prices are higher at the time the contract is negotiated than they were last time the wage was set and because inflation is expected between the time the wage is negotiated and the time it will actually be paid. Thus as the process of inflation gets under way, wages fixed in each successive period are higher than they would otherwise have been.

Because some wages are preset for 1 or 2 years or even more, it takes time for expectations of inflation to work their way into wage adjustments. For instance, if a new policy that will produce lower inflation comes into effect in 1991, it may take until 1994 before all the wages that will eventually be affected by that new policy are fully adjusted. And indeed, as we described in Chapter 13, if all wages are not adjusted at the same time, it may take much longer for all wages to come into line with a higher inflation rate, because the wage that is set in one firm or union or industry depends on the wages set elsewhere in the economy, not all of which are adjusting to the new conditions simultaneously.

Compensation for Past Inflation or Expected Inflation

We have described the adjustment for inflation in the expectations-augmented Phillips curve or aggregate supply curve as being for expected inflation. Another interpretation is that wage agreements compensate workers not only for expected inflation but also to some extent for past inflation.

The argument here is that when the inflation rate rises, workers who lost out because their real wages were low want compensation for the losses. Note that this argument implies that compensation would be for unexpected inflation only, that is, for inflation not taken into account when the previous contracts were negotiated.

In practice, at low inflation rates, an adjustment for expected inflation is very hard to distinguish from compensation for past inflation. If prices went up 10 percent last year, the firm is quite likely to raise wages this year. That may be compensation just for last year's inflation, or it may be compensation paid in advance for the inflation expected to take place during the coming year. Thus, it is very difficult to determine whether it is expected inflation or recent inflation that is represented by the π^e term in the expectations-augmented aggregate supply curve.

The confusion between whether it is compensation for past inflation or for expected inflation is illustrated by those contracts that contain formal *index* clauses, which adjust wages for inflation. These *COLA,* or cost-of-living adjustments, are contained in about 60 percent of union contracts.[2] The typical COLA clause adjusts the wage once a year, or once every 3 months, by an amount that depends on the rate of inflation since the last adjustment. For instance, if the inflation rate in the last year was 8 percent, the wage rate may go up by 6 percent.

Now, is this compensation for past inflation or for future inflation? Because it is based on the past inflation rate, it looks like compensation for past inflation. But the wage that is to be paid is that for the *coming* year. So maybe it is compensation in advance for inflation in the coming year.

Why does it matter whether wage adjustments for inflation respond to yesterday's actual inflation or tomorrow's expected inflation? The difference is very important because the explanation has different implications for how quickly it takes for the inflation rate to change. If wages for next year reflect last year's inflation and prices are based on wages, as they are, then inflation today will reflect yesterday's inflation and inflation rates will change only gradually. If it is only expected inflation that matters for wage setting, then perhaps a radical change in policy that changes expectations can also change the inflation rate quickly.

Determinants of Expected Inflation

The question of whether it is compensation for past inflation or future inflation that affects wages is further complicated when we consider how people form their expectations of inflation.

---

[2] Union membership in the United States has been steadily declining to the point at which less than 18 percent of the labor force belongs to unions in 1988. Further, the 1980s trend appears to have been for management to become stronger relative to the unions in many industries. Union contracts may nonetheless play a role in wage determination because *(a)* there is some unionization in firms employing more than 50 percent of the labor force, so that, when setting wages for their workers, those firms have to pay attention to the wages unionized workers are receiving and because *(b)* many firms desiring to keep unions out of their plants have to match or beat the terms of union contracts so that their workers will not want to unionize. On these issues, see Richard Freeman and James Medoff, *What Do Unions Do?* (New York: Basic Books, 1984).

ADAPTIVE EXPECTATIONS

One hypothesis that was used in the 1950s and 1960s, and that still commands some support, is that expectations are *adaptive;* that is, they are based on the past behavior of inflation. Thus under adaptive expectations the rate of inflation expected for next year might be the rate of inflation last year. Under this simplest adaptive expectations assumption, we would have

$$\pi^e = \pi_{-1} \tag{7}$$

Of course, the adaptive expectations assumption could be more complicated, for instance, if the expected inflation rate is the average of the last 3 years' inflation.

Note that if expectations are adaptive, it becomes virtually impossible to tell whether the π^e term in the aggregate supply curve represents expected inflation or compensation for past inflation. If $\pi^e = \pi_{-1}$, there is no difference between past inflation and expected inflation.

RATIONAL EXPECTATIONS

The rational expectations view, already introduced in Chapter 7, is more general, arguing that for the determinants of expected inflation there can be no formula that is independent of the actual behavior of inflation. The rational expectations hypothesis is the assumption that people base their expectations of inflation (or any other economic variable) on all the information economically available about the future behavior of that variable.

The rational expectations approach to macroeconomics, associated primarily with the names of Robert Lucas of the University of Chicago and Thomas Sargent of the University of Minnesota, has been extremely influential. As we have seen in Chapter 7 and shall see in Chapter 18, the approach developed by Lucas, Sargent, and others involves much more than just a theory of expectations. For now, though, we concentrate on the expectations part of the theory.

The rational expectations hypothesis implies that people do not make systematic mistakes in forming their expectations. Systematic mistakes — for instance, always underpredicting inflation — are easily spotted. According to the rational expectations hypothesis, people correct such mistakes and change the way they form expectations accordingly. On average, according to rational expectations, expectations are correct because people understand the environment in which they operate. Of course people make mistakes from time to time, but they do not make *systematic* mistakes.

For much of this chapter we work with the simple adaptive expectations assumption of (7) that the expected inflation rate is equal to the lagged inflation rate. The aggregate supply curve is thus[3]

---

[3] Recall that with the assumption $\pi^e = \pi_{-1}$ in (8) we cannot distinguish the view that the π^e term represents expected inflation from the alternative view that it represents compensation for past inflation.

$$\pi = \pi_{-1} + \lambda(Y - Y^*) \tag{8}$$

We use the aggregate supply curve (8), together with an aggregate demand curve to be introduced in the next section, to study the dynamic adjustment of the economy to changes in policy. By way of contrast, we also use the rational expectations assumption and show just how radical are its implications.

14-4 DYNAMIC AGGREGATE DEMAND

The aggregate demand curve in Chapter 13 represents combinations of the *price level* and level of output at which the goods and assets markets are simultaneously in equilibrium. In this chapter, where we are studying continuing inflation, we work with an aggregate demand curve that shows the relationship between the level of output and the *inflation rate*. The dynamic aggregate demand curve shows the relationship between the rate of inflation and the rate of change of aggregate demand.

The dynamic aggregate demand curve used in this chapter, and which is derived in the appendix,[4] is

$$Y = Y_{-1} + \phi(m - \pi) + \sigma f \tag{9}$$

In (9), m is the growth rate of the nominal money stock. Thus $(m - \pi)$ is the rate of change of real balances: when m exceeds π, the money stock is increasing faster than prices, and so real balances (M/P) are increasing. The other term, σf, denotes the impact on demand of a fiscal expansion.

The curve is most simply understood as saying that the *change* in aggregate demand $(Y - Y_{-1})$ is determined by the growth rate of real balances and by fiscal expansion. The higher the level of real balances, the lower the interest rate and the higher the level of aggregate demand; therefore, the more rapidly are real balances growing, the more rapidly is the interest rate falling, and the more rapidly is aggregate demand increasing. By the same line of argument an *increase* in government spending or a *cut* in taxes means an expansionary fiscal policy and hence an increase in demand over the previous period's level.

In the appendix to this chapter we show that the aggregate demand curve (9) is a simplified version of the aggregate demand curve obtained by using the full *IS-LM* model. The simplification is that we omit the expected rate of inflation that affects aggregate demand.[5] To start, we concentrate on presenting the aggregate demand schedule diagrammatically. For simplicity, we therefore suppress the term relating to fiscal policy changes. We return to fiscal policy changes later in the chapter.

---

[4] The parameters ϕ and σ are the money and fiscal multipliers familiar from the *IS-LM* model of Chap. 5.

[5] The expected rate of inflation enters because investment is affected by the *real* interest rate, whereas the demand for money is affected by the *nominal* interest rate. Thus when we say above that increases in real balances reduce interest rates, we should, to be more precise, say that while they reduce the nominal interest rate, whether they also reduce the real interest rate depends on how the expected inflation rate is changing.

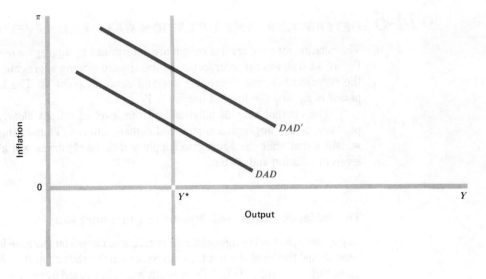

FIGURE 14-5
THE DYNAMIC AGGREGATE DEMAND SCHEDULE. The dynamic aggregate demand curve *(DAD)* is downward-sloping and drawn for a given rate of growth of money and lagged output level. The growth rate of money is higher on *DAD'* than on *DAD*.

In Figure 14-5 we plot the dynamic aggregate demand schedule (9), or *DAD*. The shape of that schedule is most clearly seen by rewriting equation (9) as[6]

$$\pi = m - \frac{1}{\phi}(Y - Y_{-1})$$

(10)

The schedule is drawn for a given growth rate of money and is downward sloping. Given the growth rate of money, a lower rate of inflation implies that real balances are higher and thus that the interest rate is lower and aggregate demand is higher. The negative slope results from this connection between lower inflation, implying higher growth in real balances, and higher spending.

The position of the aggregate demand curve depends on the level of output last period. The higher the level of output last period, the higher the inflation rate corresponding to any given level of current output on the aggregate demand curve.

A change in the growth rate of money will shift the aggregate demand curve. As we see from equation (10), a change in the growth rate of money shifts the *DAD* curve vertically by precisely the same amount as changes in the growth rate of money. Thus the dynamic aggregate demand curve, *DAD'* in Figure 14-5, lies above *DAD* by the same distance as the growth rate of money has increased between *DAD* and *DAD'*.

---

[6] As noted above we are now assuming $f = 0$, so that there is no fiscal policy change in the current period.

14-5 DETERMINING THE INFLATION RATE AND LEVEL OF OUTPUT

The inflation rate and level of output are determined by aggregate demand and supply. Figure 14-6 shows the intersection of the upward-sloping aggregate supply curve and the downward-sloping aggregate demand curve at point E. The inflation rate this period is π_0, and the level of output is Y_0.

The current rate of inflation and the level of output clearly depend on the positions of the aggregate supply and demand curves. Thus changes in any of the variables that shift the aggregate supply and demand curves will affect the current levels of inflation and output.

The Inflation Rate and Output in the Short Run

Any upward shift in the aggregate demand curve causes an increase in both the rate of inflation and the level of output, as can be seen in the shift from E to E_1 when the DAD curve shifts upward to DAD'. Such a shift would be caused by an increase in the growth rate of money. It could also be caused by an increase in government spending or a reduction in taxes, though we do not explicitly include those variables in the aggregate

FIGURE 14-6

INFLATION AND OUTPUT IN THE SHORT RUN. In the short run inflation and output are determined by the intersection of the aggregate supply and demand curves at point E. An upward shift of the aggregate demand curve raises both output and inflation. An upward shift of the aggregate supply curve increases the inflation rate while reducing the level of output.

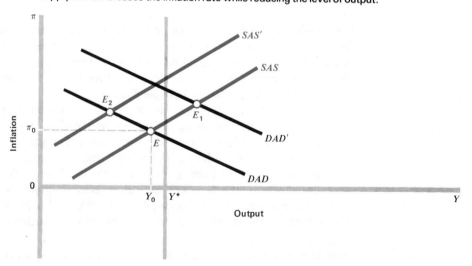

demand curve (8).[7] In addition, the position of the aggregate demand curve depends on the level of output last period. The higher the level of output last period (Y_{-1}), the higher the aggregate demand curve.

Given that an increase in the growth rate of money shifts the aggregate demand curve up by exactly the same amount as the rise in the growth rate of money, we see in Figure 14-6 that an increase in the growth rate of money causes both output and inflation to rise but that the increase in inflation is less than the increase in the growth rate of money. Thus in the short run a 1 percent increase in money growth produces a less than 1 percent increase in inflation because some of the effects of the increase in money stock show up in higher output. This is exactly the same conclusion that we reached in Chapter 13, when we showed that in the short run an increase in the money stock causes both the price level and the level of output to increase.

Shifts in the aggregate supply curve also affect the rate of inflation and the level of output. An upward shift of the aggregate supply curve, such as the shift from SAS to SAS', moves the equilibrium from E to E_2, raising the inflation rate and reducing the level of output. An increase in the expected rate of inflation would cause an upward shift such as that from SAS to SAS'. The reason is that the higher expected rate of inflation produces more rapid rises in wages that cause more rapid inflation.

Summarizing, we see that in the short run:

- An increase in the growth rate of money causes higher inflation and higher output, but inflation rises less than the growth rate of money.

- An increase in the expected rate of inflation causes higher inflation and lower output.

We also note, and leave to you to show, that the factors we have omitted here from the aggregate supply and demand curves change the inflation rate and output in the short run:

- A supply shock that shifts the aggregate supply curve upward causes higher inflation and lower output.

- An increase in expected inflation shifts the aggregate demand curve upward and to the right.[8] To understand this point note from the appendix that the analysis in the text has omitted changes in inflationary expectations as another determinant of dynamic aggregate demand.

---

[7] Recall also that changes in expected inflation will shift the aggregate demand curve.

[8] When we include inflation in the aggregate demand curve, an increase in expected inflation causes both the aggregate supply and aggregate demand curves to rise, certainly increasing the inflation rate, but producing an uncertain effect on output. The net effect on output depends on whether the aggregate demand or aggregate supply curve moves up more. Typically the aggregate supply curve would shift up more, implying higher inflation and lower output — which corresponds to the conclusion reached above when we omitted expected inflation from the aggregate demand curve.

The Inflation Rate and Output in the Long Run

From the short run, we move to the hypothetical longest run, in which the growth rate of money is and will continue to be constant, in which expectations have adjusted to actual inflation, and in which output and inflation are constant. Such a situation is called a *steady state,* obviously because nothing is changing. Returning to the aggregate demand equation,

$$\pi = m - \frac{1}{\phi}(Y - Y_{-1}) \tag{10}$$

we recognize that with output constant ($Y = Y_{-1}$), the inflation rate is equal to the growth rate of money. Thus, *in the steady state, the inflation rate is determined solely by the growth rate of money.*

On the aggregate supply side,

$$\pi = \pi^e + \lambda(Y - Y^*) \tag{5}$$

We set $\pi = \pi^e$ and recognize that output is at its potential level Y^*. Thus *in the steady state, output is at its full-employment level.*

In the steady state, then, we have very simple relationships: the growth rate of money determines the inflation rate, and output is at its potential level.

We want now to consider the real world importance of these steady-state relationships. The first thing to notice is that the economy never reaches a steady state. There are always disturbances affecting aggregate supply and demand: changes in expectations, or in the labor force, or in the prices of other factors of production, or in methods of production on the aggregate supply side; changes in fiscal policy, or in consumer tastes, or in monetary policy, on the aggregate demand side. Thus in practice the economy will not ever reach a steady state: as it starts on the route toward a steady state, some shock or disturbance will come along to bump it off that route onto another path.

Steady-state relationships are useful, though, in indicating the long-run behavior of the economy. Over long periods, we can expect the economy on average to behave as if the steady-state relationships hold. On average, we expect output to be at its potential level.[9] And on average, we expect the inflation rate to be determined by the growth rate of money. We take up the long-run relationship between inflation and output in more detail in the next chapter.

---

[9] Indeed, some economists define the natural rate of unemployment as the long-run average rate of unemployment. In that case by definition the unemployment rate is on average over long periods equal to the natural rate, to which the level of potential output corresponds.

14-6 DYNAMIC ADJUSTMENT OF OUTPUT AND INFLATION

Many factors drive the inflation rate and the level of output in the short run, whereas in the steady state, output is at its full-employment level and inflation is determined by the growth rate of money. In this section we ask how the economy moves toward the long-run equilibrium when a shock or disturbance affects aggregate supply or demand. To be specific, we examine the dynamic effects — that is, the effects that take place over time — of a change in the growth rate of money. We summarize here our two building blocks:

Dynamic aggregate supply: $$\pi = \pi_{-1} + \lambda(Y - Y^*) \tag{8}$$

Dynamic aggregate demand: $$\pi = m - \frac{1}{\phi}(Y - Y_{-1}) \tag{10}$$

Note that we have made the adaptive expectations assumption that expected inflation is equal to last period's inflation rate.

In Figure 14-7, the economy is initially at point E, with output at its potential level, Y^*, and with inflation equal to the growth rate of money, m_0, implying an initial inflation rate $\pi_0 = m_0$. Now suppose the growth rate of money increases to a new, higher level, m_1. Let the period in which the growth rate of money changes be period 1.

The immediate short-run effect is for both the inflation rate and output to rise, to π_1 and Y_1, respectively. But those changes in turn set off further changes. On the aggregate supply side, the increase in inflation causes expected inflation to increase, with the *SAS* curve shifting up to SAS_2. The new aggregate supply curve intersects the Y^* line at precisely the same rate of inflation as occurred in period 1, that is, at π_1. The aggregate demand curve also shifts upward, because the level of output was higher last period. On the new aggregate demand curve, the rate of inflation is equal to π_1 at level of output Y_1 [from equation (9)].

The period 2 equilibrium is at point E_2. Because both the aggregate supply and aggregate demand curves have shifted upward, the inflation rate in period 2, π_2, is certainly higher than π_1. However, it is not clear whether the level of output in period 2, Y_2, is higher or lower than Y_1. That depends on whether it was the aggregate demand or the aggregate supply curve that shifted more from period 1 to period 2.[10]

In Figure 14-7 we show output higher in period 2 than in period 1. The process now continues, with the aggregate supply and demand curves moving yet further upward. We show the third-period equilibrium, E_3, with a higher inflation rate and lower level of output than in the previous period.

It is not worth following the shifts of the aggregate supply and demand curves during the adjustment process in much further detail. Figure 14-8 shows the pattern of adjustment as the economy moves from E_1, the first-period equilibrium, to the eventual steady-state equilibrium at E'. So as to keep the diagram clear, we do not include

---

[10] If $\lambda\phi < 1$, then output rises in period 2 relative to period 1. If ϕ is small, the aggregate demand curve moves up a great deal, thereby tending to cause output in period 2 to be higher than Y_1.

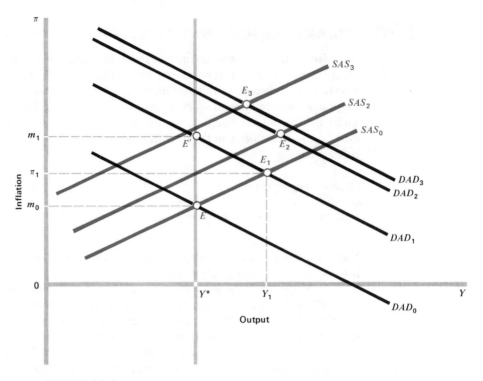

FIGURE 14-7
ADJUSTMENT TO A CHANGE IN THE GROWTH RATE OF MONEY. The
increased growth rate of money shifts the aggregate demand curve up,
from DAD_0 to DAD_1, raising the inflation rate and output. These
changes in turn cause both the supply and demand curves to shift
upward in the next period, raising the inflation rate. The process
continues until the economy reaches the new steady state.

the shifting supply and demand curves that underlie the pattern of adjustment shown.
And we have, for convenience, smoothed the time path of adjustment. The first few
points that we traced in Figure 14-7, E_1, E_2, and E_3, are also shown in Figure 14-8.

Stagflation

Two special features of the adjustment process can be seen in Figure 14-8. First, there
are times when output decreases while the inflation rate increases. For instance,
between E_2 and E_3 in Figures 14-7 and 14-8, the inflation rate increases while output
decreases. This inverse relationship between the rate of inflation and output is a result
of the shifts of the aggregate supply curve caused by changes in expected inflation.

The inverse relationship between the rate of inflation and output is important, for

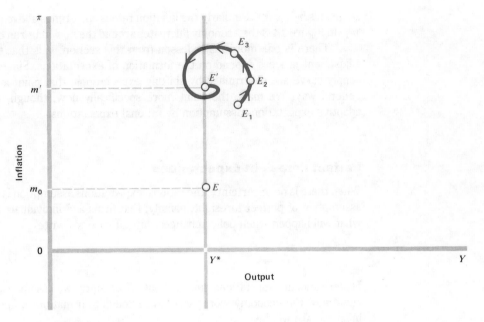

FIGURE 14-8
THE FULL ADJUSTMENT PATH. The full adjustment path moves from E_1 to
E', but with fluctuations. During the adjustment process there are
periods in which output is falling while inflation is rising.

it often occurs in practice and is widely believed not to be consistent with accepted macroeconomics. This is *stagflation.* Stagflation occurs when inflation rises while output is either falling or at least not rising.

If one ignores the role of expected inflation in the Phillips curve, it is easy to conclude that periods in which output and inflation move in opposite directions — equivalently, periods in which both inflation and unemployment increase at the same time — are impossible. Indeed, it is not only changes in expectations, but any supply shock, such as an increase in oil prices, that shifts the aggregate supply curve that can produce stagflation. Nonetheless, during periods of stagflation, such as 1973–1974 and 1980, there are articles in the newspapers that the laws of economics are not working as they should because inflation is high or rising while output is falling.

Overshooting

The most striking feature of Figure 14-8 is that the economy does not move directly to a new, higher inflation rate following the increase in the growth rate of money. Rather, given the adaptive expectations assumption we are making, the level of output at some stage falls below Y^*. Similarly the inflation rate is sometimes above its long-run level, m_1. In Figure 14-8 the economy fluctuates around the new long-run equilibrium at E'.

There is one more major lesson from this section. It is that the details of the adjustment process depend on the formation of expectations. Since the shifts in the supply curve are determined by shifting expectations, that point is easy to see in a general way. We make the point more specifically now, though, by replacing the adaptive expectations assumption by rational expectations.

Perfect Foresight Expectations

When there is no uncertainty, the rational expectations assumption is equivalent to the assumption of perfect foresight, namely, that firms and individuals correctly predict what will happen when policy changes. In that case we write

$$\pi^e = \pi \tag{11}$$

Under rational expectations, and without uncertainty, we assume that people understand how the economy works and have enough information to figure out what the inflation rate will be.

Substituting the perfect foresight assumption into aggregate supply curve (5), we obtain

$$Y = Y^* \tag{12}$$

This is a radical result, for it means that, under perfect foresight, the economy is always at potential output. It is as if under rational expectations the long-run results take place in the short run.

How can it be? The underlying assumption of the Phillips curve mechanism that includes expected inflation is that firms and workers are trying to set wages at a level such that there will be full employment. In the Friedman-Phelps version of the Phillips curve, the only reason they might not achieve that is errors in expectations. If by assumption we remove errors in expectations, the economy will then always be at full employment.

Expected and Unexpected Changes in Monetary Policy

The timing of policy actions and the formation of expectations become very important under rational expectations. The Friedman-Phelps Phillips curve assumes that wages are set before the period begins. That would mean that wages cannot react to changes in the growth rate of money that are made after wages are set. So the rational expectations assumption would leave open the possibility that an *unexpected* change in monetary policy could affect output.

The logic of rational expectations implies that people base their expectations of inflation on the policies they believe the government is following. Suppose the growth rate of money has been m_0 for a long time. Then we will have under rational expectations $\pi^e = m_0$, as long as m_0 is the expected growth rate of money.

Then if the Fed unexpectedly changes the growth rate of money to m_1, the initial impact will be exactly as in Figure 14-7, with the economy moving to point E_1, because the terms of wage contracts have not yet been changed. But one period later the adjustment under rational expectations will be very different from that in Figure 14-7. Namely, if everyone believes the Fed has indeed changed the growth rate of money, then the aggregate supply curve will move up by just that amount necessary for the economy to go back immediately to full employment, at Y^*.[11] One period later the economy will be in the steady state, with output equal to Y^* and inflation equal to m_1.[12] Thus as noted in Chapters 7 and 13, the rational expectations assumption implies that monetary policy will not have real effects unless changes in monetary policy are unexpected.

Inflationary Inertia

At this point we should note that the issue of how π^e gets into the aggregate supply function is clearly crucial. If instead of expected inflation, the π^e term reflects compensation for past inflation, or if it takes a period of years for changed inflation rates to be reflected in labor contracts, then the adjustment pattern seen in Figures 14-7 and 14-8 is more representative of what will happen than is the rapid adjustment that takes place under rational expectations.

The adjustment pattern in Figures 14-7 and 14-8 displays *inflationary inertia*. Inflationary inertia occurs when the inflation rate reacts slowly to changes in policy (particularly monetary policy) that reduce the steady-state inflation rate.

The key question for policy makers seeking to reduce the inflation rate is whether the economy displays inflationary inertia (as it does if the π^e term in the aggregate supply curve reflects compensation for past inflation, or slow adjustment of wage setting because of long-term contracts) or does not (as it would not if there were rational expectations *and* very quick readjustment of wages and prices).

Summary

1. If inflationary expectations are based on last period's inflation rate — or in general are adaptive, that is, based on past inflation — an increase in the growth rate of money increases both the inflation rate and the level of output in the short run.

---

[11] Using the aggregate supply and demand equations, it can be shown that the period 1 inflation rate under the perfect foresight assumption is given by the expression

$$\pi_1 = \frac{m_0 + \lambda \phi m_1}{1 + \lambda \phi}$$

[12] This is essentially the dynamic adjustment to a change in the money stock that was examined in Chaps. 7 and 13 when considering the approaches of rational expectations equilibrium and formal contracting aggregate supply.

Both the inflation rate and the level of output continue to fluctuate thereafter, tending eventually to move to the long-run equilibrium of the economy.

2. In the process of adjustment to a change in the growth rate of money, there are stages at which inflation and output move in opposite directions. This is because the aggregate supply curve is shifting. Stagflation occurs when output is falling while inflation stays high or rises.

3. Adjustment patterns are radically different under rational expectations. A fully expected change in the growth rate of money does not affect the level of output at all, and affects only inflation. Even if the change in money growth was not expected, output is affected only until expectations adjust to the new growth rate of money. The question of how expectations translate into wages is thus crucial to the dynamics. If it takes time for changed expectations to affect wages, then even with rational expectations, the process of adjustment to a change in the growth rate of money will be lengthy, and the economy is said to display inflationary inertia.

14-7 THE ADJUSTMENT TO A FISCAL EXPANSION

In this section we consider how inflation and output respond to a permanent fiscal expansion. We saw in Chapter 13 that a sustained fiscal expansion leads to a cumulative increase in prices and a decline in the real money stock that raises interest rates until crowding out returns the economy to the initial equilibrium. We now establish exactly the same result in the dynamic framework.

Since we now focus on a fiscal expansion we return to (9) above and rewrite the equation, moving the inflation rate to the left-hand side:

$$\pi = m - \frac{1}{\phi}(Y - Y_{-1}) + \frac{\sigma}{\phi} f \tag{10a}$$

This equation differs from (10) only in that it includes the current fiscal expansion as an extra term on the right-hand side of the equation. Given output and given the growth rate of money, a fiscal expansion ($f > 0$) will increase the rate of inflation or shift the aggregate demand schedule upward and to the right. Conversely, a current fiscal contraction ($f < 0$) shifts the aggregate demand schedule downward and to the left.

Suppose now that we have a given growth rate of money, m_0, and that the economy is in an initial steady state such that $Y = Y^*$ and $\pi = \pi^e = m$. Now a permanent fiscal expansion takes place, meaning that in the current period, f in (10a) is positive and for every period after, f is zero because government spending now remains constant at the higher level. In Figure 14-9 we show the fiscal expansion as the rightward shift of the aggregate demand schedule from DAD to DAD_1. In the short run the economy moves to point E_1. Output unambiguously expands and inflation rises.

The subsequent adjustment process can be understood from (10a). Note that in the second period $f = 0$. Hence the aggregate demand schedule will shift downward to DAD_2. Because Y_1 exceeds Y^*, DAD_2 lies above DAD. On the supply side, using (8)

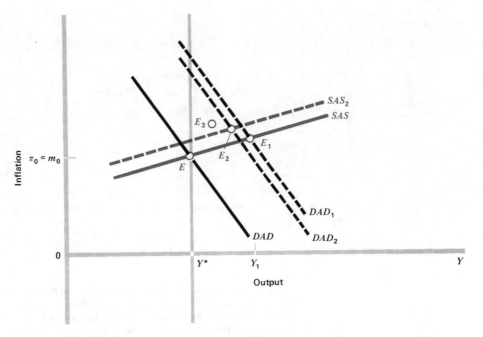

FIGURE 14-9

ADJUSTMENT TO A SUSTAINED FISCAL EXPANSION. Starting from the steady state at E, a fiscal expansion shifts aggregate demand to DAD_1 so that in the short run the economy moves to E_1. In the subsequent adjustment the aggregate demand schedule shifts back while the aggregate supply schedule shifts up and to the left as inflationary expectations increase. The economy thus suffers stagflation along a path shown by points E_2 and E_3.

the aggregate supply curve shifts upward to SAS_2. The new equilibrium, in period 2, already involves a return of output toward full employment. Inflation may be higher or lower than in period 1, depending on the relative shifts of the two schedules. This process continues over time, with the demand curve shifting inward and the aggregate supply curve shifting upward and to the left. The economy returns to full employment and then overshoots, as in Figure 14-8.

But there is an important difference. In this case the growth rate of money is not changed and hence, in the long run, we return to the initial rate of inflation, $\pi = m_0$. The typical path of the adjustment to a sustained fiscal expansion would then look like that shown in Figure 14-10. In the transition period inflation will have been higher than the growth rate of money and, as a result, real balances decline, interest rates rise, and real spending declines. The fact that the economy returns to full-employment output, with government spending higher, means that private demand has been crowded out. Once again we note the stagflation syndrome. After the initial expansion, at point E_1 output is falling, but inflation is increasing.

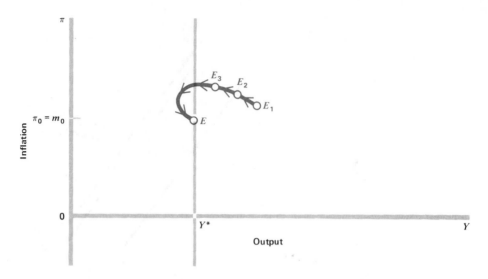

FIGURE 14-10
THE SMOOTHED ADJUSTMENT PATH FOR A SUSTAINED FISCAL EXPANSION.
The smoothed adjustment path shows that following an initial
expansion to point E_1 inflation rises further, but output falls. In the long
run, following a period of unemployment, output returns to full
employment, Y^*, and inflation to the level determined by the rate of
money growth, m_0.

The dynamics of adjustment are also affected by the impact of the fiscal expansion on the exchange rate. As the domestic interest rate rises along with the fiscal expansion, the currency tends to appreciate (as seen in Chapter 6), thus tending to reduce the prices of imported commodities. This appreciation tends to shift the aggregate supply curve down, thereby reducing the inflationary impact of the expansion. It is widely believed that the appreciation of the dollar in the period up to 1985 played an important role in the U.S. disinflation at the start of the 1980s.

Fiscal expansion, just as increased monetary growth, cannot *permanently* raise output above normal. Of course, output will be above normal for a time, and that may be enough of a motive, at the right time, for a government to implement a fiscal expansion.

14-8 ALTERNATIVE STRATEGIES TO REDUCE INFLATION

Suppose the inflation rate in the economy is 10 percent, and the government decides to fight high inflation, intending to try to get the economy down to inflation rates of around 2 to 3 percent. This is the decision that was made in the United States in 1979, and it took effect most seriously in 1982. By the mid-1980s the inflation rate was down to the 3 to 4 percent range. In the meantime the economy went through two recessions, in 1980 and again in 1981–1982. The problem of how to disinflate is one that faces governments recurrently—and occasionally the problem is how to end a hyper-inflation in which the *monthly* inflation rate is well into the double digits.

The key question for any government contemplating disinflation is how to disinflate as cheaply as possible—that is, with as small a recession as possible. In this section we consider alternative strategies for disinflation. The basic method of disinflation should be clear from the previous section: It is to reduce the growth rate of aggregate demand, shifting the *DAD* curve downward. In the model we are using, that can be done by cutting back on money growth and, in the short run, by using fiscal policy. In this section we consider only monetary policy.

Gradualism

Figure 14-11 shows the choices. A policy of gradualism—in panel *(a)*—attempts a slow and steady return to low inflation. The gradualist policy in Figure 14-11*a* begins

FIGURE 14-11
ALTERNATIVE DISINFLATION STRATEGIES. In panel *(a)* policy reduces the inflation rate gradually from 10 to 3 percent, seeking to keep output from falling much below the potential level. In panel *(b)*, by contrast, the decision is made to try to end the inflation rapidly by starting with a large cut in the growth rate of money, which produces much lower inflation at the cost of a large recession.

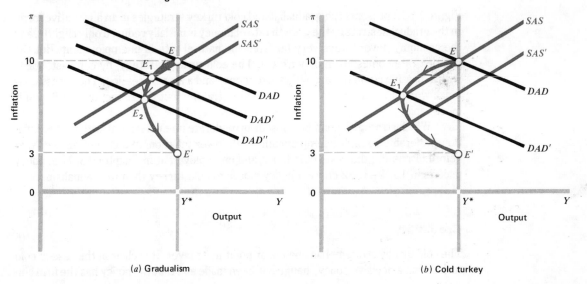

(a) Gradualism   *(b)* Cold turkey

with a small reduction in the money growth rate that shifts the aggregate demand curve down from *DAD* to *DAD'*, moving the economy a little way along the short-run aggregate supply curve, *SAS*, from E to E_1. In response to the lower inflation at E_1, the short-run aggregate supply curve shifts downward to *SAS'*. A further small cut in the money growth moves the economy to E_2, the aggregate supply curve shifts down again, and the process continues.

Eventually output returns to its potential level, at point E', at a lower inflation rate. There is no massive recession during the adjustment process, although unemployment is above normal throughout.

Cold Turkey

Panel *(b)* of Figure 14-11 shows the alternative. *The cold turkey strategy tries to cut the inflation rate fast.* The strategy starts with an immediate sharp cutback in money growth, shifting the aggregate demand curve from *DAD* to *DAD'* and moving the economy from E to E_1. There is a large recession, but because the aggregate supply curve is relatively flat, the reduction in inflation is small to begin with.

By creating a larger fall in the inflation rate than when gradualism is used, the cold turkey strategy causes the short-run supply curve to move down faster than it does in Figure 14-11*a*. The cold turkey strategy keeps up the pressure by holding the rate of money growth low. Eventually the rate of inflation falls enough that output and employment begin to grow again. The economy returns to point E' with full employment and a lower rate of inflation.

Gradualism versus Cold Turkey

Figure 14-12 presents the gradualist and cold turkey strategies in an alternative form. In the gradualist strategy the growth rate of money is initially reduced only slightly, and the economy never strays very far from the natural rate of unemployment. But the inflation rate comes down only slowly. The cold turkey strategy, by contrast, starts with a massive cut in the growth rate of money and a large recession. The recession is much worse than it ever is in the gradualist strategy, but the reduction in inflation is more rapid.

Which strategy should be chosen? Is moderate unemployment with higher inflation preferable to high unemployment with lower inflation? We cannot answer that before discussing the costs of inflation and unemployment in Chapter 15. U.S. policy makers in 1981–1982 chose a policy closer to cold turkey than to gradualism.

Credibility

The cold turkey strategy has one major point in its favor. It is clear in the case of cold turkey that a decisive policy change has been made and that the policy has the firm aim

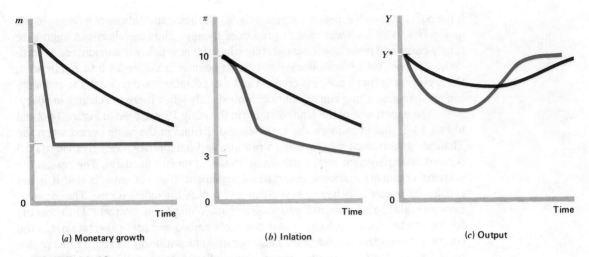

FIGURE 14-12
COLD TURKEY VERSUS GRADUALISM. This is an alternative way of
comparing the two strategies. Cold turkey (colored curves) cuts the
growth rate of money sharply, producing a massive but shorter
recession. The gradualist strategy (black curves) produces much less
unemployment, but also a much less rapid reduction in the inflation rate.

of driving down the inflation rate. The gradualist strategy, which takes a long time to be
implemented, is more likely to be abandoned if it seems to be producing more unemployment than expected, or if the policy-making team changes.

Thus people forming their expectations rationally will be more likely to believe
policy has changed under the cold turkey strategy than under gradualism. A belief that
policy has changed will by itself drive down the expected rate of inflation and for that
reason cause the short-run Phillips curve to shift down. A credible policy is one that the
public believes will be kept up and succeed. The cold turkey policy gets a *credibility
bonus* that gradualism does not.

Credibility and Rapid Deflation

Throughout the period of disinflation in the United States, starting with the Fed's
change in policy in October 1979, there was strong emphasis on the credibility of
policy. Some proponents of rational expectations even believed that if policy could only
be made credible, it would be possible to disinflate practically without causing any
recession at all.

The argument went like this. The expectations-augmented aggregate supply
curve, equation (5), is

$$\pi = \pi^e + \lambda(Y - Y^*) \tag{5}$$

If the policy is credible, people immediately adjust their expectations of inflation to the new policy, with its lower rate of growth of money. Thus the short-run aggregate supply curve will move down immediately when the new policy is announced. Accordingly, it is possible to move immediately from point E in Figure 14-8 to E'. In brief, the argument is that if policy is credible and if expectations are rational, the economy can move to a new long-run equilibrium immediately when there is a change in policy.

The experience of the United States in the early 1980s, seen in Figure 14-2 and in Box 14-1, and even more the experience of Britain in the same period when the Thatcher government was pursuing a resolute anti-inflationary policy that led to a 13 percent unemployment rate, casts doubt on this optimistic scenario. The reason the extreme credibility–rational expectations argument does not work is that it is not enough for people to believe a new policy will reduce the inflation rate. The expectations must also be incorporated into wage and other long-term contracts. The economy has, at any time, an overhang of past contracts embodying past expectations, as the contract renegotiations take time. Thus, because of inflationary inertia, a rapid return to lower inflation in economies experiencing inflation rates in the 10 to 20 percent range is unlikely.

It is easiest to change the inflation rate when there are no long-term contracts in the economy. There will be a few contracts of that kind if inflation is high and variable, for instance, in a hyperinflation. Under such conditions negotiators will not want to sign an agreement in nominal terms because they will be gambling too much on the future behavior of the price level. Long-term contracts disappear, and wages and prices are frequently reset. A credible policy will have rapid effects. But such rapid success cannot be expected in an economy in which the structure of contracts has not yet been destroyed by extreme inflation.

It remains true, though, that whatever the structure of contracts, the more credible a policy that aims to disinflate the economy is, the more successful that policy will be.[13]

Is There a Better Way?

The treatments for the inflation disease summarized in Figure 14-11 are painful and have led to a search for better ways. The most frequent alternative involves an attempt to control prices and wages directly.

INCOMES POLICY (OR WAGE AND PRICE CONTROLS)

Inflation stabilization takes time and involves unemployment because that is what is needed to get the rate of wage change down. Incomes policies try to short-circuit that slow process by getting the rate of wage change down fast, either by law (wage-price

---

[13] The credibility issue is treated in several interesting papers in "Anti-inflation Policies and the Problem of Credibility," *American Economic Review,* Papers and Proceedings, May 1982.

controls) or by persuasion. *Incomes policies* are policies that attempt to reduce the rate of wage and price increases by direct action. Either wages and prices are controlled, or the government tries to persuade labor leaders and business to raise wages and prices more slowly than they otherwise would. Incomes policies, if successful, shift the short-run aggregate supply curve down.

Wage and price controls are typically used in wartime in many countries and were used in the United States in the period 1971–1974. The 1971 controls were imposed in an effort to break the back of an inflation that for 2 years had shown little sign of responding to restrictive monetary and fiscal policy. The controls began with a 90-day wage-price *freeze.* For 3 months firms were forbidden to raise prices or pay higher wages. The freeze applied to the prices of most goods, with some exceptions, for example, agricultural goods.

A wage-price freeze certainly brings the inflation rate down. So why not get rid of inflation that way? The reason is that wages and prices have to change if resources are to be allocated efficiently in the economy. Anti-inflationary policy has to try to reduce the average rate of price increase without interfering with the role of prices in allocating resources.[14]

Over a short period, misallocations of resources from frozen wages and prices will be small and not costly. But if wages and prices are kept fixed for a long time, shortages of labor and particular goods will develop. The problem then is to find a way out of controls that does not reignite inflation. The United States did not avoid that problem when, after many policy shifts, controls were lifted in 1973–1974 — at the time when the oil price shock hit the economy.

One reason incomes policies have rarely been successful is that they are not combined with appropriate aggregate demand policies.[15] Incomes policies, or wage and price controls, aim to move the aggregate supply curve down, thereby reducing the inflation rate. So long as the aggregate demand curve moves down at the same time, the inflation rate will fall and can stay low. But if there is no accompanying change in the aggregate demand curve, the wage and price controls will only build up inflationary pressures that will eventually explode.

An interesting recent development is the use of wage and price controls as part of a complete package of economic policy measures taken to end extremely high inflation episodes. In 1985 in Argentina and Israel, and in 1986 in Brazil, policy packages were put into effect to reduce the inflation rate from several hundred percent per year to figures in the low double digits per annum. In each case the policy measures involved cuts in the budget deficit and measures to control monetary growth. Controls on wages and prices, also, were involved as central parts of the package.

---

[14] During the 1970s there was considerable interest in using *tax incentive plans* (or TIPs) to help reduce inflation. Under such a plan, firms could reduce their taxes by reducing the increase in their prices, or would have to pay higher taxes if their rate of price increase was higher. Aside from their technical complexity, TIPs also face the problem that they may hinder the efficiency of the price system. The *Brookings Papers on Economic Activity,* 1978:2, contains several articles and discussions of TIPs.

[15] For a careful account of wage and price controls, see Hugh Rockoff, *Drastic Measures, A History of Wage and Price Controls in the United States* (London: Cambridge University Press, 1984).

box 14-1 **DISINFLATION AND THE SACRIFICE RATIO**

Given that it is not in practice possible to reduce the inflation rate without a recession, the question arises, How much output is lost through different methods of disinflation, such as cold turkey and gradualism? Discussion of the costs of disinflation makes extensive use of the concept of the *sacrifice ratio*. The sacrifice ratio is the ratio of the cumulative percentage loss of GNP (as a result of a disinflation policy) to the reduction in inflation that is actually achieved.

Thus, suppose a policy reduces the inflation rate from 10 to 4 percent over a 3-year period, at the cost of levels of output that are 10 percent below potential in the first year, 8 percent below potential in the second year, and 6 percent below potential in the third year. The total loss of GNP is 24 percent (10 + 8 + 6), the reduction in inflation is 6 percent (10 − 4), and the sacrifice ratio is 4.

Before the disinflation of the 1980s, economists estimated sacrifice ratios that would apply if a disinflation program were undertaken. Estimates ranged between 5 and 10. In Table 1 we show the elements needed to calculate the sacrifice ratio, based on estimates of the level of output at full employment, and assuming that the disinfla-

TABLE 1

ACTUAL AND POTENTIAL OUTPUT AND INFLATION (percent)

Year	Actual/potential GNP*	Output loss	Inflation†
1980	97.4	2.6	9.0
1981	96.9	3.1	9.7
1982	92.4	7.6	6.4
1983	93.7	6.3	3.8
1984	97.8	2.2	4.1
1985	97.9	2.1	3.3
1986	98.4	1.6	2.7
1987	99.8	0.2	3.3
Total		25.7	

* Potential GNP series is calculated for an unemployment rate of 6 percent.

† Inflation rate is for GNP deflator.

Source: Potential GNP: from *Survey of Current Business*, March 1986, p. 13, updated using series for full-employment GNP from DRI/McGraw-Hill.

Although all three programs showed early signs of success, only the Israeli program succeeded in keeping the inflation rate low over the next 3 years. The failures of the Argentinian and Brazilian policies can clearly be laid at the door of fiscal policy, for promised cuts in fiscal deficits were not maintained. In 1988 Mexico inaugurated a similar package, which appears to be succeeding, at least through mid-1989. Whether such policy packages ultimately succeed in reducing the inflation rate without causing large increases in unemployment depends essentially on whether the accompanying

tionary period ended by the time the economy returned to 6 percent unemployment in 1987.

Taking the accumulated output loss as 25.7 percent of a year's potential GNP and the reduction in inflation as 6.4 percent (from 9.7 to 3.3 percent), the sacrifice ratio is 4.0. This is a low number relative to previous estimates, but clearly in line with them. The calculation is only an estimate, particularly because we do not know potential output for sure. The estimate may underestimate the true cost of disinflation because events favorable for disinflation, such as declining oil prices and the strong dollar, have influenced the path of actual inflation.

We can also use our theory of the aggregate supply curve to calculate sacrifice ratios. Suppose first that expectations are rational, and that all it takes to reduce the inflation rate is an announcement that the growth rate of money will be reduced next year. Then according to the simplest rational expectations view, if the announcement is believed, the sacrifice ratio will be zero, because the inflation rate will fall without a recession.

Alternatively, suppose that aggregate supply curve (8), based on adaptive expectations, applies:

$$\pi = \pi_{-1} + \lambda(Y - Y^*) \tag{8}$$

This has a very strong implication. Namely that to reduce the inflation rate by 1 percent, over any length of time, costs $1/\lambda$ units of GNP. It is clear that to reduce the inflation rate in one period by 1 percent costs $1/\lambda$ of GNP. Now suppose we did it in two steps: 0.5 percent in each of 2 years. In the first year, the output loss would be $0.5/\lambda$; the loss in the second year would also be $0.5/\lambda$. The total would again be $1/\lambda$. The same conclusion would be reached however long the period over which the adjustment was spread.

The conclusion is that with adaptive expectations, and given certain other conditions, the sacrifice ratio is independent of how rapidly the inflation rate is reduced. That does not mean of course that it does not matter whether a government undertakes a cold turkey or a gradualist policy. It may be that a short, very deep recession (cold turkey) has greater costs than a long period of only slightly greater than usual unemployment (gradualism).

The analysis also makes the role of credibility clear: To the extent that expectations of inflation can be reduced by announcements about policy, the sacrifice ratio is reduced—in the extreme (but unrealistic), simplest rational expectations case it is theoretically even possible to disinflate with no output cost at all. ∎

aggregate demand reduction measures are taken.

All attempts to control inflation through direct means run into the same difficulty. The difficulty is that relative wages and prices in the economy do have to change if the price mechanism is to work. Policies that operate directly on wages and prices have to try to prevent the overall price level from rising while permitting relative prices to change. This is either impossible or extremely difficult over any extended period.

Is There Hope?

The disinflation that started in the United States at the beginning of the 1980s was still operating successfully in 1989. The inflation rate had come down and stayed down. In part that was a result of the fall in the price of oil. But it was also a result of a cautious monetary policy. Only in 1988, 6 years after the recovery started, did the unemployment rate finally fall back close to the natural rate. At that point, the inflation rate began to edge up again, close to 5 percent, and in early 1989 the Fed was engaged in a delicate attempt to slow inflation without creating a recession. Whether or not the Fed succeeds, the record of the 1980s provides cause for hope that steady economic growth with low inflation is possible for the U.S. economy.

14-9 SUMMARY

1. The aggregate supply and demand curves introduced in this chapter differ from those of Chapter 13 by showing the relationship between output and the inflation rate rather than output and the price level.

2. The aggregate supply curve is modified further to include expected inflation. Wages increase more rapidly when inflation is expected, thus shifting the aggregate supply curve upward. Expected inflation enters prices through wages, which are changed as new wage terms are set. Thus the process through which a change in the expected inflation rate works its way into the aggregate supply curve may be quite slow. For this reason, the inflation process is often said to display inflationary inertia.

3. The short-run aggregate supply curve with constant expected rate of inflation has a small, positive slope — in fact, the curve is nearly flat — because in the short run changes in output do not cause large changes in prices. In the short run there is a tradeoff between inflation and output. The long-run aggregate supply curve, with the actual and expected inflation rates equal, is vertical: There is no long-run tradeoff between inflation and output.

4. Under adaptive expectations, expected inflation is based on the recent behavior of the inflation rate. For most of the chapter we make the particular adaptive expectations assumption that the expected inflation rate is equal to last period's inflation rate. Under rational expectations, there is no simple formula for determining expectations. Rather, people are assumed to form expectations using all the information that is available about the determinants of the inflation rate. Whereas under adaptive expectations a change in policy would not affect expectations until the actual inflation rate is affected, under rational expectations people knowing that policy will change will adjust their expectations immediately.

5. The dynamic aggregate demand curve is a negatively sloped relationship between the inflation rate and the level of output. Its position is determined by the growth rate of money and by last period's level of output. The basic relationship follows from the link between aggregate demand and real balances: The more rapidly are real balances growing, the more rapidly is aggregate demand increas-

ing. The dynamic aggregate demand curve is also shifted by changes in the aggregate demand curve and by fiscal policy changes.

6. The inflation rate and level of output are determined by the intersection of the aggregate supply and demand curves. In the short run, changes in the growth rate of money affect both output and inflation. In the long run, a change in the growth rate of money affects only the inflation rate.

7. During the process of adjustment to a change in the growth rate of money, assuming adaptive expectations, there are periods of stagflation during which inflation is increasing while output falls. Typically, there is also overshooting of the new inflation rate in the sense that on average during the adjustment process the increase in the inflation rate exceeds the increase in the growth rate of money.

8. The adjustment pattern is much more rapid under rational expectations. If the change in the growth rate of money is anticipated, then only the inflation rate changes when the money growth rate changes. If the change in monetary policy is unexpected, it does affect both the level of output and the inflation rate in the short run, but output returns to its potential level as soon as the new policy is understood.

9. There are two basic strategies to reduce the inflation rate. The gradualist strategy aims to bring the inflation rate down slowly, thereby avoiding any large recession. The cold turkey strategy cuts the growth rate of money by a large amount up front, thereby trying to reduce inflation fast at the cost of a larger recession. The cold turkey strategy may gain from a credibility bonus in that the government reduces expected inflation more rapidly by demonstrating its willingness to pay the price of disinflation.

KEY TERMS

Expectations-augmented aggregate supply
  curve
Short-run aggregate supply curve
Long-run aggregate supply curve
Adaptive expectations
Rational expectations
Dynamic aggregate demand curve
Stagflation
Overshooting

Inflationary inertia
Gradualism
Cold turkey
Credibility
Sacrifice ratio
Incomes policies
Wage and price controls
TIP

PROBLEMS

1. Explain why the expected rate of inflation affects the position of the expectations-augmented aggregate supply curve.

2. (a) Define the long-run aggregate supply curve.
   (b) Explain why the expectations-augmented long-run supply curve is vertical.
   (c) Does the economy ever reach the long run?

3. (a) In Figures 14-7 and 14-8 we show how the economy reaches a higher rate of inflation. Starting at a steady state with 10 percent inflation, show how inflation would shift back to 4 percent if the growth rate of money were reduced immediately to 4 percent.
   (b) Comment on whether inflation displays inertia during this adjustment process.

4. Consider the adjustment to a *transitory* fiscal expansion. For one period only government spending increases. In the next period it falls back to the initial level. Use equations (8) and (10*a*) to trace the adjustment path of inflation and of output. (*Note:* This is different from the analysis of Section 14-7. Here we have $f > 0$ in period 1 and $f < 0$ in period 2.)

5. Using the assumptions $\pi^e = \pi_{-1}$, $\lambda = 0.4$, and $\phi = 0.5$, and starting from a steady state with money growth equal to the inflation rate equal to 4 percent, calculate the inflation rate and output in the first three periods following an increase in the growth rate of money to 8 percent.

6. Suppose that in problem 5, expectations are rational instead of adaptive.
   (a) Suppose the change in money growth is announced before it happens, and everyone believes it will take place. What happens to inflation and output?
   (b) Suppose that money growth is unexpectedly increased from 4 percent to 8 percent in period 1, but that people believe from period 2 on that money growth will be 8 percent. Calculate the inflation rate in period 1 and in subsequent periods.

7. Calculate the sacrifice ratio using the assumptions of problem 5. Confirm that the sacrifice ratio is greater the flatter the aggregate supply curve.

8. Consider an economy that experiences an adverse supply shock. We can model this by introducing into equation (8) a one-time shock, which we denote by x:

$$\pi = \pi_{-1} + \lambda(Y - Y^*) + x$$

The term x is positive during the supply shock. Show the adjustment process to such a disturbance.

9. The economy finds itself in a recession as a result of an adverse supply shock. Show that either a fiscal expansion or increased monetary growth can speed the return of the economy to full employment.

10. Suppose that a new policy mix of fiscal expansion and a permanent reduction in money growth goes into effect.
    (a) What are the long-run effects of output and inflation?
    (b) How does the fiscal expansion affect the adjustment relative to that you discussed in answering problem 3?

APPENDIX: DYNAMIC AGGREGATE DEMAND

In the text we use the simplified dynamic aggregate demand curve

$$Y = Y_{-1} + \phi(m - \pi) \tag{A1}$$

In (A1), m is the growth rate of the nominal money stock. In this appendix we derive the dynamic aggregate demand curve carefully from the *IS-LM* model of aggregate demand and show exactly where (A1) simplifies matters.

To derive the aggregate demand curve we return to the goods market equilibrium condition

$$Y = \alpha(\overline{A} - br) \tag{A2}$$

where $\overline{A}$ denotes autonomous spending, α is the multiplier, and r denotes the *real* rate of interest. Recall that investment demand is determined by the *real* and not the nominal interest rate.

Recognizing that the real interest rate is equal to the nominal interest rate, i, minus the expected rate of inflation, we rewrite (A2) as

$$Y = \alpha(\overline{A} - bi + b\pi^e) \tag{A3}$$

In this form we recognize that the goods market equilibrium depends on both the nominal interest rate *and* the expected inflation rate. Given the nominal interest rate, an increase in the expected rate of inflation increases aggregate demand — because the increase implies a lower real interest rate and larger investment demand.

Now we bring in the asset markets by rewriting the condition that the supply of real balances is equal to the demand. Putting the interest rate on the left-hand side, as we did in equation (4) of Chapter 5, we obtain

$$i = \frac{1}{h}\left(kY - \frac{M}{P}\right) \tag{A4}$$

Substituting (A4) into (A3), we find that the level of output at which both the goods and assets markets are in equilibrium can be written as

$$Y = \alpha\left[\overline{A} - \frac{b}{h}\left(kY - \frac{M}{P}\right) + b\pi^e\right] \quad \text{or}$$

$$Y = \gamma\left(\overline{A} + \frac{b}{h}\frac{M}{P} + b\pi^e\right) \tag{A5}$$

where $\gamma = \alpha/[1 + (\alpha bk/h)]$.

The aggregate demand curve (A5) shows that the *level* of aggregate demand is determined by autonomous demand (including fiscal policy), real balances, and the expected inflation rate. An increase in any of these three factors will increase the level of aggregate demand. Note that the only difference between the aggregate demand curve here and in the previous chapter is that we are now including the expected inflation rate — and that it enters because, given the nominal interest rate, a higher expected rate of inflation means a lower real interest rate.

It follows that the *change* in aggregate demand is determined by *changes* in autonomous demand, real balances, and the expected inflation rate. Assuming that the only change in autonomous demand comes from fiscal policy, we write

$$\Delta Y = \sigma f + \phi(m - \pi) + \eta(\Delta\pi^e) \tag{A6}$$

where Δ indicates the change in a variable and f is the *change* in fiscal policy.

As described in the text, the term $(m - \pi)$ is the change in real balances, the difference between the growth rate of money and the rate of inflation: when money is growing faster than prices, real balances are increasing, and when money is growing more slowly than prices, real balances are decreasing.

Rewriting (A6) by recognizing that $\Delta Y = Y - Y_{-1}$,

$$Y = Y_{-1} + \sigma f + \phi(m - \pi) + \eta(\Delta \pi^e) \qquad \text{(A7)}$$

Equation (A7) is the complete aggregate demand relationship between the level of output and the inflation rate. Given last period's income, expectations, the change in fiscal policy, and the growth rate of money, higher inflation rates imply lower aggregate demand.

In the text we simplify by omitting the change in expected inflation, $\Delta \pi^e$.

15

THE TRADEOFFS BETWEEN
INFLATION AND UNEMPLOYMENT

Since the 1930s, the Gallup Organization has conducted opinion polls asking what is the most important problem facing the country. The answer, which is not restricted to economics, could include drugs, crime, pollution, or nuclear war. In 1981, with the inflation rate in double digits, a majority named inflation as the most important problem facing the country. Two years later, with the unemployment rate in double digits and at its highest level since the great depression, the majority declared unemployment to be the most important problem facing the nation, as can be seen in Table 15-1. By 1989, after 7 years of expansion with low inflation, neither inflation nor unemployment was perceived as a major issue, just as had been the case in the very stable period of the 1960s.

Figure 15-1 shows the *misery index*—the sum of the inflation and unemployment rates—invented by the late Arthur Okun. Whenever the index is high, as in the early 1980s, we can be sure that inflation and/or unemployment will score high as the most important problem facing the country. Table 15-1 makes the point that when inflation and/or unemployment are high, they are seen as *the* national issue, and they affect the election results. When they are low, they practically disappear from the list of concerns.

For most of this chapter we study the characteristics and costs of inflation and unemployment. We also take up the cost-benefit analysis of alternative disinflation strategies. In Chapter 14 we saw that it is necessary to go through a period of higher unemployment to reduce the inflation rate significantly. How should policy makers weigh the relative costs of producing a recession versus continuing with higher inflation.[1] And how do they in practice deal with the tradeoff? One answer is given by the

---

[1] The policy tradeoff is emphasized in Edmund Phelps, *Inflation Policy and Unemployment Theory: The Cost Benefit Approach to Monetary Planning* (New York: Norton, 1972). See also Arthur Okun's collected essays edited by J. Pechman, entitled *Economics for Policy Making* (Washington, D.C.: The Brookings Institution, 1983).

TABLE 15-1
THE MOST IMPORTANT PROBLEM FACING THE COUNTRY?

	INFLATION		UNEMPLOYMENT	
	Rate, %	Problem #1, %*	Rate, %	Problem #1, %*
1981	10.4	73	7.5	8
1982	6.2	49	9.6	28
1983	3.2	18	9.5	53
1984	4.4	10	7.4	28
1985	3.6	7	7.1	24
1986	1.9	4	6.9	23
1987	3.7	5	6.1	13
1988	4.1	2	5.4	9

* Percent of respondents.

SOURCE: *Gallup Report*, various issues, and DRI/McGraw-Hill.

TABLE 15-2
U.S. LABOR FORCE AND UNEMPLOYMENT IN 1988
(in millions of persons 16 years and over)

Working age population	186.3
Labor force	123.4
Employed	116.7
Unemployed	6.7
Not in the labor force	62.9

SOURCE: *Economic Indicators*, March 1989.

FIGURE 15-1
THE MISERY INDEX, 1960–1989. The misery index is the sum of the inflation rate and the unemployment rate. (SOURCE: DRI/McGraw-Hill.)

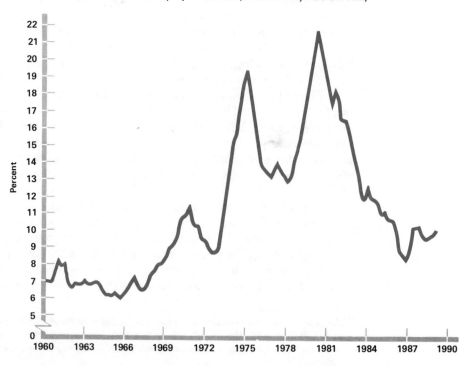

theory of the *political business cycle,* described at the end of the chapter. According to political business cycle theory, policy makers time policy moves so that the inflation and unemployment results will come out just right at the time of elections. Of course, the inflation (or the recession to stop it) will come later, after the election.

We start with a discussion of unemployment. The main point of the discussion is to distinguish between *cyclical* and *structural* unemployment and to develop the concept of the natural rate of unemployment. The discussion proceeds from there to the costs of inflation and to the cost-benefit analysis of inflation stabilization.

15-1 THE ANATOMY OF UNEMPLOYMENT

Extensive research on the U.S. labor market has revealed five key characteristics:

- There are large variations in unemployment rates across groups defined by age, sex, or experience.

- There is high turnover in the labor market. Flows in and out of employment and unemployment are high relative to the numbers of employed or unemployed.

- A significant part of this turnover is cyclical: Layoffs and separations are high during recessions, and voluntary quits are high during booms.

- Most people who become unemployed in any given month remain unemployed for only a short time.

- Much of U.S. unemployment comprises people who will be unemployed for quite a long time.

These facts are critical in understanding what unemployment means and what can or should be done about it.

The starting point for a discussion of unemployment is given in Table 15-2.[2] Working age population of the United States is given as 186 million people, of whom 66.2 percent were *in the labor force.* The size of the labor force is determined from surveys. Included in the labor force are those who respond that they are employed and those who respond that they are unemployed. An unemployed person in these surveys is defined as one who is out of work *and* who (1) has actively looked for work during the previous 4 weeks, or (2) is waiting to be recalled to a job after having been laid off, or (3) is waiting to report to a new job within 4 weeks. The requirement of having looked for a job in the past 4 weeks tests that the person is actively interested in a job, and not merely pretending or expressing an interest if a job should happen to show up.

---

[2] For a recent review see Kevin Murphy and Robert Topel, "The Evolution of Unemployment in the United States," *NBER Macroeconomics Annual,* 1987. See, too, G. Johnson and R. Layard, "The Natural Rate of Unemployment: Explanation and Policy," in O. Ashenfelter and R. Layard (eds.), *Handbook of Labor Economics* (Amsterdam: Elsevier Science Publishers, 1986).

The Unemployment Pool

Those who are of working age, but are not in the labor force (as defined above), might be old people, spouses working in the home, or people who would like to work but are discouraged by lack of success in locating a job. We now concentrate on that part of the labor force that is unemployed. At any point in time there is a given number, or *pool*, of unemployed people and there are flows in and out of the *unemployment pool*.

A person may become unemployed for one of four reasons: (1) He or she may be a new entrant into the labor force — someone looking for work for the first time — or else be a reentrant — someone returning to the labor force after not having looked for work for more than 4 weeks. (2) A person may quit a job in order to look for other employment and register as unemployed while searching. (3) The person may be laid off. The definition of *layoff* is a suspension without pay lasting or expected to last more than 7 consecutive days, initiated by the employer "without prejudice to the worker." [3] (4) A worker may lose a job to which there is no hope of returning, either because of being fired or because the firm closes down. This last way of becoming unemployed is referred to as *involuntary quits* or simply a job loss.

These sources of inflow into the pool of unemployment have a counterpart in the outflow from the unemployment pool. There are essentially three ways of moving out of the pool of unemployment. (1) A person may be hired into a new job. (2) Someone laid off may be recalled. (3) An unemployed person may stop looking for a job and thus, by definition, leave the labor force. Such a person may plan to look for a job again soon. Table 15-3 gives a breakdown of the reasons for which persons became unemployed or the way in which they joined the unemployment pool. It is interesting to observe the differences between 1979 and 1988, on the one hand, and 1983, on the other. The former were years of low unemployment, the latter a year of very high unemployment.

The key labor market facts emphasize that the labor market is in a constant state of movement. We can now ask about the factors changing the rate of unemployment and those determining the overall level of unemployment. Figure 15-2 makes it clear that unemployment increases when the flow into unemployment exceeds that out of the pool. Thus, increases in quits and layoffs increase unemployment, as does an increase in the flow of new entrants into the labor market, since new entrants typically take time to find a job once they decide to become employed. Unemployment is reduced by increases in hiring rates and by unemployed workers leaving the labor force.

---

[3] The latter qualification means that the worker was not fired but rather, will return to the old job if demand for the firm's product recovers. A firm will typically adjust to a decline in product demand by laying off some labor. A firm may also rotate layoffs among its labor force so that the individual laid-off worker may expect a recall even before product demand has fully recovered. In manufacturing, it appears that over 75 percent of laid-off workers return to jobs with their original employers. See Martin Feldstein, "Temporary Layoffs in the Theory of Unemployment," *Journal of Political Economy*, October 1976.

Variation in Unemployment across Groups

At any point in time there is a given aggregate level of unemployment, or expressed as a fraction of the labor force, an unemployment rate. For example, in March 1989, the unemployment rate was 4.9 percent. But this aggregate number conceals wide variations across sex and age groups.

The variation of unemployment rates across different groups in the labor force can be examined using the relationship between the overall unemployment rate, u, and the unemployment rates, u_i, of groups within the labor force. The overall rate is a weighted average of the unemployment rates of the groups:

$$u = w_1 u_1 + w_2 u_2 + \cdots + w_n u_n \tag{1}$$

TABLE 15-3

REASON FOR UNEMPLOYMENT (percent of unemployed persons)

	Job losers	Job leavers	Reentrants	New entrants
1979	42.9	14.3	29.4	13.3
1983	58.4	7.7	22.5	11.3
1988	46.1	14.7	27.0	12.2

SOURCE: *Employment and Earnings,* various issues.

FIGURE 15-2
THE UNEMPLOYMENT POOL.

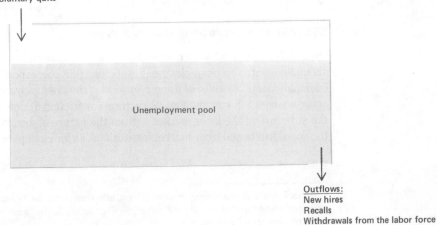

Inflow:
Entrants to the labor force
Quits
Layoffs
Involuntary quits

Unemployment pool

Outflows:
New hires
Recalls
Withdrawals from the labor force

TABLE 15-4
UNEMPLOYMENT RATES BY AGE AND RACE
(percent of group unemployed)

	1983	1988
Total	9.6	5.5
White	8.4	4.7
Black and other	17.8	10.4
Age 16–19	22.4	15.3
Men, 20 years and over	8.9	4.8

SOURCE: *Economic Indicators*, May 1989.

The w_i weights are the fraction of the civilian labor force that falls within a specific group, say, black teenagers.

Equation (1) makes it clear that the overall unemployment rate either could be made up of unemployment rates that are much the same for different groups in the labor force or could conceal dramatic differences in unemployment rates among groups categorized, say, by age, race, and sex.

Table 15-4 shows data for 1983, when unemployment was high, and 1988, when unemployment was low. Large variations in unemployment rates across groups show two common characteristics: high unemployment rates for young people and low unemployment rates for white workers. The table reveals extraordinary differences in the unemployment rates for the four groups. In 1983 nearly 1 in every 10 nonwhite workers was unemployed, but "only" 1 in every 20 white workers. By 1988 unemployment rates were lower, but the racial and age differences were still extremely large.[4]

Cyclical and Structural Unemployment

Table 15-4 can also be used to make a distinction between *cyclical* and *structural* unemployment. The unemployment rates for 1988 correspond, roughly, to structural unemployment. *Structural unemployment* is the unemployment that exists when the economy is at full employment. Structural (or frictional) unemployment results from the structure of the labor market — from the nature of jobs in the economy and from the social habits and labor market institutions, as for example unemployment benefits,

---

[4] To check your understanding of equation (1), you may want to use the data in Table 15-4 to verify that the aggregate unemployment rate in 1988 corresponds to that implied by equation (1), given that whites made up 86 percent of the labor force.

TABLE 15-5
LABOR TURNOVER RATES IN MANUFACTURING IN 1981
(per 100 employees; average of monthly data)

ACCESSIONS			SEPARATIONS			
Total	New hires	Recalls	Total	Quits	Layoffs	Other
3.2	2.0	1.0	3.6	1.3	1.8	0.7

NOTE: Components do not add to totals due to averaging and rounding. "Other" includes involuntary separations.

SOURCE: *Employment and Earnings,* March 1982.

which affect the behavior of workers and firms. The structural unemployment rate is the same as the natural unemployment rate, which we discuss in more detail below. *Cyclical unemployment* is unemployment in excess of structural unemployment; it occurs when output is below its full-employment level.

With this preliminary discussion in mind, we now turn to a closer examination of unemployment.

Labor Market Flows

The labor market presents an image of substantial turnover; firms continue to hire some new workers even as they are reducing total employment. Workers leave jobs voluntarily and locate new jobs or wind up unemployed. Research has concentrated on these flows into and out of employment and unemployment. The research starts from the recognition that the flows are large relative to the average level of employment or unemployment.[5] Thus there is considerable *turnover*.

One way of looking at the flows in the labor market is by obtaining direct estimates of the rate at which the labor force turns over in establishments. Table 15-5 shows the average of monthly flows in 1981 into and out of employment. These data (which, unfortunately, are no longer collected), show the movement, or turnover, in the labor market by splitting net employment changes into the different components. They support our conclusion about large flows into and out of the pool of unemployment.

Accessions are names added to the payroll of a company in a given month. Thus, in 1981, manufacturing companies on average added 3.2 names to their payrolls per 100 employees. *Separations* are names removed from payrolls during the month. In 1981 manufacturing companies each month on average removed 3.6 names from their

[5] Robert E. Hall, "Why Is the Unemployment Rate So High at Full Employment?" *Brookings Papers on Economic Activity,* 3:1970; Stephen T. Marston, "Employment Instability and High Unemployment Rates," *Brookings Papers on Economic Activity,* 1:1976; and Kim B. Clark and Lawrence H. Summers, "Labor Market Dynamics and Unemployment: A Reconsideration," *Brookings Papers on Economic Activity,* 1:1979. See, too, Murphy and Topel, "The Evolution of Unemployment in the United States."

TABLE 15-6

SEPARATIONS AND DESTINATIONS, MANUFACTURING, 1969–1971

	Annual moves per 100 employees	FRACTION OF MOVES ENDING IN*		
		J	U	O
All separations	9.4	0.47	0.39	0.14
Quits	3.5	0.77	0.15	0.07
Job Losses	5.9	0.29	0.53	0.18

* A move can end in a new job (J), unemployment (U), or departure from the labor force (O). Numbers may not add to 1.

SOURCE: Adapted from G. Akerlof, A. Rose, and J. Yellen, "Job Switching, Job Satisfaction and the U.S. Labor Market," *Brookings Papers on Economic Activity*, 2:1988, Table 4.

payrolls per 100 employees. Note that the levels of accessions and separations (per 100 employees) are consistently high, each above 3 percent *per month.*

Consider, too, that even though the unemployment rate was at 7.5 percent, accessions were equal to 3.2 percent of the manufacturing work force. Firms were hiring new people and calling back workers who had earlier been laid off, despite the high unemployment rate. Perhaps even more surprising, 1.3 percent of the workers in manufacturing quit their jobs voluntarily. Table 15-5 presents a remarkable picture of the movement in the labor force. People are taking *and* leaving jobs even during times of high unemployment.

Table 15-6 shows a breakdown of what happened in 1969–1971 to those workers who left manufacturing jobs, either as a result of quits or of job losses. Here the moves are classified by the way in which they ended: in new jobs (J), in unemployment (U), or in departure from the labor force (O). Nearly half of the job losses resulted in the worker's becoming unemployed and that fact is perhaps not surprising. But the interesting point revealed by the table is the behavior of quits: a third of the separations are voluntary and more than two-thirds of these quits take the worker right into a new job. Only one-fourth of the workers who quit voluntarily became unemployed or wound up out of the labor force.

Duration of Unemployment

A second way of looking at flows in and out of unemployment is to consider the *duration of spells of unemployment.* A spell of unemployment is defined as a period in which an individual remains continuously unemployed. The duration of unemployment is the average length of time a person remains unemployed. Given the unemployment rate, the shorter the duration of unemployment—the time the individual is unemployed—the larger the flows.

An essential distinction must be made between *completed* spells of unemployment and those that are still *in progress*. At any point in time there is a given number of unemployed, and we can ask how long they have been unemployed. Table 15-7 shows the data for 1983 and 1988, years of high and low unemployment. For example, in 1983 about 40 percent of the unemployed had been unemployed for more than 15 weeks against only 24 percent in 1988. These data refer to spells of unemployment in progress. For some unemployed they are about to end; for others the spells will last much longer. The obvious fact that emerges is that following a recession the duration of unemployment (measured by the mean or median) is high and it is relatively low after many years of boom, as in 1988–1989. Figure 15-3 shows the median duration of those unemployed, highlighting that duration is sensitive to the business cycle.

TABLE 15-7

UNEMPLOYMENT BY DURATION
(percent of unemployed by number
of weeks)

	1983	1988
Less than 5 weeks	33.3	46.0
5–14 weeks	27.4	30.0
15–26 weeks	15.4	12.0
27 weeks and over	23.9	12.1
Mean	20.0	13.5
Median	10.1	5.9

SOURCE: *Economic Indicators*, various issues.

FIGURE 15-3
THE MEDIAN DURATION OF UNEMPLOYMENT SPELLS, 1967–1989.
(SOURCE: DRI/McGraw-Hill.)

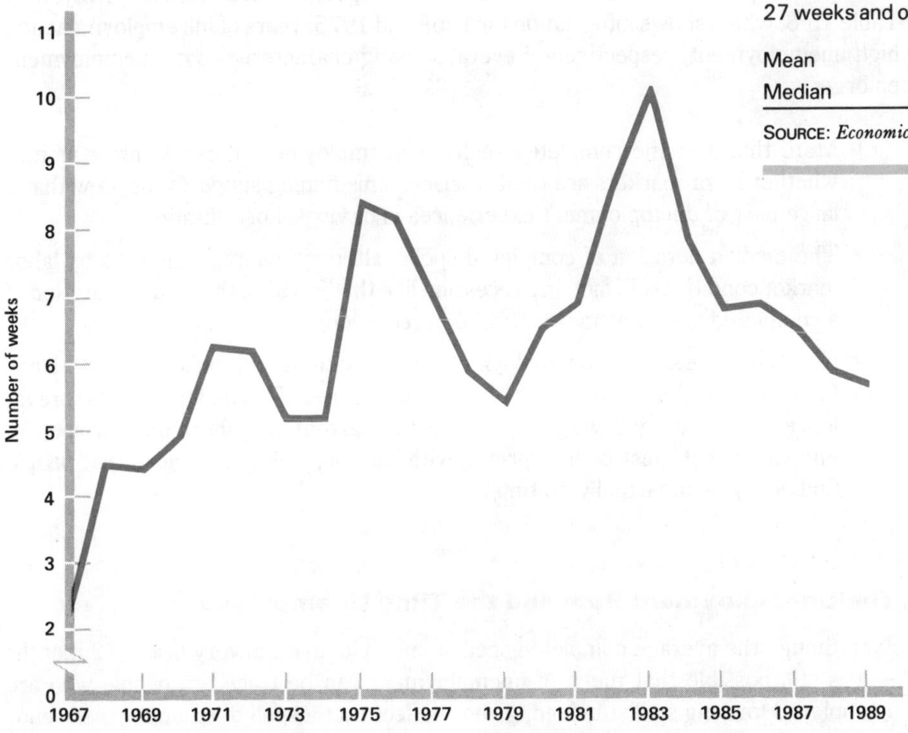

TABLE 15-8

COMPLETED SPELLS OF UNEMPLOYMENT

	1969	1975
Percent of spells ending within 1 month	79	55
Mean duration, months	1.42	2.22
Percent ending in withdrawal from the labor force	44	46

SOURCE: Adapted from Kim B. Clark and Lawrence H. Summers, "Labor Market Dynamics and Unemployment: A Reconsideration," *Brookings Papers on Economic Activity*, 1:1979. Copyright by The Brookings Institution, Washington, D.C.

TABLE 15-9

PERCENTAGE OF UNEMPLOYMENT ACCOUNTED FOR BY THE LONG-TERM UNEMPLOYED

All groups	1974	1975
Unemployment rate	5.6	8.5
Weeks of unemployment		
1–4	4.2	2.6
5–14	22.4	15.6
15–26	31.7	27.0
27–39	21.1	22.3
40 or more	20.7	32.5
	100.0	100.0

SOURCE: Adapted from Kim B. Clark and Lawrence H. Summers, "Labor Market Dynamics and Unemployment: A Reconsideration," *Brookings Papers on Economic Activity*, 1:1979. Copyright by The Brookings Institution, Washington, D.C.

But we are also interested in describing what is the duration of the typical spell of unemployment, and for that information we have to look at *completed* spells rather than spells in progress. These data are no longer reported, but an idea is conveyed by Table 15-8, which shows information for 1969 and 1975, years of full employment and high unemployment, respectively. Several striking characteristics of unemployment emerge:

- More than half the completed spells of unemployment finish within a month, whether labor markets are tight or slack. This finding supports the view that a large part of unemployment experiences is of very short duration.

- The median duration of completed spells, although short, is affected by labor market conditions. In fact, in a recession like that in 1975, the median duration of a completed spell was more than 50 percent longer than in a boom year.

- Nearly half the spells of unemployment end up with the person's leaving the labor force, independent of the state of the labor market. This may reflect the prevalence of discouraged workers, and to that extent the short median spell of unemployment must be interpreted with caution; it does not mean that people find new jobs in virtually no time.

The Unemployment Rate and the Time Unemployed

Even though the average completed spell of unemployment is very brief — 2 months — it is still possible that much of unemployment can be traced to people who are unemployed for long spells. Indeed, given the fact that a spell of unemployment ends when someone either finds a job or else withdraws from the labor force, it is possible for a person to have several spells of unemployment within the year and not actually work at all that year. A worker might move between being in the unemployment pool and being out of the labor force as a discouraged worker and back into unemployment.

Table 15-9 provides information about the proportion of unemployment that consists of people who are unemployed for different lengths of time within the year. The total amount of time unemployed (over all spells of unemployment) is counted for those individuals who experience more than one spell in a given year. In 1974, only 4.2 percent of total unemployment within the year was accounted for by people who were unemployed for 1 to 4 weeks, even though most spells of unemployment ended within a month. Nearly 42 percent of unemployment (the sum of the last two rows in Table 15-9) was accounted for by people who were unemployed for 27 weeks or more, or more than 6 months.

If instead of looking at unemployment we looked at nonemployment data—adding together the time individuals are unemployed and the time they are not in the labor force—we would find long-term *nonemployment* to be even more important than long-term unemployment. For instance, in 1974, over half of the total time not employed of all individuals taken together could be attributed to those not employed for 40 or more weeks.

These data establish that despite the substantial flows into and out of unemployment, much of aggregate unemployment is accounted for by people who remain unemployed for a substantial time. Thus, if one believes that unemployment is a more serious problem when it affects only a few people intensely, rather than many people a little, these data suggest that unemployment is a more severe problem than the aggregate unemployment rate indicates.

The duration of unemployment differs across groups in the labor force, lengthening particularly with age.[6] Spells of unemployment are more likely to end in withdrawal from the labor force among young males than among older males; this difference does not exist between younger and older females.

Despite the greater movement of young workers among jobs, unemployment, and being out of the labor force, a significant part of teenage unemployment is accounted for by long-term unemployment, just as it is for older workers.[7]

---

[6] *Technical note:* If you consult one of the sources of labor market data, such as *Monthly Labor Review* or *Employment and Earnings,* you will find figures on the duration of unemployment by characteristic, along with overall rates of unemployment. These duration data refer to the length of time the individual has been unemployed to date, *not* to the length of a *completed spell* of unemployment. Duration data in the official sources would show five people unemployed for 1 month, one person unemployed for 2 months, and one each unemployed for 3, 4, 5, and 6 months. The average duration would be computed as $[(5 \times 1) + (1 \times 2) + (1 \times 3) + \cdots + (1 \times 6)]/10 = 2.5$ months. The average duration computed as in Table 15-7 would be 2 months $(= [(4 \times 1) + (1 \times 6)]/5$. Of course, the duration as reported in the official sources would increase together with the duration of completed spells. Thus the comparative duration rates shown in the official sources agree fully with the statements here, and are well worth examining.

[7] See Kim B. Clark and Lawrence H. Summers, "The Dynamics of Youth Unemployment," in Richard B. Freeman and David A. Wise (eds.), *The Youth Labor Market Problem: Its Nature, Causes, and Consequences* (Chicago: University of Chicago Press, 1982).

The evidence tells an unambiguous story. Unemployment is much higher among the young than among the older. But the nature of the unemployment is different. The young tend to be unemployed more often and for shorter spells, whereas older workers are unemployed less often but for longer periods. It should also be noted that about half the teenagers unemployed are, in fact, at school and looking for part-time work.

15-2 FULL EMPLOYMENT

A critical question for economic policy is to know when the economy is at full employment — at an unemployment rate of 5 percent, at 4 percent, or at 6 percent? Should policy makers faced with a 6 percent unemployment rate try to sustain demand growth above trend to push unemployment down? The question arises in recoveries, once unemployment has declined from peak levels, and there is never a satisfactory answer. Some argue that there is little risk, if any, in pushing unemployment down to below 5 percent. At worst there could be an increase in inflation, but even that may not happen. Others start worrying as soon as the unemployment rate falls below 7 percent, warning that sharp acceleration of inflation is the inevitable result of overheating the economy with tightening labor markets.

In early 1986 the unemployment rate fell below 7 percent and since then the question of exactly where full employment is has been debated. There is no single, correct answer. One pragmatic answer is to choose a benchmark. This approach is somewhat arbitrary and is most commonly applied by using the 1960s as a reference point, as we shall now see.

Estimates of the Natural Rate of Unemployment

The full-employment rate of unemployment, the natural rate, and the structural rate of unemployment are all the same concept. Estimates of the natural rate generally start from some period when the labor market was thought to be in equilibrium and when the aggregate unemployment rate and the unemployment rates of the groups in equation (2) were at their natural levels. This period is usually taken to be the mid-1950s, and the aggregate natural rate for that period is assumed to be 4 percent. There is then an adjustment for changes in the composition of the labor force and, perhaps, for changes in the natural rate of unemployment of the various groups in the labor force. We can write an equation very similar to equation (1) for the natural rate, u^*:

$$u^* = w_1 u_1^* + w_2 u_2^* + \cdots + w_n u_n^* \tag{2}$$

Equation (2) says that the natural rate is the weighted average of the natural rates of unemployment of the subgroups in the labor force. The natural rate estimated for each group will differ from 4 percent: for teenagers it will be much higher, for prime-age males it will be lower, and so on.

To extrapolate the 4 percent benchmark to later periods, the first adjustment follows from the fact that the composition of the labor force has been changing since the mid-1950s. The weights of teenagers and women in the labor force have been rising. Holding the u_i constant, the changing composition of the labor force is taken into account by changing the weights, w_i, in equation (2) to reflect the current composition of the labor force rather than that of the mid-1950s. The result is a rise in the natural rate.

The second adjustment that is typically undertaken is to assume that the natural rate for each group may depend on the relative size of that group in the labor force, that is, on the group weights, w_i. The idea here is that one type of labor is not a perfect substitute for another and that the more of some type of labor there is, the higher the unemployment rate for that group. There are other estimates of the natural rate; they differ in their method of calculation, but they all include adjustments for the composition of the labor force, and they all show the natural rate rising substantially since the fifties.

Until recently there was an official full-employment–unemployment rate estimate. In the 1960s it was 4 percent. Adjustments for changes in the composition of the labor force raised the estimate to 4.9 percent in the early 1970s. Extrapolating to the 1980s and 1990s, the 4 percent rate of the 1960s corresponds to a range of 5 to 6 percent. Figure 15-4 shows the actual unemployment rate as well as the DRI estimate of a full-employment rate developed in this benchmark fashion. It is important to recognize that this full-employment rate, u^*, is nothing but a benchmark and it should properly be viewed as a band at least a percentage point wide.[8]

Determinants of the Natural Rate

The determinants of the natural rate of unemployment, u^*, can be thought of in terms of the *duration* and *frequency* of unemployment. The duration of unemployment (the average length of time a person remains unemployed) depends on cyclical factors and in addition on the following structural characteristics of the labor market:

- The organization of the labor market, including the presence or absence of employment agencies, youth employment services, etc.

- The demographic makeup of the labor force, as discussed above

- The ability and desire of the unemployed to keep looking for a better job

- The availability of unemployment benefits

The last two points deserve special notice. A person may quit a job in order to

---

[8] An alternative estimate of the natural rate of unemployment is described as the NAIRU, or *nonaccelerating inflation rate of unemployment*. This terrible terminology arises from the use of a Phillips curve like $\pi = \pi_{-1} - \epsilon(u - u^*)$, where π_{-1} may represent the expected inflation rate. It is then possible to get an estimate of u^* — the natural rate, or NAIRU — by looking for that unemployment rate at which inflation is neither accelerating nor decelerating (i.e., where $\pi = \pi_{-1}$). These estimates also tend to show an increasing NAIRU over time.

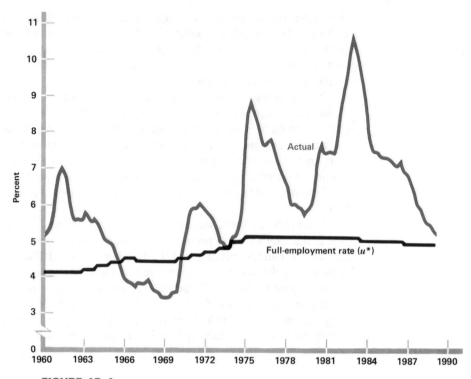

FIGURE 15-4
THE ACTUAL AND NATURAL RATES OF UNEMPLOYMENT, 1960–1989.
(SOURCE: DRI/McGraw-Hill).

have more time to look for a new and better job. We refer to this kind of unemployment as *search* unemployment. If all jobs are the same, an unemployed person will take the first one offered. If some jobs are better than others, it is worthwhile searching and waiting for a good one. If it is very expensive to remain unemployed, say because there are no unemployment benefits, an unemployed person is more likely to accept a job offer than to continue looking for a better one. If unemployment benefits are high, then it may be worthwhile for the unemployed person to continue looking for a better job rather than to accept a poor job when one is offered. Furthermore, the higher unemployment benefits are, the less costly is searching compared to continued work.

The behavior of workers who have been laid off is also important when considering the duration of unemployment. Typically, a worker who has been laid off returns to the original job and does not search for another job. The reason is quite simple: A worker who has been with a firm for a long time has special expertise in the way that firm works, which makes that worker valuable to that firm but is not of great benefit to another employer. In addition, the worker may have built up seniority rights, including a pension. Hence, such an individual could not expect to find as good a job if he or she searched for a new one. The best course of action may be to wait to be recalled, particularly if the individual is eligible for unemployment benefits while waiting.

Frequency of Unemployment

The *frequency of unemployment* is the average number of times, per period, that workers become unemployed. There are two basic determinants of the frequency of unemployment. The first is the variability of the demand for labor across different firms in the economy. Even when aggregate demand is constant, some firms are growing and some are contracting. The contracting firms lose labor, and the growing firms hire more labor. The greater this variability of the demand for labor across different firms, the higher the unemployment rate. Further, the variability of aggregate demand itself will affect the variability of the demand for labor. The second determinant is the rate at which new workers enter the labor force: The more rapidly new workers enter the labor force — the faster the growth rate of the labor force — the higher the natural rate of unemployment.

The four factors affecting duration and the two factors affecting frequency of unemployment are the basic determinants of the natural rate of unemployment.

The factors determining the level of the natural rate of unemployment are not immutable. The structure of the labor market and the labor force can change. The willingness of workers to remain unemployed while looking for, or waiting for, a new job can change. The variability of the demand for labor by differing firms can shift. As Edmund Phelps has noted, the natural rate is *not* "an intertemporal constant, something like the speed of light, independent of everything under the sun." [9] Indeed, as we see from Figure 15-4, estimates of the natural rate keep changing, from about 4 percent in the 1960s to around 5 to 6 percent at the end of the eighties.

Efficiency Wages

Many economists find it hard to believe that normal frictional unemployment — people between jobs, newcomers, and reentrants searching for new jobs — can amount to as much as 5 to 6 percent of the total labor force. After a burst of research in the 1970s on unemployment and the determinants of the natural rate, there was relatively little advance in the first half of the eighties.

New theoretical developments are now rapidly occurring. A particularly interesting possibility is *efficiency wage theory,* which argues that many firms may pay above-market clearing wages in order to obtain the loyalty of the work force or to provide workers with the incentive to work hard to avoid being fired. With the real wage set high, there will tend to be excess unemployment.

---

[9] See E. Phelps, "Economic Policy and Unemployment in the Sixties," *Public Interest,* Winter 1974.

The Rising Natural Rate of Unemployment

From 1973 to 1988 the unemployment rate stayed well above the natural rate estimated using the demographic adjustment method that underlies Figure 15-4. Some economists argued that the natural rate — regarded as the equilibrium rate of unemployment in the labor market — must for that period be higher than shown in the figure. One possible explanation of the difference is that extended periods of high unemployment raise the natural rate, making it difficult to return to previously low levels of unemployment.

UNEMPLOYMENT HYSTERESIS

The argument that high rates of unemployment have a way of perpetuating themselves is called *unemployment hysteresis.*[10] There are various ways in which this could happen. The unemployed might become accustomed to that state of life. They might find out about unemployment benefits, how to obtain them and how to spend the day doing odd jobs. But it is also possible that the unemployed, rather than finding unemployment acceptable, actually become discouraged and do not apply full effort to locating a job.

On the side of potential employers there are also effects at work that tend to make them hesitant to recruit the unemployed. The most straightforward reason is that the longer a person has been unemployed, the more plausible it may seem to the employer that the person lacks either the energy or the qualifications to work. Long unemployment spells thus *signal* to firms the possibility (not the certainty!) that the worker is undesirable, and accordingly firms shy away from hiring such workers. Firms may also simply feel that someone who has been unemployed for a very long period has lost work habits and training and thus is not a good risk. Hence, the higher the unemployment rate (and therefore the longer unemployment spells), the more unbreakable the vicious circle lengthening unemployment spells.

Reducing the Natural Rate of Unemployment

Discussion of methods for reducing the natural rate of unemployment tends to focus on the high unemployment rates of teenagers and on the very high proportion of total unemployment accounted for by the long-term unemployed.[11]

We start with teenage unemployment. Many of the unemployed teenagers are new entrants to the labor force, and teenagers are also more likely than adults to be reentrants into the labor force. Thus unemployment among teenagers could be re-

---

[10] See James Tobin, "Stabilization Policy Ten Years After," *Brookings Papers on Economic Activity,* 1:1980, and Olivier Blanchard and Lawrence Summers, "Hysteresis in the Unemployment Rate," *NBER Macroeconomics Annual,* 1986.

[11] See the *Economic Report of the President,* 1983, chap. 2.

duced if the length of time teenagers take to find a first job was reduced. In order to reduce delays in the finding of jobs, it has been suggested that a youth employment service be set up to help those who leave school locate jobs.

One of the main reasons teenagers enter and leave the labor force often is that the jobs they hold when they are working are not particularly attractive. It is a matter of some controversy as to how to improve existing jobs. The emphasis in some European countries, especially Germany, is to provide technical training for teenagers and thus make holding on to a job more rewarding.

THE MINIMUM WAGE

Because teenagers on average earn less than other workers, their wages are closer to the minimum wage than are those of more experienced workers. Many teenagers earn the minimum wage, and some would earn less if that were permissible. Accordingly, reducing the minimum wage might be one way of reducing the teenage unemployment rate. There have, in fact, been a variety of programs, including a "summer special" that reduces the minimum wage by 25 percent during the summer months, designed to reduce the impact of the minimum wage on teenage unemployment.[12]

THE SECONDARY LABOR MARKET

Peter Doeringer and Michael Piore doubt that measures such as reducing the minimum wage will do much to improve the nature of jobs in what they call the *secondary labor market*.[13] Jobs in the secondary labor market are typically for nonskilled workers and have very little security; thus such jobs carry with them higher unemployment compared to jobs in other markets.

Doeringer and Piore argue that the instability of aggregate demand is the major reason firms rely on temporary labor and subcontracting, that is, on the secondary labor market, to meet high levels of demand. If demand were maintained at a high *and* stable level, firms would have more incentive to create good, stable jobs for their entire work force. The same policies that might increase the stability of teenage employment should be expected to work for groups in the secondary market as well. The measures would include policies to provide such workers with more training, perhaps in government-run training schemes. There have been many such programs, the success of which is difficult to evaluate. The measures would also include attempts to create "job banks" that would make it possible to match the characteristics of available jobs with those of workers looking for jobs. Better day-care facilities would also contribute to more stable labor market participation.

---

[12] Charles Brown, "Minimum Wages Laws: Are They Overrated," *Journal of Economic Perspectives*, Summer 1988, finds little evidence that these measures have affected teenage unemployment.

[13] Peter B. Doeringer and Michael J. Piore, "Unemployment and the 'Dual Labor Market'," *Public Interest* 38 (Winter 1975). See, too, Robert Ullrich and Rand Araskog (eds.), *The American Work Force: Labor and Employment in the 1980s* (Auburn, 1984).

Unemployment Benefits

We come next to the implication of unemployment benefits for unemployment. The effects of changes in unemployment benefits, and in the tax treatment of benefits, on the unemployment rate remain an important current research issue. Researchers focus on the role of the *replacement ratio* in determining how likely workers are to become unemployed and how long they may remain unemployed. The replacement ratio is the ratio of after-tax income while unemployed to after-tax income while employed.

Unemployment benefits add in three separate ways to the *measured* rate of unemployment. First, the presence of unemployment benefits allows a longer job search. A high level of unemployment benefits makes it less urgent for an unemployed person to obtain a job: The higher the replacement ratio, the less urgent is the need to take a job. Feldstein and Poterba have shown that high replacement ratios significantly affect the *reservation wage*, the wage at which a person receiving unemployment benefits is willing to take a new job.[14]

The issue of the effect of unemployment compensation on unemployment rates is particularly live in Europe. Many observers of the very high levels of European unemployment (Box 15-1) regard the explanation as being that replacement ratios there are so high. Patrick Minford argues:[15]

> The picture presented is a grim one from the point of view of incentives to participate in employment. The replacement ratios are such that, should a person "work the system," incentives to have a job are, on the whole, rather small for a family man.

The second channel through which unemployment benefits raise the *measured* unemployment rate is through *reporting effects*. To collect unemployment benefits people have to be "in the labor force," looking for work even if they do not really want a job. They therefore get counted as unemployed. In the absence of unemployment benefits some people might not be in the labor force, and hence measured unemployment rates would be lower. An estimate for 1978 suggests that elimination of unemployment insurance would have reduced the unemployment rate by more than half a percentage point below the 6 percent level of that year.[16]

The third channel is *employment stability*. With unemployment insurance, the consequences of being in and out of jobs are less severe, and accordingly workers and firms do not find it as much in their interest to create highly stable employment. Further, the fact that a laid-off worker will not suffer a large loss from being unemployed makes it more attractive for an employer to lay off workers temporarily than to attempt to keep them on the job.

---

[14] Martin Feldstein and James Poterba, "Unemployment Insurance and Reservation Wages," *Journal of Public Economics*, February-March 1984.

[15] Patrick Minford, *Unemployment, Causes and Cures* (Oxford: Blackwell, 1985), p. 39.

[16] See K. Clark and L. Summers, "Unemployment Insurance and Labor Market Transitions," in M. Bailey (ed.), *Workers, Jobs and Inflation* (Washington, D.C.: The Brookings Institution, 1982), pp. 314–315.

There seems to be little doubt that unemployment compensation does add to the natural rate of unemployment.[17] This does not imply, though, that unemployment compensation should be abolished. Individuals need time to do some searching if the economy is to allocate people efficiently among jobs. It would not make sense to put a skilled worker in an unskilled job the moment she loses her previous job just because the worker cannot afford to search. Thus even from the viewpoint of economic efficiency, zero is not the ideal level of unemployment benefits. Beyond that, society may be willing to give up some efficiency so that the unemployed can maintain a minimal standard of living. What is appropriate is a scheme that will create less incentive for firms to lay off labor while at the same time ensuring that the unemployed are not exposed to economic distress. This is obviously difficult to carry off.

It has become fashionable to argue that unemployment does not present a serious social problem because the unemployed choose to be unemployed and live off unemployment compensation. This argument is wrong in assuming that all unemployed people are covered by unemployment benefits. In fact, insured unemployment is less than two-thirds of total unemployment.

15-3 THE COSTS OF UNEMPLOYMENT

The costs of unemployment are so obvious that this section might seem superfluous. Society on the whole loses from unemployment because total output is below its potential level. The unemployed as individuals suffer both from their income loss while unemployed and from the low level of self-esteem that long periods of unemployment cause.[18]

This section provides some estimates of the costs of forgone output resulting from unemployment, and clarifies some of the issues connected with the costs of unemployment and the potential benefits from reducing unemployment. We distinguish between cyclical unemployment, associated with short-run deviations of the unemployment rate from the natural rate, and "permanent," or structural, unemployment that exists at the natural rate.

The Costs of Cyclical Unemployment

We now discuss the costs that arise from cyclical unemployment. The problem here is to identify the costs to society of the output forgone because the economy is not operating at full employment. A first measure of the cost is provided by a calculation

---

[17] Among the most convincing evidence is a finding that unemployment spells tend to end, with the worker going back to a job, at precisely the time that unemployment benefits run out (typically after 26 or 39 weeks of unemployment). See Lawrence Katz and Bruce Meyer, "Unemployment Insurance, Recall Expectations, and Unemployment Outcomes," National Bureau of Economic Research, Working Paper 2594, 1988.

[18] See Harry Maurer, *Not Working* (New York: Holt, Rinehart & Winston, 1979), and Kay L. Schlozman and Sidney Verba, *Injury to Insult* (Cambridge, Mass.: Harvard University Press, 1979).

box 15-1 UNEMPLOYMENT IN INTERNATIONAL
PERSPECTIVE

At the end of the 1980s the U.S. unemployment rate had fallen well into the range of full employment; but that was not the case in Europe, as can be seen in Table 1 and Figure 1. European unemployment in the 1980s averaged more than twice its 1970s level, and was still very high at the end of the decade.

In Europe, just as in the United States, high unemployment became a public issue and a topic of academic research. Among the reasons prominently cited were the *inflexibility* of labor markets and specifically the downward inflexibility of real wages and the high firing costs imposed by law. It was argued that these firing costs stood in the way of firms' taking the risk of hiring new workers. And because firms were reluctant to hire extra workers in response to demand, governments were reluctant to promote strong demand growth, fearing that it would lead to inflation rather than to reductions in unemployment.*

The less than perfect working of labor markets is also attributed to the strength of unions. The argument is cast in terms of *insiders* and *outsiders*. The workers who hold jobs are the insiders, the unemployed are the outsiders. Firms negotiate with the insiders and the latter have few incentives to cut their own wages to create jobs for the unemployed.†

Another important argument, already encountered above, focuses on unemployment benefits. There was clearly evidence that high replacement ratios implied that some workers were better off unemployed than if they held a regular job. This would be particularly true if they had some (untaxed) work in the unofficial economy to supplement their benefits.

The European unemployment rates, high by contrast with the United States and extreme by comparison with Japan, are particularly problematic because of their incidence. The share of youth among the unemployed is very high, as is the share of the

TABLE 1

UNEMPLOYMENT RATES IN INDUSTRIAL COUNTRIES

	1971–1980	1980–1985	1986–1989
United States	6.4	8.1	6.1
Europe	4.2	9.8	10.2
Japan	1.8	2.6	2.6

SOURCE: OECD, *Economic Outlook*, various issues.

---

* See Edmond Malinvaud, *Mass Unemployment* (Oxford, Engl.: Basil Blackwell, 1988); Charles Bean, Richard Layard, and Stephen Nickell (eds.), *Unemployment* (Oxford, Engl.: Basil Blackwell, 1987); and Robert Lawrence and Charles Schultze (eds.), *Barriers to European Growth* (Washington, D.C.: The Brookings Institution, 1987).

† See Assar Lindbeck and Dennis Snower, *The Insider-Outsider Theory* (Cambridge, Mass.: MIT Press, 1989).

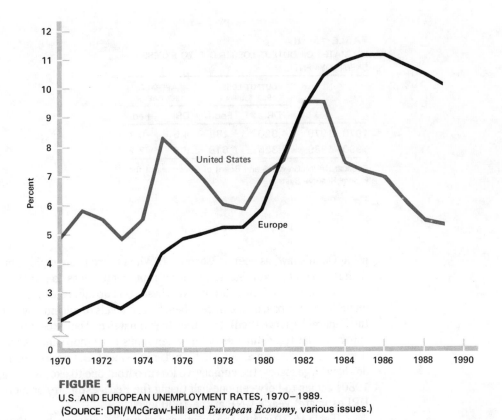

FIGURE 1
U.S. AND EUROPEAN UNEMPLOYMENT RATES, 1970–1989.
(SOURCE: DRI/McGraw-Hill and *European Economy*, various issues.)

unemployed who experience long-term unemployment. The long-term unemployment has for many gone on so long that most have greatly reduced their lifetime earnings potential. For example, in 1988, 20 percent of youth were unemployed in Europe compared with 11.5 percent in the United States. As regards long-term unemployment, the share of the unemployed experiencing a spell of more than a year in the United States was 8.7 percent. This compared with 41 percent in Britain, 32 percent in France, and 69 percent in Belgium![‡] The extraordinary incidence of European unemployment clearly called for *some* policy action. Among the measures proposed was not only demand expansion but also the idea of *work sharing*—everybody working fewer hours per day to create opportunities for more people to find employment. Others believe that the Japanese example points to profit sharing as a helpful strategy.[§] ■

[‡] For comparative data, see the annual *Employment Outlook*, published by the OECD.

[§] Jacques Dreze, "Work Sharing: Some Theory and Recent European Experience," *Economic Policy*, October 1986, and Martin Weitzman "Macroeconomic Implications of Profit Sharing." *NBER Macroeconomics Annual*, 1986.

TABLE 15-10

ESTIMATES OF OUTPUT LOSSES DUE TO EXCESS
UNEMPLOYMENT

	OUTPUT LOSS, 1982 $ billions		AVERAGE GNP GAP, %	
	DRI	Fed	DRI	Fed
1970–1979	4,920	–188	4.5	–0.1
1980–1989	8,325	2,618	6.8	2.2

SOURCE: DRI/McGraw-Hill and Board of Governors of the
Federal Reserve System.

using Okun's law, as seen in Chapter 1. When there is unemployment, output is less than it could be, and this loss in output represents a loss to society.

Table 15-10 shows output losses based on two different estimates of full employment. They are based on different benchmark levels of full employment. One is due to the Federal Reserve (Fed), the other to estimates by Data Resources, Inc. (DRI). It is apparent that the estimates differ widely, thus once more underscoring the fact that there is disagreement about what is full employment. But both estimates for the 1980s do show large losses; the cumulative loss in output due to excess unemployment in the 1980s comes to between one-half (using the Fed's estimate) or more than a full (the DRI estimate) year's GNP at the 1990 level!

Table 15-10 invites the question of why policy makers should have tolerated such high unemployment, given the staggering costs as reflected in these estimates of output lost because of unemployment.

Other Costs and Benefits

Are there any other costs of unemployment or, for that matter, offsetting benefits? It is possible to imagine offsetting benefits. We do not discuss here the benefit arising from a temporary reduction in the inflation rate accompanying a temporary increase in unemployment, but rather focus on the costs of unemployment taken by itself. A possible offsetting benefit occurs because the unemployed are not working and have more leisure. However, the value that can be placed on that leisure is small. In the first place, much of it is unwanted leisure.

Second, there is a fairly subtle issue that we shall have to explore. If people were free to set their hours of work, they would work up to the point at which the marginal value of leisure to themselves was equal to the marginal return from working an extra hour. We would then be able to conclude that if their workday were slightly reduced, the overall loss to them would be extremely small. The reason is that they acquire extra leisure from working less at the cost of having less income. But they were previously at the point at which the marginal value of leisure was equal to the after-tax marginal wage, so that the benefit of the increased leisure almost exactly offsets the private loss of income. However, the net marginal wage is less than the value of the marginal product of an employed person to the economy. The major reason is that society taxes the income of the employed person, so that society as a whole takes a share of the marginal product of the employed person. When the employed people in our example stop working, they lose for themselves only the *net*-of-tax wage they have been receiving. But society also loses the taxes they have been paying. The unemployed value their leisure at the net-of-tax wage, and that value is smaller than the value of their marginal product for society as a whole. Therefore, the value of increased leisure provides only a partial offset to the Okun's law estimate of the cost of cyclical unemployment.

Note that we do not count both the individual's personal loss of income and the Okun's law estimate of forgone output as part of the cost of unemployment. The reason is that the Okun's law estimate implicitly includes the individual's own loss of income — the law estimates the total loss of output to the economy as a whole as a result of the reduction of employment. That loss could in principle be distributed among different people in the economy in many different ways. For instance, one could imagine that the unemployed continue to receive benefit payments totaling close to their previous income while employed, with the benefit payments financed through taxes on working individuals. In that case, the unemployed would not suffer an income loss from being unemployed, but society would still lose from the reduction in total output available.

However, the effects of an increase in unemployment are, in fact, borne heavily by the unemployed themselves. There is thus an extra cost to society of unemployment that is very difficult to quantify. The cost arises from the uneven distribution of the burden of unemployment across the population. Unemployment tends to be concentrated among the poor, and that makes the distributional aspect of unemployment a serious matter. It is not one we can easily quantify, but it should not be overlooked. Further, the adverse psychological effects of unemployment, while not easy to quantify, should not be ignored (see the works cited in footnote 18).

Structural Unemployment

The benefits of reducing the natural rate of unemployment are more difficult to estimate than the costs of cyclical unemployment. It is clear that the Okun's law estimate of a 2.5 percent change in output resulting from a change of one percentage point in the unemployment rate is not appropriate here. The reason is that the increase in output associated with cyclical changes in unemployment results in part from the fact that the labor put back to work in the short run is able to use capital that has not been fully utilized when unemployment was high. However, in the long run, which is relevant when considering a reduction in the natural rate of unemployment, it would be necessary to invest to provide for the capital with which the newly employed would work. The Okun ratio of Chapter 1 is therefore too high for the long-run benefits of reducing the natural rate of unemployment.

The available estimates of the social benefits of a reduction in long-run unemployment cannot be narrowed down to very solid numbers. Even more difficult is the estimate of an "optimal" long-run unemployment rate. Here we ask the question whether any — and, if so, how much — unemployment is desirable in the long run. A first guess at the answer to that question is that all unemployment is wasteful, since the unemployed labor could usefully be employed. However, that answer is not right. Those people who are unemployed in order to look for a better job are performing a valuable service not only for themselves. They are also performing a service for society by attempting to put themselves into a position in which they earn the most and are the most valuable.

Because the composition of demand shifts over time, we can expect always to have some firms expanding and some contracting. This is true even with a stable level of aggregate demand. Those who lose their jobs will be unemployed, and they benefit both society and themselves by not taking the very first job that comes along but, rather, searching for the optimal employment. Accordingly, we can conclude that some unemployment is a good thing in an economy in which the composition of demand changes over time. It is one thing to recognize this and quite another to pin down the optimal rate of unemployment numerically.

QUITS IN A HIGH-PRESSURE ECONOMY

We conclude this section by bringing in an important argument for running an economy at high levels of demand. In Table 15-6, above, we saw that in periods of high demand quit rates are high: When demand is high and unemployment is low, workers are more willing to risk giving up a job to try to locate a better one. In this sense an economy in slack times may trap workers in poorer jobs than they might locate in periods of high employment.

This argument is due to George Akerlof, Andrew Rose, and Janet Yellen, all of the University of California at Berkeley. An essential link in their case is the relationship between quits and *vacancies*. Few workers would quit a job to look for another if they didn't think they were likely to find another job. It is precisely the existence of job vacancies that encourages workers to look for better jobs and to quit, for that purpose, the existing job. They conclude their study by observing:[19]

> Quits are cyclical because vacancy chains are longer and thus job opportunities are more abundant in a high-pressure economy; most job quits do not involve large wage increases; most job quits do result in significant nonpecuniary gains; . . . there exists an inverse relationship between vacancies and unemployment. . . . Okun's Law understates the benefits of running a high-pressure economy.

---

[19] George Akerlof, Andrew Rose, and Janet Yellen, "Job Switching and Job Satisfaction in the US Labor Market," *Brookings Papers on Economic Activity*, 2:1988.

15-4 THE COSTS OF INFLATION

The costs of inflation are much less obvious than those of unemployment. There is no direct loss of output from inflation, as there is from unemployment. In studying the costs of inflation, we again want to distinguish the short run from the long run. In the case of inflation, though, the relevant distinction is between inflation that is *perfectly anticipated*, and taken into account in economic transactions, and *imperfectly anticipated*, or unexpected. We start with perfectly anticipated inflation because that case provides a useful benchmark against which to judge unanticipated inflation.

Perfectly Anticipated Inflation

Suppose that an economy has been experiencing a given rate of inflation, say 5 percent, for a long time, and that it is correctly anticipated that the rate of inflation will continue to be 5 percent. In such an economy, all contracts would build in the expected 5 percent inflation. Both borrowers and lenders would know and agree that the dollars in which a loan will be repaid will be worth less than the dollars which are given up by the lender when making the loan. Nominal interest rates would be 5 percent higher than they would be in the absence of inflation. Long-term wage contracts would increase wages at 5 percent per year to take account of the inflation, and then build in whatever changes in real wages are agreed to. Long-term leases would take account of the inflation. In brief, any contracts in which the passage of time is involved would take the inflation into account. In that category we include the tax laws, which we are assuming would be indexed. The tax brackets themselves would be increased at the rate of 5 percent per year.[20] Inflation has no real costs in such an economy, except for a minor qualification.

That qualification arises because the interest rate that is paid on money might not adjust to the inflation rate. No interest is paid on currency—notes and coins—throughout the world, and no interest is paid on demand deposits in many countries. It is very difficult to pay interest on currency, so it is likely that the interest rate on currency will continue to be zero, independent of the perfectly anticipated inflation rate. It is reasonable to expect that in a fully anticipated inflation, interest would be paid even on demand deposits, and the interest rate paid on demand deposits would adjust to the inflation rate. If so, the only cost of perfectly anticipated inflation is that the inflation makes it more costly to hold currency.

The cost to the individual of holding currency is the interest forgone by not holding an interest-bearing asset. When the inflation rate rises, the nominal interest rate rises, the interest lost by holding currency increases, and the cost of holding currency therefore increases. Accordingly, the demand for currency falls. In practice, this means that individuals economize on the use of currency by carrying less in their wallets and making more trips to the bank to cash smaller checks than they did before.

---

[20] The taxation of interest would have to be on the *real* (after-inflation) return on assets for the tax system to be properly indexed.

The costs of these trips to the bank are often described as the "shoeleather" costs of inflation. They are related to the amount by which the demand for currency is reduced by an increase in the anticipated inflation rate, and they are small.

We should add that throughout this discussion we are assuming inflation rates that are not so high as to effectively disrupt the payments system. This disruption was a real problem in some instances of hyperinflation, but it need not concern us here. We are abstracting, too, from the cost of "menu change." This cost arises simply from the fact that with inflation—as opposed to price stability—people have to devote real resources to marking up prices and changing pay telephones and vending machines as well as cash registers. Those costs are there, but one cannot get too excited about them. On balance, the costs of fully anticipated inflation are small.

The notion that the costs of fully anticipated inflation are small does not square well with the strong aversion to inflation reflected in policy making and politics. The most important reason for that aversion is probably that inflations in the United States have not been steady, and that the inflationary experience of the United States is one of imperfectly anticipated inflation, the costs of which are substantially different from those discussed in this section.

There is a further line of argument that explains the public aversion to inflation, even of the fully anticipated, steady kind. The arguments are that it is a mirage to believe that policy makers could and would maintain a steady inflation rate at any level other than zero and that policy makers are reluctant to use restrictive policy to compensate for transitory increases in the inflation rate. Rather than maintain a constant rate of inflation in the face of inflation shocks, the authorities would accommodate these shocks and therefore validate them. Any inflationary shock would add to the inflation rate rather than being compensated by restrictive policy. In this manner, inflation, far from being constant, would, in fact, be rising as policy makers validate any and every disturbance rather than use policy to rigidly enforce the inflation target. Zero inflation, it is argued, is the only target that can be defended without this risk.[21]

Imperfectly Anticipated Inflation

The idyllic scenario of full adjustment to inflation drawn here does not describe economies that we know. Modern economies include a variety of institutional features representing different degrees of adjustment to inflation. Economies with long inflationary histories, such as those of Brazil and Israel, have made substantial adjustments to inflation through the use of indexing. Others, in which inflation has been episodic, such as the U.S. economy, have made only small adjustments for inflation.[22]

---

[21] See William J. Fellner, introductory essay in William J. Fellner (ed.), *Contemporary Economic Problems* (Washington, D.C.: American Enterprise Institute, 1973). See, too, the symposium on credibility in the *American Economic Review,* Papers and Proceedings, May 1982.

[22] In 1985 and 1986 Israel and Brazil, respectively, undertook major stabilization programs to reduce inflation. Many economists in both countries blamed indexing for the inflationary momentum that had made it difficult to stop inflation earlier. Accordingly, the stabilization packages reduced the extent of indexing in the economies. Israel's stabilization was successful; that of Brazil failed.

WEALTH REDISTRIBUTION THROUGH INFLATION

One important effect of inflation is to change the real value of assets fixed in nominal terms. A tripling of the price level, such as the United States experienced in the period from 1966 to 1990, cuts the purchasing power of all claims or assets fixed in money terms to one-third. Thus, someone who bought a 20-year government bond in 1970 and expected to receive a principal of, say, $100 in constant purchasing power at the 1990 maturity date actually winds up with a $100 principal that has a purchasing power of $33 in 1970 dollars. The more than tripling of the price level has transferred wealth from creditors — holders of bonds — to debtors.

This redistribution effect operates with respect to all assets fixed in nominal terms, in particular, money, bonds, savings accounts, insurance contracts, and some pensions. It implies that *realized real interest rates* are much lower than nominal interest rates on assets and even possibly negative. Obviously, it is an extremely important effect since it can wipe out the purchasing power of a lifetime's saving that is supposed to finance retirement consumption. Table 15-11 shows real returns on various assets. We note that for money balances ($M2$), for example, there are negative real returns in the 1960s and 1970s, since few components paid interest and the rates were low relative to inflation.

Table 15-12 shows the asset and liability positions by sector in the U.S. economy.

TABLE 15-11
REAL ASSET RETURNS (percent per year)

	1960–1969	1970–1979	1980–1988
$M2$	−0.29*	−3.3	1.75
Treasury bills	1.38	−1.08	4.04
Bonds	1.9	−0.5	5.7

* 1963–1969.
SOURCE: DRI/McGraw-Hill.

TABLE 15-12
NET NOMINAL CREDITOR STATUS (billions of dollars; year-end 1988)

	ASSETS			Liabilities (nominal)
	Tangible	Financial (nominal)	Real	
Households	6,538	4,331	7,723	3,188
Farm and unincorporated business	742	41	⋯	157
Nonfinancial corporate business	4,662	2,709	⋯	2,709
Financial business	255	8,493	1,153	9,369
Public sector (net)*				−2,097

* Net public sector financial liabilities.
SOURCE: Federal Reserve Board, *Balance Sheets for the US Economy, 1949–88.*

We treat all liabilities as nominal liabilities, and therefore the *net* nominal creditor status is just equal to nominal assets less nominal liabilities. With this definition the household sector is a creditor in nominal terms with the government the offsetting major monetary debtor. As such, households are concerned about the erosion of the real value of their net nominal creditor position by inflation. Nonfinancial corporations are to a large extent monetary debtors, reflecting their debt-financed capital structure. Similarly, financial corporations are net monetary debtors. For example, the banks' net debtor position is reflected by their liabilities in the form of debt and deposits, while their assets include some real assets, such as land and structures.

In 1988 the total value of assets fixed in nominal terms held by households was about $4.3 trillion. An increase of one percentage point in the price level would reduce the real value of these assets by $43 billion, or an amount equal to 1 percent of GNP. Those figures by themselves seem to explain the public concern over inflation. There appears to be a lot riding on each percentage-point change in the price level. That impression is slightly misleading. Many individuals are both debtors and creditors in nominal assets. Almost everyone has some money and is thus a creditor in nominal terms. Many of the middle class own housing, financed through mortgages whose values are fixed in nominal terms.

Mortgage debtors benefit from an unanticipated inflation because it reduces the real value of their mortgage. Of course, it could also turn out that someone borrows at a fixed rate for a long period and then finds that inflation sharply declines, leading to an unanticipated increase in the *real* cost of carrying the loan. But the redistribution of the 1960s and 1970s mostly went the other way, since inflation increased. Other individuals have borrowed in nominal terms to buy consumer durables, such as cars, and to that extent also have their real indebtedness reduced by inflation.

A change in the price level brings about a major *redistribution of wealth* among sectors. Obviously, we must be careful in assessing the implications of that statement. A redistribution of wealth from corporations to the household sector, for example, means that as a household the average person has gained, but as an owner of a corporate stock, the average household has lost. This singles out transfers between the government and the private sector as particularly important because here the offset is much less immediate.

We must go beyond Table 15-12 in two respects. First, that table really indicates the vulnerability of different sectors to inflation. It does not tell us to what extent inflation was anticipated when the contracts behind the figures in Table 15-12 were drawn. Inflation might have been correctly anticipated, so the wealth transfers occurring as a result of the inflation would not cause any surprises. Second, the gains and losses from these wealth transfers basically cancel out over the economy as a whole. When the government gains from inflation, the private sector may have to pay lower taxes later. When the corporate sector gains from inflation, owners of corporations benefit at the expense of others. If we really did not care about the distribution of wealth among individuals, the costs of unanticipated inflation would be negligible. Included in the individuals of the previous sentence are those belonging to different generations, since the current owners of the national debt might be harmed by inflation — to the benefit of future taxpayers.

The costs of unanticipated inflation are thus largely distributional costs. There is a presumption that the old are more vulnerable to inflation than the young in that they own more nominal assets. Offsetting this, however, is the fact that Social Security benefits are indexed, so that a substantial part of the wealth of those about to retire is protected from unanticipated inflation. There appears to be little evidence supporting the view that the poor suffer especially from unanticipated inflation.[23]

Inflation redistributes wealth between debtors and creditors because changes in the price level change the purchasing power of assets fixed in money terms. There is room, too, for inflation to affect income positions by changing the distribution of income. A popular line of argument has always been that inflation benefits capitalists or recipients of profit income at the expense of wage earners. Unanticipated inflation, it is argued, means that prices rise faster than wages and therefore allow profits to expand. For the United States in the post-World War II period, there is no persuasive evidence to this effect. There is evidence that the real return on common stocks — that is, the real value of dividends and capital gains on equity — is reduced by unanticipated inflation. Thus, equity holders appear to be adversely affected by unanticipated inflation.[24]

The last important distributional effect of inflation concerns the real value of tax liabilities. A failure to index the tax structure implies that inflation moves the public into higher tax brackets and thus raises the real value of its tax payments or reduces real disposable income. Inflation acts as though Congress had voted an increase in tax schedules. Tax brackets in the United States have been indexed since 1985.

The fact that unanticipated inflation acts mainly to redistribute wealth and that the net effects of wealth redistribution should be close to zero has lead to some questioning of the reasons for public concern over inflation. The gainers, it seems, do not shout as loudly as the losers. Since some of the gainers (future taxpayers) have yet to be born, this is hardly surprising. There is also a notion that the average wage earner is subject to an illusion when both the nominal wage and the price level increase. Wage earners are thought to attribute increases in nominal wages to their own merit rather than to inflation, while the general inflation of prices is seen as causing an unwarranted reduction in the real wage they would otherwise have received. It is hard to know how to test the validity of this argument. Nonetheless, it does appear that the redistributive effects of unanticipated inflation are large, and that, accordingly, some parts of the population could be seriously affected by it.

---

[23] See Rebecca Blank and Alan Blinder, "Macroeconomics, Income Disatribution and Poverty," in Sheldon Danziger and Daniel Weinberg (eds.), *Fighting Poverty* (Cambridge, Mass.: Harvard University Press, 1986).

[24] See Charles R. Nelson, "Inflation and Rates of Return on Common Stocks," *Journal of Finance*, May 1976. See also Franco Modigliani and Richard Cohn, "Inflation, Rational Valuation and the Market," *Financial Analysts Journal*, March – April 1979, for a controversial view of the reasons inflation affects the stock market.

15-5 INFLATION, INTEREST RATES, AND WAGE INDEXATION

In this section we look at two kinds of contracts that are especially affected by inflation. These are long-term loan contracts and wage contracts. In each case payments are fixed in nominal terms over some length of time ahead. But the future price level is not known ahead of time, and hence the *real* value of the payments can turn out to be very different from what borrowers and lenders, or workers and firms, had anticipated.

Inflation and Interest Rates

One of the areas where inflation plays an important role is the capital market. Here borrowers and lenders make loan contracts that specify fixed dollar payments. For example, a firm may sell 20-year bonds in the capital markets at an interest rate of 10 percent per year. Whether the real interest rate on the bonds turns out to be high or low depends on what the inflation rate will be over the next 20 years. The borrower and lender will each have some idea of what inflation will be. They may even agree, but they may also turn out to be wrong. Inflation has major effects particularly in the area of fixed interest home financing, where loans are made for 25 to 35 years.

Inflation and Housing

Investment in housing is one of the areas where errors in inflation expectations can bring about large redistributions between borrowers and lenders. The typical household buys a home by borrowing from a bank or savings and loan institution. The mortgage — this is the term for the home loan — used to be a fixed nominal interest rate loan for a duration of 25 or 30 years. The interest payments are deductible in calculating federal income taxes, and accordingly, the effective cost of the loan is less than the actual interest by an amount that depends on the household's marginal tax rate. Suppose the marginal tax rate is 30 percent; then the nominal interest cost is 70 percent of the actual mortgage rate.

Now consider the economics of investing in a home, comparing the interest cost with the capital gains that arise from inflation. With inflation, the value of the home rises over time. Therefore if the interest cost falls short of the capital gains, investing in a house is a good idea, even leaving aside noneconomic considerations of owning versus renting.

Consider, for example, someone buying a home in 1963 and financing it with a 25-year fixed interest mortgage. The mortgage rate was then 5.9 percent, but the rate of inflation over the next 25 years averaged 5.4 percent. Thus the pretax actual real interest cost of borrowing was 0.5 percent. In addition, the home buyer was allowed to deduct the interest paid on the mortgage from his or her taxable income. At an interest rate of 5.9 percent and a tax rate of 30 percent, the tax reduction is worth another 1.77 percent a year (30 percent of 5.9 percent), so the after-tax real cost of borrowing was

TABLE 15-13
DECLINES IN THE REAL VALUE OF THE NATIONAL DEBT
(dollars in billions)

	DEBT		DEBT REDUCTION, %	
	Nominal	Real*	Surpluses	Inflation
1945	$235.1	$235.1		
1955	226.6	130.8	3.6	57.7

* 1945 prices.
SOURCE: DRI/McGraw Hill.

minus 1.3 percent, not a bad deal![25] But of course inflation could have turned out to be lower than expected, and then the borrowers would have done worse than they expected to.

Uncertainty about the outlook for inflation was one of the reasons a new financial instrument made its appearance: *the adjustable rate mortgage*, which is a particular example of a *floating rate* loan. These are long-term loans with an interest rate that is periodically (every year, for example) adjusted in line with prevailing short-term interest rates. To the extent that nominal interest rates roughly reflect inflation trends, adjustable rate mortgages reduce the effects of inflation on the long-term costs of financing home purchases. There are thus less likely to be large unanticipated capital gains (and losses) for borrowers who use adjustable rate mortgages than for those borrowing with the conventional long-term fixed interest mortgage, which still continues in use.

Inflation and the Public Debt

There are many instances, especially in the aftermath of wars, in which governments have allowed inflation to reduce the *real* value of public debt. This was the case in Europe in the 1920s and also in the United States in the late 1940s. Interest rates then were very low and inflation very high. As a result the government paid *negative* real interest rates on the public debt, or the real value of debt outstanding declined.

Table 15-13 shows that between 1945 and 1955 the real value of the public debt declined by 55.6 percent. Of this reduction in real government indebtedness only 3.6 percent was due to debt retirement by budget surpluses. The remaining 58 percent corresponded to inflationary erosion of the public debt.

Today the scope for erosion of the debt by inflation is far more limited because a much larger share of the debt is short-term. As a result the interest rate on debt will rise (though perhaps not fully) with inflation, thus preventing inflation from reducing

---

[25] For a further discussion see L. Summers, "Inflation, the Stock Market and Owner-Occupied Housing," *American Economic Review*, May 1981.

the real value of the debt. Moreover, inflation today is far more of an established fact than it was in the 1940s (following the experience of falling prices in the 1930s), and hence interest rates reflect inflation more rapidly and more fully now than then.

Indexation of Wages

In Chapter 14 we discussed the role of automatic cost-of-living adjustment (COLA) provisions in wage contracts. COLA provisions link increases in money wages to increases in the price level. The adjustment may be complete — 100 percent indexation — or only partial. Partial indexation takes one of two forms. There may be a *threshold* or a *cap*. A threshold specifies a minimum increase in the price level before indexation comes into play. This implies that small price increases are not compensated, while larger ones are. A cap puts a limit on the extent to which price increases are compensated, say, 10 percent per year. COLA clauses are designed to allow workers to recover purchasing power lost through price increases.

WHY INDEXATION?

Indexation in some form is a quite common feature of labor markets in many countries. Indexation strikes a balance between the advantages of long-term wage contracts and the interests of workers and firms in not having *real* wages get too far out of line. Bargaining for wages is costly because workers (unions) and firms have to devote time and effort to arrive at a settlement and, often, work is disrupted through strikes. It is in the common interest of workers and firms therefore to hold to a minimum the number of times these negotiations take place.

Thus wages are not negotiated once a week or once a month, but rather they are negotiated in the form of 2- or 3-year contracts. But over the term of these contracts the evolution of prices — consumer prices and the prices at which firms sell their output — is not known with certainty. Therefore real wages paid by firms or received by workers are not known even if money wages are. To remedy this uncertainty, some provision is made to adjust wages for inflation. Broadly, there are two possibilities. One is to index wages to the CPI and in periodic, say quarterly, reviews, increase wages by the increase in prices over the period. The other is to schedule periodic, preannounced wage increases based on the expected rate of price increase. If inflation were known with certainty, the two methods would come to the same thing. But since inflation can differ from expectations, there will be discrepancies. Prefixed wage increases may turn out to be high or low relative to actual inflation. On that account indexation on the basis of actual inflation offers greater assurance of stable real wages for workers than do scheduled increases.

SUPPLY SHOCKS AND INDEXATION

Suppose real material prices increase, and firms pass these cost increases on into higher prices of final goods. Consumer prices will rise, and under a system of 100 percent indexation, wages would rise. This leads to further price, material costs, and wage increases. Indexation here leads to an inflation spiral that would be avoided under a system of prefixed wage increases because then real wages could fall as a consequence of higher material prices.

The example makes it clear that we must distinguish two possibilities in considering the effects of wage indexing, monetary disturbances and real disturbances. In the case of a monetary disturbance (a shift in the *LM* schedule), there is a "pure" inflation disturbance, and firms can afford to pay the same real wages and therefore would not mind 100 percent indexation. In the case of adverse real disturbances, however, real wages must fall, and full indexation is entirely the wrong system because it stands in the way of downward real wage flexibility.

From the two cases it is apparent that neither completely prefixed wage increases nor complete indexation is likely to be optimal. The best arrangement will depend on the relative importance of monetary and real shocks. Countries that had practiced 100 percent indexation — for example, Italy and Brazil — found in the 1970s that it was difficult to adjust to real shocks and that the indexation led to a wage-price spiral that pushed up inflation with great speed.

WAGE INDEXATION IN THE UNITED STATES

In the U.S. economy more than 50 percent of workers who are covered in major collective bargaining agreements have contract provisions for automatic cost-of-living adjustments. Table 15-14 shows that these provisions were much more common after 1973 than before, but have again declined along with inflation. The increase in the level and variability of the rate of inflation is the explanation for the increase after 1973 and the decline in the 1980s.

Table 15-14 might give the impression that indexation is a very common feature of the U.S. labor market. But that is not the case once we note that major bargaining agreements cover only a small part of the labor force. In 1985, for example, about 10 million workers out of a total labor force pool of 110 million were covered by COLA provisions.

The role of indexation is further limited because 100 percent indexation is not the rule. For example, a common rule adjusts the wage by $0.01 per hour for each 0.2

TABLE 15-14

INFLATION AND COLA PROVISIONS (percent)

Rate	Average inflation rate	Workers with COLA coverage[*]
1963–1972	3.5	27
1973–1982	8.2	55
1983–1988	3.5	50
1988	4.1	38

[*] Percentage of all workers covered in major collective bargaining agreements.

SOURCE: *Monthly Labor Review*, various issues, and DRI/McGraw-Hill.

percent increase in the CPI. With an hourly wage of $10 and an inflation rate of 5 percent, the adjustment is $0.25 (= $0.01 × 5 percent/0.2 percent) per hour, or 2.5 percent (= $0.25/$10). Under this rule, indexation compensates for just 50 percent of the inflation.

We noted above that a system of 100 percent indexation is difficult to manage when there are supply shocks such as occurred in the 1970s. The U.S. system is clearly very far from full indexation. Some observers see in this fact the reason that the U.S. economy more easily adjusted to the oil shocks than did countries in Europe where full indexation is more common.[26]

15-6 THE POLITICAL ECONOMY OF INFLATION AND UNEMPLOYMENT

We have seen the costs of unemployment and the problems that arise from inflation. The final question is how policy makers strike a balance, deciding how much unemployment to live with and how much inflation to accept. It is clear from the outset that the best of all worlds is one without either inflation or excess unemployment. But disturbances in the economy do occur, and in the absence of full wage-price flexibility, it will not be possible to restore full employment with stable prices instantly. Policy makers therefore face a tradeoff: Should they try to maintain the economy close to or at full employment, even if that involves risks of inflation bursts when shocks do occur? Or should they opt for policies that are much less accommodating and therefore involve larger swings in unemployment but more stable prices?

Alternative Policy Paths

What should be done when a disturbance, say a supply shock, creates both high unemployment and inflation? Should the return to full employment be rapid, even at the cost of high inflation? Or should stopping inflation be the first priority even if that means an extended period of unemployment? Policy makers must reach decisions on these matters. Even if their control of the economy is not perfect, there is still a need to set policy instruments to move the economy in the desired direction.

Figure 15-5 shows a long-run Phillips curve, *LPC,* which indicates that in the long run there is no tradeoff between inflation and unemployment. Suppose now that as a consequence of a disturbance, say an oil shock, the economy finds itself at point *A*, with high inflation and high unemployment. We show two possible adjustment paths. The solid path shows higher inflation rates in the transition and corresponds to a policy choice of rapid restoration of low unemployment levels and then a long period of decelerating inflation. An alternative is the dashed path along which there is an immediate reaction in inflation. Along this path inflation is falling, but the cost is that the reduction in unemployment is more gradual.

Figure 15-5 makes the point that policy makers do not choose between inflation

---

[26] See Michael Bruno and Jeffrey Sachs, *The Economics of Worldwide Stagflation* (Cambridge, Mass.: Harvard University Press, 1985).

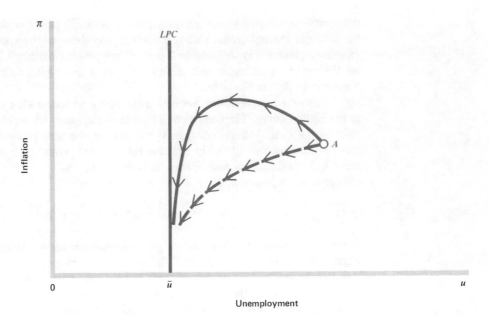

FIGURE 15-5

ALTERNATIVE PATHS OF INFLATION AND UNEMPLOYMENT. A disturbance
moves the economy to point *A*, at which there is high inflation and high
unemployment. There are alternative strategies for returning to full
employment. The upper path emphasizes a rapid elimination of
unemployment, the lower path a more rapid disinflation.

and unemployment, but rather between *adjustment paths* that differ in the inflation-
unemployment mix. The solid-line path corresponds to the gradualist disinflation policy
in Chapter 14; the broken-line path is more like the cold turkey policy.

The Extended Phillips Curve

To see more precisely the options open to policy makers, we look at the expectations-
augmented Phillips curve of Chapter 14, expressed now in terms of unemployment
rather than output:

$$\pi = \pi^e - \epsilon(u - u^*) \tag{3}$$

where, as a reminder, π denotes the inflation rate and π^e the trend or expected inflation
rate. In this form the Phillips curve states that inflation will decline relative to the
previous trend if the actual unemployment rate exceeds the natural rate, u^*. But often
it is argued that the rate of inflation depends not only on the expected inflation rate, π^e,
and on the *level* of the unemployment rate but also on the *change* in the unemployment
rate. The argument is that at the same level of the unemployment rate, inflation will be

different depending on whether unemployment is rapidly falling or sharply increasing. Suppose the unemployment rate is 8 percent, and there are two possibilities. In one case unemployment is declining by 2 percent per year; in another it is not declining at all. We would expect higher inflationary pressure or less rapidly falling inflation in the former case than in the latter.

This extension is shown in equation (4), where we add another term, $\beta(u - u_{-1})$, to the Phillips curve. The coefficient β measures the extent to which changing unemployment $(u - u_{-1})$ affects inflation. The larger is β, the more important is the effect of changing unemployment on the inflation rate. In this extended form high unemployment still exerts dampening effects on inflation, but they are now modified by the change-in-unemployment effect.

$$\pi = \pi^e - \epsilon(u - u^*) - \beta(u - u_{-1}) \tag{4}$$

Equation (4) is immediately useful for policy decisions because it suggests that there is a concrete tradeoff. The more rapid the reduction in unemployment, the less disinflation is achieved at each unemployment level. Even if unemployment is very high, inflation falls little if the economy is moving too rapidly out of the recession. Conversely, a slow recovery reinforces the inflation-dampening effects of high unemployment.

The Policy Tradeoff

We can now return to the policy problem posed in Figure 15-5. The problem is to reduce unemployment but at the same time produce a long-run reduction in inflation. Okun's law suggests that reducing unemployment requires a sustained high-growth strategy. But the extended Phillips curve in equation (4) shows that a strategy of rapidly reducing unemployment will tend to increase the inflation rate. There is a choice to be made between a *high-growth recovery* that rapidly reduces unemployment and a *slow-growth recovery* that cuts into inflation, but at the cost of sustained unemployment.

What Do Policy Makers Do?

How do policy makers actually choose between paths such as those shown in Figure 15-5, and what typically is the choice?[27] There are two ways of thinking about this problem. One is to assume that policy makers act in the interest of society. They form estimates of the social costs associated with alternative paths of inflation and unemployment and choose the path that minimizes the total cost of stabilization to society. That is the approach a benevolent dictator would choose.

In a democracy, policy makers respond to the electorate and choose policies that

---

[27] On the general topic see Herbert Stein, *Presidential Economics* (New York: Simon & Schuster, 1984).

will maximize their chances of being kept in office. This may or may not result in their choosing the socially optimal path. This second approach has given rise to an extensive literature in economics and political science that is classified as political business cycle theory.

THE POLITICAL BUSINESS CYCLE

Policy makers who hold office in a democracy choose policies that contribute to their reelection. It is therefore important for them to determine the issues that voters are concerned with, the relative importance of the issues, and the ease and degree of risk or certainty with which macroeconomic policy can be used to help secure reelection. The theory of the *political business cycle* predicts that the path of the macroeconomy mirrors the timetable of the election cycle. We now review the building blocks of that theory.[28]

We have already discussed the first building block: the tradeoffs from which a policy maker can choose. There are two more building blocks: first, how voters rate the issues — inflation versus unemployment — and second, what the optimal timing is for influencing election results.

OPINION POLLS

Voters are concerned with both inflation and unemployment. Table 15-1 showed responses to Gallup opinion polls. In virtually every poll between 1973 and 1983, more than 50 percent of the respondents rated either inflation or unemployment as the most serious problem facing the country. The same pattern emerges from almost all public opinion polls.

There is an important further lesson to be drawn from opinion polls: The public is concerned less with the level of unemployment than with the direction of change. *Rising* unemployment brings about sharply increased concern over unemployment. Concern over inflation depends on the expectation of rising inflation as well as on the level of inflation.

The evidence is thus that voters worry about both the *level* and the *rate of change* of the inflation and unemployment rates. For instance, the public is less worried about a high but *falling* unemployment rate than it is about a medium but constant unemployment rate. These facts influence the types of policies politicians will choose.

THE TIMING ISSUE

The policy maker wants to be sure that at election time the economy is pointed in the right direction to yield a maximum of voter approval. The inflation rate and unemploy-

---

[28] For a survey see Alberto Alesina, "Macroeconomics and Politics," *NBER Macroeconomics Annual*, 1988; and William Nordhaus "Alternative Approaches to the Political Business Cycle," *Brookings Papers on Economic Activity*, 2, 1989. For a critical view, see K. Alec Chrystal and David A. Peel, "What Can Economics Learn from Political Science, and Vice Versa," *American Economic Review*, May 1986.

ment rate should be falling if possible — and should not be too high if that can be managed. The problem is how to use the period from inauguration to election to bring the economy into just the right position.

The answer of the political business cycle hypothesis is that politicians will use restraint early in an administration, raising unemployment but reducing inflation. The need for restraint can often be blamed on a previous administration. But as the election approaches, expansion takes over to assure that falling unemployment brings voter approval even while the level of unemployment still checks inflation. In this hypothesis then there is a systematic cycle in unemployment, rising in the first part of a presidential term and declining in the second. There is a matching cycle, of course, in the policy instruments. Thus in the first part of the term, policy would tighten to create slack and disinflation; in the second part, expansion takes over to reduce unemployment.

The empirical evidence on the political business cycle remains mixed. The U.S. data do not show as clear a pattern over the 4-year presidential cycle in the United States as the theory would lead us to expect. Every now and then, though, as in 1969–1972 and 1981–1984, the facts seem to accord with the theory. Similarly, the Republican victory in 1988 is almost a textbook case in applying political business cycle theory (see Box 15-2).

In any event, there are factors that work against the political business cycle. One is that the President cannot use the business cycle fully because of midterm congressional election. The second is that a President cannot indulge too openly in staging recessions and recoveries timed solely with a view to the election. There are risks to being caught in cynical manipulation of macroeconomic policies. Third, large macroshocks — oil shocks and wars — may on occasion overshadow the election cycle. Fourth, the executive does not control the full range of instruments. Specifically the Fed, in principle at least, is independent and therefore need not accommodate an attempt to move the economy in an election cycle. In fact, though, the Fed, has not always spoiled the game. At least on one occasion, in 1972, the Fed very obviously provided expansion just at the right time. Fifth, if expectations are rational, then monetary policy expansions staged just for the elections will have only small real effects and will mainly produce inflation. Fiscal expansions could still have real effects even if perfectly anticipated.

Thus we should not be surprised that the electoral cycle is not completely regular. Nonetheless, the hypothesis should not be entirely dismissed. For instance, other things being equal, we should be surprised to see an administration staging a recession in an election year to sharply reduce the inflation rate — with the falls in inflation to come only later.

15-7 SUMMARY

1. The anatomy of unemployment in the United States reveals frequent and short spells of unemployment. Nonetheless, a substantial fraction of U.S. unemployment is accounted for by those who are unemployed for a large portion of the time.

box 15-2 — THE POLITICAL BUSINESS CYCLE IN 1988

Presidential elections offer a highly visible opportunity to test the theory of the political business cycle. The 1988 elections are a case in point. With low inflation and the sixth year of uninterrupted growth taking unemployment to record low levels, the incumbent party had a strong edge.

Ray Fair of Yale University has developed an equation that predicts the election outcome based on past inflation and per capita income growth in the election year. He concludes:*

> The present results suggest that voters look back between six and nine months regarding the real [per capita] growth rate and about two years regarding the inflation rate. This rather short horizon leaves room for an administration to increase the chances of its party getting reelected. Whether administrations in fact behave this way, thus creating "political business cycles," is, of course, a different question. . . . The only point here is that voters seem to behave in a way that provides an incentive for such manipulation.

How well does this approach perform? In only three of the past 19 presidential elections was the wrong winner predicted (Nixon rather than Kennedy in 1960, Humphrey rather than Nixon in 1972, and Ford rather than Carter in 1976). But in each case the prediction equation warned that the elections were very close, well within the error of the equation. Based on these findings the winner in 1992 will have to aim for low inflation in 1991-1992 and strong growth at the 1992 finish line. And, according to Fair's regressions, the incumbent has a significant advantage. ■

* Ray C. Fair, "The Effect of Economic Events on Votes for President: 1984 Update," *Political Behavior* 10, no. 2 (1988). See, too, Alberto Alesina, "Politics and Business Cycles in Industrial Democracies," *Economic Policy*, April 1989, and the references in footnote 28.

2. There are significant differences in unemployment rates across age groups and race. Unemployment among black teenagers is highest, and that of white adults is lowest. The young and minorities have significantly higher unemployment rates than middle-aged whites.
3. The concept of the natural, or structural, rate of unemployment singles out that part of unemployment which would exist even at full employment. This unemployment arises in part because of the high frequency of job changes, in particular for teenagers. The high frequency of teenage unemployment is explained partly by the poor quality of jobs available to people without training. The natural rate of unemployment is hard to conceptualize and even harder to measure. The consensus is to estimate it in the range of 5 to 6 percent, up from the 4 percent of the mid-1950s.
4. Policies to reduce the natural rate of unemployment involve labor market and aggregate demand policies. The economy needs a stable, high level of aggregate

demand. Disincentives to employment and training, such as minimum wages, and incentives to extended job search, such as untaxed unemployment benefits, also tend to raise the natural rate.

5. The cost of unemployment is the psychological and financial distress of the unemployed as well as the loss of output. The loss of output is little compensated for by the unemployed's enjoying leisure. For one thing, a large part of unemployment is involuntary. For another, the social product of labor exceeds the wage rate received by the employee, because of income taxes.

6. The economy can adjust to perfectly anticipated inflation by moving to a system of indexed taxes and to nominal interest rates that reflect the expected rate of inflation. In the absence of regulations that prevent these adjustments (such as usury laws or interest rate ceilings), there are no important costs to perfectly anticipated inflation. The only costs are those incurred in changing price tags periodically and in holding suboptimal amounts of currency.

7. Imperfectly anticipated inflation has important redistributive effects among sectors. Unanticipated inflation benefits monetary debtors and hurts monetary creditors. The government gains real tax revenue, and the real value of government debt declines.

8. In the U.S. housing market, unanticipated increases in inflation combined with the tax deductibility of interest made housing a particularly good investment over the 1960–1980 period.

9. In the U.S. economy, wage indexation is neither very widespread nor complete. This absence of strong indexation probably eased the adjustment to supply shocks.

10. Stabilization policy involves choosing an optimal path of inflation and unemployment. The choice is between more or less rapid paths of recovery. The more rapid path reduces unemployment rapidly but does so without making large inroads on inflation. To reduce inflation quickly, unemployment must be high and/or recovery slow.

11. The political business cycle hypothesis emphasizes the direction of change of the economy. For incumbents to win an election, the unemployment rate should be falling and the inflation rate not worsening.

KEY TERMS

Unemployment pool
Layoffs
Structural unemployment
Quits
Cyclical unemployment
Accessions
Separations
Duration of spells of unemployment
Natural rate of unemployment
NAIRU

Frequency of unemployment
Replacement ratio
Costs of cyclical unemployment
Anticipated inflation
Redistribution of wealth
Indexation
COLA
Extended Phillips curve
Political business cycle

PROBLEMS

1. Discuss strategies whereby the government (federal, state, or local) could reduce unemployment in or among (a) depressed industries, (b) unskilled workers, (c) depressed geographical regions, (d) teenagers. Include comments on the *type* of unemployment you would expect in these various groups (that is, relative durations of unemployment spells).

2. Discuss how the following changes would affect the natural or structural rate of unemployment. Comment also on the side effects of these changes.
   (a) Elimination of unions
   (b) Increased participation of women in the labor market
   (c) Larger fluctuations in the *level* of aggregate demand
   (d) An increase in unemployment benefits
   (e) Elimination of minimum wages
   (f) Larger fluctuations in the *composition* of aggregate demand

3. Discuss the differences in unemployment between adults and teenagers. What does this imply about the types of jobs (on average) the different groups are getting?

4. Some people say that inflation can be reduced in the long run without an increase in unemployment, and so we should reduce inflation to zero. Others say a steady rate of inflation at, say 4 percent, is not so bad, and that should be our goal. Evaluate these two arguments and describe what, in your opinion, are good long-run goals for reducing inflation and unemployment. How would these be achieved?

5. The following information is to be used for calculations of the unemployment rate. There are two major groups: adults and teenagers. Teenagers account for 10 percent of the labor force, and adults for 90 percent. Adults are divided into men and women. Women account for 35 percent of the adult labor force. The following table shows the unemployment rates for the groups.

Group	Unemployment rate (μ), %
Teenagers	19
Adults	
Men	6
Women	7

   (a) How do the numbers in this table compare (roughly) with the numbers for the U.S. economy?
   (b) Calculate the aggregate unemployment rate.
   (c) Assume the unemployment rate for teenagers rises from 19 to 29 percent. What is the effect on the male unemployment rate? (Assume 60 percent of the teenagers are males.) What is the effect on the aggregate unemployment rate?
   (d) Assume the share of women in the adult labor force increases to 40 percent. What is the effect on the adult unemployment rate? What is the effect on the aggregate unemployment rate?
   (e) Relate your answers to methods of estimating the natural rate of unemployment.

6. Use the *Economic Report of the President* to find the unemployment data for the years 1975, 1979, and 1989. Use as labor force groups, males and females, 16 to 19 years of age

and 20 and older (that is, four groups). Calculate what 1975 and 1989 unemployment would have been if each group in 1975 and 1989 had the unemployment rate of the group in 1979. What does the answer tell you?

7. In the *Economic Report of the President*, you will find data on the duration of unemployment. Compare the distribution of unemployment by duration in 1982 and 1989. What relationship do you find between duration and the overall unemployment rate?

8. (a) What are the economic costs of inflation? Distinguish between anticipated and unanticipated inflation.
   (b) Do you think anything is missing from the list of costs of inflation that economists present? If so, what?

9. A reduction in minimum wages during summer months reduces the cost of labor to firms, but it also reduces the income per hour that a teenager receives.
   (a) Who benefits from the measure, firms that have access to cheaper labor, teenagers who otherwise would not have a job, or both?
   (b) Who "pays" for the program, teenagers who would have a job anyway but who now receive less pay than they would have, and/or other workers who are displaced by the cheaper labor resulting from reduced minimum wages? Spell out what you think is the answer to these questions and decide whether you think the program is a good idea.

10. Evaluate the following argument that attempts to dispose of the notion of the political business cycle. "The public is too sophisticated to think that it makes much difference which party is running the economy. Both the Democrats and Republicans want the economy to boom, and want to keep inflation low. Both have access to the best economists available. Why would anyone think economic performance would be different with one party than with the other?"

11. When employment grows rapidly, in a recovery, it is frequently observed that unemployment rates decline only slowly. Relate this observation to the behavior of discouraged workers.

12. Contrast the implications of fixed and floating rate debt in how they protect creditors when there is inflation.

13. Suppose the economy is initially at an unemployment rate of 7 percent and that the aim is to get the rate down to 5 percent. Suppose that expectations are adaptive, with $\pi^e = \pi_{-1}$, and that the inflation rate last period was 7 percent. Using Okun's law from Chapter 1 combined with the extended Phillips curve [equation (4)], and assuming $\beta = 0.5$:
   (a) Compare the inflationary effects of reducing the unemployment rate to 5 percent within a year to those of aiming to bring it down to 5 percent within 3 years.
   (b) Show the paths of output growth corresponding to the two paths in part a.

16

BUDGET DEFICITS AND THE PUBLIC DEBT

*I*n the 1980s the United States experienced the largest string of deficits not only of peacetime but overall in this century. But even though deficits were large, in the 1988 campaign it was clear that balancing the budget was not a winning strategy. Raising taxes was completely ruled out by President Bush, whose "read my lips" was a rock-hard commitment that rightly read the mood of an electorate firmly attached to moderate levels of taxes. In fact, in a February 1989 Gallup survey 42 percent of the respondents identified an increase in taxes as their chief economic worry! With so firm a movement against taxes, and with spending cuts having already gone very far in the Reagan administrations, there seemed to be a prospect of open-ended deficits. A political stalemate on how to bring the deficits under control threatened potentially explosive growth in the national, or public, debt. That scenario sharply focused the national debate on the question, Can a country run a long string of budget deficits and what, if any, is the economic cost of those deficits?

Until the mid-1970s the public debt had been declining steadily relative to GNP. From a level of more than 100 percent in the immediate post-World War II period the debt-GNP ratio fell to less than 15 percent in 1974. But thereafter the debt grew relative to GNP—and growth accelerated sharply with the large budget deficits of the period after 1982. Figure 16-1, which shows the public debt as a percentage of GNP, highlights the sharp increase in the debt-to-income ratio since 1975.

This chapter focuses on debts and deficits. We ask how budget deficits are financed, whether the public debt is a burden, and what implications there are in deficit financing for interest rates and growth. Important questions in this discussion revolve around a surprising question: Does it make any difference whether the government pays for its expenditures by raising taxes or by issuing debt? An important group in the profession believes in the *Barro-Ricardo* view, which holds that there is basically no difference between these two ways of financing. The reason, they argue, is that debt issue involves future taxes to service the debt and that there is no difference (after

FIGURE 16-1
THE RATIO OF PUBLIC DEBT TO GNP, 1930–1994. Figures for 1989–1994
are estimates. (SOURCE: Congressional Budget Office and *Economic
Report of the President.*)

proper discounting) between present and future taxes. Of course, that view is not
universally shared, and it stands in sharp contrast to the discussion in earlier chapters,
in which we stated that tax increases lower aggregate demand. One central question
we discuss, therefore, is whether budget deficits do or do not crowd out investment.

A second question is under what conditions a deficit policy can involve the risk of
an evergrowing ratio of debt to GNP which ultimately ends either in debt repudiation
or in inflationary liquidation of debt.

In this chapter we focus on budget deficits and the public debt. The next chapter
deals with the links among budget deficits, money, and inflation. We start our discussion by examining the financing of budget deficits. From that we proceed to the causes
of recent U.S. deficits. In the following section we look at the impact of deficit finance
and issues connected with the public debt. The chapter concludes with a discussion of
the size of government.

16-1 THE MECHANICS OF FINANCING THE BUDGET

In this section we examine how the federal government finances its spending. We are particularly interested in the relationship between the federal government's deficit and changes in the stocks of money and government debt. The Treasury is the agency of the federal government that collects government receipts and makes payments for the government. The government's accounts at the Federal Reserve System are held and operated by the Treasury. The Treasury receives the bulk of its receipts from taxes. When outlays exceed receipts, there is a budget deficit. And when there is a budget deficit, the question is, How will it be financed? Figure 16-2 shows the possibilities.

How does the government pay for its spending? Directly, it pays for most of its spending with checks drawn on a Federal Reserve bank. Like an individual, the federal government must have funds in the accounts on which it writes checks. When tax receipts are insufficient to cover its expenditures, the Treasury has to borrow. Treasury borrowing means that public debt is issued. This debt is sold either to the public or to the central bank. In the United States the Treasury rarely sells securities *directly* to the Fed; but especially in developing countries, deficit financing often takes the form of direct borrowing from central banks and, as we shall see, inflationary financing.

Debt-financed Deficits

When the Treasury finances its deficit by borrowing from the public, it engages in *debt financing.* Individuals and firms, including commercial banks or other financial institutions, pay for the securities with checks. The checks are deposited either in Treasury accounts at private banks ("tax and loan accounts") or at the central bank. The funds can then be spent by the Treasury in the same way as tax receipts.

FIGURE 16-2
BUDGET DEFICITS AND THEIR FINANCING.

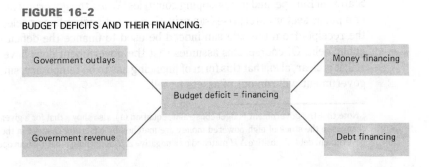

Money-financed Deficits

When the Treasury borrows from the central bank to finance its deficit, it engages in *money financing.* In the case of money financing, the central bank purchases some of the debt of the Treasury.

The distinction between money and debt financing can be further clarified by noting that Treasury sales of securities to the central bank are referred to as *monetizing the debt,* meaning that the central bank creates (high-powered) money to finance the debt purchase. Since the stock of high-powered money is an important macroeconomic variable, there is an essential distinction between selling debt to the public and selling it to the central bank.

Of course, the government may have a surplus rather than a deficit. In that case, instead of selling bonds or increasing the amount of high-powered money, the government is retiring debt (reducing the outstanding stock of government bonds) or reducing the supply of high-powered money.

BUDGET DEFICIT FINANCING

We can show how the government finances its deficit by using an equation. Let ΔB_p be the value of sales of government bonds to the private sector and ΔB_f be the value of sales of bonds to the central bank. Let H be the stock of high-powered money, and recall that BD is the budget deficit measured in *real* terms. P is the price level. The last term, ΔA, represents government asset sales. We thus have

$$P \cdot BD = \Delta B_f + \Delta B_p = \Delta H + \Delta B_p + \Delta A \tag{1}$$

Equation (1) is called the government's budget constraint. It states that the nominal budget deficit is financed by borrowing either from the central bank (ΔB_f) or from the private sector (ΔB_p) or by selling assets. The change in the central bank's holdings of Treasury debts causes a corresponding change in high-powered money (ΔH), so that we can say that the budget deficit is financed either by selling debt to the public or by increasing the stock of high-powered money. It is in this sense that the central bank "monetizes" the debt.[1]

Financing by debt and money are the common ways of financing deficits; asset sales are much less common but have become important in the 1980s in the United States, in Europe, and in developing countries. When the government sells public lands or a public sector enterprise (say privatizing a national airline or telephone company), the receipts from the sale can indeed be used to finance the deficit or else to retire public debt. Of course, this assumes that the government does have public assets to sell; it is clear, also, that this form of financing has to be temporary, since ultimately the government will run out of assets to sell.

---

[1] Note that the government budget constraint, equation (1), also shows that for a given value of the deficit, changes in the stock of high-powered money are matched by offsetting changes in the public's holdings of government debt. A positive ΔH matched by a negative ΔB_p is nothing other than an open market purchase.

The Fed and the Treasury

In many countries it is useful to think of the government sector as a whole, without bothering to distinguish between the actions of the Treasury and the central bank. However, in the United States the Fed retains considerable power and independence. Indeed, the Fed does not generally buy debt directly from the Treasury, and so does not directly finance the deficit in the way just described. The great bulk of Fed purchases of debt are made directly from the public. However, that should be thought of as only an institutional detail. For although the Fed by and large does not buy directly from the Treasury, it can do so indirectly by buying securities from the public. Suppose that the Fed is conducting open market purchases at the same time as the Treasury is selling debt to the public. The net effect of the combined Treasury sale of debt and Fed open market purchase is that the Fed ends up holding more Treasury debt, which is precisely what would happen if it bought directly from the Treasury.

The Fed on its own initiative determines how much high-powered money to create. As a result, there is no necessary association between the size of the government deficit in the United States and increases in the stock of high-powered money. If the Fed does not choose to conduct open market purchases when the Treasury is borrowing, the stock of high-powered money is not affected by the Treasury's deficit.

Nonetheless, there have been occasions in the past when there was a more or less automatic association between Fed open market purchases and Treasury borrowing. This link was most direct when the Fed was committed to maintaining constant nominal interest rates on government bonds, in the period from 1941 to 1951. An increase in the government deficit tends to increase the nominal interest rate. If the Fed were committed to maintaining a constant nominal interest rate, an increase in the deficit would force the Fed to conduct an open market purchase to keep the nominal interest rate from rising. Only in this very special way would there be a direct link between Treasury borrowing and Fed open market purchases.

The Fed's commitment to maintain constant nominal interest rates on government bonds ended formally in 1951 in the "Accord" between the Fed and the Treasury. Even though, after 1951, the Fed had no formal commitment to maintain constant nominal interest rates, its long-time policy of having target nominal interest rates — which could change from time to time — also led to an association between deficits and Fed open market purchases. Given the Fed's target interest rates, Treasury borrowing which would have led to interest rate increases triggered Fed open market purchases to keep the interest rate from rising above its target level. Thus, for much of the 1950s and 1960s, there was a link between increased Treasury borrowing and Fed open market purchases.

Once the Fed targets a strictly monetary aggregate rather than interest rates, there is no longer any *automatic* link between budget deficits and the monetary base. In the 1979–1982 period the Federal Reserve emphasized monetary targets, and even though budget deficits pushed interest rates extremely high, there was no automatic response of monetizing the deficits. Whereas interest rate targets would have led to a huge expansion in the money stock, the emphasis on monetary targets prevented a highly inflationary monetary accommodation of the deficit. We return to this issue in Chapter 17, where we discuss the evidence on the deficit-money link as part of our discussion of links between budget deficits and inflation.

Deficits and the National Debt

It follows from equation (1) that when the budget is not balanced, the Treasury changes the net amount of claims on it held by the private sector and the Fed. Those claims are the securities the Treasury sells to the private sector and (indirectly) the Fed, and they represent claims for future interest payments. The total stock of government bonds (or claims on the government) outstanding constitutes the *national,* or *public,* debt. When the budget is in deficit, the national debt increases — the stock of claims against the Treasury increases. When the budget is in surplus, the national debt decreases. The Treasury takes in more taxes than it pays out, and it can use the excess to retire (or buy back) previously issued debt.

The national debt is the result of past federal budget deficits. The Treasury sells securities more or less continuously. There is, for instance, a weekly Treasury bill auction, at which prospective buyers of Treasury bills (lenders to the federal government) submit sealed bids specifying how much they are prepared to lend at different interest rates. The Treasury sells the amount of Treasury bills it has offered at the auction to the bidders who offer the highest prices, or the lowest interest rates.[2] Longer-term debt issues are less frequent. Issues of Treasury debt are not all made for the purpose of financing the budget deficit. Most debt issues are made to refinance parts of the national debt that are maturing. For example, 6 months after a 180-day Treasury bill is issued, the Treasury has to pay the face amount of the Treasury bill to the holder. Typically, the Treasury obtains the funds to make those payments by further borrowing. The process by which the Treasury (with the help and advice of the Fed) finances and refinances the national debt is known as *debt management.* Only a minor part of debt management is concerned with financing the current budget deficit, that is, with net debt issue as opposed to refinancing the large existing stock.

We have discussed in this section the financing of the budget deficit. The same principles apply in the case of a budget surplus. When the government has an excess of tax revenues over outlays, there is a surplus. Rather than having to borrow, the Treasury is in a position to *retire debt.* Practically, what happens is the following. The excess of tax receipts over outlays means that the government's tax and loan accounts and accounts at the Fed are building up. The Treasury responds by not renewing maturing debt but, rather, by paying off bonds or Treasury bills that are coming due. Thus the stock of public debt outstanding declines. There is little risk of the U.S.

---

[2] Technically, no interest is paid on Treasury bills. Instead, a Treasury bill is a promise by the Treasury to pay a given amount on a given date, say $100 on June 30. Before June 30, the Treasury bill sells at a discount, that is, at less than $100, with the discount implying a rate of interest. For instance, if the Treasury bill just described sold for $97.50 on January 1, the holder of the bill for 6 months would earn a little more than 5 percent per annum, or 2.5 percent for 6 months.

Treasury's retiring debt in the next few years, but in Great Britain large asset sales put the government in a position to actually reduce the public debt.

Summary

1. Federal government spending is financed through taxes and through borrowing; the latter is necessary when the budget is in deficit.
2. Borrowing may be from the private sector or indirectly from the Federal Reserve System.
3. Lending by the Fed to the Treasury changes the stock of high-powered money, whereas lending by the private sector to the Treasury does not affect the stock of high-powered money.
4. The stock of claims held by the Fed and the private sector against the Treasury — the national debt — changes with the budget deficit. The national debt increases when there is a budget deficit and decreases when there is a budget surplus.
5. Because the deficit can be financed in two ways, there is no *necessary* connection between the budget deficit and changes in the stock of high-powered money. Equation (1), the government budget constraint, says only that the *sum* of changes in the stock of debt and changes in high-powered money is approximately equal to the budget deficit.

16-2 THE SIZE AND DETERMINANTS OF DEFICITS

Figure 16-3 shows the budget surplus of the federal government as a percent of GNP. Throughout the period the surplus fluctuates with the business cycle, but there is also a definite trend of a decreasing surplus or increasing deficit. Whereas deficits and surpluses alternated up to the end of the 1960s, there has been a deficit in every year since 1970. In the 1980s the deficit reached its highest levels for the entire period.

Table 16-1 reviews the averages of the budget deficit as a percent of GNP in successive 5-year periods. The table highlights the high and persistent deficits in the 1970s and the 1980s, with no major change anticipated before the end of the 1980s. Underlying the behavior of the deficit are changes in government outlays and/or revenues.

We now look at the more or less automatic effects on the budget of cyclical fluctuations, inflation, and growth. In the next section we turn to a consideration of the tax and spending changes that produced the shift toward persistent deficits.

The Business Cycle and Deficits

The distinction between the actual and the *structural* deficit is widely used. The structural deficit, or the full-employment or high-employment or cyclically adjusted deficit, is the deficit calculated as if the economy were at a full- or high-employment

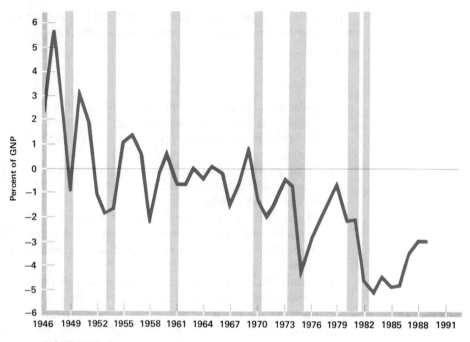

FIGURE 16-3

THE BUDGET SURPLUS AS A PERCENT OF GNP, 1946–1988. Shaded bars
mark periods of recession. (SOURCE: DRI/McGraw-Hill.)

level, typically 5 to 6 percent unemployment. The actual deficit differs from the
structural deficit by a cyclical component, which is that part of the deficit that occurs
purely because the economy is not currently at the high-employment level of output.
Figure 16-3 shows the large deficit resulting in 1980–1983 from the deep recession.
By 1988 the economy was at full employment and consequently the deficit of the late
1980s must be interpreted as structural.[3]

The difference between the structural and actual deficits occurs because both
government revenues and government spending respond systematically to the business cycle. *Given tax rates,* increases in the level of income produce larger revenues
for the government. And because the government pays unemployment benefits, its
spending rises when the economy goes into recession.

We now look at quantitative estimates of the impact of the business cycle on the
budget. The estimate we report serves as a rough rule of thumb, and as such is well

[3] For a discussion of the Reagan budgets and the evolution of the deficit see Keith Carlson, "Federal Budget
Trends and the 1981 Reagan Economic Plan," Federal Reserve Bank of St. Louis *Review,* January/February
1989.

TABLE 16-1

FEDERAL BUDGET AND DEBT RATIOS* (percent of GNP; fiscal year)

Period	Budget	Debt	Period	Budget	Debt
1946–1949	2.4	96.0	1980–1984	−3.7	30.3
1950–1954	0.1	66.7	1985–1989	−3.8	41.5
1955–1959	−0.1	51.4	1985	−4.9	37.9
1960–1964	−0.3	43.9	1986	−4.8	41.5
1965–1969	−0.5	34.9	1987	−3.5	42.6
1970–1974	−0.8	27.4	1988	−2.9	42.9
1975–1979	−2.9	27.5	1989	−2.9	42.7

* Estimate by CBO, debt ratio on a fiscal-year basis.

SOURCE: Congressional Budget Office, *The Economic and Budget Outlook*, January 1989, and *Economic Report of the President*.

TABLE 16-2

RULES OF THUMB: MACROECONOMIC EFFECTS ON THE BUDGET (per year average over 3 years)

	Percent of GNP	Billions of dollars
One-percentage-point reduction in growth	−0.86	−48.3
One-percentage-point rise in unemployment	−1.04	−56.7
One-percentage-point rise in rates	−0.26	−15.7
One-percentage-point rise in inflation	−0.0	−1.3

SOURCE: Congressional Budget Office, *The Economic and Budget Outlook*, January 1989.

worth knowing. The Congressional Budget Office (CBO) has explored the effects of alternative macroeconomic shocks to budget predictions. The rules of thumb they use are set out in Table 16-2:[4]

- A one-percentage-point reduction in GNP growth reduces the tax base in every future period relative to what it would have been otherwise. This implies a falloff in revenues of about $50 billion per year on average in the first 3 years. The losses grow cumulatively.

- Higher unemployment works just like lower growth in reducing the tax base and in increasing the amount of unemployment benefits that must be paid. A percent-

[4] See Congressional Budget Office, *The Economic and Budget Outlook*, January 1989, p. 51.

age point rise in unemployment worsens the budget by about 1 percent of GNP and thus has a massive impact.

- Because the tax system is indexed, inflation now has virtually no impact on the budget. This was not the case before the 1985 tax indexation. Prior to 1985 an increase in inflation would move taxpayers more rapidly into higher tax brackets and thus generate extra revenue, which is known as the bracket creep or the inflation tax. The disappearance of this *automatic* revenue source is a major difficulty in balancing the budget today.

- Higher interest rates increase the interest cost on the public debt. For every percentage point increase in interest rates the deficit widens by about a quarter of a percent of GNP.

These rules of thumb help in understanding some of the budget problems of the 1980s. In the early 1980s there were record high interest rates and very high unemployment. The combined effect, using the rules of thumb above, was a very large budget deficit. A major recession — such as that of 1982, with an increase in unemployment from 6 to 11 percent — would give rise to a cyclical increase in the budget deficit amounting to more than 3 percent of GNP. Extremely high interest rates would compound the effect. The very rapid debt growth of the early 1980s shown in Figure 16-1 is the consequence of this interest rate and recession shock to the budget.

The rules of thumb also have a bearing on the question whether it is possible to "grow out of deficits," that is, whether strong growth, by expanding the tax base and revenues, will eliminate the deficit in the early 1990s. Two percentage points of extra growth per year for 4 to 5 years would solve the problem, but two *extra* points of growth, starting at full employment are extremely unlikely. Hence the deficit will not disappear as a result of growth. An alternative solution might be a decline in interest rates. But the economy is at full employment, and therefore a fall in interest rates is unlikely unless there is a *structural* shift in the budget; monetary policy cannot lower interest rates at full employment! With neither growth nor lower interest rates able to solve the budget deficit problem, deficit reduction needs to be tackled by *structural* measures, such as spending cuts or higher taxes.

Discretionary Fiscal Policy Changes

Throughout the previous chapters we have talked about the effects of *discretionary* fiscal policy changes on aggregate demand. For example, how does a tax cut or an increase in government spending affect aggregate demand, and do the results depend on the measure's being temporary or permanent? In interpreting macroeconomic history it would be useful to have a simple summary measure of the direction and magnitude of fiscal stimulus or restraint. It turns out that this is not a simple issue.

The difficulty is that such a measure requires summing up in a single number the impact of a change in government spending as well as changes in corporate tax rates, personal income tax rates, and transfers. Each has to be given a weight, and the

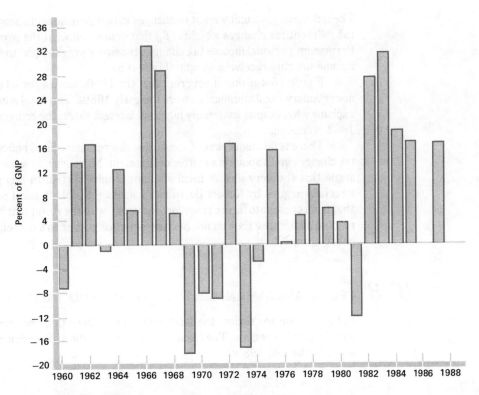

FIGURE 16-4
DISCRETIONARY FISCAL POLICY CHANGES, 1960–1988. (SOURCE: Data
kindly provided by Darrel Cohen of the Board of Governors of the
Federal Reserve.)

weight will depend on what one believes are the effects of these measures on demand. Figure 16-4 shows a measure constructed by Darrel Cohen of the Federal Reserve Board and referred to as $F1$.[5] The index measures, as equation (2) shows, the net effect of spending and tax changes, with the β_i being the weights assigned to various tax changes. The index is expressed as a fraction of real GNP, so that we can interpret it as the impact on aggregate demand, in percentage terms, of the change in fiscal stance.

$$F1 = \frac{\Delta G - \Sigma \beta_i T_i}{Y} \tag{2}$$

[5] See Darrel Cohen, "Models and Measures of Fiscal Policy," Board of Governors of the Federal Reserve System, Working Paper Series, no. 70, March 1988. See, too, P. Heller, R. Haas, and A. Mansur, *A Review of the Fiscal Impulse Measure,* IMF Occasional Paper 44 (Washington, D.C.: International Monetary Fund, 1986).

The index assigns a unit weight to changes in real government spending and assigns to the different tax changes weights (β_i) that depend on what the particular measure is. Permanent personal income tax changes receive a weight equal to 0.9, but transitory income tax cuts receive a weight of only 0.5.

Figure 16-4 makes it apparent that the 1960s were a period of very substantial discretionary fiscal stimulus, as were the early 1980s. The fiscal stimulus of the 1980s explains why, despite extremely high real interest rates, the economy came out of the 1982 recession.

There is no unique way of measuring discretionary fiscal policy; the weighting of tax changes in (2) above is a matter of judgment. Moreover, as we will see below, some argue that the very idea of fiscal stimulus is misdirected. In this perspective, most forcefully argued by Robert Barro and Laurence Kotlikoff, fiscal policy represents a shift from present to future taxes, or vice versa, with the result that households will not react at all because they do not become richer or poorer as a consequence of the fiscal policy change.[6]

16-3 FEDERAL GOVERNMENT RECEIPTS AND OUTLAYS

In this section we review the facts about the composition and trend of government spending and revenues. The main question is why the U.S. deficit reached such high levels in the mid-1980s.

Outlays

Table 16-3 shows the outlays of the federal government over the past 20 years. The table introduces some special terminology. There is a distinction between *mandatory* and *discretionary* outlays. The former are outlays that the government is committed to make under existing laws. These payments have to be made under *entitlement programs* under which the law specifies that a person meeting certain requirements is automatically entitled to receive payments. Mandatory spending includes, for example, Medicaid and Social Security. Discretionary spending, by contrast, is governed by the congressional appropriation process and includes, for example, defense expenditures, outlays for the administration of justice, and foreign aid.

Three points in Table 16-3 are of particular interest. First, over the past 20 years, defense expenditures have declined significantly as a fraction of income. Second, entitlement programs have nearly doubled. This reflects a growing involvement of the government in social programs. Third, interest payments by the government have become an important part of government outlays. The share of interest payments in total outlays has more than doubled over the past 30 years.

[6] See Laurence Kotlikoff, "From Deficit Delusion to the Fiscal Balance Rule: Looking for an Economically Meaningful Way to Assess Economic Policy," National Bureau of Economic Research, Working Paper 2841, February 1989.

TABLE 16-3

FEDERAL GOVERNMENT OUTLAYS (percent of GNP; fiscal year; unified budget)

	1960–1969	1970–1979	1980–1988	1989
National defense	8.9	6.0	6.0	5.8
Entitlements and other mandatory spending	4.8*	9.2	10.9	10.6
Nondefense discretionary spending	4.8*	5.1	4.6	3.7
Net interest	1.3	1.7	2.8	3.3
Total outlays	19.0	20.5	23.2	22.2

* 1962–1969.

SOURCE: Congressional Budget Office, *The Economic and Budget Outlook*, January 1989, and *Historical Tables, Budget of the United States Government*, fiscal-year 1990.

TABLE 16-4

SOURCES OF FEDERAL REVENUE (percent of GNP; period average)

	1960–1969	1970–1979	1980–1988	1989
Individual income tax	8.0	8.3	8.8	8.4
Corporate income tax	3.9	2.8	1.7	2.0
Social insurance taxes and contributions	3.5	5.2	6.5	7.1
Other*	2.8	2.1	2.0	1.7
Total revenue	18.2	18.4	19.0	19.2

* This entry lumps together excise, or sales, taxes; estate and gift taxes; customs duties; and miscellaneous receipts.

SOURCE: Congressional Budget Office, *The Economic and Budget Outlook*, January 1989.

For macroeconomic purposes there is an important distinction between the government's purchases of goods and services and transfer payments. The former are a component of aggregate demand—the G term in Chapter 3—whereas the latter affect aggregate demand indirectly, via changes in disposable income. By the late 1980s only a third of federal government outlays (less than 10 percent of GNP) represented spending on goods and services, while transfer payments accounted for two-thirds.

Receipts

The federal government receives most of its revenues from collection. The sources of revenue and the total are shown in Table 16-4. Each of the revenue sources is self-explanatory, except perhaps for social insurance taxes. These are taxes on wages paid by employers and by wage earners.

First, note from Table 16-4 that total revenue as a share of GNP has changed very little over the past 30 years. Second, we observe a shift in the sources of revenue. Social Security taxes and contributions have become a substantially higher source of revenue, corporate income taxes have declined moderately, and personal income taxes have remained broadly unchanged. Note that the much discussed cut in personal income tax *rates* in the 1980s has not in fact reduced the share of revenue from income taxes. The reason is that there was an offsetting closing of tax loopholes.

The Deficit Problem

In Table 16-5 we combine outlays, revenues, and the deficit. The table shows strikingly that rising outlays rather than falling taxes are responsible for the growing deficits. Revenue, as we saw above, has remained steady, but outlays have sharply increased. Moreover, the increase in outlays is almost equal to the rise in one single component, net interest paid by the government on the public debt. We now focus on the interaction between deficits and rising interest payments.

Interest Payments and Deficits

It is useful to distinguish between two components of the budget deficit: the *primary, or noninterest, deficit* and interest payments on the public debt.

$$\text{Total deficit} \equiv \text{primary deficit} + \text{interest payments} \tag{3}$$

The primary deficit (or surplus) represents all government outlays, except interest

TABLE 16-5
COMPOSITION OF THE BUDGET DEFICIT (percent of GNP; fiscal year; unified budget)

	1960–1969	1970–1979	1980–1989	1989
Outlays	19.0	20.5	23.1	22.2
Interest	1.3	1.7	2.9	3.3
Revenues	18.2	18.4	19.0	19.2
Deficit	0.8	2.1	4.1	3.0

SOURCE: Congressional Budget Office.

payments, less all government revenue. The primary deficit is also called the *noninterest* deficit.

$$\text{Primary deficit} \equiv \text{noninterest outlays} - \text{total revenue} \qquad (4)$$

The distinction between the two components highlights the role of the public debt in the budget. Interest has to be paid when there is debt outstanding. The overall budget will be in deficit unless the interest payments on the debt are more than matched by a primary surplus. Table 16-6 shows the total deficit and the two components.

Consider first the period 1960–1964; here the interest payments amount to 1.2 percent of GNP, but the total or overall budget shows a deficit of only 0.2 percent. The reason is that the budget excepting interest shows a surplus of 1 percent. By contrast in 1980–1984 interest payments amount to 2.6 percent of GNP, and the overall budget deficit is equal to more than 4 percent of GNP. The noninterest budget in this period is in deficit and thus adds to the interest payments in creating a huge deficit.

Table 16-6 draws attention to a key problem in deficit financing. *If there is a primary deficit in the budget, then the total budget deficit will keep growing as the debt grows because of the deficit, and interest payments rise because the debt is growing.* The problem is exactly the same for an individual as for a country: Someone who is spending more than he or she earns, and borrowing to cover the difference, will find a need to borrow more and more each year just because the interest on past borrowings keeps rising. This potential instability of debt financing is studied in more detail in the next section and in the appendix to this chapter.

The United States in the mid-1980s faced the dilemma that unless budget deficits were brought under control, the public debt would explode. That meant that either the government had to collect more in taxes or else spending had to be cut.

TABLE 16-6
THE PRIMARY DEFICIT (percent of GNP; fiscal year; unified budget)

	Total deficit	Primary deficit	Interest payments
1960–1964	0.2	−1.0	1.2
1965–1969	0.9	−0.4	1.3
1970–1974	1.2	−0.2	1.4
1975–1979	3.0	1.1	1.9
1980–1984	4.2	1.6	2.6
1985–1989	4.1	0.9	3.2
1989	3.0	−0.3	3.3

SOURCE: Congressional Budget Office, *The Economic and Budget Outlook*, January 1989.

Supply-Side Economics, Tax Rates, and Deficits

In 1981 – 1983 tax rates were cut by 30 percent in a three-stage process known as the Kemp-Roth tax cuts. Under 1989 tax laws there are only two marginal income tax rates, 15 and 28 percent. These tax-cutting and simplification measures were passed on the basis of efficiency arguments: High rates of taxation, it was argued, were a disincentive to effort, saving, and investment. Low rates of taxation would lead to higher growth and thus to higher, not lower, tax revenues. This kind of argument was pushed hard in the 1980s by supply-siders.[7]

No political candidate or officeholder is in favor of deficits. How, then, did the tax rate cuts of the 1980s pass when they resulted in such large deficits? There are two explanations. The first is that supply-side economists argued that the tax cuts would produce *more,* not less, revenue for the government. The other is an argument of political economy that says that Congress will spend whatever revenue it receives and that therefore the only way to get it to cut its spending is to cut its revenue. We take up the two arguments in turn.

Tax Cuts and Government Revenue

Much of the controversy surrounding the tax cuts in the 1980s centered on a highly unusual proposition advanced by supply-side economists: A *cut* in income tax rates will *raise* tax revenues. The idea was highly controversial because it had until then been accepted that lower tax rates usually mean lower government revenues. For example, we saw in Chapter 3 that a tax cut would increase the budget deficit, even when we took into account the expansion in output induced by lower taxes.

But the supply-side economists, some of whom were installed in the U.S. Treasury by the Reagan administration, were certainly not thinking in terms of the simple Keynesian analysis of Chapter 3. Rather, they were concentrating on the *incentive effects* of tax cuts. Take the income tax as an example. Anyone who is taxed, say at a 25 percent marginal rate, on income earned receives only 75 percent of the wage for working an extra hour. Supply-siders argued that a cut in income taxes, say from 25 to 15 percent, would encourage such a person to work harder. For instance, suppose the wage rate is $10 per hour. Before the tax cut a person working 1 extra hour earns, after taxes, $7.50; after the tax cut the same extra hour brings in $8.50. Surely, supply-siders argued, such a person would want to work more hours.

Up to this point the analysis is relatively uncontroversial. There is some question whether cuts in tax rates encourage people to work more, because conflicting effects are operating. The cut in the tax rate raises the after-tax wage and therefore makes work more desirable, relative to leisure. But with a higher after-tax wage, a worker needs to work less to support the same standard of living. Perhaps when the after-tax wage rises, the response is to work less, earn more income, and have more leisure. For

---

[7] See Paul Craig Roberts, "Supply Side Economics, Theory and Results: An Assessment of American Experience in the 1980s" (Washington, D.C.: Institute for Political Economy, 1989).

example, suppose someone is working 40 hours at an after-tax wage of $7.50, earning $300 per week. Now the after-tax wage rises to $8.50. By working 38 hours, the worker earns $323 per week — income and leisure have both risen.[8] However, empirical evidence suggests that a given worker will work more when the after-tax wage rises. Further, there is an unambiguous increase in the number of people working when wages rise — people who used to stay home now enter the labor force to find work. So on balance a cut in tax rates will increase output through supply-side incentive effects.

But the strength of the supply-side position lay in more than the claim that a cut in income tax rates would motivate people to work more. The supply-side claim was that, despite the cut in the tax rate, total tax revenue would rise because a lot more work would be done. To illustrate the problem with the supply-side position, we use the simple formula

$$\text{Income tax revenue} = \text{income tax rate} \times \text{income} \qquad (5)$$

The supply-side claim was that when the tax rate fell, income would rise enough that total income tax revenue would increase. For instance, suppose the tax rate was cut from 20 to 15 percent. Suppose income was originally equal to $2 trillion. Taxes would thus be $400 billion to begin with. With a tax rate of 15 percent, income would have to rise to $2,667 billion for total revenue from the income tax to increase. It is rare, indeed, that income rises by one-third within a short time — but that is the size of the increase that would be needed if taxes were cut by one-quarter, as in the example of this paragraph. Thus this supply-side claim was implausible (see Box 16-1).

Tax Cuts and Government Spending

Another motive besides supply-side arguments also led the Reagan administration to cut tax rates, despite the high deficits that would probably result over the next few years. That was the argument that the only way to get Congress to cut government spending is to reduce the revenue it receives.

The administration believed that unless tax rates were cut, and tax revenues reduced, the Congress would continue to spend. One of the major aims of the Reagan administration was to cut government spending, and so it was willing to have deficits for some time to put pressure on the Congress to reduce spending.

Gramm-Rudman-Hollings Act

There was a stalemate between Congress and the President on the budget in 1985. President Reagan insisted on maintaining the tax rate cuts of the early 1980s. He was

---

[8] If you have taken a course in microeconomics, you will recognize that the substitution effect of the increase in the after-tax wage causes the worker to work more, while the income effect reduces work. The net effect is therefore ambiguous.

box 16-1 **THE LAFFER CURVE**

Arthur Laffer, a former professor of economics and now an economics consultant in California, is among the best known of the supply-side economists. Figure 1 shows the *Laffer curve*, which relates tax revenues to the tax rate. The curve shows total tax revenue first increasing as the tax rate rises and then eventually decreasing.

The argument supporting the shape of the curve is as follows. Assume that we are discussing the income tax rate. When the tax rate is zero, government tax revenue is certainly zero. Hence we have point A on the curve. Further, suppose the tax rate were 100 percent. Then the government would be taking all the income that people earn. There would be no point in working if the government took all earnings, and so income in that case too would be zero. Then tax revenue would also be zero. Accordingly, point B is also a point on the Laffer curve.

Between A and B, though, the government certainly takes in some revenue from

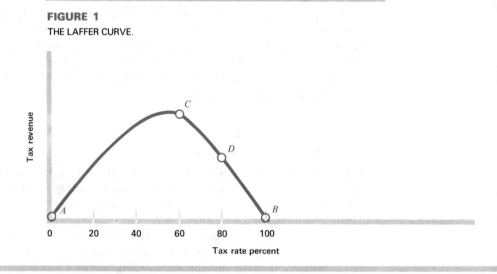

FIGURE 1
THE LAFFER CURVE.

adamantly opposed to higher taxes, insisting that expenditure cuts, outside the defense area, were the only acceptable means of eliminating the deficit. But cutting nondefense spending, as is clear from Table 16-3, meant cutting social programs. This in turn was difficult for Congress to accept, and it certainly seemed impossible to put together an assortment of budget cuts that would fill the budget gap.

A decisive change in the budget outlook occurred in late 1985. Faced with the risk of an unending string of deficits and a mounting public debt, Congress passed the Balanced Budget and Emergency Deficit Control Act, better known as the Gramm-

taxes. Thus we expect the curve to start to rise from point *A* as the tax rate is increased from zero to some very small rate, such as 3 percent. Eventually, though, the curve has to come back down to *B*. Thus at some point it will turn around—perhaps at a tax rate of 60 percent, as shown in Figure 1. Point *C* is the dividing line: At tax rates below 60 percent, any increase in the tax rate *raises* total tax revenue. At tax rates above 60 percent, any increase in the tax rate *reduces* total revenue. Looking at the same relationship in the opposite direction, we find that at any tax rate above 60 percent a *cut* in the tax rate will *increase* total tax revenue.

Supply-siders were thus arguing in 1981 that the U.S. economy was to the right of the point at which the Laffer curve turns down—say, at some point such as *D*. There was no evidence to support this assertion, and it does not appear to have been right. But it is a theoretical possibility.

Supply-siders made a similar claim about the effects of cuts in taxes on savings. When tax rates on savings are cut, the after-tax rate of return rises. For instance, suppose someone is earning 9 percent before taxes on savings. The tax rate is 25 percent, implying an after-tax rate of return on savings of 6.75 percent ($= 0.75 \times 9$ percent). Now suppose the tax rate is cut to 20 percent. The after-tax rate of return rises to 7.2 ($= 0.8 \times 9$ percent). Surely, supply-siders argued, such a person will save more.* Then there will be more investment, a larger capital stock, and higher output. With output higher, total tax revenue could be higher despite the cut in the tax rate.

Whatever the theoretical possibilities, the Kemp-Roth tax cuts did not lead to an increase in government revenue. Even if we concentrate on the full-employment budget, we do not see an increase in government revenue resulting from the tax cuts. This excessively optimistic element in supply-side economics was never believed by any but a small minority of economists, and it is now totally dismissed.† The emphasis on the role of incentives, though, is a valuable component of supply-side analysis and is discussed further in Chapter 19. ■

---

* There are conflicting income and substitution effects at work in this case, too, and the theoretical effect of the cut in the tax rate on saving is uncertain.

† On the supply-side story, see Jude Wanniski, *The Way the World Works* (New York: Touchstone, 1978); Paul Craig Roberts, *The Supply-Side Revolution* (Cambridge, Mass.: Harvard University Press, 1984); and Richard H. Fink (ed.), *Supply-Side Economics* (University Publications of America, 1982). For a critical view, see Robert Lekachman, *Greed Is Not Enough: Reagonomics* (New York: Pantheon, 1982); Olivier Blanchard, "Reagonomics," *Economic Policy*, October 1987; and Barry Bosworth, *Tax Incentives and Economic Growth* (Washington, D.C.: The Brookings Institution, 1984).

Rudman-Hollings Act (GRH), after the sponsors of the legislation.[9] With modifications regarding its implementation, GRH now is part of the budget process. Under GRH the budget deficit is to decline over time and disappear by 1993 altogether: the targets are $136 billion for 1989, $100 billion for 1990, and falling to $50 billion and $25 billion in

---

[9] See D. West, "Gramm-Rudman and the Politics of Debt Reduction," *Annals of the American Academy of Political and Social Science*, September 1988; and P. Miller, "Gramm-Rudman-Hollings' Hold on the Budget Policy: Losing the Grip," Federal Reserve Bank of St. Louis *Quarterly Review*, Winter 1989.

the following 2 years. By 1994 the budget is to be balanced. The across-the-board cuts were the congressional response to a political stalemate in which nobody was willing to cut preferred programs and the President was unwilling to see increased taxes cover the deficits.

The fiscal process under GRH requires (except under conditions of slow growth or recession) *across-the-board* cutbacks in spending if the deficit is likely to exceed the targets set by the act. For fiscal 1990, for example, the target is $100 billion, with a $10 billion margin. If the deficit projection exceeds that amount, cutbacks must be undertaken. One-half of these cutbacks is to come from defense (except if the President exempts defense), the other half, from those nondefense spending categories that are not explicitly exempted. The exempted categories are Social Security, net interest, and certain benefit programs.

If a large deficit is to be trimmed by cutting a narrow area of programs across the board, there is a political problem. As a result Congress and the President attempt last-minute budget agreements to avoid the GRH automatic cuts. These agreements increasingly involve asset sales as an important component. At the end of 1989, the deficit forecasts for the early 1990s made it seem very unlikely that the deficit reduction targets would be met.

16-4 DEBT-FINANCED DEFICITS

This is the section in which we discuss the consequences of deficits. We concentrate here on debt-financed deficits and leave money financing for the next chapter. We draw a distinction between transitory and persistent deficits.

A Debt-financed Transitory Deficit

Figure 16-5 presents the aggregate demand and supply diagram. We consider the effects of a tax cut. The tax cut is temporary, and the budget deficit is financed by selling debt to the private sector.

The initial effect of the cut in taxes is to shift the aggregate demand curve out from AD to AD_1. Because the private sector is buying bonds during the period of the deficit, it ends up holding a higher stock of government bonds. What effect does that higher stock of government debt held by the private sector have on aggregate demand?

Suppose that individuals holding government bonds regard those bonds as part of their wealth. Thus it would seem that, given the level of income, aggregate demand should rise when the stock of government bonds rises because individuals holding those bonds have higher wealth. The higher wealth increases consumption demand.[10] Accordingly, the aggregate demand curve would shift out to the right as a result of the increase in privately held wealth. Hence, we show the final aggregate demand curve

---

[10] Recall the discussion of the effect of wealth on consumption in Chap. 8.

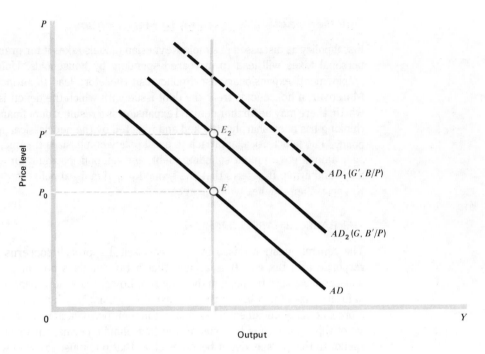

FIGURE 16-5

A TRANSITORY DEBT-FINANCED DEFICIT. A cut in taxes shifts the
aggregate demand curve from AD to AD_1. In the short run, aggregate
demand expands. Because the deficit is transitory, the tax cut is later
reversed. The rise in public debt that financed the transitory deficit
raises the wealth of the debtholders. Once the deficit has returned to
normal, the effect of increased debt outstanding implies higher
aggregate demand. AD_1 shifts back only to AD_2 rather than to AD.
There is a permanent increase in the price level and, given nominal
money, a rise in interest rates.

—after government spending has returned to its original level—at AD_2, above the
initial AD curve. The difference between the two aggregate demand schedules, AD
and AD_2, arises from the higher stock of government bonds, B', compared with B on
the initial aggregate demand curve. Since the effects of the higher wealth on consumption demand are likely to be small, we show the final aggregate demand curve, AD_2,
below the aggregate demand curve AD_1.

There are two complications to this analysis. The first is that the existence of the
higher stock of debt raises the amount of interest payments in the federal budget. If the
budget was originally balanced at point E, it may not be balanced at E_2. Of course, since
the price level at E_2 is higher than at E, bracket creep may have balanced the budget. If
it has not, then further financing of the deficit would have to be undertaken, and that
would have subsequent effects on the equilibrium.

The Neoclassical Approach to Fiscal Policy

Fiscal policy as discussed in simple Keynesian models takes it for granted that a cut in personal taxes will lead to increased spending by households. Unless there is full employment, expansionary fiscal policy can therefore lead to an increase in output. Moreover, if households treat the debt issue with which the deficit is financed as net worth, there may be further demand expansion as a result of debt financing. This line of thinking has been sharply attacked and rejected by the neoclassical approach to fiscal policy. The neoclassical approach to fiscal policy emphasizes the microeconomic linkages among government spending, debt, and tax policies and their effects on households and firms. It asserts that the scope for active fiscal policy is radically less than Keynesian approaches would suggest.

THE BARRO-RICARDO PROBLEM

The central question raised by the neoclassical approach concerns the household's response to a tax cut. It is argued that a tax cut does not, in general, affect the household's ability to spend in the long run: Lower taxes now mean an *equal* increase in future taxes (on a present value basis). Accordingly, why would households spend more if nothing fundamental has changed in their permanent income? The basic emphasis of this approach is to focus on the household's permanent income and ability to spend. In this perspective it becomes clear that one must ask who will pay the taxes that must *ultimately* service the debt that is issued to finance the *current* tax cut. And if it is the same household that must pay, then it becomes far from obvious that the present tax cut is a bonus.

It is possible, in fact, that in calculating their wealth or permanent income, households take into account the tax payments they will have to make in the future. Suppose that everyone believed that the national debt would eventually be paid off. Then everyone would know that at some point in the future the federal government would have to run a surplus. Individuals might think the federal government would at some future date have to raise taxes in order to pay off the debt. In that case an increase in the debt would increase individuals' wealth and at the same time suggest to them that their taxes would be higher in the future. The net effect on aggregate demand might then be zero. The issue raised by this argument is sometimes posed by the question, Are government bonds wealth?

The question whether government bonds are net wealth goes back at least to the classical English economist David Ricardo. It has been given prominence in the work of the new classical economists, in particular Robert Barro.[11] Hence it is known as the

---

[11] The original article is Robert Barro, "Are Government Bonds Net Wealth?" *Journal of Political Economy,* December 1974. Recent statements by the same author are "The Ricardian Approach to Budget Deficits," *Economic Perspectives,* Spring 1989, and "The Neoclassical Approach to Fiscal Policy," in R. Barro (ed.), *Modern Business Cycle Theory* (Cambridge, Mass.: Harvard University Press, 1989). Recent theoretical challenges to the Barro-Ricardo view are Olivier Blanchard, "Debts, Deficits and Finite Horizons," *Journal of Political Economy,* April 1985, and Douglas Bergheim, "A Neoclassical Perspective on Budget Deficits," *Economic Perspectives,* Spring 1989. For a discussion in the context of the 1980s see Franco Modigliani, "Reagan's Economic Policies," *Oxford Economic Papers,* October 1988, and Benjamin Friedman, *The Day of Reckoning* (New York: Random House, 1988).

Barro-Ricardo equivalence proposition. The proposition is that debt financing by bond issue merely postpones taxation, and therefore, in many instances is strictly equivalent to current taxation.

The strict Barro-Ricardo proposition that government bonds are not net wealth turns on the argument that people realize their bonds will have to be paid off with future increases in taxes. (Incidentally, after raising this as a theoretical possibility, Ricardo rejected its practical significance.) If so, an increase in the budget deficit unaccompanied by cuts in government spending should lead to an increase in savings that precisely matches the deficit.

When the government reduces taxes to run a deficit, the public recognizes that their taxes will be higher in the future. Their permanent income is thus unaffected by the government's switch from taxes today to taxes tomorrow. Their consumption is accordingly also unchanged. Since the tax cut increased disposable income, but consumption has not risen, saving must rise. The Barro-Ricardo proposition thus implies that a cut in current taxes that carries with it an implied increase in future taxes should lead to an increase in saving.

The sharp decline of the U.S. private saving rate in the 1980s is one piece of evidence against the proposition. Less casual empirical research continues in an attempt to settle the issue of whether the debt is wealth.[12] The issue is not yet closed. The theoretical arguments are not conclusive, and it is difficult to isolate the effects of changes in debt on consumption demand in empirical studies . We believe the evidence to date is on balance unfavorable to the Barro-Ricardo proposition, but recognize that the issue has not yet been decisively settled.

Money and Debt Financing

There is one important difference between debt and money financing of a given short-run budget deficit. Compared with debt financing, money financing of the deficit tends to reduce the interest rate in the short run. That is because money financing increases the nominal money stock (shifting upward the *LM* curve in the *IS-LM* model), whereas debt financing does not. In the short run, then, debt financing reduces the level of investment compared with money financing. That is an issue connected with the crowding out question.

We want also to compare the effects on the price level of money and debt financing of a temporary increase in government spending. The price level is higher with money financing than with debt financing. There are two reasons. First, money financing increases the money stock, and debt financing does not. The higher the money stock, the greater the aggregate demand at any given price level. Second, we

---

[12] Intensive empirical work on this issue is taking place. See, for example, Paul Evans "Are Consumers Ricardian? Evidence for the United States," *Journal of Political Economy,* October 1988; Leonardo Leiderman and Mario Blejer, "Modelling and Testing Ricardian Equivalence: A Survey," *IMF Staff Papers,* March 1988; James Poterba and Lawrence Summers, "Finite Lifetimes and the Savings Effect of Budget Deficits," *Journal of Monetary Economics,* September 1987; and Barro, "The Neoclassical Approach to Fiscal Policy."

attributed a price level rise in the case of debt financing to the wealth effect of a greater stock of debt on consumption. While there is some argument about whether bonds are wealth, there is no question that money is wealth. So the wealth effect on consumption is larger in the case of money financing than of debt financing. That, too, means that aggregate demand at any given price level will be higher with money than with debt financing.

We now summarize the effects of a temporary budget deficit financed by debt creation. Such financing probably increases aggregate demand, but because of the possible effects of anticipated future tax liabilities on consumption, that is not certain. Debt financing, starting from a balanced budget and not compensated for by higher taxes or reductions in other transfer payments, leads to a permanent deficit in the budget because interest has to be paid on the debt. Debt financing raises the interest rate and reduces investment in the short run as compared with the effects of money financing.[13]

Debt-financed Persistent Deficits

We turn now to a persistent real deficit. Suppose, to begin with, that the economy is not growing. Then any attempt to run a permanent primary deficit financed by debt will fail. For as the debt accumulates over time, interest payments on the debt increase, and keep on increasing. Thus attempts to finance a given primary deficit purely through debt financing cannot be viable in the long run in an economy that is not growing.

Debt, Growth, and Instability

The impossibility of running a permanent debt-financed primary deficit in a nongrowing economy is a dramatic conclusion, which certainly seems to justify concern over the massive deficits the U.S. economy faces for the next decade. It is therefore worth emphasizing what the problem is, and also showing why the problem is less serious in a growing economy.

Suppose the economy is not growing and the government is running a budget deficit. It can finance the deficit by issuing debt. But next period it has to pay interest on all the debt that existed in the past, *and also on the new debt issued to cover last period's deficit.* How can the government pay this interest? One way is to borrow some more. But then next period the interest needed to service the debt is even larger, and hence even more debt needs to be issued, and so on. This is the potential instability referred to in the previous section.

The national debt in the United States has typically risen year after year for the past 50 years. Does that mean the government budget is bound to get out of hand, with

---

[13] On the link between deficits and interest rates see the extensive review in George Iden and John Sturrock, "Deficits and Interest Rates: Theoretical Issues and Empirical Evidence," *Congressional Budget Office, Staff Working Paper, January 1989.*

interest payments rising so high that taxes have to keep rising, until eventually something terrible happens? The answer is no, because the economy has been growing.

Figure 16-6 shows the U.S. public debt as a fraction of GNP for a long stretch of time, starting in the early nineteenth century. The most striking fact is that the debt rises sharply as a result of large wartime deficits. Then, in each postwar period it declines. Over most of the period from World War II to 1974 the debt-income ratio was falling even though the debt itself was rising as the result of budget deficits. How could this happen? It is helpful to look at the definition of the debt-income ratio: Formally the ratio of debt to GNP is

$$\text{Debt ratio} = \frac{\text{debt}}{PY} \tag{6}$$

where PY represents nominal GNP. The answer is that the ratio of debt to GNP falls when nominal GNP grows more rapidly than the debt. To see this point it is useful to look separately at the numerator and denominator of the debt-GNP ratio. The numerator, the debt, grows because of deficits. The denominator, nominal GNP, grows as a result of both inflation and real GNP growth. If the debt is growing more rapidly than GNP, the debt-GNP ratio is rising. If the debt is growing less rapidly than GNP, the debt-GNP ratio is falling.

Why is it useful to look at the ratio of debt to income rather than at the absolute value of the debt? The reason is that GNP is a measure of the size of the economy, and the debt-GNP ratio is thus a measure of the magnitude of the debt relative to the size of the economy. A national debt of $2 trillion would have been overwhelming in 1929 when U.S. GNP was about $100 billion — even if the interest rate had been only 1

FIGURE 16-6

THE U.S. DEBT-INCOME RATIO IN HISTORICAL PERSPECTIVE. (SOURCE: Congressional Budget Office, from material cited in James R. Barth and Stephen O. Morrell, "A Primer on Budget Deficits," Federal Reserve Bank of Atlanta *Economic Review*, August 1982.)

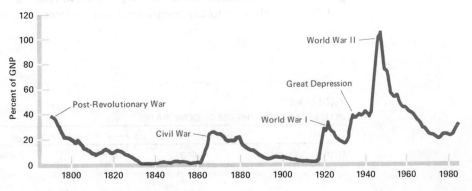

percent, the government would have had to raise 20 percent of GNP in taxes to pay interest on the debt. But when GNP is more than $4 trillion, a $2 trillion debt is not so overwhelming.

We can formalize this discussion by writing the equation for the debt-income ratio and considering explicitly how it changes over time. We define the following symbols:

r = real, or inflation-adjusted, interest rate

x = noninterest or primary budget surplus measured as a fraction of nominal income

y = growth rate of real GNP

b = debt-income ratio

In the appendix we show that the debt-income ratio is rising over time if

$$\Delta b = b(r - y) - x > 0 \tag{7}$$

The evolution of the debt-income ratio thus depends on the relationship among the real interest rate, the growth rate of output, and the noninterest budget surplus. The higher the interest rate and the lower the growth rate of output, the more likely the debt-income ratio is to be rising. A large noninterest surplus tends to make the debt-income ratio fall. Table 16-7 summarizes the conditions derived in the appendix that determine whether the debt-GNP ratio is rising or falling.

The table brings out the reason why over the 1950s and 1960s the debt-income ratio was falling. The real interest rate was practically zero, output grew steadily, and the noninterest budget was in surplus or near balance. In these circumstances debt grows less rapidly than nominal income, and hence the debt-income ratio fell. By contrast, in the 1980s the opposite was the case. Real interest rates were very high, growth was sluggish, and the noninterest budget was in deficit. As a result the debt-income ratio was rising. In a period of slow growth and high real interest rates, deficits therefore translate into a rapidly rising debt-income ratio. That was, indeed, the case in 1979 – 1983.

What would happen if the deficit were too large, so that debt relative to income grew seemingly without bounds? Such a process can really not go on forever. Ultimately, the public debt totally overshadows and displaces other assets, and crowding

TABLE 16-7

DETERMINANTS OF THE DEBT-INCOME RATIO

	$b(r - y) - x > 0$	$b(r - y) - x = 0$	$b(r - y) - x < 0$
Debt-income ratio is	Rising	Constant	Falling

out becomes so pervasive that the public comes to expect *some* action to balance the budget. This might involve inflation, special taxes, or cuts in government spending.[14]

How does inflation help solve the deficit problem? First, the inflation tax (discussed in Chapter 17) can make some small contribution to financing the deficit. But more importantly, a large, *unanticipated* inflation will reduce the real value of the outstanding stock of government debt. The national debt in most countries is *nominal,* meaning that the government is obliged to pay only a certain number of dollars to the holders of the debt. A policy that raises the price level thus reduces the real value of the payments the government is obliged to make. The debt can therefore virtually be wiped out by a large enough unanticipated inflation—so long as the debt is a nominal debt.

It is important to have some perspective on the relevance of these extreme conditions to the world today. The United States in the mid-1980s was not close to facing a massive debt crisis in which the national debt was so large as to overshadow other macroeconomic problems and in which the government could not finance its deficit by borrowing from the public. But it did face the prospect of a rapid rise in the ratio of debt to income, back toward the levels of the 1950s. The prospect was sufficient to make the political system respond with the Gramm-Rudman-Hollings bill as a way to bring deficits down to lower levels within a short time.

There are, though, a number of countries even today where many years of deficits have cumulated into a large public debt that ultimately becomes unmanageable. Often that outcome is clearly visible ahead of time, but on occasion a sharp increase in real interest rates together with a major loss in tax revenues, perhaps because of a world recession, can suddenly make the debt problem much more immediate. In particular, that problem was faced by many developing countries that had borrowed abroad during the seventies and in 1980–1981, when the real interest rate was still low. When the real interest rate rose, their heavy indebtedness meant that they had to make large interest payments to foreigners, which for many of the countries was extremely difficult to do. The result was the developing countries' debt crisis of the 1980s.

16-5 THE BURDEN OF THE DEBT

As deficits continue, the national debt piles up. The U.S. national debt now exceeds $1.5 trillion, an amount that is enough to get anyone worried. In per capita terms, the national debt now exceeds $6,000 per person in the United States. That seems to be a

---

[14] See T. Sargent and N. Wallace, "Some Unpleasant Monetarist Arithmetic," Federal Reserve Bank of Minnesota *Quarterly Review,* Fall 1981. As the title suggests, the treatment is technical. The main point the authors make is that debt problems ultimately become inflation problems. We return to this issue in Chap. 17. See Alberto Alesina, "The End of Large Public Debts," in Francesco Giavazzi and Luigi Spaventa (eds.), *High Public Debt* (Cambridge, Engl.: Cambridge University Press, 1988) for a historical discussion. An early discussion of inflationary liquidation of debts can be found in John M. Keynes, *A Tract on Monetary Reform* (London: Macmillan, 1924) and Colin Clark, "Public Finance and Changes in the Value of Money," *Economic Journal,* June 1945.

heavy debt for each individual to bear. It is the notion that every person in the country has a large debt that makes the existence of the debt seem so serious.

However, we should realize that corresponding to the share of the taxes that individuals have, there are Treasury bonds and bills that individuals also have. By and large, we owe the national debt to ourselves. Each individual shares in the public debt, but many individuals own claims on the government that are the other side of the national debt. To a first approximation, one could think of the liability that the debt represents as canceling out the asset that the debt represents to the individuals who hold claims on the government.

You will recognize that we are now discussing the question of whether the debt is counted as part of wealth for the population as a whole. Earlier, we started from the view that the government bonds and Treasury bills that individuals hold are part of their wealth. We then asked whether the possibility that all individuals take into account the future tax liabilities connected with the hypothetical paying off of the debt at some future date meant that on balance the debt was not part of the wealth. In this section we started from the other side: We first talked of the national debt as a debt and then pointed out that there were assets corresponding to that debt that were held by individuals. We pointed out earlier that it was not yet certain whether individuals taken together in fact count the national debt as part of wealth. There certainly does not seem to be any argument that the liability represented by some possible paying off of the debt at some unknown future time outweighs the value of the assets that individuals hold at present. At this level, then, there is no persuasive argument that the debt is a burden in the sense that the economy as a whole regards the national debt as a reduction in its wealth.

The only factor ignored in the previous paragraph is that part of the debt is owned by foreigners. In that case, for the U.S. economy as a whole, part of the asset represented by the debt is held by foreigners, while the future tax liability accrues entirely to residents. Then that part of the debt held by foreigners represents a net reduction in the wealth of U.S. residents.

Although the debt is not a burden in the fairly crude sense in which one asks whether individuals regard themselves as being poorer because of the existence of the debt (leaving aside the part of the debt owned by foreigners), there are more sophisticated senses in which it might be a burden. The most important sense in which there is a possible burden arises from the potential long-run effects of the debt on the capital stock. We saw earlier that debt financing increases the interest rate and reduces investment.[15] That would mean that the capital stock would be lower with debt financing than otherwise. If individuals regard the debt as part of their wealth, then they tend to increase their consumption at a given level of income, which results in a smaller proportion of GNP being invested, in a lower capital stock, and thus in lower output. This is a real burden.

Further, the debt might be a burden because debt servicing in the long run could

---

[15] Recall that the real interest rate will not rise when the debt increases if individuals do not regard the debt as net wealth.

require higher tax rates. If those tax rates have adverse effects on the amount of work that individuals do, then real output would be reduced.

Thus, if the debt is a burden, it is a burden for reasons very different from those suggested by the statement that every person in the United States has a debt of $6,000 as a share of the national debt. The major source of burden arises from the possible effects of the national debt on the country's net national worth: Increasing public debt can affect either the capital stock or the external debt.

Government Assets

It is important to recognize that the government has assets as well as debts. Imagine a government that runs a deficit, borrowing from the public, in order to add to the capital stock. For example, the government builds roads, post offices, or universities. The real capital acquired by the government should be treated as an offset against the debt issued. But in public discussions it is often forgotten that government spending is not all consumption or transfers.

Robert Eisner of Northwestern University has strongly emphasized this point in presenting government balance sheets in which both government debts and assets are listed.[16] For example, in 1984 the federal government owned tangible assets (valued at replacement cost) of $1,118 billion, but had debts of $1,175 billion. Thus the government had a net debt of only $57.9 billion, far less than the size of the debt itself would suggest.

There are serious issues of how to value government assets. Unquestionably, the government can sell a school, a post office, a jet fighter, or an offshore oil lease. But if it does not plan to do so, and if — as in the case of a jet fighter — the government will more likely have to continue to spend large amounts to keep the asset operating, it is not entirely clear whether that item should count as a government asset in calculating the government's net worth. Whatever the details, though, Eisner's calculations drive home one message: Concentrating only on government debt rather than on all the government's potential sources of future income and outlays in analyzing its financial position is likely to be misleading.

The Budget Deficits of the 1980s

The U.S. budget deficits of the 1980s were not, however, a result of a large increase in government spending on capital goods such as roads and schools. The 1980s deficits will increase the burden on future generations. They have been accompanied by very large deficits in the U.S. current account, and thus by borrowing from foreigners. And

---

[16] See Robert Eisner, *How Real Is the Federal Deficit?* (New York: Free Press, 1986), and "Budget Deficits: Rhetoric and Reality," *Economic Perspectives,* Spring 1989.

TABLE 16-8
NET SAVING AND INVESTMENT (percent of GNP)

	Net private saving	Net domestic saving	Net investment
1950–1959	7.5	7.4	7.5
1960–1969	8.1	7.9	7.9
1970–1979	8.1	7.1	6.9
1980–1988	5.6	3.1	6.1
1988	4.6	2.8	4.7

SOURCE: DRI/McGraw-Hill.

on the domestic side, the deficits have not been matched by an increase in saving. On the contrary, they were matched primarily by higher consumption spending.

Simplifying somewhat, we can say that the government offered consumers lower present taxes, financing the deficit by borrowing abroad. Someone will ultimately have to pay the taxes that finance the interest on those loans from abroad. In this respect the United States is no different from many developing countries, such as Mexico or Brazil, that have incurred a public debt by borrowing abroad.

We can see that point from the basic relation among saving in the private sector (S_p) and the public sector (S_g), investment (I), and the current account (CA):

$$I + CA \equiv S_p + S_g \qquad (8)$$

Budget deficits (negative public sector saving, $S_g < 0$), with unchanged private saving, translate either into reduced investment and hence a lower capital stock or else into a reduced current account surplus (or increased deficit). In the 1980s, as Table 16-8 shows, national net saving fell sharply, in part as a result of the budget deficit, in part as a consequence of reduced private saving. There has been a decline in net investment and also a worsening of the external balance. Clearly the rate of increase of net national wealth has fallen as a result of the sharp fall in the net national saving rate shown in Figure 16-7.

Since the U.S. economy did not increase its investment when the deficit increased, there is no prospect that the federal deficit will somehow generate extra earnings in the economy to pay the interest on the debt. Accordingly, a growing external debt burden is clearly on the horizon. This is part of the case for deficit correction.[17]

---

[17] See Charles Schultze, "Of Wolves, Termites, and Pussycats," *Brookings Review,* Summer 1989.

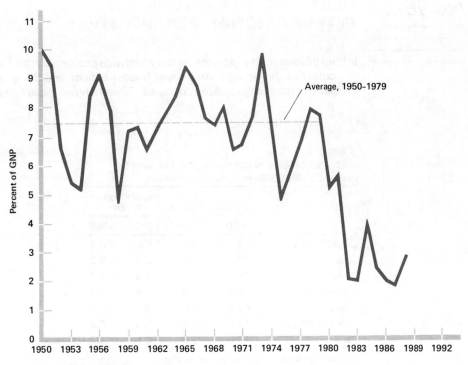

FIGURE 16-7
THE NET NATIONAL SAVING RATE, 1950–1988. (SOURCE: DRI/McGraw-Hill.)

Optimal Deficits

Figure 16-6 shows that the national debt as a percentage of GNP has typically increased during wartime and then declined in peacetime. This seems to be a sensible way for the debt to behave, reflecting large wartime deficits and peacetime surpluses or peacetime deficits that are small enough for the debt-to-income ratio to decline.

Is it possible to go beyond the general good sense of this behavior to something more specific, to ask about optimal behavior of the budget deficit over time? If the Barro-Ricardo hypothesis that current and future taxation have the same effects on current behavior were correct, then it would not matter how budgets were financed. If a government ran a large deficit in wartime, people would recognize that the large deficit meant higher taxation in the future and would consume the same amount as if they were taxed during the war.

There are in fact two main theories of optimal deficit financing. Their prescriptions depend on the assumed reason that the timing of taxes matters.

box 16-2 ## DEBT AND DEFICITS IN AN
INTERNATIONAL PERSPECTIVE

In the 1980s high interest rates were a worldwide problem and so was the recession at the outset of the decade. As a result budget deficits and rising debt ratios were a problem for most industrialized countries. Table 1 shows these facts. The data shown

TABLE 1

DEBT AND DEFICITS IN INDUSTRIALIZED COUNTRIES
(percent of GNP/GDP; general government)

	NET PUBLIC DEBT		PRIMARY BUDGET DEFICIT*	
	1980	1989	1980	1989
United States	19.0	30.3	+0.0	+0.7
Japan	17.3	19.4	−3.4	+3.2
Europe	26.3	41.4	−1.4	+1.1
Germany	14.3	22.8	−1.6	+1.7
Italy	53.6	94.6	−3.9	−1.5
United Kingdom	47.5	33.5	−0.3	+3.6
Canada	13.0	39.6	−0.9	+1.2

* A plus sign denotes a primary budget surplus.

SOURCE: OECD, *Economic Outlook*, June 1989.

MINIMIZING INTERTEMPORAL TAX DISTORTIONS

One theory, developed by Finn Kydland of Carnegie-Mellon University and Edward Prescott of the University of Chicago, focuses on tax distortions, or *tax wedges*.[18] These distortions occur because taxes create a difference between the market price of commodities and their value to consumers and producers. For instance, the income tax means that workers, who take home only an after-tax wage, place a lower value on their work than the employer, who has to pay a pretax wage.

[18] "A Competitive Theory of Fluctuations and the Feasibility and Desirability of Stabilization Policy," in Stanley Fischer (ed.), *Rational Expectations and Economic Policy* (Chicago: University of Chicago Press, 1980). See, too, Robert Lucas, "Principles of Fiscal and Monetary Policy," *Journal of Monetary Economics* 2 (1986). An alternative view is developed in David Romer, "What Are the Costs of Excessive Deficits?" *NBER Macroeconomics Annual,* 1988.

here refer to *net* public debt of the *general* government. The net measure assures that we adjust debt outstanding for any holdings by the government sector, for example, state pension funds. The general government includes federal, state, and local government units.

Two interesting patterns emerge from these data. First, with the exception of the United Kingdom, every country experienced a very substantial increase in debt ratios. Second, every single country moved toward a substantial primary budget surplus. Fiscal retrenchment thus has been the rule. The reason is that mounting interest costs in the budget meant ever larger deficits unless the *non*interest part of the budget were cut. In the pre-1980 period governments carefully avoided building up debt during peacetime; since 1980, at least in the United States, that strategy has been less than successful.*

Italy is a case of *unsustainable deficits*. The debt ratio is already very high by international standards, and the primary budget remains in deficit. Because the government is borrowing more than the entire interest bill (with real interest rates above the growth rate), the debt ratio is rising steadily. While there is no immediate issue of bankruptcy, it is also clear that the deficit strategy cannot continue forever or even for very long. Spending cuts, higher taxes, or more efficient tax collection are necessary to avoid a snowballing of the debt.

The United Kingdom presents a very interesting case in that the debt ratio actually declined in the 1980s. In fact, at the end of the decade there was even a discussion of what the U.K. government might do when all the public debt has been retired as a result of budget surpluses. A major part in the surplus strategy has been the sale of public assets. ■

---

* See Jerome Kremers, "US Federal Indebtedness and the Conduct of Fiscal Policy," *Journal of Monetary Economics*, March 1989, and IMF, *World Economic Outlook*, April 1989.

Kydland and Prescott show that in order to minimize these distortions over time tax *rates* should be kept constant. To see why, suppose that on the contrary taxes were high during war and low during peace. Then according to that policy, which is based on supply-side theory, individuals would work less during the war and more during peace. Rather than have labor supply moving perversely in that way, Kydland and Prescott show that under their assumptions tax rates should be kept constant.

The government budget constraint says that the present value of government spending has to be equal to the present value of taxes. If tax rates are constant, deficits will be high when government spending is *temporarily* high and surpluses will occur when government spending is temporarily low. The reason is that on average the budget has to be balanced. If tax rates are kept constant, then revenues will change relatively little. Government spending can fluctuate more, and when it is high, there will be a deficit. This tax-smoothing argument indeed suggests that the typical pattern of large wartime deficits is the correct one.

INTERGENERATIONAL FAIRNESS

In discussing the burden of the national debt, we showed that when Barro-Ricardo equivalence does not hold, the national debt creates a burden on future generations by reducing their capital stock. That would mean that a government that runs a deficit and creates a larger debt shifts some of the burden of current government spending to future generations.

In that case, the criterion on which decisions on budget deficits have to be made is one of intergenerational fairness. For instance, when a country is in a war, it might be thought fair that future generations should share the economic burden with those facing the burdens of both fighting and economic hardship. By that criterion, deficit financing would probably be widely agreed to be justified in wartime.

Of course, there is no hard-and-fast economic principle that describes what is fair and not fair in allocating burdens over time. Nonetheless politicians and the average person probably have little trouble basing their decisions on their views about the fair sharing of burdens across generations.

16-6 THE SIZE-OF-GOVERNMENT CONTROVERSY

There has been a worldwide trend over the last 25 years toward an increased share of government in GNP. Figure 16-8 shows the share of government outlays (all levels of government) as a percent of GNP for the total government sector and the federal government. The share was far higher in 1980 than it had been in 1960 in the United States, and this pattern was even more evident abroad. This increase reflects in large measure the broadening of government social programs, especially the growth of transfer programs discussed above. Since 1981, growth in spending has been under sharp attack.

A vocal part of the electorate and the government argues that much of government spending is wasteful, that the tax burden is excessive, and that the role of government in the economy should be reduced. In the United States the response to the growth of government has been a tax revolt, leading to limitations on taxes in several states, and an attempt to secure a constitutional amendment that would both prevent government spending from rising and require budgets to be balanced, or almost so. The balanced budget amendment had the support of the Reagan administration, despite the administration's introducing extremely unbalanced budgets.

How large should the government be? That is, of course, a difficult question. Clearly, some government programs are widely regarded as desirable; for instance, few dispute the need for an adequate national defense. Other programs, such as the Social Security program, also command wide assent, though just how large such programs should be is controversial.[19] To conservatives government is far too large, and, hence, the deficit — and the pressures it puts on interest rates and financial

---

[19] See Milton Friedman, "Why the Twin Deficits Are a Blessing," *Wall Street Journal,* December 1988, and Robert Barro, "Budget Deficits: Only a Minor Crisis," *Wall Street Journal,* January 1988.

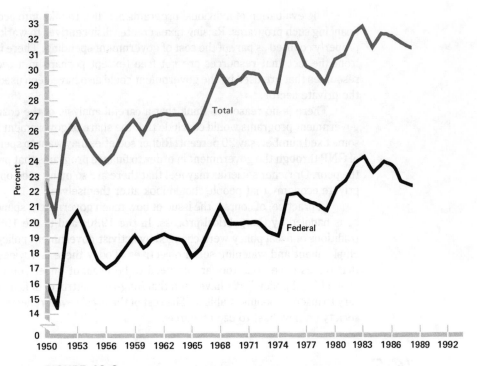

FIGURE 16-8
THE SHARE OF GOVERNMENT OUTLAYS IN GNP, 1950–1988. (SOURCE:
Historical Tables, Budget of the Government of the United States.)

stability—is desirable. The reason is that for the first time, as a result of the deficit pressure, cuts in spending are practiced seriously, year after year.[20]

But there is no simple test that will tell us whether we get our money's worth from government spending in general. There have been a number of studies of particular government programs showing that they work less effectively than was originally expected, perhaps very badly, and arguing that it would be better if the programs were abandoned and the problem left to the free market to handle. Even the Social Security system and the food stamp program have received substantial criticism. The approach that looks at individual programs to examine their success and suggest changes is clearly the most careful way to evaluate government spending.

---

[20] These issues are in no way special to the United States. In fact, they are being debated in all industrial countries. See Peter Saunders and Friedrich Klau, "The Role of the Public Sector," *OECD Economic Studies,* Spring 1985, and Dennis Mueller, "The Growth of Government," *IMF Staff Papers,* March 1987. For an evaluation of the productivity of public spending see David Aschauer, "Is Public Expenditure Productive?" *Journal of Monetary Economics,* March 1989.

The evaluation of individual programs has also to take into account the costs of financing such programs. Raising taxes creates disincentives to work and save that are properly counted as part of the cost of government spending. There is no getting away from the fact that resources are not free (except perhaps in a recession) and that resources that are used by the government could also have been used in other ways by the private sector.

There is no reason to think that a careful analysis of the costs and benefits of government programs would conclude that the share of government in GNP should be some fixed number, say 20 percent. Richer societies may want to spend a greater share of GNP through the government in order to finance programs that provide support for the poor. Or richer societies may feel that there are so many good opportunities in the private economy that people should look after themselves.

In practice, of course, the issue of how much government spending there should be is handled by the political process. In the 1930s and in the 1960s the rules and traditions of fiscal policy were changed by activist government policy in pursuit of full employment and widening social objectives. Today there is a widespread sentiment that things have gone too far and need to be brought under control by a return to "sound fiscal policy." We have seen that long-run control of deficits is, indeed, necessary to macroeconomic stability. The rest of the fiscal revolt reflects a disagreement in society on how best to use resources.

16-7 SUMMARY

1. Federal government expenditures are financed through taxes and borrowing. The borrowing takes place directly from the public and, maybe indirectly, from the Fed.
2. Under present institutional arrangements, there is no necessary link between Treasury borrowing and changes in the stock of high-powered money. Federal Reserve financing of the deficit increases the stock of high-powered money.
3. When the Fed tries to control the level of interest rates, it creates an automatic link between Treasury borrowing and the creation of high-powered money.
4. Federal government receipts come chiefly from the individual income tax and from social insurance taxes and contributions. The share of the last category has increased rapidly in the postwar period, especially since the 1960s.
5. Federal government expenditures are chiefly for defense and transfer payments to individuals. The share of defense in federal expenditure has fallen over the past 25 years, while the share of transfers has risen.
6. A temporary increase in government spending or a cut in taxes financed by debt will raise the price level and increase the interest rate.
7. The Barro-Ricardo equivalence proposition notes that debt represents future taxes. Accordingly it asserts that debt-financed tax cuts will not have any effect on aggregate demand.
8. The debt-income ratio rises if the growth rate of debt — determined by interest payments and the primary deficit — exceeds the growth rate of nominal income.

box 16-3

SOCIAL SECURITY AND THE BUDGET

In the United States the Social Security system collects contributions from workers and firms and disburses benefits to retirees. The system works on a "pay-as-you-go" basis, meaning that current revenues from contributions are used to pay current benefits. Such a system works well when inflows from contributions exceed outflows, and it has a crisis when payments to beneficiaries exceed current contributions. The net surplus or deficit of the Social Security system is part of the federal government budget in that general government resources must make up for any shortfall of the system or that any surplus of the system can be used to finance a deficit in the budget.

The financing of social security systems has become highly controversial in the United States and in other industrialized countries because demographic trends foretell serious difficulties 20 to 30 years from now. At the present time the Social Security system runs a surplus — contributions are high because the postwar baby boom is in the labor market. As a result the Social Security surplus helps reduce the size of the budget deficit, as shown in Table 1. But over time, starting in the late 1990s, the demographic balance starts deteriorating: The number of retirees will rise relative to the contributing population and the surplus will turn into a deficit. In 1990 there were about five contributors for every retiree, and in the year 2020 there will only be four. In Japan the aging of the population is much more dramatic: from six workers per retiree in 1990 the drop is to only three in 2020. The emerging imbalance means that benefits have to be trimmed or retirement age has to be raised or taxes have to increase. Given that prospect many argue that early budget balancing is an important step to avoid a far sharper increase in taxes later.*   ■

TABLE 1

SOCIAL SECURITY AND THE BUDGET DEFICIT (percent of GNP; fiscal year; unified budget)

	1988	1990	1992	1994
On-budget deficit	4.1	3.7	3.4	3.3
Off-budget deficit*	−0.8	−1.2	−1.4	−1.6
Combined deficit	3.2	2.5	2.0	1.7

* Social Security system.

SOURCE: Congressional Budget Office.

* See Henry Aaron, Barry Bosworth, and Gary Burtless, *Can America Afford To Grow Old?* (Washington, D.C.: The Brookings Institution, 1989); Robert Hagemann and Guiseppe Nicoletti, "Population Ageing: Economic Effects and Some Policy Implications for Financing Public Pensions," *OECD Economic Studies,* Spring 1989; and Alan Auerbach et al., "The Economic Dynamics of an Ageing Population: The Case of Four OECD Countries," *OECD Economic Studies,* Spring 1989.

9. Debt financing of a permanent increase in government spending is not viable if the economy is not growing. The interest payments on the debt would continually increase, making for a rising deficit that has to be funded by ever-increasing borrowing. In a growing economy, small deficits can be run permanently without causing the debt-GNP ratio to rise.

10. The major sense in which the national debt may be a burden is that it may lead to a decline in the capital stock in the long run.

11. The balance sheet of the government shows government real assets as an offset to the public debt.

12. The U.S. deficits of the 1980s have consumption as their primary counterpart, and they are financed by external borrowing. They accordingly represent exactly the kind of deficit that does give rise to a debt burden.

13. The increase in government spending in the 1960–1985 period led to the imposition of limits on taxes and spending in several states and a proposed constitutional amendment in the United States to require a balanced budget and limits on government spending as a share of GNP.

KEY TERMS

Public debt

Debt financing

Money financing

Entitlement spending

Discretionary spending

Bracket creep

Tax indexation

Transfers

Debt-income ratio

Laffer curve

Gramm-Rudman-Hollings Act

Barro-Ricardo equivalence

Primary deficit

Noninterest deficit

Burden of the debt

PROBLEMS

1. What effect does a federal government surplus have on the stock of money and the stock of debt? Explain in detail the mechanics of how the stocks of money and bonds are affected.

2. Suppose the Treasury issues $1 billion in Treasury bills that are bought by the public. Then the Fed carries out an open market purchase of $300 million. Effectively, how has the debt been financed?

3. Under what circumstances are fiscal and monetary policy related rather than existing as two completely independent instruments in the hands of the government?

4. Trace the path the economy follows when there is a permanent increase in government spending that is financed by borrowing from the public. Assume the economy is growing. Evaluate the argument that the budget should be balanced every period.

5. Analyze the difference in the impact on the interest rate, investment, and the price level of a temporary change in government spending financed by borrowing.

6. What would be the bracket creep effect of inflation on real income taxes if income taxation was (a) regressive, (b) proportional, (c) indexed?

7. Suppose the real interest rate is 3 percent, output growth is 7 percent, the debt-income ratio is 50 percent, and the primary budget shows a deficit of 7 percent of GNP. Will the debt-income ratio increase or fall?

8. Explain in words why a high growth rate of output will tend, other things being equal, to reduce the debt-income ratio. How does your answer help explain Figure 16-6?

9. A government increases spending by building a dam. The spending is financed by issuing debt. Does the debt issue create a debt burden? Would your answer be different if the government had bought a fleet of automobiles for the Pentagon?

10. The Kemp-Roth tax cuts of the early 1980s cut government receipts from an average of 19.7 percent of GNP in 1980–1982 to only 18.6 percent in 1985. Are these tax cuts the main explanation for the budget deficit problem of the 1980s?

11. "The unsustainable deficits of the 1980s urgently call for a new approach to fiscal policy. Budgets need to be balanced year by year so that today's taxpayers pay the full bill of what they want the government to do for them." Comment on this statement.

12. "The United States faces a fiscal crisis because mounting deficits are driving the debt-income ratio far beyond the range that this country has experienced. From these high debt levels there is no return except by years of high taxes to pay off the debt." Comment on this statement.

APPENDIX: THE POTENTIAL INSTABILITY OF DEBT FINANCING

In this appendix we develop a framework to assess the instability problem associated with debt financing. We focus on the debt-income ratio and ask under what conditions the debt-income ratio will rise over time. Instability arises if the debt-income ratio rises year after year without limits.[21]

The derivation uses definitions, addition, and subtraction, and avoids calculus. Its main purpose is for you see where Table 16-7 comes from and to understand the discussion of explosive debt situations and unsustainable deficits.

B = nominal stock of debt outstanding

i = nominal interest rate

$r \equiv i - \pi$ = real interest rate

P = price level

Y = level of real output

x = noninterest, or primary, budget surplus (as a share of GNP)

b = debt-income ratio

y = growth rate of output

---

[21] The discussion of debt-income ratios draws on James Tobin, "Budget Deficits, Federal Debt and Inflation in the Short and Long Run," in The Conference Board, *Toward a Reconstruction of Federal Budgeting,* 1982; Robert Eisner and Paul Pieper, "A New View of the Federal Debt and Budget Deficits," *American Economic Review,* March 1984; Willem Buiter, "A Guide to Public Sector Debt and Deficits," *Economic Policy,* November 1985; and Luigi Spaventa, "The Growth of Public Debt," *IMF Staff Papers,* June 1987.

The debt-income ratio is defined as the ratio of debt outstanding relative to nominal GNP:

$$\text{Debt-income ratio} = b = \frac{B}{PY} \tag{A1}$$

Over time the debt-income ratio changes by Δb. From equation (A1) the change over time can be calculated (we assert rather than derive here the well-known "fraction rule" of calculus) as[22]

$$\Delta b = \frac{\Delta B}{PY} - b\left(\frac{\Delta P}{P} + \frac{\Delta Y}{Y}\right) = \frac{\Delta B}{PY} - b(\pi + y) \tag{A2}$$

We next simplify this expression by substituting an expression for the increase in the nominal debt outstanding. The increase in debt from one year to the next is the result of the budget deficit. It therefore is equal to interest payments, which are equal to the debt outstanding times the interest rate, iB, less the noninterest budget surplus, x, which we can write as the primary budget share times nominal GNP, xPY:

$$\Delta B \equiv iB - xPY \tag{A3}$$

The final step is to substitute (A3) into (A2) to obtain

$$\Delta b = ib - x - b(\pi + y)$$

In this form the increase in the debt ratio has three components: nominal interest payments less the contribution to debt stabilization from noninterest surpluses less the contribution from growing nominal income. The former two tell us about the growth of the numerator in (A1) and the latter about the growth of the denominator.

A more useful form of this equation is obtained by collecting terms and writing

$$\Delta b = b(r - y) - x$$

where we have used the definition of the real interest rate, $r \equiv i - \pi$. In this form, which is commonly used, we see that the debt ratio rises whenever the real interest rate exceeds the growth rate, or $r > y$, *and* the primary budget is balanced or in deficit. But, as Table 16-7 showed, there are other combinations that maintain a stable or falling debt ratio, for example, a negative real interest rate (as in the 1970s) combined with noninterest deficits.

Deficits are called unsustainable if on the current path of future fiscal policy the debt ratio rises without bounds. "Unsustainable" simply means that at some point fiscal policy must change to avoid a snowballing of the debt ratio. Note, too, that the higher the debt ratio, b, the more important becomes the real interest component. If real interest rates exceed the growth rate, as in the 1980s though not before, debt problems become worse by themselves, without a country even running primary deficits.

---

[22] See, for example, Luigi Spaventa, "The Growth of Public Debt: Sustainability. Fiscal Rules and Monetary Rules," *IMF Staff Papers,* June 1987.

DATA APPENDIX

All data refer to the federal government and are expressed as fractions of GNP. The full-employment deficit is the series developed by DRI, Inc.; $F1$ measures the discretionary *change* in fiscal policy; a plus sign signifies expansion.

Year	Budget total	Deficit excluding Social Security	Net interest	Debt	Full-employment budget deficit	$F1$
1960	−0.6	−0.3	1.3	46.8	−0.9	−0.0
1961	0.7	0.5	1.2	46.0	−0.6	0.8
1962	0.7	0.9	1.2	44.5	−0.3	0.9
1963	−0.0	0.3	1.2	43.2	−0.5	−0.1
1964	0.5	0.9	1.2	40.8	−0.1	0.6
1965	−0.1	0.2	1.2	38.8	−0.1	0.3
1966	0.2	1.2	1.2	35.7	0.2	1.5
1967	1.6	2.4	1.2	33.6	0.7	1.3
1968	0.7	1.3	1.3	34.1	0.4	0.2
1969	−0.9	−0.1	1.3	29.9	−0.3	−0.8
1970	1.2	1.6	1.4	28.6	0.2	−0.3
1971	2.0	2.0	1.3	28.7	0.4	−0.4
1972	1.4	1.6	1.2	28.0	0.3	0.6
1973	0.4	1.1	1.3	26.6	0.1	−0.6
1974	0.8	1.2	1.4	24.3	−0.2	−0.1
1975	4.3	3.5	1.4	25.9	1.2	0.6
1976	3.0	2.3	1.5	28.1	0.7	0.1
1977	2.3	1.8	1.5	28.4	0.7	0.2
1978	1.3	1.2	1.6	28.0	0.4	0.3
1979	0.6	0.8	1.7	26.1	−0.1	0.2
1980	2.2	1.8	2.0	26.6	0.4	0.1
1981	2.1	1.7	2.4	26.3	0.0	−0.4
1982	4.6	3.6	2.7	29.3	1.1	0.9
1983	5.2	4.2	2.8	34.0	2.1	1.0
1984	4.5	4.5	3.1	35.3	3.0	0.5
1985	4.9	5.2	3.2	37.9	3.9	0.5
1986	4.8	5.3	3.2	41.5	4.1	0.0
1987	3.5	4.1	3.2	42.6	3.0	0.4
1988	2.9	4.0	3.2	42.9	2.9	0.0

SOURCE: DRI, Inc., and Federal Reserve Board.

MONEY, DEFICITS, AND INFLATION

*I*n this chapter we concentrate on the effect of money growth on inflation and interest rates. We take up four main topics. First, we examine the monetarist proposition that inflation is a monetary phenomenon, which means that inflation is entirely, or at least primarily, due to excessive money growth. Second, we study the linkages among interest rates, inflation, and money growth. The question is whether increased money growth raises or lowers interest rates. Third, we look at the links between budget deficits and money growth, asking whether or under what circumstances budget deficits generate money growth. Finally, we describe hyperinflations and the role of money growth in them.

We establish some basic results in this chapter. The most important is that really high inflation is indeed primarily a monetary phenomenon in the sense that inflation could not continue without continued money growth. But typically in conditions of high inflation there are also high budget deficits underlying the rapid money growth. Such was the case, for instance, in the hyperinflations in 1984–1985 in Israel and Bolivia and in the continuing hyperinflations in Argentina, Brazil, Nicaragua, and Peru. Similarly in conditions of high inflation nominal interest rates become very high, as expected inflation becomes incorporated into nominal rates.

The real world application and significance of these results is quite striking and can be seen in many high-inflation countries around the world. However, when inflation rates are lower, in the single-digit or low-double-digit range, real disturbances like supply shocks may well be playing a relatively larger role, and the simple results isolating the role of money become less dominant. Similarly, the role of the deficit in causing money growth becomes less definite; for instance, there was no acceleration in money growth in the United States in the early 1980s despite growing budget deficits.

We start out in Section 17-1 with the linkages between money growth and inflation. Then, in Section 17-2, we discuss evidence on the links between money and inflation, and between inflation and interest rates. In Section 17-3 we analyze the relationship between budget deficits and money growth in the U.S. economy. We conclude, in Section 17-4, with a discussion of hyperinflation.

17-1 MONEY AND INFLATION

In this section we develop the Chapter 14 analysis of the dynamics of inflation to show exactly the role played by money growth. Our task is to make sense of the monetarist claim that inflation is always and everywhere a monetary phenomenon.

To obtain a firm understanding of these points, two distinctions have to be kept in mind. The first is between the short run and the long run. The second is the distinction between monetary and other disturbances (fiscal, for example, or oil shocks) to the economy.

Monetarists tend to concentrate on the long run and on economies in which changes in money growth are the primary disturbances. Not surprisingly they tend to be right, *for that special case,* when they argue that money explains most of what is happening to inflation. But as one moves away from the long run and from monetary disturbances toward short-run inflation determination and alternative shocks, it becomes necessary to be much more eclectic. In the short run, disturbances other than changes in the money stock affect inflation and, conversely, changes in the money stock do have real effects. Even if the disturbances are purely monetary it will still generally take a while before they are fully reflected in inflation and only in inflation.

A key point in the distinction between the short run and the long run and in determining the dynamics of inflation is the role of expectations. Increased money growth will have real effects as long as inflationary expectations have not fully adapted. Milton Friedman has put this point as follows:[1]

> Monetarist analysis goes on to say that any changes in the nominal quantity of money that are anticipated in advance will be fully embedded in inflationary and other expectations, but that unanticipated changes in the quantity of money will not be. An unanticipated increase or decrease in the quantity of money tends to affect total nominal spending some six to nine months later in countries like the United States, Japan or Great Britain. The initial effect is primarily on output rather than on prices. Prices tend to be affected only some 18 months to two years later. This does not mean that there is no further effect on real quantities. On the contrary, the delayed impact on prices means an overshooting of output — up or down depending on the initial stimulus — which will then require an overshooting in the opposite direction to allow the price level to reach its appropriate level. As a result the cyclical reaction pattern in both output and prices tends to last for a considerable period — years, not months. . . .

While using the model of Chapter 14 to develop these ideas, we shift the exposition to focus on dynamics. Our task is to highlight a number of relationships involving money, interest rates, and inflation.

---

[1] See Milton Friedman, "Monetarism in Rhetoric and Practice," Bank of Japan, *Monetary and Economic Studies,* October 1983, p. 2.

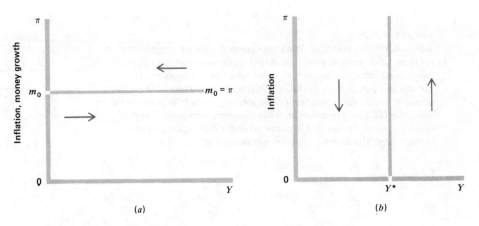

FIGURE 17-1

THE DYNAMICS OF INFLATION AND OUTPUT. Panel (*a*) shows the response of output to real balances. When inflation exceeds the growth rate of money, real balances are falling and hence demand and output are declining. Conversely, when inflation falls short of money growth, output is rising. Panel (*b*) shows that at output levels above Y^* inflation rises and at output levels below Y^* inflation declines.

The Model

The starting point is the aggregate demand equation derived in Chapter 14. Aggregate demand and output will rise whenever real balances are increasing. Conversely, when real balances are falling, so, too, are aggregate demand and output.[2] We write this relation in equation (1), using the notation $\Delta Y = Y - Y_{-1}$, $m =$ growth rate of money, and $\pi =$ inflation rate:

$$\Delta Y = f(m - \pi) \tag{1}$$

Assume now a given growth rate of money, m_0. In Figure 17-1*a* we show the schedule $\pi = m_0$ along which output is neither rising nor falling. Now we consider how output is changing at different points in Figure 17-1*a*. For points above the $\pi = m_0$ schedule, inflation exceeds the given growth rate of money. Hence real balances are

---

[2] In the appendix to Chap. 14 we developed the aggregate demand curve, taking account of the role of inflationary expectations in determining the real interest rate. In that case there is an additional term in the aggregate demand relationship equation (1). Under the assumption to be made for much of this section that $\pi = \pi_{-1}$, i.e., that the expected inflation rate is equal to last period's inflation rate, current aggregate demand increases with the lagged inflation rate. In order to simplify, we do not include this term on the aggregate demand side in this section. The omission does not affect the general results obtained except possibly if the expectations effect on aggregate demand were very large.

FIGURE 17-2

THE ADJUSTMENT PROCESS. The upper panel combines the information in Figure 17-1 to show how output and inflation evolve over time. The long-run equilibrium is at point E, at which inflation equals money growth and output is at the full-employment level. The lower panel shows the real rate of interest corresponding to each level of output along the IS curve. For example, if the economy is at point A in the upper panel, point A on the IS curve gives the corresponding real interest rate. The long-run equilibrium real interest rate is r^*.

TABLE 17-1
THE DETERMINANTS OF OUTPUT AND INFLATION

	$m > \pi$	$m < \pi$
$Y > Y^*$	I	II
	Y is ↑	Y is ↓
	π is ↑	π is ↑
$Y < Y^*$	III	IV
	Y is ↑	Y is ↓
	π is ↓	π is ↓

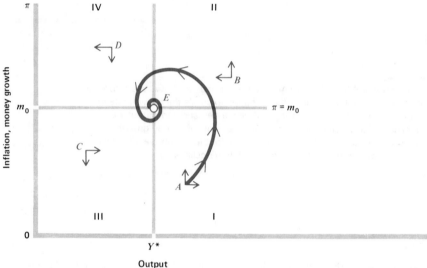

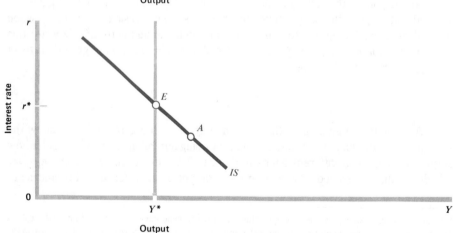

falling and so, according to equation (1), is output. This is indicated by the arrow showing falling output. Conversely, below the schedule, inflation is lower than money growth, and hence real balances are increasing, interest rates are falling, and demand and output are growing.

The second relationship is the aggregate supply curve:

$$\pi = \pi^e + \lambda(Y - Y^*) \tag{2a}$$

In equation $(2\,a)$ Y^* is the full-employment level of output, assumed in this section to be constant. For most of this section we make the simplest adaptive expectations assumption, which is that inflation expectations are given by last period's inflation rate, that is, $\pi^e = \pi_{-1}$.[3] Making that substitution in equation $(2\,a)$, the change in inflation over time, denoted by $\Delta\pi = \pi - \pi_{-1}$, depends on the output gap and is given by

$$\Delta\pi = \lambda(Y - Y^*) \tag{2}$$

Focusing again on dynamics, in Figure 17-1b we show the arrows that indicate the direction in which inflation is moving. When output is below the full-employment level, inflation is falling, and when output is above the full-employment level, inflation is rising.

Table 17-1 and Figure 17-2 combine the information in the two parts of Figure 17-1. The table shows the direction in which output and inflation are moving in each of the four regions of Figure 17-2. We use the arrows to show the combined movement or the path of inflation and output at each point.

Suppose the economy is at point A in region I. Because output is above the full-employment level, inflation is rising. But inflation is below money growth. Therefore, real balances are increasing, and hence demand and output are rising. Thus at point A output is rising as is inflation so that the economy moves in a northeastward direction. We can establish the direction of movement at points B, C, and D in a similar fashion. Note that point E is the only point in the diagram at which *both* output and inflation are constant. This is the long-run equilibrium to which the economy ultimately converges.

In Figure 17-2 we complete the model by bringing in the *IS* schedule. On the vertical axis in the lower diagram we show the *real,* or *inflation-adjusted,* interest rate. Real aggregate demand, as we saw in previous chapters, depends on the real interest rate. A higher real interest rate lowers aggregate demand and hence reduces equilibrium output, as shown by the *IS* schedule. The lower part of Figure 17-2 helps us track the real interest rate in the adjustment process. For each level of output in the upper part we can find the corresponding equilibrium real interest rate on the *IS* schedule. Thus we can follow output, inflation, and the real interest rate at the same time.

---

[3] We discuss behavior under rational expectations of inflation later in this section.

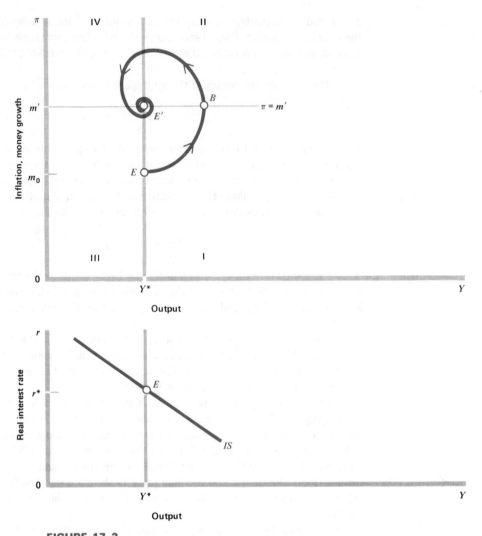

FIGURE 17-3

THE ADJUSTMENT TO AN INCREASE IN MONEY GROWTH. A sustained increase in money growth from m_0 to m' leads the economy along a path from E to E'. Output first expands, and inflation gradually builds up. In the long run, inflation rises to equal the growth rate of money. The economy returns to full employment at the real interest rate, r^*.

In Figure 17-2 we show a typical adjustment path starting at point *A*. The corresponding point is also labeled *A* in the lower part of Figure 17-2. At *A* inflation is rising because of overemployment. But because inflation is low relative to money growth, real balances are rising and hence demand and output are growing. The economy thus moves in a northeasterly direction. The driving force is the increasing level of real balances, which reduces interest rates and pushes up demand and output. Over time, as the economy cycles back to point *E*, the real interest rate first declines and then, as the economy enters region II, starts rising. The interest rate overshoots the long-run equilibrium level, r^*, several times before it ultimately settles there.

An Increase in Money Growth

We now use this framework to examine once more the effects of a sustained increase in money growth. We start in long-run equilibrium at point *E* in Figure 17-3, where money growth is initially m_0. The inflation rate is equal to the growth rate of money, and output is at its full-employment level. Now the growth rate of money is permanently raised to m'. The new $\pi = m'$ schedule lies above the previous one (which is not drawn to avoid cluttering up the diagram). The arrows on the path show the direction in which inflation and output are moving. The path starting at *E* shows the evolution of the economy.

At point *E* the growth rate of money, m', now exceeds the initial inflation rate $\pi = m_0$. As a result, the real money stock is increasing. Interest rates are pushed down, and thus aggregate demand and output will be rising. At the very beginning of the adjustment process the economy therefore moves horizontally to the right with output rising. But the moment output starts exceeding the full-employment level, inflation increases. Now the path starts pointing in a northeasterly direction with rising output because inflation, although rising, remains low relative to money growth.

Over time the economy moves to point *B*. Here real balances are constant because now inflation has risen to the level of money growth. But output is above the full-employment level. Therefore inflation is still increasing, and the economy is thus pushed into region II. We do not describe the whole path, but it is apparent that the economy will cycle its way gradually to point *E'*.

Rational Expectations

The exact details of the adjustment path chosen in Figure 17-3 depend on the assumptions about expectations. But the general pattern — that increased monetary growth first raises output and ultimately is fully reflected in higher inflation — is valid for (almost) any assumption about expectations.

Only in a world of complete flexibility of wages and prices combined with rational expectations would the adjustment occur instantly without any dynamics whatsoever. In that case, if a change in the growth rate of money is expected, π^e in equation (2a) will be equal to *m'* at the time the growth rate of money changes, and output will remain at its full-employment level throughout.[4]

Once we move away from that extreme case — which requires both rational expectations and full flexibility of prices and wages — the pattern of adjustment is that shown in Figure 17-3. Alternative assumptions about expectations and the adjustment of wages and prices will primarily influence the speed of adjustment and the movement of nominal interest rates, but will generally imply a slow adjustment pattern of the type seen in Figure 17-3.

Before going further we want to summarize the main results so far. There are four characteristics of the adjustment process and the new long-run equilibrium that are important to keep in mind:

- A sustained increase in the growth rate of money will, in the long run when all adjustments have taken place, lead to an equal increase in the rate of inflation. If money growth rises by 5 percent, so, too, ultimately will the inflation rate.

- A sustained change in money growth will have no long-run effects on the level of output. Thus there is no long-run tradeoff between inflation and output.

- In the short run, during the adjustment process, increased monetary growth will affect the real interest rate, aggregate demand, and output. Specifically, in the initial stages there will be an expansion in output while inflation builds up.

- In the short run, increased money growth will reduce the real interest rate. But in the long run, after all adjustments have taken place, the real interest rate will return to its initial level.

We ask you in Problem 1 at the end of the chapter to demonstrate the corresponding results for a sustained reduction in the growth rate of money. To complete our analysis, we now turn to the behavior of real balances and the nominal interest rate.

The Fisher Equation

We have noted at various points in this book the relationship between nominal interest rates, real rates, and the expected rate of inflation. The (expected) real rate of interest is the nominal rate less the expected rate of inflation:

$$r^e \equiv i - \pi^e \tag{3}$$

Equation (3) is the Fisher equation, named after Irving Fisher (1867–1947), the most

---

[4] Remarkably, in this case the inflation rate would generally start to rise before the growth rate of money increases, because people's expectations of inflation in the future reduce the quantity of real balances demanded, and the price level therefore starts moving up.

famous American economist of the first third of this century, who drew attention to the inflation–interest rate linkage.[5]

The Fisher equation immediately draws attention to a very important finding about money growth, inflation, and interest rates. We saw above that in the long run the real interest rate returns to the full-employment level, r^*, and that actual and expected inflation converge. Using these two facts ($r^e = r^*$, $\pi^e \equiv \pi$) we write the long-run relationship as

$$i \equiv r^* + \pi \tag{4}$$

With r^* constant, equation (4) implies a central result: *In the long run when all adjustments have occurred, an increase in inflation is reflected fully in nominal interest rates.* Nominal interest rates rise one for one with the increase in inflation. The reason we have such a strong inflation – nominal interest rate link is that in the long run the real interest rate is unaffected by purely monetary disturbances.

Of course, we already saw in Figure 17-3 that the constancy of the real interest rate holds only in long-run equilibrium. During the adjustment process the real interest rate does change, and hence changes in the nominal interest rate reflect both changes in real rates and changes in inflationary expectations.

Alternative Expectations Assumptions

The way in which expectations of inflation are formed will influence the adjustment path of the interest rate, real and nominal, to a change in money growth, though not the long-run implication of the Fisher equation. Depending on expectations, there are different paths for interest rates. The nominal rate may start out rising, or it may first decline and then later rise.

Figure 17-4 shows a possible pattern, which has received considerable attention in empirical work. In response to increased growth in nominal money, at time T_0 the real money stock grows and initially pushes down the nominal interest rate. Then, as output rises and with it inflation, the nominal interest rate is pushed up until, ultimately, after some cycling it has increased by the full increase in money growth and inflation.

The declining phase of the nominal interest rate path is called the *liquidity effect* to denote the impact of increased real balances (liquidity) on the interest rate. The phase of increasing nominal interest rates just after the bottom is reached is called the *income effect*. In this phase increasing nominal income pushes up interest rates by

---

[5] See Irving Fisher, *The Rate of Interest* (New York: Macmillan, 1907). Fisher taught at Yale and was an effective and sophisticated developer of the quantity theory of money. He had other interests, too; he was the inventor of the card index file still used for keeping addresses, and was a health food enthusiast who wrote several books on the subject. Fisher was an early, if long forgotten, discoverer of the Phillips curve. See the reprinted version of his 1926 article, "A Statistical Relation between Unemployment and Price Changes," under the heading "Lost and Found," *Journal of Political Economy,* March/April 1973, pp. 496–502.

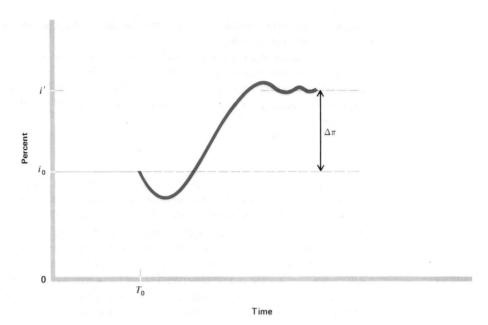

FIGURE 17-4

THE FISHER EFFECT. A sustained increase in money growth leads first to a reduction in nominal interest rates. Then, as output and inflation both increase, the interest rate gradually rises. In the long run it increases by the same amount as money growth and inflation.

increasing the quantity of real balances demanded. The long-run effect is called the *Fisher effect*, or *expectations effect*, to represent the impact of an increase in inflationary expectations, at a constant real interest rate, on the nominal interest rate. These names are suggestive of the three phases of adjustment as the economy is initially surprised by increased money growth and gradually adjusts to it.[6]

Real Balances and Inflation

In Figure 17-5 we present the demand for real balances as a function of the nominal interest rate. We now study the effect of a sustained change in the growth rate of money on the long-run equilibrium level of real balances.

For that purpose we simply combine two of our results. We saw that in the long

---

[6] For an extensive discussion see Milton Friedman and Anna Schwartz, *Monetary Trends in the United States and the United Kingdom* (Cambridge, Mass.: National Bureau of Economic Research, 1982), chap. 10.

run a sustained change in monetary growth changes the rate of inflation and the nominal interest rate in the same direction and by the same amount. A three-percentage-point increase in money growth raises the nominal interest rate by three percentage points in the long run. We therefore conclude from Figure 17-5 that *a sustained increase in money growth and in inflation ultimately leads to a reduction in the real money stock.*

Here is a very important result that might seem a bit puzzling: Increased *nominal* money growth reduces the long-run *real* money stock. Conversely, reduced nominal money growth raises the long-run real money stock. The reason is that higher inflation raises the nominal interest rate and hence raises the opportunity cost of holding money. Hence money holders will reduce the amount of real balances they choose to hold. This reduction in real balances is an important part of the adjustment process to an increase in money growth. It means that, *on average, in the period of adjustment to an increase in money growth, prices must rise faster than money.*

Figure 17-6, which shows the time paths of inflation and money growth, helps explain the adjustment of real balances. At time T_0 money growth rises from m_0 to m'. At the very beginning, as we saw in Figure 17-3, nothing happens to inflation. Inflation builds up gradually until, with overshooting and cycling, it settles down at the higher

FIGURE 17-5

THE DEMAND FOR REAL BALANCES. An increase in inflation and accordingly in the nominal interest rate will reduce the equilibrium stock of real balances. As the interest rate increases in long-run equilibrium from i_0 to i', real balances decline from E to E'.

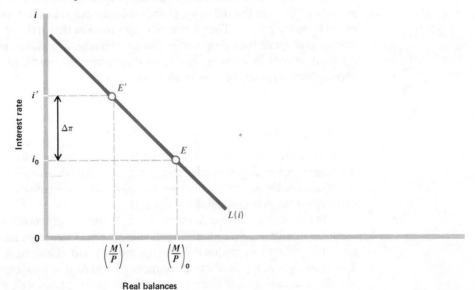

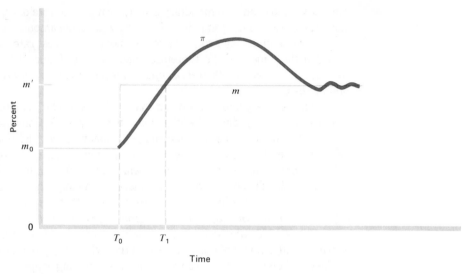

FIGURE 17-6

MONEY GROWTH AND INFLATION. An increase in money growth from m_0 to m' only gradually translates into increased inflation. In the adjustment process prices rise cumulatively more than money, as shown by the overshooting of inflation. This implies that real balances will be reduced in the long run.

level m'. In the phase up to time T_1 money growth exceeds inflation and real balances are rising. Then in the following phase real balances are falling as the inflation rate exceeds money growth. The diagram is drawn to show that in the phase of decline, real balances fall more than they rise in the initial phase. This is the phase in which the economy adjusts in a major way to increased money growth as rising output and expectations push up the rate of inflation.

Alternative Expectations Assumptions

Once again, the long-run reduction in real balances in response to higher money growth is a general result. A sustained increase in money growth *must* in the long run reduce the equilibrium level of real balances. The particulars of how expectations are formed determine the particular details of the path.

In the extreme case of full wage-price flexibility and rational expectations there would be an instant adjustment. The announcement of increased money growth would lead to an instant recognition that the opportunity cost of holding money is increased. The public would try to shift out of money because it is now expected to be more expensive to hold. But, of course, the economy in the aggregate cannot get rid of the existing nominal money stock. People trying to spend fast to get rid of their real balances would cause prices to jump, thereby reducing real balances to the lower desired level. Following the jump, prices and money would start rising at the long-run equilibrium rate, m', and the nominal interest rate would have increased to i'. All adjustments would occur literally in no time.

This case of rational expectations with full flexibility of wages and prices may sound implausible, but it serves as a useful benchmark for comparison. On one side there is a world with only gradual adjustment of inflation and inflationary expectations. In that world increased money growth takes time to find itself translated fully into inflation and interest rates, as described by Friedman in the quote above. In the other world all adjustments are instantaneous.

How exactly the real world adjustment takes place depends in good part on people's experience with inflation. In economies in which inflation is the number one issue — because of hyperinflation — it takes very little time for adjustment to occur, as we will see later in this chapter. But in the U.S. economy, in which inflation never became a complete way of life, the path of Figure 17-3 is a lot more likely.

$17\text{-}2$ EMPIRICAL EVIDENCE

We now turn to evidence on the links between money growth and inflation and between money growth and interest rates.

The Money-Inflation Link

To start we note the often-made statement that inflation is a monetary phenomenon. The claim that inflation is a monetary phenomenon means that sustained high rates of money growth produce high rates of inflation. Further, the statement that inflation is a monetary phenomenon means that high rates of inflation cannot long continue without high rates of money growth; this is an implication of the quantity theory of money and is the backbone of monetarist macroeconomics.

The quantity theory, as we saw in Chapter 10, relates the level of nominal income, PY, the money stock (M), and the velocity of money (V):

$$MV = PY \tag{5}$$

and it can also be written in terms of the percentage change over time of each of the four terms in (5):

$$m + v = \pi + y \tag{6a}$$

or, taking the inflation rate to the left, we obtain the central result:

$$\pi = m - y - v \tag{6b}$$

where m is money growth, v is the percentage change in velocity, π is the inflation rate, and y is the growth rate of output.

Equation (6b) can be used to account for the sources of inflation, that is, for what part is due to velocity changes or to money growth or to output growth. The monetarist position is that inflation is predominantly a monetary phenomenon, which implies that velocity changes are not significant. Consider now the link between inflation and money growth. Figure 17-7 shows annual $M2$ growth and the inflation rate of the GNP deflator. We see that the inflation rate and the growth rate of money have more or less moved together over the period since 1960 in the United States. But the relationship is *very* rough, especially in the first part of the 1970s. Equation (6b) suggests that the relation need not be exact because both output growth and velocity changes appear as additional factors. Specifically, if velocity is rising, other things equal, inflation will be higher than money growth, and if output is rising, inflation will be less than money growth.

Table 17-2 explores how well the link between money growth and inflation holds once we allow for growth in output. At the same time we shift to a longer time horizon, namely, averages over a decade. Here the relation is much more striking when we look

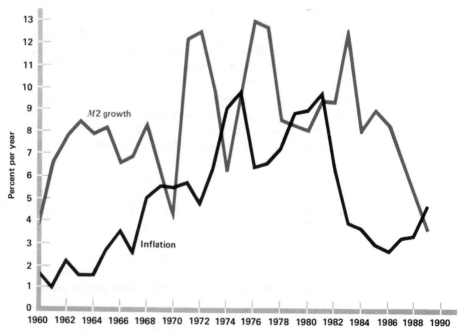

FIGURE 17-7

MONEY GROWTH AND INFLATION, 1960–1989. Inflation is depicted by the GNP deflator, and money growth by $M2$. (SOURCE: DRI/McGraw-Hill.)

TABLE 17-2
MONEY, INFLATION, AND GROWTH (percent per year)

	M1	M2	Inflation*	GNP growth
1960–1969	3.8	7.1	2.7	4.0
1970–1979	6.5	9.8	7.1	2.8
1980–1989	8.4	8.0	5.0	2.6
1960–1989	6.1	8.2	4.9	3.2

* Inflation rate of the deflator.
SOURCE: DRI/McGraw-Hill.

at $M2$: In Chapter 10 we saw that the demand for real money balances ($M2$) has an income elasticity of about unity. Thus the long-run relationship between money growth and inflation should be approximately 1:1 except for changes in velocity unrelated to income growth.[7]

We find that this relationship holds in fact quite tightly. For example, in the 1960s money growth less real growth was 3.1 percent and actual inflation averaged 2.7 percent, not far off the mark. Likewise in the 1970s equation ($6b$) predicts 7 percent whereas actual inflation was 7.1 percent. And the same close forecast is evident once more in the 1980s, with a predicted inflation rate of 5.2 percent versus an actual rate of 5.0 percent.

Note that the relation between money growth, adjusted for growth in real money demand because of income growth, and the rate of inflation holds well for $M2$, but does not hold in the same way for $M1$. This is a reflection, especially in the 1980s, of the instability of $M1$ money demand. To obtain a stable relationship between money growth and inflation we need a stable real money demand. That seems to be the case for $M2$, at least through the 1980s.

FLUCTUATIONS OF VELOCITY

We can now step back and ask why the year-to-year relationship is so poor while the 10-year average money-inflation relation works much better. One reason, of course, is that we have adjusted for output growth in Table 17-2. But the more important reason is fluctuations in velocity. Figure 17-8 shows the year-to-year percentage change in $M2$ velocity — the v term in equation ($6a$). It is clear that there is a lot of movement and that as a result there cannot plausibly be a tight link between money and inflation in the short run.

---

[7] In the text we assume an income elasticity of real money demand of unity. Let η be the income elasticity. Then the relation between inflation and money growth is: $\pi = m - \eta y$. Thus if the income elasticity is less than unity, growth works less to reduce inflation in the face of a given growth of nominal money.

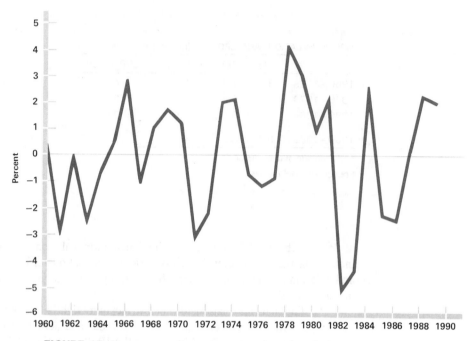

FIGURE 17-8

YEAR-TO-YEAR CHANGE IN VELOCITY, 1960–1989. Percent change in the velocity of *M2*. (SOURCE: DRI/McGraw-Hill.)

In the short run, as Figure 17-8 shows, velocity moves a lot. In the short run, variations in output and interest rates affect the velocity of *M2*. For example, because the short-run income elasticity is much less than unity, a sharp fall in real income will reduce velocity. A sharp rise in interest rates will raise velocity. In the short run, this happens because the own rate of interest on *M2* responds very slowly to market interest rates such as Treasury bill rates or CD rates. But even in the longer run a rise in interest rates raises velocity because at higher interest rates the rise in deposit rates does not fully match what happens to CD and Treasury bill rates.

The role of money growth in determining inflation is well summarized in a passage from the 1986 *Economic Report of the President* (p. 27):

> There is a well-established causal link between money growth and inflation over the long run that has been supported by empirical evidence for the United States as well as many other countries. The exact nature of this relationship varies with time and institutions, but the long-run relationship between appropriately defined money growth and inflation is difficult to refute . . .

With a lag of 1 to 2 years, most significant slowdowns in money growth are also reflected in subsequent movements in the inflation rate. There are, however, several periods, notably the period since 1982, when the inflation rate has diverged from the trend rate of money growth . . .

There are several reasons why the inflation rate may not track money growth closely in the short run. The short-run impact of a change in money growth may differ, depending on the state of inflation expectations. If, for example, an increase in money growth occurs when current inflation rates are already high or when monetary or fiscal actions are already perceived as inflationary, the rise in money growth is likely to show up in the inflation rate more quickly. The immediate effect of a given change in money growth also depends on whether it is perceived as permanent or as just a temporary deviation from a long-term policy path. An acceleration of money growth that is perceived to be a permanent move toward a more inflationary policy is likely to translate more immediately into a higher inflation rate.

Other causes of inflation in the short run will shift the aggregate supply or demand curves and cause changes in both output and inflation. In the 1970s, the major other cause of inflation was supply shocks, particularly the oil price increases of 1973–1974 and 1979–1980 that shifted the aggregate supply curve upward, causing more rapid inflation and recessions. In the 1980s declining oil and commodity prices and the strengthening of the dollar helped bring down inflation. In terms of our accounting framework above these changes are captured as short-run movements in velocity.

Figure 17-9 further focuses on medium-term velocity movements. To eliminate very short run fluctuations, we look at 5-year averages (i.e., the 1963 observation, for example, is the average for the years 1959–1963). The figure highlights how in the early 1980s, with interest rates extremely high, velocity was at a peak. By contrast, in the late 1980s, with lower interest rates, velocity had fallen to very low levels. But part of the decline in velocity since the early 1980s is, no doubt, a reflection of financial deregulation. The introduction of interest payments on a large range of deposits increased the attractiveness of assets included in $M2$, raised the real demand for these assets at each level of income, and hence brought about a reduction in velocity.

We observed above that the constancy of velocity across decades is somewhat of a surprise rather than something to be predicted as a long-run characteristic of velocity. The statement reflects the fact that financial deregulation presumably played an important part in making the averages come out right.

A warning is in order: There is no economic rule that says velocity in the long run tends to be constant; in fact, if the income elasticity of real money demand is not unity, velocity will change for that reason alone. With an income elasticity of, say 0.5, velocity would be rising with real income. The other critical factor is financial innovation. If innovation introduces substitutes for the particular monetary aggregate whose velocity we study, we expect a fall in real money demand and hence a rise in velocity. Conversely, if features of the aggregate (interest payments, liquidity) become more attractive, we expect a fall in velocity. Over long periods of time a constant velocity is therefore somewhat surprising.

box 17-1 **FEDERAL RESERVE MONETARISM**

Recent work at the Federal Reserve has revived a very strong form of monetarism. The research supports the view that changes in the inflation rate over time can be predicted on the basis of actual $M2$ money growth relative to the growth of potential output.[*]

The starting point is the distinction between a virtual price level, P^*, and the actual price level. The virtual price level is defined using the quantity theory as the level of prices that would prevail if output were at the full-employment level (that is, if $Y = Y^*$) and velocity of $M2$ were equal to its long-run average value, $V2 = 1.6527$:

$$P^* = 1.6527 \frac{M2}{Y^*} \tag{B1}$$

Define next as the *price gap* the percentage difference between the virtual price level and the actual price level at any point in time:

$$\text{Price gap} = \frac{P^* - P}{P} \tag{B2}$$

The empirical finding that supports the new monetarism is the following: Changes in the inflation rate over time are better predicted by the price gap than they are by unemployment or the GNP gap. Specifically, researchers at the Fed report the following relationship in annual data between changes:

$$\pi = \pi_{-1} + 0.18 \text{ price gap} \tag{B3}$$

Thus when the virtual price level exceeds the actual level, inflation accelerates; conversely, when the virtual price level is less than the actual price level, inflation decelerates. To make the idea concrete suppose we had a situation of 5 percent money growth and 2.5 percent growth in potential output. Inflation then will settle down in the long run at 2.5 percent. Now we raise the growth rate of money permanently to 10 percent. What is the path of inflation? The results reported by the Federal Reserve suggest that inflation follows the pattern shown in Figure 17-6.

The central feature of this approach is the reliance on a constant velocity of $M2$. We have seen earlier that the constancy of velocity is certainly influenced by financial innovations. Accordingly, it is not obvious whether the low levels of velocity in 1988–1989 are permanent or soon to be reversed to move velocity up to the historical average. That uncertainty about the behavior of velocity translates into uncertainty about whether this monetarist approach would over- or underpredict inflation developments. ∎

---

[*] See Jeffrey Hallman, Richard Porter, and David Small, "M2 Per Unit of Potential Output as an Anchor for the Price Level," Board of Governors of the Federal Reserve System, *Staff Papers*, no. 117, April 1989.

FIGURE 17-9
MEDIUM-TERM VELOCITY MOVEMENTS, 1963–1989. Five-year moving
average of the velocity of $M2$. (SOURCE: DRI/McGraw-Hill.)

HISTORICAL AND FOREIGN TRENDS

In fact, in the United States for the case of $M2$ the money-inflation link has not always
been as tight as in the past 3 decades. In problem 11 we provide data for decadal
averages in the period 1860 to 1989 and ask you to investigate the money-inflation link
for that period. It is clear that some periods, for example, the 1890s or the 1950s, are
not well captured by equation (6*b*). There are clearly some outliers, for example, the
1890s, when money growth (adjusted for real income growth) was high but prices were
falling. Thus, constancy of velocity, even in the very long run, is not a safe assumption.

It is also interesting to note that in international data there is no very close link
between inflation and money growth. Table 17-3 shows average growth rates for long
periods for several industrialized countries. While it is clearly true that countries with
higher money growth (adjusted for real income growth) also have higher inflation, once
more the relationship is not 1:1. Among the reasons for departures from a 1:1 relation
is, once again, the effect of financial deregulation on velocity, changes in interest rates

TABLE 17-3

MONEY AND INFLATION IN INTERNATIONAL PERSPECTIVE, 1973–1987 (percent per year)

	Money growth*	Output growth	Inflation
Canada†	11.0	2.6	5.0
United States	9.9	2.5	6.7
Japan	10.5	3.7	5.3
Germany	6.7	1.9	2.7
France†	9.1	1.7	8.1
Italy	16.9	3.6	15.3
United Kingdom	13.4	1.6	13.6

* $M1$ plus quasi-money.

† For 1979–1987 only, previous data being unavailable for broad monetary aggregates.

SOURCE: OECD, *Historical Statistics*, 1989.

that affect velocity, and income elasticities of money demand that are different from unity.[8]

Table 17-3 confirms that, other things equal, higher money growth implies higher rates of inflation. But beyond that prediction the relationship is quite loose. For Canada (just as in the United States) very high money growth in the 1980s has not led to high inflation because financial deregulation helped raise real money demand. In some countries, for example the United Kingdom and France, inflation exceeded the prediction of equation (6b). In others, notably Canada, the United States, and Japan, inflation fell short of what the equation of money growth adjusted for output growth would have predicted.

SUMMARY: IS INFLATION A MONETARY PHENOMENON?

The answer to the question of whether inflation is a monetary phenomenon *in the long run* is yes. No major inflation can take place without rapid money growth, and rapid money growth will cause rapid inflation. Further, any policy that determinedly keeps the growth rate of money low will lead eventually to a low rate of inflation.

But at the same time the long-run link between money growth and inflation is not precise. There are three reasons for that.

---

[8] Definitions of monetary aggregates differ substantially among countries. The term money plus quasi-money, or broad as opposed to narrow aggregates, describes the closest aggregate corresponding to $M2$ in the United States.

- Increases in output increase the demand for real balances and reduce the inflation rate corresponding to a given rate of money growth.

- Changes in interest rates change the alternative cost of holding money and hence affect the desired ratio of income to money.

- Financial institutions change, the definition of money changes, and the demand for money may shift over time.

The first two reasons explain short-run instability of the money-inflation relationship. The third factor, financial innovation, has become very important in the 1980s in most industrialized countries. The payment of competitive interest on a wide range of $M2$ items has raised the demand for $M2$ and hence reduced in the transition period inflation associated with a given money growth.

Inflation and Interest Rates

The Fisher equation asserts a positive link between nominal interest rates and inflation. With the real interest rate approximately constant in the long run, and with expectations of inflation adjusting to actual inflation, the nominal interest rate adjusts to the prevailing rate of inflation.

Figure 17-10 shows quarterly averages of the nominal interest rate on 3-month Treasury bills and the rate of inflation over the period for which the bills are outstanding. The *realized* real interest rate, then, is the difference between the nominal interest rate and the actual rate of inflation or, in symbols

$$r \equiv i - \pi \tag{7}$$

We do not have data on expected inflation and hence can reliably report only realized *actual* rates rather than expected real rates of interest. But in the short term, with inflation quite predictable there are no big discrepancies between expected and actual real rates.

Note from Figure 17-10 that in the 1970s there were several episodes of negative real rates, particularly in 1974–1975 when inflation increased sharply and exceeded the interest rate by a significant margin. By contrast, in the period since 1980 the real rate of interest has been *persistently* positive, and by a good margin. This is a quite new experience if we look back only a few years, but it certainly has precedents in U.S. experience in the past 100 years, during which real interest rates were significantly positive in several decades. Table 17-4 shows the real rate of return on Treasury bills or their equivalent over different periods. The shift toward positive real interest rates reflects the presence of full-employment budget deficits.

Clearly there have been decades with positive and even high real interest rates. But the average real rate has been low for well over half a century. Imagine an investor who put money into Treasury bills in the mid-1920s and reinvested (tax free) all the

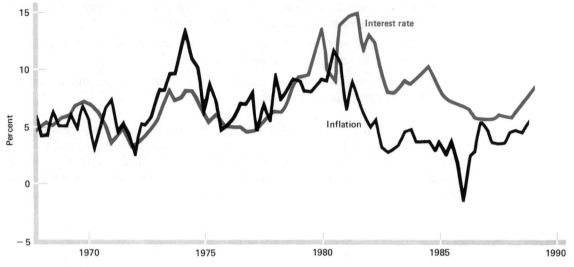

FIGURE 17-10

INFLATION AND NOMINAL INTEREST RATES, 1959–1988. The interest rate
is the yield on 3-month Treasury bills. The inflation rate is the rate of
inflation of the CPI over the following quarter. (SOURCE: DRI/McGraw-Hill.)

TABLE 17-4

THE REAL INTEREST RATE, UNITED STATES
(average annual percent)

Period	Rate	Period	Rate
1860–1869	1.5	1930–1939	3.6
1870–1879	9.8	1940–1949	−4.6
1880–1889	7.2	1950–1959	0.4
1890–1891	4.2	1960–1969	2.1
1900–1909	2.3	1970–1979	−0.2
1910–1919	−3.6	1980–1989	4.1
1920–1929	6.0		

SOURCE: Lawrence Summers, "The Non-Adjustment of
Nominal Interest Rates: A Study of the Fisher Effect," in J.
Tobin (ed.), *Macroeconomics, Prices and Quantities* (Washington, D.C.: The Brookings Institution, 1983), updated
by the authors.

TABLE 17-5

INTEREST RATES AND INFLATION, 1988*

Country	Interest rate, % per annum	Inflation rate
Australia	11.9	7.7
Canada	9.4	4.0
France	7.5	3.1
Germany	4.0	1.6
Mexico	66.3	51.7
Italy	11.3	4.8
Switzerland	2.2	2.0
United Kingdom	10.3	6.8
United States	7.6	4.4

* Interest rates are short-term market rates except as noted. The inflation
rate is the average from December to December.

SOURCE: International Financial Statistics, various issues.

earnings every time the bills matured. The real return over the period 1925–1989 would have been barely positive, just 0.5 percent.[9]

Table 17-5 shows international evidence on the interest rate–inflation link. The table conveys clearly the notion of a positive relationship between the *nominal* interest rate and inflation. The link is especially clear for countries like Mexico, Argentina, and Brazil, which had both exceptionally high inflation rates and also extremely high interest rates. If that were not the case, real interest rates would be spectacularly negative.

The evidence we have seen does tend to show that inflation and interest rates move together, within a country over time and across countries. But the evidence does not support a very strict Fisher equation. Year-to-year changes in inflation are not reflected one for one in nominal interest rates. The real rate does move, and hence the Fisher equation is primarily a guide to interest rates when inflationary disturbances are large relative to all other factors determining interest rates.

17-3 DEFICITS, MONEY GROWTH, AND THE INFLATION TAX

We have seen that a sustained increase in money growth ultimately translates into increased inflation. But that still leaves the question of what determines the money growth rate. A frequent argument is that money growth is the result of government budget deficits. In this section we examine several possible relationships between the budget deficit and inflation.

The Government's Budget Constraint

The Federal government as a whole, consisting of the Treasury plus the Fed, can finance its budget deficit in two ways. It can either sell bonds or "print money." By printing money we mean that the Fed increases the stock of high-powered money, typically through open market purchases that buy up part of the debt that the Treasury is selling.

The government budget constraint[10] (from Chapter 16) is

$$\text{Budget deficit} = \text{sales of bonds} + \text{increase in money base} \tag{8}$$

There are two types of possible links between budget deficits and money growth. First,

---

[9] See Roger G. Ibbotson and Rex A. Sinquefield, *Stocks, Bonds, Bills and Inflation: The Past and the Future* (Charlottesville, Va.: Financial Analysts Research Foundation, 1982), updated by the authors.

[10] We show here the government's *flow,* or year-by-year budget constraint. In addition, the government faces a stock budget constraint that says the present value of all the government's future outlays has to be equal to the present value of all its future receipts. Technically, the stock budget constraint can be obtained by integrating the year-by-year flow constraints.

in the short run, an increase in the deficit caused by expansionary fiscal policy will tend to raise nominal and real interest rates. If the Fed is targeting interest rates in any way, it may increase the growth rate of money in an attempt to keep the interest rate from rising. Second, the government may deliberately be increasing the stock of money as a means of obtaining government revenue over the long term.

In the remainder of this section we examine first the short-run links between money and deficits that come from central bank policy and then the use of money printing as a means of financing government budgets. Finally, we link the short- and long-run aspects.

The Fed's Dilemma

The Fed is said to monetize deficits whenever it purchases a part of the debt sold by the Treasury to finance the deficit. In the United States the monetary authorities enjoy independence from the Treasury and therefore can choose whether to monetize or not.[11]

The Fed typically faces a dilemma in deciding whether to monetize a deficit. If it does not finance the deficit, the fiscal expansion, not being accompanied by accommodating monetary policy, raises interest rates and thus crowds out private expenditure. There is accordingly a temptation for the Fed to prevent crowding out by buying securities, thereby increasing the money supply and hence allowing an expansion in income without a rise in interest rates.

But such a policy of accommodation or monetization runs a risk. If the monetization leads to excessive money growth, then the policy ultimately will feed inflation. Eventually higher aggregate demand will raise the real interest rate; crowding out will occur in any event. Thus the policy fails in its objective of preventing crowding out, but it does have a cost in terms of higher inflation.

Much discussion of Fed policy centers on this question: Should the Fed control monetary aggregates or interest rates? In the context of an increase in budget deficits the answer must often be that the Fed should *not* accommodate; that is, it should let the interest rate increase and keep the growth rate of money constant. If the economy is close to full employment, an accommodating policy would simply feed inflation. An unwise fiscal expansion would be made even more potent by fueling it with a monetary expansion.

There are other circumstances, though, in which the risks of igniting inflation are much more remote. Certainly in a deep recession there is no reason to shy away from accommodating a fiscal expansion with higher money growth.

In any particular case, the Fed has to judge whether to pursue on accommodating monetary policy or whether, rather, to stay with an unchanged monetary target or even offset a fiscal expansion by a tightening of monetary policy. To make that decision,

---

[11] In other countries the central bank may enjoy much less independence; for instance, it might be under the control of the Treasury, and then it may simply be ordered to finance part or all of the deficit by creating high-powered money.

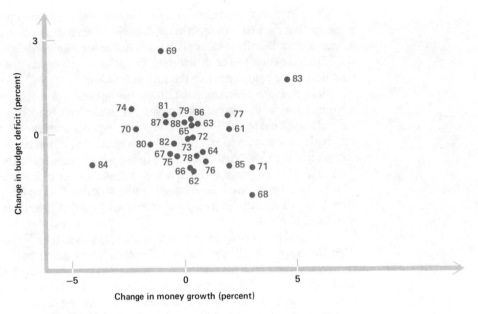

FIGURE 17-11
BUDGET DEFICITS AND MONEY ACCOMMODATION, 1960–1988. The
diagram shows the change in the cyclically adjusted budget expressed
as a fraction of GNP and the change in the growth rate of high-powered
money. (SOURCE: DRI/McGraw-Hill.)

the Fed must decide what relative weight it attaches to inflation and to unemployment
whenever expansionary policy threatens to cause inflation.

The U.S. Evidence

A number of studies have tried to determine how the Fed reacts to deficits in practice.
The question here is whether there is a systematic link between monetary policy and
the budget. Specifically, does the Fed allow money growth to rise when the budget
deficit increases?

Figure 17-11 shows a scatter diagram of the change in the growth rate of the
monetary base[12] and the change in the cyclically adjusted budget (expressed as a
percent of GNP). There is no very clear pattern of accommodation. Nor does a diagram
relating money growth to the *level* of the deficit show a closer relationship.

---

[12] The monetary base is the relevant aggregate because, as noted in Chap. 16, the deficit can be financed
either by the sale of bonds or by the creation of high-powered money (or monetary base).

The empirical evidence on this question thus remains open. There is some evidence that the Fed does react in the direction of accommodation, monetizing deficits at least in part. But the evidence is not conclusive because it is difficult to know whether the Fed is reacting to the deficit itself or rather to other macroeconomic variables, specifically unemployment and the rate of inflation.[13]

The question of accommodation and the monetary-fiscal policy mix was certainly a major issue in the discussion leading up to the Gramm-Rudman-Hollings deficit control legislation of 1985. Fiscal and monetary policy combined in the early 1980s to take real interest rates to exceptionally high levels. As a result the dollar remained very strong, hurting U.S. trade and hurting debtors both here and in the developing countries. The Fed was seen to be in a very unusual position: holding out on monetary accommodation, it raised the economic and political cost of an excessive fiscal expansion. It thus made the economy experience a "lopsided" recovery in which imports increased and exports fell.

Federal Reserve Chairman Paul Volcker, first, and then his successor, Chairman Alan Greenspan, explicitly held out the promise of easier money to continue the recovery if the Congress and the administration would cut the budget deficit. They increasingly insisted that at full employment the Federal Reserve could no longer help keep interest rates low; accommodation of continuing high demand growth would simply mean inflation, not high real growth. Starting in 1988 interest rates were pushed up gradually to cool an overheating economy.

By 1988–1989 opinion was divided on what was suitable monetary policy. Monetarists argued that the Fed had allowed too high money growth for too long — an annual growth rate of 7 percent since 1983, far above the 2.5 percent trend growth. And, in the face of a sharp deceleration of money growth in 1989 to only 3.6 percent they were quick to argue that the Fed followed the usual pattern of too much expansion and then a dramatic slamming on the brakes. Others saw the high growth of money in the 1980s as fully appropriate, given the initial recession and financial deregulation, and they also felt that at full employment much slower money growth was altogether appropriate. Of course, the resulting increase in interest rates and the slower growth of output would make budget problems worse, but it was not for monetary policy to push the economy any further. Fiscal policy had to take over to avoid crowding out.

The Inflation Tax

In discussing monetization of deficits in the United States we paid no attention to the fact that financing government spending through the creation of high-powered money

---

[13] See Alan Blinder, "Issues in the Coordination of Monetary and Fiscal Policy," Federal Reserve Bank of Kansas City, *Monetary Policy Issues in the 1980s*, 1983; and "On the Monetization of Deficits," in Laurence Meyer, *The Economic Consequences of Government Deficits* (Kluwer-Hijhoff, 1983); Gerald Dwyer, "Federal Deficits, Interest Rates and Monetary Policy," *Journal of Money, Credit and Banking*, November 1985; and Douglas Jones, "Deficits and Money Growth in the United States: 1872–1983," *Journal of Monetary Economics*, November 1985.

is an alternative to explicit taxation. Governments can — and some do — obtain significant amounts of resources year after year by printing money, that is, by increasing
high-powered money. This source of revenue is sometimes known as *seigniorage,*
which is the government's ability to raise revenue through its right to create money.

When the government finances a deficit by creating money, it in effect keeps
printing money, period after period, which it uses to pay for the goods and services it
buys. This money is absorbed by the public. But why would the public choose to
increase its holdings of nominal money balances period after period?

The only reason, real income growth aside, for the public's adding to its holdings
of nominal money balances would be to offset the effects of inflation. Assuming there is
no real income growth, in the long run the public will hold a constant level of *real*
balances. But if prices are rising, the purchasing power of a given stock of *nominal
balances* is falling. To maintain the real value of its money balances constant, the public
has to be adding to its stock of nominal balances at the rate that will exactly offset the
effects of inflation.

When the public is adding to its stock of nominal balances in order to offset the
effects of inflation on holdings of real balances, it is using part of its income to increase
holdings of nominal money. For instance, suppose someone has an income of $20,000
(nominal) this year. Over the course of the year, inflation reduces the value of that
person's real balances. He or she therefore has to add, say, $300, to a bank account just
to maintain the real value of his or her money holdings constant. That $300 is not
available for spending. The person seems to be saving $300 in the form of money
holdings, but in fact in real terms is not increasing his or her wealth by adding the $300
to nominal balances. All that person is doing is preventing his or her wealth from falling
as a result of inflation.

*Inflation acts just like a tax because people are forced to spend less than their
income and pay the difference to the government in exchange for extra money.*[14] The
government thus can spend more resources, and the public less, just as if the government had raised taxes to finance extra spending. When the government finances its
deficit by issuing money, which the public adds to its holdings of nominal balances to
maintain the real value of money balances constant, we say the government is financing
itself through the inflation tax.[15]

How much revenue can the government collect through the inflation tax? Table
17-6 shows data for Latin American countries in the 1983–1988 period. Clearly the
amounts are very significant. The amount of revenue produced is the product of the tax

---

[14] There is one complication in this analysis. As noted above, the amount that is received by the government
is the increase in the stock of *high-powered* money, because the Fed is buying Treasury debt with high-powered money. But the public is increasing its holdings of both bank deposits and currency, and thus part of the
increase in the public's holdings of money does not go to the government to finance the deficit. This
complication in no way changes the essence of the analysis.

[15] Inflation is often referred to as the "cruelest tax." This does not refer to the above analysis of the inflation
tax, but rather to the redistribution of wealth and income associated with unanticipated inflation, which is
discussed in Chap. 15.

TABLE 17-6
INFLATION AND INFLATION TAX, 1983–1988 (percent)

Country	AVERAGE, 1983–1988		Peak-year tax/GDP
	Tax/GDP*	Inflation	
Argentina	3.7	359	5.2
Bolivia	3.5	1,797	7.2
Brazil	3.5	341	4.3
Chile	0.9	21	1.1
Colombia	1.9	22	2.0
Mexico	2.6	87	3.5
Peru	4.7	382	4.5

* Inflation tax.

SOURCE: M. Selowsky, "Preconditions Necessary for the Recovery of Latin America's Growth," The World Bank, June 1989 (mimeographed).

rate (the inflation rate) and the object of taxation (the real monetary base). When real output is constant, inflation tax revenue is given by

$$\text{Inflation tax revenue} = \text{inflation rate} \times \text{real money base} \tag{9}$$

The amount of revenue the government can raise through the inflation tax is shown by the curve AA in Figure 17-12. When the inflation rate is zero, the government gets no revenue from inflation.[16] As the inflation rate rises, the amount of inflation tax received by the government increases. But, of course, as the inflation rate rises, people reduce their real holdings of the money base—because the base is becoming increasingly costly to hold. Individuals hold less currency, and banks hold as little excess reserves as possible. Eventually the real monetary base falls so much that the total amount of inflation tax revenue received by the government falls. That starts to happen at point C and signifies that there is a maximum amount of revenue the government can raise through the inflation tax: the maximum is shown as amount IR^* in the figure. There is a corresponding inflation rate, denoted π^*: the steady-state inflation rate at which the inflation tax is at its maximum.

We can now look back to Figure 17-3 to study the long-run effects of money-financed deficits. We start at point E. Now the government cuts taxes and finances the deficit by printing money. We assume that the deficit is equal to amount IR' in Figure 17-12, and thus it can be financed entirely through the inflation tax. Now money

---

[16] When the economy is growing, the government obtains some revenue from seigniorage even if there is no inflation. That is because when the demand for real monetary base is growing, the government can create some base without producing inflation.

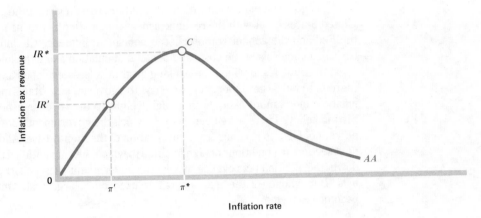

FIGURE 17-12

THE INFLATION TAX. At a zero inflation rate, the inflation tax revenue is
zero. As the inflation rate rises, the government receives more revenue
from inflation, up to point *C*, at which the tax revenue reaches its
maximum of *IR**. The corresponding inflation rate is π^*. Beyond point *C*
the demand for real balances is falling so much as the inflation rate
increases that total tax revenues decline.

growth has been permanently increased, and inflation in the long run moves to the rate
π', corresponding to the inflation tax revenue *IR'*.

In the long run the economy reached point *E'*. In that equilibrium expectations
have fully adjusted to the inflation, and output is at the full-employment level. Inflation
equals the growth rate of money,[17] and the inflation rate depends on the size of the
deficit. The larger the deficit, the higher the inflation rate. Figure 17-12 raises the
question of what happens if the government tries to finance a deficit larger than *IR** by
printing money. That cannot be done. We take up that issue in Section 17-4 on
hyperinflation.

Inflation Tax Revenue

How much revenue can governments in practice obtain from the printing of money?
The amount is quite small in developed economies in which the real money base is small
relative to the size of the economy. For instance, in the United States the base is
slightly above 5 percent of GNP even with the current low rates of inflation. At a 10
percent inflation rate the government would, from equation (9), be collecting about 0.5
percent of GNP in inflation tax revenue. That is not a trivial amount, but it is not a major

---

[17] Except for an adjustment that takes account of growth in real output.

source of government revenue either.[18] It is hard to believe that the inflation rate in the United States is set with the revenue aspects of inflation as the main criterion. Rather the Fed and the administration choose policies to influence the inflation rate on the basis of an analysis of the costs and benefits of inflation along the lines of Chapter 16.

In countries in which the banking system is less developed and in which people therefore hold large amounts of currency, the government obtains more revenue from inflation and is more likely to give high weight to the revenue aspects of inflation in setting policy. There have been cases in which the government obtains as much as 10 percent of GNP in revenue from the creation of the money base. And, as we see in the next section, in conditions of high inflation in which the conventional tax system breaks down, the inflation tax revenue may be the government's last resort to keep paying its bills. But whenever the inflation tax is used on a large scale, inflation invariably becomes extreme.

Unpleasant Monetarist Arithmetic

In a well-known article, Thomas Sargent and Neil Wallace of the University of Minnesota have pointed to an important implication of the government budget constraint, equation (8).[19] Specifically, *debt-financing of a deficit may in the long run be more inflationary than money financing.*

The argument turns on the fact that when a government finances a current deficit through debt, it incurs the obligation to pay interest on that debt in future. Recall the distinction in Chapter 16 between the primary, noninterest deficit and the total budget deficit:

$$\text{Total deficit} \equiv \text{primary deficit} + \text{interest payments} \tag{10}$$

Combining equation (10) with equation (8), we obtain

$$\text{Bond sales} + \text{money base creation} \equiv \text{primary deficit} + \text{interest payments} \tag{11}$$

Consider now the choice between debt financing (bond sales) and money financing of a given deficit. If money financing is used, interest payments will be no larger in the future than they are now. But if the government turns to debt financing, it will have a larger deficit in the future. That in turn will have to be financed through either money finance or debt finance.

---

[18] A measure of seigniorage different from the value of the printing of high-powered money is sometimes used in the United States. It is the value of the interest payments the Fed earns on its portfolio. Since the Fed's securities were obtained through open market purchases that increased the high-powered money stock, this is a measure of how much interest the Treasury saves (since the Fed pays its profits to the Treasury) as a result of *previous* Fed money printing. The printing of high-powered money is a measure of the current command over resources obtained as a result of money printing this period.

[19] "Some Unpleasant Monetarist Arithmetic," Federal Reserve Bank of Minneapolis *Quarterly Review,* Fall 1981.

Now imagine the following circumstances. The government has a given national debt today. The primary deficits today and in the future are, by assumption, given at some constant level; for example, the primary deficit may be zero. The government is considering whether to finance its current deficit by borrowing or by printing money. If it finances by borrowing, it intends to stop borrowing and switch to money financing in 5 years.

Under which alternative will the inflation rate ultimately be higher? The answer can be worked out from the following considerations. If the government starts money financing today, it will have to create money at a rate that finances the interest payments on the *existing* national debt. But if it waits 5 years to start money financing, it will have to create money at a rate that finances the interest payments on the national debt that will exist 5 years from now. Because interest on the debt will have accumulated in the meantime, the debt will be larger 5 years from now and, therefore, so will the inflation rate.

This example shows that, because of the accumulation of interest, short-run debt financing that ends in money financing will generally ultimately be more inflationary than immediate money financing of a given deficit. The arithmetic is unpleasant for monetarists because it suggests that budget deficits may have more to do with the eventual inflation rate than with the current growth rate of money.

The main question raised by this example is whether the government will be eventually forced into money financing of a given deficit or whether it can continue debt financing forever. That depends on the relationship between the growth rate of output and the real interest rate. As we saw in Chapter 16, if the real interest rate is above the growth rate of output, and given a zero primary deficit, debt financing cannot continue forever because the debt becomes a larger and larger part of GNP and interest payments keep mounting up. At some point, in that case, the government will have to turn to money financing. The turn to money financing will both provide some revenue, and, if the debt is nominal, perhaps reduce the value of the outstanding debt through unanticipated inflation.

If the real interest rate is below the growth rate of output, with a zero primary deficit, then the government can continue debt financing without a resulting rise in the debt-GNP ratio. In that case debt finance is viable for the long term, and the hard choice posed by the Sargent-Wallace example can be avoided. Note also though that the tight link examined by Sargent and Wallace takes future primary deficits as given. If the government is willing to raise taxes at some future date to pay higher interest bills, there is no necessary link between current deficits and future money growth.

The Sargent-Wallace analysis does make clear why permanent deficits cause concern. If the national debt is growing relative to GNP, then ultimately the government will have to raise taxes or raise the inflation rate to meet its debt obligations. That is the long-run threat that leads people to worry about deficits. But the long run in this case may be decades away.

There is a further important point. The Sargent-Wallace concern is about *primary* deficits; if the total deficit is constant as a percentage of GNP, then ultimately the debt-GNP ratio will stabilize, provided the economy is growing at all. For instance, a statement that the deficit in the United States would be 5 percent of GNP forever would not mean that the debt would explode as a percentage of GNP. Rather if the deficit were financed through debt, the debt-GNP ratio would eventually reach a steady state.[20] The explanation is that when the deficit is measured to *include* interest payments, a statement that the deficit will be constant forever means that behind the scenes the primary deficit or surplus is being adjusted to ensure that interest payments are being made without the debt-GNP ratio's exploding.

NOMINAL INTEREST AND THE BUDGET DEFICIT

Nominal interest rates rise with the inflation rate and increase the measured budget deficit. To make this point we repeat equation (10):

$$\text{Total deficit} \equiv \text{primary deficit} + \text{interest payments} \qquad (10)$$

Suppose now that the government debt is at the relatively low level of just 20 percent of GNP. With an interest rate of, say 10 percent, total interest payments are 2 percent of GNP (10 percent interest rate × 20 percent of GNP debt). Let the inflation rate rise by 90 percent, with the real interest rate remaining unchanged, so that the nominal interest rate goes up to 100 percent. Then total interest payments amount to 20 percent of GNP (100 percent interest rate × 20 percent of GNP debt), and the budget deficit measured as in (10) rises by no less than 18 percent of GNP. The data in this example are essentially those of Mexico in 1986, where the budget deficit during the inflation looked very large, despite the noninterest part of the budget's being in surplus.

The problem here is that the conventional way of measuring the deficit includes *nominal* interest on the debt. This can give a distorted impression of the size of the deficit because in fact the government is paying the high interest to offset the effect of inflation in reducing the value of its outstanding debt. We should recognize that at the same time as the government has to pay high interest, it also receives revenue from the decline in the value of its outstanding debt, owing to inflation. And indeed, in the 1970s many economists began to calculate inflation-corrected budget deficits that took account of the government's gain from inflation because the value of its debt fell. The inflation-corrected budget deficit is calculated taking into account the effect of inflation in reducing the outstanding value of the government's debt.

We return to the previous example for an illustrative calculation. Suppose the real interest rate is 5 percent and the primary deficit is zero. Then, with a debt-GNP

---

[20] This is a fairly technical but important point. If the total deficit is kept at a constant ratio to GNP, say 5 percent, that means that behind the scenes increasing interest payments are being met by higher taxes or lower government spending. Suppose that the debt-GNP ratio is denoted b, that GNP is growing at a real rate y, and that the total deficit as a percentage of GNP is denoted td. In a steady-state economy, debt is being issued at just the rate that keeps the debt-GNP ratio constant. That means that in steady state $td = y \cdot b$. Then the steady-state debt-GNP ratio is just equal to td/y. For instance, if the deficit is 5 percent of GNP forever, and the growth rate of GNP is 4 percent, then the debt-GNP ratio will be 1.25, or 125 percent in steady state. At that point interest payments are a constant proportion of GNP.

ratio of 20 percent, the budget deficit at a zero inflation rate is only 1 percent of GNP. When the inflation rate hits 95 percent, with a nominal interest rate of 100 percent, the calculated nominal deficit becomes 20 percent of GNP. But the inflation-corrected deficit is still only 1 percent of GNP as long as the real interest rate remains at 5 percent.

Although the principle of the calculation of inflation-corrected deficits is clear, there is some controversy about whether they should be used. The question that should be asked is whether the private sector wants to maintain the value of the debt-to-GNP ratio. If so, it will willingly finance the apparently increased nominal deficit by purchases of bonds — people need to step up bond purchases precisely because the real value of their existing bonds is being reduced through inflation. If on the other hand the inflation rate is high as a result of unexpectedly high printing of money, then the inflation-corrected deficit does not give a good measure of the extent to which people are willing to continue financing the existing deficit at the existing real interest rate by purchasing bonds.

17-4 HYPERINFLATION

Large budget deficits are inevitably part of the extreme inflations of 50 to 100 or even 500 percent per year that took place in the mid-1980s in Latin America and Israel. They are also part of the even more extreme cases of *hyperinflation*. Although there is no precise definition of the rate of inflation that deserves the star ranking of hyper- rather than high inflation, a working definition takes 1,000 percent per annum as the rate that marks a hyperinflation. When inflation becomes very high, inflation is reckoned in terms of *monthly* rates, not inflation per year. The power of compound interest is apparent when we look at the correspondence between monthly inflation rates and the same rate annualized. For example, a 20 percent inflation per month corresponds to an annualized rate of 791 percent. Table 17-7 shows recent extreme inflation experiences.

TABLE 17-7
RECENT HIGH-INFLATION EXPERIENCES (percent per year)

	1984	1985	1986	1987	1988	1989*
Argentina	627	672	90	131	343	1,470
Bolivia	1,231	11,750	276	15	16	15
Brazil	65	58	86	132	682	820
Israel	374	305	48	20	16	19
Mexico	68	58	86	132	114	18
Nicaragua	35	220	681	911	10,205	23,710
Peru	110	163	78	86	825	3,564

* Latest 12-month data available.

It seems difficult to believe that countries can function for any length of time with extremely high inflation rates of several hundred percent or more. In fact, they do not function well, and sooner or later they will stabilize a high inflation simply because the economy turns chaotic. Thus, Israel successfully stabilized in 1985 as did Bolivia (see Box 17-2). But other countries, such as Argentina, Brazil, or Peru, and obviously Nicaragua, are in the midst of explosive inflation.

In a hyperinflationary economy, inflation is so pervasive and such a problem that it completely dominates daily economic life. People spend significant amounts of resources minimizing the inflationary damage. They have to shop often so as to get to the stores before the prices go up; their main concern in saving or investing is how to protect themselves against inflation; they reduce holdings of real balances to a remarkable extent to avoid the inflation tax, but have to compensate by going to the bank more often — daily or hourly instead of weekly, for example, to get currency.

The classic hyperinflations have taken place in the aftermath of wars. The most famous of all — though not the most rapid — was the German hyperinflation of 1922 – 1923. The average inflation rate during the hyperinflation was 322 percent *per month.* The highest rate of inflation was in October 1923, just before the end of the hyperinflation, when prices rose by over 29,000 percent. In dollars that means that something that cost $1 at the beginning of the month would have cost $290 at the end of the month. The most rapid hyperinflation was that in Hungary at the end of World War II: The *average* rate of inflation from August 1945 to July 1946 was 19,800 percent per month, and the maximum monthly rate was 41.9 quadrillion percent.[21]

Keynes, in a masterful description of the hyperinflation process in Austria after World War II, tells of how people would order two beers at a time because they grew stale at a rate slower than that at which the price was rising.[22] This and similar stories appear in all hyperinflations. They include the woman who carried her (almost worthless) currency in a basket and found that when she set it down for a moment, the basket was stolen but the money left behind. And, it was said, it was cheaper to take a taxi than a bus because in the taxi you pay at the end of the ride and in the bus at the beginning.

Hyperinflationary economies are typically marked by widespread indexing, more to the foreign exchange rate than to the price level. That is because it becomes difficult to keep measuring prices on a current basis when they change so fast. So prices might be specified in terms of dollars, and the actual amount of the local currency (marks in the German case) that has to be paid in each transaction is calculated from the dollar

---

[21] At least, so we think. The price level rose 41.9×10^{15} percent in July 1946. Data are from Phillip Cagan, "The Monetary Dynamics of Hyperinflation," in Milton Friedman (ed.), *Studies in the Quantity Theory of Money* (Chicago: University of Chicago Press, 1956). This classic paper contains data on seven hyperinflations.

[22] John Maynard Keynes, *A Tract on Monetary Reform* (New York: Macmillan, 1923). This remains one of the most readable accounts of inflation. See also Thomas William Guttmann and Patricia Meehan, *The Great Inflation* (Gordon and Cremonsi, 1975), and Leland Yeager and associates, *Experiences with Stopping Inflation* (Washington, D.C.: American Enterprise Institute, 1981).

price and the exchange rate. Wages are paid very often — at the end of the German hyperinflation, several times a day.

Deficits and Hyperinflation

The hyperinflationary economies all suffered from large budget deficits and from rapid money printing. In several cases the origin of the budget deficit was wartime spending, which generated large national debts and also destroyed the tax-gathering apparatus of the country.

But there is a two-way interaction between budget deficits and inflation. Large budget deficits can lead to rapid inflation by causing governments to print money to finance the deficit. In turn, high inflation increases the measured deficit. There are two main mechanisms whereby inflation increases budget deficits.

THE TAX-COLLECTION SYSTEM

As the inflation rate rises, the real revenue raised from taxation falls. The reason is that there are lags in both the calculation and payment of taxes. Suppose, to take an extreme example, that people pay taxes on April 15 on the income they earned the previous year. Consider someone who earned $50,000 last year and has a tax bill of $10,000 due on April 15. If prices have in the meantime gone up by a factor of 10, as they might in hyperinflation, the real value of the taxes is only one-tenth of what it should be. The budget deficit can rapidly get out of hand. This impact of inflation on the real value of tax revenues is called the Tanzi-Olivera effect, so named after two economists who independently documented it.[23]

In principle the tax system can be indexed to adjust for the inflation. But that is difficult, especially for business taxation, and in any event even indexing lags behind. For example, if the monthly rate of inflation is 20 percent (equivalent to an annual rate of nearly 800 percent), then even if the amount that has to be paid is fixed according to the most recent price index and it takes a month to collect taxes, inflation causes the government to lose 20 percent of the value of its taxes.

The Inflation Tax and Accelerating Hyperinflation

Rates of money growth are also very high during hyperinflations, of the same order of magnitude as the inflation rate.[24] The high rates of money growth originate in attempts to finance government spending.

---

[23] Vito Tanzi of the IMF and Julio Olivera of the University of Buenos Aires.

[24] On average, though, the growth rate of money is below the inflation rate. That is because people are reducing their holdings of real balances during hyperinflation: If M/P is falling, then P has on average to be growing faster than M.

box 17-2 **BOLIVIAN HYPERINFLATION AND STABILIZATION**

In the 1920s, Europe experienced hyperinflation, and the experience is reviewed in an important paper by Sargent.* Latin America followed in the 1980s. In 1985 Bolivia experienced a full-fledged hyperinflation, as can be seen in Figure 1. At the peak, in mid-1985, inflation was, at an annual rate, 35,000 percent! There were three main reasons for the hyperinflation. First, like other Latin American countries, Bolivia had overborrowed in the 1970s. When, in the early 1980s, interest rates increased in world markets, debts could no longer be serviced by taking out new loans for the purpose of paying the interest on the old loans. But the country was not in a position to service easily the very large external debt. The attempt to do so strained the budget and led to high rates of money creation. Second, commodity prices, especially of tin, fell sharply. For Bolivia this meant a large fall in real income and in revenues for the government. Third, the substantial political instability led to capital flight. The combination of factors set off an inflationary spiral that forced increasing depreciation of the currency and opened an ever wider gap between government outlays and revenues. Tax collection sharply dropped by more than half, as can be seen in Table 1.

FIGURE 1

BOLIVIAN HYPERINFLATION, 1981–1988. Percent per month. (SOURCE: Banco Central de Bolivia.)

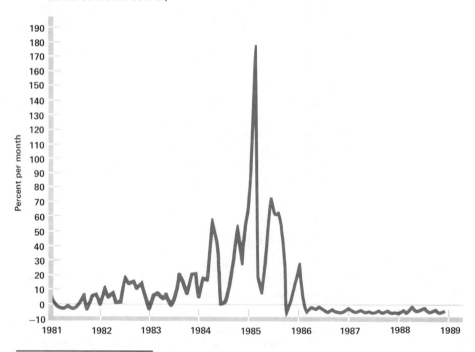

* See Thomas Sargent, "The End of Four Big Inflations," in R. Hall (ed.), *Inflation* (Chicago: University of Chicago Press, 1982).

TABLE 1
THE BOLIVIAN HYPERINFLATION

	1980–1983	1984	1985	1986
Budget deficit*	11.9	26.5	10.8	3.0
Tax collection*	6.7	2.3	3.1	6.6
Inflation†	123	1,282	11,750	276

* Percent of GDP.

† Percent per year.

SOURCE: World Bank and Banco Central de Bolivia.

By 1984–1985 the government was attempting to finance nearly 25 percent of GNP with money creation, but, of course, by this time the demand for real balances had fallen to negligible levels because of the hyperinflation. It took ever-larger rates of inflation to finance the ever-growing deficit.

In August–September 1985 a new government came into power and, in a short time, imposed a drastic stabilization plan. By stopping external debt service and raising taxes the drain in the budget was brought under control; money creation was reduced from the extreme rates of the past years; and the exchange rate was stabilized. Within half a year the inflation rate had come down to less than 50 percent. Moreover, because the decrease in budget deficit was maintained and reinforced, the gain in disinflation continued; and by 1989, inflation rates had fallen to less than 10 percent per year.

The Bolivian stabilization is a good example of how a sharp turn toward fiscal deficit can stop a major inflation.† But there should be no illusion about the costs. As a result of austerity (and of poor export prices) Bolivian per capita income in 1989 was 35 percent less than it had been 10 years earlier, at its peak. Inflation had been brought under control, but confidence was not sufficient to bring back growth on a significant scale.

While Bolivia succeeded in controlling inflation, in several other Latin American countries inflation was exploding. An important question for these countries was whether wage-price controls (called *heterodox* programs) would be a helpful supplement to the *orthodox* medicine of fiscal austerity. The stabilization attempts, demonstrated several times in 1985–1989 in Argentina and Brazil, were long on the former and short on the latter.‡   ■

---

† See Juan A. Morales, "Inflation Stabilization in Bolivia," in M. Bruno et al. (eds.), *Inflation Stabilization* (Cambridge, Mass.: MIT Press, 1988), and J. Sachs, "The Bolivian Hyperinflation and Stabilization," *American Economic Review*, May 1987.

‡ See E. Helpman and L. Leiderman, "Stabilization in High Inflation Countries: Analytical Foundations of Recent Experience," *Carnegie Rochester Conference Series on Public Policy*, no. 28 (1988); M. Kiguel and N. Liviatan, "Inflationary Rigidities and Orthodox Stabilization Policies: Lessons from Latin America," *The World Bank Economic Review*, no. 3 (1988); M. Blejer and N. Liviatan, "Fighting Hyperinflation," *IMF Staff Papers*, September 1987; as well as Bruno et al. (eds.), *Inflation Stabilization*.

But as the inflation progresses and the tax collection system breaks down, the government reaches a point at which it tries to raise more revenue through money printing than the maximum amount, IR^*, that it can (see Figure 17-12). It can succeed in raising more than IR^* *temporarily* by printing money even faster than people expected. That increased money growth causes the inflation rate to increase. And as the government continues to try to spend more than IR^*, it continues driving up the inflation rate. The amount of real money base that people hold becomes smaller and smaller, as they try to flee the inflation tax, and the government prints even more rapidly to try to finance its expenditure. In the end the process will break down.

Stopping Hyperinflations

All hyperinflations come to an end. The dislocation of the economy becomes too great for the public to bear, and the government finds a way of reforming its budget process. Often a new money is introduced, and the tax system is reformed. Typically, too, the exchange rate of the new money is pegged to that of a foreign currency in order to provide an anchor for prices and expectations. Frequently, there are unsuccessful attempts at stabilization before the final success.

The presence of so many destabilizing factors in inflation, particularly the collapse of the tax system as the inflation proceeds, together with an economy that is extremely dislocated by inflation, raises a fascinating possibility. A coordinated attack on inflation may stop the inflation with relatively little unemployment cost. This approach was used in Argentina and Israel in 1985 and in Brazil in 1986, when the governments froze wages and prices. That stopped the inflation at a single blow. They also fixed their exchange rates, and there were significant changes in fiscal policy in order to put the budget closer to long-run balances. In each case there was little increase in unemployment. Despite the early encouraging signs, the ultimate success of these stabilization programs remains to be established.

One more important feature of the stabilizations should be brought out. *Money growth rates following stabilization are very high.* Why? Because as people expect less inflation, nominal interest rates decline, and the demand for real balances rises. With the demand for real balances increasing, the government can create more money without creating inflation. Thus at the beginning of a successful stabilization there may be a bonus for the government: It can temporarily finance part of the deficit through the printing of money, without renewing inflation. But it certainly cannot do so for very long periods without reigniting inflation.

17-5 SUMMARY

1. A sustained monetary expansion typically expands output in the short run. In the long run higher money growth is translated fully into inflation. Real interest rates and output return to the full-employment level. Only under rational expectations

and with full wage and price flexibility does a monetary expansion translate instantly into an increased rate of inflation with no impact on output.

2. A sustained change in money growth ultimately raises the nominal interest rate by the same amount. This positive association between inflation and nominal interest rates is called the Fisher effect.

3. In the short run, increased money growth will lead to lower nominal interest rates if expectations adjust slowly. This is called the liquidity effect.

4. A sustained monetary expansion ultimately raises nominal interest rates and hence reduces the demand for real balances. That means that prices must on average rise faster than money in the transition to the new long-run equilibrium.

5. In the U.S. economy, broad trends in money growth and in inflation do coincide. Money growth does affect inflation, but the effects occur with a lag that is not very precise. In the short term, inflation is affected by other than monetary shocks, for example, fiscal policy changes and supply shocks.

6. Nominal interest rates tend to reflect the rate of inflation in the U.S. economy. But the real interest rate is definitely not constant. In the early 1980s the real rate increased sharply compared with the levels of the 1970s and long-term average rates.

7. When fiscal policy turns expansionary, the Fed has to decide whether to monetize the deficit, printing money in order to prevent a rise in interest rates and crowding out; to keep the growth rate of money constant; or even to tighten monetary policy. If the government monetizes the deficit, it runs the risk of increasing the inflation rate. The evidence on deficit monetization in the United States remains ambiguous.

8. Inflation is a tax on real balances. To keep constant the purchasing power of holdings of money in the face of rising prices, a person has to add to nominal balances. In this fashion resources are transferred from money holders to money issuers, specifically the government.

9. A decision to finance a deficit through bond sales today may mean a higher inflation rate in the future if the government eventually has to finance the deficit through money printing. That is because the interest payments on the debt accumulate to increase future deficits, given a fixed primary deficit. This tradeoff exists when the interest rate exceeds the growth rate of output.

10. Hyperinflations have generally taken place in the aftermaths of wars. Large deficits are typical in hyperinflations. Governments can use the inflation tax to finance deficits to a limited extent, but if too large a deficit has to be financed, inflation explodes.

11. There is a two-way interaction between inflation and budget deficits. Higher inflation rates raise the deficit by reducing the real value of tax collection. Higher nominal interest rates raise the measured deficit by increasing the value of nominal interest payments in the budget. The inflation-corrected deficit adjusts for this latter effect.

12. Money growth rates are very high following a successful inflation stabilization, as people increase their holdings of real balances.

KEY TERMS

Fisher effect
Liquidity effect
Expectations effect
Monetization of deficits

Hyperinflation
Inflation tax
Seigniorage
Inflation-corrected deficit

PROBLEMS

1. (a) Show graphically the effects of a reduction in the growth rate of money on output and inflation.
  (b) Show also how the real interest rate adjusts over time. Be specific about the expectations assumption you are using.

2. In the above example show how the nominal interest rate adjusts to lower inflation.

3. We stated in the text that under rational expectations and with full price and wage flexibility, the inflation rate rises immediately to its new steady-state level when the growth rate of money increases. We also stated that real balance holdings decline when the expected inflation rate rises. How can the level of real balances fall under rational expectations if the inflation rate is equal to the growth rate of money? (*Hint:* With prices fully flexible, they can change all at once when new information becomes available.)

4. (a) Study the growth rate of money and the inflation rate in the last 5 years in the tables on the inside covers of the book. How closely are they linked?
  (b) Calculate the real rate of interest on Treasury bills during the last 2 years and compare with the historical average.
  (c) What is the explanation for the high levels of real rates in the early 1980s relative to the historical average?

5. Suppose the ratio of money base to GNP is 10 percent. The government is considering raising the inflation rate from the current 0 rate to 10 percent per annum and believes it will obtain an increase in government revenue of 1 percent of GNP by doing so. Explain why that calculation overestimates the inflation tax the government will receive at a 10 percent inflation rate.

6. During 1981–1990 the U.S. government has added massively to the national debt.
  (a) Explain why you might worry that this is inflationary.
  (b) Explain whether you actually worry that the high deficits of the early 1980s will lead to high inflation later.

7. At the height of the German hyperinflation, the government was covering only 1 percent of its spending with taxes.
  (a) What happened to the rest?
  (b) How could the German government possibly finance the remaining 99 percent of its spending? Refer to Figure 17-12.

8. (a) If the debt-GNP ratio is 30 percent, the nominal interest rate is 12 percent, the inflation rate is 7 percent, and the total budget deficit is 4 percent of GNP, calculate the inflation-adjusted deficit.
  (b) Suppose you were to discover in an inflationary economy that the inflation-corrected budget was in surplus. Explain why in that case the government might be able to sustain

a low inflation rate if it could only find a way of getting the rate down to start with.

(c) Then explain why governments in the mid-1980s used wage and price controls in trying to stop high inflations.

9. Explain how, following the end of hyperinflation, it was possible for the nominal money stock in Germany to increase by a factor of nearly 20 without restarting the inflation.

10. Why do budget deficits create such alarm? Distinguish the short from the long run in developing your answer.

11. The accompanying table shows growth rates of *M2*, inflation, and real growth for decadal averages since 1870. Discuss the extent to which money growth adjusted for output growth helps explain inflation.

	Money growth	Output growth	Inflation
1870–1879	2.3%	5.5%	−3.0%
1880–1889	6.6	1.4	−1.1
1890–1899	5.0	3.7	−2.2
1900–1909	7.3	4.0	1.9
1910–1919	9.8	3.5	6.6
1920–1929	3.3	4.2	2.2
1930–1939	0.8	1.5	−1.9
1940–1949	11.5	3.4	5.6
1950–1959	3.8	3.3	2.5
1960–1969	7.1	4.0	2.7
1970–1979	9.8	2.8	7.1
1980–1989	8.0	2.6	5.4

NOTE: Money refers to *M2* and inflation to the GNP deflator.

SOURCE: Until 1959, Milton Friedman and Anna Schwartz, *Monetary Trends in the United States and the United Kingdom* (Chicago: University of Chicago Press, 1982); thereafter, DRI/McGraw-Hill.

MACROECONOMICS: THE INTERACTION OF EVENTS AND IDEAS

The ideas of economists and political philosophers, both when they are right and when they are wrong, are more powerful than is commonly understood. Indeed, the world is ruled by little else.

John Maynard Keynes, 1936

As an advice-giving profession we are in way over our heads.

Robert E. Lucas, Jr., 1980[1]

Gone are attempts to smooth fluctuations in aggregate demand through frequent changes in government expenditure and tax policies and efforts to find a balanced mix of fiscal and monetary actions.

Economic Report of the President, 1989

Macroeconomics, more than microeconomics, seems to be subject to changing fashions and beliefs. In 1971, 35 years after the appearance of the *General Theory*, President Nixon announced, "I am a Keynesian." Since then, monetarism, rational expectations, supply-side economics, and Reaganomics have all, at one time or another, been confidently prescribed as the solution for the economy's problems. And during that same period, none of the different approaches delivered what it promised.

---

[1] The first quote is from Keynes's, *The General Theory of Employment, Interest and Money* (London: Macmillan, 1936), p. 383, and the second is from Lucas's, "Rules, Discretion, and the Role of the Economic Adviser," in his *Studies in Business Cycle Theory* (Cambridge, Mass.: MIT Press, 1981).

In this chapter we describe the major currents of thought in macroeconomics since the 1960s, when the monetarist challenge to mainstream Keynesian economics first gathered strength. Because policy and ideas are intertwined, in discussing the main macroeconomic currents we refer also to economic events of the time. We show how theories influence policies, and how the results of policies influence views about theory.

The success of Keynesian economics was itself the result of the great depression, from which it showed the way out. Support for Keynesian economics or the New Economics (described in Chapter 12) strengthened after the successful 1964 tax cut. Support weakened as inflation worsened in the second half of the 1960s. Monetarism promised to deal with inflation — but the 1969 – 1971 failure of slower money growth to stem inflation weakened support for monetarism. In the early 1980s supply-side economists promised that disinflation was possible without unemployment. The 1981 – 1982 recession punctured that hope. But supply-side economics made a partial comeback because the recovery from that deep recession was both rapid and pro-longed.

Any student should wonder about a field in which opinions and policy prescriptions change so often. And you should worry, too, about the differences in views among macroeconomists at a given time. For instance, what should you conclude about budget deficits when one group of economists claims deficits have no real effects and another group blames deficits for high real interest rates and the large trade deficit?

There certainly are disagreements among economists. But it is also true that those disagreements, and the distinguishing features of different points of view, are systematically exaggerated by the media. Macroeconomic controversies are always in the newspapers because macroeconomics concerns some of the most important issues of daily life — whether jobs are hard or easy to find, whether prices are rising slowly or fast, whether living standards will rise fast or hardly at all. The disagreements are systematically exaggerated because disagreements are news.

Behind the rapidly changing macroeconomic fashions of the media is a more balanced macroeconomic analysis that addresses current economic problems while at the same time weighing carefully the evidence that leads to changes — mostly small, but sometimes, as when the aggregate supply side was remodeled to include expected inflation, large — in macroeconomic theories.

We start the chapter by providing the necessary background of economic events from the 1960s to the end of the 1980s. In Section 18-2 we describe monetarism. In Section 18-3 we extend the discussion of the rational expectations equilibrium approach, which was introduced in Chapters 7 and 14. We go on to supply-side economics and Reaganomics, and then to the New Keynesianism of the 1980s, ending by discussing how to make sense of the different views and approaches. Much of the material in this chapter has already appeared earlier in the book, for our aim throughout has been to use the best available theories to analyze the problems of the real world rather than to present the views of a particular school. This chapter can be viewed as primarily drawing together and explaining the origins of many theories and views that are by now part of a balanced approach to modern macroeconomics — but also as setting out some views that have achieved prominence but that are more controversial.

TABLE 18-1
COMPARATIVE ECONOMIC PERFORMANCE (percent)

	Growth rate of real GNP	Unemployment rate	Inflation (CPI)	MONEY GROWTH	
				M1	M2
1961–1968	4.9	4.8	2.2	4.3	8.9
1969–1982	2.3	6.4	7.5	6.4	9.7
1982–1988	4.0	7.2	3.5	8.8	7.8

SOURCE: *Economic Report of the President*, 1989, and *Economic Indicators.*

18-1 THE ECONOMY: 1969–1989

The 1960s was a period of generally rising inflation and falling unemployment. It was also a period of rapid growth of real GNP. Table 18-1 presents data on comparative economic performances in the 1960s, in the period 1969–1982, and in the period 1982–1988. Growth in the 1960s was substantially higher, and inflation and unemployment were lower, than in subsequent years. In the period since 1982 growth was significantly higher and inflation significantly lower than in the 1970s. Indeed, the period since 1982 has been more like the 1960s than the 1970s not only in combining high growth with low inflation but also in combining declining unemployment with rising inflation.

Figure 18-1 shows the unemployment and inflation rates over the period since 1969. Figure 18-2 shows the full-employment surplus (as a percentage of potential GNP) and the growth rate of M1 for the period. There were four recessions (shaded) during this period, in contrast with none during the previous 8 years.[2] The 1973–1975 and 1981–1982 recessions were each in turn the deepest since World War II.

The period opened with restrictive monetary and fiscal policies designed to reduce the inflation rate below the 5 percent level it had reached at the end of 1968. The restrictive policies were kept in place for more than 2 years. But when the inflation rate proved resistant to conventional aggregate demand policies, the Nixon administration turned in 1971 to wage and price controls, aiming to bring the inflation rate down rapidly through direct measures.

From 1971 to 1973 the economy boomed, with the encouragement of expansionary monetary and fiscal policies. During 1973 food and raw materials prices rose sharply, and then at the end of 1973, the first oil price shock hit the economy. The rapid rises in food and raw materials — particularly oil — prices constituted the first serious supply shock to hit the economy in the post–World War II period. Policy makers and

---

[2] Some economists argue that the period 1980–1982 should count as one long recession rather than two recessions interrupted by a recovery. In support of this argument, note that the decline in unemployment following the 1980 recession was very small.

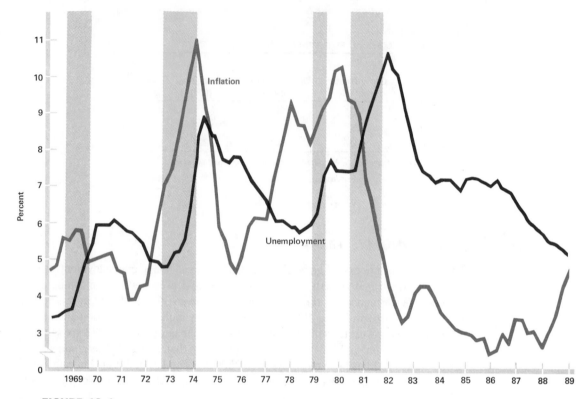

FIGURE 18-1
INFLATION AND UNEMPLOYMENT, 1969–1989. The inflation rate is for the
GNP deflator, current quarter relative to the same quarter a year before.
Shaded bars mark periods of recession. (SOURCE: DRI/McGraw-Hill.)

economists were perplexed about how to respond to the shock. The high inflation rate
seemed to call for restrictive monetary and fiscal policy, but the supply shock was
reducing output; so perhaps policy should have been expansionary or at least accommodating of the shock. In any event, monetary policy became restrictive to fight the
inflation. As late as the end of 1974, with the recession well under way, the administration was still considering a tax *increase* to fight inflation. By early 1975, though, fiscal
policy became expansionary; consumers were given a rebate on their 1974 taxes, and
the investment tax credit was increased.

The 1973–1975 recession reduced the inflation rate. Consumer prices rose less
than 5 percent during 1976. From the relatively low-inflation–high-unemployment
situation at the beginning of 1975, the economy grew rapidly. The growth rate of GNP
was 4.7 percent or more per year in each year from 1976 to 1978. This was a strong
recovery from the recession, as can be seen in the rapid fall of the unemployment rate

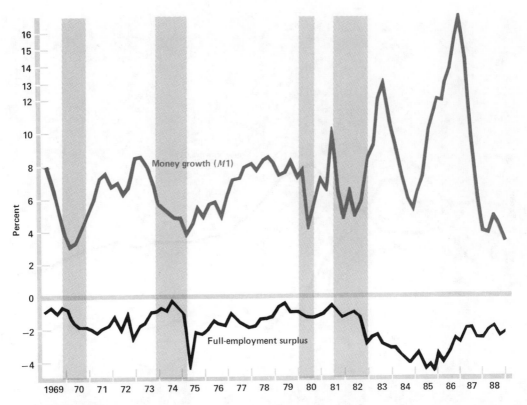

FIGURE 18-2
MONEY GROWTH (*M*1) AND THE FULL-EMPLOYMENT SURPLUS, 1969–1989.
The full-employment surplus is shown as a percentage of potential
GNP. Shaded bars mark periods of recession. (SOURCE: DRI/McGraw-Hill.)

from 1975 to 1979 in Figure 18-1. The only fly in the ointment — and it was no small fly — was the rising inflation rate. In 1979 a second oil price shock caused the inflation rate to rise sharply again.

In response to the high inflation, the Fed in October 1979 adopted its new monetary policy, described as intended to concentrate on keeping the growth rate of money under control and on target. Exceptionally high inflation at the beginning of 1980 led the Fed and the administration to panic and impose credit controls in March 1980, probably after a recession had already begun (see Box 12-1).

The Reagan administration took office in 1981 with a commitment to sharply reducing taxes and the size of the government, while also building up national defense. The administration's major fiscal move was the phased-in 3-year Kemp-Roth tax cut. Government revenues as a percentage of GNP fell, but spending did not. The result was a large increase in the full-employment deficit, which can be seen in Figure 18-2.

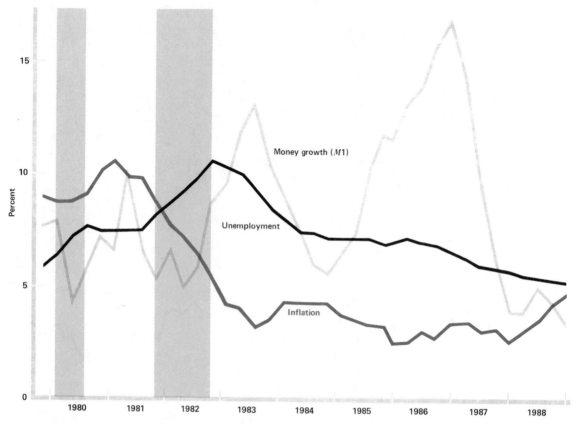

FIGURE 18-3

INFLATION, UNEMPLOYMENT, AND MONEY GROWTH, 1979–1989. The
inflation rate is for the GNP deflator, money growth is for $M1$, and each
is for the given quarter over the same quarter a year before. Shaded
bars mark periods of recession. (SOURCE: DRI/McGraw-Hill.)

With the Fed still attempting to control money growth to reduce inflation, a second
recession began in the middle of 1981 and continued to the end of 1982. Measured by
the unemployment it created, this was the worst recession since the great depression.
In the fall of 1982, the Fed in effect abandoned its money-targeting procedures,
permitting very rapid growth in money to try to fight the deepening recession and high
interest rates (see Figure 18-3).

The economy began to recover at the end of 1982. Real GNP growth was
exceptionally rapid during 1983 and into 1984. The rapid decline in unemployment
from 1983 to 1985 seen in Figure 18-1 reflects that GNP growth. Inflation continued
to fall despite the falling unemployment—a result of the continuing high *level* of

unemployment. Growth slowed substantially in 1985 and 1986, as can be seen in Figure 18-3 in which the unemployment rate was essentially unchanged over the period, but growth then resumed, reaching nearly 4 percent in 1988, in part benefiting from the favorable supply shock in 1986, when the price of oil declined sharply (see Figure 13-13). The unemployment rate fell throughout 1988, briefly touching 4.9 percent in early 1989, a rate well below estimates of the natural rate that had been common only 3 years before. By the end of 1988 the U.S. economy was, by any reasonable definition, back at full employment.

The first half of the 1980s was marked by exceptionally high real interest rates and current account deficits; the data are in Table 18-2, which also presents an index of the dollar exchange rate. The dollar depreciated sharply from the beginning of 1985, and real interest rates fell somewhat, but the current account deficit stayed high. The cause of both the high real interest rate and the trade deficit became the subject of dispute. One view, consistent with the *IS-LM* model and the extended version that includes foreign trade (developed in Chapter 6) is that both high interest rates and a current account deficit are implied by the policy mix of exceptionally easy fiscal policy and tight monetary policy. It has also been argued, though, that the fiscal deficit has nothing to do with either the real interest rate or the current account deficit. On the current account deficit the argument goes as follows: The U.S. economy became a more attractive place in which to invest; foreigners therefore bought U.S. assets,

TABLE 18-2
BUDGET AND CURRENT ACCOUNT DEFICITS AND REAL INTEREST AND EXCHANGE RATES

	Actual deficit	Full-employment deficit	Current-account deficit	Real interest rate	Real exchange rate
1980	2.2	0.5	−0.0	2.4	89.5
1981	2.1	0.2	−0.2	6.0	100.6
1982	4.6	1.0	0.3	6.2	109.9
1983	5.2	1.8	1.4	5.8	112.7
1984	4.5	2.6	2.8	8.4	118.2
1985	4.9	3.3	2.9	6.5	121.3
1986	4.8	3.4	3.3	4.1	107.6
1987	3.5	2.4	3.4	4.7	97.8
1988	2.9	2.3	2.8	4.7	92.4

NOTE:

1. Actual and current account deficits are percentages of actual GNP; the full-employment deficit is a percentage of potential GNP as calculated by DRI/McGraw-Hill.

2. Actual budget deficit of the federal government (on national income accounts basis) and current account budget deficit are from *Economic Report of the President*, 1989, and *Economic Indicators*.

3. Real interest rate is nominal rate on 3-year Treasury bonds minus expected inflation calculated as average inflation rate of GNP deflator for last year, current year, and next year (assuming 3.9 percent for 1989).

4. Dollar real exchange rate is an index (1980–1982 = 100) and is from *World Financial Markets*, Morgan Guaranty.

raising the value of the dollar, which made importing cheaper and exporting more difficult (because foreigners had to pay more for U.S. goods), thereby creating a current account deficit.

The poor economic performance of the 1969–1982 period and the improvements since raise interesting and important questions. Why was performance so disappointing in the 1970s? Are supply shocks mainly to blame? If so, are there better ways of dealing with them? Does part of the blame go to excessively expansionary monetary policy? The low growth of the 1970s raises the essential issue of whether there is any way of ensuring that the economy keeps growing at rates close to those of the 1960s. Is the improved performance of the 1980s sustainable into the last decade of this century?

In searching for answers to these questions, macroeconomics developed and moved away from the New Economics of the 1960s. The emphasis in 1969 was on monetarism, which promised control of inflation by controlling the money supply.

18-2 MONETARISM

Milton Friedman and monetarism are almost synonymous. Monetarism — which we have already discussed — appears, however, in many shades and covers quite a spectrum: from a hard monetarism, beyond the Friedman variety, to eclectic Keynesianism. In that spectrum one would include the late Karl Brunner of the University of Rochester, Allan Meltzer and Bennett McCallum of Carnegie-Mellon, Thomas Mayer of the University of California at Davis, Phillip Cagan of Columbia University, David Laidler and Michael Parkin of the University of Western Ontario, and William Poole of Brown University, to name only some of the most prominent. Monetarism is not confined to academic economists. Indeed, the Federal Reserve Bank of St. Louis has long been a haven of a monetarist perspective on macroeconomics, as have congressional committees, and Beryl Sprinkel, chairman of President Reagan's Council of Economic Advisers from 1984 to 1989, was also a monetarist.

If monetarism admits of some diversity, it nevertheless comes down to the proposition that money is extremely important for macroeconomics, that money is more important than other things such as fiscal policy, and, in some variants, that money is virtually all that matters.

We define monetarism by describing Friedman's view, but we should warn you that in so doing we overemphasize Friedman's role in developing and sustaining monetarism. Friedman's views on macroeconomics have been laid out in a series of scholarly articles, books, and popular writings.[3] Outstanding among his publications is

---

[3] In addition to the books referred to earlier see *The Optimum Quantity of Money* (Chicago: Aldine, 1969); *A Program for Monetary Stability* (New York: Fordham University Press, 1959), and, coauthored with Anna J. Schwartz, *Monetary Trends in the United States and the United Kingdom* (Chicago: University of Chicago Press, 1982). His journalistic writings are reprinted in *There's No Such Thing as a Free Lunch* (La Salle, Ill.: Open Court Publishing, 1975), and *Bright Promises, Dismal Performance* (New York: Harcourt Brace Jovanovich, 1983).

A Monetary History of the United States, 1867–1960, written jointly with Anna J. Schwartz of the National Bureau of Economic Research. We have already noted the influential monetary explanation of the great depression in *Monetary History.* More generally, *Monetary History* is an absorbing book that skillfully relates the behavior of the economy to the behavior of the stock of money.

What are the main features of monetarism?[4]

Emphasis on the Stock of Money

Monetarism emphasizes the importance of the behavior of the money stock in determining (1) the rate of inflation in the long run and (2) the behavior of real GNP in the short run. Friedman has said:[5]

> I regard the description of our position as "money is all that matters for changes in *nominal* income and for *short-run* changes in real income" as an exaggeration but one that gives the right flavor of our conclusions.

The view that the behavior of the money stock is crucial for determining the rate of inflation in the long run is consistent with the analysis of Chapter 14, as we noted there. The view that the behavior of the money stock — by which Friedman usually means the *growth rate* of the money stock — is of primary importance in determining the behavior of nominal and real GNP in the short run is not one we have accepted, nor one to which the evidence of the 1980s has been kind (see Chapter 11). Our treatment has given emphasis to *both* monetary and fiscal variables in determining the short-run behavior of nominal and real GNP. But there is no doubt that monetary variables play an important role in determining nominal and real GNP in the short run.

An important part of monetarism is the insistence that instability in monetary growth is mirrored in variability in economic activity. Monetarists point to a number of economic expansions and recessions as being caused by monetary accelerations and decelerations. These would certainly include the 1966 slowdown of economic activity in response to the credit crunch, the failure of the 1968 tax surcharge due to its being swamped by expansionary monetary policy, and the 1970, 1980, and 1981–1982 recessions.

Friedman's view of the primary importance of money is based in part on careful historical studies, in which he and Anna Schwartz were able to relate the booms and recessions of U.S. economic history to the behavior of the money stock. In general, it

---

[4] For recent contributions, see James Dorn and Anna J. Schwartz (eds.), *The Search for Stable Money* (Chicago: University of Chicago Press, 1988).

[5] "A Theoretical Framework for Monetary Analysis," *Journal of Political Economy,* March/April 1970, p. 217.

appeared that increases of the growth rate of money produced booms and inflations, and decreases in money stock produced recessions and sometimes deflations.[6]

Long and Variable Lags

Monetarism has emphasized that the effects of changes in the growth rate of money on the subsequent behavior of GNP occur with long and variable lags. On average, it takes a long time for a change in the growth rate of money to affect GNP, and so the lag is long. In addition, the time it takes for this change to affect GNP varies from one historical episode to another — the lags are variable. These arguments are based on empirical and not theoretical evidence. Friedman estimates the lags may be as short as 6 months and as long as 2 years.

The Monetary Rule

Combining the preceding arguments, Friedman argues against the use of active monetary policy. He suggests that because the behavior of the money stock is of critical importance for the behavior of real and nominal GNP, and because money operates with a long and variable lag, monetary policy should not be used to "fine-tune" the economy. The active use of monetary policy might actually destabilize the economy, because an action taken in 1990, say, might affect the economy at any of various future dates, such as in 1991 or 1992. By 1992, the action taken in 1990 might be inappropriate for the stabilization of GNP. Besides, there is no certainty that the policy will take effect in 1992 rather than 1991.[7]

Thus monetarists argue that although monetary policy has powerful effects on GNP, it should not be actively used lest it destabilize the economy. Accordingly, their view is that the money supply should be kept growing at a constant rate, to minimize the potential damage that inappropriate policy can cause.[8]

Interest Rates versus Monetary Targets

In the *IS-LM* model, changes in the money stock affect the economy primarily by changing interest rates, which, in turn, affect aggregate demand and thus GNP. Since the Fed can control the level of interest rates, and since interest rates provide a guide

---

[6] Strong supporting evidence from the post–World War II period for the view that money matters is provided by Christina Romer and David Romer, "Does Monetary Policy Matter? A New Test in the Spirit of Friedman and Schwartz," *NBER Macroeconomics Annual*, 1989.

[7] For a concise statement, see Milton Friedman, "The Case for a Monetary Rule," *Newsweek,* Feb. 7, 1972, reprinted in *Bright Promises, Dismal Performance*, pp. 225–227. See, too, his article, "The Role of Monetary Policy," *American Economic Review*, March 1968.

[8] In Chap. 12 we discussed the case for a monetary rule that arises from the problem of dynamic inconsistency. This argument was not typically made by monetarists; rather, it is a later argument more associated with the rational expectations equilibrium approach to macroeconomics.

to the effects of monetary policy on the economy, it seems perfectly sensible for the Fed to carry out monetary policy by controlling interest rates. Through the 1950s and most of the 1960s, the Fed did carry out its monetary policy by attempting to set the level of interest rates.

Friedman and monetarism presented two serious criticisms of the Fed procedure of attempting to set interest rates as the basis for the conduct of monetary policy. The first is that the behavior of nominal interest rates is not a good guide to the direction — whether expansionary or contractionary — of monetary policy. The *real* interest rate (i.e., the nominal interest rate minus the expected rate of inflation) is the rate relevant for determining the level of investment. But a high nominal interest rate, together with a high expected rate of inflation, means a low real rate of interest. Thus monetary policy might be quite expansionary in its effects on investment spending even when nominal interest rates are high.

The second criticism is that the Fed's attempts to control nominal interest rates might be destabilizing. Suppose the Fed decides that monetary policy should be expansionary and that the interest rate should be lowered. To achieve these goals, the Fed buys bonds in the open market, increasing the money supply. The expansionary monetary policy itself tends to raise the inflation rate. It thus tends to raise the nominal interest rate as investors adjust their expectation of inflation in response to the behavior of the actual inflation rate. But then the Fed would have to engage in a further open market purchase in an attempt to keep the nominal interest rate low . . . and so on. The end result could be that an attempt to keep nominal interest rates low leads to increasing inflation. For both these reasons, Friedman argues, the Fed should not pay attention to the behavior of nominal interest rates in the conduct of monetary policy, and should, rather, keep the money supply growing at a constant rate.

Each of these arguments on the dangers of conducting monetary policy by reference to nominal interests rates is important. It is indeed correct that real, and not nominal, interest rates provide the appropriate measures of the effects of monetary policy on aggregate demand. It is also true that the Fed could, by attempting to keep nominal interest rates low forever, destabilize the economy. However, once the latter danger has been pointed out, the probability that the Fed will destabilize the economy by operating with reference to interest rates is reduced. The use of interest rates as a guide to the direction of monetary policy does not mean that the Fed has to attempt to keep the interest rate fixed forever at some level. Instead, it may aim each month or quarter for an interest rate target that it regards as appropriate for the current and predicted economic situation.

The strength of the monetarist case for concentrating on the behavior of the money stock in the conduct of monetary policy depends on the stability of the demand-for-money function. As discussed in Chapter 10, there has been substantial instability in the money demand function in the United States. The problem of shifts in the demand-for-money function became particularly acute in the early 1980s, following the change in Federal Reserve monetary policy in October 1979. The policy change was intended to place more emphasis on keeping the growth rate of money under control. But with a shifting demand function it became unclear what the right rate of growth of money to keep the economy on track was.

At the end of 1982 the Fed announced that it was temporarily abandoning its $M1$ money growth rate targets until the shifts in the demand function for money were completed. While the Fed does continue to publish money supply targets, the widespread belief — as noted in Chapter 11 — is that the Fed is not paying them a great deal of attention.[9] Nonetheless, the Fed does continue to search for useful quantitative guides to monetary policy, and during 1988 argued that there was a stable demand function for $M2$ (see Box 17-1). It remains to be seen whether that demand function will remain stable if the Fed does begin to pursue $M2$ money targets more closely than it has in the 1980s.

Indeed, the low inflation of the 1980s was achieved with relatively high growth rates of money, as can be seen from Table 18-1 and Figure 18-3. Money growth was especially high during 1983 and 1985. During the 1980s, velocity, which had seemed to be steadily rising, began to fall, and lower inflation rates were thus achieved despite high money growth.

Because of shifts in the demand for money, the behavior of the money stock is not a perfect guide to the conduct of monetary policy. Neither is the behavior of nominal interest rates. However, the behavior of *both* the nominal money stock *and* nominal interest rates provides some information about the direction in which monetary policy is pushing the economy, imperfect as each measure is. Accordingly, the Fed should, and does, pay attention to the behavior of both interest rates and the quantity of money in the conduct of its monetary policy.[10]

The Importance of Fiscal Policy

Friedman has frequently, if tongue in cheek, said that fiscal policy is very important. Although we noted earlier that he argues fiscal policy itself is not important for the behavior of GNP, he does contend that it is of vital importance in setting the size of government and the role of government in the economy. Friedman, like former President Reagan, is an opponent of big government. He has made the interesting argument that government spending increases to match the revenues available. The government will spend the full tax collection — and some more. Accordingly, he is in favor of tax cuts as a way of reducing government spending. This argument was probably influential in the Reagan administration's 1981 decision to pass tax cuts well before it had figured out how to cut government spending.

Friedman stands out in arguing that fiscal policy does not have strong effects on

---

[9] The monetary lessons of the 1980s are discussed by Benjamin M. Friedman, a well-known critic of monetarism, and William Poole, in *Journal of Economic Perspectives*, Summer 1988. Friedman argues that the events of the 1980s discredited monetarist monetary policy prescriptions; Poole concludes his article by expressing doubts about sticking closely to monetary targets during a disinflationary process, but argues that a monetary rule would still work well once low inflation was established.

[10] This argument is demonstrated in Benjamin M. Friedman, "Targets, Instruments, and Indicators of Monetary Policy," *Journal of Monetary Economics*, October 1975.

the economy except to the extent that it affects the behavior of money. Thus he has remarked:[11]

> To have a significant impact on the economy, a tax increase must somehow affect monetary policy — the quantity of money and its rate of growth. . . .
>
>   The level of taxes is important — because it affects how much of our resources we use through the government and how much we use as individuals. It is not important as a sensitive and powerful device to control the short-run course of income and prices.

The Inherent Stability of the Private Sector

The final aspect of monetarism we consider here is the monetarist view that the economy, left to itself, is more stable than when the government manages it with discretionary policy and that the major cause of economic fluctuations lies in inappropriate government actions. This view is quite fundamental to the monetarist position. It is because the point is so fundamental that a major stage in the acceptance of monetarism occurred when Friedman and Schwartz published their *Monetary History of the United States.* In it they provided evidence for the view that the great depression was the result of bad monetary policy rather than private sector instability arising, say, from autonomous shifts in consumption or investment demand.

Summary: We Are Almost All Partly Monetarists

From the viewpoint of the conduct of economic policy, the major monetarist themes are (1) an emphasis on the growth rate of the money stock, (2) arguments against fine tuning and in favor of a monetary rule, and (3) a greater weight that monetarists, as compared, for example, with Keynesians, place on the costs of inflation relative to those of unemployment.

Although we describe these as the major monetarist propositions relating to policy, it is not true that macroeconomists can be neatly divided into groups, some subscribing to the monetarist religion and some to other faiths. Most of the arguments advanced by Friedman and his associates are technical and susceptible to economic analysis and the application of empirical evidence. Many of those propositions are now widely accepted and are no longer particularly associated with monetarism. As Franco Modigliani has remarked, "We are all monetarists now." He adds that we are monetarists in the sense that all (or most) macroeconomists believe in the importance of money — a point repeatedly stressed in this book.

The second monetarist proposition — against activist policy — is echoed in the quotation from the 1989 *Economic Report of the President* at the beginning of this chapter. Fiscal policy was not actively used for stabilization purposes in the United

---

[11] Milton Friedman, "Higher Taxes? No," *Newsweek,* Jan. 23, 1967. Reprinted in *There's No Such Thing as a Free Lunch,* p. 89.

States during the 1980s. But monetary policy continues to be carried out actively, and there is a good case for the view that the sustained low-inflation growth of the 1980s owes much to the Fed's skill in conducting discretionary monetary policy. Although monetary authorities around the world announce monetary targets — and thus seem to have become more monetarist — the authorities do not stick to the targets when they believe there is good reason to change.[12]

The third proposition noted above, that inflation matters, is one that has gained increasing assent among both economists and policy makers.

Slow Adjustment of Wages and Prices

Keynesians and monetarists agree on one fundamental issue, that the economy adjusts only slowly to changes in policy, and that policy changes usually affect output first and inflation later. Accordingly, monetarists, like Keynesians, argued that an inflation could not be reduced without producing a recession. Although both monetarists and Keynesians relied on much the same analysis to explain why disinflation could not come cheaply — the aggregate supply-demand analysis of Chapter 14 — that explanation left many economists dissatisfied. They worried that the slow adjustment of wages and prices assumed in those models lacked a firm theoretical basis. Early in the 1970s, a radical new development in macroeconomics seemed to promise improved understanding of the effects of policy measures on the economy. This was the rational expectations equilibrium approach.

18-3   THE RATIONAL EXPECTATIONS EQUILIBRIUM APPROACH

The failure to reduce inflation in the 1970s and the apparent inability of macro policy to achieve its goals led to a reconsideration of the premises of modern macroeconomics. The reconstruction, called the *rational expectations equilibrium approach,* emphasizes as central three elements:

- The need to model explicitly the microeconomic motives and incentives that underlie the actions and responses of individuals

- The role of expectations and the adjustment to new information

- The limited scope for discretionary stabilization policies

These are among the hallmarks of the rational expectations equilibrium approach to macroeconomics, which we have discussed in earlier chapters, but to which we now give systematic consideration.

Among the leading members of the school are Robert Lucas of the University of

---

[12] These targets for the major countries are published in the OECD's *Economic Outlook,* which appears twice a year.

Chicago, Thomas Sargent of the Hoover Institution, Edward Prescott and Neil Wallace of the University of Minnesota, and Robert Barro of Harvard.[13]

The rational expectations approach acquired that name because the assumption of rational expectations in the context of the expectations augmented aggregate supply curve of Chapter 14 has such striking implications. Recall that in Chapters 7 and 14 we defined the rational expectations hypothesis as assuming that *individuals form expectations using information efficiently and do not make systematic mistakes in expectations.*

We saw in Chapter 14 that rational expectations applied to the expectations-augmented aggregate supply curve implied that an expected reduction in the growth rate of money would reduce the inflation rate without causing a recession. We also noted in the same context that only unexpected changes in monetary policy would have real effects, and we discussed the important role of credibility of the intentions of policy makers.

But the group known as the rational expectations school has a broader aim. The rational expectations equilibrium approach aims to build all of macroeconomics on explicit microeconomic foundations, that is, on the assumption that individuals maximize utility, firms maximize profits, and markets are in equilibrium. *The emphasis on markets' being in equilibrium is far more fundamental than just the rational expectations assumption.* It is for that reason that we add "equilibrium" in referring to the approach as the rational expectations equilibrium approach.

In the remainder of this section we briefly take up the rational expectations part of the approach. In the next section we turn to the equilibrium approach.

Rational Expectations as a Theory of Expectations

The assumption that expectations are rational, that they are based on the efficient use of information, and that they are not systematically incorrect is made on occasion by almost all macroeconomists. Use of the assumption does not automatically qualify the user as a member of the rational expectations equilibrium school.

The question of whether individuals make systematic mistakes in expectations is an empirical one. Indeed, there is some evidence that individuals do make systematic mistakes.[14] At the level of the individual firm forecasting sales, some firms seem to be

---

[13] For an introduction, see Thomas Sargent and Neil Wallace, "Rational Expectations and the Theory of Economic Policy," *Journal of Monetary Economics,* April 1976. See also Robert E. Lucas, "Understanding Business Cycles," in Lucas (ed.), *Studies in Business Cycle Theory.* Two textbooks review the tools and propositions: Steven Sheffrin, *Rational Expectations* (Cambridge, Engl.: Cambridge University Press, 1983), and David Begg, *The Rational Expectations Revolution in Macroeconomics* (Baltimore: John Hopkins University Press, 1983). For recent developments, see Robert J. Barro (ed.), *Modern Business Cycle Theory* (Cambridge, Mass.: Harvard University Press, 1989).

[14] See Michael C. Lovell, "Tests of the Rational Expectations Hypothesis," *American Economic Review,* March 1986. See, too, the challenging paper by Amos Tversky and Daniel Kahneman, "Judgment Under Uncertainty: Heuristics and Biases," 185 *Science* (1984), pp. 1124–1131.

perpetual optimists, others perpetual pessimists. It has to be recognized that firms or individuals may make mistakes in forecasts for long periods. In normal times, they may use simple rules of thumb for forecasting. Nonetheless, the rational expectations approach suggests that if forecast errors are expensive to the forecaster, any systematic errors will eventually be corrected by the people making them.

Beyond that, rational expectations as a theory of expectations implies that policy cannot rely for its effectiveness on systematic misunderstandings by the public. For instance, if at first the public does not understand that countercyclical tax changes are transitory, those changes will have powerful effects on the economy. But as people begin to realize that tax changes are reversed as the economy reaches full employment, such a policy comes to have less powerful effects because the tax changes are understood to be transitory. The expectations part of rational expectations suggests that it is best, in formulating policy, to assume that the public will soon understand how a particular policy is working. It also implies that any policy that works for some time only because the public does not correctly anticipate its effects is doomed to eventual failure.

18-4 THE EQUILIBRIUM APPROACH

The equilibrium component of the rational expectations equilibrium approach is also known as the *new classical macroeconomics*.[15] The approach accepts as its basic challenge the need to explain the fluctuations in output and employment that take place in the business cycle.

Money and Business Cycles

The early work in this area was done by Robert Lucas. Lucas saw the Phillips curve, the tradeoff between inflation and unemployment, as the central empirical fact that had to be explained. And he aimed to explain it in a model in which prices can move to make supply equal to demand.[16]

Why is the Phillips curve a central problem for an equilibrium approach to macroeconomics? In the first place, there is evidence, provided by Friedman and Schwartz, and by many others, that changes in monetary policy affect the real economy. Thus, any serious theory would have to try to account for that fact. But we showed in Chapter 7 that when prices are flexible, an increase in the money stock is fully neutral, raising prices but not output. If prices are not assumed to be sticky — and the essence of the equilibrium approach is to assume that prices are free to move so as to clear markets — it is necessary to explain why an increase in the money stock that

---

[15] See Kevin Hoover, *The New Classical Macroeconomics* (Oxford, Engl.: Basil Blackwell, 1988).

[16] The most influential single article is Robert E. Lucas, "Some International Evidence on Output-Inflation Tradeoffs," *American Economic Review*, September 1973.

raises prices appears to be accompanied by higher output. Equivalently, it has to be explained why reducing the inflation rate without creating a recession appears to be impossible.

We have already outlined (in Chapter 7) Lucas's explanation for the tradeoff between output (rather than unemployment) and inflation. We go into more detail here to show precisely how Lucas builds up his supply curve from microeconomic foundations. The explanation assumes that individuals have imperfect information about the current price level and thus mistake movements in *absolute* prices for *relative* price changes.

The model starts from the supply of a particular good, i; quantity supplied increases with the *relative* price of that good. This is simple microeconomics. The aggregate price level (P_t) is not known at the time suppliers have to decide how much to produce and sell. Instead, suppliers base their output decisions on the estimated, or expected, aggregate price level, P_t^e. *The price of the particular good, i, is P_{it}.* The supply curve of good i is

$$Y_{it} = f\frac{P_{it}}{P_t^e} \tag{1}$$

where Y_{it} is the output of the ith good, and f is a constant.

In a competitive market each supplier knows the price in his or her market. But because information is imperfect, suppliers know only P_{it} in their individual market, not any other prices or the aggregate price level. On the basis of P_{it} and the price level they expected, P_t^e, they have to make a best estimate of the actual relative price of good i, that is, of P_{it}/P_t.

Individuals know that there are two types of shocks in the economy. Some shocks are *relative,* or specific to individual markets. These relative shocks sum to zero across the markets, some markets having higher than average demand, others having less than the average. There are also *aggregate* shocks, which raise quantity demanded at a given price in every market. An unexpected increase in the money stock is one such shock.

Consider the supplier who has some expectation of the aggregate price level, P_t^e, and who now learns the relative price in the market. Suppose the relative price is high. The supplier has to decide whether that is because there has been an increase in demand in all markets, raising the aggregate price level, or just in his or her market, raising the relative price. If the high price in market i is a result of a shock to the money stock that affects all markets, the supplier will not want to raise output. If the shock is specific to market i, the supplier will want to raise output.

The key result that Lucas establishes is this: The rational calculation is to assume that when price in market i is high, that is partly because the aggregate price level is high and partly because there has been a relative shock in market i. The statistically best guess that individuals in the market can make assigns responsibility for the high price between its two possible sources. When seeing a price that seems high relative to the expected aggregate price level, suppliers will react to the higher price by producing more — though the reaction is less than if the suppliers were certain the relative price in their market was high.

The next step is to look at all markets together. If there has been no shock to the money supply, the relative shocks will cancel out in their total effects on output. Output will be higher than average in some markets, lower than average in others. But if there has been an unexpected increase in the money stock, output will on average be higher than normal — because everyone partly mistook the increase in aggregate demand as a shift in relative demand and produced more than average. The sum of output across markets, that is, total production, will be higher when the money stock has unexpectedly increased. And on average prices will be higher because demand in each market was greater.

Lucas thus succeeded in producing a Phillips curve type of tradeoff in which a higher average price level would be accompanied by higher output. The Lucas demonstration of a possible Phillips curve based on incomplete information attracted much attention, particularly the demonstration that with regard to monetary policy, only unexpected changes in the stock of money affect the price level. Under these circumstances, there appears to be no role for monetary policy to systematically affect output or unemployment.[17] Any systematic policy, such as increased monetary expansion in a recession (remember that recessions are possible as a result of surprises), would be predicted by market participants, and wages and prices would be set accordingly. Unless the Fed had better information, or shorter reaction lags than the market, it could not, according to this history, have a systematic *real* effect.

Empirical Testing

The proposition that only monetary *surprises* affect output was the subject of intense empirical research, which was noted in Chapter 7. At this stage, the evidence does not support the strong implication of the equilibrium approach that only unanticipated changes in the money stock affect output. Accordingly, the evidence also does not support the view that systematic monetary policy does not affect the behavior of output.

Equilibrium Real Business Cycles

The weakness of the empirical evidence for the view that only unanticipated money affects real output led to two reactions. Some economists believed that better explanations would have to be found for the role of money in the business cycle. Others questioned the evidence linking money with the business cycle at all.

In particular, economists working on the equilibrium approach developed *equilibrium real business cycle* theory, the view that fluctuations in output and employment are the result of a variety of real shocks hitting the economy. They explained the apparent link between money and output as a result of the money stock's accommodat-

---

[17] The Lucas supply curve held so much attraction for many economists not only because of its striking implications, but especially because it was derived from an explicit microeconomic basis.

ing movements in output. Thus money could be correlated with changes in output, but would not necessarily cause them.[18]

With monetary causes of the business cycle assumed out of the way, real business cycle theory is left with two tasks. The first is to explain the *shocks,* or *disturbances,* that hit the economy, causing fluctuations in the first place. The second is to explain the *propagation mechanisms.* A propagation mechanism is the means through which a disturbance is spread through the economy. In particular, the aim is to explain why shocks to the economy seem to have long-lived effects.

Propagation Mechanisms

Many of the mechanisms that real business cycle theory relies on to explain why a shock to the economy affects output for several years have already been discussed. Among these are inventory adjustments and changes in investment caused by shifts in profitability. These are part of anyone's theory of the business cycle.

The one mechanism that is most associated with equilibrium business cycles, though, is *the intertemporal substitution of leisure.* Any theory of the business cycle has to explain why people work more at some times than at others; during booms employment is high and jobs are easy to find; during recessions people work less.

A simple equilibrium explanation would be that people work more in booms because wages are higher. That way they would voluntarily be supplying more labor in response to a higher wage. (Remember that the equilibrium approach requires people to be on their supply-and-demand curves at all times.) However, the facts are not strongly in favor of that argument because the real wage changes very little over the business cycle. People are thus not obviously working more in response to higher wages.

The Keynesian or monetarist approaches explain these movements in output by saying that the demand for labor shifts as aggregate demand shifts, and that people may be unemployed in recessions because they cannot get work despite their willingness to work at the going wage.[19] But the equilibrium approach constrains itself to assume

---

[18] This view is developed in a technically very advanced paper by Robert King and Charles Plosser, "Money, Credit and Prices in a Real Business Cycle Model," *American Economic Review,* June 1984. A non-technical review is in Carl Walsh, "New Views of the Business Cycle," Federal Reserve Bank of Philadelphia *Business Review,* January–February 1986. Bennett T. McCallum, "Real Business Cycles," in Barro (ed.), *Modern Business Cycle Theory,* provides a high-level review of this literature. See, also, Charles Plosser, "Understanding Real Business Cycles," and N. Gregory Manhiw, "Real Business Cycles: A New Keynesian Perspective," both in *Economic Perspectives,* Summer 1989, for a recent discussion of the topic.

[19] In some versions of the Keynesian model, including that of Keynes in the *General Theory,* it is assumed that firms move up and down the labor demand curve over the course of the business cycle (see the neoclassical labor demand curve in the appendix to Chap. 13). That implies the real wage would be higher in recessions than in booms. Since the real wage does not move much over the cycle, this explanation, too, cannot be correct. In the model developed in Chaps. 13 and 14, the real wage is constant as a result of markup pricing, and employment changes with aggregate demand. Constancy of the real wage is a reasonable approximation to actual wage behavior.

markets are in equilibrium. The explanation for the large movements in output with small movements in wages is the following: There is a high elasticity of labor supply in response to temporary changes in the wage. Or, as the argument is put, people are willing to substitute leisure intertemporally.

The argument is that people care very little about when in any given period of a year or two they work. Suppose that within a 2-year period they plan to work 4,000 hours at the going wage (50 weeks each year for 40 hours a week). If wages are equal in the 2 years, they would work 2,000 hours each year. But if wages were just 2 percent higher in one year than the other, they might prefer to work, say, 2,200 hours in one year, foregoing vacations and working overtime, and 1,800 hours in the other. That way they work the same total amount and earn more total income.

This intertemporal substitution of leisure is clearly capable of generating large movements in the amount of work done in response to small shifts in wages — and thus could account for large output effects in the cycle accompanied by small changes in wages. However, there has not been strong empirical support for this view either.

Similar intertemporal substitution arguments have been advanced to explain fluctuations in consumption over the course of the business cycle. In this case the real interest rate is assumed to change, with individuals reducing current levels of consumption when the interest rate is high in order to take advantage of the higher rate of return on saving. Again, the evidence for this proposition is very weak.

Disturbances

The most important disturbances isolated by equilibrium business cycle theorists are shocks to *productivity*, or supply shocks, and shocks to *government spending*.

A productivity shock raises output in relation to a given level of input. Good weather and new methods of production are examples. Suppose there is a temporary favorable productivity shock this period. Then individuals will want to work harder to take advantage of the higher productivity. In working more this period they raise output. They will also invest more, thus spreading the productivity shock into future periods by raising the stock of capital. If the effect of the intertemporal substitution of leisure is strong, even a small productivity shock could have a relatively large effect on output.

Increased government spending is another type of shock. To provide the extra goods the government needs, individuals will work harder if the real wage rises, and save more if the real interest rate rises. Thus we should expect an increase in government spending to raise the real interest rate and the real wage.[20]

There is less certainty in the real business cycle approach about the effects of a cut in taxes than about the effects of an increase in government spending. As we discussed earlier, the Ricardian view is that individuals recognize that a cut in taxes

---

[20] Note that increased government spending raises the real interest rate in the *IS-LM* model, too, though there the crowding out is more of investment than consumption.

today is just an increase in taxes tomorrow, and that they therefore should not increase consumption when taxes are cut.

Summary

The equilibrium real business cycle approach is still a subject of intense research. Its goal of building macroeconomics on sound microeconomic foundations is surely widely shared. There is no doubt, too, that some of the mechanisms, such as inventory accumulation and investment dynamics, that underlie its explanation of the dynamics of the business cycle will form part of future business cycle models, as they have of past and current business cycle models. But there is room for doubt that the attempt to build business cycle models in which there is no role for monetary factors will be ultimately successful.

18-5 THE RATIONAL EXPECTATIONS EQUILIBRIUM APPROACH TO POLICY

The rational expectations approach has led to a sophisticated view of policy making, in at least two respects. First, there is the sophisticated treatment of expectations. The rational expectations approach emphasizes that economic agents do not react mechanically to every policy change. Rather, they try to figure out what the policy change means for the behavior of the economy and for future changes in policy. And they behave accordingly. For instance, as we noted in Chapter 8, economic agents adjust their consumption more in response to a permanent income tax cut than to a transitory tax cut of the same size. Second, by attempting to build macroeconomics on microeconomic foundations, the rational expectations equilibrium approach has brought a new perspective to the principles of fiscal and monetary policy.

Credibility

The emphasis on expectations leads naturally to a concern with the credibility of policy. Under rational expectations individuals' reactions to current policy decisions depend on what they believe the current decisions mean about future decisions. Thus, believability of policy becomes crucial.[21]

Suppose the Fed announces a reduction in the growth rate of money. If people believe the Fed, the rate of wage increase will slow and the Fed will be able to reduce the growth rate of money without any significant output cost. Suppose they do not believe the Fed. Then the Fed is faced with the decision of whether to do what it said

---

[21] See for instance, Torsten Persson, "Credibility of Macroeconomic Policy: An Introduction and a Broad Survey," *European Economic Review*, 1988, pp. 519–532, and K. Blackburn and M. Christensen, "Monetary Theory and Policy Credibility: Theories and Evidence," *Journal of Economic Literature*, March 1989.

and create a recession, or not to do it, thereby avoiding the recession but losing credibility.

Indeed, it is even possible to see how under rational expectations individuals' beliefs can be self-justifying. Suppose the Fed announces that it will reduce money growth. Suppose people believe it and wage increases slow. Then the Fed will reduce money growth, and the expectations were right. Suppose people do not believe the Fed and wages go on rising as before. Then if the Fed fears a recession, it will not cut the growth rate of money. The people were right again. This example illustrates the value of credibility.

ENDING INFLATIONS

Is there evidence that credibility — the extent to which people believe the government's policy announcements — does in practice affect the outcome of policies? In a famous paper, Thomas Sargent sought to establish that four of the hyperinflations of the 1920s — in Germany, Poland, Austria, and Czechoslovakia — ended quickly and at a relatively low unemployment cost because government policies were credible.[22] While Sargent's evidence is extremely interesting, it is not conclusive, in part because it does not clearly show that the hyperinflations did end with relatively little unemployment.

Calculations showing that the sacrifice ratio for ending the inflation of 1980–1981 was lower than expected have also been used to support the view that credibility mattered in that case. But because credibility is so hard to measure, there is as yet no definitive evidence of its role in practice. That does not mean the concept is not useful, nor does it mean that the concept does not matter. Many governments and particularly central banks take explicit account of the effects of their decisions on their credibility, seeking to establish a reputation for toughness and steadfastness in the fight against inflation. That way they hope in the long run to be able to maintain low inflation without having to create recessions every time a supply shock hits the economy.

Fiscal and Monetary Policy Rules

We have already seen in the discussion of Ricardian equivalence one way in which the rational expectations approach sheds fresh light on the analysis of fiscal policy. Similarly, other insights into fiscal policy have been provided by members of the rational expectations school who start their analysis from microeconomic foundations.

There is a well-established microeconomics-based neoclassical analysis of fiscal policy that concerns itself with optimal rates of taxation of different goods and factors of production. The optimal tax rates are chosen to minimize the economic distortions created by the taxes needed to finance a given level of government spending. By

---

[22] Thomas J. Sargent, "The Ends of Four Big Inflations," in Robert E. Hall (ed.), *Inflation* (Chicago: University of Chicago Press, 1982).

developing this theory, Kydland and Prescott and Barro have shown that economic distortions would be minimized over time if tax *rates* were kept quite stable over the business cycle.[23] This is known as the *tax-smoothing* result, with the smoothing referring to the need for smooth tax rates. One implication is that government revenues should be higher in booms than recessions, thus suggesting that on microeconomic grounds the budget surplus should tend to be larger during booms than recessions.[24]

The approach leads also to an emphasis on institutional changes as ways of altering the behavior of the economy. Members of the rational expectations school are less interested in what policy should be *now* than they are in ways of making it possible for policy to operate better in general. The quote from Lucas at the beginning of this chapter shows a general attitude toward attempts to predict the effects of a particular policy action. Members of the rational expectations school doubt that we know enough to predict how the public will respond in the short run to a particular policy change, because the response depends on how the policy measure affects expectations. But in the long run the public will catch on to the effects of any policy change, and it thus becomes possible to predict the long-run effects of long-run policy changes. A member of the rational expectations school would support a constitutional amendment to balance the budget, in part because a constitutional amendment should have a very strong, predictable effect on expectations, in part because he or she fears that policy makers not bound by rules may do anything — and despite the fact that microeconomics might suggest a more sophisticated fiscal policy.[25]

Similarly, a rational expectations economist confronted with the inflationary experience of the 1970s would argue that the best way to change the behavior of the Fed is to change the institutional environment in which it works. Accordingly, such an economist is likely to support a monetary rule for the Fed, for example, requiring the money supply to grow at 4 percent per year.[26]

---

[23] Finn E. Kydland and Edward C. Prescott, "A Competitive Theory of Fluctuations and the Feasibility and Desirability of Stabilization Policy," in S. Fischer (ed.), *Rational Expectations and Economic Policy* (Chicago: University of Chicago Press, 1980), Robert J. Barro, "The Neoclassical Approach to Fiscal Policy," in Barro (ed.), *Modern Business Cycle Theory*, and S. Rao Aiyagari, "How Should Taxes Be Set?" Federal Reserve Bank of Minneapolis, *Quarterly Review*, Winter 1989.

[24] We say "suggesting" because we have not specified the optimal cyclical pattern of government expenditures; if that were highly procyclical, the budget surplus could optimally be countercyclical.

[25] Robert Lucas, "Principles of Fiscal and Monetary Policy," *Journal of Monetary Economics*, January 1986, takes this position.

[26] You might wonder why members of the rational expectations school should care at all about monetary policy if they believe that (1) only unexpected changes in money affect real output and (2) the public's expectations eventually catch up with reality. The two assumptions — (1) and (2) — seem to suggest that whatever the Fed is doing will eventually have no effect on real output. However, the strong form of rational expectations does not imply that monetary policy is irrelevant to the behavior of *prices*. Thus members of the rational expectations school concerned about keeping inflation low can logically be in favor of a monetary rule that will prevent the average rate of growth of money from becoming high.

The Rational Expectations Equilibrium Approach, Monetarism, and Macroeconomics

There is considerable overlap between the policy views of monetarists and those of members of the rational expectations school. The similarity extends to the usually conservative views of policy held by members of both groups. But there are important differences between the monetarist and rational expectations approaches to macroeconomics. Monetarists are willing to assume that expectations may be systematically wrong and that markets are very slow to clear, whereas a member of the rational expectations school would not make such assumptions. Monetarism can be viewed as operating within the same framework and model as Keynesianism, while disagreeing over the relative importance of monetary and fiscal policy. The rational expectations school believes that the standard framework is fundamentally flawed and thus has developed the equilibrium approach, which argues that imperfect information is responsible for the business cycle. It thus offers a far more radical restructuring of macroeconomics than does monetarism.

Where will the rational expectations equilibrium alternative to conventional macroeconomics lead? It has already had a substantial influence on the way all macroeconomists think. First, rational expectations is widely used as a theory of expectations. Second, the sophisticated view of policy, in which responses to policy depend on the public's analysis of what policy measures will do to current and future behavior of the economy, has been widely adopted.[27] The equilibrium approach, however, is more controversial than other components of the rational expectations view and seems to be inconsistent with the slow reaction of the economy to policy measures.[28]

18-6 SUPPLY-SIDE ECONOMICS

Supply-side economics was all the rage in the United States in 1981, the first year of the Reagan administration. And so-called supply-siders still run a very active publicity machine, proclaiming the correctness of their views in the press (particularly in the *Wall Street Journal*) and in books.[29]

Supply-side economists lay heavy stress on the incentive effects of taxation in determining the behavior of the economy. Beyond that broad agreement there are really two separate supply-side groups. The mainstream group includes economists such as Martin Feldstein of Harvard, president of the National Bureau of Economic Research and, from 1982 to 1984, chairman of the Council of Economic Advisers, and

---

[27] The development of the rational expectations approach to policy has led to much game-theoretical (the mathematical theory of games) research on policy. For an introduction, see John Driffill, "Macroeconomic Policy Games with Incomplete Information: A Survey," *European Economic Review*, 1988, pp. 533–541.

[28] See the discussion in the special issue of the *Journal of Money, Credit and Banking*, November 1980.

[29] Paul Craig Roberts, *The Supply-Side Revolution* (Cambridge, Mass.: Harvard University Press, 1984) presents an insider's view of the supply-side impact on U.S. economic policy in the first Reagan administration. Various supply-side arguments are brought together in the collection edited by Richard Fink, *Supply Side Economics* (Washington, D.C.: University Publications of America, 1982).

Michael Boskin of Stanford University, who was appointed chairman of President Bush's Council of Economic Advisers in 1989. This group stresses the importance of tax incentives in promoting growth, especially by their effect on saving and investment. Similarly, it analyzes the effects of tax changes on labor supply, the effects of Social Security on saving and retirement decisions, and a host of other important issues.

The mainstream group has been presenting the results of its research in scholarly journals for many years and is influential and active within the economics profession. There are few serious economists of any school or group who believe incentives are unimportant. Indeed, it was the New Economics that was sufficiently concerned about growth in 1962 to introduce investment incentives through the investment tax credit.

But it was the radical fringe of the supply-side group that received most of the publicity during the early 1980s, when the Reagan tax cut that determined fiscal policy for the entire decade was put in place.[30] This group made exaggerated claims for the effects of tax cuts on saving, investment, and labor supply and for the effects of tax cuts on total government revenue from taxation. Among the intellectual leaders of the fringe are Arthur Laffer, whose curve was described in Chapter 16. Radical supply-siders were installed in the Treasury, and there was an active supply-side group in Congress. The radical fringe argued that (1) tax rate reductions would have such powerful effects on work effort that total tax revenues would rise and (2) the supply-side effects of the tax cuts would have a powerful effect in reducing inflation by increasing the growth rate of output.

In 1981 the Reagan administration presented an optimistic scenario for growth with low inflation that was supposedly justified by supply-side considerations. Tax rates were to be cut significantly but, it was claimed, the rapid increase in growth would keep the budget close to balance. That at least was the public claim.

Radical supply-side economics was thus an essential part of the rhetoric supporting *Reaganomics*. There is no precise definition of Reaganomics other than that it is the economic policies pursued by President Reagan throughout his presidency, but especially in 1981–1982. The most important factor in these policies was the President's determination to cut taxes. This was done in the belief that the government was too large and that government spending could be cut by denying Congress tax revenue to spend. Arguments by supply-siders that tax cuts would rapidly increase economic growth and reduce inflation were certainly welcome, but it is quite likely that President Reagan would have proceeded with his policies even had he known they would result in massive budget deficits, so long as they would reduce the size of government.

Supply-side predictions were criticized at the time by mainstream macroeconomists. The evidence is that tax reductions do affect incentives and that tax cuts

---

[30] The distinction between mainstream and radical groups is drawn by Harold McClure and Thomas Willett, "Understanding the Supply Siders," in W. C. Stubblebine and T. D. Willett (eds.), *Reaganomics: A Midterm Report* (San Francisco: Institute of Contemporary Studies, 1983). See this paper and a paper by Richard Rahn in the same volume for more details on supply-side economics and for lists of the players in the two groups.

increase output.[31] But there is no evidence that the incentives would be so strong as to result in higher government revenue after a tax cut. Similarly, an increase in the growth rate of output will contribute to reducing the inflation rate — but the effects are unlikely to be powerful.[32]

The events of the 2 years following the Reagan tax cuts do not support the views of the radical supply-siders. Inflation was indeed reduced, but the reduction was a result of tight monetary policy and not of expansionary fiscal policy. Output fell rapidly; it did not increase. These events led to the departure of the radical supply-siders from responsible policy-making positions, but did not slow down their claims that supply-side economics (of the radical branch) was the solution for the economy's problem.

The extremely rapid recovery from the recession that took place in 1983 and 1984 refueled the claims of supply-siders that incentives were crucial to growth. An alternative explanation is that the rapid growth of the money stock seen in Figure 18-3 and the large increases in the full-employment deficit seen in Figure 18-2 are mainly responsible for the rapid recovery. That recovery ran out of steam in 1985 and 1986 and was then reinvigorated, in part by the decline in oil prices, in 1986, in 1987, and in1988. While one cannot disagree that incentives matter, there is no strong case that they played any special role in the macroeconomy in the 1980s.

An interesting sidelight on supply-side economics comes from considering the relationship between supply-side economics and monetarism. Both approaches are often associated with conservative political positions. But the two groups of economists are critical of each other, and competed for influence in the Reagan administration. In their policy positions, favoring tax cuts in almost all circumstances and believing also that the Fed should allow rapid money growth to foster rapid output growth, the supply-siders are closer to Keynesianism than to monetarism.

18-7 THE NEW KEYNESIANISM

Under the challenge of the rational expectations equilibrium approach there has been substantial research since 1973 that attempts to explain why wages and prices are sticky. We have already discussed in Chapters 13 and 14 the approach that builds on the existence of long-term and perhaps overlapping labor contracts to explain wage and price stickiness and inflationary momentum. Because the coverage in Chapters 13 and 14 is quite full, we shall not review that approach further, even though it is one major strand that attempts to account for wage and price stickiness even when expectations are rational.

More recently a *New Keynesian* school has developed.[33] The New Keynesians

---

[31] Some of the evidence is examined in Chap. 19. The effects of cuts in tax rates on tax revenue were discussed in Chap. 16.

[32] See Chap. 12, footnote 18.

[33] See Julio Rotemberg, "The New Keynesian Microfoundations," in *NBER Macroeconomics Annual*, 1987.

combine the Keynesian recognition that the economy does not adjust instantly and smoothly to shocks, including monetary shocks, with an insistence on building their explanations on microeconomic foundations. Among the leading New Keynesians are George Akerlof and Janet Yellen of Berkeley, Olivier Blanchard and Julio Rotemberg of MIT, Joseph Stiglitz of Stanford, Mark Gertler of Wisconsin – Madison, Ben Bernanke of Princeton, and Gregory Mankiw of Harvard.

New Keynesianism is built on three main microfoundations:

- Efficiency wage theory
- The connection between monopolistic or imperfect competition and traditional Keynesian macroeconomic propositions
- The role of imperfect information in financial markets

We discuss the first two here.[34]

Efficiency Wages

As we have noted, the basic question to answer is why wages and prices do not move quickly to clear markets when there is unemployment. *Efficiency wage theory argues that wages are not cut because doing so reduces a firm's profits.*[35]

There are several explanations for this assumption. The simplest occurs in very poor countries, where individuals cannot feed themselves adequately unless they receive a reasonable wage. Cutting wages in such a country would reduce the physical ability of the workers to perform their tasks. Even if there were substantial unemployment, it would not pay an employer to cut wages because doing so would reduce profits as the efficiency of workers fell owing to poor nutrition.

Physical efficiency is not the problem in developed countries. Efficiency wage theory for such countries argues that firms pay above market-clearing wages in order either to attract the more efficient workers or to ensure that workers on the job do not shirk. The shirking version starts from the fact that it is often difficult to observe the amount of effort put out by workers. To create the right incentive to work, there has to be a benefit to having this particular job. To create the benefit, so that the worker really wants to keep the job, the firm pays above-market wages. Then anyone found to be

---

[34] The New Keynesian approach to the financial markets was discussed in Chap. 11, where we examined credit rationing and the role of financial intermediation in the transmission mechanism of monetary policy.

[35] See Janet Yellen, "Efficiency Wage Models of Unemployment," *American Economic Review,* May 1984. For a more extensive examination, see Lawrence Katz, "Efficiency Wage Theories: A Partial Evaluation," *NBER Macroeconomics Annual,* 1986. Alan B. Krueger and Lawrence H. Summers, "Efficiency Wages and the Inter-Industry Wage Structure," *Econometrica,* March 1988, present evidence for the view that wage differentials in U.S. industry are more consistent with efficiency wage theory than with standard competitive theory that would ascribe wage differences to the characteristics of jobs and the people who hold them. For a related approach, see Assar Lindbeck and Dennis Snower, "Wage Setting, Unemployment and Insider-Outsider Relations," *American Economic Review,* May 1986.

shirking is fired and has to return to the labor market to look for a lower-paid job.

This view suggests that there may be two types of jobs — high-paying, desirable jobs that are difficult to find because the wage is above the market equilibrium wage and other jobs, at a lower wage, that are easy to find and for which firms can easily observe workers' effort. That description brings to mind such jobs as driving a cab, in which there are almost always available positions, even when there is unemployment.[36]

Alternatively, there may simply be a social custom that wages are not cut. If workers whose wages are cut regard that as unfair and reduce their work effort in response, then wage cutting will not take place. This fairness argument, although it has the ring of truth, is not fully satisfactory, because there is no explanation of how the custom developed.

Efficiency wage theory explains why some firms would want to pay above-market real wages. Whether it can account for unemployment depends on the size and role of the secondary market and on whether there are always alternative jobs in that market that any unemployed person would take rather than remain unemployed. It is quite possible that many who are unemployed are waiting for primary market (high-paying) jobs. If so, efficiency wage theory can account for some unemployment. It is a further question whether such unemployment would vary cyclically, and particularly whether it would vary as monetary shocks hit the economy. To see whether this can be the case, we turn to possible causes of price and wage stickiness.

The Small Menu Cost—Monopolistic Competition Approach

There is a puzzling aspect of business cycle theories based on the assumption that wages are slow to adjust. Unemployment is a very serious problem creating large costs for society. Changing a wage or price is a relatively simple and apparently cheap matter. The payroll has to be reprogrammed, or a new price tag has to be put on. The puzzle is why these apparently small costs stand in the way of adjusting prices so as to get rid of unemployment.

The so-called *small menu cost approach* argues that small costs of changing prices can have large effects.[37] The argument is technical, but asserts that when firms set prices optimally, they lose very little by meeting increases or decreases in demand by producing more or less without changing prices. Then if there is some small cost for the firm of changing its prices or wages, a small shift in demand will not trigger a price or wage change. But if firms do not change prices in response to shifts in demand, then the economy exhibits price (and/or wage) stickiness. The researchers in this area show

---

[36] Sometimes the two types of jobs are described as primary and secondary, primary jobs being the better ones. This is the *dual labor market hypothesis.*

[37] The simplest such model is N. Gregory Mankiw, "Small Menu Costs and Large Business Cycles: A Macroeconomic Model of Monopoly," *Quarterly Journal of Economics,* May 1985. A more complete model is developed in George Akerlof and Janet Yellen, "A Near-Rational Model of the Business Cycle, with Wage and Price Inertia," *Quarterly Journal of Economics,* Supplement, 1985.

that extremely small costs of changing prices can generate enough wage and price stickiness to give changes in the money stock substantial real effects.

MONOPOLISTIC COMPETITION AND KEYNESIAN MACROECONOMICS

It is essential to the small menu cost result that firms be monopolistic competitors that set wages and prices, rather than taking them as given by the market. The key to understanding the small menu cost argument is this: *For a monopolist or monopolistic competitor, price is always above marginal cost.* If offered the opportunity to sell more at the current price, a monopolist will be willing to do so. Thus monopolistic competitors that find the menu costs of changing prices too high will nonetheless willingly sell more when the demand curve they face shifts, perhaps as a result of an increase in the money stock. Further, because price (which is equal to the marginal value of the good to the consumer) exceeds marginal cost, society benefits from the increase in output.

If firms were competitive, price would be equal to marginal cost, and firms would not be willing to increase output if price remained constant, even if the demand curve facing the industry shifted.[38] Thus one major achievement of the new Keynesians has been the demonstration of a close link between imperfect competition on the microeconomics side and Keynesian propositions in macroeconomics — particularly the proposition that an increase in aggregate demand will lead to an increase in output.[39]

COORDINATION AND MULTIPLE EQUILIBRIA

Under imperfect competition the profits of one firm depend on the actions of other firms; but at the time one firm has to make its decisions about prices or output, it does not know with certainty what other firms will do. The actions of other firms are a matter of conjecture or expectations. These facts have two extremely important implications: First, there is inevitably *interdependence* among firms; they simply have to form expectations (or guess) about other firms' behavior. Second, depending on what firms assume about other firms' actions, the economy may reach different equilibria. Some of these may be "good" equilibria, in the sense that output is high because everybody believes that everyone else also believes this is a good year; but it is also possible that firms form pessimistic views about other firms' actions and a "bad" or low production equilibrium results.

Multiple equilibria may also result from small menu costs. Consider many monop-

---

[38] Robert E. Hall, "The Relation Between Price and Marginal Cost in U.S. Industry," *Journal of Political Economy*, October 1988, shows that price is above marginal cost for much of U.S. industry.

[39] The imperfect competition revolution in microeconomics took place at about the same time as the Keynesian revolution in macroeconomics, in the 1930s. Although many had argued that Keynesian macroeconomic propositions depended on the existence of imperfect, or monopolistic, competition, that link was not really established until recently. For a fully worked out model, see for instance Olivier Blanchard and Nobu Kiyotake, "Monopolistic Competition and the Effects of Aggregate Demand," *American Economic Review*, September 1987.

box 18-1

DISEQUILIBRIUM ECONOMICS AND POST-KEYNESIAN ECONOMICS

In the main text we developed the history of ideas as running from Keynesian economics to monetarism and the rational expectations equilibrium challenge, together with the New Keynesian response—with supply-side economics as a flashy side-show. However, two other strands of macroeconomics are sufficiently distinct and fruitful to deserve attention.

THE DISEQUILIBRIUM APPROACH

As early as the 1950s economists recognized the implications of disequilibrium in one market for supply or demand in other markets. If workers cannot sell all the labor they wish at the going wage, and cannot borrow, how will this affect their consumption decision? If they cannot buy all the goods they wish at the going prices, how does this affect their supply of labor or their demands for money and other assets? If firms cannot sell at the going price all the output they would like to produce, how does this affect their demand for labor?*

The disequilibrium approach answers these questions by constructing a model of the economy that explicitly takes into account the *quantity constraints* on the decisions which households and firms face. Quantity constraints are present when households or firms cannot buy or sell all the quantities they wish at the going wages or prices. Central to the approach is the assumption that wages and prices do not move rapidly, and thus, they leave markets in disequilibrium, which gives rise to quantity adjustments. These quantity adjustments in different markets are interdependent through the quantity constraints under which households and firms make their optimal decisions.

The most interesting contribution of the disequilibrium approach so far has been to influence empirical work. For example, studies of consumption pay close attention to the role of income and wealth, reflecting the possibility that individuals cannot borrow against future income, so that *liquidity constraints* affect spending behavior. In studies of the labor market the approach suggests the important distinction between "high-wage"—or classical—unemployment, on one side, and Keynesian—or "lack-of-demand"—unemployment, on the other.

This difference is illustrated in Figure 1. The figure shows the labor demand schedule—the marginal product of labor (MPN)—with the real wage on the vertical axis and N as the full-employment labor supply. The full-employment real wage is $(w/P)_0$. Suppose the economy is at a point such as A, with real wage $(w/P)'$. At point A firms hire only an amount of labor N', which falls short of full employment because the real wage is too high. The economy suffers from *classical*, or *real wage, unemployment*. The cure is either a reduction in the real wage to $(w/P)_0$ or else productivity growth or increased investment that shifts the MPN schedule out and to the right and thus reduces unemployment.

---

* The early reference is D. Patinkin, *Money, Interest and Prices* (New York: Row, Peterson, 1956), Chap. 13. The complete working out of these ideas can be found in R. Barro and H. Grossman, *Money, Employment and Inflation* (Oxford, Engl.: Cambridge University Press, 1976), and E. Malinvaud, *The Theory of Unemployment Reconsidered* (Oxford, Engl.: Basil Blackwell, 1977), and *Profitability and Unemployment* (Oxford, Engl.: Basil Blackwell, 1981).

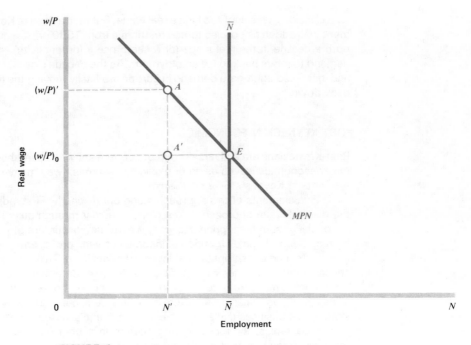

FIGURE 1

CLASSICAL OR KEYNESIAN UNEMPLOYMENT? The schedule MPN is the marginal product of labor or the demand curve for labor. The full-employment labor supply is $\overline{NN}$. At a real wage $(w/P)'$ there is "high real wage" unemployment because firms want to hire only a labor force of N', which falls short of the equilibrium supply, $\overline{N}$. But it is also possible that even at the lower wage—$(w/P)_0$—firms want to hire only N' of labor because they cannot sell the output that would be produced by a larger labor force.

Alternatively, suppose that the economy was at a point such as A'. Again there is unemployment, but this time the real wage is not the problem. Firms are not willing to hire more workers than N' because they cannot sell the output. Aggregate demand is insufficient to absorb more output than is produced by an employment level N'. Therefore firms do not hire more workers, and accordingly, there is *Keynesian unemployment*. The cure, in this case, is not a cut in real wages but rather an expansion in aggregate demand through monetary or fiscal stimulus.

In both cases there is unemployment. In both cases it is unprofitable for firms to hire more labor than N'. In one case the problem is that labor is too expensive; in the other there is no market for the increased output. But it is essential to identify the kind of unemployment the economy faces before designing policy action.

This analysis was used in diagnosing the high European unemployment of the 1980s. There were many who argued that European unemployment in the early 1980s was classical, a result of too high a real wage. But then a dose of Keynesian unemployment was added as policies turned restrictive from 1980 on. It would thus have taken both a decline in the real wage (or a sharp rise in productivity) and an expansion in demand to move back to full employment. As the decade closes, productivity growth and increased aggregate demand in Europe are finally moving the unemployment rate back down.

POST-KEYNESIAN ECONOMICS

Post-Keynesians are a diverse group of economists who share the belief that modern macroeconomics leaves aside or explicitly assumes away many of the most central elements of Keynes's *General Theory*.†

Five elements of this approach stand out distinctly. First, adjustment, just as in the disequilibrium approach, takes place primarily through quantity adjustment, not price changes. Indeed, price changes, where they occur, are often seen as disequilibrating. Second, the distribution of income between profits and wages plays a central role in affecting consumption and investment decision. Third, expectations (Keynes's animal spirits), together with profits, are the chief determinant of investment plans. Fourth, institutional features — credit constraints on households and self-finance by firms, as well as a financial structure involving credit creation in a pyramid — interact in shaping the business cycle and on occasion financial crises. Finally, unlike in classical macroeconomics, the focus of post-Keynesian economics is on explaining why the economy does not work well. Several of these elements are of course shared with regular Keynesianism.

Post-Keynesian economics remains an eclectic collection of ideas, not a systematic challenge like, for example, the rational expectations equilibrium approach. The former has influenced economists in their research program. But the deliberate downplaying, indeed rejection, of individual rationality and maximization as a basis of behavior by firms and households by post-Keynesians has kept the approach at odds with the mainstream of the profession, which has been attempting to bring macroeconomics into closer touch with microeconomics. ∎

---

† For an introduction see A. Eichner (ed.), *A Guide to Post-Keynesian Economics* (White Plains, N.Y.: M. E. Sharpe, 1979), and the essays on post-Keynesian economics in the *American Economic Review*, May 1980.

---

olistically competitive firms confronted by a shift in the demand curves facing them. Suppose that all but one of them chooses not to change the price charged for the firm's output, and consider the decision facing the last firm. If it increases its price, it will lose many customers; the marginal revenue from raising the price would be small, and hence would not outweigh the small menu cost. Therefore, if all but one firm does not raise the price, the last firm will not do so either.

Now suppose, instead, that all but one firm have raised their price. The marginal revenue the last firm faces is larger than in the previous case, and may therefore be larger than the small menu cost. Therefore, the firm would raise its price.

It follows that there may be two possible equilibria. Either all firms raise their price, or none does. In the first case we have a neoclassical or rational expectations equilibrium response to an increase in the money supply; in the latter case we have a Keynesian response. There may even be more possible responses.[40]

One way of viewing the possibility of multiple equilibria is that difficulties of *coordinating* responses to economic shocks may produce slow adjustment of wages and prices. From the viewpoint of the firms taken as a group, the best response to an increase in the money stock may be for all to raise prices together. But because they cannot get together to make that decision, each will make its decision while having to guess what the others will do—and they may start off by not raising the price. Similarly, when there is unemployment, all firms together could reduce wages. But because of efficiency wages, it would not pay one firm to reduce wages if the others do not. Again the problem of coordination prevents an instant return to a full-employment equilibrium.

The difficulty of coordinating responses to a shock points to one possible answer to the question with which this section started: Why, if unemployment has such large social costs, do firms not lower wages to reduce unemployment? The answer may be that no individual firm can do much about the unemployment problem: acting in its own interest it may not reduce wages; but if other firms would reduce wages at the same time, so would this firm.[41]

Summary

The New Keynesian ideas are still being worked out, and it is not clear whether they will succeed in providing a convincing account of the microeconomic foundations of Keynesian macroeconomics. The small menu cost notion in particular fails to convince many economists. But it does seem likely that efficiency wage theory, the role of imperfect competition, and the difficulties of coordinating responses to disturbances will play important roles in macroeconomics in the future.

18-8 WHERE DOES IT ALL LEAD?

At the start of this chapter we asked why macroeconomics suffers from such rapidly changing opinions. The answer is that it does not. There has been an evolution from simple Keynesianism toward a more sophisticated approach, not a series of rapidly changing beliefs. Macroeconomics has evolved, and it now gives more weight to monetary factors and to aggregate supply, emphasizing the roles of both expectations and labor market institutions. The New Keynesianism reviewed in Section 18-7 does

---

[40] This is shown by Rotemberg, "The New Keynesian Microfoundations."

[41] Interestingly, the difficulty of coordinating wage reductions was mentioned by Keynes in the *General Theory* as one reason for wage stickiness.

not lead to a significantly different overall view of the economy — rather, it should be viewed as attempting to develop microeconomic foundations for existing macroeconomics.

The rational expectations equilibrium approach does pose a more radical challenge to the standard way of viewing the economy, and it has already had a major impact on mainstream macroeconomics. As of now, it remains far from a major empirical success, though it has more theoretical appeal. Whether it will lead to the replacement of current mainstream macroeconomics with a new standard model remains to be seen — and time and evidence will determine that.

If there have not in fact been frequent changes of opinion in macroeconomics, why does it still seem that way? Because macroeconomic issues are important: Macroeconomics is both news and politically useful. Politicians look for economists with arguments that will support the politicians' positions. For instance, supply-side economists had an influential role in the Reagan administration because the President wanted to cut taxes and needed professional support. No matter that the radical supply-side arguments were accepted by only a very small part of the profession: they provided at least some intellectual support for a policy that was based more on the President's ideology than on a detailed analysis of the potential effects of the tax cuts.

It is hoped that careful study will cumulate over the years to improved knowledge. Opinions, of course, change as new evidence accumulates, but genuine revolutions in thinking are rare. There was a Keynesian revolution in the thirties and a significant shift toward monetarism in the 1950s and 1960s — which was easily accommodated by expanding the Keynesian framework. There may be a rational expectations revolution in progress. Even if it succeeds, it will build on much of the existing structure of macroeconomics. And even if it does not radically reshape macroeconomics, it will, nonetheless, make for serious changes in our understanding of the formation of expectations and the operation of economic policy. It has already set new standards in demanding that macroeconomics be based on microeconomic foundations.

The hope is that study of existing macroeconomics combined with the right degree of skepticism and questioning will make it possible for you to reach your own conclusions when the next brand of economics hits the headlines.

18-9 SUMMARY

1. Economic performance in the United States (and other countries) was much worse from 1969 to 1982 than during the 1960s. There were four recessions in the latter period and none in the 1961–1969 period. The poor economic performance led to a search for explanations and cures. Economic performance since 1982 has been better than that of the 1970s, and closer to that of the 1960s.
2. Monetarism lays heavy stress on the money stock as determining the level of output in the short run and the inflation rate in the long run. The essential step in the advance of monetarism was the Friedman-Schwartz analysis of the great depression as having been significantly worsened by extremely poor monetary policy.

3. Monetarists generally view the money supply as having powerful, but not easily predictable, effects on the economy. Money works with long and variable lags. For that reason monetarists favor a monetary rule. Monetarists argue that interest rates are a poor guide to the direction of monetary policy. They also believe that the private economy is inherently stable.

4. Monetarism's influence on economic policy can be seen in the adoption of money targeting in major countries. Monetarism has also been influential in several policy episodes in which tight money was used to bring down the inflation rate. This takes a long time and works by creating a recession that puts pressure on wages and prices.

5. The rational expectations equilibrium approach to macroeconomics has two components. The first is a theory of expectations. It argues that people form expectations using all available information and do not make systematic mistakes. The second is the equilibrium approach. This assumes that markets are in equilibrium each period and attributes deviations of output from normal levels to imperfect information.

6. Equilibrium real business cycle theory denies any causal role for money in the business cycle. Rather, the cycle is seen as resulting from real shocks that hit the economy and are then distributed throughout it currently and also into future periods by a variety of propagation mechanisms. The main real shocks are to productivity and government spending. The main propagation mechanism is intertemporal substitution of leisure and consumption. More standard mechanisms, such as inventory accumulation and investment in physical capital, also play a role.

7. The rational expectations approach to policy making emphasizes the credibility of policies as an important factor in determining policy success or failure. The approach views institutional reform as the main way to get better policy.

8. Supply-side economics focuses on the incentive effects of taxation. There are two groups — mainstream and radical. The radical group attracted much attention at the time the new Reagan fiscal policy was going into effect in 1981. That group argued that the incentive effects of taxes were powerful enough to prevent tax cuts from causing a major budget deficit and would have a powerful supply-side effect on inflation. Neither argument was supported by later events. Mainstream supply-siders continue to be influential in both policy making and economics.

9. The approach to wage stickiness of Chapters 13 and 14 achieves one synthesis of Keynesian and rational expectations approaches by basing the slow adjustment of wages and prices to changes in monetary policy on the existence of long-term labor contracts.

10. The New Keynesianism has accepted the challenge of the rational expectations equilibrium approach to develop microeconomic foundations for Keynesian macroeconomics. For this purpose it has built on efficiency wage theory, the small menu cost – monopolistic competition approach, and the role of imperfect information in the capital markets.

11. Efficiency wage theories explain real wage stickiness as being a result of losses in productivity that would occur if firms cut wages. In combination with small menu

costs, efficiency wage theory can account for sticky wages and prices as well as unemployment.

12. The small menu cost – monopolistic competition approach shows that even small costs of changing prices may keep prices from changing. In that case, an increase in the money stock will lead to an increase in output. The approach also shows the close link between Keynesian macroeconomics and imperfect, or monopolistic, competition. It further shows that coordination difficulties may help account for the slow adjustment of the economy to shocks.

KEY TERMS

Monetary rule

Rational expectations equilibrium approach

Credibility

Imperfect information

Real business cycles

Propagation mechanism

Intertemporal substitution of leisure

Productivity shock

Supply-side economics

Reaganomics

New Keynesians

Efficiency wages

Small menu costs

Coordination difficulties

Multiple equilibria

Disequilibrium approach

PROBLEMS

1. Figure 18-3 shows the growth rate of money for the 1979 – 1988 period. To what extent do those data justify the view that inflation is caused by money growth? (Explain your answer.)

2. Using the *IS-LM* model, examine the effects of a combination of tight money and easy fiscal policy on the real interest rate. To what extent is that analysis supported by the data in Table 18-2?

3. (a) In what ways is monetarism closer to Keynesianism than to the rational expectations equilibrium approach?

   (b) In what ways is monetarism closer to the rational expectations equilibrium approach than to Keynesianism?

4. Distinguish and define the two components of the rational expectations equilibrium approach to macroeconomics.

5. Suppose that people did not believe the Fed was serious about stopping inflation in 1979, 1980, and 1981. Can you then reconcile the 1981 – 1982 recession with the rational expectations approach? Explain.

6. (a) Explain why, in the aggregate supply and demand model of Chapter 14, more work is done in booms than recessions.

   (b) Contrast this with the real business cycle explanation.

7. Supply-side economics points, appropriately, to the importance of incentives in determining economic behavior. Why then have mainstream macroeconomists generally been critical of radical supply-side economics?

8. (a) Why according to efficiency wage theory are employers reluctant to cut wages?

   (b) Suppose there were always some jobs available at a low enough wage. Could efficiency wages still help explain why high unemployment can continue year after year?

*9. Explain why there appears to be a link between Keynesian macroeconomics and monopolistic competition, using the impact of an increase in the money stock on output as an example.

*10. Suppose the money stock is reduced. Explain why if everyone could coordinate the reduction in his or her wages and prices, the economy would be more likely to move smoothly to a new full-employment equilibrium than if everyone had to guess what other people would do.

11. Evaluate the quote of Keynes with which this chapter begins.

12. In the introduction we note contradictory views on the budget deficit. One group of economists believes that large deficits cause high real interest rates and a balance of trade deficit. Another group believes that the budget deficit has no real effects. Going back to Chapter 17, trace the key point that leads to this difference of opinion. What is your opinion of this issue in light of Chapters 17 and 18?

13. At the end of Section 18-1 of this chapter, we raised a set of questions about the performance of the economy, including what accounts for its superior economic performance from 1982 to 1988 relative to the previous 13 years. Among the possibilities are (a) the absence of supply shocks, (b) improved monetary policy, and (c) less active use of fiscal policy. Using what you have learned in earlier chapters, assess the importance of each of these factors.

---

* An asterisk denotes a more difficult problem.

19

LONG-TERM GROWTH AND PRODUCTIVITY

*I*n this chapter we turn our attention away from short-run problems of the business cycle to look at long-run growth — at where the economy has been and where it may be heading in the long term. Figure 19-1 shows U.S. real GNP for the century since 1889. Over long periods output shows roughly steady growth. The business cycle appears as short-run fluctuations around the trend path of output.

From 1889 to 1989 real GNP grew at an average annual rate of 3.2 percent in the United States. At that rate of growth, real GNP doubles every 22 years. As Table 19-1 shows, *per capita* real GNP grew at the slower rate of 1.8 percent, doubling every 39 years. At that rate, a 20-year-old college student could anticipate per capita GNP doubling before she reaches retirement — and thus to the extent that per capita GNP measures the material standard of living, that the material standard of living will roughly double during her working life. The difference between the growth rate of total real GNP and that of per capita real GNP is the result of population growth, which averaged 1.4 percent per annum over the period.

What determines the growth rate of output over long periods? The answer to that question helps in understanding the prospects for rising living standards in the decades ahead. In analyzing long-run growth, it is important to recognize that small differences in the *growth rate* of output cumulate over time to large differences in the *level* of per capita GNP and hence in the standard of living. With a growth rate of per capita income of 2 percent per year it takes 35 years for per capita GNP to double. But if the growth rate is only 1.0 percent, it takes 70 years to achieve a doubling of output per head.[1] If two economies start off at the same level of per capita real GNP, an economy growing at 2 percent per capita will have double the per capita GNP of one

---

[1] The so-called rule of 70 says that to calculate the (approximate) length of time it takes for a variable to double, divide 70 by the percentage growth rate of the variable.

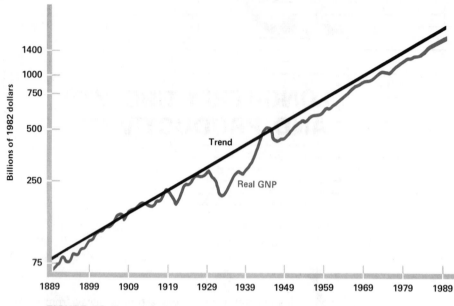

FIGURE 19-1

REAL GNP IN THE UNITED STATES, 1889–1989. (SOURCE: DRI/McGraw-Hill and *Historical Statistics of the United States.*)

TABLE 19-1

U.S. AVERAGE ANNUAL GROWTH RATES

	1889–1989		1964–1989	
	GNP	GNP per capita	GNP	GNP per capita
GNP growth, % per year	3.2	1.8	3.0	2.0

SOURCE: U.S. Department of Commerce, *Long-term Economic Growth, 1860–1970; Economic Report of the President*, 1973; and DRI/McGraw-Hill.

growing at 1 percent within 70 years. Whatever the shortcomings of real GNP as a measure of welfare, the residents of the faster-growing country will be materially much better off as time goes on.

International comparisons of per capita income are presented in Table 19-2. The first row shows per capita incomes in dollars in 1987 for the United States, Japan, and several developing countries. The incomes are translated to a common base through an exchange rate between the local currency and the dollar (e.g., the yen in Japan and the peso in Mexico). There are two problems with this method: First, real exchange rates

TABLE 19-2
COMPARATIVE PER CAPITA INCOME LEVELS

	U.S.	Japan	Korea	Brazil	Mexico	India
Per capita income (1987), 1987 $	18,530	15,760	2,690	2,020	1,830	300
Growth rate (1965–1987), % per year	1.5	4.2	6.4	4.1	2.5	1.8
Per capita income, ICP method (1985), U.S. = 100	100	71.5	24.3	. . .	. . .	4.7

SOURCE: World Bank, *World Development Report,* 1989.

fluctuate a great deal, and thus the comparisons would look very different depending on the exchange rate used.[2] To attempt to deal with this problem the exchange rate used in the top row of Table 19-2 is the average exchange rate for the period 1985–1987.

The second problem is more fundamental. Consider the data for India and the United States in the top row of Table 19-2. Per capita income in India is shown as $300. People could literally not live on such an income in the United States, but on average Indians do survive. Thus in terms of U.S. income, the Indian income level cannot be $300. It must be that incorrect prices (i.e., an incorrect exchange rate) are being used to compare per capita incomes in the two countries in the top row of the table.

The third row of Table 19-2 presents results of the *International Comparisons Project,* which uses a common set of prices to compare incomes across countries.[3] Whereas the income data in the first row imply that per capita income in India is 1.6 percent of U.S. per capita income, measuring those incomes at the *same* set of prices suggests per capita income in India is 4.7 percent of that in the United States. However, that amount is still incredibly low (4.7 percent of U.S. 1987 per capita income is only $870), in fact far below the poverty line in the United States.

Table 19-2 shows that U.S. *growth* in per capita income is much lower than that of the other countries, but that its *level* of per capita income is much higher. However, if Korea, for example, maintains a high growth rate long enough it will ultimately catch up with and even surpass the U.S. level of income. Using the growth rates in Table 19-2, we can calculate that it would take less than 41 years to get there. That may seem to be a long period, but Japan did just that in the post–World War II period. In the past 40 years U.S. real income per capita only doubled but that of Japan increased by a factor of more than 10. From that perspective some of the newly industrialized countries in Asia

---

[2] For historical international comparisons see Angus Maddison, *Phases of Capitalist Development* (London: Oxford University Press, 1982). However, it is difficult to compare incomes both across time and across countries. The difficulties of comparing incomes across countries and a methodology for these comparisons are presented in Irving Kravis et al., *World Product and Income* (Baltimore, Md.: Johns Hopkins University Press, 1982). See, too, A. Bergson, "Comparative Productivity," *American Economic Review,* June 1987.

[3] See, too, A. Maddison, *The World in the Twentieth Century,* Paris: OECD, 1989, and the data from that publication presented on the first back endpaper of this book.

and Latin America may well get within reach of the old and established nations, such as the United Kingdom, Germany, or even the United States, within the next 30 to 50 years.

To answer questions about the long-run growth rate of output, we go back to fundamentals. With the unemployment rate constant, there are only two possible sources of growth:[4] *Factor supplies may grow, or the productivity of factors of production may increase.* This, in turn, raises the questions of what determines the growth of factor supplies and their productivity, and what the quantitative link is between growth in factor supplies and productivity, on the one side, and output growth, on the other.

There are two complementary approaches to these questions. One is *growth theory,* which models the interactions among factor supplies, output growth, saving, and investment in the process of growth. The other is *growth accounting,* which attempts to quantify the contribution of different determinants of output growth. The two approaches draw on a common analytical framework, which we now outline.

19-1 SOURCES OF GROWTH IN REAL INCOME

In this section we use the production function to study the *sources of growth.* We show that growth in labor, growth in capital, and improved technical efficiency are the three sources of growth.

The Production Function

In earlier chapters we introduced the concept of a production function. The *production function* links the amount of output produced in an economy to the inputs of factors of production and to the state of technical knowledge. Equation (1) represents the production function in symbols:

$$Y = AF(K, N) \tag{1}$$

where K and N denote the inputs of capital and labor and A denotes the state of technology. The production function $AF(K, N)$ in (1) states that the output produced depends on factor inputs K and N and on the state of technology. Increases in factor inputs and improved technology lead to an increase in output supply.

The next step is to make these links more precise by looking at an expression for the growth rate of output. In equation (2), which is derived in the appendix, we show the determinants of output growth.[5]

---

[4] It is not essential for what follows that the average unemployment rate be the same as the natural rate; we make that assumption purely to simplify the exposition.

[5] Equation (2) applies when there are *constant returns to scale* in production; that is, increases in both inputs, in the same proportion, increase output in that proportion.

$$\Delta Y / Y = (1 - \theta) \times \Delta N / N + \quad \theta \quad \times \Delta K / K + \quad \Delta A / A \tag{2}$$

$$\frac{\text{Output}}{\text{growth}} = \frac{\text{labor}}{\text{share}} \times \frac{\text{labor}}{\text{growth}} + \frac{\text{capital}}{\text{share}} \times \frac{\text{capital}}{\text{growth}} + \frac{\text{technical}}{\text{progress}}$$

where $(1 - \theta)$ and θ are weights equal to the income shares of labor and of capital in production.

Equation (2) summarizes the contributions of growth of inputs and of improved productivity to growth of output:

1. The contribution of the growth of factor inputs is seen in the first two terms. Labor and capital each contribute an amount equal to their individual growth rates *multiplied by the share of that input in income.*
2. The rate of improvement of technology, called *technical progress,* or the *growth of total factor productivity,* is the third term in equation (2). The growth rate of total factor productivity is the amount by which output would increase as a result of improvements in methods of production, with all inputs unchanged. In other words, there is growth in total factor productivity when we get more output from the same factors of production.[6]

EXAMPLE: Suppose the income share of capital is 0.25 and that of labor is 0.75. These values correspond approximately to the actual values for the U.S. economy. Furthermore, let labor force growth be 1.2 percent and growth of the capital stock be 3 percent, and suppose total factor productivity to grow at the rate of 1.5 percent per annum. What is the growth rate of output? Applying equation (2) we obtain a growth rate of $\Delta Y / Y = 3.2$ percent ($= 0.75 \times 1.2$ percent $+ 0.25 \times 3$ percent $+ 1.5$ percent).

An important point in equation (2) is that the growth rates of capital and labor are weighted by the respective income shares. The reason for these weights is that the importance to production of, say a one-percentage-point change in labor differs from the same percentage-point change in capital, and that difference in importance is measured by the relative income shares of each factor. Specifically, if labor has a larger share than capital, output rises more when labor increases by, say 10 percent, than if capital increases by 10 percent.

Returning to our example, if labor alone grows by 1 percent, output will grow by 0.75 percent, using the 0.75 percent income share for labor. If capital alone grows by 1 percent, output will grow by only 0.25 percent, reflecting the smaller importance of capital in production. But if each grows by 1 percent, so does output.[7]

---

[6] There is a distinction between *labor productivity* and total factor productivity. Labor productivity is just the ratio of output to labor input, Y/N. Labor productivity certainly grows as a result of technical progress, but it also grows because of the accumulation of capital per worker.

[7] This result holds only when there are constant returns to scale in production; if there are increasing returns to scale, an increase in each input by 1 percent will increase output by more than 1 percent — as explained in the next subsection.

This point — that growth in inputs is weighted by factor shares — turns out to be quite critical when we ask how much extra growth we get by raising the rate of growth of the capital stock, say by supply-side policies. Suppose in the example above, with everything else the same, capital growth had been twice as high — 6 percent instead of 3 percent. Doing the calculations with the help of equation (2), we find that output growth would increase to 3.9 percent, rising by less than a percentage point even though capital growth rose by three percentage points.

INCREASING RETURNS TO SCALE

The result cited in the preceding paragraphs — namely, if each input grows by 1 percent, so does output — holds only when there are constant returns to scale. If there are increasing returns to scale, then a 1 percent increase in each input results in a greater than 1 percent increase in output. Whether there are increasing or constant returns to scale is a matter of fact, with much of the evidence suggesting that returns to scale are roughly constant. We now turn to the evidence.

19-2 EMPIRICAL ESTIMATES OF THE SOURCES OF GROWTH

The previous section prepares us for an analysis of empirical studies that deal with sources of growth. Equation (2) suggests that the growth in output can be explained by growth in factor inputs, weighted by their shares in income, and by technical progress. An early and famous study by Nobel prizewinner Robert Solow of MIT dealt with the

TABLE 19-3
SOURCES OF GROWTH OF TOTAL NATIONAL INCOME,
1929–1982

Source of growth	Growth rate, % per year
Total factor input	1.90
Labor: 1.34	
Capital: 0.56	
Output per unit of input	1.02
Knowledge: 0.66	
Resource allocation: 0.23	
Economies of scale: 0.26	
Other: 0.03	
National income	$\overline{2.92}$

SOURCE: Edward Denison, *Trends in American Economic Growth,*
1929–1982 (Washington, D.C.: The Brookings Institution, 1985),
Table 8-1.

period 1909–1949 in the United States.[8] Solow's surprising conclusion was that over 80 percent of the growth in output per labor hour over that period was due to technical progress, that is, to factors other than growth in the input of capital per labor hour. Specifically, Solow estimated an equation for the United States similar to equation (2) that identifies capital and labor growth along with technical progress as the sources of output growth. Of the average annual growth of total GNP of 2.9 percent per year over that period, he concluded that 0.32 percent was attributable to capital accumulation, 1.09 percent per annum was due to increases in the input of labor, and the remaining 1.49 percent was due to technical progress. Per capita output grew at 1.81 percent, with 1.49 percent of that increase resulting from technical progress.

The very large part of growth that is explained by technical progress makes that term really a catchall for omitted factors and poor measurement of the capital and labor inputs. Further work therefore turned quite naturally to explore this residual, that is, growth not explained by capital accumulation or increased labor input.

One of the most comprehensive of the subsequent studies is that by Edward Denison.[9] Using data for the period 1929–1982, Denison attributed 1.9 percent of the 2.9 percent annual rate of increase in real output to increased factor inputs. Output per labor hour grew at the rate of 1.58 percent, of which 1.02 percent was due to technical progress. Denison's findings thus support Solow's estimate that most of the growth in output per labor hour is due to technical progress. Table 19-3 shows Denison's breakdown of the sources of U.S. growth over the period 1929–1982.

Technical progress explains one-third of the growth in output, with growth in total factor inputs accounting for the other two-thirds of growth. Consider now the breakdown among the various components of increased factor use. Here increases in the labor force get a very large credit for their contribution to growth. Why? Because labor grows very fast? The answer is provided by equation (2), which suggests that labor's growth rate has a relatively large weight mainly because labor's share of income is relatively large. The counterpart is obviously the relatively low share of capital. As noted above, even if capital and labor grew at the same rate, the fact that they have different shares in income — labor having a share of about 75 percent and capital having a share of about 25 percent — implies that labor would be credited with a larger contribution toward growth.

Next we look at the various sources of increased factor productivity or increased output per unit of factor input. Here the striking fact is the importance of advances in knowledge, which account for almost two-thirds of the contribution of technical progress toward growth. Two other sources of increased factor productivity are worth recording. One is the increase in productivity that stems from improved resource

[8] "Technical Change and the Aggregate Production Function," *Review of Economics and Statistics,* August 1957.

[9] *Accounting for United States Economic Growth, 1929–1969* (Washington, D.C.: The Brookings Institution, 1974). See also Denison's *Accounting for Slower Economic Growth: The United States in the 1970s* (Washington, D.C.: The Brookings Institution, 1980); *Trends in American Economic Growth, 1929–1982* (Washington, D.C.: The Brookings Institution, 1985); and *Estimates of Productivity Change by Industry* (Washington, D.C.: The Brookings Institution, 1989).

allocation. Here we can think of people leaving low-paying jobs or low-income areas and moving to better jobs or locations, thus contributing to increased output or income growth. An important element is relocation from farms to cities.

The remaining significant part of technical progress is *economies of scale*. This is a bit troublesome because we explicitly assumed constant returns to scale in deriving equation (2), but we find now that more than 10 percent of the average annual growth in income is attributed to the expanding scale of operation in the economy. As the scale of operation of the economy expands, fewer inputs are required per unit of output, presumably because we can avail ourselves of techniques that are economically inefficient at a small-scale level but yield factor savings at a larger scale of production.

The major significance of Denison's work, and the work in this area of others, including Nobel laureate Simon Kuznets (1901 – 1985) and J. W. Kendrick, is to point out that there is no single critical source of real income growth. The early finding by Solow that growth in the capital stock makes a minor, though not negligible, contribution to growth stands up well to the test of later research.[10] Capital investment is certainly necessary — particularly because some technological improvements require the use of new types of machines — but it is clear that other sources of growth can make an important contribution. Furthermore, since for many purposes we are interested in output per head, we have to recognize that we are left with only technical progress and growth in capital to achieve increased output per head. Here we have to ask, What are the components of technical progress? *Advances in knowledge and efficiency stand out as the major sources and point to the roles of research, education, and training as important sources of growth.*[11]

The Decline of Growth

U.S. output growth declined in the 1970s. The decline in growth was not limited to the United States, as can be seen in Table 19-4, which shows the growth rates of output for the five largest (non-Soviet) industrial economies. In each of these countries there was a major decline in GNP growth after 1973, and in each of them there was an increase in the 1980s. But only for the United Kingdom does the growth rate for the last four years

[10] The major exception is in work by Dale Jorgenson and his associates. The results of a massive study are presented in Dale Jorgenson, Frank Gollop, and Barbara Fraumeni, *Productivity and U.S. Economic Growth* (Cambridge, Mass.: Harvard University Press, 1987). Working with data for the period 1948– 1979, for which the overall growth rate was 3.4 percent, Jorgenson et al. estimate that capital inputs contributed 1.6 percentage points of that growth, labor inputs 1.05 percentage points, and productivity growth only 0.8 percentage points. One-quarter of the increased capital input is attributed to quality improvements, and thus fully 1.2 percentage points of growth are attributed to an increased input of capital — significantly more than Denison's estimate. Understanding of the sources of the difference between the Jorgenson et al. and other measures of the contribution of improved technical knowledge to growth will have to wait for a more advanced course.

[11] A collection of useful papers on the sources of growth are contained in Edmund Phelps (ed.), *The Goal of Economics Growth* (New York: Norton, 1969), and Dennis C. Mueller (ed.), *The Political Economy of Growth* (New Haven, Conn.: Yale University Press, 1983).

TABLE 19-4

GROWTH PERFORMANCE IN MAJOR ECONOMIES (percent per year)*

	U.S.	Japan	Germany	France	U.K.
1960–1973	4.0	9.6	4.4	5.7	3.1
1973–1979	2.4	3.6	2.3	3.0	1.5
1979–1986	2.4	3.8	1.4	1.6	1.4
1986–1990†	3.2	4.6	2.7	2.6	3.4

* Data are for GDP through 1986; for GNP, 1986–1990.

† Data include projections by OECD.

SOURCE: OECD, *Historical Statistics*, 1960–1986, and *Economic Outlook*, December 1988.

TABLE 19-5

PRODUCTIVITY TRENDS IN MAJOR ECONOMIES (business sector total factor productivity*; percent per year)

	U.S.	Japan	Germany	France	U.K.
1960–1973	1.5	6.3†	2.6	3.9	1.9
1973–1979	−0.1	1.8	1.8	1.8	0.2
1979–1986	0.1	1.7	0.8	1.2	1.0
1986–1990‡	0.8	2.2	1.3	1.8	1.8

* The rate of increase of total factor productivity corresponds to $\Delta A/A$, the rate of technical progress, in equation (2).

† For the period 1966–1973.

‡ Data include projections by the OECD.

SOURCE: OECD, *Economic Outlook*, December 1988, p. 46.

of the 1980s match that for 1960–1973; interestingly, the decline in growth is greater the higher the growth rate for 1960–1973.

Table 19-5 spotlights the cause of the worsened growth performance: In the 1970s average growth rates of productivity declined throughout the industrialized world. There was a slight improvement in the United States and the United Kingdom between 1980 and 1986, with continued worsening in that period in Japan, Germany, and France. The OECD projects more rapid productivity growth for the period 1986–1990, but for none of the five largest economies is the growth rate of productivity projected to return to anywhere close to the growth rate of 1960–1973.

Pinpointing the exact source of the decline in productivity growth in the 1970s remains a controversial issue—and a crucial one, because lower growth means a

box 19-1 PRODUCTIVITY GROWTH ACROSS SECTORS

Growth rates of total factor productivity differ widely across sectors. Manufacturing invariably stands out as having especially high rates; in the nonmanufacturing business sector, by contrast, *measured* productivity growth is much lower. This is particularly striking in the 1980s.

Table 1 shows data for U.S. total factor productivity growth for the private economy and for manufacturing. Manufacturing accounts for about 22 percent of GNP and 27 percent of business output.

The data raise questions especially about the measurement of productivity; in part this is a question about the classification of industries. In part it raises doubts about how effectively we measure output in some service industries, such as banks or the government or telecommunications. Some argue that in fact in some areas in the service sector productivity growth is significantly underestimated. ∎

TABLE 1

TOTAL FACTOR PRODUCTIVITY GROWTH (percent per year)

	Total private business	Manufacturing
1948–1973	2.0	2.0
1973–1979	0.1	0.5
1979–1986	0.5	2.6

SOURCE: Edward Denison, *Estimates of Productivity Change by Industry* (Washington, D.C.: The Brookings Institution, 1989).

slower rate of improvement in the standard of living. Explanations for lower productivity growth include[12]

- A worsened age-skill mix of the labor force (the baby-boom generation and more part-timers coming into the labor force)

- The costs of "nuisance" outputs such as investment in pollution abatement and crime prevention

- The very sharp increases in the price of oil during this period

- A slowdown in the rate of innovation[13]

- An increase in government regulation

---

[12] For detailed accounting of the decline in growth see Denison's works, cited in footnote 9, and J. W. Kendrick, "The Implications of Growth Accounting Models," in Charles Hulten and Isabel Sawhill (eds.), *The Legacy of Reaganomics* (Washington, D.C.: Urban Institute Press, 1984).

[13] A. Steven Englander, Robert Evenson, and Masaharu Hanazaki, "R&D, Innovation and the Total Factor Productivity Slowdown," *OECD Economic Studies*, no. 11 (Autumn 1988), present evidence that the large slowdown in innovation in the 1970s contributed significantly to the slowdown in economic growth.

The rise in the price of oil would have had an effect by making much existing capital (gas-guzzlers, for example) obsolete and requiring new investment to be used to replace existing capital rather than to expand productive capacity.[14]

Increased government regulation includes antipollution requirements as well as rules that make it very expensive to fire workers and therefore increase the costs of reallocating labor in response to changing prices and opportunities. Government regulations (and labor unions) have been especially blamed for the European growth slow-down, also called "Eurosclerosis." In J. W. Kendrick's international comparison of the sources of growth slowdown, government regulation appears uniformly as a negative contribution to growth.[15] In principle, government regulation could be a source of increased efficiency and therefore of growth. But in none of the nine countries and two subperiods studied by Kendrick is this the case. Government regulation, from this account, appears harmful to growth. But in interpreting that finding we must bear in mind that the regulation that reduced pollution brought improvements in the quality of the environment. These improvements make us better off but do not show up in GNP.

The period of the productivity slowdown from 1973 to roughly 1983 was also a period in which the use of computers spread rapidly and an electronic revolution took place. Many find it difficult to believe that the rate of productivity growth slowed at that time — after all, isn't life better as a result of the invention and spread of the personal computer, VCRs, compact disks, and other electronic equipment? — and some believe that the slowdown may be purely a result of the fact that we do not measure output correctly. Careful examination of the data suggests that mismeasurement is unlikely to explain the slowdown.[16]

Many of the causes given for the productivity slowdown — the entry of the baby boomers into the labor force, the rise in the price of oil, the spread of government regulation — have been reversed. The rate of increase of productivity has risen since the early 1980s, and may well increase a bit further, as projected in Table 19-5. But there are few who project an increase in the rate of productivity growth to pre-1973 rates. Increasingly, the period from the end of World War II to 1973 is being seen as a golden age of rapid growth, perhaps a period of catch-up from the effects of the great depression and World War II. As the time since 1973 passes, it looks as if we have to get used to the idea that productivity growth is not what it used to be. And, remembering the importance of changes in the growth rate, we can anticipate that this change in productivity growth will have huge consequences for likely future standards of living.

---

[14] See "Symposium on the Slowdown in Productivity Growth," *Journal of Economic Literature,* Fall 1988, as well as A. Maddison, "Growth and Slowdown in Advanced Capitalist Economies: Techniques of Quantitative Assessment," *Journal of Economic Literature,* June 1987.

[15] See J. W. Kendrick, "International Comparisons of Recent Productivity Trends," in W. Fellner (ed.), *Contemporary Economic Problems* (Washington, D.C.: American Enterprise Institute, 1981).

[16] See Martin Neil Baily and Robert J. Gordon, "The Productivity Slowdown, Measurement Issues, and the Explosion of Computer Power," *Brookings Papers on Economic Activity,* no. 2 (1988). Martin Bailey and Alok Chakrabarti, *Innovation and the Productivity Crisis* (Washington, D.C.: The Brookings Institution, 1988), and Edward Denison, *Estimates of Productivity Change by Industry* (Washington, D.C.: The Brookings Institution, 1989).

19-3 OUTPUT GROWTH AND SUPPLY-SIDE ECONOMICS

In the early 1980s, partly as a result of disappointment with slow growth and generally poor macroeconomic performance, *supply-side economics* (discussed in Chapter 18) attracted much attention. We now concentrate on the solid aspect, which argues that the level and/or the growth rate of output could be significantly increased through policies designed to promote greater efficiency, reduced regulation, greater willingness to work, and greater willingness to save and invest.[17]

In discussing full-employment output in earlier chapters we took the labor supply to be given and independent of the real wage, and similarly, we assumed a given stock of capital. But the basic premise of supply-side economics is that capital and labor supplies are not given, independent of incentives to work, save, and invest. On the contrary, it is argued that the labor-leisure choice is strongly affected by the *after-tax* real wage and that the willingness to save and invest is likewise affected by the *after-tax* rates of return on assets. This perspective directs attention to fiscal policy as influencing factor supplies and hence the level and rate of increase of output.

Labor Supply

Households have to choose how much labor to supply. In practice that means choosing how many members of the family work and for how many hours per week or month. At first sight there appears to be little choice, since the typical job comes with a given number of working hours per week. But that is not quite the case once we take into account the possibility that more than one family member might work or the possibilities of working overtime hours or holding part-time jobs. A household's labor supply can thus vary in response to incentives.

The main determinant of labor supply is the after-tax real wage. Suppose it rises. Then some family members who had preferred to stay home may now be tempted into the labor force. But for those already working, the real wage increase has ambiguous effects on labor supply. The *income effect* of the wage increase tends to reduce labor supply because it is now possible to work less and earn more. But because every hour of leisure is now more costly, the *substitution effect* tends to increase the labor supply. The outcome of conflicting income and substitution effects is thus a matter for empirical study. In addition, of course, higher participation in the labor force will tend to increase the labor supply when the after-tax real wage rises.

---

[17] On supply-side economics see particularly Barry Bosworth, *Tax Incentives and Economic Growth* (Washington, D.C.: The Brookings Institution, 1984); Hulten and Sawhill (eds.), *The Legacy of Reaganomics;* Laurence Meyer (ed.), *The Supply Side Effects of Economic Policy* (Federal Reserve Bank of St. Louis, 1981); and Martin Feldstein, "Supply Side Economics: Old Truths and New Claims," *American Economic Review,* May 1986. For a historical treatment see Nathan Roisenberg and L. E. Birdzell, *How the West Grew Rich* (New York: Basic Books, 1987).

Empirical Evidence

Jerry Hausman of MIT has shown in a number of studies that the household labor supply increases *significantly* in response to increased after-tax real wages.[18] This implies that changes in the tax structure that increase the after-tax real wage would increase labor supply and output. Hausman finds that the progressivity of income taxes reduces the labor supply of someone already working. The magnitude of the effect can be judged from the following experiment. Suppose the progressive income tax structure were eliminated and replaced by a flat 15 percent income tax that would lead to the same amount of revenue. What would happen to labor supply? Hausman estimates that total labor supply would rise by 5 percent. With an income share of 0.75, a 5 percent growth in labor supply would increase the level of full-employment output by 3.75 percent. This is certainly a nonnegligible gain, although the policy experiment — the move to a flat income tax — is quite radical.

Supply of Capital

The supply of capital represents the cumulation of past investment. The capital stock grows if additions to the stock more than offset the depreciation due to wear and tear and to obsolescence.

A supply-side point of view emphasizes the links between saving and investment. Recall that when the goods market clears and when net exports are zero, investment minus saving equals the budget surplus, or

$$I = S + (T - G) \tag{3}$$

Equation (3) shows that to raise investment, and thus the growth of the capital stock, we require increased saving or reduced government budget deficits. Supply-side economics has focused on the incentives to save and invest. Supply-side economists argue that regulation has reduced the productivity of investment and that corporate and personal income taxes further reduce the rate of return eventually received by the savers who provide the funds needed to finance investment. The claim of supply-siders is that if savers receive a lower rate of return as a result of taxation, they reduce saving, and therefore capital accumulation is reduced.[19]

For instance, consider an investment that yields 12 percent per year in real terms. That is, someone who undertakes the investment, costing $100 in year 1, earns $12 per year in real terms forever after (net of labor and material costs). If the income

---

[18] See J. Hausman, "Labor Supply and the Natural Unemployment Rate," in Meyer (ed.), *The Supply Side Effects,* and Henry Aaron and Joseph Pechman (eds.), *How Taxes Affect Economic Behavior* (Washington, D.C.: The Brookings Institution, 1981).

[19] In "Symposium on the Slowdown in Productivity Growth," *Journal of Economic Perspectives,* Fall 1988, the chairman of the Council of Economic Advisers, Michael Boskin, presents evidence for the view that the current tax system discriminates strongly against saving.

tax rate is 40 percent, the saver can at most earn, after tax, 60 percent of 12 percent, or 7.2 percent. As a result of taxation, the return to saving is substantially reduced. Accordingly, claim supply-siders, the higher the tax rate, the less saving there will be.

What policies could increase the yield on saving? There is considerable support for the use of a *consumption tax* rather than the income tax. A consumption tax levies taxes only on consumption spending, not on income. Since the difference between income and consumption is saving, a consumption tax effectively exempts any amount that is saved from being taxed in the year it is earned, and thereby encourages saving.

There is considerable disagreement on the issue of the response of saving to changes in its return. The contention that increased after-tax rates of return to saving will *strongly* raise saving does not have much support. Once again we have two opposing effects: With increased interest rates, less saving is needed to ensure a given future income, say for retirement. This effect (actually an income effect) reduces saving. At the same time a dollar saved today yields increased future wealth and consumption and would therefore lead households to postpone consumption and increase saving (this is the substitution effect). The balance of effects is theoretically uncertain.

The empirical evidence does not settle the issue of whether changes in the after-tax rate of return affect the rate of saving.[20] Therefore, policies that reduce taxes on saving as a means of generating more saving, capital formation, and growth have an uncertain effect on the economy.

Another line of argument questions the quantitative importance of policies to promote saving. We note from the growth equation (2) that growth in capital receives a very small weight in determining output growth. Even if policies led to a 10 percent rise in the capital-labor ratio, output per head would increase by only 2.5 percent. But to achieve a 10 percent rise in the capital-labor ratio, say over 10 years, net investment as a share of GNP would have to double.[21]

Regulation

Government regulation involves a tradeoff. Government regulations serve some social purpose (the environment, safety, conservation), but they also involve costs to firms that have to abide by them. Regulation therefore reduces business profitability. Policy makers are keenly aware that the tradeoff exists and therefore, rightly, focus on inefficient regulation and particularly costly (nonmarket) regulation as requiring re-

---

[20] Gerald A. Carlino, "Interest Rate Effects and Intertemporal Consumption," *Journal of Monetary Economics,* March 1982, reviews and extends the (ambiguous) evidence. See, too, Larry Kotlikoff, "Taxation and Savings: A Neoclassical Perspective," *Journal of Economic Literature,* December 1984.

[21] Suppose the capital stock is equal to 3 times output. Then a 10 percent increase in capital represents an amount equal to 30 percent of GNP or, over a 10-year period, an increase in net investment of 3 percent of GNP. *Net* investment is now between 2 and 5 percent of GNP. The increase therefore would imply doubling the share of net investment in GNP.

view. That process has been under way for some time, but it would be a mistake to expect major growth in output from reduced regulation.

Budget Deficits and Growth

In equation (3) we showed that private investment and capital formation will be higher when saving is higher and the government budget deficit is smaller.[22] Government budget deficits thus imply, other things equal, a reduction in full-employment output growth. Government budget deficits absorb private saving — households buy government securities rather than the stocks or bonds that firms issue to finance their investment. Therefore funds are diverted from growth toward other purposes. It is clear that if the only objective is to promote growth, the government should balance the budget or even run a surplus to free resources for investment. However, there is a tradeoff between growth and the social objectives that may lie behind a budget deficit.

Evaluating Supply-Side Economics and Growth Incentives

The emphasis on increasing incentives to work, save, and invest is the valid core of supply-side economics. There are two questions here. The first is, Will the proposed policies work, that is, increase future potential output? The second question is, If the policies do work, how far should we go in creating incentives to increase future potential output?

Policies to increase the labor supply by reducing taxes and policies to increase investment by reducing government budget deficits and by providing investment subsidies would be effective in increasing potential output today and in the future. Thus supply-side policies are available. But we can also go overboard on such policies. If we are reducing government budget deficits while reducing other taxes, we are also reducing government spending. We could reduce government spending by getting rid of the armed forces. But most people would think it better to have higher taxes and some armed forces than lower taxes and no armed forces. And similarly, the government provides many useful services through its welfare programs — consumption services that most people prefer to have — rather than aiming purely to maximize the level of investment.

Further, given government spending, and at full employment, increases in saving imply reductions in consumption. Thus in supply-side economics we are trading off current consumption for future consumption. We are trading off the consumption of those now alive for the consumption of their children and children who will come later yet. This process, also, can go too far. In the extreme, we (society) would not want to

---

[22] We implicitly assume that all investment is undertaken by the private sector, not by the government. But in many countries government investment is a large part of total investment. Larry Kotlikoff, "The Economic Impact of Deficit Financing," IMF *Staff Papers*, November 1984, shows that budget deficits have particularly strong adverse effects on long-term growth.

force the current generation to consume at a bare survival level just so that their grandchildren will be able to sit around their pools doing very little work while automated factories made possible by a huge volume of past investment produce a high level of output. Somewhere between not saving now and saving almost all of output, there is an optimal amount of saving to be done.

How can a society decide what that optimal amount of saving is? Those who will be consuming in the future are not here to vote because they have not yet been born. And those who are around now will have different views. Some may ask, as reportedly has Joan Robinson (1905–1984), the famous English economist, "What did posterity ever do for us?" Others may feel it is the duty of the parents to sacrifice for their children's sake. Ultimately the policy decisions that affect growth are settled politically.

19-4 GROWTH THEORY

We turn now from empirical issues and the historical record to the theory of economic growth. The goal of growth theory is to explain the determinants of growth rates within a country and the reasons for differences in per capita incomes across countries. One of the central results of growth theory, for example, is the proposition that between two countries with the same technology and saving rates the one that has the higher rate of population growth will eventually have lower per capita income.

We have already examined the sources of growth in equation (2), where we showed that full-employment output growth depends on the growth in factor inputs and on technical progress. In this section we pursue the issue further to ask what determines the growth of factor supplies and what is the link to long-run per capita incomes or standards of living.

We start with a rather simple formulation by assuming a given and constant rate of labor force growth, $\Delta N/N \equiv n$, and also that there is no technical progress, that is, $\Delta A/A = 0$.[23] With these assumptions the only variable element left in equation (2) is the growth rate of capital. Capital growth is determined by saving, which, in turn, depends on income. Income, or output, in turn, depends on capital. We are thus set with an interdependent system in which capital growth depends, via saving and income, on the capital stock. We now study the short-run behavior, the adjustment process, and the long-run equilibrium of that interdependent system.

Steady State

We start by discussing the steady state of the economy. Here we ask whether in an economy with population growth and saving, and therefore growth in the capital stock,

---

[23] For further simplicity we also assume that the entire population works, so that the labor force and the population are the same.

we reach a point at which output per head and capital per head become constant. In such a steady state, current saving and additions to the capital stock would be just enough to equip new entrants into the labor force with the same amount of capital as the average worker uses.

The idea of a steady state is this: If capital per head is unchanging, given technology, so is output per head. But for capital *per head* to remain unchanging even though population is growing, capital must grow at just the right rate, namely, at the same rate as population. More formally, if output per head is to remain constant, output and population must grow at the same rates, or $\Delta Y/Y = \Delta N/N = n$. Therefore, from equation (2), setting productivity growth and growth in output per capita equal to zero, we have $0 = \Delta K/K - n$, or

$$\frac{\Delta K}{K} = n \qquad (4)$$

Equation (4) states that in the steady state the growth rate of the capital stock is equal to the growth rate of population. Equivalently, in the steady state the amount of capital per head is constant.

We now show the steady state graphically in Figure 19-2. We put output per head on the vertical axis and capital per head on the horizontal axis. The production function, which is central to the understanding of growth, exhibits diminishing returns *to capital*.[24] As capital per head increases, so that workers use increasing amounts of machinery, output per head increases, but at a diminishing rate. Thus an increase in the capital-labor ratio is productive, but there are diminishing returns. In steady state, the economy settles down to a fixed capital-labor ratio, $(K/N)^*$. The production function shows the corresponding amount of output per head $(Y/N)^*$.

Saving and Growth

Now we examine the link between saving and growth in capital. We are assuming there is no government sector. Accordingly, investment, or the gross increase in capital, is equal to saving. To obtain the increase in the capital stock, however, we have to deduct depreciation. Therefore the net addition to the capital stock is equal to saving less depreciation.

$$\Delta K = \text{saving} - \text{depreciation} \qquad (5)$$

Two assumptions take us from (4) and (5) to a complete description of the steady state. In (5) we need to specify saving behavior and to make an assumption about depreciation. We assume first that saving is a constant fraction, s, of income, Y. Second, depreciation is at a constant rate of d percent of the capital stock. Concretely, we might assume that people save $s = 15$ percent of their income and that depreciation is at a

---

[24] With constant returns to scale, there are diminishing returns to either factor separately.

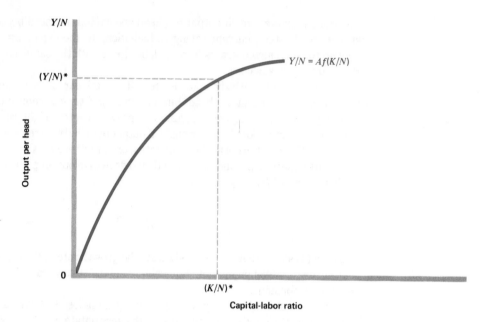

FIGURE 19-2
OUTPUT PER HEAD AND THE CAPITAL-LABOR RATIO. The production
function shows output per head as a function of the amount of capital
per head, or the capital-labor ratio. The higher the capital-labor ratio,
the higher is output per head. But the increment to output that results
from raising the capital-labor ratio grows progressively smaller as the
capital-labor ratio rises.

rate of 10 percent per year, so that every year 10 percent of the capital stock needs to
be replaced to offset wear and tear.

Substituting these assumptions in equation (5) yields

$$\Delta K = sY - dK \qquad (6)$$

or, using equation (4), we arrive at the following result, which describes the steady
state:[25]

$$sY = (n + d)K \qquad (6a)$$

Equation (6a) states that in the steady state, saving (sY) is just sufficient to
provide for enough investment to offset depreciation (dK) *and* to equip new members

---

[25] Substituting equation (6) into equation (4) yields $(sY - dK)/K = n$. By multiplying both sides by K and
collecting terms, we obtain $sY = (n + d)K$.

of the labor force with capital (nK). If saving were larger than this amount, capital per head would grow, leading to rising income per head. Conversely, if not enough were saved, capital per head would fall and with it income per head.

The Growth Process

We next study the adjustment process that leads the economy from some initial capital-labor ratio over time to the steady state. The critical element in this transition process is the rate of saving and investment compared with the rate of depreciation and population growth.

NOTATION

The argument is made easier by a bit of new notation. We define the amount of output per head as $x = Y/N$ and the amount of capital per head, or the capital-labor ratio, as $k = Y/N$. This is simply notation and in no way changes our model.

$$k \equiv \text{capital-labor ratio} = \frac{K}{N} \qquad x \equiv \text{output per head} = \frac{Y}{N} \qquad (7)$$

Thus in terms of Figure 19-2 the vertical axis is labeled x, and the horizontal axis k.

CAPITAL ACCUMULATION

We now turn to the transition to the steady state. Note from equation (2) that output per head will grow if capital per head grows and that capital per head will grow if saving is *more than sufficient* to cover depreciation of the capital stock and also to equip new members of the population with capital. This can be formalized by writing the change in the capital-labor ratio as follows:[26]

$$\Delta k = sx - (n + d)k \qquad (8)$$

The growth process can now be studied with the help of equation ($6a$) and Figure 19-3. Here we reproduce the production function from Figure 19-2, writing output per capita as a function of the capital-labor ratio.

We have added the saving function, which, for each capital-labor ratio, is simply the fraction s of output. Thus, for any capital-labor ratio, say, k_0, the corresponding

---

[26] The percentage growth rate of the capital-labor ratio is equal to the difference between the growth rate of capital and the growth rate of labor, or $\Delta k/k = \Delta K/K - n$. Now using equation (6) to replace ΔK, we have

$$\frac{\Delta k}{k} = \frac{sY}{K} - d - n = \frac{s(Y/N)}{K/N} - (d + n) = \frac{sx}{k} - (d + n)$$

Multiplying both sides by k yields equation (8) in the text.

point of the saving schedule tells us the amount of saving per head, sx_0, that will be forthcoming at that capital-labor ratio.

We know that all saving is invested, so that gross investment or gross additions to the capital stock, in per capita terms, are equal to sx_0, given a capital-labor ratio of k_0. We know, too, from equation (8) that the increase in the capital-labor ratio falls short of that gross addition for two reasons: First, depreciation reduces the capital-labor ratio, so that part of gross investment must be devoted to offsetting depreciation; and second, growth in the labor force implies that some saving has to be used to provide new members of the labor force with capital.

In particular, if the depreciation rate is d, an amount dk is required as a depreciation allowance; and if population is growing at rate n, we need to invest an amount nk in order just to maintain capital per head constant. It follows that we can write the investment required to maintain a constant capital-labor ratio in the face of depreciation and labor force growth as $(n + d)k$. When saving and hence gross investment are larger (smaller) than $(n + d)k$, the stock of capital per head is increasing (decreasing). We can therefore think of the term $(n + d)k$ as the investment requirement that will

FIGURE 19-3

SAVING, INVESTMENT, AND CAPITAL ACCUMULATION. The saving function shows the part of income that is saved, sx, at each capital-labor ratio. The straight line $(d + n)k$ shows the investment requirement. At low capital-labor ratios, saving exceeds the investment requirement, and hence output per head grows. Conversely at high capital-labor ratios, saving is less than the investment requirement, and capital per head is falling. The steady-state capital-labor ratio is k^*, at which saving is just sufficient to maintain the capital-labor ratio constant.

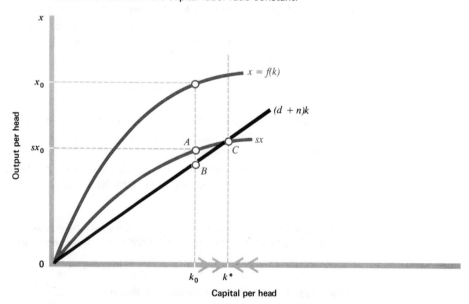

maintain constant capital per head and therefore, from Figure 19-2, output per head.

In Figure 19-3 we show this investment requirement as a positively sloped schedule. It tells us how much investment we would require at each capital-labor ratio just in order to keep that ratio constant. It is positively sloped because the higher the capital-labor ratio, the larger the amount of investment that is required to prevent the capital-labor ratio from falling.

The saving schedule tells us the amount of saving and gross investment associated with each capital-labor ratio. Thus, at a capital-labor ratio of k_0 in Figure 19-3, saving is sx_0 at point A. The investment requirement to maintain a constant capital-labor ratio at k_0 is equal to $(n + d)k_0$ at point B. Clearly, saving exceeds the investment requirement. Accordingly, the capital-labor ratio grows. Not surprisingly, the increase in the capital-labor ratio is equal to actual saving or investment less the investment requirement and is thus given by the vertical distance AB.

In the next period, capital per head will be higher. Thus on the horizontal axis we draw an arrow showing k to be increasing. You recognize the line of argument we are taking. From Figure 19-3 it is clear that with a somewhat higher capital-labor ratio, the discrepancy between saving and the investment requirement becomes smaller. Therefore the increase in the capital-labor ratio becomes smaller. However, the capital-labor ratio still increases, as indicated by the arrows.

The adjustment process comes to a halt at point C. Here we have reached a capital-labor ratio, k^*, for which saving and investment associated with that capital-labor ratio exactly match the investment requirement. Given the exact matching of actual and required investment, the capital-labor ratio neither rises nor falls. We have reached the steady state.

We can make the same argument by starting with an initial capital-labor ratio in excess of k^*. From Figure 19-3 we note that for high capital-labor ratios, the investment requirement is in excess of saving and investment. Accordingly, not enough is added to the capital stock to maintain the capital-labor ratio constant in the face of population growth and depreciation. Thus, the capital-labor ratio falls until we get to k^*, the steady-state capital-labor ratio.

To review our progress so far:

- To maintain the capital-labor ratio constant, saving and investment have to be sufficient to make up for the reduction in capital per head that arises from population growth and depreciation.

- With saving a constant fraction, s, of output, we established that the capital-labor ratio moves to a steady-state level k^* at which output and therefore saving (investment) are just sufficient to maintain a constant capital-labor ratio.

- The convergence to a steady-state capital-labor ratio, k^*, is ensured by the fact that, at low levels of the capital-labor ratio, saving (investment) exceeds the investment required to maintain capital per head constant and therefore causes the capital-labor ratio to rise, and conversely.

Now we turn to a more detailed study of the steady-state equilibrium and the adjustment process. We note that the steady-state level of capital per head is constant, and thus the steady-state level of output per head is also constant. This means that in the steady state, output, capital, and labor all grow at the same rate, which is equal to the rate of population growth.

We note two important implications of the model we are using. First, the steady-state growth rate is equal to the rate of population growth and therefore is *not* influenced by the saving rate. (Recall that we are assuming no technical progress.) Second, it follows that if two countries have the *same* capital stock and the *same* rate of population growth and have access to the same production function, they will eventually reach the same level of income. Using this model, we could interpret poor countries as being those with less capital, starting further from k^* than the rich countries, but if the former save at the same rate, and can get the same technology, they will eventually catch up.

A Change in the Saving Rate

Why should the long-run growth rate be independent of the saving rate? If people save 10 percent of their income, as opposed to 5 percent, should we not expect this to make a difference in the growth rate of output? Is it not true that an economy in which 10 percent of income is set aside for additions to the capital stock is one in which capital and therefore output grow faster than in an economy in which only 5 percent of income is saved?

We show here that an increase in the saving rate does the following: In the short run, it raises the growth rate of output. It does not affect the *long-run growth rate* of output, but *it raises the long-run level of capital and output per head.*

Figure 19-4 shows an initial steady-state equilibrium at point $C,$ at which saving precisely matches the investment requirement. Next suppose that, for some reason, people want to save a larger fraction of income, that is, there is an increase in the saving rate. The higher saving rate is reflected in an upward shift of the saving schedule. At each level of the capital-labor ratio, and hence at each level of output, saving is larger.

At point $C,$ at which we initially had a steady-state equilibrium, saving has now risen relative to the investment requirement, and as a consequence, more is saved than is required to maintain capital per head constant. Enough is saved to allow the capital stock per head to increase. In Figure 19-4 the capital stock per head will keep rising until we reach point $C'.$ At $C',$ the higher amount of saving is just enough to maintain the higher stock of capital. At point $C',$ both capital per head and output per head have risen. Saving has increased, as has the investment requirement.

Thus with this constant-returns-to-scale production function, and in the absence of technological change, an increase in the saving rate will in the long run raise only the level of output and capital per head, and not the growth rate of output per head.

In the transition process, however, the higher saving rate increases the growth rate of output and the growth rate of output per head. This follows simply from the fact that the capital-labor ratio rises from k^* at the initial steady state to k^{**} in the new steady state. The only way to achieve an increase in the capital-labor ratio is for the capital stock to grow faster than the labor force (and depreciation).

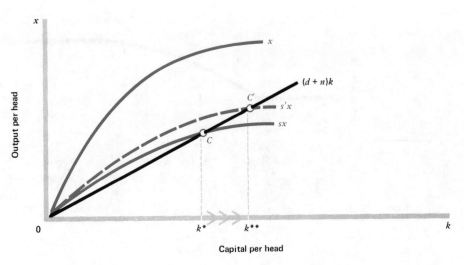

FIGURE 19-4

AN INCREASE IN THE SAVING RATE. An increase in the saving rate implies
that at each capital-labor ratio a larger fraction of output is saved. The
saving schedule shifts upward to $s'x$. At the initial steady state, saving
now exceeds the investment requirement, and hence the capital-labor
ratio rises until point C' is reached. An increase in the saving rate raises
steady-state per capita income. The growth rate rises only in the
transition from C to C'.

In summary, the long-run effect of an increase in the saving rate is to raise the
level of output and capital per head but to leave the growth rate of output and capital
unaffected. In the transition period, the rates of growth of output and capital increase
relative to the steady state. In the short run, therefore, an increase in the saving rate
means faster growth, as we would expect.

Figure 19-5 summarizes these two results. Figure 19-5 a shows the level of per
capita output. Starting from an initial long-run equilibrium at time t_0, the increase in
the saving rate causes saving and investment to increase, the stock of capital per head
grows, and so does output per head. The process will continue at a diminishing rate. In
Figure 19-5 b we focus on the growth rate of output in the initial steady state. The
increase in the saving rate immediately raises the growth rate of output because it
implies a faster growth in capital and therefore in output. As capital accumulates, the
growth rate decreases, falling back toward the level of population growth.

Population Growth

The preceding discussion of saving and the influence of the saving rate on steady-state
capital and output makes it easy to discuss the effects of increased population growth.

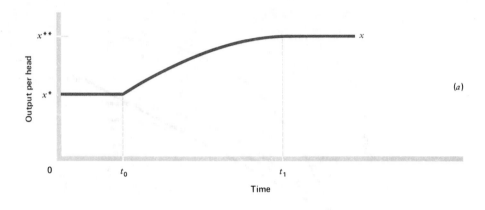

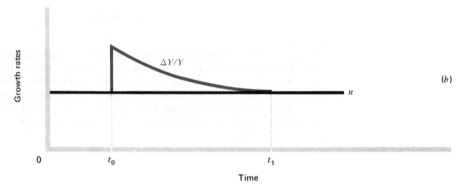

FIGURE 19-5
(*a*) THE TIME PATH OF PER CAPITA INCOME. A rise in the saving rate leads to a rising capital-labor ratio and therefore to increasing output per head until a new steady state is reached.
(*b*) THE TIME PATH OF THE GROWTH RATE OF OUTPUT. An increase in the saving rate raises investment above the investment requirement and thus leads to capital accumulation. Output growth transitorily rises and then falls back to the growth rate of population.

The question we ask is, What happens when the population growth rate increases from n to, say n' and remains at that higher level indefinitely? We will show that such an increase in the rate of population growth will *raise* the growth rate of output and *lower* the level of output per head.

The argument can be conveniently followed in Figure 19-6. Here we show the initial steady-state equilibrium at point C. The increase in the growth rate of population means that, at each level of the capital-labor ratio, it takes a larger amount of investment just to maintain the capital-labor ratio constant. Suppose we had 10 machines per head. Initially, the growth rate of population is 1 percent and depreciation is 10 percent, so that we require per year 11 percent times 10 machines, or 1.1 machines, just to offset population growth and depreciation and thus maintain capital per head constant. To maintain the capital-labor ratio constant in the face of a higher growth rate of population, say 2 percent, requires a higher level of investment, namely, 12 percent as opposed to 11 percent. This is reflected in Figure 19-6 by an upward rotation of the investment requirement schedule.

It is clear from the preceding argument that we are no longer in steady-state equilibrium at point C. At the initial equilibrium, the higher population growth with unchanged saving and investment means that capital does not grow fast enough to keep up with labor force growth and depreciation. Capital per head will keep declining until we reach the new steady-state equilibrium at point C'. Here the capital-labor ratio has declined sufficiently for saving to match the investment requirement. It is true, too, that, corresponding to the lower capital-labor ratio, we have a decline in output per head. Output per head declines from x^* to x^{**}.

The decline in output per head as a consequence of increased population growth points up the problem faced by many developing countries. Fast growth in population,

FIGURE 19-6

AN INCREASE IN THE POPULATION GROWTH RATE REDUCES PER CAPITA INCOME. Increased population growth raises the investment requirement, rotating the schedule upward to $(d + n')k$. At point C saving is insufficient to maintain capital per head constant in face of the more rapidly growing population. Capital and output per head decline until a new steady state, at C', is reached.

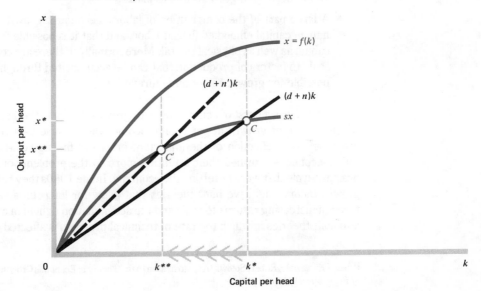

Capital per head

given the saving rate, means low levels of income per head. Indeed, in poor countries one can trace poverty, or low income per head, to the very high rate of population growth. With high population growth, saving will typically be too small to allow capital to rise relative to labor and thus to build up the capital-labor ratio to achieve a satisfactory level of income per head. In those circumstances, and barring other considerations, a reduction in the rate of population growth appears to be a way of achieving higher levels of steady-state per capita income and thus an escape from poverty.

Growth in the Steady State

The very simplified model we have presented so far has per capita income reaching a constant steady-state level, with no growth in the long run. Although it is conceivable that natural resources and environmental pressures will eventually bring an end to growth, it would be useful and more realistic to have a model that allows for the possibility of growth in the steady state. There are several reasons why growth should be expected to continue in the steady state:

- Most important is *technical progress*, which empirical work has identified as the prime source of growth. As we saw from equation (2), technical progress at the rate $\Delta A/A$ will increase the growth rate by that amount. There can be little doubt that human ingenuity will produce technical progress that will allow growth to continue if that same human ingenuity can maintain peace and political stability.

- *Increasing returns to scale* would mean that continued accumulation of factors allows per capita growth to take place.

- A large part of the contribution of labor to economic growth is a result of the human capital embodied in that labor, and that it is possible to invest in human capital as well as physical capital. More formally, if there are constant returns to scale to factors of production that can be accumulated through saving, it can be possible for growth to continue forever.

There was a burst of contributions to growth theory in the 1950s and 1960s, in which persistent growth in per capita income was possible as a result of technical progress[27] — a reflection of the important empirical findings of that period. In the 1970s economists turned their attention more to the problems of inflation and the business cycle that were besetting the economy. In the 1980s they have turned back to growth theory, and have built theories that allow for long-run steady-state growth through increasing returns to scale and the accumulation of human capital. They have also built theories in which the rate of technical progress is affected by the amount of

---

[27] See, for example, Robert Solow, "A Contribution to the Theory of Economic Growth," *Quarterly Journal of Economics*, February 1956.

box 19-2 **LIMITS TO GROWTH**

There were fears in the 1970s that the world was rapidly running out of natural resources, not only oil, but also such commodities as copper, coal, and land (under the pressure of growing populations). These shortages, it was feared, would impose *limits to growth.*

Economists argued that price increases would cause people to conserve resources, that new technologies would develop, and thus that there was not too much to worry about. The use of energy per unit of GNP has indeed declined sharply since 1973, and so has the price of oil. Most other commodity prices have also dropped. The fear that growing populations put pressure on resources and cause environmental degradation has, however, increased since then, as tropical forests begin to disappear, and there is some evidence that the global climate may be warming.* Economic mechanisms can also be used to modify the trend to global warming, for instance, by imposing taxes on the use of carbon fuels and making the proceeds available for the development of alternative technologies.† Resource limitations may nonetheless slow the rate of productivity increase. ∎

---

* United Nations Environment Project, *World Resources 1988–89* (New York: Basic Books, 1989), and S. Schneider, "The Greenhouse Effect: Science and Policy," *Science*, February 1989.

† See W. Baumol and W. Oates, *The Theory of Environmental Policy* (Cambridge, Engl.: Cambridge University Press, 1988).

---

resources devoted to research, which is another route through which steady long-run growth may be attained.[28]

One important if regrettable result that emerges from the new theories in which the long-run rate of growth can be affected by investment in human capital and in research is that these theories do not predict a convergence of income levels among countries that start from different initial capital stocks.

19-5 GROWTH AND DEVELOPMENT

What lessons does growth theory have for economic development? Table 19-2 shows an income level in India that, even after adjusting for differences in price levels, is less than 5 percent of that in the United States. Indeed, average income for the world's poorest countries, with nearly 60 percent of the world's 5 billion people, is below that

---

[28] For a useful summary, see Paul Romer, "Crazy Explanations for the Productivity Slowdown," *NBER Macroeconomics Annual*, 1987. See, too, his "Capital Accumulation in the Theory of Long Run Growth," in R. Barro (ed.), *Modern Business Cycle Theory* (Cambridge, Mass.: Harvard University Press, 1989); R. Lucas: "On The Mechanics of Economic Development," *Journal of Monetary Economics* 1 (1988); Robert Solow, "Growth Theory and After," *American Economic Review,* June 1988; and *Growth Theory: An Exposition,* 2d ed. (New York: Oxford University Press, 1988).

of India. The key question for most of the world's people is whether their economies will grow or develop sufficiently fast for them or their grandchildren ever to be able to live at the material levels enjoyed in the industrialized countries.

Economic development takes place when the economic welfare of a country's people increases over a long period. We measure the state of development by a variety of economic indicators, including primarily per capita real GNP, but also indicators such as health, literacy, and longevity.

The data in Table 19-2 also indicate the wide range of incomes among developing countries. Average income levels in many developing countries, particularly in Latin America, are at about the level in the United States a century ago. But in other developing countries, in Asia and in Africa, per capita incomes are far lower. Further, there are very big gaps in incomes within each country, with some people in those countries living very well indeed, and others at well below the very low average income level.

Growth Performance

Table 19-6 shows a number of developing countries that differed vastly in their growth performance in the 1965–1987 period. Zaire, for example, had a declining level of per capita income—by 1987, income per head was 40 percent less than it had been in 1965! But there is also Korea, whose per capita income quadrupled in the period. What accounts for the differences in performance? The production function is a good starting point for thinking about development. Economic development requires the accumulation of factors of production and the improvement of resource utilization or increases in factor productivity.

Growth theory looks for replies to questions about four decisive elements:

- How fast is population growing?
- What is the quality of the human capital input?
- How much does a country invest?
- How effectively are the given productive resources utilized?

Each of these determinants of growth is influenced in part by a country's policies. For that reason it makes sense to ask, What are policies that do or do not promote economic growth?

We review each of the four elements in turn.

POPULATION GROWTH

We saw in the model of steady-state growth that the rate of population growth affects the steady-state *level* of per capita income. Given the saving rate, higher population growth means lower per capita income. Here is an immediate and stark implication of growth theory. Two countries with the same saving rate will have radically different

TABLE 19-6

GROWTH PERFORMANCE OF DEVELOPING COUNTRIES, 1965–1987 (percent)

	Per capita income growth	Population growth	Investment/GDP
Argentina	0.1	1.5	19.1
Brazil	4.1	2.3	21.6
China	5.2	1.9	33.8*
Korea	6.4	1.8	28.2
Mexico	2.5	2.8	22.6
India	1.8	2.2	21.6
Zaire	−2.4	2.9	14.3

* For the period 1970–1987.

SOURCE: World Bank, *World Development Report*, 1989.

levels of per capita income simply because one has, say twice, the growth rate of population of the other.

Population growth affects also, of course, the transition from one steady state to another. Thus if the population growth rate is cut by government policies, holding the saving rate unchanged. the growth rate will be higher for some time, and capital per head will grow until a new, higher level of income per head is reached.[29]

One particular difficulty facing many developing countries is very high rates of *population growth*. If per capita income is to grow, there has to be enough investment in physical and human capital to equip each new worker with the tools that will make it possible to earn a higher level of income. But with a rapid rate of population growth, it takes a lot of resources to feed and educate the young. There are very poor countries in which population is growing above a rate of 3 percent per year. It thus takes income growth of 3 percent just to keep per capita income constant.

Some governments are beginning to recognize the need to reduce population growth — in the less repressive countries, by trying to persuade people to use contraceptives; in other countries, by policies of force that include sterilization. China, for example, made a decision to limit population growth drastically; from 2.2 percent in 1965–80 the rate was cut to only 1.2 percent in the 1980s. But it often turns out to be difficult to reduce the rate of population growth in very poor countries, where a large family may be acting as a social security system for the family, with the large number of children ensuring that the parents are taken care of in their old age.

HUMAN CAPITAL

In studying the sources of U.S. growth, above, we saw that physical capital is important. But *human capital* is crucial. Human capital is the value of the income-earning

---

[29] On population as a factor in economic development, see Allen Kelley, "Economic Consequences of Population Change in the Third World," *Journal of Economic Literature*, December 1988.

potential embodied in individuals. Human capital includes native ability and talent as well as education and acquired skills.

The average worker in the industrialized countries is much more productive than the average worker in the developing countries. In part that is because she works with more physical capital. But it is also because she has far more training and education.

Human capital is produced through formal education and informal training, and through on-the-job experience. The problem for the developing countries is that it is extremely difficult to accumulate factors of production, physical or human capital, at the low levels of income characteristic of developing economies. The little that is left after providing for subsistence does not buy much education or much physical capital. The choice for children between working at a very young age or going to school is a critical one for families at very low income levels. And so is the choice for a government of how to use the very limited resources it has at its command. And even if the financial resources were made available, it still takes years to build up the group of teachers who can spread education and training. Thus countries cannot leap from one level of income to a much higher income level. Growth is bound to take time as factors of production are accumulated very gradually; education is the slowest but also the most powerful growth factor.

SAVING AND INVESTMENT

Physical capital has always been at the center of explanations for economic progress simply because of the conspicuous presence of abundant and sophisticated machinery and equipment in rich countries and their scarcity or absence in poor countries. As we already noted for the United States, physical capital accumulation does contribute to growth, but its contribution is easily exaggerated.

In order to invest a country must either save or else have access to foreign saving through loans or aid. If domestic saving is the prerequisite for capital accumulation, then attention must focus on policies to promote high saving. For free market economies there is little we know about this issue, as the discussion of supply-side economics has already pointed out. The only aspect that must be mentioned is that saving does depend on the availability of saving instruments — a banking system that offers convenient deposit services, for example — and it depends on the return on saving. There is little evidence that saving is highly responsive to small variations in the return. But there is abundant evidence that extreme financial instability with large and negative real interest rates interferes with saving. When the return on saving becomes negative one of three things happens: Households sharply reduce their saving or they shift their saving abroad (which we call capital flight) or they accumulate their saving in unproductive assets, such as gold. One way or another, the financial environment for saving is an important factor in mobilizing resources for capital formation and in channeling them from households, via financial intermediaries, to investing firms.[30]

In nonmarket economies, such as China or the Soviet Union, *forced* saving is a

---

[30] See Mark Gersovitz, "Saving and Development," in H. Chenery and T. N. Srinivasan, *Handbook of Development Economics* (Amsterdam: North Holland, 1988).

powerful way of limiting consumption and raising saving. Forced saving takes the form of reducing incomes paid to workers and setting aside a large share of the output produced for capital accumulation. The extremely high saving rate in China is a demonstration of this process and is at the basis of the dramatically successful growth of the past 20 years. In market economies the equivalent policy can be achieved via the budget: If the government collects more in taxes than it spends on *current* goods and services, the resources left over can be invested by the government in infrastructure or state enterprises or that can be channeled into firms via development banks.

A developing country can tap foreign saving in three ways. One possibility is that foreign firms invest *directly* in a country. For example, in the late nineteenth century, European companies built railroads in Latin America; today, Japanese firms build plants in Indonesia. The second way a country can tap foreign resources is by borrowing in the world capital market or from institutions such as the World Bank. Third, a country may be able to receive foreign aid from industrialized countries. The importance of these three sources of external saving has varied over time and between countries. But there is little doubt that external saving has always been important in supplementing domestic saving. Of course, foreign saving is all the more important the lower per capita income. At very low income levels there is very little income to spare for accumulation —filling the most basic needs absorbs nearly all there is. At that stage foreign resources would be most beneficial, but they are also typically least available, except in the form of aid.

The huge disparities in income levels among countries have led many of the industrialized countries to provide aid, in the form of grants and loans, to developing countries. The total volume of official development assistance in 1988[31] was about $50 billion, with about $10 billion each coming from the United States and Japan. The total represents about 0.7 percent of the GNP of the donors. Aid received was more than 1.3 percent of the income of developing economies; in many sub-Saharan African countries aid amounted to more than 10 percent of their GNP.

The amount of saving, domestic and foreign, private and public, determines how much investment will take place in a country. But there is no simple relation between the share of GNP devoted to investment and the growth rate of per capita income. The reason is that the *efficiency* of investment can vary widely. Governments might invest in relatively unproductive assets or they might pursue policies that give incentives for unproductive private investments. The widely differing productivity of extra investment can be judged by means of the following question: How much must the investment-to-GNP ratio rise in order to achieve an extra percentage point of growth? For Asian countries that as a group had very successful development policies the relation is 5:1: an extra percentage point of growth requires an increase in the investment-to-GNP ratio of five percentage points. But for Latin America, where resource allocation was much inferior, the proportion might be more nearly 10:1. The large difference in the productivity of investment therefore focuses attention on development policies and strategies that affect the efficiency of resource utilization.

---

[31] This is the total from members of the OECD and OPEC, and does not include assistance from the Soviet Union and other socialist economies.

box 19-3 **DUAL TRACK DEVELOPMENT**

Development performance in the 1980s has been very different in most of Asia and in Latin America and Africa, as shown in Table 19-6. There has been extremely rapid growth in East Asia (which includes China and the NIEs) and fast growth in South Asia (which includes India). Per capita income in sub-Saharan Africa in 1988 was about 20 percent *below* its 1980 level, and in Latin America there has also been negative growth in per capita income. This is not development, but regression. Thus the developing world seems to be on two tracks, with one set of countries (with the larger population) on track toward higher income levels, and other countries heading for lower incomes rather than higher.

Among the reasons for economic decline in Latin America and sub-Saharan Africa are the fact that many of these countries export primary goods (metals and food crops) whose prices have declined sharply. Many of their governments have been unable to provide stable economic or other policies, and many of the policies that have been implemented have been expensive and inefficient.

In addition, these countries have very heavy debt burdens. The data for the seventeen HICs (highly indebted countries) are shown in Table 1. These countries have substantial debts outstanding to the commercial banks, and have had on average to pay about 5 percent of their GNP in interest to the banks during the 1980s. Most have not been able to pay and have had to increase their borrowing to pay, and have also sometimes simply not paid. The debts were incurred in the late 1970s and early 1980s, when economic growth and commodity prices were much higher. The prospects for growth in these countries without a solution to the debt crisis — which the international community is slowly moving toward — are poor. The sub-Saharan African countries are also heavily in debt, but primarily to governments. A reduction in their debt burden, too, would help their development. ∎

TABLE 1

GROWTH RATES OF PER CAPITA GNP, 1980–1988

	East Asia	South Asia	Sub-Saharan Africa	Latin America and the Caribbean	HICs*
Growth rate, % per year	6.7	2.9	−2.8	−1.1	−1.5
Population in 1987, millions	1,511	1,079	442	404	582

* HICs are the seventeen *highly indebted countries*, mostly in Latin America but including also the Ivory Coast, Morocco, and Nigeria in Africa, and the Philippines and Yugoslavia.

SOURCE: World Bank, *World Development Report*, 1989.

Development Strategies

Development is a far more complex process than the use of the production function would suggest. Economic growth in today's industrialized countries has taken place as part of the move away from an agricultural to an industrial economy. Even a century ago, the bulk of Americans lived on farms. Now the fewer than 3 percent of the population that lives on farms feeds the rest of the country and other parts of the world, too. Essential to that change has been an extraordinary increase in agricultural productivity. And, simultaneously, modern growth depended on rapid increases in manufacturing productivity.

Industrialization thus appears to be the key to development. To bring it about, agricultural productivity has to be increased, and then resources have to be used to build up industry. At a general level this is easy to understand, but it is far more difficult in practice.

IMPORT SUBSTITUTION AND OUTWARD ORIENTATION

Industries need some minimal scale if they are to produce cheaply. For that reason, established producers of internationally traded manufactures have an advantage over new producers wanting to break into the market. In the 1950s and early 1960s, it was widely believed that industrialization in the developing countries would take place if manufacturers were given secure domestic markets that would allow them to build up productive capacity. The so-called *import substitution* strategy was to protect domestic producers from foreign competition by quotas and tariffs, so that they would expand their production to replace goods that used to be imported.

By the 1980s it was clear that the import substitution strategy had failed in most countries. The domestic producers, safe from foreign competition, produced at high cost and small volume, and with very little innovation. In the 1980s most countries decided that they would try to reduce trade barriers and enter world markets. They started to liberalize imports by reducing tariffs and quotas, and to encourage exports through devaluations and more direct measures.

The *outward-oriented* development strategy sees export markets as allowing domestic producers to reach efficient scales of production, and regards exposure of domestic producers to foreign imports as a spur to greater efficiency.

THE NEWLY INDUSTRIALIZING ECONOMIES

The major impetus to the adoption of outward-oriented growth strategies is the success of the *newly industrializing economies* (NIEs) of East Asia. The so-called four tigers are Korea, Taiwan, Hong Kong, and Singapore; close behind are countries like Malaysia, Thailand, and Indonesia, which are beginning to grow fast. And ahead of them was Japan.

Each of these economies has grown extremely rapidly in the last two decades, on the basis of rapid growth of manufactured exports. They did not generally start by freely allowing imports, but rather for a time protected domestic producers, and then began to allow imports in order to make sure that the domestic producers were subjected to competitive pressures.

But of course in each of these cases outward orientation by itself is not enough. The tigers have had extremely high saving rates, sometimes as much as 40 percent, and have spent resources on education. They have also generally run very conservative fiscal policies, with the government budget remaining quite small relative to GNP.

THE ROLE OF GOVERNMENT

One of the major controversies in economic development is whether the government should play a leading role in trying to bring about development or whether it should try to stay out of the economy to the extent possible. For several decades after the 1930s what seemed to be the very rapid growth of the centrally planned Soviet Union, and later of the economies of eastern Europe, led to some support for heavy state intervention. In the 1980s the centrally planned vision of growth is dead, and there is widespread agreement that markets and prices have to be used to allocate resources. But within that broad agreement, there is also a wide range of experiences, from the almost complete laissez faire (absence of government intervention) of Hong Kong to the heavy intervention of the Korean government in its economy until the 1980s. And there is, of course, complete agreement that the government has to play its part by maintaining a stable legal and macroeconomic framework in which economic activity can take place.

It is also unfortunately the case that in many developing countries, including some of the poorest, governments are too weak and sometimes too corrupt to provide that essential input.

Convergence

Will the developing economies ever catch up to the industrialized economies? That seems remote, but growth at the rate of the NIEs would enable them to catch up fast, as Korea appears to be doing, and as Japan has done. Economic leadership changes: According to Angus Maddison of the University of Groningen in the Netherlands, the Netherlands had the highest per capita income in 1700, the United Kingdom in 1800, and the United States in 1900.[32] If present trends continue, Japan will have the highest per capita income in the year 2000.

There is nothing inevitable about the poorer countries catching up, or for that matter about the current leaders staying ahead. At the turn of this century Argentina was one of the world's richest countries; now its income is only about $2,500 per capita.[33]

---

[32] See Maddison, *Phases of Capitalist Development*. See, too, the data on the first back endpaper of this book.

[33] William Baumol, "Productivity Growth, Convergence, and Welfare," *American Economic Review*, December 1986, argues that the data do tend to show the poorer industrial countries on average catching up. His finding is disputed by J. Bradford De Long, "Population Growth, Convergence, and Welfare: Comment," *American Economic Review*, December 1988.

19-6 SUMMARY

1. A production function links factor inputs and technology to the level of output. Growth of output — changes in technology aside — is a weighted average of input growth with the weights equal to income shares. The production function directs attention to factor inputs and technological change as sources of output growth.
2. Growth theory studies the determinants of intermediate-run and long-run growth in output.
3. In U.S. history over the 1929–1969 period, growth in factor inputs and technical progress each accounted for roughly one-half of the average growth rate of 3.4 percent of output. Growth in the stock of knowledge, along with growth in labor input, was the most important source of growth.
4. Per capita output grows faster, the more rapidly the capital stock increases and the faster technical progress advances. In U.S. history since 1889, output per head has grown at an average rate of 1.8 percent.
5. The growth rate of output in the major economies decreased sharply in the 1970s and recovered somewhat in the 1980s. The slowdown reflects a decline in productivity growth, which has been ascribed to several factors most of which are reversing themselves in the late 1980s. Even so, predictions are for slower growth rates in the 1990s than earlier in the post–World War II period.
6. Supply-side economics proposes to raise the level and growth rate of full-employment output by creating improved incentives for work, saving, and investment and by reducing regulation. Empirical research suggests that incentives would be successful on the labor supply side, and that reduced government deficits would stimulate investment.
7. The concept of steady-state equilibrium points (in the absence of technical change) to the conditions required for output per head to be constant. With a growing population, saving must be just sufficient to provide new members of the population with the economywide amount of capital per head.
8. The steady-state level of income is determined by the saving rate and by population growth. In the absence of technical change, the steady-state growth rate of output is equal to the rate of population growth. An increase in the growth rate of population raises the steady-state growth rate of total output and lowers the level of steady-state output per head.
9. An increase in the saving rate transitorily raises the growth rate of output. In the new steady state, the growth rate remains unchanged, but the level of output per head is increased.
10. With technical change, per capita output in the steady state grows at the rate of technical progress. Total output grows at the sum of the rates of technical progress and population growth.
11. Persistent growth in per capita income may result not only from technical progress but also from continued accumulation of factors of production if there are constant returns to scale in these factors.
12. Economic development takes place as a result of the accumulation of factors of

production, including human capital, operating in a stable economic and political framework. It generally involves increased agricultural productivity that permits the population to be fed by only a small part of the labor force, enabling industrialization to take place.

13. A variety of development strategies have been followed in the post–World War II period. The most successful developing economies, the NIEs, have pursued outward-oriented policies that emphasize the growth of exports and, after a restricted period of protection, exposing domestic producers to foreign competition.

KEY TERMS

Production function

Growth accounting

Growth of total factor productivity

Limits to growth

Supply-side economics

Steady state

Sources of growth

Labor productivity

Technical progress

Economic development

Human capital

Import substitution

Outward-oriented strategy

Newly industrializing economies (NIEs)

Catching-up hypothesis

PROBLEMS

1. Which of the following government activities have effects on the long-term growth rate? Explain how they can do so. (a) Monetary policy, (b) labor market policies, (c) educational and research policies, (d) fiscal policy, (e) population control programs.

2. Discuss the role of government policy in raising (a) the supply of labor and (b) the supply of capital. How successful can such policies be?

3. Since 1973, the growth rate of productivity has sharply declined in most industrialized countries. List several of the factors that are responsible for this decline and discuss why the decline in productivity growth is an important issue.

4. Suppose the share of capital in income is 0.4 and the share of labor is 0.6. Capital grows by 6 percent, and labor supply declines by 2 percent. What happens to output?

5. An earthquake destroys one-quarter of the capital stock. Discuss in the context of the growth model the adjustment process of the economy, and show, using Figure 19-3, what happens to growth.

6. (a) In the absence of technical progress, what happens to output per head and total output over time? Why?

   (b) What is the long-run effect of the saving rate on the *level* of output per capita? On *growth* of output per capita?

7. Evaluate this statement: "The saving rate cannot affect the growth of output in the economy. That is determined by the growth of labor input and by technical progress."

8. Suppose we assume a production function of the form

$$Y = AF(K, N, Z)$$

where Z is a measure of the natural resources going into production. Assume this production function obeys constant returns to scale and diminishing returns to each factor [like equation (1)].

(a) What will happen to output per head if capital and labor grow together but resources are fixed?

(b) What if Z is fixed but there is technical progress?

(c) In the 1970s there were fears that we were running out of natural resources and therefore that there were limits to growth. Discuss this view using your answers to (a) and (b).

9. (a) Using the data in the two top rows of Table 19-2, calculate how long it would take for per capita income in India to reach that of the United States.

(b) How long would it take India to catch up to Korea?

(c) Explain whether you believe these answers.

*10. Use the model of long-run growth to incorporate the government. Assume that an income tax at the rate t is levied and that, accordingly, saving per head is equal to $s(1 - t)x$. The government spends the tax revenue on public consumption.

(a) Use Figure 19-3 to explore the impact of an increase in the tax rate on the steady-state output level and capital per head.

(b) Draw a chart of the time path of capital per head, output per head, and the growth rate of output.

(c) Discuss the statement: "To raise the growth rate of output, the public sector has to run a budget surplus to free resources for investment."

11. Use Figure 19-3 to explore the impact of a *once-and-for-all* improvement in technology.

(a) How does technical progress affect the level of output per head at a given capital-labor ratio?

(b) Show the new steady-state equilibrium. Has saving changed? Is income per head higher? Has the capital stock increased?

(c) Show the time path of the adjustment to the new steady state. Does technical progress transitorily raise the ratio of investment to capital?

12. Discuss the statement: "The lower the level of income, the higher the growth of output."

13. Explain the catching-up hypothesis that asserts that productivity growth is lower the higher the level of per capita income. What factors do you think are responsible for this observed pattern?

APPENDIX: PROPERTIES OF THE PRODUCTION FUNCTION

In this appendix we briefly show how the fundamental growth equation (2) is obtained. The material is presented for completeness; it is not essential to an understanding of the text.

We start with a production function that exhibits constant returns: increasing *all* inputs in the same proportion raises output in that same proportion. Thus if we double all inputs, output

---

* An asterisk denotes a more difficult problem.

will double. With that property the change in output due to technical progress and to changes in inputs can be written as

$$\Delta Y = F(K, N)\Delta A + MPK\, \Delta K + MPN\, \Delta N \tag{A1}$$

where MPK and MPN are the marginal products of capital and labor, respectively. We remember that the marginal product of a factor tells us the contribution to output made by employing one extra unit of the factor. Dividing both sides of the equation by $Y = AF(K, N)$ yields the expression

$$\frac{\Delta Y}{Y} = \frac{\Delta A}{A} + \frac{MPK}{Y}\Delta K + \frac{MPN}{Y}\Delta N \tag{A2}$$

Equation (A2) is further simplified by multiplying and dividing the second term on the right-hand side by K and the third term by N.

$$\frac{\Delta Y}{Y} = \frac{\Delta A}{A} + \left(K\frac{MPK}{Y}\right)\frac{\Delta K}{K} + \left(N\frac{MPN}{Y}\right)\frac{\Delta N}{N} \tag{A3}$$

We now argue that the terms in parentheses are the income shares of capital and labor. In a competitive market, factors are paid their marginal product. Thus the term $N(MPN/Y) = wN/Y$, where w is the real wage: the right-hand side is recognized as the ratio of labor income to total income or the share of labor in income. Similarly, the term $K(MPK/Y)$ is the share of capital in income. With constant returns and competition, factor payments exhaust the total product. Therefore the shares of capital and labor sum to unity. Denoting the share of capital in income by θ and the labor share by $1 - \theta$, we arrive at equation (2) in the text.

We note a further property of the constant returns production function. When returns to scale are constant, we can write the production function as follows:

$$Y = AF(K, N) = NAF\left(\frac{K}{N}\right) \tag{A4}$$

or using the notation $x = Y/N$ and $k = K/N$,

$$x = AF(k) \tag{A5}$$

This is the form used in the growth theory section of the text, where output per head is a function of the capital-labor ratio.

INTERNATIONAL ADJUSTMENT
AND INTERDEPENDENCE

*I*nternational economic issues — the value of the dollar in world currency markets, the large and persistent U.S. current account deficit, and the adjustment problems of heavily indebted countries, especially in Latin America — became central problems of international discussion and concern in the 1980s. In the United States the prime question was whether the current account deficit was a problem or not: could the large U.S. external deficit continue almost indefinitely, or was it and is it unsustainably large? Closely related is the question of what it would take to eliminate the current account deficit: Would it be enough to reduce the U.S. budget deficit, or would the exchange rate of the dollar also (or instead) have to change? Some argued that by 1989 the dollar was *under*valued and would have to strengthen relative to the yen. Others believed that the dollar would have to decline further in order to reduce the current account deficit.

In this chapter we amplify and develop the discussion of Chapter 6. We study balance of payments adjustment under fixed and flexible exchange rates, now taking into account the interactions of changes in prices with exchange rate changes. The short-run results developed in Chapter 6 remain essentially valid: the open economy *IS-LM* model of Chapter 6 is a sturdy workhorse for macroeconomic discussion even in an economy in which prices are flexible.

We start the chapter by discussing how adjustment to balance of payments problems takes place in an economy with a fixed exchange rate. Although exchange rates among the dollar, yen, and other major currencies have been freely flexible since 1973, the discussion remains relevant both because some smaller countries do still operate with fixed exchange rates and because exchange rates are fixed among European countries in the European Monetary System (EMS).[1] Moreover, understanding the adjustment mechanisms that operate under fixed exchanges rates helps in grasping the operation of flexible exchange rates. We then discuss the monetary approach to the balance of payments, which argues that balance of payments problems are a result of too rapid money growth.

In Section 20-3 we consider the adjustment process under flexible exchange rates when prices are flexible. This section generalizes the Chapter 6 *IS-LM* discussion of adjustment in a flexible exchange rate system with a constant price level. In the remainder of the chapter we take up aspects of the behavior of the current flexible exchange rate system: interest rate linkages among different countries; the effects of exchange rate changes on trade flows; and the interdependence among countries' economic policies that exists even in the world of flexible exchange rates.

20-1 POLICY CONFLICTS AND ADJUSTMENT UNDER FIXED EXCHANGE RATES

In the later nineteenth century, in part of the interwar period, and after World War II, until 1973, exchange rates among currencies were fixed. The Bretton Woods system that operated from the end of World War II to 1973 and the gold standard of the nineteenth and first third of the twentieth century were examples of fixed exchange rate systems. We shall now study the adjustment process when exchange rates are fixed but prices are flexible.[2]

Adjustment to a balance of payments problem can be achieved in two ways. One way is by changing economic policy. The second way is through *automatic* adjustment mechanisms. The automatic mechanisms are two: payments imbalances affect the money supply and hence spending; and unemployment affects wages and prices and thereby competitiveness. Policy measures by contrast include not only monetary and fiscal policy but also tariffs or devaluation.

The Role of Prices in the Open Economy

We start the analysis by bringing prices explicitly into the aggregate supply-demand model of Chapters 7 and 13. In Chapter 6 we assumed that the price level was constant.

---

[1] Exchange rates in the European Monetary System, which includes Germany, France, and Italy, and which Britain is thinking of joining, are held fixed for long periods of time and only occasionally adjusted. See Francesco Giavazzi, Steffano Micossi, and Marcus Miller, *The European Monetary System* (Cambridge, Engl.: Cambridge University Press, 1988), and Alberto Giovannini and Francesco Giavazzi, *The European Monetary System* (Cambridge, Mass.: MIT Press, 1989).

[2] For some history of the international monetary system see Anna Schwartz, *Money in Historical Perspective* (Chicago: University of Chicago Press, 1987), especially Chaps. 13 to 16; Leland Crabbe, "The International Gold Standard and US Monetary Policy from World War I to the New Deal," *Federal Reserve Bulletin,* June 1989; and Paul de Grauwe, *International Money. Postwar Trends and Theories* (Oxford, Engl.: Oxford University Press, 1989).

With fixed prices and a given exchange rate the *real* exchange rate was also fixed. Recall the definition of the real exchange rate:

$$R = \frac{eP_f}{P} \tag{1}$$

Here e is the exchange rate, P_f the foreign price level, and P the domestic price level. We now abandon the assumption of a fixed domestic price level, but for the time being take the exchange rate and foreign prices as given.

What does the aggregate demand and supply model look like once we allow open economy effects? In the closed economy version of the model used so far, aggregate demand depends on the level of prices: a higher level of prices implies lower real balances, higher interest rates, and lower spending. In an open economy, the relation is slightly more complicated because now an increase in our prices reduces demand for our goods for two reasons. The first is the familiar higher interest rate channel summarized above. The second is that an increase in our prices makes our goods less competitive with foreign-produced goods. When the prices of goods produced at home rise, given the exchange rate, our goods become more expensive for foreigners to buy, and their goods become *relatively* cheaper for us to buy. An increase in our prices is thus an increase in the *relative price* of the goods we produce, and shifts demand away from our goods toward imports, as well as reducing exports.

In summary, then, an increase in our price level reduces the demand for our goods both by increasing the interest rate (and reducing investment demand) and by reducing net exports — by making the goods we produce relatively more expensive than foreign-produced goods. In Figure 20-1 we show the downward-sloping demand schedule for our goods, *AD*. Demand is equal to aggregate spending by domestic residents, plus net exports, or $AD \equiv A + NX$.

The demand for domestic goods, *AD,* is drawn for a given level of foreign prices, a given nominal money supply, and given fiscal policy. Remember, too, that the exchange rate is fixed. An increase in the nominal money stock shifts the schedule upward, as does expansionary fiscal policy. We show, too, the short-run aggregate supply schedule, *AS,* and the full-employment level of output, Y^*. Initial equilibrium is at point *E,* at which we have unemployment.

Next we look at the trade balance equilibrium schedule, $NX = 0$. An increase in our income raises imports and worsens the trade balance. To restore trade balance equilibrium, domestic prices would have to be lower. This would make the home country more competitive, raise exports, and reduce imports. Thus, we show the trade balance equilibrium schedule as downward-sloping.[3] We assume that it is steeper than the demand schedule for domestic goods. The schedule is drawn for a given level of

---

[3] We assume that a decline in domestic prices improves the trade balance. This requires that exports and imports be sufficiently responsive to prices. There is a possibility that a reduction in our price level (which reduces the prices of our exports) lowers our revenue from exports — because the increased sales are not sufficient to compensate for the lower prices. We assume that this possibility does not occur. We shall assume, too, that import spending does not depend on the interest rate.

prices abroad. The short-run equilibrium at point E is one at which the home country has a trade deficit. Our prices are too high or our income is too high to have exports balance imports. To achieve trade balance equilibrium, we would have to become more competitive, thus exporting more and importing less. Alternatively, we could reduce our level of income in order to reduce import spending.

Financing and Adjustment

What does a country with a current account deficit, like that at E in Figure 20-1, do? In a fixed exchange rate system, it is possible for the central bank to use its reserves to finance temporary imbalances of payments — that is, to meet the excess demand for foreign currency at the existing exchange rate arising from balance of payments deficits. Other ways of financing temporary payments imbalances are also available. A country experiencing balance of payments difficulties can borrow foreign currencies abroad. The borrowing may be undertaken either by the government (usually the central bank) or by private individuals. Although borrowing may be undertaken to finance both current and capital account deficits, we concentrate in this section on the current account.

A current account deficit cannot be financed by borrowing from abroad without raising the question of how the borrowing will be repaid. If the counterpart of the current account deficit is productive domestic investment, there need be little concern about repaying. The investment will pay off in terms of increased output, some of which may be exported or which may replace goods that previously were imported. The investment would thus yield the foreign exchange earnings with which to *service* (make payments on) the debt. However, problems may well arise in repaying the foreign debt if borrowing is used to finance consumption spending.

The Adjustment Process

Maintaining and financing current account deficits indefinitely or for very long periods of time is impossible. The economy has to find some way of *adjusting* the deficit. Again, that can happen automatically or through policy. We examine first the important automatic adjustment mechanisms.

AUTOMATIC ADJUSTMENT

First we look at the aggregate demand side. We remember that there is a link between the central bank's holdings of foreign exchange and the domestic money supply, assuming no sterilization, as defined in Chapter 11. When a country with a fixed exchange rate runs a balance of payments deficit, the central bank has to be selling foreign exchange to those who demand it. When it sells foreign exchange, it reduces domestic high-powered money and therefore the money stock. Thus the deficit at point

E implies that the central bank is pegging the exchange rate, selling foreign exchange to keep the exchange rate from depreciating, and reducing the domestic money stock. It follows immediately that over time the aggregate demand schedule (which is drawn for a given money supply) will be shifting downward and to the left.

Point *E* in Figure 20-1 is also a point of unemployment. On the aggregate supply side, unemployment leads to a decline in wages and costs, which is reflected in a downward-shifting aggregate supply schedule. Over time, therefore, the short-run equilibrium point, *E* in Figure 20-1, moves downward as both demand and supply schedules shift (not shown). The points of short-run equilibrium move in the direction

FIGURE 20-1

OPEN ECONOMY EQUILIBRIUM WITH PRICE ADJUSTMENT. Net exports and the demand for domestic goods depend on the relative price of our goods. Demand for domestic goods also depends on the price level because this affects the real money supply and hence interest rates. *AD* is the aggregate demand schedule. It is downward-sloping because a reduction in our prices raises the real money stock, lowering interest rates, and because lower prices for our goods increase our international competitiveness. The trade balance equilibrium schedule is also downward-sloping, reflecting the increased competitiveness that we derive from a lower relative price of our goods. Macroeconomic equilibrium obtains at *E*, at which aggregate demand equals aggregate supply. This need not be a point of full employment and external balance, which obtain at *E'*.

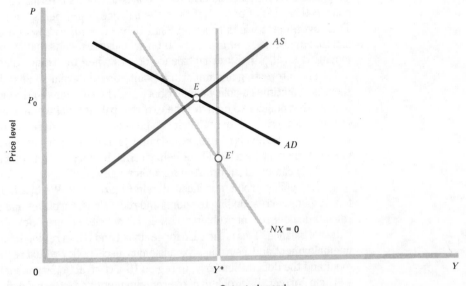

of point E', and the process will continue until that point is reached. (The approach may be cyclical, but that is not of major interest here.)

Once point E' is reached, we have achieved long-run equilibrium. Because the trade balance is in equilibrium, there is no pressure on the exchange rate and therefore no need for exchange market intervention. Accordingly, there is no influence from the trade balance on the money supply and thereby on aggregate demand. On the supply side, we have reached full employment. Therefore, wages and costs are constant, so that the supply schedule is not shifting. At point E' we have a combination of relative prices, demand, and employment that gives both internal and external balance. The adjustment of the level of prices ensures that we can — in the long run — have both full employment and trade balance equilibrium.

The adjustment process we have just described is called the *classical adjustment process*. It relies on price adjustments and an adjustment in the money supply based on the trade balance. The adjustment process "works" in the sense that it moves the economy to a long-run equilibrium of internal and external balance. However, the mechanism is far from attractive, for it may take a very long time for the effects of unemployment on wages and prices to restore the economy's equilibrium. There is no good case for a protracted recession simply in order to achieve a cut in prices. The alternative to waiting for the automatic adjustment mechanisms to work is to make policy changes that move the economy more rapidly toward balance.

Policy Conflicts and the Choice of Policies

In considering policies to adjust the balance of payments problem at point E in Figure 20-1, the government has also to take account of its internal economic problem. At point E there is not only a deficit in the balance of payments but also unemployment. The government wants to achieve not only *external balance* (in the balance of payments) but also *internal balance*. Internal balance means that output is at the full-employment level, Y^*. External balance occurs when the trade balance is zero.

The interesting and important point about internal and external balance is that there is sometimes a policy conflict between the solutions to the two problems. It can happen that policies to improve the external balance will worsen internal balance. For instance, a current account deficit can be reduced through restrictive domestic policy that reduces the levels of income and imports. But such policies will increase the rate of unemployment, which would not help internal balance from a point such as E in Figure 20-1. This can create a problem for policy makers.

The policy problem is illustrated in Figure 20-2. We break up the diagram into four regions corresponding to booms and recessions, surpluses and deficits. Two of the regions do not present problems: corrective policies bring us closer to both internal and external balance. This is the case for regions I and III. In region I, for example, we have unemployment and a surplus. Expansionary fiscal policy would reduce both unemployment and the deficit. Similarly, in region III a contractionary monetary or fiscal policy will help correct the problem of overemployment and external deficit. But in the other two regions there are policy dilemmas.

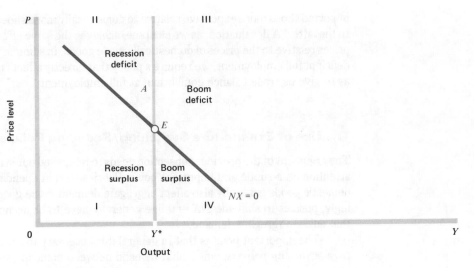

FIGURE 20-2
POLICY DILEMMAS. In regions I and III monetary or fiscal policy can move the economy toward internal and external balance. In regions II and IV there is a policy dilemma. For example, in region II unemployment calls for expansion but the deficit calls for contraction.

Policy Dilemmas

At point *A*, the economy is in a position of recession and deficit. Here we have to choose whether we want to use tight policies to achieve trade balance equilibrium or expansionary policies to achieve full employment. Not only are we unable to reach both targets simultaneously by manipulating aggregate demand, but any attempt to reach one target gets us further away from the other. Such a situation is called a *policy dilemma,* and it can always arise when there are more targets of policy than instruments with which to move the economy toward its targets. In our case we have only one policy instrument — aggregate demand policies — but we have two independent targets — external and internal balance.

The policy dilemma can be solved by finding another policy instrument to cope with the multiple targets. What is needed is some policy that shifts the trade balance schedule to the right so that, at any given price level, trade is balanced at a higher level of income. An obvious policy would be to cut down on imports at each level of income. Such a policy would reduce import spending at each level of income and thus shift the trade balance schedule to the right.

How can we cut import spending? We can use any of a number of tools, among them tariffs and exchange rate changes. Tariffs are taxes on imported goods. A tariff raises the cost of imports to domestic residents and thereby diverts demand away from imports to domestic goods. A 10 percent tariff on imported shoes, for instance, makes imported shoes more expensive relative to domestically made shoes and shifts demand to the latter. A devaluation, as we shall see, achieves the same effect by raising import prices relative to the prices of domestically made goods. In summary, if we have a trade deficit at full employment, we require a policy that directly affects the trade balance so as to give us trade balance equilibrium at full employment.

The Use of Expenditure Switching/Reducing Policies

The argument of the previous subsection needs to be spelled out in more detail to focus attention on a subtle and important point: Policies to shift spending from imports to domestic goods generally also affect aggregate demand in the goods market. Accordingly, policies to shift the $NX = 0$ line generally have to be accompanied by policies that adjust aggregate demand.

The important point is that In general it is necessary to combine both *expenditure switching policies*, which shift demand between domestic and imported goods, and *expenditure reducing* (or *expenditure increasing*) *policies* in order to cope with the targets of internal and external balance. This point is of general importance and continues to apply when we take account of capital flows and other phenomena omitted in this section.

One method of adjusting a current account deficit is through the imposition of tariffs. However, tariffs cannot be freely used to adjust the balance of trade, partly because there are international organizations and agreements such as GATT (General Agreement on Tariffs and Trade) and the IMF (International Monetary Fund) that outlaw, or at least frown on, the use of tariffs. Tariffs have generally fallen in the post–World War II period as the industrialized world has moved to desirably freer trade between countries.

Another way of adjusting a current account deficit is to use a restrictive domestic policy. These are expenditure reducing policies. In this regard, it is worth repeating that a trade deficit reflects an excess of expenditure by domestic residents and the government over income. In Chapter 2 we showed that

$$NX \equiv Y - (C + I + G) \tag{2}$$

where NX is the trade surplus and I is actual investment. Thus, a balance of trade deficit can be reduced by reducing spending $(C + I + G)$ relative to income (Y). The trade deficit can be eliminated by reducing aggregate demand, by reducing C, or G, or I, and by using restrictive monetary and/or fiscal policy.

The link between external deficit and budget deficits is shown in (2 a) where, as at the end of Chapter 2, we add and subtract taxes on the right-hand side:

$$NX \equiv S - I + T - G \tag{2a}$$

where S denotes *private* saving and $T - G$ is the budget surplus. Equation (2 a) *does* show an immediate relation between the budget and the external balance. If saving and investment were constant then changes in the budget would translate, one for one, into changes in the external balance; budget cutting would bring about equal changes in the external deficit. But budget cutting will affect saving and investment and therefore we need a more complete model to explain the way in which budget cuts affect the external balance.

Devaluation

The unemployment that typically accompanies adjustment through recession and the desirability of free trade, which argues against the use of tariffs, both suggest the need for an alternative policy for reconciling internal and external balance. The major policy instrument for dealing with payments deficits in the dilemma situation is *devaluation*, which usually has to be combined with restrictive monetary and/or fiscal policy. A devaluation, as we noted in Chapter 6, is an increase in the domestic currency price of foreign exchange. Given the nominal prices in two countries, devaluation increases the relative price of imported goods in the devaluing country and reduces the relative price of exports from the devaluing country. Devaluation is primarily an expenditure switching policy.

How does a devaluation assist in achieving internal and external balance? Let us take, first, the special case of a country that has been in full employment with balance of trade equilibrium and is at point E in Figure 20-3. Now let there be an exogenous decline in export earnings, so that the $NX = 0$ schedule shifts to the left to $NX' = 0$. At the given exchange rate the foreign demand for domestic goods is assumed to decline. In the absence of domestic policy intervention, and with fixed rates, output would decline. The AD schedule moves to the left as a result of the fall in exports, but not enough to make up for the loss of export revenue. The net effects are therefore unemployment and a trade deficit.

Next, we ask how the home country can adjust to the loss of export markets. One possibility is to go through an adjustment process of declining domestic wages and prices as the high unemployment slowly reduces wages or slows down their rate of increase. This is the automatic process described earlier. Such an adjustment would, over time, lower domestic costs and prices as compared with the prices of foreign goods. The home country would gain in competitiveness in world markets and thus restore its export earnings and employment. This is a feasible adjustment process, and, indeed, is the process that would occur by itself, given enough time.

An alternative solution is to recognize that in order to restore full employment and export earnings, the home country's pricing of exports and imports must become more competitive. To restore competitiveness, domestic costs and prices have to decline *relative* to foreign prices. That adjustment can occur in two ways: (1) through a decline in domestic costs and prices at a given exchange rate and (2) through a depreciation of the exchange rate with unchanged domestic costs and prices.

The latter strategy has the obvious advantage that it does not require a protracted recession to reduce domestic costs. The adjustment is done by the stroke of a pen — a devaluation of the currency. Why would a devaluation achieve the adjustment?

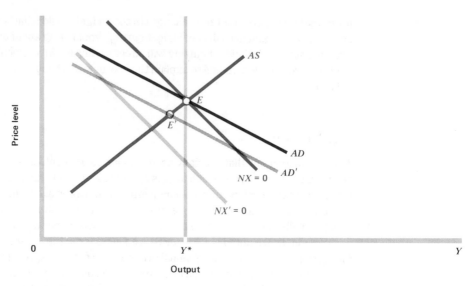

FIGURE 20-3
A LOSS OF EXPORT REVENUE. The economy starts out in full equilibrium
at point E. An export loss shifts the $NX = 0$ and AD schedules to the
left. The new short-run equilibrium is at point E' with unemployment and
a deficit.

Given prices of foreign goods in terms of foreign currency (for example, the mark
prices of German goods), a devaluation raises the relative price of foreign goods. The
effect is to induce an increased demand for American goods and a reduction in demand
for imports in the United States.

The case we have just considered is special, however, in one important respect.
The economy was initially in balance of trade equilibrium at full employment. The
disturbance of the economy took place in the trade account. Accordingly, if we could
move the $NX' = 0$ locus back to the full-employment level of income — as we could
with a devaluation — both internal and external balance would be attained. Put differently, the reason there was an internal balance problem of unemployment in Figure
20-3 was the reduction in exports and consequent external balance problem. Both
problems could thus be cured through devaluation.

In general, though, we cannot secure both external and internal balance following a disturbance by using just one instrument of policy. A general rule of policy making
is that we need to use as many policy instruments as we have policy targets.

Finally, a comment on the role of the exchange rate in a fixed rate system: In the
fixed rate system, the exchange rate is an *instrument of policy*. The central bank can
change the exchange rate for policy purposes, devaluing when the current account
looks as though it will be in for a prolonged deficit. In a system of clean floating, by
contrast, the exchange rate moves freely to equilibrate the balance of payments. In a

system of dirty floating, the central bank attempts to manipulate the exchange rate while not committing itself to any given rate. The dirty floating system is thus intermediate between a fixed rate system and a clean floating system.

Exchange Rates and Prices

A devaluation that takes place when domestic prices are constant at given foreign prices will succeed in reducing the relative price of a country's goods, and will thus improve the trade balance. However, the price level typically changes along with the exchange rate. The essential issue then is whether the country succeeds in bringing about a *real devaluation*. A country experiences a real devaluation when a devaluation brings about a reduction in the price of the country's own goods relative to the price of foreign goods.

Recalling the definition of the real exchange rate, eP_f/P, a real devaluation takes place when the *real* exchange rate is devalued. Taking the foreign price level (P_f) as given, a real devaluation occurs when e/P rises, or *when the exchange rate increases by more than the price level.*

We use Figure 20-4, and the example of Mexico, to illustrate the issues in securing a real devaluation. Let P_{US} be the price level in the United States, P the Mexican price level, and e Mexico's exchange rate, that is, the number of pesos per dollar. Mexico's competitiveness then is measured by U.S. prices relative to Mexican prices, both measured in dollars: $P_{US}/(P/e)$. A fall in the dollar prices of Mexican goods makes them more competitive in trade and thus increases Mexican net exports. We assume that the U.S. price level is given and show P/e, the Mexican price level measured in dollars, on the vertical axis in Figure 20-4. For a given U.S. price level, a rise in Mexican dollar prices worsens Mexico's net exports. Accordingly, as in Figure 20-2, points to the right of $NX = 0$ correspond to deficits.

Consider now the problem of adjustment to external shocks. Suppose that an oil price fall in world markets reduces Mexico's export earnings at each price level and thus creates a deficit. Initially we were at E, with internal and external balance, and now external balance only prevails along $NX' = 0$.

In the short run a country might absorb an external shock by staying at point E, borrowing abroad to finance the external deficit. But that is not possible forever; ultimately, adjustment must come about, with the country aiming to return to point E''. There are two ways to move to point E''. One is *deflation*. A deflation policy relies on unemployment to reduce wages and prices and thus achieve competitiveness at an unchanged exchange rate. Alternatively, the country can devalue the currency and move directly to point E''.

But the devaluation will be successful only to the extent that it is not offset by an increase in domestic prices. What matters is that a country with an external deficit (say Mexico) succeeds in reducing its prices in dollars, P/e. If devaluation leads to a rise in domestic prices, then there is no gain in competitiveness. In Box 20-1 we discuss Mexican adjustment.

Figure 20-5 shows the U.S. price level and Mexican prices in dollars. Note that

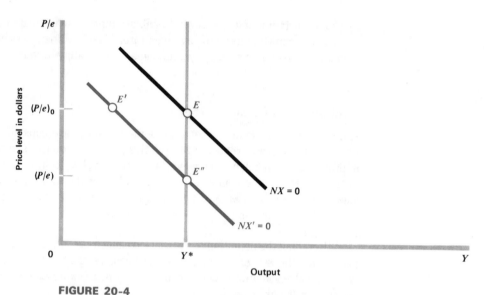

FIGURE 20-4

COMPETITIVENESS AND ADJUSTMENT. When a country faces an adverse external shock, this can be shown as a leftward shift of the *NX* schedule. On the vertical axis we show the price of the country's output measured in dollars (*P/e*). To achieve internal and external balance the economy must move to point *E"*. The price in dollars must decline to achieve an increase in competitiveness. Because it is often difficult to achieve such a gain in competitiveness, countries with external constraints will tend to be at a point like *E'*, at which there is unemployment.

exchange rate devaluations in 1982 and in 1985–1986 sharply reduced the dollar prices of Mexican goods. But the gains in competitiveness did not last. Inflation in Mexico, fueled by large government budget deficits, soon raised prices relative to the exchange rate; by 1989 the *real* exchange rate was not much more competitive than it had been in 1980. In the absence of a real devaluation, Mexico had to rely on reducing the level of demand in the economy to adjust the external accounts: thus in Figure 20-4 it was closer to *E'* than to *E"* by the end of 1988.

What would have been needed to achieve a real devaluation? That would have taken more restrictive demand policies in order to ensure that the domestic price level did not rise along with the exchange rate. It is rarely the case that a devaluation unaccompanied by restrictive domestic policies can by itself restore external balance.

CRAWLING PEG EXCHANGE RATES

When a country experiences inflation above the rate of its trading partners, holding the exchange rate fixed would imply a steady loss in competitiveness. In order to avoid the foreign exchange problems of a loss in competitiveness many countries follow a *crawling peg* exchange rate policy. Under a crawling peg exchange rate policy the exchange rate is depreciated at a rate roughly equal to the inflation differential between a country and its trading partners. A crawling peg assures that the *real* exchange rate, $R = P_f/(P/e)$, remains unchanged because depreciation offsets inflation differentials.

It is clear from Figure 20-5 that for lengthy periods, for example, in 1988, Mexico failed to offset the impact of its inflation on competitiveness. The exchange rate was not depreciated fast enough to maintain the real exchange rate. As a result competitiveness fell and foreign exchange problems remained.

Countries are often and easily tempted to use the exchange rate as a means of slowing down inflation. When the exchange rate is held constant, the prices of imports stay constant (assuming foreign prices are not rising), and therefore the prices of some

FIGURE 20-5

THE UNITED STATES AND MEXICO: DOLLAR PRICE LEVELS, 1980–1989. The U.S. price level is shown as the gradually rising line P_{US}. The Mexican price level *in dollars* is represented by the erratic schedule; devaluation by Mexico reduces prices in dollars, but inflation without offsetting depreciation raises prices in dollars. By 1989 the Mexican level of competitiveness was no higher than it had been in 1985.

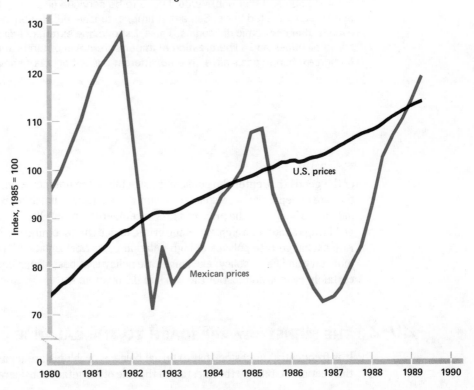

box 20-1 MEXICO: EXTERNAL DEBT, OIL, AND ADJUSTMENT PROBLEMS

In the short run, payment deficits can be financed by borrowing abroad. In the long run, they require adjustment. But politically there is never a good time for adjustment — and that is often how extreme policy difficulties arise. Mexico is a case in point.

Mexico is an oil-exporting country. It discovered and began to exploit its large oil reserves in the 1970s, when oil prices skyrocketed. Mexico enjoyed a large increase in export revenues. Even so, its domestic spending increased so fast that Mexico ran big trade deficits. These deficits were financed by borrowing abroad. Foreign banks were willing to lend to Mexico because it was oil-rich and its prospects for being able to pay interest on the debt and repay the amounts borrowed looked good. By 1982 the Mexican external debt had reached $82 billion, about 50 percent of GNP.

Mexican external balance problems came to the fore in 1982. Real interest rates in the world market increased sharply in 1981. That meant Mexico had to pay more interest on every dollar of its debt. At the same time oil prices started to fall. Losses of export revenues and higher interest bills led to a loss of confidence in the Mexican currency, which resulted in massive capital outflows. The government financed these outflows by borrowing dollars abroad to defend the exchange rate from collapse.

By 1982 external borrowing by Mexico became impossible. At the same time the nation was not earning enough dollars to pay interest on the debt. In August 1982, Mexico had to declare a moratorium — telling its creditors that it could not pay the full amounts due and that debts would have to be serviced (interest paid and debt rolled over) on an adjusted basis. Since that time, extensive adjustment has put Mexico into even further economic difficulties. Table 1 shows the extent of adjustment. However, falling oil prices and a liberalization of imports (removal of tariffs and quotas) kept the foreign exchange crisis alive. The noninterest current account showed a surplus, but

---

of the goods that enter the consumer price index are not increasing. Thus by slowing the rate of depreciation, a country can for a while reduce inflation. But the reduction in inflation is bought at the price of a loss in competitiveness. Often such a strategy in the end brings about a foreign exchange crisis, hence the recommendation to use crawling rate exchange rate policies in high-inflation countries. Inflation has to be stopped by monetary and fiscal policy; exchange rate policy is at best a supplementary tool, and it certainly cannot do most of the work in disinflation.

20-2 THE MONETARY APPROACH TO THE BALANCE OF PAYMENTS

It is frequently suggested that external balance problems are monetary in nature. In this section we take up the question of the role of monetary considerations in explaining

TABLE 1
MEXICO'S EXTERNAL BALANCE (current account in billions of U.S. dollars)

	1985	1986	1987	1988*
Current account	1.2	−1.7	3.9	−2.7
NICA†	9.6	5.1	10.1	3.4
Exports	21.7	16.0	20.7	20.6
Oil	14.7	6.3	8.6	6.7
Nonoil	7.0	9.7	12.1	14.3
Tourism and other	0.7	0.9	2.0	2.3
Imports	13.2	11.4	12.2	18.6
Interest payments	8.4	6.8	6.2	6.1
Oil price, $U.S. per barrel	25.4	17.1	16.1	12.1
Real exchange rate,‡ 1980−1982 = 100	91	65	67	80

* Estimate.

† NICA denotes the noninterest current account.

‡ Morgan Guaranty.

SOURCE: Current account data from Banco de Mexico, *Informe Anual*, various issues.

the surplus was too small to finance all the interest payments due. Thus by 1988–1989 the major issue for Mexico, and for other Latin American countries, was how to reduce the debts they owed their creditors. ∎

balance of payments problems. In particular, we consider the claim that balance of payments deficits are a reflection of an excessive money supply.

There is a simple first answer to that claim. It is obviously true that, for any given balance of payments deficit, a sufficient contraction of the money stock will restore external balance. The reason is that a monetary contraction, by raising interest rates and reducing spending, generates a contraction in economic activity, a decline in income, and therefore a decline in imports. It is equally true that this result could be achieved by tight fiscal policy, and so there is nothing especially monetary about this interpretation of remedies for external imbalance.

A more sophisticated interpretation of the problem recognizes the links among the balance of payments deficit, foreign exchange market intervention, and the money supply. The automatic mechanism is for a sale of foreign exchange — as arises in the case of a balance of payments deficit — to be reflected in an equal reduction in the stock of high-powered money. The central bank in a deficit country sells foreign exchange and in return receives high-powered money, thereby reducing the money stock. In a surplus country the central bank increases the outstanding stock of high-powered money when it buys foreign exchange, thereby expanding the money stock. Given that the money supply is thus linked to the external balance, it is obvious that this adjustment process must ultimately lead to the right money stock so that external payments will be in balance. This is the adjustment process discussed in Section 20-1.

Sterilization

The only way the automatic adjustment process can be suspended is through *sterilization operations.* We discussed this in Chapter 11 on the money supply. There we noted that central banks frequently offset, or sterilize, the impact of foreign exchange market intervention on the money supply through open market operations. Thus, a deficit country that is selling foreign exchange and correspondingly reducing its money supply may offset this reduction by open market purchases of bonds that restore the money supply.

Such a practice suspends the automatic adjustment mechanism. Persistent external deficits are possible because the link between the external imbalance and the equilibrating changes in the money stock is broken. It is in this sense that persistent external deficits are a monetary phenomenon: By sterilizing, the central bank actively maintains the stock of money too high for external balance.

The Monetary Approach and the IMF

The emphasis on monetary considerations in the interpretation of external balance problems is called the *monetary approach to the balance of payments.*[4] The monetary approach has been used extensively by the IMF in its analysis and design of economic policies for countries in balance of payments trouble. We give the flavor of the approach by describing typical IMF procedure in analyzing a balance of payments problem.

We start with the balance sheet of the monetary authority, usually the central bank, as in Table 20-1. The monetary authority's liabilities are high-powered money. But on the asset side it can hold both foreign assets — including foreign exchange reserves, gold, and claims on other central banks or governments — and domestic assets, or *domestic credit.* Domestic credit consists of the monetary authority's holdings of claims on the public sector — government debt — and on the private sector — usually loans to banks.

From the balance sheet identity, we have

---

[4] For a collection of essays on this topic, see Jacob Frenkel and Harry G. Johnson (eds.), *The Monetary Approach to the Balance of Payments* (London: Allen & Unwin, 1976). See also *The Monetary Approach to the Balance of Payments* (Washington, D.C.: International Monetary Fund, 1977).

TABLE 20-1
BALANCE SHEET OF THE MONETARY AUTHORITIES

Assets	Liabilities
Net foreign assets (*NFA*)	High-powered money (*H*)
Domestic credit (*DC*)	

$$\Delta NFA = \Delta H - \Delta DC \tag{3}$$

where ΔNFA denotes the change in net foreign assets, ΔH the change in high-powered money, and ΔDC the change in domestic credit. In words, the change in the central bank's holdings of foreign assets is equal to the change in the stock of high-powered money minus the change in domestic credit.

The important point about equation (3) is that ΔNFA is the balance of payments: Recall from Chapter 6 that official reserve transactions, which are all that ΔNFA is, are equal to the balance of payments.

The first step in developing a monetary approach type of stabilization policy package is to decide on a balance of payments target, ΔNFA^*. The IMF asks how much of a deficit the country can afford and then suggests policies to make the projected deficit no larger. The target is based largely on the availability of loans and credit from abroad and the possibility of drawing down existing reserves.

The next step is to ask how much the demand for money in the country will increase. The planned changes in the stock of high-powered money, ΔH^*, will have to be just sufficient to produce, via the money multiplier process, the right increases in the stock of money to meet the expected increase in demand. Then, given ΔNFA^* and ΔH^*, equation (3) tells the monetary authority how much domestic credit it can extend consistent with its balance of payments target and expected growth in money demand. Typically, a stabilization plan drawn up by the IMF will include a suggested limit on the expansion of domestic credit.

The limit provides a *ceiling on domestic credit expansion.* The adoption of such a ceiling helps the central bank avoid the temptation of expanding its loans to the government or private sector in the face of rising interest rates or government budget deficits.

How Does It Work?

The simplicity of equation (3) raises an obvious question. Since all it takes to improve the balance of payments is a reduction in the rate of domestic credit expansion, why not balance payments immediately and always? To answer this question, we need to understand the channels through which the curtailment of domestic credit improves the balance of payments.

Controlling domestic credit means operating tight monetary policy. Consider an economy that is growing and has some inflation, so that demand for nominal balances is rising. If domestic credit expansion is slowed, an excess demand for money develops. This, in turn, causes interest rates to rise and spending to decline. The increase in interest rates leads to a balance of payments improvement. That is, the monetary approach as used by the IMF relies on restrictive monetary policy to control the balance of payments. There is, though, a subtle difference between domestic credit ceilings and ordinary tight money. In an open economy with fixed exchange rates, the money stock is endogenous. The central bank cannot control the money stock, since it has to meet whatever demand arises for foreign currency. But it can make "money" tight by reducing the growth of domestic credit. That will imply that the only source of money growth becomes an increase in foreign exchange reserves or foreign borrowing. The economy has to go through enough of a recession or rise in interest rates to generate a balance of payments surplus.

The use of domestic credit ceilings is a crude policy to improve the balance of payments. But the simplicity of the conceptual framework, and the apparent definiteness of the policy recommendations to which it leads, frequently makes it the best policy tool available, particularly if dramatic action is needed and the credibility of the government's policies need to be restored.

The Monetary Approach and Depreciation

Proponents of the monetary approach have argued that depreciation of the exchange rate cannot improve the balance of payments except in the short run. The argument is that in the short run the depreciation does improve a country's competitive position and that this very fact gives rise to a trade surplus and therefore to an increase in the money stock. Over the course of time, the rising money supply raises aggregate demand and therefore prices until the economy returns to full employment and external balance. Devaluation thus exerts only a transitory effect on the economy, which lasts as long as prices and the money supply have not yet increased to match fully the higher import prices.

The analysis of the monetary approach is entirely correct in its insistence on a longer-run perspective in which, under fixed exchange rates, prices and the money stock adjust and the economy achieves internal and external balance. It is also correct in arguing that monetary or domestic credit restraint will improve the balance of payments. But this mechanism is not painless, since the tight money policy produced by slow domestic credit growth typically produces a recession.

The monetary approach is misdirected when it suggests that exchange rate policy cannot, even in the short run, affect a country's competitive position. More importantly, exchange rate changes frequently arise from a position of deficit and unemployment. In that case, a depreciation moves the economy toward equilibrium. It eases the adjustment mechanisms by achieving an increase in competitiveness through an increase in import prices rather than through a recession-induced decline in domestic prices.

Summary

1. Once we allow for price flexibility with fixed exchange rates, we use the analytical apparatus of Chapter 13. Price flexibility ultimately leads an economy to full employment with balanced trade. The mechanism involves changes in the domestic money supply that occur as the central bank keeps selling foreign exchange to domestic residents in exchange for domestic currency (essentially an open market sale of foreign currency). The falling money stock reduces our prices and therefore improves the balance of trade. Policy can be used actively to bring about adjustments without relying on this automatic and slow-moving mechanism.

2. Because trade does not necessarily balance in short-run equilibrium, there may be a *policy dilemma* in attempting both to move income to the potential output level and to balance trade. Increasing the level of income to move it closer to potential output may well worsen the trade balance. The use of *expenditure switching* policies, which change the relative prices of domestic and imported goods, combined with *expenditure reducing* policies, can move the economy to full employment with balanced trade.

3. Competitiveness depends on a country's prices in dollars relative to the dollar prices of its trading partners. Successful real depreciation requires a reduction of a country's *relative* price level; any domestic inflation must be more than offset by depreciation. If there is a risk that inflation will erode competitiveness, a crawling peg exchange rate policy is appropriate.

4. The monetary approach to the balance of payments emphasizes the central bank's balance sheet identity, equation (3), which shows that sufficient contraction of domestic credit will improve the balance of payments. This improvement comes about through higher interest rates and lower domestic income. Note also that the link between the balance of payments and the domestic stock of money, which is central to the monetary approach, may be broken through sterilization operations by the central bank.

20-3 FLEXIBLE EXCHANGE RATES, MONEY, AND PRICES

We now return to a flexible exchange rate world. We once again assume, just as in the Mundell-Flemming model of Chapter 6, that capital is perfectly mobile. The only difference from the earlier treatment is that now prices, too, are allowed to change. Our question now is how output, the exchange rate, and prices respond to monetary and fiscal policy and how that response evolves over time. The starting point is a discussion of the adjustment of prices and the exchange rate to the state of the economy.

The Adjustment Process

Figure 20-6 shows the interest rate and output. Full employment is shown by the vertical line Y^*. The assumption of perfect international capital mobility is reflected in the horizontal *BB* schedule. Only at an interest rate $i = i_f$ will the balance of payments be in equilibrium. If the interest rate were higher, there would be net inflows of capital. Conversely, with a lower domestic interest rate, capital would flow out and the balance of payments would turn toward a deficit position.

We make two strategic assumptions to describe the adjustment process: First, whenever output exceeds full employment, prices are falling. Second, capital is highly mobile. That implies we are always moving toward the *BB* schedule in Figure 20-6 because our interest rate cannot diverge far from that in the rest of the world. A decline in interest rates, say because of a monetary expansion, leads to an outflow of capital, depreciation, and an increase in net exports, income, money demand, and interest rates, thus moving us back toward *BB*. Conversely, a tightening in money or a fiscal expansion leads to a tendency for interest rates to rise. In response, capital flows in, and

FIGURE 20-6

ADJUSTMENT OF EXCHANGE RATES AND PRICES. Prices move in response to the deviation of the economy from full employment. When output is above potential, prices are rising (regions I and IV), and they are falling at output levels below potential (regions II and III). With capital highly mobile the balance of payments is sensitive to interest rates. If our interest rate falls below the world level, capital tends to flow out, and that leads to a deficit and depreciation of the exchange rate (regions III and IV). Conversely, a rise in interest rates leads to capital inflows, a surplus, and appreciation (regions I and II).

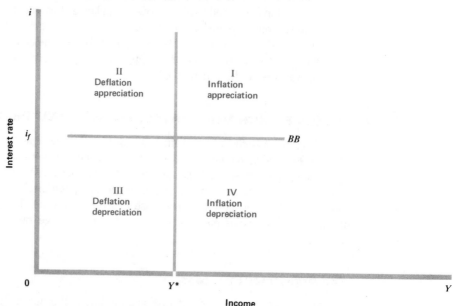

the currency appreciates. There is a loss in competitiveness and a fall in net exports, income, and money demand, and so the pressure on interest rates to rise is offset.

With these assumptions we can study the adjustment process in terms of Figure 20-6. Anywhere to the right of Y^*, prices are rising, and to the left prices are falling. Points above BB lead to capital inflows and appreciation; points below, to capital outflows and depreciation. Moreover, with capital mobility that is extremely high, the exchange rate will adjust very rapidly, so that we are practically always on the BB schedule.

A Monetary Expansion: Short- and Long-Run Effects

We saw earlier that with given prices a monetary expansion under flexible rates and perfect capital mobility leads to depreciation and increased income. We ask how that result is modified once we take adjustments in prices into account. We will show that the output adjustment is now only transitory. In the long run a monetary expansion leads to an exchange depreciation and to higher prices with no change in competitiveness. Figure 20-7 helps make these points.

In Figure 20-7 we start at an initial equilibrium with full employment, a payments balance, monetary equilibrium, and equilibrium in the domestic goods market. All this occurs at point E. Now a monetary expansion takes place and shifts the LM schedule to LM'. The new goods and money market equilibrium at E' involves an interest rate below the world level, and therefore the exchange rate immediately depreciates, raising home competitiveness and thus shifting the IS schedule to IS'. The economy moves rapidly from E via E' to E''. Output has risen, the exchange rate has depreciated, and the economy has thereby gained in external competitiveness. But that is not the end of the story.

At E'' output is above the full-employment level. Prices are therefore rising, and that implies real balances are falling. As the real money stock, M/P, declines because of rising prices, the LM schedule starts shifting to the left. Interest rates tend to rise, capital tends to flow in, and the resulting appreciation leads now to a decline in competitiveness that also shifts the IS schedule back toward the initial equilibrium. Both the IS and LM schedules thus move back toward point E. The process continues until point E is reached again.

What adjustments have taken place once the economy is back to point E? At point E, interest rates have returned to their initial level and so have relative prices, eP_f/P. In moving from E to E' the exchange rate depreciated immediately, ahead of the rise in prices. But when prices increased and real balances fell, some of that depreciation was reversed. Over the whole adjustment process, prices and exchange rates rose in the same proportion, leaving relative prices, eP_f/P, and therefore aggregate demand unchanged. In the long run money was therefore *entirely neutral*. Table 20-2 summarizes these results. Neutrality of money means, in terms of the second row of the table, that nominal money, prices, and the exchange rate all increase in the same proportion, so that the real money stock and relative prices are unchanged.

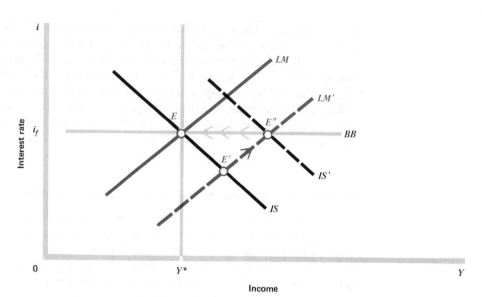

FIGURE 20-7

THE SHORT- AND LONG-RUN EFFECTS OF A MONETARY EXPANSION. The economy is in initial equilibrium at E when a monetary expansion shifts the LM schedule to LM'. The goods and money market equilibrium at E' involves an interest rate below the world level. Capital outflows now lead to immediate exchange depreciation, and therefore the IS schedule shifts to IS'. The economy thus moves rapidly from E to E''. But at E'' there is overemployment, and hence prices are rising. Rising prices reduce real balances and shift the LM schedule back toward E. As real balances decline, interest rates tend to rise, drawing in capital and leading to appreciation, which shifts the IS' schedule back toward E. In the long run, output returns to normal, and money, prices, and the exchange rate all rise in the same proportion.

TABLE 20-2

THE SHORT- AND LONG-RUN EFFECTS
OF A MONETARY EXPANSION

	$\dfrac{M}{P}$	e	P	$\dfrac{eP_f}{P}$	Y
Short run	+	+	0	+	+
Long run	0	+	+	0	0

770

Exchange Rate Overshooting

The analysis of monetary policy under flexible exchange rates, given above, leads to an important insight about the adjustment process. The important feature of the adjustment process is that *exchange rates and prices do not move at the same rate.* When a monetary expansion pushes interest rates down, the exchange rate adjusts immediately, but prices adjust only gradually. Monetary expansion therefore leads in the short run to an immediate and abrupt change in relative prices and competitiveness.

Figure 20-8 shows time paths of nominal money, the exchange rate, and the price level implied by the analysis of Figure 20-7. For each of these variables we show an

FIGURE 20-8

EXCHANGE RATE OVERSHOOTING. The diagram shows indexes for prices, money, and the exchange rate. Initially the economy is in full equilibrium, and the value of each index is chosen as 100. A permanent increase in the money stock of 50 percent takes place at time T_0, as shown by the solid line. The exchange rate immediately depreciates from A to A', more than the increase in money. Prices adjust only gradually. In the short run, the relative price of imports, eP_f/P, increases sharply. That gain in competitiveness causes a transitory income expansion. But over time prices rise and the exchange rate appreciates somewhat, undoing the initial overshooting. In the long run, nominal money, the exchange rate, and prices all rise in the same proportion (50 percent, from 100 to 150), and real balances and the relative price of imports are therefore unchanged.

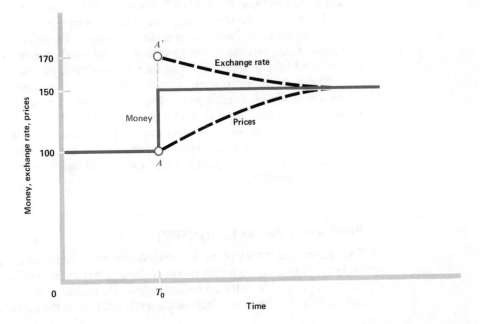

index that is initially equal to 100. The economy starts at long-run equilibrium. Then, at time T_0, the money stock is increased by 50 percent. Thus the money stock rises from 100 to 150 and stays at that higher level, as shown by the solid schedule. The exchange rate immediately depreciates. In fact the exchange rate index rises by more than money, say from the initial level of 100 at point A to a new level of 170 at point A'. Prices, by contrast, do not move rapidly.

Following the impact effect at time T_0, further adjustments take place. Because the gain in competitiveness at time T_0 has raised output above potential, there is now inflation. Prices are rising, and at the same time the exchange rate is appreciating, thus undoing part of the initial, sharp depreciation. Over time, prices rise to match the increase in money, and the exchange rate will also match the higher level of money and prices. In the long run, real variables are unchanged. The adjustment pattern for the exchange rate seen in Figure 20-8 involves *overshooting*. The exchange rate overshoots its new equilibrium level when, in response to a disturbance, it first moves *beyond* the equilibrium it ultimately will reach and then gradually returns to the long-run equilibrium position. Overshooting means that changes in monetary policy produce large changes in exchange rates.

Figure 20-9 shows an index of the DM (deutsche mark)-U.S. dollar exchange rate for the period since 1979. We notice the sharp depreciation of the DM or appreciation of the dollar from 1979 to the beginning of 1985, and the subsequent reversal, which continued well into 1988. We also show an index of the relative price, eP_f/P, using consumer prices in Germany and the United States. The diagram shows clearly that along with an appreciating dollar there occurs a loss in U.S. competitiveness as eP_f/P declines. The dollar appreciation is partly explained by the shift toward tight money in the United States, starting in late 1979. Our model predicts that, in the case of tight money and easy fiscal policy, there would be an immediate appreciation of the dollar. Moreover, in the short run, prices would respond relatively little, and therefore competitiveness would immediately decline, almost one for one, with the appreciation. The episode supports the notion that under flexible exchange rates monetary policy has powerful effects on the exchange rate, competitiveness, and net exports.

These effects are so strong that they have become a source of major concern. Those who believe that exchange rate overshooting introduces an undesirable instability into the economy argue that governments should intervene in foreign exchange markets to avoid large, excessive exchange rate fluctuations. The sharp dollar appreciation of 1980–1985 strongly reinforced the call for such intervention. In 1985 the major countries agreed in principle that they would intervene to try to prevent exchange rate instability.

Purchasing Power Parity (PPP)

The long-run neutrality of money, discussed above, illustrates the potential role of exchange rates in offsetting the effects of changes in the price level at home and abroad on the terms of trade. In the preceding analysis, the exchange rate rose by precisely the right amount to offset the effects of domestic inflation on the terms of trade. That is, the exchange depreciation maintained the *purchasing power* of our goods in terms of foreign goods between the initial and the final equilibrium points.

An important view of the determinants of the exchange rate is the theory that exchange rates move primarily as a result of differences in price level behavior between the two countries in such a way as to maintain the terms of trade constant. This is the *purchasing power parity* (PPP) theory. Purchasing power parity theory argues that exchange rate movements primarily reflect divergent rates of inflation. Examining the terms of trade, eP_f/P, the theory maintains the following: When P_f and/or P change, e changes in such a way as to maintain eP_f/P constant.

PPP is a plausible description of the trend behavior of exchange rates, especially when inflation differentials between countries are large. In particular, we have seen

FIGURE 20-9

THE EXCHANGE RATE AND RELATIVE PRICES: GERMANY AND THE UNITED STATES, 1979–1989 (index, 1985 = 100). (SOURCE: DRI/McGraw-Hill.)

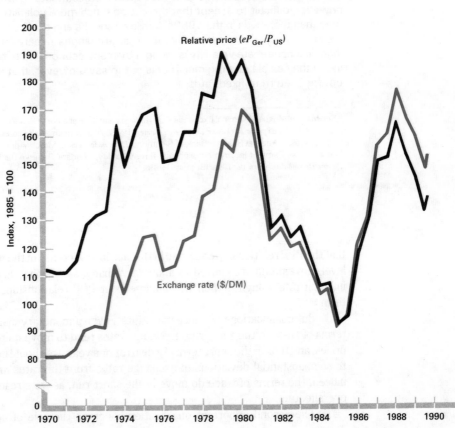

box 20-2 **EXCHANGE RATE VOLATILITY**

Figure 1 shows monthly percentage changes in the *bilateral* U.S.-German real exchange rate. In the 1960s, when exchange rates were fixed and inflation rates low, the real exchange rate moved very little. In fact, the only two spikes in that period correspond to revaluations of the deutsche mark. But in the 1970s and 1980s, under flexible exchange rates, real exchange rates were very volatile.

There are two schools of thought regarding the sharply higher real exchange rate volatility observed since the world moved to flexible exchange rates. One school holds that wages and prices are relatively sticky—certainly on a month-to-month basis. Accordingly when nominal exchange rates move, so do real exchange rates. This variability of real exchange rates is thus considered a by-product of the volatility of nominal exchange rates. The other school of thought, mostly represented by new classical economists, maintains that the increased volatility of real exchange rates reflects changes in the *equilibrium* real exchange rate. In this interpretation, the 1970s and 1980s brought much more substantial volatility in the real variables that underlie the foreign exchange market: oil price shocks, fiscal shocks, changes in trade flows.[*]

If the new classical interpretation is correct, exchange rate volatility is not an issue. Rather it is simply a reflection of volatility in real variables, and fixing nominal exchange rates would only shift the required adjustments to wages and prices. It is, however, difficult to accept that there is so much more volatility in the real economy now than there was in the 1960s. While oil shocks and the like make good examples, they hardly explain the month-by-month large changes in real exchange rates. Accordingly, exchange rate volatility is thought by many economists to be a major shortcoming of the flexible rate regime. That is not to say, however, that they would therefore opt for a return to fixed rates. ■

---

[*] See Michael Mussa, "Nominal Exchange Rate Regimes and the Behavior of Real Exchange Rates: Evidence and Implications," *Carnegie Rochester Conference Series*, 1979; Alan Stockman, "The Equilibrium Approach to Exchange Rates," Federal Reserve Bank of Richmond *Economic Review*, March/April 1987; and Jeffrey Frankel, "International Capital Mobility and Exchange Rate Volatility," Federal Reserve Bank of Boston, *International Payments Imbalances in the 1980s* (Boston, 1989).

---

that the PPP relationship does hold in the face in an increase in the money stock. If price level movements are caused by monetary changes—as they are likely to be if the inflation rate is high—then we should expect PPP relationships to hold in the long term.

But qualifications are necessary. First, even a monetary disturbance affects the terms of trade in the short run. Exchange rates tend to move quite rapidly relative to prices, and thus in the short term of a quarter or a year, we should not be at all surprised to see substantial deviations of exchange rates from the rates implied by PPP. And indeed, the terms of trade do move in the short run, as we already saw in discussing overshooting.

The second important qualification concerns the role of nonmonetary distur-

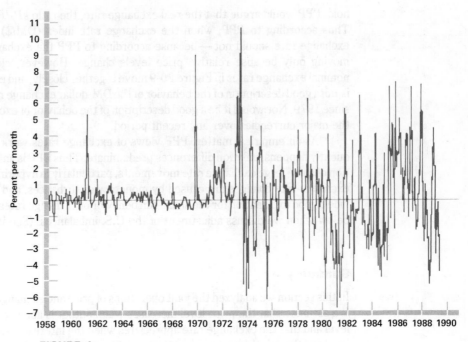

FIGURE 1

THE UNITED STATES AND GERMANY: REAL EXCHANGE RATE VOLATILITY,
1958–1989 (percent change). (SOURCE: DRI/McGraw-Hill.)

bances in affecting exchange rates. For example, we saw that an increase in exports improves our terms of trade or leads to currency appreciation at unchanged domestic prices. Or if we look at an increase in potential output as another example, we will find that the equilibrium terms of trade worsen. To absorb the increased output, demand must rise, implying a decline in the relative price of our goods. Thus, it is apparent that, over time, adjustments to *real* disturbances will affect the *equilibrium* terms of trade. In the longer run, exchange rates and prices do *not* necessarily move together, as they do in a world where all disturbances are monetary. On the contrary, we may have important changes in relative prices. Such changes run counter to the purchasing power parity view of exchange rates.

Returning to Figure 20-9, we see that the PPP theory in its strict form does not hold. PPP would argue that the real exchange rate, the ratio eP_f/P, remains consant. Thus according to PPP, when the exchange rate index (DM/\$) changes, the real exchange rate should not — because according to PPP the exchange rate should be moving only because relative price levels change. However, clearly the real and nominal exchange rates in Figure 20-9 move together closely, and equally clearly, PPP is *not* a good description of the behavior of the DM-dollar exchange rate over the period since 1979. Nor would it be a good description of the behavior of exchange rates among the major currencies over any recent period.

As an empirical matter, PPP views of exchange rates work well when, as frequently happens, inflation differences predominate. Thus PPP is an important explanation of some large exchange rate movements, particularly in hyperinflations. But not all exchange rate changes are caused by monetary disturbances, and PPP does not provide a good explanation for the short-run behavior of exchange rates. We return to PPP below when we discuss adjustment of the U.S. imbalances. (See Box 20-2.)

Summary

In this section we analyzed the joint operations of price and exchange rate adjustments. We assumed that the price level increases when output is above the full-employment level and that the exchange rate appreciates when the interest rate is above the world level and there is therefore a capital inflow. The examination of monetary disturbances under flexible prices and exchange rates gave us the following results:

1. Price level and exchange rate adjustments affect the level of income and the interest rate. An increasing price level reduces real balances, tending to increase the interest rate. Changes in the price level and the exchange rate also affect the terms of trade and thus influence the demand for our goods.
2. A monetary expansion in the long run increases the price level and the exchange rate, keeping real balances and the terms of trade constant. In the short run, though, the monetary expansion increases the level of output and reduces the interest rate, depreciating the exchange rate. The exchange rate overshoots its new equilibrium level.
3. Purchasing power parity theory argues that exchange rate changes are, in practice, caused by divergences in inflation rates between countries, with the exchange rate changing in a way that maintains the terms of trade constant. This theory is a good predictor of the behavior of the exchange rate over periods when disturbances are caused mainly by monetary factors, such as in hyperinflations. But in the short run, monetary disturbances are not neutral, and even in the long run the exchange rate can change as a result of real disturbances. Examples include changes in technology in different countries, shifts in export demand, and shifts in potential output.

We have now completed the core of this chapter. The remaining sections take up a number of issues that extend the basic analysis.

20-4 INTEREST DIFFERENTIALS AND EXCHANGE RATE EXPECTATIONS

A cornerstone of our theoretical model of exchange rate determination was international capital mobility. In particular, we argued that with capital markets sufficiently integrated, we would expect interest rates to be equated across countries. How does this assumption stand up to the facts? In Figure 20-10 we show the U.S. federal funds rate and the money market rate in Germany. It is quite apparent from the chart that these rates are certainly not equal. Thus, in 1985, the interest differential reached more than four percentage points. How do we square these facts with our theory?

FIGURE 20-10

THE U.S. FEDERAL FUNDS RATE AND GERMAN MONEY MARKET RATES, 1978–1989 (percent). (SOURCE: DRI/McGraw-Hill.)

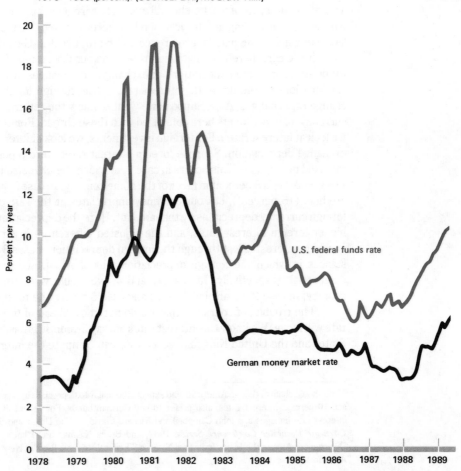

Exchange Rate Expectations

Our theoretical analysis was based on the assumption that capital flows internationally in response to nominal interest differentials. For example, if domestic interest rates were 10 percent and foreign rates were 6 percent, we would, according to the earlier sections, expect a capital inflow.

However, such a theory is incomplete in a world in which exchange rates can, do, and are expected to change. For example, consider a situation in which the deutsche mark is expected to appreciate by 5 percent over the next year relative to the dollar. Suppose the interest rate in Germany is 6 percent. Anyone buying German bonds will earn a return in deutsche marks of 6 percent. Suppose now that the U.S. interest rate is 10 percent. A German investing in the United States for a year will, at the beginning of the year, exchange deutsche marks for dollars and then earn 10 percent in dollars. At the end of the year, she will want to change the dollars back into deutsche marks to spend in Germany. But she expects that by the end of the year, each dollar will be worth 5 percent less in terms of deutsche marks as a result of the expected depreciation. Therefore, in terms of marks, she will expect to earn only 5 percent (10 percent minus 5 percent) by investing in American bonds, whereas she earns 6 percent by investing in German bonds. The natural preference will be to invest in German bonds.[5]

It is clear, therefore, that we must extend our discussion of interest rate equalization to incorporate expectations of exchange rate changes. Table 20-3 gives some combinations of the domestic interest rate, i; the foreign interest rate, i_f; and exchange rate changes, $\Delta e/e$. Suppose we want to know the return, in terms of domestic currency, of investments here compared with those abroad. For domestic investments we look at interest rate i. For foreign investments, we look at interest rate i_f and at the exchange depreciation. Suppose foreign interest rates were 5 percent and exchange rates did not change. This occurs in case 1, in which the *adjusted* interest differential, $i - i_f - \Delta e/e$, is 5 percent in favor of the home country. In case 2, interest rates abroad are high (15 percent), but our currency appreciates at the rate of 5 percent, or the foreign currency depreciates by that amount. Here the depreciation exactly offsets the higher foreign interest rates, and the adjusted differential is zero — what would be gained in interest is lost through the foreign depreciation. Cases 3 and 4 show circumstances in which the foreign depreciation falls short of, and exceeds, the interest differential, respectively. In cases 1 and 4, we would want to invest in the home country; in case 2 we are indifferent; and case 3 favors the foreign country.

The trouble, of course, is that we do not know ahead of time how the exchange rate will move. We know the interest rates on, say 3-month Treasury bills in the United States and the United Kingdom, so that we can compute the interest differential, but

---

[5] You should confirm that an American who expects the dollar to depreciate by 5 percent would, given the 6 and 10 percent interest rates, also prefer to buy German bonds. For recent literature on international interest rate linkages see John Campbell and Richard Clarida, "The Dollar and the Real Interest Rate," *Carnegie Rochester Conference Series,* 1987, and Bruce Kasman and Charles Pigott, "Interest Rate Divergences Among the Major Industrial Nations," Federal Reserve Bank of New York *Quarterly Review,* Autumn 1988.

TABLE 20-3
INTEREST RATES AND EXCHANGE DEPRECIATION (percent)

Case	Domestic interest rate (i)	Foreign interest rate (i_f)	Depreciation $(\Delta e/e)$	Adjusted interest differential, $(i - i_f - \Delta e/e)$
1	10	5	0	5
2	10	15	−5	0
3	10	15	−2	−3
4	10	15	−10	5

we do not know whether the pound will appreciate or depreciate over the next 3 months. Even if we somehow knew the direction, we would certainly not know the precise amount.

Investors then have to form *expectations* about the behavior of the exchange rate; that is, in deciding whether to invest at home or abroad, they have to make forecasts of the future behavior of the exchange rate. Given these forecasts, we would expect that, in a world of high capital mobility, the interest differentials, *adjusted for expected depreciation,* should be negligible. That means that a country that is certain to depreciate will have interest rates above the world level, and conversely, a country that is expected to appreciate will have interest rates below the world level.

The introduction of exchange rate expectations modifies our equation for the balance of payments. Now capital flows are governed by the difference between our interest rate and the foreign rate adjusted for expected depreciation: $i - i_f - \Delta e/e$. An increase in foreign interest rates or an expectation of depreciation, given our interest rates, would lead to a capital outflow. Conversely, a rise in our rates or an expectation of appreciation would bring about a capital outflow. We thus write the balance of payments as

$$BP = NX\left(Y, \frac{eP_f}{P}\right) + CF\left(i - i_f - \frac{\Delta e}{e}\right) \tag{4}$$

The adjustment for exchange rate expectations thus accounts for international differences in interest rates that persist even when capital is freely mobile among countries. When capital is completely mobile, we expect interest rates to be equalized, after adjusting for expected depreciation:

$$i = i_f + \Delta e/e \tag{4a}$$

Expected depreciation helps account for differences in interest rates among low- and high-inflation countries. When the inflation rate in a country is high, its exchange rate is expected to depreciate. In addition, the Fisher relationship of Chapter 17 suggests that the nominal interest rate in that country will be high. Thus high-inflation countries tend to have high interest rates and depreciating currencies. This is an international extension of the Fisher equation, which relies on PPP to argue that inflation differentials internationally are matched by depreciation. Our long-term relation then is

$$\text{Inflation differential} \cong \text{interest differential} \cong \text{depreciation rate} \qquad (5)$$

(The $\cong$ means "approximately equal to.") The relation is only approximate because, as we have seen — particularly in Figure 20-9 — exchange rates can move independently of prices and also because obstacles to capital flows may create long-term interest differentials.

There is another respect in which the introduction of exchange rate expectations is important, and that concerns speculative capital flows and their impact on macroeconomic equilibrium. The point is made with the help of Figure 20-11, which assumes perfect capital mobility, as specified in equation (4a). Here the *BB* schedule is drawn for a given foreign interest rate and a given expected rate of change for the exchange rate, say zero. Suppose that we start in full equilibrium at point *E* and that the market develops the expectation that the home currency will appreciate. This implies that even with a lower home interest rate, domestic assets are attractive, and so the *BB* schedule shifts downward by the amount of expected appreciation.

Point *E* is no longer an equilibrium, given the shift of the *BB* schedule to *BB'*, but rather a position of surplus with large-scale capital inflows motivated by the anticipation of appreciation. (This might well describe the case of the United Kingdom in 1979 after awareness of British oil discoveries spread in the market.) The surplus caused the exchange rate to start appreciating, and we move in a southwesterly direction, as indicated by the arrow. The speculative attack causes appreciation, a loss in competitiveness, and, consequently, falling output and employment.

This analysis confirms that exchange rate expectations, through their impact on capital flows and thus on actual exchange rates, are a potential source of disturbance to macroeconomic equilibrium.

20-5 EXCHANGE RATE CHANGES AND TRADE ADJUSTMENT: EMPIRICAL ISSUES

In this section we take up two important empirical issues related to the possibility of adjusting current account imbalances by changes in the exchange rate. The first is that wages and prices may respond to movements in the exchange rate in a way that makes it impossible or at least difficult to change relative prices through changes in the exchange rate.[6] This issue is particularly important if formal wage indexation arrangements link wage behavior to import prices and thus to the exchange rate.

The second issue we consider is whether changes in relative prices, assuming

---

[6] We examined this issue briefly in Sec. 20-1 in discussing the Mexican exchange rate experience since 1982.

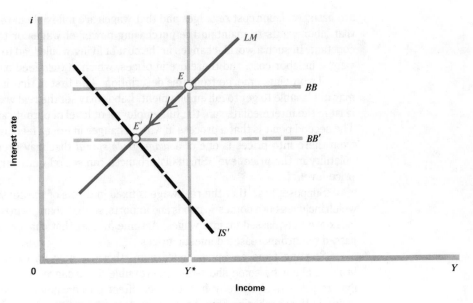

FIGURE 20-11

RESPONSE TO AN EXPECTED APPRECIATION OF THE CURRENCY. The initial equilibrium at E is disturbed by the expectation that the home currency will appreciate. The BB schedule shifts down to BB', reflecting the fact that people are willing to hold domestic assets at a reduced interest rate since they expect to be compensated for the differential by the anticipated appreciation of the currency. At E there is now a capital inflow that leads to exchange appreciation. The IS schedule (not drawn) shifts to IS', and the economy moves into a recession. The capital inflow has brought about a loss of trade competitiveness and thus unemployment at point E'.

that they are possible, will affect the current account in the direction we have assumed. The assumption, so far, has been that a decline in the relative price of our goods improves the current account. But the possibility arises that at least in the short run there might be a perverse reaction. For example, with import prices rising, import demand may not decline sufficiently to compensate for higher prices, and thus total import spending (price times quantity) may actually increase. We turn our attention now to these two issues.

Exchange Rates and Relative Price Adjustment

In studying the flexible wage-price model, we assumed that wages and prices adjust to achieve full employment. Now we consider as an alternative the possibility that prices are based on labor cost or wages and that wages are inflexible in real terms. Suppose that labor wants to maintain the purchasing power of wages or to keep real wages constant. In such a world, changes in the cost of living would lead to changes in money wages, in labor cost, and therefore in prices, which in turn feed back into wages.

Two points emerge from this description. The first is that in such a world, we may not be able to get to full employment. Labor may set the real wage too high, and at least in the intermediate run, the full-employment level of output cannot be sustained. The second point is that a process in which changes in prices feed back into wages and from there into prices is one of a *wage-price spiral* that may produce considerable volatility in the price level. Small disturbances can set off quite large changes in the price level.

Suppose, first, that the real wage is fixed in terms of the consumer price index, which includes both domestic goods and imports, so that changes in the consumer price index are fully passed on into wages. Assume further that changes in wages are fully passed on into increased domestic prices.

Starting from an initial equilibrium, there is now an exchange depreciation brought about by some short-term, reversible disturbance. The depreciation raises import prices and thereby has a direct effect on consumer prices and wages. To maintain the purchasing power of their wages, workers demand higher money wages, which firms grant and pass on by raising prices. Where are we after the process ends? Real wages are constant, which means wages and the price level (a weighted average of the prices of domestic and imported goods) have risen in the same proportion; wage increases have been fully passed on, which means that real wages *in terms of domestic output* are also unchanged. The two results imply that relative prices are unchanged, or that the exchange depreciation is fully matched by domestic inflation.

Of course, this is not really the end because we have to ask how the higher price level affects the macroeconomic equilibrium. To the extent that lower real balances lower aggregate demand, we would have a reduction in employment. To round out our story, we can imagine that the central bank steps in to prevent unemployment by raising the money stock. If nominal money rises in proportion to the price increase, then the full-employment equilibrium, at the same terms of trade, is reestablished but, of course, at a higher level of wages and prices. This is an economy in which there is very little stability in the price level because the slightest change in exchange rate expectations leads to actual exchange rate movements that are fully *validated* by domestic wage, price, and monetary developments.

A second context in which the idea of *sticky real wages* (wages that are difficult to change) is important is that of real disturbances. Suppose our export demand declines permanently because of, say, the introduction of superior technology abroad. To return to full employment, the relative price of our goods must fall so as to encourage foreign demand. But how can the relative price fall? In Section 20-3, we argued that the exchange rate will depreciate, thereby raising import prices relative to domestic prices and restoring our competitiveness. In the present context we have to recognize that import price increases would be fully passed on into price increases. Relative prices cannot change. The consequence would be, of course, protracted unemployment. Unemployment would continue until the *real* wage declines.

The empirical question, then, is, How flexible are real wages? That is, to an important extent, a question of institutional arrangements. In small, open economies with substantial cost-of-living indexation in wage agreements, it may indeed be very difficult to change real wages and relative prices through exchange rate changes.

Relative Prices and the Trade Balance: The J Curve

We come now to the second issue, the effect of changes in relative prices on the trade balance and the possibility that a depreciation *worsens* the trade balance. To make this point, we write out the trade balance, measured in terms of domestic goods, as

$$NX = X - \frac{eP_f}{P} Q \tag{6}$$

where X denotes the foreign demand for our goods or exports and Q denotes our own import quantity. The term $(eP_f/P)Q$ thus measures the *value* of our imports in terms of domestic goods.

Suppose that we now have an exchange depreciation and that in the first instance, domestic and foreign prices, P and P_f, are unchanged. Then the relative price of imports, eP_f/P, rises. This leads to two effects. First, if the physical *volume* of imports does not change, their *value* measured in domestic currency unambiguously increases because of the higher price. With unchanged physical import volume, Q, higher prices mean increased import spending (measured in terms of the domestic currency) and thus a worsening of the trade balance. This is the source for the potentially perverse response of the trade balance to exchange depreciation. However, there is an adjustment that runs in the opposite direction. The increased relative price of imports makes us more competitive and shifts demand in volume terms toward domestic goods. This *volume effect* of substitution in response to changed relative prices shows up in equation (6) in the form of increased export volume, X, and reduced import volume, Q. The volume effects thus ambiguously improve the trade balance.

The question, then, is whether the volume effects on imports and exports are sufficiently strong to outweigh the price effect, that is, whether depreciation raises or lowers net exports. The empirical evidence on this question is quite strong and shows the following result: *The short-term volume effects, say, within a year, are quite small and thus do not outweigh the price effect.*[7] *The long-term volume effects, by contrast, are quite substantial, and certainly enough to make the trade balance respond in the normal fashion to a relative price change.*

Where does this asymmetry come from, and what does it imply about trade adjustment to relative prices? First, the low short-term and high longer-term volume

---

[7] See Ellen Meade, "Exchange Rate Adjustment and the J Curve," *Federal Reserve Bulletin,* October 1988, and Ralph Bryant et al. (eds.), *Empirical Macroeconomics for Interdependent Economies* (Washington, D.C.: The Brookings Institution, 1988). See, too, Paul Krugman, "The J-Curve, the Fire Sale and the Hard Landing," *American Economic Review,* May 1989.

effects result from the time consumers and producers take to adjust to changes in relative prices. Some of these adjustments may be instantaneous, but it is clear that tourism patterns, for example, may take 6 months to a year to adjust and that relocation of production internationally in response to changes in relative costs and prices may take years. A case in point is increased foreign direct investment in the United States—say Toyota moving from Japan to California. In the long term, such direct investment leads to reduced imports by the United States, and thus to an improved trade balance, but such an adjustment takes years, not weeks or months.

The lag in the adjustment of trade flows to changes in relative prices is thus quite plausible. The next question is, What do these lags imply about the impact of relative price changes on the trade balance? Suppose that at a particular time, starting with a deficit, we have a depreciation that raises the relative price of imports. The short-term effects result primarily from increased import prices with very little offsetting volume effects. Therefore, the trade balance initially worsens. Over time, as trade volume adjusts to the changed relative prices, exports rise and import volume progressively declines. The volume effects come to dominate, and in the long run, the trade balance shows an improvement. This pattern of adjustment is referred to as the *J-curve effect,* because diagrammatically the response of the trade balance looks like a J.

The J-curve effect could be seen in the behavior of the U.S. current account after 1985. Despite a rapid depreciation of the dollar starting in February 1985, the current account continued to worsen for the next year. But the current account began to improve in 1987 and continued improving in 1988.

The medium-term problem of sticky real wages and the J-curve effect are important qualifications to the macroeconomics of flexible rates as spelled out in Section 20-3. They imply that flexible exchange rates do not provide for instant, costless flexibility of relative prices and trade flows. At the same time, these considerations provide important clues for the interpretation of macroeconomic experiences across countries, particularly in showing why depreciations typically do not lead to improvements in the current account in the short term.

HYSTERESIS EFFECTS OF OVERVALUATION

A further complication has been suggested in the aftermath of the large and persistent overvaluation of the dollar, namely *hysteresis effects.* Such effects are present, in the case of the exchange rate, when a change in the exchange rate that is later exactly reversed nonetheless leaves a long-term impact on the trade account. The very strong dollar that lasted for several years in the early 1980s put U.S. firms at a sharp disadvantage in world trade and in the U.S. market. Foreign firms experienced a reduction in their costs (measured in dollars) and as a result could afford to charge lower prices in the U.S. market. In foreign markets, U.S. firms lost out because their costs in foreign currency had been raised by the strong dollar.

These are the normal effects of a currency appreciation. The new argument is that when exchange rate changes are very large and long lasting, then they will lead to a relatively permanent change in trade patterns. Foreign firms will incur the fixed costs of entering the U.S. market; once the firms are established and consumers have become accustomed to their goods, even a reversal of the exchange rate to the initial level will not be enough to enable U.S. firms to recapture their share of the market. In foreign markets U.S. firms will have lost market share, and going back to the initial exchange rate will not be enough to bring U.S. firms back. To return to the initial trade pattern, exchange rates would have to overshoot in the opposite direction, making it profitable to incur the costs of starting up export operations and competing with foreign firms who supply imports.

The evidence on these hysteresis effects remains tentative, but the idea is certainly plausible. The continued large import penetration into the U.S. market and the failure of the U.S. external balance to correct itself, even after the 1985–1988 depreciation brought the real exchange rate back close to its 1980 level, support the idea that the damage of overvaluation may be a lasting one.

20-6 EXCHANGE RATE FLUCTUATIONS AND INTERDEPENDENCE

In the 1960s there was growing dissatisfaction with fixed exchange rates. The Bretton Woods system[8] was called a crisis system because from time to time exchange rates would get out of line and expectations of exchange rate changes would mobilize massive capital flows that often precipitated the exchange rate changes that speculators expected. Is the flexible rate system of the 1970s and 1980s better? Is it less crisis-prone, and does it provide a better framework for macroeconomic stability? Before providing an answer, we look briefly at how flexibly the system has, in fact, operated.

Dirty Floating and Intervention

Under *fully* flexible exchange rates the government takes no action in the foreign exchange market. Far from buying or selling foreign exchange at a fixed price, the government does not conduct *any* foreign exchange transactions. It stays out of the foreign exchange market, whatever happens to the exchange rate. Such a system is almost unheard of, although the United States did behave that way briefly in 1981–1982. More commonly, governments intervene in the foreign exchange market to a lesser or greater extent. Foreign exchange market *intervention* occurs when a government buys or sells foreign exchange in an attempt to influence the exchange rate. The extent to which governments intervene varies substantially. They may only try to offset short-term fluctuations and buy or sell foreign exchange to maintain "orderly markets." But they also may try to keep an overvalued exchange rate from depreciating or an undervalued exchange rate from appreciating. *Dirty floating* (as opposed to clean) is the practice of using substantial intervention to try to maintain an exchange rate against the pressure of market forces.

---

[8] This is the system of fixed exchange rates that prevailed from the end of World War II to 1973, so-called because it was designed, in 1944, in a major international conference held in Bretton Woods, New Hampshire.

During the 1973–1986 period, exchange rate floating has been of the decidedly dirty variety. Governments have intervened on a very large scale. This leads naturally to the question of why a government should try to resist market forces, to prevent an appreciation or a depreciation of the currency.

Why Governments Intervene

Central banks intervene to affect exchange rates for several reasons. Probably the main reason is the belief that many capital flows represent merely unstable expectations and that the induced movements in exchange rates move production in the economy in an unnecessarily erratic fashion. The second reason for the intervention is a central bank's attempt to move the real exchange rate in order to affect trade flows. The third reason arises from the effects of the exchange rate on domestic inflation. Central banks sometimes intervene in the exchange market to prevent the exchange rate from depreciating, with the aim of preventing a depreciation-induced increase in the inflation rate.

Should central banks intervene in the exchange market? The basic argument for such intervention is that it is possible for intervention to smooth out fluctuations in exchange rates. At one extreme, the argument would assert that any movements in exchange rates produce unnecessary fluctuations in the domestic economy and that exchange rates therefore ought to be fixed. This is the basic argument for dirty floating. The only — and overwhelming — objection to the argument that the central bank should smooth out fluctuations is that there is no simple way of telling an erratic movement from a trend movement. How can we tell whether a current appreciation in the exchange rate is merely the result of a disturbance that will soon reverse itself, rather than the beginning of a trend movement in the exchange rate? There is no way of telling at the time a change occurs, although with the benefit of hindsight one can see which exchange rate movements were later reversed.

There is one circumstance under which central bank intervention might be desirable. It is clear from our earlier analysis that one of the key determinants of exchange rate behavior consists of expectations of economic policy. It may sometimes be possible to make it clear that there has been a change in policy only by intervening in the foreign exchange market. This is a case of putting your money where your mouth is.

Should Governments Intervene?

There is disagreement on whether governments should intervene in the foreign exchange market. The United States, for example, in 1981–1982 strongly refused consideration of any kind of intervention. The reason was that policy makers in the United States, unlike those in Europe, believed the market knows better than policy makers what level the exchange rate should be at. But there is another and more interesting disagreement: it concerns the effectiveness of intervention. Does it make any difference to the exchange rate if the Bundesbank sells $1 billion from its foreign currency reserves?

To judge the effectiveness of intervention we must make a distinction between *sterilized* and *nonsterilized intervention.* In the case of sterilized intervention a central bank, say, buys foreign exchange, issuing domestic money. But then the increase in home money is reversed by an open market sale of securities. In the sterilized intervention case, therefore, the home money supply is kept unchanged. In the case of nonsterilization, by contrast, there is a change in the money stock equal to the amount of intervention.

Thus nonsterilized intervention results in a change in the money stock. It is widely agreed that nonsterilized intervention, because it changes the money supply, will affect exchange rates. There is widespread skepticism, however, about the effectiveness of sterilized intervention. In 1978–1979 the U.S. dollar was depreciating in currency markets even though there was intervention on a massive scale. But that intervention was carefully sterilized. Only in late 1979, when the dollar depreciation had come to alarm the Fed, did a change in policy take place. Monetary policy was tightened, and immediately the dollar depreciation was stopped and soon massively reversed.

That episode, and other evidence, strongly suggests the effectiveness of non-sterilized intervention and of intervention that is backed by credible policies. The earlier failure of sterilized intervention suggested that only unsterilized intervention could affect the exchange rate. But a more recent episode gives cause for rethinking that issue.

The very large appreciation of the dollar from 1980 to 1985, described in Box 20-2, was a major concern to policy makers in the United States, Europe, and Japan.[9] Many policy makers thought that the markets had pushed the dollar too high, and that only speculative forces were keeping it up. In September 1985 the finance ministers of the Group of Five (the United States, Japan, Germany, France, and the United Kingdom) announced their view that the dollar was too high, and their central banks went into action to sell dollars in order to drive the rate down. The dollar responded quickly, suggesting that concerted action can affect the exchange rate even if there is no obvious change in monetary policy. Such action is certainly not guaranteed to work, but could work if there is widespread speculation in the markets about the future course of policy and if announcements and intervention suggest that future policy will try to move the exchange rate in a particular direction.

[9] See Federal Reserve Bank of Kansas City, "The U.S. Dollar — Recent Development, Outlook and Policy Options," 1985, which includes a discussion of many of the issues raised by the strong dollar, intervention, and coordination. See also Jeffrey Frankel, "Six Possible Meanings of Over-valuation: The 1981–85 Dollar," *Essays in International Finance* (Princeton, N.J.: Princeton University Press, December 1985), and the Symposium in *Brookings Papers on Economic Activity,* I, 1986.

Interdependence

It used to be argued that under flexible exchange rates countries can pursue their own national economic policies — monetary and fiscal policy and the inflation rate — without having to worry about the balance of payments. That is certainly correct, but it is also misleading. There are important linkages between countries *whatever the exchange rate regime.*

These *spillover,* or *interdependence,* effects have been at the center of the discussion about flexible exchange rates. The effects of the tight U.S. monetary policies in 1980 – 1982 created problems for all industrialized countries. The reason is clear from our models: As the United States tightens monetary policy, our interest rates rise, and that attracts capital flows from abroad. The dollar appreciates, and foreign currencies depreciate. Table 20-4 shows the effects in other countries.

The U.S. appreciation implies a loss in competitiveness. World demand shifts from U.S. goods to those produced by our competitors. Therefore, at home, output and employment decline. Abroad, our competitors benefit from the depreciation of their currency. They become more competitive, and therefore output and employment abroad expand. Our monetary tightening thus tends to promote employment gains abroad, which come, of course, at the expense of our own employment.

There are also spillover effects through prices. When our currency appreciates, import prices in dollars fall. Therefore our inflation tends to decline quite rapidly when there is a sharp dollar appreciation. But abroad the opposite occurs. Their currency depreciates, and therefore prices in foreign currency tend to increase. Inflation abroad thus rises. Foreigners might welcome an increase in employment as a side effect of our monetary policy, but they certainly can do without the inflation that comes from currency depreciation.

In the same way, our fiscal policies exert effects abroad. A U.S. fiscal expansion such as the one in the 1980 – 1985 period will lead to dollar appreciation and a loss in competitiveness. The direct increase in our spending and the deterioration in our competitiveness are the channels through which our expansion is shared abroad. When the United States has a fiscal expansion, the rest of the world shares via increased exports. Table 20-4 summarizes these interdependence effects.[10]

Table 20-4 also shows the effects of monetary and fiscal policy on inflation. Because fiscal expansion leads to appreciation, the decline in import prices helps reduce inflation in the expanding country. But abroad import prices will rise, and that means inflation will be increased. These impacts of exchange rate movements on inflation were important factors in changing inflation rates in industrial countries in the 1980 – 1985 period.

Policy makers abroad therefore must decide whether to accept the higher employment-higher inflation effects of our policies or whether they should change their

---

[10] On interdependence see Ralph C. Bryant et al., "Domestic and Cross-Border Consequences of US Macroeconomic Policies," International Finance Discussion Paper 344, Board of Governors of the Federal Reserve System, March 1989; Pete Richardson, "The Structure and Simulation Properties of the OECD's Interlink Model," *OECD Studies,* Spring 1988; and Jeffrey Shaffer, "What the US Current Account Deficit Has Meant for Other OECD Countries," *OECD Studies,* Spring 1988.

TABLE 20-4
MONETARY AND FISCAL POLICY EFFECTS
WITH INTERDEPENDENCE

	U.S. MONETARY CONTRACTION		U.S. FISCAL EXPANSION	
	U.S.	Rest of the world	U.S.	Rest of the world
Exchange rate	$ appreciates		$ appreciates	
Output	−	+	+	+
Inflation	−	+	−	+

own policies. If inflation is already a problem abroad, or if the rest of the world is highly averse to inflation, then the policy response abroad to this *imported inflation* may well be to tighten money. A monetary contraction abroad, matching our own, ensures that exchange rates will not move or at least will move less. But it also means that our own tight money and recession become the world's tight money and recession. This was substantially what happened in the worldwide recession of 1981–1982.

Policy Synchronization

The large changes in exchange rates that arise when policies are not fully synchronized between countries pose a major threat to a world of free trade. When import prices fall by 20 or 30 percent because of a currency appreciation, large shifts in demand will occur. Domestic workers become unemployed, and they have no trouble seeing that it is foreigners who gain the jobs they just lost. Accordingly, there will be pressure for protection — tariffs or quotas — to keep out imports that are "artificially cheap" due to the currency appreciation. In the United States repeated calls for protection in the automobile industry, in steel, and in many other industries reflect in large part the side effects of a dollar that appreciated sharply in response to tight money.

On the question of independence or interdependence under flexible exchange rates, the experience of the last 14 years offers a quite unambiguous answer. Under flexible exchange rates there is as much or more interdependence as there is under fixed rates. Moreover, because exchange rates are so flexible and so ready to respond to policies (good or bad), macroeconomic management does not become easier. Further, to the extent that exchange rate overshooting causes sharp changes in competitiveness, it leads to protectionist sentiment.

On all counts then, flexible rates are far from being a perfect system. But there is no better system, for the Bretton Woods system collapsed. Therefore we can ask only whether through international coordination of interests and policies, we can make the system work better than it has in the recent past. In 1985 the leaders of the major industrial countries recognized their interdependence and agreed to work toward more coordinated policies. But there were as yet no major institutional changes that would provide a mechanism to ensure that coordination would take place.[11]

Proponents of changes argued for *target zones*. In a target zone arrangement central banks limit the fluctuations of exchange rates to a specified range. Target zones require policy coordination. Specifically, in an effective target zone arrangement governments must synchronize both their monetary and their fiscal policies.[12] The unwillingness to give up this sovereignty stands in the way of more limited exchange rate fluctuations between the United States, Europe, and Japan.

Within Europe, in the European Monetary System, important steps in this direction have already taken place. Moreover, proposals to push European exchange rate arrangements all the way to a full monetary integration in Europe are under very active consideration.[13]

20-7 U.S. ADJUSTMENT IN THE 1990s

In the 1980s the United States ran a persistent current account deficit. In earlier years the current account had always been in surplus or close to balance, with alternating surpluses and deficits. But starting in 1981, as Figure 20-12 shows, the current account deficit widened and an uninterrupted string of deficits soon made the United States the biggest net debtor in the world economy. By the early 1990s U.S. net external liabilities exceeded $700 billion.

By the late 1980s a critical question for the U.S. economy was whether these deficits could be sustained for long. And supposing that they could be financed, was it desirable to keep running these deficits even if that meant a growing external debt? It was not clear for how much longer such deficits could be sustained. But the risk that they could not be sustained and the long-run impacts of a growing U.S. debt to

---

[11] On coordination see Martin Feldstein (ed.), *International Economic Cooperation* (Chicago: University of Chicago Press, 1988); Jeffrey Frankel and Katherine Rockett, "International Macroeconomic Policy Coordination When Policy Makers Do Not Agree on the True Model," *American Economic Review*, June 1988; "To Coordinate or Not Coordinate: A Panel Discussion," Federal Reserve Bank of Boston, *International Payments Imbalances in the 1980s* (Boston, 1989); and Richard Cooper et al. (eds.), *Can Nations Agree?* (Washington, D.C.: The Brookings Institution, 1989).

[12] For a proposal on target zones see John Williamson and Marcus Miller, *Targets and Indicators: A Blueprint for the International Coordination of Economic Policy* (Washington, D.C.: Institute for International Economics, 1987); J. Williamson, "The Case for Roughly Stabilizing the Real Value of the Dollar," *American Economic Review*, May 1989; and Martin Feldstein, "The Case Against Trying to Stabilize the Dollar," *American Economic Review*, May 1989. See, too, Jacob Frenkel and Morris Goldstein, "Exchange Rate Volatility and Misalignment: Evaluating Some Proposals for Reform," in Federal Reserve Bank of Kansas City, *Financial Market Volatility* (Kansas City, 1989).

[13] On proposals for European monetary integration in the context of *Europe 92* see *European Economy*, May 1988. In early 1989 a committee headed by Jacques Delors, president of the European Commission, reported to the member governments of the European Community in favor of a process of full monetary integration. See, too, footnote 1, above.

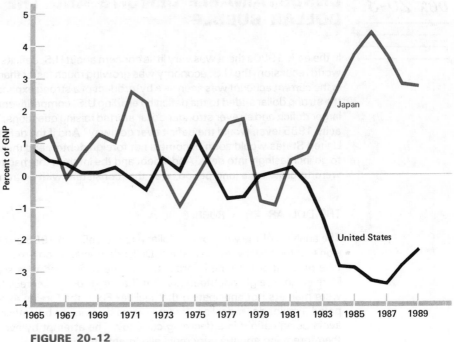

FIGURE 20-12
THE UNITED STATES AND JAPAN: CURRENT ACCOUNT IMBALANCES,
1965–1989 (percent of GNP). (SOURCE: DRI/McGraw-Hill.)

foreigners implied that early fiscal correction could not but improve the long-run prospects for financial stability and a rising standard of living. But it was also clear that if and when the United States adjusted, other countries would lose their external surpluses (as a group) and would in their turn have to make adjustments to sustain full employment. Thus the U.S. imbalances posed an international adjustment problem.[14]

The Dollar in 1989

By 1989 the U.S. current account deficit had declined somewhat, as had the current account surplus of Japan, but forecasts by international organizations predicted continuing large imbalances. In the view of some observers the imbalances would continue as

---

[14] See William Cline, *United States Adjustment and the World Economy* (Washington, D.C.: Institute for International Economics, 1989); "Studies on US External Imbalances," Federal Reserve Bank of New York *Quarterly Review,* Winter–Spring 1989; and Mark Ott, "Is America Being Sold Out?" Federal Reserve Bank of St. Louis *Review,* March/April 1989.

box 20-3

UNSUSTAINABLE DEFICITS AND THE DOLLAR BUBBLE

In the early 1980s there was very little concern about U.S. deficits: Following the 1982 world recession, the U.S. economy was growing much faster than others, and a deficit in the current account was seen as a by-product of a strong expansion. But increasingly the strong dollar added to the deficit by eroding U.S. competitiveness. By 1985 an ever larger deficit and an ever stronger dollar started raising questions: If the dollar remained at its 1985 level, would the deficit ever go away? And if the deficit did not decline, the United States would soon become a net foreign debtor, and then year after year have to go increasingly into debt. And if debt and the interest that had to be paid on the debt were to grow for a long period, was that consistent with a strong dollar?

THE DOLLAR AS A BUBBLE

The analysis of the value of the dollar and the deficit in 1985 quickly led to the conclusion that the dollar was overvalued. Dollar depreciation on a major scale would have to take place at some time in order to trim the deficit and thus slow down the rate of increase in foreign indebtedness. But if a major dollar depreciation was ahead, why were markets not anticipating the decline? For if the foreign exchange market anticipated a major dollar decline, traders would be quick to buy other currencies, trying to avoid being caught in a declining currency. The attempt by everybody to sell would therefore bring about a very rapid alignment of the dollar.

Even as the discussion of an unsustainable dollar emerged, the dollar actually started its 1985 – 1987 decline. But that left unanswered the question of why it had risen so much in the first place.

Explanations of tight U.S. monetary policy and fiscal expansion went some way in explaining the rise of the dollar, but that could not be the whole story; the timing did not match. Some observers concluded that the dollar peak of 1985 had been a speculative *bubble*, a departure of the dollar from a level justified by the fundamental factors that should determine its value, interest rates, the current account, and expected future current accounts. Once the bubble had burst, in part because of central bank cooperation in intervention, the dollar declined for 2 years to reach more realistic levels. The discussion of whether asset markets and, in particular, the foreign exchange market, are or are not rational, whether there are possibilities of future bubbles, continues unresolved.* ∎

---

* See Jeffrey Frankel and Richard Meese, "Are Exchange Rates Excessively Variable?" *NBER Macroeconomics Annual*, 1987, and Jeffrey Frankel and Ken Froot, "Using Survey Data to Test Standard Propositions Regarding Exchange Rate Expectations," *American Economic Review*, March 1987.

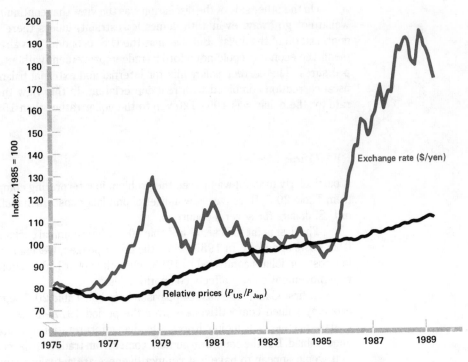

FIGURE 20-13
THE UNITED STATES AND JAPAN: WHERE SHOULD THE DOLLAR BE?
1975–1989 (index, 1985 = 100). (SOURCE: DRI/McGraw-Hill.)

long as the United States ran budget deficits and had a low saving rate and would disappear, without need for major exchange rate realignments, once those adjustments took place. Others argued that a further significant realignment of the dollar was inevitable.

The differences of view became particularly apparent in mid-1989, when the dollar strengthened for some time. Those who believed that the imbalances were driven by high levels of U.S. spending, rather than by low competitiveness, argued that the dollar was, if anything, undervalued, that is, that the dollar should move up relative to the yen. Their argument relied on purchasing power parity considerations.[15] In this interpretation the dollar had depreciated *too much* in 1985–1989, considering inflation differentials between the United States and Japan. An exchange rate of 155–175 yen to the dollar was the appropriate range, above the 145 yen then prevailing in the market (see Figure 20-13).

---

[15] See Ronald McKinnon, "Monetary and Exchange Rate Policies for International Financial Stability: A Proposal," *Journal of Economic Perspectives,* Winter 1988, and "Sound Dollar Tells Business: Think Long," *Wall Street Journal,* June 15, 1989. For an opposing view see Martin Feldstein, "Let the Market Decide," *The Economist,* December 8, 1988.

On the other side of the discussion was the view that continuing large imbalances would not go away, even with domestic restraint, unless there was a further real depreciation of the dollar. But, because the U.S. economy was already at full employment, the economy could not afford a trade improvement without risking inflationary pressures. The correct policy mix for internal and external balance was, therefore, fiscal correction combined with real depreciation. In this view the proper exchange rate for the dollar was 100–120 yen to the dollar rather than 155–175 yen.

PPP Once More

A particularly forceful way to see the problem in interpreting competitiveness comes from Table 20-5. Here we show indices of unit labor costs in manufacturing measured in U.S. dollars for several countries.

The first point to observe in Table 20-5 is how nominal exchange rates affect unit labor costs in dollars. In 1985, when the dollar peaked, Germany and Japan had very low costs in dollars compared to 1988, when the dollar had weakened. This exchange rate movement clearly affects competitiveness.

At first glance, the cost comparison based on Table 20-5 suggests that the U.S. economy gained competitiveness over the period 1977–1988 relative to all these trading partners, including Korea. On that interpretation the dollar might well be undervalued. But the counterargument comes from trade imbalances. All the countries that would appear to have lost competitiveness are actually running record current account surpluses. This suggests that a much closer scrutiny of the facts is required. One simple possibility is that the mix of products has shifted over the years in favor of the surplus countries. In that case imbalances must be corrected by expenditure changes combined with real exchange rate changes that assure a market for U.S. goods that do not sell well even when they are relatively cheap.

TABLE 20-5
UNIT LABOR COSTS IN DOLLARS (index, 1977 = 100)

	U.S.	Germany	Japan	Korea
1970	71	43	59	53
1977	100	100	100	100
1980	131	150	117	146
1985	143	101	107	130
1988	142	180	188	158

SOURCE: U.S. Department of Labor.

20-8 SUMMARY

1. External imbalances can be financed in the short term. In the long run they call for adjustment.

2. Adjustment of the external balance calls for expenditure reducing and expenditure switching policies. The former change the level of spending; the latter affect the composition of spending between domestic goods and imports and exports.

3. Under fixed exchange rates, the automatic adjustment mechanism works through prices and money. Unemployment leads to a decline in prices, a gain in competitiveness, increased net exports, and a gain in employment. Money responds to trade imbalances, affecting the level of interest rates, spending, and hence the payments deficit.

4. The monetary approach to the balance of payments draws attention to the fact that a payments deficit is always a reflection of a monetary disequilibrium and is always self-correcting. But the correction mechanism, because it involves unemployment, may be excessively painful compared with policy actions such as devaluation.

5. Exchange rate overshooting results from the rapid response of exchange rates to monetary policy and the sluggish adjustment of prices. A monetary expansion will lead to an immediate depreciation but only a gradual increase in prices. Exchange rate overshooting implies that real exchange rates are highly volatile.

6. Purchasing power parity (PPP) refers to the long-run tendency of exchange rates to offset divergent trends in national price levels. The currency of the country with the higher rate of inflation would tend to be depreciating at a rate equal to the inflation differential. If exchange rates follow PPP, then nominal exchange rate movements have no effects on competitiveness. In the short run, exchange rates certainly do not follow a PPP pattern.

7. Capital moves internationally in response to yield differentials, taking into account anticipated exchange rate movements. Interest rates in a country with a depreciating currency have to be sufficiently high to compensate asset holders for the depreciation of the assets.

8. Changes in nominal exchange rates will affect relative prices only if there are no offsetting changes in wages and prices. The real exchange rate, $R = eP_f/P$, can change only as a result of nominal exchange rate movements if P_f/P does not move in a fully offsetting manner. Among industrialized countries stickiness of wages and prices assures that real exchange rates change when nominal rates do.

9. If trade flows respond only gradually to a change in the real exchange rate, we observe a J-curve pattern. A real depreciation will worsen the trade balance in the short run, but then gradually improve it in later years as volume effects dominate.

10. Governments can intervene in exchange markets to limit the impact on output and prices of exchange rate fluctuations stemming from asset market disturbances. But intervention is very problematic when the authorities cannot determine whether the exchange rate is moving on account of fundamentals or for purely speculative reasons.

11. Even under flexible exchange rates economies are closely tied to one another. A monetary expansion at home will lead to unemployment and disinflation abroad. A fiscal expansion will cause an expansion abroad along with inflation. These interdependence effects make a case for coordinating policies.

KEY TERMS

Real exchange rate
Expenditure switching policies
Expenditure reducing policies
Internal balance
External balance
Policy dilemmas
Crawling peg
Monetary approach
Sterilization
Devaluation

Exchange rate overshooting
Exchange rate expectations
Purchasing power parity (PPP)
J curve
Intervention
Dirty floating
Exchange rate volatility
Target zones
Interdependence

PROBLEMS

1. It is sometimes said that a central bank is a necessary condition for a balance of payments deficit. What is the explanation for this argument?

2. Use the central bank balance sheet to show how a balance of payments deficit affects the stock of high-powered money under fixed exchange rates. Show, too, how sterilization operations are reflected in the central bank's balance sheet.

3. Consider a country that is in a position of full employment and balanced trade. Which of the following types of disturbance can be remedied with standard aggregate demand tools of stabilization? Indicate in each case the impact on external and internal balance as well as the appropriate policy response.
   (a) A loss of export markets
   (b) A reduction in saving and a corresponding increase in demand for domestic goods
   (c) An increase in government spending
   (d) A shift in demand from imports to domestic goods
   (e) A reduction in imports with a corresponding increase in saving

4. Discuss the manner in which income, price adjustments, and money supply adjustments interact in leading the economy ultimately to full employment and external balance. Choose as an example the case in which a country experiences a permanent increase in exports.

5. In relation to external imbalance, a distinction is frequently made between imbalances that should be "adjusted" and those that should be "financed." Give examples of disturbances that give rise, respectively, to imbalances that require adjustment and those that should more appropriately be financed.

6. Consider a world with some capital mobility: The home country's capital account improves as domestic interest rates rise relative to the world rate of interest. Initially, the home

country is in internal and external balance. (Draw the *IS, LM,* and *BB* schedules.) Assume now an increase in the rate of interest abroad.

(a) Show the effect of the foreign interest rate increase on the *BB* schedule.

(b) What policy response would immediately restore internal and external balance?

(c) If the authorities took no action, what would be the adjustment process along the lines described by the "monetary approach to the balance of payments"? (You may refer here to your answer to problem 4.)

7. Suppose in year 1 we have price levels $P = 100$ and $P_f = 100$. Suppose next that in year 2 the respective price levels are $P_2 = 180$ and $P_{2f} = 130$. Let the exchange rate initially be $2 per pound.

(a) If there were no real disturbances between year 1 and year 2, what would be the equilibrium exchange rate in year 2?

(b) If the real exchange rate, eP_f/P, had deteriorated between years 1 and 2 by 50 percent, what would the exchange rate be in year 2?

8. Explain why an expansionary fiscal policy reduces foreign income less than direct (unsterilized) intervention by the central bank in the foreign exchange markets to depreciate the exchange rate.

9. Assume that capital is perfectly mobile, the price level is fixed, and the exchange rate is flexible. Now let the government increase purchases. Explain first why the equilibrium levels of output and the interest rate are unaffected. Then show whether the current account improves or worsens as a result of the increased government purchases of goods and services.

10. Assume that there is perfect mobility of capital. How does the imposition of a tariff affect the exchange rate, output, and the current account? (*Hint:* Given the exchange rate, the tariff reduces our demand for imports.)

11. Explain how and why monetary policy retains its effectiveness when there is perfect mobility of capital.

12. Consult the *Wall Street Journal* or some other newspaper that lists foreign exchange rates on its financial pages. For some countries, such as Britain and Germany, you should find futures prices listed. That is the price to be paid today to receive one unit of the foreign currency in the future. A 30-day futures price for the pound sterling, say, is the price paid today to receive 1 pound 30 days from now. Explain why the futures prices are not generally equal to the spot prices — the price paid today to receive the foreign currency today. See whether you can explain the difference between the relationship of spot and futures prices for the pound and deutsche mark, respectively.

13. Assume you expect the pound to depreciate by 6 percent over the next year. Assume that the U.S. interest rate is 4 percent. What interest rate would be needed on pound securities — such as government bonds — for you to be willing to buy those securities with your dollars today and then sell them in a year in exchange for dollars? Can you relate your answer to this question to problem 12?

14. What considerations are relevant for a country deciding whether to borrow abroad to finance a balance of trade deficit or to adjust?

15. Explain the purchasing power parity theory of the long-run behavior of the exchange rate. Indicate whether there are any circumstances under which you would not expect the PPP relationship to hold.

INDEX

INTERNATIONAL COMPARISONS OF REAL PER CAPITA INCOME AND GROWTH, 1900–1987

	PER CAPITA INCOME IN INTERNATIONAL DOLLARS (1980 PRICES)						GROWTH RATES, 1900–1987 (ANNUAL AVERAGE)		
	1900	1913	1929	1950	1973	1987	GDP	Population	GDP per capita
Australia	2,293	3,390	3,146	4,389	7,696	9,533	3.1	1.7	1.4
Austria	1,651	1,985	2,118	2,123	6,434	8,792	2.2	0.3	1.9
Belgium	2,126	2,406	2,882	3,114	6,937	8,769	2.1	0.4	1.6
Canada	1,808	2,773	3,286	4,822	9,350	12,702	4.1	1.8	2.3
Denmark	1,732	2,246	2,913	3,895	7,845	9,949	2.8	0.8	2.0
Finland	1,024	1,295	1,667	2,610	6,804	9,500	3.3	0.7	2.6
France	1,600	1,934	2,629	2,941	7,462	9,475	2.4	0.4	2.1
Germany	1,558	1,907	2,153	2,508	7,595	9,964	2.8	0.7	2.2
Italy	1,343	1,773	2,089	2,323	6,824	9,023	2.8	0.6	2.2
Japan	677	795	1,162	1,116	6,622	9,756	4.3	1.2	3.1
Netherlands	2,146	2,400	3,373	3,554	7,754	9,197	2.9	1.2	1.7
Norway	1,218	1,573	2,184	3,436	7,071	11,653	3.4	0.7	2.6
Sweden	1,482	1,792	2,242	3,898	8,288	10,328	2.8	0.6	2.3
Switzerland	2,077	2,474	3,672	5,256	10,556	11,907	2.8	0.8	2.0
United Kingdom	2,798	3,065	3,200	4,171	7,413	9,178	1.8	0.4	1.4
United States	2,911	3,772	4,909	6,697	10,977	13,550	3.2	1.3	1.8
OECD average	1,817	2,224	2,727	3,553	7,852	10,205	2.9	0.9	2.1
Bangladesh	349	371	372	331	281	375	1.6	1.5	0.1
China	401	415	444	338	774	1,748	2.9	1.1	1.7
India	378	399	403	359	513	662	2.1	1.4	0.6
Indonesia	499	529	660	484	786	1,200	2.7	1.7	1.0
Pakistan	413	438	441	390	579	885	2.8	1.9	0.9
Philippines	718	985	1,091	898	1,400	1,519	3.3	2.4	0.9
South Korea	549[a]	610	749	564	1,790	4,143	4.2[a]	1.8	2.4[a]
Taiwan	434	453	631	526	2,087	4,744	5.1	2.2	2.8
Thailand	626	652	616	653	1,343	2,294	3.8	2.3	1.5
Asian average	485	539	601	505	1,061	1,952	3.2	1.8	1.3
Argentina	1,284	1,770	2,036	2,324	3,713	3,302	3.3	2.2	1.1
Brazil	436	521	654	1,073	2,504	3,417	4.8	2.4	2.4
Chile	956[b]	1,255	1,928	2,350	3,309	3,393	3.2[a]	1.7	1.5[a]
Colombia	610[b]	801	975	1,395	2,318	3,027	4.2[a]	2.3	1.9[a]
Mexico	649	822	835	1,169	2,349	2,667	3.7	2.1	1.6
Peru	624[b]	819	890	1,349	2,357	2,380	3.6[a]	2.0	1.6[a]
Latin American average	760	998	1,220	1,610	2,758	3,031	3.8	2.2	1.7
USSR	797	973	1,044	2,265	5,066	5,948	3.3	1.0	2.3

[a] Korean per capita GDP assumed to have moved like the average for the other eight Asian countries from 1900 to 1913.

[b] Chilean, Colombian, and Peruvian per capita GDP assumed to have moved like the average for the three other Latin American countries from 1900 to 1913.

SOURCE: A. Maddison, *The World in the 20th Century*, Paris, OECD, 1989.

THE U.S. DEBT-GNP RATIO, 1918-1989

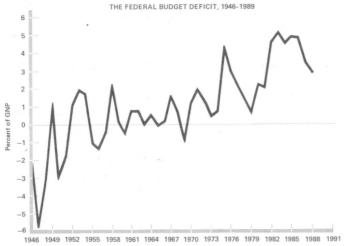

THE FEDERAL BUDGET DEFICIT, 1946-1989

U.S. DEBT AND DEFICITS (percent of GNP)

	Debt	Deficit	F.E. deficit		Debt	Deficit	F.E. deficit		Debt	Deficit	F.E. deficit
1960	46.8	−0.6	−2.8	1970	28.6	1.2	0.4	1980	26.6	2.2	0.5
1961	46.0	0.7	−1.8	1971	28.7	2.0	0.9	1981	26.3	2.1	0.0
1962	44.5	0.7	−1.0	1972	28.0	1.4	0.7	1982	29.3	4.6	1.1
1963	43.2	−0.0	−1.5	1973	26.6	0.4	0.2	1983	34.0	5.2	2.1
1964	40.8	0.5	−0.3	1974	24.3	0.8	−0.3	1984	35.3	4.5	2.8
1965	38.8	−0.1	−0.2	1975	25.9	4.3	2.0	1985	37.9	4.9	3.5
1966	35.7	0.2	0.7	1976	28.1	3.0	1.2	1986	41.5	4.9	3.6
1967	33.6	1.6	1.9	1977	28.4	2.3	1.0	1987	42.6	3.5	2.5
1968	34.1	0.7	1.0	1978	28.0	1.3	0.6	1988	42.9	2.9	2.4
1969	29.9	−0.9	−0.7	1979	26.1	0.6	−0.2				

NOTE: F.E. denotes the full-employment deficit; the deficit and debt data refer to the federal government.

SOURCE: DRI/McGraw-Hill.

WORLD OUTPUT, 1971–1989 (annual changes, in percent)

	Average, 1971–1980	1981	1982	1983	1984	1985	1986	1987	1988	1989
World	**3.9**	**1.8**	**0.7**	**2.8**	**4.5**	**3.4**	**3.2**	**3.2**	**4.1**	**3.3**
Industrial countries	**3.2**	**1.5**	**−0.3**	**2.8**	**4.9**	**3.4**	**2.6**	**3.4**	**4.1**	**3.3**
United States	2.8	1.9	−2.5	3.6	6.8	3.4	2.8	3.4	3.9	3.1
Japan	4.8	3.7	3.1	3.2	5.1	4.9	2.5	4.5	5.7	4.5
Germany, Federal Republic of	2.7	...	−1.0	1.9	3.3	1.9	2.3	1.8	3.4	2.4
Other industrial countries	3.2	0.7	0.7	2.1	3.1	3.1	2.5	3.2	3.6	2.9
Developing countries	**5.5**	**1.9**	**2.2**	**2.2**	**4.1**	**3.6**	**4.2**	**3.3**	**4.3**	**3.3**
Africa	3.8	1.9	2.5	−0.9	0.5	3.5	2.2	1.2	1.7	2.3
Asia	5.3	5.9	5.4	7.8	8.2	6.7	6.6	7.2	9.0	6.4
Europe	5.0	−0.1	1.4	2.5	4.1	2.3	4.2	2.4	2.5	2.3
Middle East	7.2	−1.3	1.3	1.7	0.1	−1.4	0.9	−1.6	3.9	2.3
Western hemisphere	5.9	0.3	−0.8	−2.7	3.7	3.6	4.1	2.6	0.9	0.8

INFLATION, 1971–1989 (percent)

	Average, 1971–1980	1981	1982	1983	1984	1985	1986	1987	1988	1989
Inflation based on GDP deflator										
Industrial countries	**8.3**	**8.7**	**7.2**	**5.0**	**4.4**	**3.5**	**3.4**	**2.9**	**3.1**	**3.8**
United States	7.4	9.6	6.4	3.8	3.7	3.0	2.7	3.3	3.4	4.7
Japan	7.4	3.3	1.8	0.8	1.2	1.4	1.8	−0.2	0.5	1.4
Germany, Federal Republic of	5.3	4.0	4.4	3.3	2.0	2.2	3.1	2.0	1.5	2.5
Other industrial countries	10.6	11.3	10.6	8.3	6.9	5.5	5.1	4.3	4.4	4.7
Inflation based on consumer prices										
Industrial countries	**8.7**	**10.1**	**7.5**	**4.9**	**4.7**	**4.1**	**2.3**	**2.9**	**3.2**	**3.8**
United States	7.8	10.4	6.1	3.2	4.4	3.5	2.0	3.6	4.1	4.7
Japan	9.0	4.9	2.7	1.9	2.3	2.0	0.6	0.1	0.7	1.3
Germany, Federal Republic of	5.1	6.3	5.3	3.3	2.4	2.2	−0.2	0.2	1.2	2.8
Other industrial countries	10.6	12.7	11.0	8.1	6.7	6.1	4.2	4.1	4.0	4.6
Developing countries	**20.5**	**25.8**	**25.2**	**32.4**	**38.2**	**39.7**	**31.1**	**40.5**	**67.1**	**45.5**
Africa	14.1	20.8	13.1	17.9	20.8	13.3	14.4	15.0	18.8	15.1
Asia	10.5	10.4	6.4	6.7	7.3	7.1	9.1	9.8	14.6	10.0
Europe	13.8	23.6	33.1	22.8	25.4	25.5	24.8	30.3	49.3	50.3
Middle East	13.5	15.1	12.9	12.0	14.4	17.0	18.2	19.3	18.8	14.6
Western hemisphere	39.8	60.8	66.8	108.6	133.0	144.9	87.8	130.0	277.6	154.9

INDUSTRIAL COUNTRIES: EMPLOYMENT AND UNEMPLOYMENT, 1971–1989 (percent)

	Average, 1971–1980	1981	1982	1983	1984	1985	1986	1987	1988	1989
Growth in employment										
Canada	3.1	2.8	−3.5	0.5	2.4	2.6	2.8	2.9	3.2	1.7
United States	2.4	1.1	−0.9	1.3	4.1	2.0	2.3	2.6	2.3	2.2
Japan	0.8	0.8	1.0	1.7	0.6	0.7	0.8	1.0	1.7	1.1
All industrial countries	**1.5**	**0.2**	**−0.7**	**0.4**	**2.1**	**1.4**	**1.6**	**1.7**	**1.8**	**1.4**
Unemployment rates										
Canada	6.9	7.6	11.0	11.8	11.2	10.5	9.5	8.8	7.8	8.0
United States	6.4	7.6	9.7	9.6	7.5	7.2	7.0	6.2	5.5	5.3
Japan	1.8	2.2	2.4	2.7	2.7	2.6	2.8	2.8	2.5	2.4
All industrial countries	**4.5**	**6.6**	**8.0**	**8.6**	**8.1**	**8.0**	**7.9**	**7.6**	**7.0**	**6.8**

SOURCE: International Monetary Fund, *World Economic Outlook*, April 1989.